T0293572

B
U
P

Gimede Gigante

PRINCIPLES OF INTERNATIONAL FINANCE

Foreword by **Matteo Arpe**

Typesetting: Laura Panigara, Cesano Boscone (Milan)
Cover: Cristina Bernasconi, Milan

Copyright © 2022 Bocconi University Press
EGEA S.p.A.

EGEA S.p.A.
Via Salasco, 5 - 20136 Milano
Tel. 02/5836.5751 – Fax 02/5836.5753
egea.edizioni@unibocconi.it – www.egeaeditore.it

First edition: June 2022

ISBN Domestic Edition   978-88-99902-90-2
ISBN International Edition   978-88-31322-47-8
ISBN Digital International Edition   978-88-31322-48-5
ISBN Digital Domestic Edition   978-88-238-8393-2

Table of Contents

Foreword

by *Matteo Arpe*

The world financial system has experienced a period of exceptional transformation in recent decades. A number of concurrent events have profoundly changed its balance and functioning. Only in the last twenty years we have seen the most serious and long-lasting global financial crisis in the history of capitalism, several speculative bubbles – from the internet to subprime mortgages, to the liquidity bubble – a true digital revolution in the form of cryptocurrencies, the rise in prominence of emerging economies, which now outweigh the so-called "advanced" ones on a global level and, more recently, an unprecedented world health emergency.

The same geo-economic equilibria have evolved and changed as a result of the interventions of regulators and the influence of public opinion. Just think of the recent movements toward nationalism after decades of economic globalization.

Even for those living through this intense and exciting period, operating in the financial and banking world, it was difficult, if not impossible, to grasp the magnitude of the evolutions that were taking place. And that continue to take place at a pace that is accelerated by a rapid digital revolution.

In such a dynamic and complex context, "Principles of International Finance" provides a valuable analytical contribution to understand the structure and functioning of world finance, dealing in an organic, clear and complete way with the structural aspects (Chapters 1, 2 and 3), the evaluative principles (Chapters 4 and 5), the flow dynamics (Chapters 6 and 7), the risk management tools (Chapters 8 and 9) and the different compartments of the system (Chapters 10, 11, 12 and 13). The last chapter closes the work by addressing a very topical issue: corporate governance. In short, this refers to the principles of behavior and functioning of economic subjects, with a particular emphasis on the increasingly important phenomenon of investor activism.

This work is the result of many years of deep theoretical contemplation in the classroom, positively influenced by the continuous contribution of experiences in the real world. The author alternates in-depth and up-to-date analyses with substantial sections dedicated to concrete cases, allowing the reader to better understand issues that have often also sparked debate in public opinion.

To all those who find themselves fascinated by this book and its analyses, who are or who will decide to enter the complex world of international finance, I recommend that you always refer to the theoretical principles clearly described here by the author, in the hope that they can inspire you to anticipate future changes in this field.

A final mention is dedicated not to the book, but to the author, Professor Gigante. On my behalf and I am sure on behalf of all the managers and the people from various financial institutions that he invited to share their expertise in his courses, I wish to express my deep appreciation for his great academic and human skills.

Introductory Remarks

Today's economic environment has reached levels of interconnectedness never imagined before. We live in a highly globalized world, where consumption, the production of goods, and the provision of services have become highly integrated. Financial markets are following similar trends: portfolios are internationally diversified and financial securities are now more cross-listed than ever on foreign exchanges.

This vibrant, global, and fast-changing context gives rise to an urgent need to evaluate how to move and act in such a complex environment. The inspiration for this book emerged from this necessity to put into writing the complexities of multinational financial management, ranging from dealing with foreign currency exposures to determining a subsidiary's capital structure, valuing an investment in a risky country, or the managerial and environmental considerations that make multinational financial decision-making so challenging. In fact, the multinational setting requires sound understanding of an array of issues, including the extension of traditional finance considerations to a more complex global setting (i.e., exchange rate effects, global CAPM), how institutional constraints can create obstacles and opportunities for multinational firms (i.e., new prospects in different markets) and the managerial objectives that can limit the relevance of traditional financial objectives or institutional opportunities. The framework developed throughout this book focuses on how to balance these three factors, showing that complex financial incentives must be integrated with institutional obstacles and opportunities as well as aligned with managerial objectives. The book aims to offer both a clear framework and a set of operational tools for analyzing the relationship between multinational firms and international financial markets. Each topic and chapter will include several real-world cases, aimed at putting international finance methodologies and practices to use around the world.

The main discussion will revolve around the features of international markets, which will be addressed from both a macroeconomic and a financial perspective. The macroeconomic component of international markets concerns currencies and market and policy variables, such as exchange rates and interest rates. The financial components of international markets include assets and financial instruments, such as cash and deposits, bonds, stocks, loans, derivatives, and insurance contracts – as well as activities like takeovers or financing that involves different players (i.e., international organizations, central banks, and supervisory authorities).

This is a panoramic overview of the main content of the book, which is intended to serve as a roadmap for readers attempting to better understand how multinational companies interact with international financial systems and to provide a clear framework and set of tools for engaging in decision-making related to these markets.

Acknowledgments

This book was possible because of the many people who have led me this far. I will try to remember them all.

I would like to start by thanking all the people who encouraged me and helped me on my path during my years at Bocconi, starting with my mentors: Stefano Caselli, first a guide and then a friend who allowed me to grow both as a person and as a professional; Stefano Gatti, who believed in me and started me off with conviction on my career in academia.

Thanks to Andrea Agnelli, always ready to share with me and my students his enlightened vision of business management and finance in international and complex organizations. An honor.

Thanks to Andrea Sironi for having followed my path in the Finance Department at Bocconi with care and attention.

Sincere thanks to Maurizio Dallocchio, always a kind and helpful source of invaluable advice that continues to shape my academic and professional career.

I would like to thank all my colleagues of the Finance Department at Bocconi and the Department Head Fulvio Ortu.

Special affection and gratitude go to Giulia Zanetello who, in the last mile of this long and important journey of writing, provided me with the support and help necessary – indispensable even – to successfully complete the revision of the final drafts. Thank you Giulia.

My gratitude also goes to all those who over the years have contributed to increasing my knowledge on the topics covered in the book. In particular Marco Alverà, Giulia Belloni, Marcella Caradonna, Emiliano Di Bartolo, Maria Teresa Iardella, Elisabetta Magistretti, Francesco Mele, Massimo Della Ragione, Riccardo Mulone, Rodolfo Pambianco, Leonardo Patroni Griffi, Giovanni Pirovano, Giovanni Tamburi, Giorgio Tinacci, Luciano Santel, Stefano Sardo.

Thanks to Andrea Cerri, Baptiste Gilliot, Maria Vittoria Venezia, Martina Montanari, Carolina Grosso and Claudia Caracciolo for the precious work of re-reading the different chapters and for contributing with suggestions, revisions, and support in exploring the various themes addressed in the book in depth.

A special thanks to Andrea Locatelli. Over the years, his help and support in organizing the course and the Principles of International Finance materials has been priceless.

A heartfelt thanks to Stefano Sardo and Maria Vittoria Venezia for their invaluable efforts in drafting and the critical re-reading of Chapter 14.

Thanks to Maria Teresa Iardella for her support with data and bibliographic material necessary for Chapter 13.

Thanks to Jill Connelly and Amanda Swain for valuable proofreading work.

Thanks to Leo Goretti, excellent and always precise in his suggestions and editorial revisions.

Thanks to Roberto Gamba, Cristina Casati and Cinzia Facchi of Egea who, with perseverance, patience and great professionalism, have always stayed by my side and have been fundamental in making this book possible.

This book would not have been possible without my students in Course 30151, Principles of International Finance, who have been my greatest source of inspiration over the years, contributing incessantly with their ideas in the classroom, during office hours, with the theses they've written and the class notes they've shared to make this publishing project possible. It is impossible to name them all, but each of you will find in the book a piece that is the result of your contribution as individuals or as a class.

In life we all have our idols and I was lucky enough to meet mine in person, and then have the absolute privilege of having him by my side in this editorial adventure with the writing of the preface to the book. I am talking about Matteo Arpe. My thanks go to him for deciding to accompany me on my path of personal as well as professional growth that began at Bocconi ten years ago since I started teaching at Bocconi in 2012, when I had the great pleasure and honor of working with him as a Visiting Professor. In all these years Matteo Arpe has been able to transfer his precious insights to his students, providing them and me with the essential tools to understand the global financial world we live in. I will never thank him enough for his continuous dedication to Università Bocconi, for all the initiatives he has financed and for his unfailing dedication, above all towards his students. Over the years, I have received numerous messages from students who have candidly confessed to me how Matteo Arpe's lessons have inspired their lives and positively influenced their professional choices. Personally, I too am grateful to him because he inspired my decision to pursue a career in finance when I was still a university student and at the time he was already the "Italian rising star" in the international financial system. The Economist had already dubbed him an *enfant prodige* of finance. To be close to Matteo Arpe, to work with Matteo Arpe is an absolute privilege since he is – and I say this with no fear of being contradicted, one of the most brilliant minds I have ever known as well as the best banker we have ever had in Italy.

Finally, an important and sincere thank you is for my wife Carlotta and my two daughters Giulia and Ginevra who, with their affection and love, have always given me their unwavering support.

Contributor

Stefano Sardo is Partner at EMIP, providing services to Elliott Advisors (UK) Ltd. Stefano has been involved in the origination and execution of the most relevant Italian investments of US-fund Elliott Management since 2017. Previously Stefano was based in London where he worked as investment analyst in TMT hedge fund DWC and M&A associate at Goldman Sachs.

1 A Global Financial System: Internationalization and MNCs

This first chapter will outline the key notions necessary to discuss the topics highlighted in the introduction.

We will begin with some provoking real-world cases that will immediately underscore the significance of the issues discussed in the book. Each example will come with questions meant to stimulate thought and offer interesting insights. After this initial icebreaking, the second section of the chapter will go on to analyze multinational companies by defining their goals and objectives and briefly reviewing the history of internationalization and multinational companies or MNCs. The chapter will then dive deeper into the rationale motivating internationalization, surveying some economic and business theories, and consider how opportunities to conduct business abroad can increase exposure to potential risks like exchange rate movements, foreign policies, or more general political risk. The chapter will conclude with a third section that broadly addresses the issue of calculating the value of a multinational company and how internationalization processes can have an impact on this calculation.

Thus, the overall objective of the chapter is to introduce the reader to the world of international finance and to the main topics of discussion throughout the book: the multinational corporation and its features, opportunities, and risks as well the challenges it faces, considering also their financial implications and the impact on valuation.

1.1 Relevance of financial markets: some examples

This section will discuss real-world cases that help showcase the relevance and importance of finance in people's daily lives. We identify several examples drawn from recent history that help illuminate key concepts discussed throughout the book. Each example is accompanied by some reflection questions. The hope is that, by the end of the book, readers will be able to come up with answers to these questions and develop their own interesting insights on topics that might at first seem complicated and confusing.

US investment banks conquer the European Banking System

Supported by healthier domestic market conditions and larger scales, US investment banks have been gaining market share in Europe over the last decade, often to the detriment of their European competitors. The latter have instead downsized their operations in response to more rigid regulations, slow growth, and negative interest rates that have been undermining their core profitability. As a result, US investment banks have consolidated their leadership position across deal types and geographic locations and are now only handling deals above a certain size threshold (large cap), which are usually more profitable in terms of fees.

- What is the background?
- What is happening to the European Banking System?
- What should we expect for the post-Covid-19 pandemic future?

Luxottica and Essilor merger

Italy's Luxottica and France's Essilor agreed to one of Europe's largest cross-border mergers in January 2017 – €46 billion deal that would have established the combined entity as the world leader in the fast-growing eyewear industry. According to Essilor, the merger was intended to meet growing global demand for corrective lenses, sunglasses, and high-end frames. In the short term, Essilor and Luxottica expected the new company to produce revenue and cost synergies ranging from $424 million to $636 million. In July 2019, the combined company, EssilorLuxottica, also agreed to buy the European competitor GrandVision for €5.49 billion ($6.1 billion), thereby cementing the Ray-Ban maker's global position as the largest eyewear and lens manufacturer and retailer. With the purchase of GrandVision, EssilorLuxottica's retail footprint was expanded by more than 7,200 locations worldwide.

"EssilorLuxottica is the largest eyewear supplier in the world and GrandVision is the largest eyewear retail chain in Europe," observed European Commission Executive Vice President Margrethe Vestager, who manages competition policy, in her comments on the transaction. The merger raised the bar for a consolidating market in which it has become necessary to carefully assess whether the proposed merger will result in higher prices or fewer options for customers. In late August 2020, the European Commission approved the acquisition of GrandVision on the condition that its Italian stores be sold to another operator. The expansion strategies of this global eyewear giant seem to have been a wise decision, since the first fruits have already been reaped: EssilorLuxottica has already ranked 17th on *Fortune* magazine's 2019 Change the World list, which honors companies that create positive social impact through actions that are central to their business strategy.

- What are the management strategies of a multinational company like Luxottica?
- What kind of synergies are involved? How are they valued in this type of cross-border acquisition?
- How will this cross-border transaction generate shareholder value?

Ferrari's IPO

Luxury carmaker Ferrari priced its initial public offering (IPO) in October 2015 at

$52, the top end of the range, in a deal to list about 10% of its shares on the New York Stock Exchange.

The company had set a price range of $48 to $52 with the aim of raising nearly $1 billion. Shares started trading on the NYSE on Wednesday, October 21, 2015.

- How might a global capital market like the US help Ferrari grow more than a segmented capital market (i.e., the Italian one)?

Alibaba's IPO dilemma: Hong Kong or New York?[1]

Alibaba's initial public offering was expected to be one of the largest in history in April 2014. With respect to its listing, Alibaba had to face several challenging choices regarding its ownership structure, trading venue, and the price and timing of its IPO. Due to geographic, cultural, and linguistic proximity, the Hong Kong Stock Exchange (HKEx) seemed an obvious choice, especially since Alibaba had generated nearly 90% of its sales in China. The New York Stock Exchange (NYSE) and NASDAQ, on the other hand, would have allowed for implementation of the ownership structure that Alibaba wanted: a dual class share structure. If Hong Kong investors were more familiar with Alibaba's business, the New York markets offered Jack Ma's company more liquidity and visibility.

- What, then, were the advantages and disadvantages in choosing to list in Hong Kong versus New York?

Investindustrial exits Ducati[2]

Ducati, an Italian motorcycle manufacturer headquartered in Bologna, had been well managed by private equity group Investindustrial, which had taken it to record-level sales – increasing them by about 40% between 2006 and 2011 in addition to increasing its EBITDA margin more than twofold. At the time of the exit, Investindustrial was evaluating an international option for the world-renowned brand Ducati: a public listing on the Hong Kong stock exchange.

- What options should Investindustrial have pursued to exit a multinational corporation like Ducati while maximizing its returns?

Globalizing the cost of capital and capital budgeting at AES[3]

A U.S. international energy company, AES operates in four business divisions (utilities, contract generation, competitive supply, and growth distribution), with opera-

---

[1] Emir Hrnjić, "Alibaba's IPO dilemma: Hong Kong or New York?" Copyright © 2014, National University of Singapore and Richard Ivey School of Business Foundation.

[2] Brochet, Francois, and Karol Misztal. "Investindustrial Exits Ducati." Harvard Business School Case 113-058, February 2013. (Revised October 2013.)

[3] Desai, Mihir A., and Douglas Kurt Schillinger. "Globalizing the Cost of Capital and Capital Budgeting at AES." Harvard Business School Case 204-109, December 2003. (Revised October 2006.)

tions in 30 countries on five continents. Since its listing in the early 1990s, the company has experienced remarkable growth thanks to its global development strategy – even though the global economic crisis of the late 2000s had a significant impact on its profitability, particularly in terms of currency devaluations in South America, falling energy prices, and changes in energy regulatory frameworks in various countries. Due to the deterioration of AES's financial performance and the subsequent precipitous drop in its stock price, the company needed to rethink its strategy. A planning group was therefore formed and tasked with determining the value of the company's assets and devising a new technique for estimating its capital expenditure on investments made around the world.

• What approach should AES have taken during its restructuring process to identify the risks of its various international projects and correctly assess their capital costs?

Dow Chemical's bid for the privatization of PBB in Argentina[4]

Intentions to privatize 51% of PBB, a company that produces ethylene and polyethylene, were revealed in 1995 by the Argentine government. Dow Chemical was one of the potential buyers.

The U.S. conglomerate Dow Chemical would gain significant dominance in Latin America and the petrochemical industry as a whole by acquiring this Argentine company and becoming that country's leading polyethylene producer. To make this huge purchase, Dow Chemical had to analyze in detail the long-term risks and opportunities of the transaction. Here are a few details of the situation it faced. First, the peso was tied to the U.S. dollar at the time of the transaction, and the local government had promised to implement economic reforms. To solidify its position in the polyethylene market, Dow believed that additional capacity expenditures would be required to upgrade PBB's production facilities. This meant that, in addition to acquiring PBB, the project would require further investments that were hard to assess.

For example, a currency crisis in Argentina might pose significant risk to the profitability of the entire project. As a result, Dow executives had to identify the project's most important risks and decide how to include them in their valuation in order to arrive at a purchase price to propose to PBB.

• When valuing cash flows in an international project, what assumptions should be established and what steps should be taken to complete the valuation (i.e., terminal value, discount rate, scenario analysis)?

---

[4] Desai, Mihir A., and Kathleen Luchs. "Dow Chemical's Bid for the Privatization of PBB in Argentina (TN)." Harvard Business School Teaching Note 206-040, December 2005.

The refinancing of Shanghai General Motors[5]

Shanghai General Motors (SGM) is a joint venture between General Motors and Shanghai Automotive Industry Corporation (SAIC) owned by the Shanghai Municipal Government. It was formed in 1997 as a 50/50 partnership. Each partner contributed equal amounts of equity, and a group of banks provided debt financing for the new business. This is how most joint ventures work. The partnership also turned out to be a lot of fun. In 1999, SGM built a profitable auto plant that helped it gain a 5% share of the Chinese market in less than two years.

SGM was first funded after the Asian financial crisis, when it was hard to get banks to invest in new Chinese businesses. SGM grew significantly in the late 2000s and began facing new strategic issues with China's planned entry into the WTO. Mark Newman, the CFO of SGM, believed it was time to refinance. There were several factors affecting the scenario. How could the company devise a new financial strategy that both the host government and SGM would like? Moreover, would the proposed refinancing be good for both SGM's American and its Chinese owners?

- What are the main reasons for seeking foreign direct investment, and what are the consequences for those who own the company?
- How should we evaluate the financing decisions of a subsidiary, especially with regards to the currency used to pay off its debt?
- How do financial decisions get made in a multinational company?

Valentino's acquisition by Permira Private Equity Fund

In 2007, the private equity fund Permira bought Valentino Fashion Group (VFG). VFG was a global brand with a retail-price turnover of over €700 million in 2006 and more than 1,250 Points of Sale (POS) in 69 countries. Immediately after the acquisition, the project faced a difficult situation, but after a few years the scenario changed completely.

- How and why do private equity firms allow businesses to obtain funding and grow?
- How is the business of private equity organized internationally?

Drilling South: Petrobras evaluates Pecom[6]

Petrobras, a Brazilian oil corporation, was considering acquiring Pecom, an Argentine oil company, in the early 2000s. This proposal presented concerns for both companies. Pecom's valuation was complicated, because of Argentina's economic crisis.

---

[5] Desai, Mihir A., and Mark Veblen. "Refinancing of Shanghai General Motors (B), The." Harvard Business School Case 204-025, July 2003. (Revised September 2003.)

[6] Desai, Mihir A., and Ricardo Reisen de Pinho. "Drilling South: Petrobras Evaluates Pecom." Harvard Business School Case 204-043, November 2003. (Revised March 2004.)

Although Pecom possessed attractive assets, the host country's financial crisis and the depreciation of the Argentine peso brought the company to the brink of bankruptcy due to its dollar-denominated debt. Country risk was also a critical issue in the transaction, since Argentina's economic crisis generated a significant increase in its country risk premium.

The CFO of Petrobras and his staff had to consider how to account for these considerations in their evaluation of Pecom. In addition to issues in Argentina, the situation in Brazil raised additional concerns, because Petrobras was majority owned by the Brazilian government. While the state's authority over Petrobras had loosened in recent years, one of the main contenders in Brazil's upcoming general election did not fully support Petrobras' growing autonomy, and a change in government could have jeopardized the company's governance and strategy.

- What are the most pressing concerns for corporate governance in developing markets?
- A valuation in an uncertain environment requires a different strategy. What effects do political factors have on a company's financial and strategic choices?
- How are enterprises affected in the event of a currency crisis?

1.2   From domestic to international markets: MNCs and their internationalization process

In the traditional finance setting, firms face issues concerning financing, cash distribution, capital structure, and commitment evaluation. If a firm has a larger, international scope, these issues become more complex. When there are foreign subsidiaries, there are further complications related to repartition policies (repatriation) and investments in different countries. These additional structural design risks and opportunities associated with internationalization underscore the need for figures who can manage and cope with them. Examples might be CFOs, general managers, or specific managers who deal with a firm's global operations or who vet investment options. The role of such figures is to provide the MNC advice in a highly complex and interconnected environment. In addition, each country has to confront more specific domestic concerns. In Italy, for instance, firms also have to cope with refinancing, NPLs, and ensuring that decisions comply with the policies imposed to lenders by the European Central Bank (EBC). These topics will be discussed in this second section of the chapter, which introduces the main protagonist of the book: the MNC. The definitions, historical context, and goals of the MNC will be outlined, as well will the main motivations, risks, and opportunities entwined with its internationalization.

1.2.1   The definition of a multinational corporation

Multinational companies are large enterprises that do business across national borders. Typically, a company starts out as a local business. With growth, it begins to expand, first internationally and in some cases also globally, with the goal of maximizing wealth creation for shareholders. A variety of opportunities and threats shape this growth process and expansion across borders.

A multinational corporation is an enterprise that engages in foreign direct investment (FDI) and that owns or controls value-added activities in more than one country (Brewer et al., 2000). In other words, an enterprise, firm, company, or economic agent is considered a "multinational" when it controls income-generating assets (subsidiaries) and produces or sells goods and services in more than one country or regional area. Implicit in this definition is the idea of *direct control* (usually 10% of its capital) over the subsidiary – control which is exerted to influence the latter's strategies and not just for the sake of capital investments. Indeed, with the parent company located in the home country, there is normally a high degree of strategic interaction among the units and foreign subsidiaries. A typical MNC works with its headquarters in one country, typically its home country, and its other subsidiaries located in other countries around the world. A plethora of taxonomies are used in the scholarly literature to categorize firms that operate on a global scale. In this book, we will focus on multinational, global, and transnational firms. Multinational firms have interests in a number of countries, but their product offerings in each country are not coordinated with each other. These companies focus on customizing their products and services for each market in relation to the needs of local consumers. Global corporations have a physical presence in a large number of countries where they have made significant investments. They offer their products in all areas and maintain a consistent image and branding strategy across the entire group. A single centralized corporate office at the parent company is often responsible for worldwide strategy and core operations, with an emphasis on volume, cost control, and efficiency. Transnational corporations are highly complex companies with significant global investments all over the world and a centralized product and service strategy but which completely delegate decision-making power as well as research and development and promotional responsibilities to each individual foreign market in which they operate. All these companies have one thing in common: they are all global in scope and complexity, which is a result of the fact that they have extended their operations across international boundaries. For the sake of consistency, we will use the same set of criteria stated above to assess whether a company is global or not.

Many MNCs engaging in FDI activities today rely heavily on foreign capital. This has been the driving force for economic development, as most economies have gradually become interdependent. Indeed, multinational enterprises have played increasingly prominent roles in international economic integration. Because of the tight link among MNCs, their activities, and FDI over time, some confusion has emerged regarding the definition of an MNC. In particular, the terms "multinational enterprise" and "foreign direct investments" have often been used interchangeably. This is a mistake, however, because foreign direct investment is just one of a multinational enterprise's many activities, albeit an essential one. In fact, without such investment there is no extension of the firm and no internationalization, which is obviously fundamental to any international business.

The first question that comes to mind might be the following: why do companies decide to operate in the international market? A substantial body of research examines the business benefits of internationalization (OECD, 2001)[7]. Host nations with larger market sizes, faster rates of economic growth, and higher levels of economic development will give firms that enter more opportunities to capitalize on their ownership advantages. Expansion into a specific foreign country may also be motivated by the presence of natural and human resources, labor costs and productivity levels, or by strategic resources such as technology and innovative assets like popular brands. Corporate governance and ethical business practices are also critical: expansion may enable enterprises to avoid additional expenses incurred by bureaucratic or restrictive administrative methods or to exploit practices that are in some cases illegal in the country of origin. Finally, policies regarding the functioning and structure of markets are also key, because the economic, political, and social stability of a host nation serves as fertile ground for the development and growth of an MNC.

There are then multiple reasons a firm might decide to internationalize, just as there are many different strategies it can use to do so:

- Export or import.
- Establish subsidiaries abroad or acquire a foreign company.
- Raise capital on foreign markets (e.g., Alibaba is a Chinese company listed on the NYSE, which started raising capital with its US IPO).

Each of these strategies is a sufficient condition to define a company as a multinational. Each must also be implemented taking the forex (foreign exchange) outlook into consideration, i.e., exchange rates, foreign interest rates, etc.

A further complication in the definition of MNCs is their evolution over time. In the US, for instance, MNCs now constitute the most powerful companies, making foreign markets of critical importance and rapidly accelerating internationalization.

As stated in Slaughter (2009), the activities of U.S. multinationals are generally focused on the United States, where their parent businesses are headquartered, rather than overseas, where their foreign affiliates are located. The perception that multinational corporations have "left" the United States is not substantiated by facts. MNCs have a large presence in America, both in terms of the overall size of the U.S. economy and the number of worldwide affiliates. International engagement is crucial to the overall success of multinational corporations in the United States, even though the United States is the world's biggest domestic market. To secure their domestic success, U.S. multinational corporations approach strategic investments and hiring decisions with a global view, privileging linkages and dynamic variety in strategies across firms and within organizations. The operations of

---

[7] OECD paper 2001, growth, technology transfer and foreign direct investment authored by Maria Maher and Hans Christiansen.

foreign affiliates often complement, rather than replace, the parent company's key activities in the United States. Global participation requires U.S. corporations to create operations overseas, expand these operations, and integrate them with their parent companies in the United States. Continuing with Slaughter the notion that global growth tends to "hollow out" domestic operations in the United States is erroneous. The development of American parent corporations and their affiliates benefits the productivity of all Americans, as well as their average quality of life. Most actions that boost America's productivity and result in high average wages for American employees are performed by American parent firms. They help U.S. businesses to be more productive, which means more money for the millions who work for them. The global operations of U.S. multinationals are mostly based in the United States, not in the other countries where they have branches and about two-thirds of the world's jobs at U.S. multinationals are in their parent companies. Foreign affiliates are mostly found in high-income countries that have similar economic structures to the United States, not in low-income countries where people have less money (Slaughter, 2009).

Of course, it is also essential to note that the weight of foreign markets and overseas operations differs among industries. The following section briefly outlines some of the factors underpinning the rise of MNCs.

Considerations that have driven the rise of MNCs over time (Shapiro, 2010):

- The main objective of the first multinationals was to look for and use the *raw resources* present in foreign countries but absent in the country of origin.
- Other companies entered markets in other countries so that they could produce and sell their goods there directly. Foreign market access may be necessary in certain industries to achieve *economies of scale*, *reduced costs*, or *opportunities for expansion*.
- Companies conducting business globally today are increasingly focused on reducing production and sourcing costs. To remain competitive both domestically and internationally, these companies seek out and invest in low-cost production locations in other nations. *Offshoring* and *outsourcing* are other terms used to describe this process (see **Table 1.1** for definitions).
- Frequently, companies decide to enter foreign markets to maintain their competitive advantage by *gaining access to new knowledge* that they lack in their home country. It is essential to keep pace with the advances made in countries at the forefront of certain sectors, especially those characterized by rapid product innovation and technological advances.

Table 1.1   **Offshoring and Outsourcing**

Location of production	Internalized	Externalized (outsourcing)
Home country	Production kept in-house at home	Production outsourced to third-party service provider at home
Foreign country (offshoring)	Production by foreign affiliate/ subsidiary	Production outsourced to third-party provider abroad (i.e., to a local company or foreign affiliate of another MNC)

- Suppliers of goods or services to multinationals often follow their clients around the world to ensure that they can guarantee a steady and efficient supply of the products they need and *avoid being replaced in favor of local suppliers* in their host countries.
- Finally, it is possible for multinationals to take advantage of *flaws in the financial system*, which can lead to lower financing costs and higher project cash flows for a multinational than might be possible for a local company.

In addition to the definitions above, many scholars use a tool created by John Dunning called the OLI model to illustrate how multinationals think about their foreign operations and strategies (Dunning, 2009). Though some think the model is too simplistic and others think the variables need to be operationalized, it still represents a useful way to think about the basics of MNC behavior. The model's acronym 'OLI' refers to ownership, location, and internalization. *Ownership* refers to how important it is for MNCs to have certain kinds of knowledge or skills in order to gain market power and grow both at home and abroad. *Location* means that in order for MNCs to work abroad, they consider a specific foreign country as better for investment than other countries or places (including the domestic market). Finally, *Internalization* refers to the desire on the part of MNCs to operate their own facilities overseas rather than merely contract with local suppliers, which leads these corporations to internationalize (Jeffrey, 2017).

1.2.2   A brief history of globalization and MNC development

The multinational corporation's history is inextricably linked to the roots of commerce within and among cultural communities. Such borders defined the boundaries between city-states in ancient Greece. In this sense, international business activity is far from being a new phenomenon. In the ancient world, the Phoenicians and Carthaginians were already heavily reliant on international trade. The Industrial Revolution, on the other hand, is credited with establishing the foundations of modern international corporate activity. Modern multinational enterprises, in particular, have their origins in this worldwide movement that occurred in the nineteenth century (Dunning, 1993).

After outlining the definition of MNCs and what factors have driven the internationalization of companies over time, we now need to consider some key aspects of the history of MNCs, globalization, and interconnectedness among companies and economies. Literature on the history of multinational enterprises is extensive and growing. There is substantial scholarly interest in this field, with academics progressively gathering new ideas and viewpoints on the topic and expanding the existing body of knowledge.

Most scholars of the history of multinational corporations agree that the contemporary MNC has dates to the mid- to late-nineteenth century and is a post-industrial revolution phenomenon. Indeed, it was only with the invention of steamships, railroads, and cables that it became possible to exert control over foreign business operations. As a result, revolutions in transportation and communication were critical to the coordination, if not the very existence, of multinational corporations. Despite this widespread agreement, some historians place the origins of MNCs significantly earlier. Early MNCs, according to Wilkins (Wilkins, 2009), date back to ancient civilizations about 2500 BC. Some scholars point to thirteenth century Italian bankers, while others refer to the East India Company (England) and the Dutch East India Company as MNCs. Most historians today agree that it is possible to distinguish earlier multinationals from the post-industrial revolution firms that have been (and continue to be) the main focus of multinational enterprise historians. Furthermore, several researchers contend that MNCs in the post-World War II period vary from those preceding them. They underscore that postwar multinational corporations are more focused on manufacturing and services than prewar corporations, which were more centered on the consumption and exploitation of raw resources and commodities. Rather than foreign portfolio investments, the latter were more often financed by a combination of FDI and local capital. Today's MNCs exhibit some additional interesting features: current MNCs are the most common owners of proprietary technology, and in the latter two decades of the twentieth century they have developed geographically distributed "value chains" to take advantage of cheaper R&D, manufacturing, and distribution costs as a result of decreased trade and investment barriers.

The history of MNCs is inextricably related to that of economic globalization. Globalization, which first appeared in the late 1990s, may be characterized as growth in the modern world economy's degree of connectivity and interdependence. MNCs and globalization are linked since they are both benefactors and agents of globalization – the former because MNC internationalization and global plans would be impossible to implement without some level of globalization, and the latter because as MNCs pursue internationalization strategies, globalization increases. Academics generally believe that globalization has three key underlying motivations. First, the involvement of international institutions (i.e., the World Trade Organization or the OECD). Second, the evolution of transportation and communication technology, which made managing international activities less expensive and difficult. Finally, the preferences of powerful national players (especially the United States), which have played a key role in globalization.

Historically, the presence of MNCs has resulted in nations becoming wealthier over time. Indeed, in addition to channeling investments and increasing globalization, the function of MNCs in national governments has been to transfer financial and physical riches or capital to states. This is clear in the United States and the United Kingdom, which lead the way for MNCs, with Japan and EU countries trailing close behind. Furthermore, Arab countries such as Saudi Arabia, Qatar, and Kuwait have lately experienced rapid globalization. Academics identify a large degree of shared interest between these firms and the US government, whose policies have historically fostered business development in foreign areas to provide protection to MNCs.

Furthermore, several experts think the presence of multinational corporations has facilitated the growth of emerging economies. The tax funds generated by multinational corporations in developing countries enable them to invest in their infrastructure, improve life and the security of property, and increase human capital. According to the United Nations, MNCs can assist in the elimination of global poverty and create positive externalities through boosting capital flow efficiency.

Recent MNC considerations and challenges in the euro area

Global corporations have grown in size and profitability in recent years. Profit-sharing activities (i.e., activities to reduce MNC tax burden by exploiting transfer pricing or shifting intra-company positions to low or no tax jurisdictions) have become more relevant as a result of the rise of multinational corporations, posing challenges to current international frameworks. For example, the OECD estimates that tax avoidance by multinational corporations (MNCs) costs the world economy $240 billion every year.

It's worth noting that the operations of huge multinational corporations have influenced and changed external imbalances and financial centers in the Eurozone over time. Indeed, the operations of huge multinational corporations have a significant impact on national accounts, making statistical compilation and economic analysis difficult. In particular, MNC strategies and operations have three effects on balance of payments data: (i) they channel profits to low-tax affiliates via, for example, manipulation of intra-firm transfer prices; (ii) they shift intra-firm debt obligations and capital linkages; and (iii) they redomicile headquarters and legal incorporations to financial centers with favorable tax situations (i.e., economies where financial activities tend to dominate domestic economic activity).

A variety of legislative initiatives at the international level have been launched to offset the escalation of MNC tax avoidance activities and the impact that MNC operations have on foreign accounts, not only in the euro area but globally. The Base Erosion and Profit Shifting (BEPS8) Project was co-sponsored by the OECD and the G20 (which includes 135 nations, including EU member states), and it included a 15-point action plan to combat tax evasion. The EU improved on the suggestions produced by the BEPS Project by enacting two Anti-Tax Avoidance Directives between 2019 and 2020. The EU reform package contains not only new standards for MNC financial reporting but also steps to minimize tax avoidance, increase tax transparency, and move towards an equal playing field for all EU enterprises. Multilateral attempts to promote MNC transparency are clearly necessary to facilitate cross-border information exchanges for tax and statistical purposes. The European Central Bank also emphasizes the importance of combining these actions with national government efforts to combat tax evasion and increase statistical compiler collaboration (including the sharing of information). To improve the accuracy and consistency of macroeconomic statistics, the latter would ensure uniform cross-border recording of MNC activity.

1.2.3   The objectives of a multinational corporation and conflicting goals

MNCs owe it to their stakeholders to consistently increase revenue, control costs, and boost profits. With offices and facilities located all over the world, multinational enterprises must be familiar with the specific needs of each market. This unique position presents the organization with distinct difficulties and possibilities. As is the case for many businesses, the fundamental goal of most MNCs is then to maximize profits and meet financial goals. However, MNCs, unlike many other businesses, must negotiate different geographic distances, cultures, and target customers to offer their goods and services.

---

[8] "Base erosion and profit shifting (BEPS) refers to tax planning strategies used by multinational enterprises that exploit gaps and mismatches in tax rules to avoid paying tax. Developing countries' higher reliance on corporate income tax means they suffer from BEPS disproportionately. BEPS practices cost countries USD 100-240 billion in lost revenue annually. Working together within OECD/G20 Inclusive Framework on BEPS, 141 countries and jurisdictions are collaborating on the implementation of 15 measures to tackle tax avoidance, improve the coherence of international tax rules and ensure a more transparent tax environment." Available at https://www.oecd.org/tax/beps/about/

The objective of an MNC is to maximize shareholders value or wealth. Some scholars view shareholder value maximization as synonymous with lowest-cost profit maximization. There are different approaches to achieving this goal, depending on the country where the MNC operates. For instance, the capacity of shareholders to influence company decisions differs between Europe and the US. In general, Europe is more block-holder oriented (stakeholders > shareholders), while the US is more market oriented (shareholder > stakeholder).

MNCs might face conflicts and difficulties in reaching the abovementioned objectives. Two particular obstacles should be emphasized: agency problems and both internal and external interfering forces and challenges.

Agency problems and how to overcome them

In this section of the chapter, we will look at how an MNC's organizational structure is vulnerable to the risk that management would prioritize its own interests above the interests of shareholders. An agency issue is a conflict of interest between principals (shareholders and the main firm) and agents (subsidiary management).

The agency's costs can be monitored through management style and corporate control

The technique for accomplishing corporate goals is known as management control. To accomplish a given aim, employees inside a business organization are limited or prevented from conducting certain actions. Different management styles in multinational businesses may have an impact on the size of agency expenditures. In some management styles, all decisions may be reserved for the holding company, allowing it to directly manage all ultimate shareholder interests and thereby reducing agency costs. In other management styles, the approach may be more collaborative between the parent company and the subsidiaries, with significant decision-making delegated to local managers, which can increase the management efficiency of the multinational while exposing it to the risk of increased agency costs. Various corporate controls may assist managers in avoiding the agency dilemma and making decisions that benefit the company's shareholders (i.e., stock options plans). In these procedures, the risk of a hostile takeover and the engagement of experienced investors are crucial. The market may be eager to acquire undervalued enterprises that have been mishandled. Furthermore, institutional investors with large shares in a multinational company's stock, such as mutual funds or pension funds, may petition the board of directors to replace the company's management. Because they have no desire to pro-actively influence company governance or management, these qualified investors are referred to as passive investors. Active shareholders, on the other hand, seek to influence business decisions via their voting rights, while passive shareholders are fundamentally governance-dependent investors. Active investors keep a close eye on their investments and are ready to persuade other shareholders to make the adjustments required to increase the value of their stock (as for example the substitution of non-aligned and underperforming managers in a distant subsidiary).

In situations in which shareholders differ from managers, agency problems may arise.[9] Agency costs are internal costs that arise because of irreconcilable conflicts of interest among managers and shareholders within a corporation. Jensen and Meckling (1976)[10] define agency costs as costs caused by the divergence of interests between owners and managers and group them as 1) monitoring expenditures by the principal, 2) bonding expenditures by the agent, and 3) residual loss.

The Enron fall

The failure of the energy company Enron in 2001 revealed how devastating the agency problem can be. Because of fraudulent accounting reports that made the stock unfairly overpriced, the company's officers and Board of directors – including the Chairman, CEO, and CFO – sold their Enron stock at higher rates. Thousands of stockholders lost millions after the scam was exposed.

Agency costs are usually larger for MNCs than for purely domestic firms, where other factors instead come into play. Communication and control issues arise in MNCs because of their vast sizes and the dispersion of their subsidiaries. If the choices made by the parent firm are at odds with the local culture, foreign managers may be tempted to hold off on implementing them. An important aspect of capital budgeting is how much to spend on a project (capital budgeting) and how much to invest in a subsidiary (subsidiary value). If subsidiaries had the option to decide on investments, their managers might come to different conclusions than those of their parent company: value created locally may not always be appreciable from a multinational perspective, since the NPV (*Net Present Value*) of a project has to be translated into the currency of the parent and some value may be offset by exchange rate costs (Madura, 2008).

When a business expands into a multinational organization, one of the most critical decisions it must make is how to structure its management between the parent company and its subsidiaries. There are two types of management systems: centralized and decentralized (regionalized) authority. Centralized management is an organizational system in which a small number of managers make the majority of choices that affect the subsidiaries located in diverse foreign nations. Decentralized organizations instead allow subsidiary company managers to define the strategic objectives followed in their nation. While the parent company's management retains overall power and create rules that impact the company's

---

[9] On the definition of Agency Theory, consider the following quote from Adam Smith: "The directors of such [joint-stock] companies, however, being the managers rather of other people's money than of their own, it cannot well be expected, that they should watch over it with the same anxious vigilance with which the partners in a private copartnery frequently watch over their own. Like the stewards of a rich man, they are apt to consider attention to small matters as not for their master's honour, and very easily give themselves a dispensation from having it. Negligence and profusion, therefore, must always prevail, more or less, in the management of the affairs of such a company." — Adam Smith (1776).

[10] Jensen, M. and Meckling, W. (1976): "Theory of the firm: managerial behavior, agency costs and ownership structure", *Journal of Financial Economics* 3, 305–360.

important choices, the majority of decision-making authority is given to the enterprise's decentralized departments.

There are many compelling reasons for businesses to centralize management, but there are also significant risks to going too far. A centralized company's senior management will have total control over training and product offerings and will be more likely to guarantee that the company's aims and basic values are upheld. Businesses often centralize when they wish to increase the consistency of their product's quality and standardize manufacturing. With an high degree of centralization, the managers of the parent company may make sub-optimal choices due to their lack of knowledge and proximity to the local markets and needs of the subsidiaries. Decentralization enables subsidiaries in other nations to be more accessible to their consumers. This results in more effective management choices since local managers have greater direct control over their daily responsibilities and may reward or discipline personnel to accomplish objectives. However, if some managers at lower-level subsidiaries lack the necessary skills, experience, education, or competence to run the firm, the multinational as a whole may suffer. Given the advantages and disadvantages of both models, most established businesses strive to blend both. This balance permits branches to make important decisions while requiring parent management to review and approve big expenditures on a frequent basis.

Source: Sageder, M. & Feldbauer-Durstmüller, B. (2019). *Management control in multinational companies: a systematic literature review. Rev Manag Sci*, 13, 875-918. https://doi.org/10.1007/s11846-018-0276-1

The magnitude of agency costs varies significantly with a MNC's management style, since there are different ways to organize such companies and each organizational structure has inherent trade-offs (Madura, 2008):

- *Centralized Model*: All decisions (cash management, finance, investments) are made by the parent company. This obviously reduces agency problems, since more control is given to the central component of the company. Yet it might be impossible to correctly assess the potential benefits of projects because local management has more thorough knowledge of the environment and culture.
- *Regionalized Model*: In this model, a business maintains its headquarters in one nation and controls a network of offices situated in other countries. In contrast to the centralized model, the regionalized model has subsidiaries and affiliates that all report to the corporate headquarters. Corporate decisions are made directly by subsidiaries, but this might increase agency costs. There could be a trade-off between creating value abroad and the difficulties in repatriating that value
- *Balance between the two models*: Analysis of potential projects is performed by the subsidiary without the need of approval up to a certain amount of money. This allows subsidiary managers to make key decisions for their respective operations, but these decisions are monitored by parent company management. Recent developments in technologies and network solutions make this monitoring activity by the parent company easier and more feasible. The main advantage of centralization for multinational companies is the ability to adopt a global strategy. In contrast, regionalization affords subsidiaries a high degree of autonomy. An efficient business strategy is probably one that takes advantage of both centralized and decentralized approaches to business.

Acting on structural drivers could represent a solution to the above-mentioned problems. Corporate control for instance might indirectly reduce agency problems (Madura, 2008).

- MNCs might provide incentives to align the interests of subsidiary managers with those of parent company executives. Stock options are often provided to senior management, members of a company's board of directors, or workers as an incentive tool. These plans provide the employee the right to acquire (or dispose of) securities representing the company's risk capital if previously issued stock is used or to subscribe to securities representing the company's risk capital if freshly issued stock is used. Employee options are comparable to American-style call options in that they offer the right to acquire stocks within a certain time period (option expiry) and at a predetermined price (strike price). The manager who gets the option offer, which is usually at or below the strike price, has the chance to make a financial gain if the stock price rises above the strike price at some time after the options are given. Otherwise, the alternatives lose their entire worth. Stock option programs often involve many phases in which the employee may select whether or not to exercise his or her option and acquire the shares provided at a specified price. Three major phases can be identified: i) the granting phase, in which the company grants its employees the right to purchase a certain number of shares in a predetermined future time frame and at a predetermined price; ii) vesting, which is the period between the offer of the stock option and the start of the period for exercising the option right; and iii) exercise, the phase during which the choice right is used[11].

- Undermanaged companies are at risk of being targeted for hostile takeover. A hostile takeover occurs when one company (referred to as the acquiring company or "acquirer") decides to buy another company (referred to as the target company or "target") despite objections from the target company's board of directors. A hostile takeover is the inverse of a friendly takeover, in which all parties are amicable and work collectively toward a same goal. Acquiring businesses conducting a hostile takeover use a variety of strategies to win control of their targets. Making a direct tender offer to shareholders or participating in a proxy war to change the target company's management are two examples. The possibility of hostile takeovers grows more intense when the market recognizes that a certain firm is poorly managed; hence, this risk is greater in publicly traded corporations. If a firm fails to produce value for its shareholders, the market will reduce its valuation and it may be vulnerable to hostile takeovers. Out of fear of losing their employment, management will attempt to give a firm a high value. Some nations have legislation in place to safeguard indigenous firms against hostile takeovers. Sophisticated shareholders and institutional investors are able to indirectly influence the way a corporation is managed when they do not control the company.

---

[11] https://www.borsaitaliana.it/notizie/sotto-la-lente/stockoption203.htm

This practice began in the United States in the 1980s with corporate raiders, who are regarded as the forefathers of today's activists. Aggressive, ruthless, and asset strippers, they used to acquire businesses, dismantle them, and profit from the resulting trades. Nowadays, activists confront management and strive to alter the status quo without affecting the firm's control (Gigante et al., 2021).

Additional interfering forces and challenges

Aside from agency problems, an MNC might encounter additional challenges or forces that prevent or limit its expansionary designs. These constraints can be grouped in two categories: internal challenges and external challenges (Fox, 2017).

- *In-house difficulties:* An example would be investor activism, or the influence of hedge funds, institutional investors, and other sophisticated shareholders over minority stockholders. For instance, the sale of a significant stake in the company to a competitor may trigger a tender offer. Shareholder activism is most common in the US, whereas it is less frequent in Europe.
- *External problems:* These include regulatory restrictions (taxes, currency convertibility, etc.) imposed by domestic policies or regimes in host countries. They may also include ethical issues, since there is no standard business conduct that applies in all cases all over the world, or environmental issues (building codes, pollution caps, etc.). In terms of ethical issues, it is important to take into account interference relating to corruption. Such issues augment a firm's costs of doing business. Moreover, if these external limitations are not respected, the reputation of the company, an MNC's most important asset, could be jeopardized. For instance, if an MNC is accused of destructive practices such as polluting, environmental negligence, or corruption, the damage to the company can be highly detrimental.
    - A further external problem that can become an obstacle for MNCs in globalization activities is distance, which also magnifies the cost of activities abroad. Distance is not just measured in terms of geography but also in terms of culture (including language, ethnicity, religion, etc.). Investment flows or operations in different countries are more likely to occur in companies or among investors in countries that are relatively less distant. For instance, in two countries where the majority of the population speaks the same language.
    - Host country governments, policies, and regulations can be quite complex to navigate. It is worth noting that there is ongoing debate over the fact that MNCs in certain sectors can easily secure greater levels of protection for themselves than in other industries. For instance, if they are important to the economy of a specific host nation, elected governments may make economic and political decisions to ensure stable environments for their activities. Moreover, some MNCs have higher bargaining power with some national governments (especially in developing countries), where they may be able to influence and sometimes control domestic policy outcomes by threatening to move jobs elsewhere.

Environmental, cultural, ethical, and legal differences among the parent and the various subsidiaries

Interactions between headquarters and subsidiaries can be sought and controlled along a number of dimensions, including knowledge exchange and resource allocation within the company, decision making and strategy creation, and coordination and control of activities.

Collaboration with managers in the various subsidiaries, as well as understanding of the environmental, cultural, ethical, and legal differences among the home and host countries of the various subsidiaries are important to developing, acquiring, synthesizing, learning, sharing, and applying knowledge in a manner that achieves the company's overall goals and provides competitive advantage.

To successfully expand businesses, it is crucial to understand the environmental factors that influence international business. Environmental forces pertain to the economic, natural, technological, political, and legal environment (Ball & McCulloch, 1996). These forces are uncontrollable since they are externally driven factors. Therefore, it is necessary to investigate how such issues affect the operation of the company.

Mahoney et al. (2001) state that the term "culture" refers to the set of values, attitudes, beliefs, behaviors, and conventions that define a civilization. Culture is acquired and shared by members of the same social group, and the components of culture are inextricably linked. Culture clearly defines the boundaries of a group. Any large civilization may have several subcultures that share a common environment. Culture influences decision making, strategic management actions, and even negotiations. As mentioned above, cultural differences pose problems for MNCs when it comes to managing staff and interacting with the host country government. The MNC therefore must keep its business in line with the norms of the local culture to be successful. Cross-cultural literacy is the ability to understand another culture. Business professionals must not only understand the foreign cultures where they operate but also adjust and adapt their conduct to fit them. Cultural differences can generate ethical dilemmas. For example, what is considered acceptable behavior in one culture may be considered unethical in another (Mahoney et al., 2001).

According to Mayer et al. (2010), corporations must also address the legal issues presented by domestic and foreign laws, regional regulations or directives, bilateral and multilateral treaties, and international standards and certifications. The defining characteristics of international law are fairly straightforward: firms operating around the world are subject to bilateral and multilateral treaties ratified by states engaged in global trade, as well as the specific laws of the host countries in which they operate. When companies do business in host countries, they may also be forced to follow the laws of their own countries. In addition to the power to establish and enforce laws within their borders, all nation states retain the right to enact and enforce laws that apply to their residents (or "citizens") regardless of where they reside or do business. This means that for U.S.-based multinational corporations, U.S. antitrust, anti-corruption, and equal employment opportunity laws often apply to their international operations. The political and legal systems in which a company works are important to its performance, as MNC managers often learn in host nations where they face "public officials," chaotic or nonexistent systems of property rights, or complicated (or opaque) rules (Mayer et al., 2010).

A well-designed MNC control system should therefore allow for adaptability and responsiveness to the environment of the foreign country in which the subsidiary operates. A challenging task for senior management in MNCs is to create a control structure that helps both the parent company and its subsidiaries, while keeping the overall competitiveness of the group high. In other words, if the subsidiaries feel that a strategic process and associated control mechanism are acceptable, they will be more inclined to accept it. Branch managers see a business strategy as more attractive when it reflects the diverse interests of the branches, which are not completely ignored for the greater good represented by the business objectives of the group as a whole. In this way, the planning process is seen as fairer and easier to execute in subsidiaries, which simplifies monitoring activities by the parent company.

Case MNCs in China in the long run

Over the years, China has been an extremely attractive hotspot for MNCs to kick off new business opportunities and grow. However, as the Chinese economy develops, MNCs are slowly dis-
covering that some of the advantages they once found particularly attractive about that market
are diminishing. Indeed, China needs to find new ways to attract MNCs – the question is, will
MNCs still go to China for the same reasons as in the past, or for new ones?
Below is a description of the negative and positive changes MNCs face in China:

- *Negative changes*: As China's economy and populations are growing, two trends are negatively impacting MNCs. The first is the rising cost of labor, and hence of production, due to
  an uptick in national minimum wages. As a result, MNCs that sought to enter China for its
  relatively cheaper labor will find the situation is changing. A further shift is represented by
  the steep and astonishing growth of local Chinese firms, which, because of the establishment
  of MNCs over the years, have been able to glean knowledge and expertise. The rise of local
  Chinese firms is thus making it harder for MNCs to compete.
- *Positive changes*: On the contrary, while the above-mentioned trends have a negative impact
  on MNC activity in China, the country has also experienced some positive changes which
  might alter the reasons why MNCs decide to do business there in the future. Firstly, China is
  starting to become less lenient with regulations: as the government enforces control and seizure of counterfeit goods – closing counterfeit garment markets and imposing heavier fines
  and accountability for e-commerce websites selling counterfeit goods – MNCs are better
  protected and can operate in China more safely. A further improvement that might encourage
  more MNC business in China in the long run are the country's massive investments to improve infrastructure and transportation. Indeed, the urbanization of non-populated areas will
  make them more accessible, opening up more markets for MNCs.

1.2.4   Rationale behind internationalization: Theories of international business

As should now be clear, there is no one-size-fits-all approach to studying internationalization and there
is no single success formula that can be applied to a company. The most recent models for internationalization attempt to identify consensus in the literature and in the business sector and to identify features
that seem to be vital. However, no one model accounts for the many realities and demands that exist in
businesses, especially at a time when markets and challenges are ever changing.

According to the most important and widely accepted scholarly literature on the topic, theories supporting the internationalization of a firm can be considered "*classical*," or based on nation states, or "*modern*," based on the strategies of the enterprises.

a) Classical theories (pre-Hymer)

These theories developed in sixteenth century Europe with the establishment of the first "nation states"
and emphasize individual nations. They were conceived to explain international movements of products
and capital and intended to depict trade in goods based on price differentials. According to absolute
advantage theory (Smith, 1776), a nation should export products and services where it has a higher
productivity (output per hour), and it should import goods and services where it has a lower productivity.
According to Ricardo's (1911) fundamental theory of comparative advantage, a nation benefits by exporting products and services where it has a comparative productivity advantage and purchase goods and

services from countries with a comparable comparative advantage with respect to it. This is the opportunity cost, or the value forfeited in order to get a product. Each nation has the benefit of specializing in its
area of expertise. Ricardo's comparative advantage is thus contrasted with Smith's absolute advantage.
Absolute advantage refers to the ability to produce more or better goods and services than someone else.
Comparative advantage refers to the ability to produce goods and services at a lower opportunity cost,
not necessarily at a higher volume or quality. Ricardo's theory implies that comparative advantage rather
than absolute advantage is responsible for much of international trade.

We will discuss the classical theories of comparative advantage[12] and the imperfect
market.[13] The theory of *comparative advantage* rests on the idea that each nation
should specialize in the production and exportation of the goods it can produce with
highest relative efficiency and that it should import the goods that other nations can
produce relatively more efficiently. The underlying idea is to take into account national and economic factors when making an internationalization decision. For example, it is widely acknowledged that some countries are better than others at certain activities: the United States is a forerunner in innovation and technology, Asian
countries are pioneers in importing raw materials and providing low-cost manufacturing, etc. This is the foundation of the comparative advantage theory, which holds
that country specialization can increase production efficiency.

This theory has some limitations in today's world. To begin with, the theory is
based on the assumption that while goods and services can move internationally,
production factors such as capital, labor, and land are relatively immobile. It also
deals with commodity trading (undifferentiated products), ignoring the impact of uncertainty, economies of scale, transportation costs, and technology in international
trade. Furthermore, nations are becoming increasingly homogeneous in terms of living standards, lifestyles, and economic organization, while natural resources have
diminished in importance, capital moves at incredible speeds around the world, and
labor skills can no longer be considered fundamentally different. As a result, the
ability of corporations of all sizes to use these globally available factors of production is a far more important determinant of international competitiveness than broad
macroeconomic differences between countries.

Of course, the value added in a specific country is determined by differences in
labor costs as well as by unique national characteristics or skills. Although trade in
goods, capital, and services, as well as the ability to shift production, help to limit
cost and skill disparities among nations, differences persist due to cultural preferences, historical accidents, and government policies. Each of these factors can have
an impact on the nature of the competitive advantages enjoyed by various countries
and their businesses.

---

[12] In economics, a comparative advantage occurs when a country can produce and offer a good or
service at a lower opportunity cost than another country. The theory of comparative advantage is attributed to political economist David Ricardo, who wrote the book *Principles of Political Economy and
Taxation* (1817).

[13] Because of imperfect markets, resources cannot be easily and freely accessed by the MNC. Consequently, the MNC must sometimes go to the resources rather than retrieve resources.

The *imperfect markets theory* holds that factors of production are immobile, and countries specialize in what they have. The focus here lies more on the idea that markets for the various resources used in production are "imperfect." As such, these markets are characterized by information asymmetry, government intervention, barriers to the entry and exit of firms, and differentiated products. Leveraging on this "imperfectness" is presented as a key to success.

In the past, MNCs were also discussed within the broader scope of *trade theories*, since these enterprises were regarded as components in the long-term capital section of a country's balance of payments and seen as facilitating one type of capital export (i.e., FDI). However, one of the limitations of this approach to MNCs is the fact that there is no exact match between FDI and MNC growth.

b) Modern theories (post-Hymer)

These theories were developed after World War II, with the emergence of major global enterprises. The emphasis in these theories shifted to individual enterprises and the idea of corporate advantage took on central importance. Here the focus is on the trade of distinct items with the corporate brand playing a significant role in the purchase process. According to Vernon (1966), enterprises based in countries with a highly developed outlet market have an "innovation edge" that enables them to predict demand from other countries. Vernon identifies different stages to this life cycle.

The first stage (product introduction to the domestic market) involves the introduction of a novel and non-standardized product where the product's design is currently unknown, and production procedures are being investigated, with cost optimization being a major concern. At this stage, there is considerable ambiguity about the market's eventual size, its competitiveness, and the product specifications that will prevail. It is critical for the company to be adaptable, to experiment with different models and raw resources, and to learn.

The second stage (development) involves the establishment of a fundamental standard, though this does not guarantee uniformity, since product varieties and variants might grow. Demand increases at a fast pace. Scale economies are sought and established. Cost becomes critical. Other nations begin to see an increase in demand for the product and exports increase along with foreign investment in production facilities established in those countries where demand for the product has become significant.

Domestic sales stabilize in the third stage (maturity), with costs that become crucial and the manufacture is relocated to countries with low labor cost. Additionally, imitation processes grow in other nations, allowing local companies to join the industry.

Finally, in the fourth and final stage (decline), demand for the product reaches its peak and becomes stable or declining around the world. Imitation processes are now complete, both in the country of origin and in foreign countries, and the technology is fully mature, standardized, and completely accessible to local imitators.

Source: Melin, L. (1992). Internationalization as a strategy process. *Strategic Management Journal*, 13(S2), 99-118.

Modern theories, like the product cycle theory, turn attention to the life cycle of a firm. The premise is that at the beginning a firm is mainly focused on the domestic market and meeting local demand. As foreign demand increases, and as the firm continues to be successful, the company will start expanding abroad to better meet demand. Most companies start their foreign production in a country with a good reputation for cheaper manufacturing, like in China and India.

Hymer's *industrial organization theories* similarly shifted focus from the nation to the firm. Hymer considered what happened in a world dominated by domestic monopolists when lower transportation costs and trade barriers bring two of them into contact. He argued that competition between these two firms would generate (pecuniary) externalities, which a merger of these two firms or the acquisition of one by the other (the creation of a firm spanning the two countries, i.e., an MNC) would internalize. This could explain the creation of MNCs.

Hymer's model (1960)

In his doctoral dissertation, Hymer (1960) clearly identifies the main causes of internationalization for companies, citing in particular the possibility of exerting control over other enterprises, thus making it possible to reduce competition, and the exploitation of certain competitive advantages which the multinational holds and which it can leverage by expanding abroad. Hymer's approach, unlike Vernon's, focuses then on the company rather than the product. In the first phase of its lifecycle, the firm expands domestically through a process of concentration which enables it to make increasing profits. When home country investment opportunities are exhausted, a multinational could exploit its advantages related to market imperfections.

Hymer lists a number of potential advantages for MNCs, including, among others, scale economies, knowledge advantages, distribution networks, credit advantage, product diversification and innovativeness. Given these benefits, the company will choose between exporting or producing locally, depending on the market circumstances in which it will operate. Foreign market obstacles, such as high transportation costs, tend to tip the scales in favor of local producers. The multinational will have to decide whether to intervene directly or offer licenses to local producers. Direct intervention will be recommended especially if the multinational's competitive advantages are based on ownership of specialized know-how and other intangible assets that are difficult to transfer properly with licenses. The extension of the company to a foreign country is therefore for Hymer nothing other than a phase in the development in the geographic and economic growth of the company itself. He proposes the theory of oligopoly and the modern theory of the formation and development of large multi-divisional firms as interpretative keys. To sum up then, the doctoral thesis of the Canadian economist Stephen Hymer entitled *The International Operations of National Firms: A Study of Foreign Direct Investment*, can be considered as the beginning of the development of a modern theory on multinational firms, as it had the merit of shifting the discussion from foreign direct investment based on a neoclassical financial theory to a model mainly based on the firm itself and on the analysis of its strategic investments abroad.[14]

---

[14] ".... Two main causes of international operations are given in this thesis. (1) Firms control enterprices in many countries in order to remove competition between them when the enterprices sell in the same market or sell to each other under conditions of imperfect competition, (2) Firms undertake operations in a foreign country in order to appreciate fully the returns to certain abilities which they possess. They choose this method rather than an alternative method such as licensing because the imperfections in the market prevent the fullest realization of profits unlsess the firm excercises some control. These two causes help explain the extent of international operations, but they do not predict it exactly..." from the abstract of Hymer, S. (1960). *The International Operations of National Firms: A Study of Foreign Direct Investment.* Ph.D. dissertation, MIT, published by MIT Press under the same title in 1976.

Hymer's thesis was therefore that MNCs internalize externalities due to competition in markets for final products. In other words, as firms compete with one another, they lower the price they can charge consumers and end up giving up their monopoly profits. While there is no doubt that in some cases an MNC is set up to limit competition (via M&As or greenfield investments), Hymer's theory does not provide a set of necessary and sufficient reasons for the emergence and development of MNCs.

Another interesting theory to explain the rise of MNCs is the *transaction cost theory*. Transaction cost theory centers on the problem of organizing interdependencies among individuals. These individuals can generate rents by pooling together different or similar capabilities. Transaction cost theory argues that firms arise when they are the most efficient institutions to organize these interdependencies. Likewise, MNCs thrive when they are more efficient than markets and contracts in organizing interdependencies among agents located in different countries, and, if the benefits of organizing interdependencies within the firm are higher than their costs. These interdependencies can involve know-how and knowledge, reputation, raw materials, and components.

Theory of internalization and transaction costs

Contributions from several authors over the years have investigated the many reasons why exploiting the advantage of internalizing activities within the firm was superior to exploiting the advantage through market-based activities. In the late 1930s, Coase (1937) introduced a notion of the firm as an efficient structure that replaced the market in the organization of economic commerce under certain circumstances. Buckley and Casson (1976) similarly see the MNC as an "internal market," or mechanism for allocating resources among internationally decentralized units that facilitate the removal of economic, social, and international defects and impediments. Thus, MNCs can increase the overall efficiency of the production system when their internal coordination costs are lower than those of the market. Hennart (1982) concentrated on corporations' greater capacity to coordinate and manage international resources, especially labor. Williamson, Caves, and Teece (1985) included internationalization in a broader theory of transaction costs and explained how the market can be an inefficient transaction governance structure compared to non-market mechanisms which, in extreme situations, lead to the complete internalization of transactions, with the emergence of the multinational firm that is efficient because of its ability to coordinate, control, adapt, and monitor relational activities and behaviors.

Source: Pitelis, C.N. & Teece, D.J. (2018). The new MNE: 'Orchestration' theory as envelope of 'internalisation' theory. *Management International Review*, 58(4), 523-539.

1.2.5   Global business strategies

So far, this chapter has discussed different taxonomies for considering firms operating abroad, but nothing has been mentioned yet about the methods a firm can use to conduct international business. Before looking into the different methodologies listed below (Madura, 2008), it is important to note that studies of corporate expansion abroad indicate that firms become multinationals by degree – with foreign direct investment being a later step in a process that begins with exports. Indeed, companies usually gradually intensify their commitment to international business, developing strategies that are progressively more elaborate and sophisticated.

> Walmart is an American retailer whose operations are spread across the globe. In fact, from the beginning the company chose to expand its operations not only across the United States but also globally. Currently, the company is present in 28 countries, operating over 11,000 outlets and aligning its strategies with globalization forces. This US firm thus sells products around the world at cheap prices, importing from China and being connected with manufacturing companies abroad.

- *International trade* is defined as the sale and purchase of goods and services across national borders. Businesses that want to take a cautious and low-cost approach to international commerce might do so by merely exporting or importing items rather than investing in foreign markets. The internet has made international trading easier by enabling companies to market and handle orders on their websites. Exporting has several benefits, including, as previously said, cheap capital needs, low risk, instant earnings, and the chance to learn about the market in preparation for greater future investments. The inability to fulfill a product's full sales potential, on the other hand, might be a big disadvantage.

> Nike Inc. (formerly Blue Ribbon Sports) is a well-known American athletic shoe, equipment, and apparel company. Nike products are produced employing 1.1 million people. Most of Nike's factories are outsourced, which means that they do not own them but rather 'contract' them to produce. This produces the question: Where on Earth is Nike Made? The answer is in 41 nations and 533 different factories in Vietnam, China, Japan, Indonesia, Thailand, and Italy, among other nations. Because of the inexpensive cost of labor in Asia, Nike has all of its key plants there.

- *Overseas Production* instead refers to a manufacturing process carried out in another nation. Among the positives to this strategy are a company's capacity to respond to market changes, modify its products and production schedules to changing local tastes and conditions, and provide quicker and more complete after-sales service. Additionally, this approach displays a greater commitment to the worldwide market. Naturally, the issue of whether a firm should develop its own affiliates or acquire them is a consequence of worldwide production. Despite the benefits, manufacturing in other nations has drawbacks. Though manufacturing abroad is often a financially viable option, it does entail some obstacles. Since overseas manufacturers often demand an additional fee for distribution outside their home country, shipping costs tend to be greater, delivery times might be lengthy, and import taxes may be higher. When items are created abroad, quality control and human contact are harmed, and Covid, which has made international mobility more difficult, has exacerbated several problems. Negotiating contracts and price, comprehending processes and ethics, and recognizing other cultural differences may also be challenging. Having on-site representation, whether a local resident or someone fluent in the language and intimately connected with the local culture, enables firms to more effectively monitor their interests.

"(a) An example would include Walt Disney granting McDonalds a license for McDonalds to co-brand its Happy Meals with a Disney trademarked character; (b) A license where a technology company, as licensor, grants a license to an individual or company, as licensee, to use a particular technology."[15]

- *Licensing* entails no major investment abroad but rather the sale of patents, copyrights, or trademarks in exchange for fees and royalties. It allows a firm to provide its technology in exchange for fees or some other benefits. This method is widely used by pharmaceutical companies, which can sell the right to produce a drug to foreign companies in exchange for royalties. This approach, apart from requiring minimal investment, also enables faster market-entry time and fewer financial and legal risks. However, the maintenance of quality standards and controls can be an issue.

The French supermarket chain and international corporation Carrefour, founded in 1959, is one of Europe's largest supermarket chains. To open a Carrefour franchise, the following requirements must be met:
- *Experience in management*, ideally gained in the distribution sector;
- Desire to become an *independent entrepreneur* and business owner;
- High availability and geographical *mobility*;
- An *initial investment*.
The franchise agreement is usually signed for a *duration* of 7 years and is automatically renewable.

- *Franchising* requires no initial investment but obliges a firm to provide specialized sales or service strategy, support assistance, and possibly a small initial investment in the franchise in exchange for periodic fees.

Honda, for example, started the sale of scooters in India by establishing a joint venture with a local company.

- Firms may also go international by engaging in a *joint venture* with firms in target markets, i.e., creating a company with joint ownership and operation. This can be advantageous for firms wanting to expand in a country where there are no other alternatives. For example, if a company is not incorporated in China but wants to operate in the country, it has to start a joint venture with a local partner, usually owned or influenced by the government.

Luxottica is an Italian company that decided in 1999 to expand internationally, specifically to the US market. To do so, it could opt to either establish subsidiaries or acquire an American company and list its stock on the NYSE. The latter option was chosen as it was considered a quicker path to growth. Luxottica acquired Ray-Ban and was listed on the NYSE, which was also seen as a way to support its aim of growth in the US market. A company has to pass various tests by regulators before being listed on this exchange.

- *Acquisitions of existing operations* in foreign countries allow firms to quickly gain control over foreign operations as well as a share of the foreign market. This

---

[15] https://www.franchiselawsolutions.com

is a quick way to expand in a new market, offering full control of a company in-corporated abroad. However, this option also gives rise to issues linked to the val-uation of the target company (i.e., synergies, premiums for control, cross-border issues) if a company is multinational.

> Setting up a subsidiary in a foreign nation may offer a number of advantages, including increased brand recognition, access to new markets, and cost management via the use of efficient manufac-turing processes. Increased income and corporate development may be achievable in a new location that would not be viable in the home nation.

- The *establishment of foreign subsidiaries* is another way to penetrate distant mar-kets. Unlike M&As, this approach does not involve the risk of destroying val-ue (in most cases acquisitions turn out to be excessively expensive). Establishing foreign subsidiaries is a tailor-made transaction over which the parent has full control. However, it is a slow process. Nevertheless, in order to begin a viable en-deavor in a new nation, a firm must examine aspects such as the costs and effort required to create a foreign subsidiary, its policy for remuneration and other HR concerns, and compliance risks for payroll, taxes, and citizenship requirements. It must also establish safe office buildings, staff housing, and checking balances, evaluate growth opportunities against the needed expenditures, and stabilize in-stallation difficulties.

> The purchase of Tetley by Tata Tea in early 2000 was the first big LBO (perhaps the first ever LBO) established by an Indian corporation. Tata Tea established Tata Tea (GB) Limited in the UK, a special purpose vehicle (SPV). Tata Tea Limited invested GBP 71 million in this SPV.

- The incorporation of a *Special Purpose Vehicle* (SPV) is an alternative to an M&A and or the establishment of subsidiaries and consists of the creation of a new company that is separate from the original corporation. Since in this case there is no control by the parent company, the parent company is also not affected if something goes wrong. SPVs are extensively engaged in LBO transactions.

In general, any method of conducting business that requires a direct investment in foreign operations is referred to as a foreign direct investment (FDI[16]). More precise-ly, an FDI could create an SPV or acquire or establish subsidiaries. To be defined as FDI, ownership interest of at least 10% is required. The optimal international busi-ness method to be used may depend on the characteristics of the MNC.

---

[16] "Foreign direct investment (FDI) is a category of cross-border investment in which an investor resident in one economy establishes a lasting interest in and a significant degree of influence over an enterprise resident in another economy. Ownership of 10 percent or more of the voting power in an enter-prise in one economy by an investor in another economy is evidence of such a relationship. FDI is a key element in international economic integration because it creates stable and long-lasting links between economies. FDI is an essential channel for the transfer of technology between countries, it promotes international trade through access to foreign markets, and can be an important vehicle for economic development. The indicators covered in this group are inward and outward values for stocks, flows and income, by partner country and by industry and FDI restrictiveness." Cited from the OECD Library.

1.2.6   International opportunities and risks

In general, there are two types of financial management opportunities for an MNC with regards to foreign expansion:

- *Investment opportunities*: Because of the expanded opportunity set of possible projects from which to choose, the marginal return on projects for an MNC is higher than for purely domestic firms. The allocation of funds over time to maximize shareholder wealth is the focus of investment decisions.
- *Financing opportunities*: Because of its larger opportunity set of funding sources around the world, an MNC can obtain capital funding at a lower cost. Financing decisions involve generating funds from internal or external sources at the lowest possible long-run cost.

In some cases, macroeconomic conditions may encourage international opportunities to materialize. In Europe, for example, the Single European Act (1987), the fall of the Berlin Wall (1989), and the introduction of the euro (1999) were all significant events that accelerated internationalization. In America, the North American Free Trade Agreement (NAFTA, 1993) and the General Agreement on Tariffs and Trade (GATT, 1947) played similar roles. In Asia, the 1990s liberalization of investment restrictions, the Chinese growth potential, and the Asian economic crisis of 1997–98 were all critical.

Nonetheless, it is important to remember that while implementing internationalization plans, MNCs must adopt suitable financial and promote maximum shareholder value (the main objective of the firm, measured via its share price). Risks accompany opportunities. International business often increases an MNC's exposure to exchange rate swings (which may affect cash flows and overseas demand), foreign economic circumstances (which can also affect demand), and political risk (which can impact cash flows).

These risks, which we will describe in detail in the next chapters, must be included in a DCF (*Discounted Cash Flow*) valuation. In this scenario, the first two factors are represented by the modification of expected cash flows, while the last is reflected in the discount rate. It is critical to assess these factors and include them in the valuation model, since improper or incorrect assessment of such risks may result in misrepresentative outcomes.

In addition to the concerns stated above, it is important to consider the function of geographical benefits. MNCs may have location disadvantages compared to indigenous enterprises in host nations (for example, linguistic and cultural obstacles, a lack of understanding of the local socioeconomic and business system, expropriation threats, and so on), which may be summed up as liability of foreignness (Hymer, 1968).

1.3   The implications of internationalization for the valuation of MNCs

The scope of business valuation goes beyond valuing a domestic corporation to include placing a value on a multinational corporation. This section of the chapter examines aspects key to the valuation of a multinational corporation. The formulation of a discount rate and the cost of capital will be discussed in chapters 4 and 5 of the book.

Recognizing the relevance of the three pillars of growth, risk, and profitability is foundational to any business valuation and even more important for companies that operate internationally. When evaluating a multinational company, the due diligence process should be expanded to include lines of inquiry that seek information in all countries that are part of the company's scope of operations. A due diligence framework should consider analysis of the country, currency, industry, and country risk of each individual subsidiary. The multinational company will also inevitably be exposed to foreign exchange gains or losses because of its portfolio of offshore subsidiaries, which sometimes will have operations in emerging markets, exposing it even more to the volatility of various local currencies. Currency is a significant contributor to risk, and the multinational firm might strategically decide to accumulate some type of strong, stable currency in its offshore affiliates while at least partially reducing its exposure to foreign country risk.

Now that we have introduced the topic of multinational companies, the challenges they face, and the objectives that drive their internationalization strategies, we need to discuss what internationalization means from a financial standpoint and how it affects the valuation of MNCs compared to domestic firms.

Like domestic projects, foreign ones involve investment and financing decisions. When managers make multinational financial decisions that maximize a firm's overall present value of cash flows, they maximize its value and therefore shareholder wealth.

There are two methods that can be used to calculate firm value: intrinsic firm value (DCF) and value derived from comparables (multiples).

Intrinsic valuation refers to the process of determining the value of something from the inside out, performing an analysis of the cash flows produced by the company (DCF). Multinational companies are valued based on the same factors that determine the value of any other type of company: cash flows from existing assets, expected growth rate, associated risk, and the expected time period for the analysis.

As stated in Damodaran (2009), when valuing the outstanding assets of a multinational corporation, three types of problems are common:

- Aggregate profits arise from investments made for activities carried out by subsidiaries in different countries around the world with their own currencies, risk characteristics, and investment opportunities.
- Earnings, broken down by branch, are influenced by expense allocation decisions that usually involve a centrally decided budget and not just the unique characteristics of each local branch. Not only can growth rates vary significantly across branches in different countries, but the quality of growth can also change significantly.
- We need information on two essential factors to provide an accurate assessment of the value of growth: the amounts (and rates) of reinvestment made by each for-

eign subsidiary and the returns earned on the capital invested in each company. While obtaining this information for a single company is difficult enough, it is even more so in complex companies where capital expenditures are often aggregated at the corporate level and the book values of capital at the divisional and foreign subsidiary levels are difficult to reconstruct.

There are two challenges in measuring risk (and the cost of capital) for a global company if different businesses have distinct risk characteristics and if operating in different regions of the world exposes companies to distinct national risks. The first step is to develop risk measures that are specific to each segment of the business, company, or country rather than to the multinational corporation as a whole (this problem will be explored further in Chapter 5). The second step is to determine the weights that should be assigned to each aspect of the business to arrive at a risk score for the overall organization. As the growth rates of various businesses fluctuate, the weights of those businesses will also fluctuate. Last but not least, a global company will produce cash flows in multiple currencies and often issue debt in numerous currencies, which creates complications for both discount rates and forecasting expected cash flows.

Moreover, the use of multiples will not easily allow for the identification of companies with a similar mix of assets and regional operations that could be used for comparison with the multinational whose enterprise value we are calculating (Damodaran, 2009).

Internationalization, like other strategic investments, may be then highly appealing. However, the risks that need to be taken into account in the valuation of enterprises and their investments vary depending on its business scope and degree of internationalization, since MNCs are exposed to a variety of risks related to their global positioning. Currency exchange swings, political uncertainty, financial issues, increased expenses, and a lack of understanding of new markets and customer expectations represent just a few of the numerous hazards.

For a domestic company, no adjustment for the aforementioned risks is required.

On the other hand, in an international environment, additional risks need to be kept in mind. Simply estimating cash flows for an international opportunity can be especially hard due to the challenges posed by foreign markets. One method for making this estimation is the home currency approach. In this case, a measure of exchange rate risk must be incorporated.

A second method is the foreign currency approach, which requires calculating the NPV based on the foreign country cost of capital. The foreign currency NPV then needs to be converted into the local currency using a spot exchange rate.

In either case, the cost of capital should reflect the perceived levels of risks involved and be adjusted accordingly. In addition to adjusting the cost of capital, scenario planning (i.e., creating a best, normal and worst-case scenario) is often a best-practice approach when dealing with uncertainty deriving from international foreign markets.

Comparing the international valuation and domestic valuation, it is clear that the net present value of the firm in the international context is going to factor in additional risks that are not present in a domestic environment such as the exposure to foreign economies, the exchange rate risk, and the political risk (Madura, 2008).

More considerations concerning the impact of internationalization on a company's valuation, financing, and investing decisions will be highlighted in subsequent chapters, particularly in Chapter 5, where the topic of cost of capital for multinational corporations will be analyzed in more detail.

1.4   Conclusions

By now the reader should have an initial overview of multinational companies (MNCs), foreign direct investment (FDI), and also the evolution of globalization with reference to both practical examples and theory. As we have seen, there is a wide range of classifications for enterprises that have business operations outside the country of their headquarters: international companies, multinational companies, global companies, and transnational companies. Each enterprise might have different drivers for operating in the international market and may adopt different strategies. MNCs may also face problems, including agency costs and internal and external challenges. Finally, MNCs are also exposed to additional risks, such as the exchange rate, which impact their overall valuation.

2   International Financial Markets

The growth of international businesses made evident the need to create several international financial markets where the new multinational corporations (MNCs) discussed in the previous chapter could operate. MNC managers now have access to a variety of international financial markets, and the funding they source there is a pivotal asset not only in cross-border transactions but also in terms of realizing the benefits of diversification. For example, MNCs use the foreign exchange market to exchange currencies. In this market, they can either exchange currencies for immediate delivery in the spot market or negotiate forward contracts in order to purchase or sell currencies at a future point in time in the forward market. Moreover, they also have access to both local and international money markets, credit markets, and stock and bond markets for borrowing short-term, medium-term, and/or long-term funds.

Each of these markets has different characteristics. Managers of MNCs should understand the differences among these various international financial markets available to them if they want to facilitate international business transactions and maximize the value of their corporations. Divergences among the various international financial markets (differing interest rates, currencies, regulations) create opportunities for MNC managers to lower their financing costs as much as possible. This line of reasoning hails back to the issue of imperfect markets and the asymmetry of information mentioned in the previous chapter. Effectively leveraging financial opportunities pivots upon exploiting such asymmetries. For example, an MNC could borrow on the international market when it expects foreign currencies to depreciate against its own or if it wants to capitalize on lower foreign interest rates. On the other hand, lenders provide credit in international financial markets to capitalize on higher interest rates, when they expect foreign currencies to appreciate against their own, or to reap the benefits of international diversification.

Note that differences among markets, and thus opportunities, are even more evident when dealing with specific geographic markets, since markets for real and financial assets are prevented from complete integration by various barriers (tax differentials, tariffs, quotas, labor immobility, communication costs, cultural diversity, and financial reporting differences). These markets attract foreign investors and creditors. Indeed, investors put their money in international financial markets to take advantage of favorable economic conditions when they expect foreign currencies to appreciate against their own or to reap the benefits of international diversification.

This chapter will dive deeper into the different financial markets that the manager of an MNC might have access to, exploring how these markets are structured and how to leverage them to identify the best possible source of financing. The chapter will begin by discussing the role of the foreign exchange market, its history, transactions, and interpretation. Finally, it will focus on the international money market for short term funds and analyze the European and Asian money markets. In addition, it will consider the international credit market for medium-term loans and the international stocks and bonds markets for long-term funds. Yet before addressing any of these topics, it will first touch upon two general notions that precede the consideration of any specific financial markets: the recent standardization of banking regulations around the world and the general MNC cash flow movements that require the use of different foreign markets.

2.1   The standardization of global banking regulations

With the development of international businesses and international financial markets, banking regulation became necessary to ensure the standardization of regulations across regions and promote the globalization of the banking industry. The two most significant regulatory events allowing for a more competitive global banking industry were the Single European Act and the Basel Accord.

2.1.1   The Single European Act

The European Union passed the Single European Act in 1992, thereby liberalizing the European banking sector. This legislation paved the way for greater market efficiency in the European banking industry by allowing banks to operate in other European nations without being bound by country-specific laws, as had previously been the case. The following provisions were particularly significant for the banking industry: money could move freely across Europe; banks could engage in a wide range of lending, leasing, and securities transactions across the European Union (EU); competition, mergers, and tax laws became consistent across the EU; and a bank incorporated in any EU nation had the freedom to expand into any or all other EU countries (Madura, 2008).

Moreover, in 2012, the European Council outlined proposals to create a Banking Union. This was part of a program with the dual aims of helping to resolve problems in Europe's financial system and creating a more resilient financial system. There were two main underlying ideas behind the proposals. First, the belief that the responsibility for bank supervision should be managed at a European level (i.e., with the European Central Bank [ECB]). Second, the idea that standard mechanisms should be put in place to facilitate bank resolutions and insure customer deposits. The three main proposals included the establishment of a:

• *Single Supervisory Mechanism* (SSM) bearing both an EU and a national dimension. Part of the process of moving towards an SSM involved regulatory reform of the European Banking Authority (EBA) to adapt it to the new situation, establishment of new rules on capital regulation (the EU's Capital Requirements Regulation), and adoption of the fourth Capital Requirements Directive (CRD IV). The objective here was to implement a single harmonized supervisory rulebook based on Basel III rather than on divergent national arrangements.

- *European resolution scheme* (ERS) mainly funded by banks. This framework could provide assistance and/or support in applying measures to banks subject to European supervision. The key objective was to provide a mechanism for the orderly shutdown of non-viable banks, in order to protect taxpayer bailouts.
- *European deposit insurance scheme* (EDIS) to ensure that bank deposits are seen as equally safe in any EU or Euro member country, since if capital is mobile, deposits will flee to safe havens in the moments of crisis. This proposal, however, was controversial, as it implies a form of debt mutualization within the EU or Eurozone whereby deposit protection funded by a member with an orderly banking system can be used to protect depositors in a country with a failing banking system. Many member states are opposed to this third proposal.

2.1.2 Basel Accord

The Basel Committee (formerly called the Committee on Banking and Supervisory Practices) was formed in late 1974 by the central bank governors of 10 nations in response to severe disruptions in international banking and currencies. Since the establishment of the Basel Committee, its membership has expanded to 45 institutions from 28 different jurisdictions. The primary objective of the committee is to promote financial stability globally by improving the quality of banking supervision and serve as a forum for frequent collaboration among member nations on banking supervision issues. The committee became known over time for issuing a series of global banking standards known as the Basel I, II, III, and IV Accords.

Prior to 1987, capital requirements for banks varied from country to country, allowing certain institutions to have a competitive advantage over others globally. In addition, in the early 1980s, the Latin American debt crisis increased the Committee's concern that the capital ratios of the world's largest banks were deteriorating at a time of increasing international risks.

In July 1988, the Committee sought to reconcile the differences among national minimum capital requirements by presenting a set of standardized recommendations called the Basel Capital Accord, or Basel I. According to these standards, banks were obliged to maintain a particular ratio of required capital depending on the riskiness of their assets. This effectively led to the need for banks with riskier assets to maintain a higher ratio of required capital. In fact, the Accord mandated that a minimum capital ratio of 8% be established for risk-weighted assets by the end of 1992. Over time, the Basel I framework has been updated to cover market risks, including foreign currency exposures, equities, and other products provided by banks.

In June 1999, the Committee proposed replacing Basel I with a new capital adequacy framework. This led to the publication in 2004 of Basel II, a revised capital framework with three main pillars: (1) the development and expansion of minimum capital requirements; (2) the introduction of a supervisory review of institutions' capital adequacy and internal assessment processes; and (3) indications for the effective use of disclosure as a lever to strengthen market discipline and promote sound and transparent banking practices.

At the onset of the global financial crisis in 2008, it became clear that the Basel II framework needed to be strengthened. The banking sector entered the financial crisis with excessive debt levels and insufficient liquidity buffers, as well as weak governance and risk management. In 2010, a new reform package known as Basel III was agreed upon. It included an increase in minimum capital levels for banks and strengthened existing pillars, in addition to changing some Basel II rules. The main contributions of Basel III were the following: (1) more stringent requirements for the quality and quantity of regulatory capital, with an emphasis on the central role of common equity through the capital conservation buffer (i.e., when this requirement is breached, payouts are restricted to help meet minimum common equity requirements); (2) the establishment of a leverage ratio and liquidity requirements to address periods of stress; and (3) additional requirements for banks important across the European system. Many of these changes proposed by Basel III were implemented during the post-crisis era.

More recently, in 2017 *Basel IV* was ratified by the Basel Committee, with a start date of January 2022. The Basel IV agreement included substantial amendments to the capital treatment of credit risk, operational risk, and the credit valuation adjustment, as well as higher capital requirements, revisions to the definition of the leverage ratio, and parameters for the application of this ratio to global banks.

Now that we have outlined the international regulatory framework, we can shift our focus back to MNCs and see how financial markets can facilitate their functions and operations. We will discuss the variety of financing options these companies have at their disposal.

2.1.3   MNC functioning and cash flow movements

The foreign cash flow movements of a classic MNC can be classified into four distinct business functions, all of which involve the use of foreign exchange markets: first, Import and Export, with exports creating foreign currency inflows and imports requiring foreign cash outflows; then Foreign Direct Investment (FDI), where financial outflows to acquire foreign assets produce future inflows through profits remitted to the MNC. Those two functions involve the use of International Money Markets, since the MNC has inflows and outflows denominated in foreign currencies that need to be hedged against exchange rate fluctuations. The last two business functions related to foreign exchange markets are Short-term Foreign Securities Investment or Financing, which often takes place in the eurocurrency market,

Figure 2.1   **MNC and the International Financial Markets**

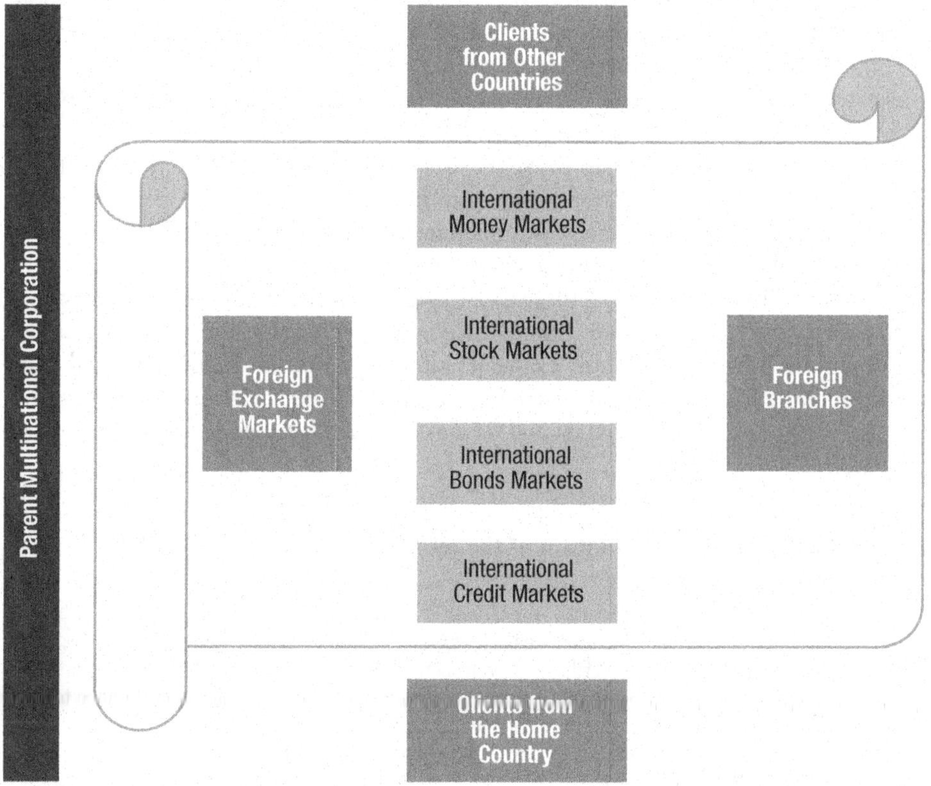

and Long-term Financing on Eurocredit, Eurobonds, or International Equity Markets (Madura, 2008).

The next stage is then to analyze the worldwide financial marketplaces from which they might get cash, including (**Figure 2.1**): the *Foreign Exchange Market* for currency exchanges; the *International Money Market* for short-term funding; the *International Credit Market* for medium-term loans; and the *International Stock or Bond Market* for long-term loans.

2.2   The foreign exchange market and monetary system: currency exchanges

International monetary and financial systems revolve around exchange rates, i.e., the rates at which the currencies from different countries are exchanged. An exchange rate is simply the price of one currency in relation to another. The foreign exchange market (i.e., forex or FX) makes currency exchange possible; this is the market where exchange rates are determined.

Just as individuals rely on the foreign exchange market to change their money when they travel to foreign countries, MNCs exchange currencies to purchase supplies from manufacturers located in foreign countries. These companies also convert the earnings of their foreign subsidiaries into the currency of the parent company.

Large commercial banks allow MNCs to exchange currencies by holding inventories of each currency. For one currency to be exchanged with another one, commercial banks (or other financial intermediaries) need to quote the exchange rate which specifies the rate at which one currency can be exchanged for another.

The system for establishing these exchange rates has evolved tremendously over time – from the so-called Gold Standard to agreement about fixed exchange rates, and finally, to the current floating exchange rate system. In this section, we will learn more about the history of foreign exchange, as well as about foreign exchange transactions, foreign exchange markets, and how to interpret foreign exchange transaction quotations.

2.2.1   The history and evolution of the monetary system and foreign exchange

The great differences in climate and resources in the different European regions, the geographic configuration of the European continent, and the legal protections of commercial activities provided by different European countries during the Middle Ages favored the development of large-scale, long-distance trade organized in relation to a dense network of commercial centers. By the late Middle Ages, the decrease in monetary fragmentation enabled by monetary unions was playing a crucial role in market integration and expansion (Epstein, 2001). Trade would have been severely limited by market friction in the absence of foreign payments and capital transfers. To move cash through banking locations linked by branch networks of international trading firms and merchant banks, coin-like instruments such as bills of exchange, obligatory letters, and promissory notes were devised. This network of monetary connections among cities created a "geography of money" in mid-eighteenth-century Europe characterized by agglomeration in Amsterdam, London, and Paris.

Prior to 1914, the sterling-denominated "London bill of exchange" became the primary vehicle for international trade. Once the Bretton Woods system restored external convertibility after the Second World War, however, an international money market of global scope re-emerged in the 1960s. This market, which was again concentrated in London but linked financial centers around the world, was now based upon several currency-like instruments (short-term bank deposits) denominated predominantly (but not entirely) in terms of U.S. dollars (Battilossi, 2020).

The dominance of the British pound and the U.S. dollar in international money markets in the nineteenth and twentieth centuries reflects their positions as the most important international currencies. Taking a longer view, however, the international monetary and financial system has always been multipolar. The size of the issuing country's economy and its military capability are structural elements that explain the global stature achieved by various currencies over the centuries. This paradigm can be effectively applied to the British pound in the nineteenth century and the U.S. dollar in the twentieth century (Eichengreen, 2001).

The Gold Standard and the gold exchange standard

The classical Gold Standard is the most well-known monetary system in history, with its golden period spanning around a third of a century until the outbreak of World War I. During that period, it was the world's dominant national and international monetary system. The years 1876-1913 are often regarded as "the heyday of the gold standard" owing to the existence of the "system's key nations" (Great Britain, France, Germany, and the United States), as well as Scandinavia and numerous Western European countries. Britain established the first gold standard, and the country's involvement was critical to this system's expansion and functioning. London housed the world's biggest gold, commodity, and finance markets. There were numerous sterling-denominated assets, and several nations used sterling as their international reserve currency instead of gold (Bordo, 1993). It is debatable whether the United States should be recognized as having played a prominent role from the start. Yet evaluating in terms of the substantial circulation of gold coins (Gallarotti, 1995), the United States unquestionably should be recognized as an important national player. Some areas, including China, Persia, and portions of Latin America, never followed the traditional gold standard and instead used silver or bimetallic standards.

By 1914, practically every economically significant nation in the world accepted the gold standard, but after World War I the system crumbled and the major purpose of gold money became reserves for the Treasury, central banks, and commercial banks, rather than for financial circulation.

From 1876 to 1913, exchange rates were dictated by the Gold Standard. Currencies were convertible into gold at a specified rate, and thus the exchange rate between two currencies was determined by their relative convertibility rates per ounce of gold. Under this system, exchange rates were fixed. Indeed, with the gold standard countries agreed to convert paper money into a fixed amount of gold, that then could be bought or sold in unlimited quantities at a fixed price. That fixed price was used to determine the value of the currency.

However, when World War I (WWI) began in 1914, a period of instability followed, and the Gold Standard system was suspended. After WWI, a gold exchange standard was adopted because there was an inadequate supply of gold for reserve purposes. Under this system, a nation's currency could be converted into bills of exchange drawn on a country whose currency was convertible into gold at a stable exchange rate. The convertibility required was no more in gold, but in convertible-gold currencies of specific countries such as USA and England. In this way, countries did not need to hold just gold, but they could also have foreign currencies as reserves. A nation on the gold exchange standard was thus able to keep its currency at parity with gold without having to maintain as large a gold reserve as was required under the Gold Standard. In parallel, some countries such as the UK returned to the Gold Standard in the 1920s, but most then abandoned it as a result of the banking panic caused by the Great Depression.

Bretton Woods Agreement: fixed exchange rates

As reported in Kugler (2016), the Bretton Woods system was a global monetary system with fixed exchange rates based on the cooperation of central banks and administered by a newly formed international entity, the International Monetary Fund (IMF). The system was based on twenty principles that were agreed upon at the Bretton Woods meeting of the Allied countries in July 1944. Its purpose was to restore exchange rate stability without the need for deflationary adjustments for deficit countries.

It did this by introducing rules that distinguished it from the Gold Standard. Central banks assumed an interventionist role in the forex market. The IMF was supposed to help members with current account deficits. Only current transactions required free convertibility at a fixed rate, and capital movements were permitted. Devaluations were possible if a "fundamental imbalance" was detected. The Gold Standard, on the other hand, had involved no cooperation among central banks, was not supervised by an international authority, required full convertibility for both current and capital transactions, and did not allow devaluations. Despite its flaws, the Bretton Woods system helped rebuild the international economy after World War II. Delaying convertibility for current transactions until December 1958 allowed for greater flexibility in domestic monetary and fiscal policy. After convertibility was restored, however, the system's flaws became apparent. Three issues arose: the adjustment process, liquidity, and the stability of gold and dollar prices. As stated by Kugler et al. (2020), the Bretton Woods system ended in 1968 when the pound was devalued in November 1967 and gold reserves fell by $3 billion in four months. Gold prices rose in London based on private demand but remained at $35 an ounce for official transactions. In May 1968, strikes and student demonstrations destabilized France, prompting the government to adopt expansionary fiscal and monetary policies, causing a flight of capital. The United States depreciated its currency by 8% in 1971, causing the price of gold to rise from $35 to $38 an ounce. Places such as the Benelux countries and Germany revalued their currencies. In April 1972, members of the European Community (EC) reduced their exchange margins, anticipating the end of the Bretton Woods system. In March 1973, EC members agreed to float their currencies against the dollar. The Bretton Woods era came to an end. (Kugler et al., 2020).

Some nations sought to peg their currencies to the US dollar or the British pound when the Gold Standard collapsed in the 1930s. In 1944, independent nations such as the United States, Canada, most Western European countries, Australia, and Japan signed an international agreement (known as the Bretton Woods Agreement) that stipulated, among other things, fixed currency exchange rates. International financial arrangements were examined by participating nations that established (1) an exchange rate stabilization scheme, (2) the International Monetary Fund, and (3) the World Bank.

As mentioned above, members established an external or "par value" for their currencies, expressed either in terms of gold or the US dollar, in order to achieve exchange rate stability. The US dollar was denominated in gold and was intimately tied to it (at $35 per ounce, the dollar could be converted to gold on demand). All other member nations, on the other hand, anchored their currencies to the dollar (they were hence indirectly linked to gold via the dollar). A more organized gold exchange standard was used in this arrangement.

During this time, currency exchange rates were set at a predetermined level, known as the par value. Member nations' governments and central banks had to intervene in foreign currency markets to keep their exchange rates against the dollar from drifting more than 1% above or below the previously set threshold. When their currencies threatened to climb beyond 1%, member nations sold their currency (buying dollars) and bought their currency when it threatened to fall below 1%.

The Bretton Woods Agreement, as previously stated, also created the International Monetary Fund (IMF), which began operations in 1946. One of the IMF's key goals was to avoid a return to the interwar period's restricted international trade climate and volatile exchange rate movements. The IMF's mandate also included promoting international monetary cooperation via the establishment and maintenance of exchange rate stability. Indeed, the IMF's primary responsibility was to oversee a fixed-rate regime. It also offered its members the opportunity to borrow money.

Finally, in 1945, the World Bank was established with the goal of assisting in the rebuilding of war-torn Europe by granting long-term loans. It also provided loans for economic development in newly independent African, Asian, and Caribbean countries. The World Bank's current emphasis is on assisting less developed countries (LDCs) in growing their economies.

The Bretton Woods Agreement remained in effect until 1971, when the US dollar appeared overvalued due to a large gap between international demand for dollars and the quantity available for sale. Furthermore, the dollar was under tremendous pressure, due in part to the high cost of the Vietnam War. As a consequence, politicians from economically powerful countries (particularly members of the EU single market) were afraid that free-floating rates might jeopardize the Common Agricultural Policy's existing standing. As a result, they drafted the Smithsonian Agreement, commonly known as the "Snake," in which the US dollar was depreciated compared to other major currencies and exchange rates were permitted to vary by 2.25% in each direction relative to the newly established values.

Floating exchange rate system

1972-1978: The Snake

US President Richard M. Nixon unilaterally suspended the dollar's convertibility to gold in August 1971. The so-called gold window closure basically brought the Bretton Woods system to an end. The Smithsonian agreement established fluctuation bands of 2.25% between each currency's central rate and the US dollar (the "Snake" agreement). This approach provided a "tunnel" for the fluctuations of European currencies. Between 1971 and 1976, the transition to the post-Bretton Woods system was a watershed point in the European Economic Community's (EEC) currency cooperation, as it compelled the EEC to rethink the foundation upon which its monetary ties had previously been established. On March 21, 1972, as a first step in gradually reducing exchange rates within the EEC, the so-called European currency snake was enacted, limiting the fluctuation margins between EEC currencies to 2.25%. However, it quickly became evident that the snake was not an appropriate exchange rate mechanism for all EEC member nations. For instance, the majority of the EEC's biggest member nations – including founding members Italy, France, and the United Kingdom – had escaped the snake. As an EEC-wide exchange rate mechanism, the snake did not seem well-suited to the disparate economic realities of EEC member states (Mourlon-Druol, 2020).

Even after the Smithsonian Agreement, which expanded the range of exchange rate fluctuations, governments still had difficulties maintaining exchange rates within stated boundaries. In March 1973, more widely traded currencies were allowed to fluctuate in relation to market forces, and the official exchange rate boundaries were eliminated. The floating exchange rate system thus came into effect. In this period, central banks did not need to intervene in the currency market to the same extent and did not need the IMF to make similar interventions. Throughout this time, the dollar proved to be a volatile currency. However, since foreign trade is much smaller proportion of GDP in the US than in many other countries, it seems able to live with wild fluctuations that would wreak havoc elsewhere.

European Economic and Monetary Union

1979-1992: The European Monetary System

As presented in Mourlon-Druol (2012), during the Brussels European Council in December 1978, the various EEC member countries agreed on the European Monetary System (EMS) after months of talks. The British government had unequivocally stated that it would not participate in the Exchange Rate Mechanism (ERM) but would officially join the EMS. In March 1979, the ERM went into effect. The European Monetary System (EMS) talks focused largely on the function of the European Currency Unit (ECU) in the exchange rate.

The EMS implemented a so-called divergence indicator to distribute the cost of adjustment more equitably across nations with strong and weak currencies. The goal of this indicator was to determine which currencies were diverging from the ECU, either upwards or downwards. After 1979, the ECU's usage in private markets expanded, which assisted in debates regarding the prospect of converting it into a rival currency. In short, the EMS functioned quite similarly to the snake.

The ECU launched in 1979 had the same value (at par) as the European Unit of Account (EUA)[1] in 1975. The major change was the new economic policy consensus backing the EMS, particularly between the French and German governments, During the initial years of the EMS's functioning, European politicians and central bankers explored prospective EMS upgrades. The Basel-Nyborg Agreement, signed on September 12, 1987, formalized the outcome of a long-running discussion over the use of intramarginal intervention in the EMS that codified the Monetary Committee's and Board of Governors' monitoring of policy discrepancies among EMS members with a set of indicators and predictions, as well as the possibility of deploying intramarginal interventions (Mourlon-Druol, 2020).

Further developments occurred in the late 1970s. For example, in 1979 the ERM was introduced (i.e., the European Exchange Rate Mechanism).

The birth of the Euro

At their meeting in Hanover on June 27 and 28, 1988, the European Economic Community EEC heads of government decided to reintroduce the issue of the Economic and Monetary Union (EMU) and the European Council commissioned Jacques Delors, head of the committee, to develop a road map for establishing it (James, 2012). The Delors committee consisted of all the central bankers of the EEC, as well as a few other economic specialists.

---

[1] The European Unit of Account (EUA) was a unit of account most notably used in the European Communities from 1975 to 1979, when it was replaced at parity by the European Currency Unit (ECU), in turn replaced at parity in 1999 by the euro.

While the Delors report detailed the steps necessary to establish a single European currency, a political decision had to be reached before the single currency could be implemented. The EEC heads of state and government supported the Delors Report, but the establishment of the EMU required amendment of the treaties and the convening of an international conference (the Inter-governmental Conference, IGC).

In December 1989, the European Council in Strasbourg decided to convene the IGC, which began its work in December 1990. In February 1992, the Maastricht Treaty was signed and entered into force on January 1, 1993.

As per Mourlon-Druol (2020), the Maastricht Treaty established four convergence requirements for euro membership, namely price stability, fiscal sustainability, exchange rate stability, and interest rate convergence. The Maastricht Treaty established three phases for the creation of the EMU, based on the findings of the Delors Report. Stage 1 (July 1, 1990 to December 31, 1993) was mostly preparatory in nature and included measures to increase economic convergence, central bank cooperation, free movement of capital, and free use of the ECU. Phase 2 (January 1, 1994 to December 1998) included more tangible institutional changes, such as the creation of the European Monetary Institute and the independence of national central banks. Phase 3 (beginning January 1, 1999) culminated the single currency creation process with the establishment of the European System of Central Banks and the European Central Bank to conduct a single monetary policy, irreversibly setting exchange rates, ratifying the Stability and Growth Pact, and, of course, introducing euro bills and coins. Just when the EMU seemed to be on the right track, the EMS was shaken by two significant currency crises in 1992 and 1993 (James, 2012). Both stemmed from currency speculation and posed a danger to the very survival of the European exchange rate system. The first decade of the euro was a success on several fronts although not without some issues. The adoption of the euro was accompanied, in fact, by a rapid adjustment of prices. The onset of the so-called Eurozone crisis in 2008 and 2009 exposed the inherent flaws of the Eurozone (Mourlon-Druol, 2014), showing that the Maastricht Treaty did not mark the end of the path of European monetary unity and resulting in significant adjustments in terms of monetary policy (Claeys, 2017). Some of the most notable include secondary market purchases of government bonds in 2011, long-term refinancing operations (LTROs) in 2012 to support bank lending and liquidity, outright monetary operations (OMTs) in 2012, and the public sector purchase program (PSPP) – dubbed "quantitative easing" – in 2015. In addition, the ECB has expanded its function as a transnational banking regulator over the years as part of the European Banking Union (Mourlon-Druol, 2020).

In addition, in 1999, 11 countries adopted a single currency, the Euro. Both initiatives were implemented to reduce exchange rate fluctuations and attempt to achieve monetary stability in the EU.

Current exchange rate scenario

Currently, the IMF sets out a series of categories of different exchange rate mechanisms that are used by different countries. Countries establish their monetary systems based on their own preferences. The mechanisms used are stated by the IMF as follows:

a) *Exchange agreement with no separate legal tender*: Members of a currency union share a common currency (i.e., the Economic and Monetary Union), and countries adopt the currency of another country.

b) *Currency Board Agreement*: Members have a legislative commitment to exchange their domestic currency against a fixed exchange rate.

c) *Conventional Fixed Peg Agreement*: Similar to the Bretton Woods Agreement, a country pegs its currency to another or to a set of currencies with a fluctuation that remains within +/−1%.

d) *Pegged Exchange Rates with Horizontal Bands*: A country's currency fluctuates around a central par with greater flexibility (i.e., a wider band).

e) *Crawling Peg*: A country's currency is pegged to another or to a set of currencies with the peg adjusted periodically.

f) *Crawling Bands*: A country's currency is kept within a specific margin around a central par which "crawls" depending on a series of indicators.

g) *Managed Float*: The country's central bank manages the foreign exchange market by buying and selling foreign currencies against the home currency.

h) *Independently Floating*: Exchange rates are determined by market forces and are free – the central bank is responsible for preventing an excessive supply of foreign exchange but not for bringing it to a desired level.

2.2.2   Foreign exchange transactions

The trade of one currency for another is known as foreign exchange (forex or FX). One may, for example, exchange the US dollar for the euro. The foreign exchange market, often known as the forex market, is where foreign currency transactions are made.

With billions of dollars changing hands every day, the FX market is the world's biggest and most liquid market. There is no centralized location for this service. Rather, the forex market is an electronic network of banks, brokers, institutions, and individual traders (mostly trading through brokers or banks). As reported in Lessambo (2021), Forex (FX) market dates back over 500 years, when it was originally brought to a financial center thus signing the beginning of Forex transactions. The financial hub of London was one of the most active financial centers around the turn of the twentieth century, accounting for almost half of all Forex transactions involving sterling at the time. After the US Dollar, the Euro, and the Japanese Yen, Sterling is the fourth most traded currency in the twenty-first century. Because it is structured as an over-the-counter (OTC) market, based on credit connections outside of an established market, the global FX market is opaque (Lessambo, 2021). The foreign exchange market is often used by governments and central banks. To aid their governments in international commerce, central banks retain official reserves or international reserves. Central banks purchase and sell foreign currencies when their balances of payments are in deficit or excess. Central bank involvement is often highly scrutinized, since it might provide insight about a country's financial fortunes.

Global investment banks and commercial banks are key participants in FX markets, where they act as on-demand brokers to serve their customers, particularly multinational organizations that do business across the globe. Commercial and investment banks trade in interbank FX in addition to servicing their customers by acting as dealers though FX arbitrage in pursuit of a spread. Hundreds of worldwide commercial and investment banks have FX desks that actively participate in FX markets. Transactions are carried out over the phone with brokers or via electronic trading terminal connections with counterparties. Brokers generally serve as matchmakers in foreign exchange markets, bringing together dealers to purchase and sell currencies. They are compensated for their participation through commissions. Multinational firms that operate globally and need to make or receive payments in foreign currencies use foreign exchange markets to hedge their risks and balance foreign currency credits and the debits of their transactions.

Hedge funds, private equity companies, major institutional investors, and other FX market players are examples of non-commercial financial institutions. In FX, there are various hedging strategies, each with its own unique set of features. Foreign exchange options are used by some traders to hedge foreign exchange risk, while "delta hedging" is used by others to hedge option-type risk or to synthetically produce foreign currency options. The forward rate may be used as a prediction of the future spot rate if the proper measure of risk is connected to variances between actual and predicted exchange rates. Yet, the forward rate does not totally reduce volatility risk for two reasons: (a) the forward rate is not a strong predictor of future exchange rates; and (b) quotations are only accessible for large currencies (Lessambo, 2021).

The average daily volume of foreign exchange around the world exceeds \$6.6 trillion (Triennial Central Bank Survey; BIS calculations, 2019). Even though hundreds of banks facilitate those foreign exchange transactions, the top 20 banks handle about half of them (Fox et al., 2017). Profits generated from foreign exchange transactions are important to major banks. The banks handling the majority of forex transactions operate in the leading financial markets, including Tokyo, New York, and London (Bekaert & Hodrick, 2018).

As a minimum requirement, banks must maintain a certain inventory of U.S. dollars, Euros or other currencies to facilitate exchange transactions (Gray, 2011). If a bank falls short of a given currency, it can purchase it from another bank through the interbank market (trading between banks). Although commercial banks handle most foreign exchange transactions directly with MNCs, other intermediaries exist. For instance, some MNCs deal with brokers or traders who act as intermediaries between them and the commercial banks. This makes the process more transparent compared to traditional transactions, since the MNCs can assess quotes from multiple banks to keep costs at a minimum and avoid being overcharged. Notably, competing banks offer different exchange rates for various currencies (Bekaert & Hodrick, 2018). Foreign exchange trading is conducted during normal business hours in a given location. These hours vary among locations due to different time zones. At any given time on a weekday, somewhere around the world a bank is open and ready to accommodate foreign exchange requests. Arbitrage ensures that exchange rates are similar across banks and countries. In other words, at any given point in time, the exchange rate between currencies should be similar across the various banks providing foreign exchange services. If there is a large discrepancy, customers or other banks will purchase large amounts of a currency from whatever bank quotes a relatively low price and immediately sell that currency to whatever bank quotes a relatively high price. Such actions cause adjustments in the exchange rate quotations that eliminate discrepancies.

When corporations need a foreign currency, they request quotations from different commercial banks; this allows them to assess and choose the banks offering the most convenient exchange rates. Multinationals basically prefer buying currencies with the lowest possible quotes to minimize costs. However, a lower price is not the only factor MNCs consider when selecting a bank; critical bank-specific characteristics must also be considered for a successful exchange. Firstly, MNCs must take into consideration the performance of the current price relative to the domestic or foreign prices; for instance, how much of the domestic currency equals

$1. Secondly, they must evaluate the businesses associated with the bank: some banks may offer money management services and go the extra mile in accessing hard to locate currencies for the MNC. The third consideration revolves around the efficiency of the transaction; some MNCs prefer banks that handle orders promptly and efficiently to avoid unnecessary delays, which might become costly. Fourthly, MNCs must consider a bank's outlook on different foreign market trends and how such trends relate to customers. Lastly, the bank must be able to offer accurate and reliable projections regarding the expected future state of global economies and exchange rates (Madura, 2008).

It is worth mentioning that multinational corporations are not always compelled to convert currencies. Some currencies are acceptable beyond national boundaries. The US dollar, for example, is widely utilized as a medium of exchange by merchants in many countries, particularly in areas where the local currency is either weak or subject to foreign exchange restrictions. Because US dollars may be used to buy items from other nations, many shops accept them (Madura, 2008).

As outlined above, currencies are traded worldwide for potential profits. The two main financial strategies (speculation and arbitrage) that traders use to do so differ greatly. In using a speculation strategy, the trader takes a position in the exchange market with expectations that the price will change in their favor. In this case, the trader can take a long (i.e., buy the currency today with the expectation of benefiting from future appreciation) or a short position (i.e., selling the currency today and buying it back when the price drops). On the other hand, arbitrage is a risk-free strategy that allows traders to simultaneously buy and sell currencies taking advantage of discrepancies.

2.2.3 Foreign exchange markets

Foreign Exchange (FX) is a market that operates around-the-clock, seven days a week. Currencies are quoted throughout the globe on a constant basis. Quotes posted on data service provider platforms by currency dealers serve as advertisements for their readiness to transact at a certain pricing. When a bank dealer publishes a quotation, the quote may be seen on the computer screens of other market players across the globe who participate in the foreign currency market. This public quotation informs the rest of the market of the pricing at which the dealer who published it is willing to trade. There is still direct bilateral trading in the market, such as when a person speaks to a dealer at a bank to arrange an exchange, in addition to computerized trading sites. As far as market prices are concerned, the best publicly accessible data comes from quotes on the electronic trading network. A small number of geographic places account for most foreign currency trading activity. More than half of all global commerce is carried out between the United Kingdom and the United States. Historically, London, New York, and Tokyo have been the world's three largest financial hubs for dealing in foreign currency, and the volume of trade in these cities follows fairly consistent trends (Melvin et al., 2017).

The foreign exchange market is then technically open 24 hours a day and is split over three time zones. Trading begins each day in Sydney and moves around the world as the business day begins in each financial center, opening first in Tokyo, then in London, and finally New York.

There is no building or physical location where traders exchange currencies. MNCs exchange currencies through commercial banks or over a telecommunication network in either the *spot market* or the *forward market*, depending on their respective needs.

The spot market

A spot exchange rate is the current price of one currency in terms of another. Spot exchange rates are given at a particular time because prices vary during the day as supply and demand for currencies change. Spot exchange rates are calculated considering quantities exchanged at more than $1 million, which is the standard threshold used. The cost of a foreign currency would be a lot higher if the quantities exchanged were less than that value. The greater the price, the lower the amount of foreign currency acquired. As a result, if you go to a foreign nation as a tourist, the exchange rate will be significantly less advantageous to you. We can always convert the Renminbi China (CNY) price of the Euro (EUR) into a Euro (EUR) price of the Renminbi China (CNY) by taking the reciprocal of the exchange rate, or 1/exchange rate. For example, an exchange rate of 7,28 CNY per euro is translated into Renminbi China by using the reciprocal: $1/7,28 = 0,14$ EUR.

The spot rate is always comprised of two rates. Banks bid (purchase) foreign currencies at lower rates than they offer (sell), and the spread is the difference between the selling and the purchasing prices. The mid-price is the sum of the purchasing and selling prices. The bid/offer prices are given such that the bid (buy) price can be seen, and the offer (sell) price can be found by removing the final three digits of the purchase quotation and replacing them with the second number. The gap (bank profit) between purchase and sell rates is quite modest, and it may be expressed in a percentage as ask-bid/mid-price. The present spread in any currency will vary depending on the particular currency trader, the currency being traded, and the trading bank's general perspective regarding the foreign exchange market. Quoted spread tends to rise for more sparsely traded currencies or when the bank feels that the risks involved with trading in a currency at a certain moment are growing. Quotes for exchange rates are normally accessible for all nations where currencies may be freely exchanged. In the absence of free markets, the state normally conducts all foreign currency trade at an official exchange rate, regardless of current market circumstances. The spot market refers to the purchasing and selling of foreign currency for delivery on the spot. When the value of the exchange rate rises, we say the currency has appreciated. If the value of the currency declines, it is said to have depreciated. The Euro/Dollar exchange rate, abbreviated EUR/USD, is one of the most prominent currency pairings, indicating how many dollars are required to purchase one euro. This signifies that the euro is the base currency, while the dollar is the quoted currency. There are various elements that influence the trajectory of the EUR/USD exchange rate that are not necessarily related to the two currencies; in fact, interactions with other currencies also have an effect. Because exchange rates are reciprocal, a falling dollar indicates that the euro has risen in value against it (Melvin et al., 2017).

When an MNC needs immediate delivery of a foreign currency to instantly purchase supplies abroad or convert earnings from a foreign subsidiary, it purchases or sells the currency in the spot market at the so-called *spot rate*. The spot or current exchange rate is the rate paid for immediate delivery of a currency. The spot market is made up of financial institutions (e.g., commercial and investment banks, pension funds, hedge funds, money market funds, insurance companies, financial government entities) and non-financial institutions (e.g., corporations, non-financial government entities, private individuals) involved in buying and selling foreign currencies.

The forward market

The forward exchange market refers to the purchase and sale of currencies for delivery at a later date. Most nations have forward markets, and maturities and quantities are specified in each transaction. Because 1-month and 6-month forward rates are routinely traded maturities, they are often mentioned as well.

The benefit of the forward market is that there is a fixed exchange rate between the euro and the Chinese renminbi and the purchase of the Chinese renminbi can take place within 90 days. This may be preferable to the alternative of purchasing Chinese renminbi now and investing them for three months, since neither cash nor knowledge of investment prospects in Chinese renminbi are required. With a forward rate, the importer knows exactly how much the imported items will cost in 90 days. Furthermore, the importer pays only a tiny premium over the market exchange rate for this forward contract.

A currency is considered to be selling at a forward premium if its future exchange price surpasses its current spot price. When the future rate is less than the current spot rate, a currency is selling at a forward discount. In order to comparable to interest rates, forward premiums or discounts are presented in annualized percent figures (Melvin et al., 2017).

The forward market allows multinationals to negotiate and lock exchange rates for future/forward contracts that will go into effect on a specified future date. In such cases, negotiations are done through the futures, forward, and options markets. In forward contracts, the exchange rate is agreed upon in the present, but the exchange occurs at a specified future date. Generally, involved parties agree on the exchange rate during the making of the contract, and no payment is made until the contract reaches maturity.

Most MNCs use forward contracts to hedge payments expected to be received in the future using a foreign currency. This reduces financial risks related to fluctuations in spot/current exchange rates, potentially affecting future payments. Generally, a forward contract specifies the quoted price with respect to the currency bought or sold by the trader; specifically, it specifies the exchange rate and date of maturity. As in spot markets, banks also accommodate multinationals interested in 'forward' contracts (Madura, 2008).

The futures market

The foreign currency market (spot and forward) that we have described is a worldwide market. Commercial banks, corporations, and governments in many regions purchase and sell foreign currency through telephone and computer systems, with no centralized geographical market location. However, there are several institutions that have yet to be addressed, one of which is the foreign currency futures market. In the futures market foreign currency may be purchased and sold for delivery at a later date. The futures market varies from the forward market in that it only trades a few currencies; trading moreover takes place through standardized contracts and in a defined geographic region (Melvin et al., 2017). Futures contracts are exchanged on regulated exchanges such as the Chicago Mercantile Exchange's (CME) International Monetary Market (IMM), which is the world's biggest currency futures market. An exchange allows buying and selling while also ensuring that all promises are met. CME futures are traded in the following currencies: the British pound, the Canadian dollar, the Japanese yen, the Swiss franc, the Australian dollar, the Mexican peso, and the euro. The contracts require that a specified quantity of money be delivered on certain dates. Contracts expire on the third Wednesday of March, June, September, and December of each year. Contracts in the forward market are commonly 30, 90, or 180 days long but may be for any duration agreed upon by the parties and can mature on any day of the year. Forward market contracts may be formed for any amount that the parties involved agree on. Contracts for fixed quantities are written in the CME futures market. The futures table displays the dollar values reported for each contract unit. Futures markets provide enterprises engaged in international commerce a hedging option as well as a speculative opportunity. Speculators benefit when they correctly predict a future price for a currency that varies considerably (by more than the transaction cost) from the present contract price. Because the futures market guarantees the fulfillment of all contracts, participants are asked to deposit cash to ensure that the contract is fulfilled. A September contract in our possession will be quoted in the futures market every day until the maturity date, meaning the contract's value will alter on a daily basis. Notably, the security deposit is refunded if we sell the contract. A reduction in the value of the pound in August, on the other hand, will harm our financial situation. The original purchaser need not hold a futures contract to maturity. Only the final contract holder is required to take possession of the foreign exchange. As a result, the futures market may be utilized to hedge risk as well as exploited by speculators. With a tiny initial investment, speculators can obtain ownership of large contracts. As a result, speculators may be heavily leveraged, with futures contracts valued at much more than their possessor's net worth (Melvin et al., 2017).

A currency future, or FX future, is a futures contract used to exchange one currency for another at a given date in the future at a price (exchange rate) that is fixed on the purchase date. Some MNCs involved in international trade use the currency futures markets to hedge their positions. Indeed, futures contracts are somewhat similar to forward contracts except that they are sold within an organized exchange market, whereas forward contracts are offered by commercial banks. A currency futures contract specifies the standard volume of a particular currency to be exchanged on a specific settlement date.

The options market

In addition to forward and futures contracts, the options market is another way to hedge foreign currency future assets and liabilities. It is possible to buy or sell a certain amount of currency at a fixed exchange rate on or before a specific expiration date. When the transaction could occur before the date, it is called "American" options; "European" options can only be used at the expiration date. A call option allows you to acquire currency, while a put option allows you to sell it. The striking price is the price at which a currency may be purchased or sold. The use of options for hedging is straightforward. Assume a European importer is purchasing equipment from a US manufacturer, with a payment of $2 million due in December. The importer may protect against currency appreciation by purchasing a call option that enables them to acquire dollars at a fixed price until the December maturity date. To protect against these risks, large multinational corporations often acquire options directly from banks. These personalized options may be of any agreed-upon size or for any date, which allows for greater flexibility than in scheduled exchanges. For instance, a trader with a $2 million payment due in December would cost the corporation EUR 1,748,370 ($1 = EUR 0.87). If the dollar were to appreciate to $1 per 1 EUR during the following three months, however, the value would change to 2,000,000 EUR ($2,000,000 1EUR), resulting in a 251,630 EUR rise in the cost (Melvin et al., 2017). A call option protects against this possibility. However, there are other solutions to consider. If we are simply interested in a significant rise in the value of the dollar, a higher strike price is preferable since it is less expensive. We should pick a lower strike price but be prepared to pay a greater initial cost if we cannot accept considerable fluctuation. For instance, if we want to hedge against a significant change in the value of the dollar, we may use 0.90 as our strike price. We would be able to purchase dollars at 0.90 if we used this strike price and would have to pay $0.03 for each euro. Yet we could prevent any rise in the currency's cost over 0.90 by using an options contract. If the dollar goes below 0.90, however, we would not be able to execute the option and would forfeit the premium. When the striking price of a call option is lower than the current spot rate, or when the strike price of a put option is higher than the current spot rate, the option is said to be "in the money." If we know the future exchange rate with certainty, no market for options, futures, or forward contracts would exist. Risk-averse merchants readily pay to prevent the possible losses associated with unfavorable exchange rate changes in uncertain environments. Options provide greater flexibility than futures or forwards. An option is a contract that gives the right to purchase or sell something in the future. It is not an obligation like it is in the case of futures and forward contracts (Melvin et al., 2017).

A currency option, or FX option, is a contract that grants the holder the right, but not the obligation, to buy or sell a currency at a pre-agreed price (exchange rate) for a specified period of time. Currency call and put options can be purchased through exchange and offer more flexibility than forward or futures contracts, because they do not entail any obligation (i.e., they grant the right to buy or sell but imply no obligation).

Currency options contracts grant the right to buy or sell a specific currency at a specific price within a specific period of time. These contracts can be either *call contracts* (which give the right to buy a currency at a specific price, called the strike price or exercise price) or *put contracts* (which give the right to sell at a specific price, which is also called the strike price or exercise price).

Call contracts are commonly used by MNCs to hedge their future payables. For example, if a European MNC knows that in one year it will need to pay its Japanese suppliers, it can buy a call contract to fix the exchange rate at which it will be able to convert its euros into Japanese yen one year from that date. On the contrary, put contracts are usually used to hedge receivables.

Note that hedging is used by companies, financial investors, and other economic agents to insure against the foreign exchange risk inherent to all international transactions. Hence, in contrast to speculation, hedging is the activity of covering an open position.

2.2.4   Foreign exchange dealing

The foreign exchange or Forex (FX) market is where exchange rates are determined. An exchange rate is a price, specifically the price of one currency in relation to another. It is the mechanism by which world currencies are linked together in the global marketplace.

Foreign exchange quotations

Exchange rate quotations for widely traded currencies are listed in the news media daily. Those quotations normally reflect the ask price for large transactions, which may differ from the price quoted to an individual investor who wants to purchase low volumes. In addition, since exchange rates vary throughout the day, the exchange rates quoted in a newspaper only reflect the price of the currency at one specific point of time during the day.

How should we interet exchange quotations? Below are some important features.

1) Direct *vs* Indirect quotations

The most common methods of representing currency exchange rates are direct and indirect quotes. Multinationals need to consider a number of factors while performing foreign transactions. They must first analyze the direct quotation, which represents the exchange rate as the price of the foreign currency in proportion to the domestic currency: the number of units of local currency required to acquire one foreign currency unit. When a price for EUR/US$ is presented as 0.84, it means that 0.84 euro units are required to purchase one US dollar unit. Second, they should note how the exchange rate is stated in the indirect quotation, which represents the price of the home currency versus the foreign currency. For example, if the US$/EUR quote is 1.14, it means that it takes 1.14 units of dollars to purchase one unit of euro. The indirect quote is defined as the reciprocal of the direct quotation, using the following general formula (Fox et al., 2017):

$$Indirect\ quotation = \frac{1}{Direct\ quotation}$$

Thus, the indirect quotation is the reciprocal of the corresponding direct quotation.

2) Bid/Ask spread of banks

To perform foreign currency transactions, commercial banks charge a fee known as the bid/ask spread. A bank's bid quotation (the price at which it is ready to purchase) for a foreign currency will always be lower than its ask quote (the price at which the bank is willing to sell) at any given moment. The bid/ask spread is the difference between bid and ask quotations, and it is meant to cover the expenses of receiving currency exchange requests:

$$Bid/Ask\ spread = Ask\ rate - Bid\ rate$$

It's worth noting that the difference between a bid and an ask quotation will seem to be considerably lower for currencies with a lower value. As a result, MNCs may standardize the bid/ask spreads of multiple currencies by measuring them as a percentage of the currency's spot rate: the bid/ask percentage spread.

$$Bid/Ask\ \%\ spread = \frac{Ask\ rate - Bid\ rate}{Ask\ rate}$$

The bid/ask percentage spread, on the other hand, might vary in a variety of circumstances. The gap will be substantially less for bigger "wholesale" transactions between banks or between banks and major enterprises than it will be for retail transactions servicing individual clients. Furthermore, since commercial banks are exposed to additional exchange rate risk when retaining non-liquid currencies that are traded less frequently, the gap is generally bigger.

The difference in currency quotes is influenced by a number of variables. One is the order spend, which includes the costs of processing orders, such as clearing and documenting transactions, as well as the costs of providing customer service. The cost of maintaining a currency's inventory is also taken into account. To balance the opportunity cost of maintaining inventory, it is generally considered best to divert the same amount of money to another purpose. Maintaining a high interest rate stock results in a significant loss of opportunity.

The less competition there is, the lower the spread provided by brokers is likely to be. More liquid currencies are less prone to rapid price changes because of the higher volume of transactions. High trading volume indicates that there are many buyers and sellers at any given time, making these currencies more liquid than others. Some currencies are more volatile than others due to economic or political factors that cause supply and demand to change more rapidly than for other currencies. Currency markets in nations with frequent political upheaval, for example, are more prone to price volatility. This implies that the value of these currencies can vary drastically, causing huge losses for brokers who are willing to buy or sell them on the open market (Fox et al., 2017).

An example will allow for better understanding.

Let's assume that the following are the respective bid rates and ask rates for the euro and the Japanese yen:

Currency	Bid rate	Ask rate	$\dfrac{\text{Ask rate} - \text{Bid rate}}{\text{Ask rate}}$	Bid/Ask % spread
British Pound	€1.16	€1.22	$\dfrac{€1.22 - €1.16}{€1.22}$	4.92%
Japanese Yen	€0.0080	€0.0086	$\dfrac{€0.0086 - €0.0080}{€0.0086}$	6.97%

Even though the differential between the bid and the ask quote for the Japanese yen seems much smaller than for the British pound, the bid/ask percentage spread for the Japanese yen is actually greater than that of the British pound.

Cross exchange quotations

Most currency rates are stated in euros or US dollars. Nevertheless, in some cases individuals or businesses may be interested in non-euro or non-US dollar conversion rates. A cross-exchange rate might be employed in this scenario. It refers to the exchange rate of one foreign currency against another. By using a table like the one in **Figure 2.2**, a multinational firm can easily calculate the rate it will be able to use to convert the profits of its Japanese subsidiary and fund the operations of its Swedish subsidiary.

Figure 2.2   Spot rates as of 20/02/2020

	USD	EUR	JPY	GBP	CAD	AUD	NZD	CHF	DKK	NOK	SEK
SEK	9.8117	10.5880	0.0876	12.6430	7.4014	6.4928	6.2161	9.9703	1.4178	1.0531	
NOK	9.3169	10.0540	0.0832	12.0060	7.0281	6.1653	5.9026	9.4674	1.3663		0.9496
DKK	6.9204	7.4676	0.0618	8.9175	5.2203	4.5795	4.3843	7.0322		0.7428	0.7053
CHF	0.9841	1.0619	0.0088	1.2681	0.7423	0.6512	0.6235		0.1422	0.1056	0.1003
NZD	1.5784	1.7033	0.0141	2.0340	1.1907	1.0445		1.6040	0.2281	0.1694	0.1609
AUD	1.5112	1.6307	0.0135	1.9473	1.1399		0.9574	1.5356	0.2184	0.1622	0.1540
CAD	1.3257	1.4305	0.0118	1.7082		0.9872	0.8399	1.3471	0.1916	0.1422	0.1351
GBP	0.7760	0.8370	0.0069		0.5854	0.5135	0.4917	0.7886	0.1121	0.0833	0.0791
JPY	112.0500	120.9100		144.3900	84.5230	74.1470	70.9870	113.8600	16.1910	12.0260	11.4300
EUR	0.9267		0.0083	1.1942	0.6991	0.6133	0.5871	0.9417	0.1339	0.0995	0.0945
USD		1.0791	0.0089	1.2886	0.7543	0.6617	0.6335	1.0162	0.1445	0,1073	0,1029

% Change on Day Range
■ *Below –2.5%*   ■ *–0.5% to –2.5%*   ■ *-0.05% to –5%*   *–0.05 to 0.05%*   ■ *0.05% to 0.5%*   ■ *0.5% to 2.5%*   ■ *Above 2.5%*

Source: Bloomberg.com

Foreign exchange swaps

As stated in Melvin et al. (2017), SWAPSA foreign exchange swap is an agreement in which two currencies are exchanged simultaneously on a certain day at a rate agreed upon at the time of the contract, and the same two currencies are then later re-exchanged in the reverse direction at a rate agreed upon at the time of the contract. Swaps are a cost-effective approach to satisfying foreign currency needs, since they consolidate two distinct transactions into one, thus halving transaction costs. The corporation avoids foreign exchange risk by matching the liability created by borrowing foreign currencies with the asset created by lending local currency, both of which get repaid at the same future exchange rate. This is called hedging foreign currency risk. Let's say Profile Bank needs funds right now and wants to keep them for three months. Rather than borrowing dollars, Profile Bank might engage in a swap deal, exchanging euros for dollars now and dollars for euros in three months. The swap rates will be established by discounts or premiums in the forward foreign exchange market. The parameters of the arrangement are therefore inextricably linked to future market circumstances (Melvin et al., 2017).

Foreign currency swaps are a kind of transaction that combines two different types of transactions: spot and forward. The bank buys a currency spot in the market and concurrently sells an equal amount forward to deliver in the future. At a later period, the bank will return to its previous position. It is also worth noting that foreign exchange swaps are often short-term, lasting as little as two days.

2.2.5   Foreign exchange market players

The players in foreign exchange markets who perform speculation or arbitrage activities are businesses, international investors, multinational corporations, and others who seek to profit from trading in the market. Among the main players and their activities, there are:

a) *Commercial and investment banks*: These are leading players who buy and sell currencies from each other in what is known as the interbank market. Commercial and investment banks not only trade for their customers and on their own behalf through proprietary desks (proprietary trading) but also are the channel which all other market participants must use to trade. They account for the largest proportion of total trading volume by far, thus playing the vital role of catalysts in international financial markets.

b) *Foreign Exchange Brokers*: Forex brokers are intermediaries that make it easier to connect traders in the interbank market. Typically, a forex broker offers quotations for most currencies from the banks it has relationships with, showing the best rates. A trader is likely to incur a small cost when dealing through a broker. This is known as a brokerage fee, which is a commission charged by brokers for every currency pair offered on their trading platforms.

c) *Retail clients*: These include consumers and travellers, businesses, investors, and others who need foreign currencies for personal use or business purposes. They normally do not buy and sell currencies directly with one another, but rather they operate through brokers and commercial banks.

d) *Central Banks*: These are institutions delegated to manage exchange rates and foreign reserves. Central banks play a very important role in foreign exchange market. However, they normally do not do a significant volume of trading. They enter the FX markets to trade with other central banks, various international institutions, and to maintain the financial stability of exchange rates.

2.2.6   Foreign exchange risk for corporations

MNCs operating in the international marketplace are vulnerable to exchange rate changes. This exposure derives from three main types of risks:

1. *Transaction Risk*: This is the most common risk and occurs when an importer from Country A needs to pay for dollar imports within 6 months of the order date. If Country A's currency weakens against the dollar, the imports will cost more. If a Country A exporter has also sold goods to someone in the US to be paid for in dollars, by the time the goods are shipped and paid for in 9 months, Country A's currency may have strengthened against the dollar, making the dollar earnings worth less.

2. *Translation Risk*: This risk occurs when holding a property in a foreign country in foreign currency; if that currency weakens, the property will be worth less in the domestic currency in the company's annual report.
3. *Economic Risk*: This is less straightforward than the former two types. Economic risk occurs when a Country A firm and its main competitor from Country B sell goods to Country C. If Country B's currency weakens, then the Country A company may lose its competitive advantage in selling goods to Country C.

The topic of foreign exchange risk and risk management will be discussed extensively in Chapter 9.

2.3   International money market: short-term financing

Money market: what is it exactly?
The money market refers to the set of negotiations concerning monetary loans with terms of less than 12 months – or 18 months in cases where the distinction between short and medium term serves to differentiate different fiscal regimes.

Introduction to the money market
The money market differs from the capital market primarily in terms of the maturity of the instruments, which is longer in the latter. One of the purposes of the money market is to manage liquidity flows because of the short duration of contracts and presence of a secondary market that allows institutional and individual investors to invest temporary surplus funds and governments and businesses to solve temporary needs through short-term loans.

The money market's characteristics
The following are the primary characteristics of the money market:

* Variable risk in relation to issuer solvency; the higher the issuer's solvency, the lower the degree of risk.
* Investments with a high degree of liquidity that are easy to negotiate due to their short maturity.
* Impersonal trading and a continuity of exchanges.
* The prices of the traded instruments are determined by short-term interest rates.

(*Source*: Borsa Italiana https://www.borsaitaliana.it/notizie/sotto-la-lente/mercato-monetario.htm)

The Money Market serves to transfer short-term funds denominated in a certain currency from investors with surplus units (savers) to borrowers with unit deficits. In most countries, local corporations and governments commonly use the money market to borrow short-term funds to support their operations and finance their budget deficits. At the same time, individuals or local institutional investors provide funds through short-term deposits at commercial banks.

Expansion of international businesses, corporations, and state actors in a particular country producing need for short-term funds denominated in a currency different from that of the home currency is what gave birth to International Money Markets.

Operations in the money market

Money market operations are classified based on the goals each operator seeks to achieve. Key operations include:

- Investment of cash surplus: one of the most important functions of the money market is to allow for optimal liquidity management. Indeed, families, businesses, and institutional investors (banks, insurance companies, Sim, pension funds, and mutual funds) can use their excess liquidity to generate an economic return.
- Financing: The money market also enables institutions and businesses to deal with temporary money shortages at a cost. The Public Administration can find financial resources to cover the Treasury's cash requirements through short-term securities, such as ordinary Treasury bills. As a result, these instruments have a lifespan of three, six, or twelve months. The investor receives a sum of money equal to the total nominal value of the securities held at maturity. In other words, the maturity collection is known at the time the securities are purchased. Banks can obtain funds to deal with temporary cash flow imbalances by engaging in very short-term funding operations and issuing certificates of deposit. Companies, on the other hand, use the issuance of bankers' acceptances and bills of exchange to accomplish the same thing.
- Intermediation: This refers to the money market activities of securities brokerage firms, banks, and brokers on the behalf of other operators.
- Liquidity control: the Bank of Italy conducts money market operations in conjunction with the banking system, using an auction procedure managed by the Bank of Italy on behalf of the Ministry of Economy and Finance (MEF) and/or bilateral negotiations managed directly by the MEF or by the Bank of Italy on behalf of the MEF. The Bank of Italy intends to regulate the system's liquidity through these operations.

(*Source*: Borsa Italiana https://www.borsaitaliana.it/notizie/sotto-la-lente/mercato-monetario.htm)

The international money market refers to the market for short-term financing and investment instruments that are issued or traded on a global scale. At its core, the Euro currency market is where bank deposits are issued and sold outside the country that issued the currency. Other products, such as Euro commercial paper and floating rate notes, have a variety of uses and are marketed to a diverse range of clients. Each instrument, however, is a partial substitute for the others, and its output and price are subject to many of the same forces. This allows us to group them together in something called a market. The fact that many other international money market products are priced using LIBOR (London Interbank Offered Rate), the eurodollar deposit interest rate, indicates that the same market participants see the various instruments in the same light.

The two most famous International Money Markets are the *European Money Market* (or *Eurocurrency market*) and the *Asian Money Market* (or *Asian dollar market*).

International money market instruments

Interbank deposits

These are short-term funds transferred (lent or borrowed without collateral) between financial intermediaries.

- These transactions take place only between financial intermediaries;
- They allow banks to manage the daily liquidity imbalances inherent to their business;
- The market allows for the redistribution of liquidity across the main European financial centers and reflects the high level of integration achieved within the countries of the Euro zone.

Repurchase agreements

These are loans equivalent to interbank deposits but with a guarantee which takes the form of securities (BOTs and other government bonds):

- The high use of bonds is linked to their function as a guarantee to provide spot resources;
- In the event of the non-repayment of the forward funds, the resource provider can retaliate by selling the securities on the market;
- The guarantee is generally made up of widely distributed securities listed on an official market (government securities, and in particular government instruments);
- Most of the transactions under consideration are short-term (Tomorrow next and Spot next);
- Transactions with a maturity of less than one week have high average amounts (25 million euros or more);
- Transactions with longer maturities have lower average values (approximately 10 million euros).

Certificates of Deposit (CDs)

These are registered or bearer securities issued by a bank that document a deposit, the interest rate (fixed or variable), and the maturity date:

- They have a maturity date, so they are considered term securities rather than demand deposits (term securities have a specified maturity date, while demand deposits can be withdrawn at any time);
- They take the form of bearer securities;
- They can be bought and sold until maturity;
- Certificate denominations range from $100,000 to $10 million (few have denominations less than $1 million);
- Why such large denominations? Banks in the U.S. have a minimum trading size of $1 million in order to reduce transaction costs;
- Maturity typically ranges from one to four months.

Commercial Paper

These are unsecured notes (promissory notes) issued by businesses with a maximum maturity of 270 days:

- These are unsecured notes;
- They are issued by the largest and most creditworthy companies;
- The interest rate offered reflects the issuer's level of risk;
- Maturities in the United States are concentrated between 20 and 45 days;
- They are sold net of discount;
- The majority of them are usually placed directly by the issuer to the investor, without intermediaries;
- In the event of disinvestment by an investor, the placing bank buys them back;
- The liquidity obtained is used to guarantee loans to consumers.

2.3.1   European Money Market (or Eurocurrency market)

Eurocurrencies are worldwide marketplaces for wholesale bank deposits and loans that are held for a limited period of time. A eurocurrency is a type of bank money consisting of unsecured short-term bank debt denominated in a currency (e.g., US dollars) but issued by banks operating offshore, in a physical area or legal space outside the authority of the national authorities in charge of that currency (e.g., the Federal Reserve). Banks generally act as intermediaries between foreign residents in eurocurrency markets. They borrow money by "accepting" foreign currency deposits and lend it out by "placing" deposits with other banks, providing short-term loans, or investing in other liquid assets in foreign currency (Battilossi et al., 2020).

The Eurodollar market, now referred to as the Eurocurrency market, emerged in the late 1940s and 1950s when large amounts of US dollars ended up outside of the US. This included deposit of US dollars in US bank branches outside of the country, large multinational corporations headquartered in the US which were building factories in other countries, and Cold War funds and efforts to reconstruct post-war European economy through the Marshall Plan – all cases which resulted in public dollar flows, particularly into EU nations. The rise of the Eurodollar market was one of the most significant developments in the post-war period. The Eurodollar market developed further during the 1960s and 1970s to accommodate the rise of international businesses and bypass stricter regulations on banks in the United States (Fox et al., 2017).

Since the US dollar was used widely even by foreign countries as a medium for international trade, thus there was a consistent need for dollars in Europe and elsewhere. To conduct international trade with European countries, corporations in the United States deposited US dollars into European banks. These dollar deposits in banks in Europe came to be known as Eurodollars, and the market for Eurodollars came to be known as the Eurocurrency market. Eurocurrencies are currencies held outside their home country. For instance, Eurodollars are dollar deposits outside the US. To put it simply, the Eurodollar market is an international money market focused on short-term credit flows.

Eurodollars and associated Eurocurrencies were a novel form of wholesale banking (transactions with large clients – including other banks – involving huge quantities), which resulted in the establishment of an international money market with a distinct microstructure and independent interest rate settings (Battilossi et al., 2020).

Indeed, the development of the Eurodollar market since the 1950s has been significant for a number of reasons: (1) the market served as a source of short-term funds for the trade financing activities of international banks; (2) the Eurocurrency market facilitated foreign exchange transactions by banks and provided short-term money market trading opportunities; (3) international banks used the market as an outlet for placing surplus funds temporarily at attractive yields; and (4) the Eurocurrency interbank market became the central mechanism channeling flows of international funds among banks. This gave birth to the London Interbank Offered Rate (i.e., LIBOR), which became one of the key benchmarks for international interest rates.

The rise of OPEC (Organization of Petroleum Exporting Countries) also played a major role in the growth of the Eurodollar market. Generally, oil-producing countries operating under OPEC were required to transact using the dollar, which increased savings from oil sale revenues. Notably, traders deposited some of their revenues in money markets to gain interest. Deposits from oil product sales became referred to as "Petrodollars" (Fox et al., 2017).

2.3.2 Asian Money Market (or Asian dollar market)

Bank of America's Singapore branch established the Asian dollar market, and for a period following its institution in September 1968, it was that market's sole bank.

Eventually, however, Bank of America approached Hong Kong rather than Singapore with the proposal to create an Eurodollar market. The rationale was straightforward: it was Asia's international financial hub, with the advantages of proximity to the City of London, British legacies such as common law and the English language, and a tiny city. With the backing of the Bank of England, Singapore also had a long history of foreign banking. Bank of America proposed the development of the Asian Eurodollar market to Hong Kong's colonial authorities. Nonetheless, the local government unexpectedly declined the offer. It had imposed limitations on the financial sector since the 1950s and refused to eliminate the interest withholding tax on foreign currency deposits, a necessary condition for effectively attracting foreign capital (Palan 2010, p. 172). Schenk also notes that Hong Kong's Financial Secretary J. J. Cowperthwaite feared that his jurisdiction would become a tax haven and foresaw that the new foreign currency market bore the threat of suffocating the local market (Schenk 2017, p. 12). Furthermore, unlike Singapore, Hong Kong was directly controlled by the United Kingdom, which had a strong commitment to the sterling (Kim 2018). Singapore's government, on the other hand, was eager to embrace a plan to establish an international financial hub within its borders. Interestingly, the Asian Dollar's geopolitical roots parallel those of the Eurodollar: during the Korean War, Communist China transferred its US dollar assets to a Soviet-owned bank in Paris; the Soviet Union followed suit in the 1950s, notably following its invasion of Hungary in 1956 (Kim, 2018). There was business opportunity in Southeast Asia's refugee funds, and Bank of America developed a positive connection with the Singapore government. For instance, as mentioned above, the bank gained a fortune for the Singapore government during the 1967 Sterling Crisis by operating a sterling overdraft in London. The bank then requested permission from the government to collect dollar deposits from Southeast Asia, recommending that the government establish an Asian currency market with Singapore as its core (Kim, 2020). Additional banks, such as First National City Bank, Chase Manhattan Bank, Chartered Bank, Hong Kong and Shanghai Bank, General Bank of the Netherlands, and Bank of Tokyo gradually joined.

Banks operating in the Asian dollar market accept deposits in specified convertible currencies from foreigners (individuals and entities). When it was created, Asian Currency Units were used to refer to the deposits, just as European Currency Units were used to refer to Euro-dollar deposits. Residents of Singapore were permitted to make deposits with the authorization of the Singapore Exchange control authorities. Banks were not required to acquire approval from Exchange control authorities prior to opening individual bank accounts, nor were they obligated to report on individual accounts. Despite the market name of the Asian dollar, minor deposits of Deutsche mark, Dutch guilders, and Swiss francs were also made. The majority of deposits were made for a fixed period of time, typically little more than three months. The minimum deposit amount that could be accepted from one party was US$25,000 or its equivalent in any other convertible currency. The relatively small size of this minimal amount was a crucial factor in the market's development. Deposits in the

Asian dollar market had a minimum maturity of one month. For those with a limit-ed amount of US dollars or other convertible funds who were unable to engage in the Eurodollar market, the minimum deposit was US$100,000. The Asian dollar market represented an enormous opportunity, and within a few years, the industry boomed, reaching an estimated value of about US$200 million by the 1970s (Pandit, 1971).

As a regional hub for Eurodollars, the Asian Dollar Market's history and evolu-tion are akin to and part of the history of worldwide financial centers, most notably the City of London - the primary market for Eurodollar activity. Additionally, the Asian Dollar Market shares characteristics with Eurodollar transactions, such as an unknown end user and double counting, which complicate determination of its actual size (Kim, 2019). In this context, the term "Asian" only refers to the market's geo-graphical location.

Initially, the Asian money market was similar to its European equivalent in that it was dominated by deposits denominated in United States dollars. Later, the Asian dollar market was officially recognized for the first time. A new market was formed to fulfill the desires of firms aiming to facilitate international trade using the U.S. dollar (Solnik et al., 2009). An essential function of banks in the Asian dollar market is the transmission of funds from depositors such as multinational businesses and government agencies to borrowers such as manufacturing companies. The Asian money market is now primarily centered in Hong Kong and Singapore, where large banks accept deposits and make loans in a variety of currencies.

2.4   International credit market: medium-term financing

The global debt market is a component of the global financial market (the loan capital market). It is an area of market relations that involves the circulation of debt obligations, allowing creditors to recover debts from debtors. These include the international credit market (market for bank loan obligations) and the international debt securities market (bonds, notes, commercial papers, etc.). Its main feature is the possibility of free purchase and sale of financial obligations or financial instruments (transactions based on the exchange of current costs for future costs designed as securities, which can be freely purchased and sold, unlike credit transactions, i.e., the obligations of borrowers to creditors). It constitutes part of the worldwide loan capital market, the Euromarket (Shengelia & Temur, 2016). Financial intermediaries, nonbank financial organizations (insurance firms and pension funds), central banks and other public bodies, governments, regional international development banks, and international financial institutes are participants in the international credit markets (Shengelia & Temur, 2016). International credit transac-tions include bank-to-bank loans and credits, nonbank loans and credits, and new interbank deposits. Basic elements of bank international transactions are three: first, the fact that transactions take into account currency, credit and regional risks; secondly, the fact that areas of the short-term crediting are more various geographically than those of the long-term crediting. Finally, the credit operations of most international banks are directed toward foreign banks that are not their branches, since international crediting is mostly focused on granting short-term credits to foreign banks that are not their branches (Shengelia & Temur, 2016).

When MNCs need to obtain medium-term funds, they have a number of alternatives. They can either take out loans from local financial institutions or raise cash flows through the issuance of notes in their local markets or access medium-term funds through banks located in foreign markets. Loans of one year or longer that are granted by banks to MNCs or government agencies in Europe are commonly called *Eurocredit loans*. These loans are provided in the *Eurocredit market*.

Banks commonly use floating rate loans. In these loans, the rate floats in relation to the movement of some market interest rates, such as the rate commonly charged for loans between banks. This is because banks want to avoid the risk that they incur when authorizing such loans. Indeed, as banks accept short-term deposits and provide longer-term loans, the maturity of their assets and liabilities does not match. This can adversely affect a bank's performance during periods of rising interest rates, since the bank may have fixed a rate on long-term loans while the rate it pays on short-term deposits rises over time. To avoid this risk, they propose floating rates. For example, a Eurocredit loan may have a rate that adjusts every six months and is set at "LIBOR plus 3%". The premium paid above the LIBOR (London Interbank Offer Rate) will depend on the credit risk of the borrower.

2.4.1   Syndicated loans

A syndicated loan is a single loan from a group of banks to a borrower. As with bonds, syndicated loans are offered on the market via an underwriting procedure comparable to bonds, but with a significant element which is peculiar to those type of contracts, that is the connection established between the banks who form the syndicate. Not all loans are acceptable for syndicating; they are more likely to be syndicated when the borrower's information is clear, and the originating institution is credible. Borrowers benefit from cheaper expenses than bond offerings or bilateral loans. Multiple bank ties help the borrower avoid long-term relationship loan hold-up issues and increase funding sources. Creating a syndicate also entails giving other banks a portion of present earnings and client relationships, giving them the opportunity to eventually steal future revenues and market shares.
In summary:

- a syndicated loan is a single loan from a group of banks to a borrower;
- many corporations rely on syndicated bank loans to finance new investment projects, since they lack independent fund raising skills;
- loans are a major source of company or project finance in emerging nations, where bond markets are less developed (Thia, 2019). Syndicated loans have grown in popularity and market share due to their advantages for both parties;
- participating in a syndicated loan helps members to increase credit availability, overcome financial limits, and reduce single borrower risk (Thia, 2019);
- in terms of monitoring, lone lenders can better supervise borrowers, whereas many bank connections (as syndicates) are subject to duplications of transaction costs and reduced efficiency (Godlewski, Lobez, Statnik, & Ziane, 2010).

Sometimes a single bank is unwilling or unable to lend the amount needed by a particular corporation or government agency. In this case, a *syndicate of banks* may be created in which each bank participates in a certain amount of the total lending. Syndicate loans not only reduce the default risk that each bank is exposed to (as they share the amount lent), but they also add extra incentive for the borrower to repay the loan (in case of default, all the participating banks will know that the borrower is not trustworthy).

Borrowers that receive a syndicated loan incur various fees besides the interest rate on the loan. Front-end management fees are paid to cover the cost of organizing the syndicate and underwriting the loan. In addition, a commitment fee is charged annually on the unused portion of the available credit extended by the syndicate.

> Fees are an important part of syndicated loan compensation, with over 80% of loan contracts containing at least one fee type. Mills & Terrell (1984) find a strong statistical relationship between fees and syndicate spreads. Fees are more convenient for borrowers because they do not usually need to be disclosed. The arrangement fee or praecipium is paid upfront to facilitate the deal. Front-end fees are either fixed or calculated as a percentage of the arranger's funding commitment.
> The underwriter is paid an underwriting fee to guarantee funds. This is a reward for committing funds during the first stage of syndication. The arrangement fee is paid upfront when joining the facility. Other syndicate members, especially managers and co-managers, receive a participation fee. This latter fee is usually related to the degree of commitment (Gadanecz, 2004). It also attracts the number and quality of lenders required by the borrower (Steinhauer, Mahler, Kronat, & Weitkamp, 2015).
> If the loan contract specifies a security agent, the security agent is also entitled to a fee. The security agent is appointed and paid for by the borrower, but it represents the syndicate. Since this agent works for the benefit of the syndicate, it could be argued that the security agency fee should be paid by the lenders rather than the borrowers. The market shows that Euribor-based loans have higher fees than Libor-based loans (recall that the Euribor is the average interbank interest rate at which European banks lend to one another, while Libor is the rate at which selected banks on the London money market usually lend. The main difference between the two rates is that Libor rates come in different currencies). Fees are higher for industrialized market borrowers than for emerging market borrowers. Other fees can be paid to entities involved in loan management, such as legal fees.

2.5 International stock and bond market: long-term financing

2.5.1 Sources of long-term funds

There are a number of ways in which an MNC can raise funds in the long run; in fact, there are not only multiple agencies that can be involved but also various instruments that companies can choose to use. Sources of long-term funds can be divided into official and non-official sources. Official sources comprise international development banks, regional development banks, and bilateral agencies. Non-official sources comprise borrowing and lending markets involving international banks, debt securities (such as the international bond market), and equity securities (such as the international stock market). The international stock and bond markets will be addressed in the following sections, while a deeper dive into international banks will provided in the next chapter.

In any discussion of the long-term official sources of funds available for MNCs, it is significant to take note of the following:

a) *Multilateral Agencies*: These institutions were established after the 1940s as the result of large-scale economic development programs, increasing international trade, and the rise of multinational companies. In 1945, the International Bank for Reconstruction and Development (IBRD) was founded for lending with government guarantees; in 1956, the International Finance Corporation (IFC) was established for loans even without government guarantees. In 1960, the International Development Association (IDA) was created for the benefit of relatively poorer nations and institutions, and 1988 saw the establishment of the Multilateral Investment Guarantee Agency (MIGA) to cover the non-commercial risks of foreign investors. Together, all four institutions are known as the World Bank Group (WBG). The World Bank Group is further supported by the work of regional development banks that support the requirements and conditions of different countries and regions.

b) *Bilateral Agencies*: These institutions were first established in 1951 by US President Truman to politically and economically support the Cold War by creating close ties among developing economies through the provision of funds. In the late 1950s, many other governments of the OECD (i.e., the Organization of Economic Cooperation and Development) announced external assistance programs and bilateral lending which peaked in the 1960s.

2.5.2   International bond market

The bond market comprises a wide variety of debt instruments that can differ considerably with respect to various features.

A straight bond pays a fixed rate of interest (the coupon interest) at predetermined intervals (e.g., every six months) and a maturity payment (the maturity or face value) at some predetermined future point in time. A callable bond allows the issuer to call back, or buy back, the bond at a predetermined price.

Bonds are classified as investment grade or noninvestment grade based on the ratings they receive from rating agencies such as Moody's and Standard & Poor's. The risk of an investment grade bond defaulting on the interest and/or maturity value is moderate to very low.

The global corporate bond market is valued at approximately €128.3 trillion (Bloomberg data, May 2020), with 68.1% made up of bonds issued by Sovereigns, Supranationals, and Agencies worth approximately €79.5 trillion. 53% of these bonds are issued globally by financial companies, while the remaining 47% are issued by non-financial companies. The U.S. and China lead the corporate Bond market with a combined 45% share of the global market. If Europe, the third largest market in the world, is included, the size of the share of the three markets reaches over 59%. On its own, Europe has an overall share of 15% of the global market. This reflects not only the market's relative immaturity (the European market is still developing) but also cultural differences and approaches to this source of capital.

MNCs can obtain long-term debt issuing bonds in their local markets.

MNCs can also access long-term funds in foreign markets, given the international nature of their business and the asymmetry of information we have already discussed. MNCs may choose to issue bonds in the international bond market for different reasons:

1. The issuers recognize that they may be able to attract a stronger demand by issuing their bonds in a particular foreign country rather than in their home country. Some countries have a limited investor base, so MNCs in those countries seek financing elsewhere.

2. The MNCs prefer to finance a specific foreign project or subsidiary in a particular currency and therefore attempt to obtain funds where that currency is widely used.
3. Financing in a foreign currency with a lower interest rate may enable an MNC to reduce its financing costs, although it may be exposed to exchange rate risks.

> International bond issues are bonds issued and traded outside the country where the issuer is headquartered. Foreign (exotic) bonds are bonds issued by foreign issuers on the stock exchange of a foreign country and denominated in the currency of that country's market. The issuance of foreign bonds is governed by the rules of the host country's bond market. A foreign bond, for example, is a bond denominated in US dollars issued by a German company in the United States. Foreign bonds are identified by distinct "street" names that allow them to be identified as having originated in a specific country.
> For instance, Yankee bonds traded in the United States, Bulldog bonds traded in the United Kingdom, Samurai bonds traded in Japan, and Matador bonds traded in Spain are all examples of foreign bonds. The term "Eurobond" refers to a bond issued outside the issuer's home country through an international syndicate and sold to investors residing in a number of different countries. A Eurobond is denominated in US dollars that have been issued by a US company and placed in European and/or Asian countries because of the global financial crisis. The Eurobond market is frequently referred to as a supranational market, since Eurobonds are issued simultaneously by international syndicates of underwriters facing lax regulation in a number of countries at the same time. Eurobonds are traded on multiple exchanges, the majority of which are located in London (George et al, 2017).

When an MNC opts to source financing by selling bonds internationally, it has to make decisions about the type of issuance. International bonds are typically classified as Eurobonds, Foreign bonds, or parallel bonds and fully hedged bonds, floating rate notes, foreign currency futures, foreign currency convertible bonds.

a) *Eurobonds*: These are bonds sold in countries other than the one represented by the currency denominating them. For example, a US MNC might issue a bond denominated in Japanese yen but sell it to investors in the United States. For simplicity's sake, we can say that the Eurobond market is an international capital market dealing with long-term bonds (debt), where bonds can be issued in a foreign currency. For this reason, Eurobonds are also called external bonds. Eurobonds take the name from the currency in which they are denominated. For instance, when they are emitted outside the US in US dollars, they are called Eurodollar bonds. This market emerged in the early 1960s, catalyzed by a mandate from the US Commerce Department that US companies investing abroad had to raise money outside of the US. The Eurobond market was born as an alternative to issuing debt in the US. Interest rates and credit conditions in the Eurobond market change constantly, causing the popularity of the market to vary. MNCs typically prefer to issue bonds in the country in which the cost of financing is lowest (i.e., with a lower interest rate or expected depreciation of the foreign currency). Nonetheless, about 70% of Eurobonds are denominated in US dollars. They are underwritten by a multinational syndicate of investment banks and simultaneously placed in many countries through second-stage, and in many cases, third-stages underwriters. In the secondary market, market makers are often the same underwriters who sell the primary issues. Generally, Eurobonds have very distinct features. They are issued in bearer form, which means no record of ownership is kept. Coupon payments are made yearly. They carry a convertibility clause allowing them to be converted into a specific number of shares of common stock and have few, if any, protective covenants. Sometimes they include call provisions, whereas others, called "floating rate notes," have variable rate provisions that adjust the coupon rate over time according to prevailing market rates.

b) *Foreign Bond*: Bonds denominated in the currency of the country where they are placed but issued by borrowers foreign to that country. For example, a US MNC might issue a bond denominated in Japanese yen, then sell it to investors in Japan.

c) *Parallel Bonds*: These represent a blend of the previous two types. Indeed, by using a parallel bond, an MNC can split the same issuance by selling bonds in different currencies at the same time in order to target a wider spectrum of investors worldwide.

d) *Fully Hedged Bonds*: These bonds allow MNCs to sell foreign bonds that eliminate the risk of currency fluctuations by selling the stream of interest and principal payments on forward markets.

e) *Floating Rate Notes*: On these instruments, interest rates are adjusted according to exchange rates and are generally less expensive than foreign loans.

f) *Foreign Currency Futures*: These are obligations to buy or sell a specific currency today for a agreed upon amount at a future date.

g) *Foreign Currency Convertible Bonds*: These bonds are convertible into equity shares by the issuing company either in whole or in part and on the basis of the related agreement.

Before concluding our overview of the international bond market, it is important to emphasize a key characteristic of interest rates: they can vary substantially among currencies. This is due to differences in the interaction between the total supply of funds available in a specific country in relation and the total demand by borrowers in that country. If there is an ample supply of savings relative to the demand, the interest rate for that country will be relatively low. These divergences are crucial for MNCs, since they impact their financing costs. Moreover, interest rates continuously fluctuate depending on credit conditions in the Eurobond market, leading to shifts in the use of this market.

Case Prada and its financing concerns

Developed countries, in particular the United States, were the primary drivers of the global luxury sector before the 2008 financial crisis. The 2008 mortgage crisis, which significantly impacted the economy of most industrialized nations, halted this rising tendency. The global luxury goods market seemed to enter a new era of expansion in 2010, with developing economies leading the way. For example, growth estimates for Japan for the following five years were about 1%-2% per year, but 4%-5% per year for Europe and the Americas, and over 10%-11% per year in Asia – with 15%-20% anticipated for China alone. Prada chose Asia as a prospective growth region in 2011. Prada projected sales in Asia to expand at a considerably greater pace than in Europe at the time since Asia was seeing substantially stronger growth than the rest of the globe. Prada intended to increase its presence in this important sector to profit from this fast expansion. Yet despite its apparent success in terms of increasing income and market presence, Prada ended up significantly in debt and struggled to pay it off. As a result, its board concluded that if Prada wanted to extend its activities in Asia, it would need to raise more than 1 billion euros. The €1 billion would be used to support Prada's expansion in Asia as well as settle a large portion of the company's long-term debt, which was due in a year.

What were Prada's options?
- Issue bonds locally (in the euromarkets), as investors began to rekindle their interest in financing reputable companies. Bulgari was successful in placing a €130 million five-year bond at LIBOR + 2.75% in 2010. LVMH also issued four-year and seven-year notes with LIBOR + 1.85% and 2.00%, respectively. Though Prada did not have a rating, it was predicted that it would have been rated somewhere between Bulgari and LVMH and that there would have been enough demand to produce around 750 million euros in five-year notes at LIBOR + 2.25%-2.50%.
- Issue "dim sum bonds" in Hong Kong, which are bonds denominated in Chinese yuan. McDonald's was one of the first firms to issue this form of bond in October 2010 (a three-year bond at 3%). However, Prada anticipated the Chinese yuan to strengthen against the US currency and the euro, so this alternative was not especially appealing.
- Issue Eurobonds, which are bonds that are sold in countries other than the one in whose currency they are denominated. Prada could have offered bonds in Hong Kong denominated in US dollars. Following this approach, Prada could have profited from Asia's high demand for bonds while avoiding the danger posed by the Chinese yuan depreciating versus the euro.

Which of the options was the best fit for Prada?

2.5.3   The international stock market

The new issue markets for raising equity capital are the market for initial public offerings (IPOs) and the market for seasoned equity offerings (SEOs). An IPO refers to the initial sale of equity (stock) into the public market by a corporation that has no publicly traded equity. SEOs have the advantage that the issuer is already a publicly traded corporation with a history of information disclosure and presence in the public markets.

When an MNC wants to borrow long-term funds, it can either issue bonds in local or international bond markets or issue stocks in local or international stock markets. In fact, MCNs commonly obtain long-term funding by issuing stock locally. Yet, they can also attract funds from foreign investors by issuing stocks on international stock markets.

Although more complex and therefore also more expensive, there are four main reasons why MNCs might choose to issue stocks in a foreign market rather than in their local market:

1. An international listing can create the chance to exploit a potentially more sophisticated, financially educated, and more efficient foreign stock exchange market.
2. The stock offering may be more easily digested when it is issued in larger markets such as, for example, the U.S. Stock Exchange.
3. The issuance of stock in a foreign country can enhance the firm's image and name recognition in that foreign country by serving as a kind of marketing tool to reach investors who may also ultimately become customers of the issuer.

4. Issuing stock in a foreign market diversifies the MNC's shareholder base by attracting investors located abroad in the country where the stock market is located.

Typically, an MNC will issue stocks in a location where it is likely to generate enough future cash flows to cover dividend payments. When an MNC needs to select a foreign stock exchange, it must investigate and assess various features of each potential market. Indeed, MNCs consider the different characteristics of each foreign stock market: its size, trading activity level, regulatory requirements, taxation rate, legal protections for shareholders, and proportion of individual versus institutional share owners. Companies have to keep in mind that, when operating in a foreign international stock market, it is mandatory to comply with the legislation of that stock exchange. As a result, the MNC will likely incur extra expenses to abide by such requirements, including fiscal, legal, and auditing fees.

Examples of stock issuing in the United States by foreign MNCs

A foreign equity issue is the sale of equity in a national market that is not the issuer's home country. Typically, such issues are denominated in the currency of the country in which they are traded.
American Depository Receipts are a special type of foreign equity issue (ADRs). ADRs are certificates that represent ownership of foreign companies' stocks.
Euro-equity issues are equity issues denominated in a currency other than the currency of the country of placement and distributed in multiple national markets at the same time. They are typically underwritten by international syndicates and listed and traded in multiple markets outside the issuer's home country (George et al., 2017).

1) Issuance of foreign stocks in the United States
Non-US corporations that need large amounts of funds sometimes issue stock in the United States. Large businesses usually prefer to list their shares on the US Stock market, since their local stock market may not be large enough to digest the stock offerings. If a large foreign business lists its stock in its local market, and that stock exchange is relatively small or the number of institutional investors is limited, its shareholder base will be limited to few large local institutional investors. The latter will own most of the firm's shares and may cause high price volatility if one starts selling shares. Therefore, to ensure easy stock issuance and diversify their shareholders base, MNCs may choose to issue stocks in the United States.

It is worth mentioning that firms issuing stock in the United States are typically required to satisfy more stringent disclosure rules regarding their financial conditions than they would in their local market. Those obligations might increase the cost of the IPO, since they probably imply additional regulatory costs in the future.

2) American Depositary Receipts (ADRs)

American Depositary Receipts (ADRs) were first introduced to financial markets in 1927 and have since become widely used. They were initially intended to make it possible for American citizens to invest directly in foreign securities on U.S. stock exchanges. A century later, there are nearly 2,000 ADR programs worldwide, representing shares of companies based in more than 70 different countries. American

Depositary Receipts (ADRs) are a type of share certificate/receipt issued by an overseas company to investors in the United States who want to invest in that company's stock. ADRs require the participation of four different parties: a company, an overseas depositary bank, a domestic custodian, and two intermediaries. It is possible to categorize the advantages of American Depositary Receipts (ADRs) into three main categories. First, companies based outside the United States can raise equity capital on the most developed and efficient financial market in the world using these vehicles. Secondly, they also facilitate the activities of mergers and acquisitions, because they are a desirable and sought-after stock-swap "acquisition currency." Third, it is simple and convenient to purchase and hold shares of foreign corporations using American Depositary Receipts (ADRs). Foreign securities deposited with an American depositary are represented by a specific number of American Depositary Receipts (ADRs). It is common for them to be expressed as a ratio (e.g., 1:10, 1:1, 2:1), which has a direct effect on the price. One ADR is equal to one ordinary share of the company (ratio 1:1). The market forces of demand and supply determine the price of ADRs.

Non-US listed firms can also obtain equity financing from the US market using *American Depository Receipts* (ADRs), certificates representing bundles of foreign stocks. ADRs enable firms listed in foreign markets to tap the US market for funds while circumventing some of the disclosure requirements imposed on stock offerings in the United States.

Italian firms go global

JP Morgan issued the first Italian ADR in 1956 for Montecatini, a major mining and chemical company. In recent years, the US Securities and Exchange Commission has allowed banks and depository institutions to establish ADR programs without requiring a non-US issuer. Currently, 54 Italian companies are using American Depositary Receipts to access the US equity market. These include manufacturers (e.g., Leonardo, Atlantia, Prysmian), textile companies (e.g. Moncler, Salvatore Ferragamo, Tod's), and Commercial Banks (e.g. Intesa SanPaolo, Unicredit, Banco BPM). The over-the-counter (OTC) market represents 50 out of 54 programs. The 50 OTC ADR programs are divided into 46 unsponsored ADR programs and 4 Level-I ADRS. The aim of those instruments was, in the plan of the 50 Italian companies who issued them, to increase existing shareholder bases. The remaining 4 ADRs that are not OTC are traded on the New York Stock Exchange and are Level-III, which allows for new share issuance. Ferrari, STMicroelectronics, Eni, and Natuzzi are all listed on the New York Stock Exchange.

Since ADRs represent bundles of stocks, they are traded just like normal shares. The price of an ADR changes constantly in response to supply and demand. However, the intrinsic value of an ADR should move in tandem with the value of the corresponding stock listed on the foreign stock exchange, after adjusting for exchange rate effects.

If there is a discrepancy between the price of the ADR and the price of the foreign stock after adjusting for the exchange rate, investors can use arbitrage to capitalize on the discrepancy between the prices of the two assets until that price reaches an equilibrium.

Alternatives to ADRs

GDRs
A Global Depositary Receipt (GDR) represents ownership of foreign company shares on two or more global markets. It is based on American Depositary Receipts, but unlike ADRs can be traded in multiple countries. GDRs allow companies to tap into international capital pools (with the obvious exclusion of the United States). Global Depositary Receipts programs provide non-U.S. corporations access to capital that would be otherwise unavailable in their home markets, as well as with increased visibility and recognition in international markets, which may lead to future capital raising.

Secondary and dual listings
Dual listing occurs when a company's securities are listed on two or more exchanges, each with its own primary listing requirements. The main reasons why companies use this instrument are to access a larger capital base and benefit from increased share liquidity due to increased market participants. A longer trading period is possible when the time zones of the exchanges do not coincide. Dual listing is not the same as secondary listing. Cross listing refers to a company's listing on stock exchanges other than the primary exchange where its securities are listed. Because it is less expensive to maintain than dual listing, cross listing is commonly used when the listing requirements or geographical reach of the two exchanges are similar. Secondary listing is used to gain access to new markets or to maintain a presence on a company's former primary market.

Global shares
A Global Registered Share (GRS) trades in multiple currencies and can be transferred across borders without conversion. For example, a global registered share bought on the New York Stock Exchange can be sold on the London Stock Exchange for pounds. The securities are identical regardless of the exchange on which they trade, and shareholders have the same rights (voting, dividends, etc.) as the company. Both Global Registered Shares and American Depositary Receipts share the same goals of buying foreign securities without having to trade them. Whereas an ADR is held by the U.S. Depositary Bank, a GRS is held directly by the investor.

Case Prada and the potential IPO in 2011

As we saw earlier, Prada considered raising the €1 billion it required for expansion in Asia by issuing bonds in the different bond markets. However, many outsiders suggested that the stock market was a better option for Prada to raise the capital it required to pay off its debts and finance its expansion plans. Prada has had serious issues with IPO plans in the past. Indeed, in 2001, Prada was slated to list 30% of its stocks on the Milan Stock Exchange to raise more than $850 million. Unfortunately, the offering was put on hold as investor interest in Prada declined in relation to intensifying fears of a recession and the later drop in spending on luxury goods in two of Prada's largest markets: the United States and Japan. Following this postponement, the IPO was moved to the United States, where it was believed to have a better chance of success under these market conditions. The new date was set for September 18, 2001. After the terrorist attacks of September 11th, however, it was impossible to move forward, and the IPO was again rescheduled. In June 2002, the IPO again had to be cancelled – this time because of the WorldCom scandal. In May 2008, there was serious talk of an imminent IPO, but market turmoil following the collapse of Lehman Brothers resulted in a further postponement. In 2011, the market was more stable, and Prada analyzed the possibility of raising funds through an Initial Public Offering. What were the different options for Prada's IPO?

1. Issuing stock on the Hong Kong Stock Exchange (HKEX). In 2011, Asia was dominating the global IPO market with US$48.7 billion raised through IPOs. For Prada, the advantage of listing its shares in Hong Kong was that it could benefit from a substantially higher valuation than if it were listed in Europe.
2. Do a primary listing in Milan and later issue a Hong Kong depositary receipt (HKDR) which could be bought and sold by investors in Asia.

In the end, Prada did not opt for an IPO. In fact, although conditions in financial markets appeared more stable in early 2011, it was unclear what would happen in the next 6 to 12 months. Significant uncertainty in the world's equity markets would have resulted in Prada being undervalued if it were to go public.

2.6   Conclusions

In this chapter, we surveyed the development of international markets. We saw the steps taken to integrate international regulation at EU level (with the SSM, ERS, and EDIS) and the international level (with the Basel Accord). Another important aspect for MNCs is the exchange rate market. We examined the evolution of the monetary and exchange rate system from the Gold Standard until today. Currently, a wide range of banks facilitate foreigner exchange transactions and engage in international trade. There is also a foreign exchange market where MNCs can exchange currencies through banks or telecommunication networks, on the spot, or in forward, future, or options markets, depending on their needs.

Exchange rates are determined in the Forex market. We discussed how to interpret exchange quotations (direct vs. indirect quotations and bid/ask spread). We also outlined the main players in this market and the major risks they present for enterprises. Finally, we analyzed different financing options based on their duration: international money markets (short-term), international credit markets (medium-term), and international stock and bond markets (long-term).

3 International Banks

Reading up until this point, you may have already realized how essential financial intermediaries are, as they help the MNC and its managers navigate the many complicated markets. The topic of asymmetries of information is just an example of the importance of knowhow, an excellent track record and an extensive network, all things that any financial intermediary should have. This is precisely the objective of this chapter: to familiarize the reader with the definition and the business of the financial intermediary. First, we will define financial intermediaries, then outline a taxonomy and touch upon the history of this professional position. Then we will dive directly into the six (or seven) businesses of an international investment bank, namely capital markets, corporate finance, private equity, structured finance, risk and asset management (and lending as a seventh).

3.1 Introductory definitions and history

There are several names for financial intermediaries that specialize in the financial environment, according to different traditions. The US historically defined *international investment banks* as institutions whose main business is underwriting activities. The UK tradition names *merchant banks* those that focus on active trading. The European tradition considers instead *universal banks* those which mainly engage in corporate banking. Nowadays, however, there is no longer a clear distinction, therefore from now on, we will adopt only one label: international investment bank.

3.1.1 Definition of international investment bank (IB)

According to the dictionary, an IB is "a bank whose function is provision of long-term equity and loan finance for industrial and other companies, particularly new securities." While this definition is accurate, it hardly covers the full range of activities in which IBs are involved.

Indeed, an IB is a system of different businesses, with a consultancy and advisory approach. Still, remember that IBs do not take part in strategic growth decisions and do not manage corporations. These institutions see strong interaction with the customer's financial structure, and are specialized in medium-big tickets with an international scope. In addition, international investment banking is a higher risk business compared with traditional commercial banking.

In few words, IBs are international banks which aim to offer a system of financial services for special kinds of clients: public administrations or public authorities, other financial institutions and MNCs.

IBs and commercial banks can be unified into a Unique Universal Bank which has the following pros and cons:

* integration and economies of scale; universal offering; higher capability to satisfy customers;
* conflict of interest (selling issues that the bank has underwritten); higher risk.

What does "medium-big ticket" mean? Imagine receiving a call from Prada, an MNC that needs to raise $1 billion. This is what we would usually refer to as a medium-big ticket referring to the large size of this type of transactions.

There are seven business areas that an IB can be involved in:

1. Capital markets
2. Corporate finance
3. Private equity
4. Structured finance
5. Risk management
6. Asset management
7. Lending.

We include lending services here, but we will never find an IB specialized in lending services alone. This is because, as mentioned above, these banks focus on medium-big tickets, so it would not be economically convenient to offer lending services only, due to the high regulatory capital requirements briefly discussed at the very beginning of Chapter 2. As a reminder, these requirements, which apply both for commercial and international investment banks, state that the higher the amount invested in a single transaction, the higher the risk exposure and therefore the higher the regulatory capital costs.

3.1.2   Core functions

Before moving on, let's look at an IB's core functions – functions that tie into each of the business lines presented above.

As presented in Hughes et al. (2002), the purpose of an IB is to offer services pertaining to underwriting and the selling of bonds and securities and to create markets around these securities for investors wanting to buy or sell them. Underwriting is a big business that saw massive expansion during the 1980s and 1990s. A typical underwriting transaction entails either commitment by an IB to purchasing a whole issue (full underwriting commitment) or its decision to take the entire deal on a best effort basis, which means selling as much as the market will absorb but without guarantees. An IB devotes a considerable amount of time and energy to developing relationships in the underwriting process. If the relationship is a solid one, the IB can win the mandate to manage the issuance of equity or debts. To win such a mandate, the bank must demonstrate an understanding of the client's strategic and operational plans, be ready to assist with credit rating issues, and contemplate the aftermarket services (if needed in the secondary market). Underwriting is sometimes also called primary market making, because the primary market is the first market in which a just-issued security trades, while the secondary market is exclusively devoted to seasoned securities.

In addition, an IB will also provide advisory services for any kind of extraordinary or non-extraordinary financial operations that the customer may be a part of. An advisory service is any activity in which an IB gives advice, recommendations, or options in exchange for a fee. Usually this involves the field of corporate finance, with operations like takeovers, mergers, or leveraged buyouts.

Lastly, IBs can offer other services beyond underwriting and advisory. These can be supplementary business streams, such as foreign currency trading, bridge financing (lending for a short duration to cover a financial gap), financial engineering, and leasing. Financial engineering, for example, occurs when derivatives are applied to manage risk and entails the packaging and sale of zero-coupon securities, asset-backed securities, and so on; this activity offers high rewards but often also high risks.

Given the wide range of activities and functions that IBs can perform, international banking is a much higher-risk business than traditional commercial banking and is heavily reliant on stock markets, interest rates, and other macro-economic factors – all of which are subject to intense speculation. The next section will outline the history of this complex business and then discuss the specificities of its business areas.

3.1.3   History

The roots and origins of the international banking system as we know it today lie in Europe, though other regions have made significant contributions to the field. To step into the past and look back at the origins of banking requires looking closely at the origins of money and the various kinds of regulations establishing codes and rules for its use. According to Hughes et al. (2002), two historical events are significant: the first references to banking can be found in the legal code of Hammurabi, the King of the Babylonian Empire (1728-1686 BC), while money was allegedly created by the Chinese, who were very trade-oriented and saw huge benefits in currency standardization. We cannot forget about Italy or the importance of money and rudimentary forms of banking for the Roman Empire, especially under the Pax Romana,[1]

---

[1] The Pax Romana was a period of relative stability that characterized the Roman Empire for over 200 years, beginning with the reign of Augustus.

or in the early Italian city states, which had strong commercial and financial capabilities. Florence, for instance, coined the florin in 1252, while Venice had the ducat. The merchants of Genoa, Milan, Venice, and Florence formed the first international financial networks, and Italians played a key role in the development of international banking.

From roughly 1350 to 1600, international banking advanced significantly, with German, Flemish, and Dutch peoples seeing international banking as a legitimate profession with a tight connection to commerce. Antwerp[2] was the epicenter of European investment banking in the sixteenth century, thanks to its strategic location between the Baltic, the Atlantic, and the Spice Islands. Antwerp had a stock market where credit was available for royal borrowers in return for guaranteed tax revenues or promises of other forms of reimbursements. The major players in this period were two major German families, the Fuggers and the Welsers, who financed long-distance expeditions that set sail from the city. After Antwerp, Amsterdam became an economic center as the Dutch began dominating trade in the Baltic region. The Dutch established a particularly organized system and founded the Amsterdam Exchange Bank in 1609 and the Amsterdam Stock Exchange in 1611.

During the 1700s and 1800s, London succeeded Amsterdam as Europe's financial center through the establishment of the Bank of England, which was owned by private investors but represented the government's interest in preserving control over the nation's finances. As the most powerful country at the time, Britain imposed a free-trade regime as well as the gold standard. The global financial and trade system was built on the premise that national currencies were tied to the world gold price, which was established by the British from that point forward. This era also saw the rise of a famous banking dynasty, the Rothschilds, which came to symbolize the ideal combination of political and financial power (Hughes et al., 2002).

After London, American banks rose to prominence between the 1800s and the turn of the twentieth century, as the U.S. economy underwent a major structural shift. From its rural and agricultural roots, America grew into the world's most powerful industrialized, urban, and market-oriented economy. The origins of international investment banks as we know them today date back exactly to the early nineteenth century in the United States. In those years, the American government and various sectors of industry needed a large amount of capital to support large projects and investments. Soon there was a shortage of supply of financial resources given the huge demand for capital. Consequently, several investment banks, leveraging their international network, began to seek and collect the necessary funds from the old continent (Europe) by selling to European investors the financial instruments issued by large American companies that needed them to support their large development projects.

American banks' power began to erode in the 1980s as European and Japanese competitive institutions grew in the form of universal banks that began to gain trac-

---

[2] Antwerp, city in the Flanders region of Belgium that is one of the world's major seaports and the international center of the diamond industry.

tion and offered the possibility of providing a range of financial services– including commercial banking, securities issuance and trading, and insurance product sales – all under one roof, as we will see below.

Important banking families

Hughes et al. (2002) offer a brief history of the most important banking families throughout history: the Medici of Florence, the Fuggers of Germany, the Rothschilds of Frankfurt, and the Morgans from the United States.

The Medici of Florence

This family started out as farmers and eventually expanded into commerce and banking, becoming one of the most well-known names in early international banking. The Banco dei Medici (1397-1494) was the greatest and most renowned bank in fifteenth century Europe.
According to several academics, the Medici were once Europe's richest family. The family amassed political influence via this money, initially in Florence and subsequently across Italy and Europe.
The Medici made a great contribution to accounting progress by improving the ledger introducing the double entry method, which made credits and debits more visible.
Giovanni di Bicci de' Medici was the first Medici to establish his own bank, but it was under the reign of Lorenzo il Magnifico (1449–1492) that the family achieved its pinnacle of dominance. The dynasty was also intimately tied to the politics of the Roman Catholic Church. Its authority and prosperity gradually began to wane in the 1500s and disappeared completely by the 1700s.

The Fuggers of Germany

The Fuggers of Augsburg borrowed money from Cardinal Melchior von Brixen in South Tyrol and made loans to Holy Roman Emperor Maximilian, for which they received mortgages on gold and silver mines in Hungary, in the Tyrol, and in the Erzgebirge. By 1508, the Fuggers had established a presence across Europe by investing in textiles, pepper, real estate, and silver being active in long-distance trade, mining, state finance, and overseas ventures. They had a large enough network to serve the Hapsburg court by assisting in the collection of money from vassal nations and giving credit through printed credit notes. However, their prosperity was inextricably linked to the Hapsburg family's deeds, and as that dynasty declined, so did the Fuggers.

The Rothschilds from Frankfurt

The Rothschilds trace their origins back to the Frankfurt Jewish ghetto of the mid-eighteenth century. Mayer Rothschild, the family's founder, began by exchanging fabric and antique coins, sending his five sons around Europe (to Paris, Vienna, Naples, London, and Frankfurt) to establish a worldwide banking network. In 1798, Nathan (1777-1836), the most renowned, is sent to London, Solomon (1774-1855) to Vienna, Carlmann (1788-1855) to Naples, and Jakob (1792-1868), the youngest, to Paris. In less than half a century, starting in the early 1800s, the Rothschilds brothers traded favors and information, expanding abroad and multiplying their money from 3 million francs in 1812 to over 100 million in 1825. Their specialty was moving money, not necessarily their own, but particularly that of the major ruling houses, towards the most profitable activities, which were essentially two: high-interest loans to countries preparing to enter the war and high-yield public debt securities purchased by countries preparing to rebuild after the war. The Rothschilds built a reputation for themselves in Europe during the Napoleonic period, owing to Nathan's competence, who had a large sum of money and established a bank in

London where he invested, specializing in war loans and government bonds. Although his major business was the funding of England and its satellite nations, he granted money to everyone, even Napoleon's France. Rothschild's remains today a significant global bank, with a big London branch, a Swiss holding company with a local presence also in Italy.

J.P. Morgan from the United States

The Morgan family made its fortune with the development of the U.S. railroad industry: in order to raise the funds needed to finance the expansion of the railroad, John Pierpont Morgan's father (1837-1913) moved to London to sell stock to European investors. J.P. Morgan started his career in New York City as a finance and investment agent for his father, where he gained knowledge of both the U.K. and U.S. financial systems. In 1871, he founded Drexel, Morgan & Co., which later became J.P. Morgan & Co. Morgan became extensively involved in loans for railroads and rail lines in the Eastern United States during the 1893 financial crisis. As a result, he became more broadly engaged in the country's reconstruction during a time of volatile economic growth. Morgan was a staunch advocate for establishing a more stable financial system. Throughout his life, he coordinated a significant private sector rescue effort, restoring trust in the financial system and advocating for the establishment of a central bank. Today, JP Morgan Chase & Co. is a market leader in corporate and investment banking financial services, providing solutions to the world's largest enterprises, governments, and organizations.

3.1.4   International investment banks after the credit crisis

The Glass-Steagall Act separated investment and commercial banks in the United States, but the Federal Reserve's activities undermined the law's restrictions, and it was abolished in 1999. Since the repeal of the Glass-Steagall Act, various U.S. commercial banks have absorbed investment banks. As a result, banks are now able to provide both commercial and investment banking services. Both commercial and investment banks have been heavily involved in the securitization sector, which includes trading and investing in property-backed securities, such as prime and sub-prime mortgage-backed securities, as well as in different collateralized debt obligations. Defaults on sub-prime mortgages began to rise in 2006 and property values in the United States began to plummet, escalating even more rapidly in 2007. Valdez et al. (2012) notes that at this point banks had massive portfolios of securities backed by deteriorating collateral on their balance sheets – securities which they were unable to liquidate due to their complex structures and uncertain collateral. Consequently, interbank lending almost came to a halt, since many banks held these securities but had no idea what losses these investments had suffered or how many similar holdings were housed in different banks. This freeze in interbank lending and collapse of liquidity in the system (which needed liquidity to fund their holding of medium- and long-term securitized assets) culminated in crisis. As a result, Bear Stearns and Lehman Brothers failed in 2008, and Merrill Lynch merged with the Bank of America.

From 2008 to 2009, international investment banking slowed substantially. This trend recovered in 2010, only to fall again from 2011 through 2013 as these banks performed poorly. IBs were therefore under considerable pressure to increase their capital, which resulted in a significant consolidation of the industry. Since that time,

U.S. investment banks have increased their market share also in Europe, while the shares of their European counterparts have decreased. According to Caselli et al. (2020), U.S. investment banks enjoy a significant competitive advantage over their European peers. They have a high degree of concentration, constant price discipline, and a vast and lucrative domestic market; their service quality is also generally quite strong. Consequently, they have grown their market share in European investment banking at the cost of local rivals, and this trend is unlikely to change. It seems improbable that European players would join hands in cross-border mergers to establish stronger European investment banking entities in the absence of a fresh campaign for a true European banking union.

3.2 Capital markets

Capital markets support customers in raising money from financial markets by issuing and trading in securities in exchange for fees. Securities include different financial instruments, such as debt, equity, and currency instruments. The type of services offered depends on when and where assistance is offered: *primary* vs *secondary market*.

The *primary market* services deals involving the first issuance of securities. There are four phases to this process: Origination, Advising, Selling and Underwriting. The IB assists customers in originating the deal, thanks to its competences and knowledge of the financial system (e.g., choosing the best foreign country with the lowest interest rate). Once the deal is originated, the IB advises its customers on the valuation of the issue and determines the prices for selling the issue (debt or equity). Finally, the IB sells the issue to international investors. Underwriting is an additional service offered by IBs to guarantee that the company will receive the agreed-upon payment. Underwriting is a commitment to buy any securities that investors cannot be persuaded to buy. If the underwriting service is not utilized and the IB is not committed to purchasing the issue, the bank deals only on a best effort basis, meaning that they will attempt to sell as much as the market will absorb with no guarantees. Therefore, with underwriting, the IB bears the risk of losing both its money (because of the unsold shares) and its reputation. Usually, however, the risk is shared among other merchant banks and investment institutions. Indeed, in this process, depending on the size of the issue, many players can be involved: the bulge bracket (the largest IBs in the deal), the major bracket (second tier of IBs) and mezzanine or submajor bracket (smaller third tier banks).

The *secondary market* instead assists deals by providing advisory services and support for the sale of securities that have already been issued. Brokerage and dealing are two additional services within this domain.

Table 3.1 clearly divides the tasks of both the primary and secondary market services.

a) Primary market activities: advisory and support for initial issuing of securities.
b) Secondary market activities: advisory and support offered post issuing.

Table 3.1   **Primary and Secondary market services**

	DCM	ECM
Primary market	IPO SEO PP → advisory, placement & selling, underwriting	
Secondary market	Brokerage & dealing	

To clarify further, observe the matrix in **Table 3.1**, which answers two crucial questions:

1. Which securities? Financing via bonds (debt capital markets) or equities (equity capital markets).
2. How are these securities used? With a liability approach (primary market) or an asset approach (secondary market).

Depending on the answers to these questions, the IB might be doing different jobs and activities, as illustrated in the matrix. The deals that this bank could run in the primary market are:

- *Initial Public Offering* (IPO), namely helping customers change their legal status as they start issuing securities on the stock exchange. This is the only business that will help customers transform from a private company to a public (listed) one. The process requires help from the bank in due diligence, pricing of the issue, setting calendar dates, delivering a prospectus and selling the offer securities, among other things.
- *Seasoned Offering* (SEO) is similar to the IPO, but differs in the sense that the issuer is already listed in the stock exchange and simply has to issue additional securities.
- *Private Placement* (PP) means issuing securities for a company that is not listed and intends to stay that way. The securities will be sold to one or more institutional buyers in this case, a rather complicated and difficult task.

The jobs that banks could do are the same for the three businesses listed above, which all constitute sources of revenues (as we will summarize at the end of the chapter in a table). The first possible job is *advisory*, meaning advising customers, helping them understand whether a primary issuance would make sense, or if corporate lending would be a more appropriate solution. Advisory fees usually range between 0.5 and 5%, and are usually the subject of a long one-to-one negotiation: the bigger the deal, the higher the fee, the happier the bank. After advisory, the second job could be *placement and selling*, namely selling the securities in the market, i.e. finding customers that want to buy them. In this case too, the remuneration for the bank comes in the form of fees. Last comes *underwriting*, which we already mentioned in the introduction. To underwrite means to buy securities. But why would a bank want to buy the securities it is issuing? There are two main reasons: to send a signal to the market regarding the strength and value of the securities in question, and as a parachute deal with the customer, who feels reassured that if all securities are not placed, the bank will intervene and buy the remaining ones. Revenues in this specific case come from fees but also from any possible capital gains on the securities sold on the market. At this point banks must be careful as matters of regulatory capital might enter into the discussion. In fact, if a bank underwrites securities, it ends up having additional assets on its balance sheet. So adjustments must be made accordingly to the regulatory capital which is calculated based on risk-weighted assets, as seen in the section on the Basel Accord in the previous chapter. The final profit from underwriting will be the capital gains plus the fees minus the cost of regulatory capital incurred.

As for the *secondary market*, instead, as illustrated in the matrix above, there are two relevant jobs: brokerage and dealing. When talking about *brokerage*, it is the IB that acts as a broker, becoming the official agent of the customer and placing its securities with buyers. In the *dealing* activity instead, the IB completes a rather delicate transaction. The end goal is still to sell securities, but in this case the bank has a ten-day window to prepare the deal, study the transaction and find the customers. Once the ten days are up, the IB will push the button starting the countdown and open a 24-hour window, within which the IB has to place all the securities to close the deal. In the first case, with brokerage, profit comes from fees, while for dealing banks earn from both fees and capital gains. Remember that dealing does not involve any considerations of regulatory capital, unlike with the underwriting process. Indeed, the deal should be completed within the 24-hour window and as such, no increase in assets is recorded in the balance sheets, resulting in no alteration of the regulatory capital levels. Thus, this type of job is highly remunerative and highly coveted. But on the other hand, dealing is very difficult and entails huge risks if the banker does not manage to complete the deal within the timeframe.

3.3 Corporate finance

The role of corporate finance in an IB is to give financial assistance to clients (MNCs in this case) in order to implement their strategic decisions (to grow, or acquire new businesses, or restructure). The revenue model is based on fees obtained for the services provided.

Let's take the case of an MNC whose strategic priority is acquisition. Here, again, we have the initial *origination services*, which refer to searching for a potential target, studying the market and deciding when to grow, and then the *arranging the deal* and *offering advisory services*. Once the best target has been found, the client needs help in evaluating that target, for instance by addressing the question of how exposure to international risk can be represented directly in the discount rate, or how it can be reflected in the cash-flow assumptions valuation. Based on the outcomes of this valuation, the corporate finance division of the IB will define an acquisition price, which must be negotiated with the target shareholders. Note that there is a difference between evaluating a corporation on a stand-alone basis and directly proposing an acquisition price. We must determine the value of synergies and control first, to take this into account in setting the price. The last service is *financing*, helping the client raise the funds necessary to finance the acquisition price. We might suggest that the client pay the acquisition price with cash or with stocks. Usually, payment is made with a combination of the two.

Corporate finance services are deeply involved with consultancy to enhance customers' ability to achieve:

1. Growth
2. Acquisitions
3. Restructuring
4. Privatization.

As we mentioned, corporate finance activities entail advising clients who take part in M&A transactions. M&A covers a wide spectrum of services involving corporate governance, strategy and financing of consumers. The most common deals are:

- *Mergers*: A merger occurs when two companies join together to form a new one.
- Acquisitions: In an acquisition, one company takes over the ownership of another by purchasing its shares.
- *Spin offs*: A spin-off is the process whereby a company (the spinning-off company) transfers part of its activities to a newly created independent company (the spun-off company).
- *Joint ventures*: An agreement whereby two or more parties, usually companies, undertake to collaborate on a common project by jointly exploiting their synergies, know-how or capital.
- *Carve Out*: Particular type of Spin-Off put in place mainly for the purpose of obtaining financial resources from the market through the contribution of a company branch in a vehicle destined to be listed through an IPO.

Firms planning a takeover will turn to an IB for help and advice regarding price, timing, tactics and so on. Likewise, the target of the takeover will turn to these bankers for help in fending off the predator or negotiating the fair price at which it makes sense to sell the control. The fees for these services can be substantial, and in a large takeover there may be three investment bankers or more on each side. Typically, M&A fees average between 0.125% and 0.5% of the target's value. Some fees depend on success, whereas others are linked to the premium achieved over the stock price of the customer-company.

When talking about M&A transactions, battles and strategies to overcome a hostile bid or takeover are relevant to keep in mind. Indeed, over the years, companies and advisors have devised a large number of strategies to attempt to avoid unwanted takeovers. Some strategies include the selection of a *white knight*. In this case, if a takeover seems inevitable, the bank may find a rival bidder who is preferable to the original predator. Moreover, sometimes one or two investors can be found who will take a substantial minority holding and block the takeover; they are called *white squires*. Alternatively, a company might decide to implement a *Pacman defence*, where the target firm turns around and tries to acquire the company that made the hostile takeover attempt. *Greenmail* can be an additional strategy, when the company persuades the bidder to withdraw by buying back the shares at a higher price. Finally, companies can implement a *poison pill*, where, once one shareholder's stake rises above a given percentage (usually 20%), this device is triggered, allowing the company to give all shareholders (apart from the 20% holder) the right to buy new shares at a substantial discount, often 50%. The greater the number of shareholders who buy additional shares, the more diluted the acquiring company's interest becomes. This makes the bid prohibitively expensive.

3.4   Private equity

Private equity is the equity investment by a bank that wants to provide financing by buying shares in a customer (in this case the customer is the MNC). Imagine a little roleplay, with two participants: an MNC that needs funds and a sophisticated investor, that is, a private equity investor willing to enter into the equity of a corporation that is not listed. Therefore, private equity is a way to raise funds for an MNC. The MNC will accept funds in exchange for a part of its equity and a say in corporate governance by the investor. This is how private equity differs from bank funding.

As one might imagine, public equity and private equity differ significantly. First, there are several distinguishing aspects that can be managed only by sophisticated investors: liquidity, pricing and monitoring. Moreover, private equity goes hand in hand with corporate governance, which, from the MNC side, is partially relinquished for a series of benefits: financial benefits, networking benefits, knowledge benefits and certification benefits. Lastly, another difference between private and public equity is that with the latter, we expect both dividends and capital gain as returns; with the former we get only capital gains.

Private equity means financing a customer by providing equity capital. When sales growth is stable, a private equity investment is called a *replacement*. If instead the company is in decline, then investment by private equity is called vulture financing. Private equity can be managed directly by the bank or by a dedicated vehicle like a closed-end fund in Europe and venture capital fund in US and UK.

Private equity can be handled by the bank in two different ways. Before describing them, it should be stressed that from the customers' perspective, nothing changes: they still receive financing, which can be done directly, or by using funds.

If done directly, clients get financed because the bank buys directly their shares. As a consequence, the shares in question will remain on the balance sheet of the bank, so they have an impact in terms of regulatory capital. The profit model in this case is capital gains minus the cost of the additional regulatory capital to be held by the bank. If done indirectly, instead, the bank uses its investors' money to buy the shares of the client. Whenever the bank uses funds raised from investors, it has to create an Asset Management Company in Europe (AMC) or a limited partnership (LP) in US and UK to manage private equity funds. The idea here is that the bank does not want to incur the onus of additional regulatory capital by using its own funds; instead it will provide a service in order to raise funds of others investors to finance the company. The AMC/LP is nothing more than a vehicle for managing funds, owned 100% by the bank. Its purpose is to create private equity funds, i.e. bank accounts in which investors deposit their money. The revenues for the bank come only in the form of fees (the higher the financing, the higher the fees), and there is a small portion of regulatory capital to keep in mind. Indeed, to create the AMC/LP, the bank has to invest at least 2% in the equity of the vehicle, thus resulting in slight adjustments to the regulatory capital.

3.5 Structured finance

A structured finance transaction is a deal that always has three features:

1. An asset or a system of assets able to generate cash flows;
2. The creation of a SPV (Special Purpose Vehicle), namely a new corporation established with the intention of implementing the transaction (the SPV is created to isolate the asset);
3. The transaction is always financed with an enormous amount of debt, which is contractually repaid by the SPV with the cash flows produced by the asset.

Examples of structured finance transactions are *securitization, project finance* and *leveraged buyout.*

3.5.1 Securitization

Securitization is a structured finance transaction where the asset or system of assets can be represented by a real estate property, mortgage, commercial credit, etc. It is often used to create marketable instruments based on illiquid assets. How does securitization work? Consider an MNC's balance sheet and assume that on the asset side there is a real estate property which is not the core business of the MNC. In this case, we can apply a securitization transaction to a non-core asset with the goal of extracting additional value. All that we need to do is to create an SPV (in which the bank invests a token 1% in equity). As shown in **Figure 3.1** equity is invested in this vehicle, which will raise funds in the form of debt from the banking system (usually consisting of syndicated loans or bonds from the market). So the SPV has assets, and the bank's job is to manage these assets and create cash flows that will repay the loans.

Figure 3.1   Securitization process

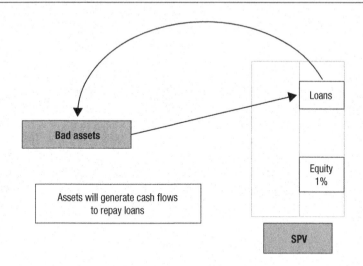

When the project comes to an end, the SPV is shut down; in other words, it is a one-deal vehicle. In order to raise debt through an empty shell, no collateral is needed. And since there is no collateral, lenders only rely on the fact that after the transaction is implemented, the real estate property will be transferred to the asset side of the SPV.

Lenders are willing to finance this transaction because they rely on the reputation of the IB involved in the deal. The role of the IB in this sense is crucial. In fact, the MNC can depend on the ability of the IB to properly manage the SPV's assets and to entice the market in order to give investors higher returns. It is important to remember that there is a legal separation between the MNC and the SPV; in other words, if the MNC collapses the SPV could still exist and vice versa. In case the securitization fails to produce enough cash to repay the debt, participation in the control governance is cancelled, so the equity invested is lost. There is a huge amount of debt in an SPV, with a debt-equity ratio usually made up of 10% equity and 90% debt. So we have a highly leveraged company.

It is worth spending few words on the profit model of securitizations. If all the steps and the mechanisms behind them are clear, one might agree with this list of revenue sources:

a) Fees from the advisory business;
b) Fees from the establishment of the SPV;
c) Fees and capital gains (from Capital Markets division) by raising money through loans;
d) Fees from asset management;
e) Capital gains from private equity.

We can understand very well that if five sources of revenues pop up from one deal, the reasons for excessive securitization before the 2008 crisis appear more than clear.

3.5.2   Project finance

In project finance, the system of assets is represented by a large project (infrastructure, for example). Let's take an MNC and the creation of an SPV, where equity is invested as we know; the SPV raises debt to sustain construction costs for a large project. Again, there is a legal separation between the MNC and the SPV. The reason why project finance is implemented here is that it is far too risky for the company to undertake the project on its own (e.g., there are political and external/environmental risks). The sectors where the best projects are to be found are usually hospitals and prisons.

3.5.3   Leveraged Buyout

A Leveraged Buyout (LBO) is a deal where the asset generating cash flows is a company bought thanks to the transaction (the target). Imagine a customer wants to buy a company. An IB would organize and set up the deal, creating an SPV from scratch (where just a small amount of equity is invested by the sponsor of the initiative). The IB looks also for loan sponsors that invest in this deal because of the bank's reputation and good standing as an IB. Many other banks jump on board with loans, and now the bank knows it has the money to buy the target company that its customer wants. If the target company is not on sale, a hostile takeover must be launched. In an LBO, this job is a very aggressive one, as the bank supports its customer in buying another company. In this case, the future cash flows of the target company will be used to repay the SPV. This is a different job from M&A operations, in which the bank does not use any of the target's money to repay the acquisition. The diagram in **Figure 3.2** might help the reader better understand the process.

An example: an MNC (let's say Pirelli) decides to buy a target company (Telecom). Pirelli can decide either to buy its target directly or with an LBO transaction, which works as follows: the MNC builds an SPV, invests equity, and relies on an IB to raise debt, with the aim of cash generation. This cash will then be used by the SPV to acquire the equity of the target company. The target will have its own debt (Dt) and assets (At) and will be merged with the SPV. The SPV gains control of the target equity using the MNC capital invested in the SPV (equity) and the debt raised for the deal, so the new equity will be the SPV's equity and the new total debt is equal to the debt of the target (Dt) plus the debt raised by the SPV, while the new assets (At) are the assets of the target. If in project finance the object of the transaction was the project, in this case the object is the target company, whose cash flows are used to repay the debt. Again, there is a legal separation between the MNC and the risks associated

Figure 3.2   **Leverage buyout process**

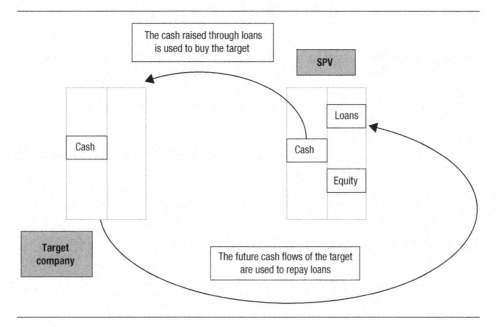

with the transaction. An LBO is an important deal for an international investment bank in terms of potential profits, as the bank gets remunerated for originating the transaction, and for arranging it (if a syndicated loan is used); or for being a global coordinator (if bonds are issued). Since the bank usually provides equity, it will also earn money from capital gains.

3.6   Asset management

Being an asset manager means managing the wealth of one's own customers, thus the IB will offer services in terms of *allocating*, *protecting* and *investing* financial or non-financial assets. The fundamental objective of the asset management service is to provide superior returns by utilizing the best relative-value global credit strategies in an interest-rate-neutral framework. Customers may include high-net-worth individuals, corporates, pension funds and mutual funds. In particular, looking at potential customers more in detail:

- *High-net-worth individuals* may approach the bank to handle all their affairs, including investments. Keep in mind that this can also be part of private banking division within a commercial bank.
- *Corporates* may either have good cash flow and wish to pay someone else to

handle their investments, or they may be building up a large amount of funds, anticipating some later takeover activity, and temporarily pay an IB to handle this.

- *Pension Funds.* In some economies, administrators may feel that they lack the proper management skills to run pension funds and may pay others to do so. In these circumstances, pension funds are usually the biggest clients of the investment management department.
- *Mutual Funds* (i.e., collective investments in money market instruments, bonds or equities). In this case, the bank may run its own fund and advertise it to small investors. In addition, the bank will manage mutual funds for others. Typically, fund managers will charge a small percentage fee for handling the fund and the client will cover costs such as the broker's commission.

Dealing with financial assets means not only specializing in cash management strategies but also having taxation/legal expertise and country-specific knowledge, given the possibilities of exploring deals in different countries. Indeed, considerable care is given to ensure diversification among credit risk profiles, industry sectors, geography and asset classes.

Asset management can refer to *financial* or *non-financial assets*. There could be two different jobs involved in this activity:

- *Advisory on portfolio creation* and *asset allocation*: The IB fixes guidelines and suggests actions, but it is the customer who has the last word when it comes to taking a decision. The revenue model in this case is fees only.
- *Advisory* (as above) and *asset management*: In this case, the IB is in charge of the final decisions too. The profit model is still based on fees that come from advisory (fixed fees) as well as from management (fees here can also be negotiated contingent to portfolio performance).

However, important to note is that for an IB, it is often difficult to break into investment management; in fact, not all institutions participate in this line of business. One of the main reasons for this is the distinct danger of losing money. In particular, if an IB loses money in asset management, this does not project the proper image of an institution capable of making money, which in turn can damage the more traditional capital-raising role of the bank.

3.7   Risk management

This division of the IB offers services to protect customers from several risks, which can be financial and/or pure risks. When facing pure risks (e.g., risks that always have a negative outcome when they arise, such as industrial risks), one option is to take out an insurance contract. With financial risks, the focus is on analyzing derivatives (options, futures, forwards).

Two questions are salient when dealing with risk management:

- What kind of risk is it, financial or non-financial?
- What kind of instruments should be used to manage this risk, derivatives or insurance contracts?

What kind of risk is it?

Financial risks are always linked to the volatility of something; as such they can generate both losses and capital gains. Non-financial risks instead are linked to the probability of some event, e.g. the CEO leaving the company. In this case only losses can result.

What instruments?

In order to manage risk, IBs provide supplementary services. These services are also known as financial engineering, which can be defined as the application of derivatives to manage risk. This entails the packaging and sale of zero-coupon securities, mortgage-backed securities, other asset-backed securities and derivatives.

Derivatives can only be used to manage financial risks (futures, options, swaps). A derivative is a financial instrument based on another more elementary financial instrument. The value of the derivative derives from this second instrument, which is usually a cash market financial instrument, such as a stock or bond. The utilization of derivative instruments in investment banking is associated with securities trading. In particular, traders who are experts in this instrument can act both on behalf of clients or take positions of their own for the IB (i.e., proprietary trading). Although there is much hype over financial engineering, and derivatives in particular, it is essential to keep in mind that these instruments offer high rewards, but often with high risk. Derivatives are not for the financially unsophisticated banks, as they entail buying and selling credit risk.

In this case a bank is faced with a make-or-buy decision: whether to produce a derivative or buy one on the market. When buying on the market, the profit model lies in fees because the bank is acting like a broker. When producing a derivative instead, profit will come from capital gains and regulatory capital, as the bank is generating a contract to hold on the asset side of its balance sheet. As for insurance contracts, they can cover both financial and non-financial risks. These contracts are not issued by a bank but by specific intermediaries, insurance companies, and the profit model for the bank is fee-based only.

3.8   Lending

As mentioned earlier, corporate lending is not considered a typical business of an IB. Still, it is worth mentioning a few lines on this too. Corporate lending means providing loans to companies. Traditionally, loans can be classified in different families: treasury loans (from 1 to maximum 7 days maturity), short-term loans (max 18 months maturity) and mortgages or leasing (more than 18 months maturity). It is very common for a pool of banks to create these loans, in which case they are called "syndicated" (see Chapters 1 and 13 for more details on syndicated loans).

Both investment and commercial banks can also accept bills of exchange. A bill of exchange in the past was mainly used for export/import businesses, but can be utilized nowadays in several other ways. A bill of exchange used to mean an exporter drawing up the bill stating that payment would be due for goods and services within a given time frame, and the importer would sign it. Given that the exporter might need compensation immediately, this party would either ask the bank for a loan, or sell the bill of exchange to the bank at a discount (i.e., selling it at lower price that what was due, to compensate for the risk and the cost of money). Today, the whole procedure for trade finance is tied up by arrangements between the importer's bank and the exporter's bank.

3.9   Revenue model per division within an international investment bank

Following the previous descriptions of all the different businesses of an IB, you should now be able to accurately identify all the revenue models for all the businesses and fill in this table. For the sake of clarity, and because understanding the sources of revenue is crucial in these businesses, the complete table with the cells that correspond to each source of revenue can be found below (Caselli et al., 2021). Try and take the time to fill in this table without looking at the solution and see whether you have understood everything correctly concerning the specificities of the six businesses previously described. This is an excellent exercise to consolidate your knowledge and reveal potential doubts, if there are any.

Now, let's discuss **Table 3.2**. As we can see, in the capital markets division a distinction has been made between primary and secondary market as well as particular deals like proprietary trading, market making and specialist. Associated with each of these deals, there is the specific job to be considered. For example, as explained in the previous sections, whenever there is a primary market deal, there are two activities that the IB can perform, namely placement and selling, and underwriting. No impact on the balance sheet of the bank means no impact on the regulatory capital, as in placement and selling. The other job is underwriting. Here, not only does the IB get paid fees for its work, but it also has the chance to earn capital gains if it manages to sell the securities for more than the purchase price. However, if these securities remain unsold, they will end up in the balance sheet of the bank, and impact the regulatory capital requirements. This is the way to look at this table. Now, apply the same reasoning to all the other divisions.

Table 3.2   **Revenue model for international investment banks**

Business	Relevant Deals	Activities	Revenue Model			Regulatory Capital Impact
			Capital Gains	Fees	Interest Margin	
Capital Market	Primary	Placement and Selling		Yes		
		Underwriting	Yes	Yes		Yes
	Secondary	Brokerage		Yes		
		Dealing	Yes	Yes		Yes, only if on books
	Proprietary Trading	Trading	Yes			Yes
	Market Making	Pricing		Yes		
	Specialist	Pricing and Trading	Yes	Yes		
Corporate Finance	M&A	Advisory		Yes		
	Restructuring	Advisory		Yes		
Private Equity	Direct Investment	Investing	Yes			Yes
	Managing of Funds	Managing		Yes		Yes, but marginal
Structured Finance	Project Finance	Advisory		Yes		
	Securitization	Advisory		Yes		
	LBO	Advisory		Yes		
Asset Management	Financial Asset	Advisory & Management		Yes		
	Non-Financial Asset	Advisory & Management		Yes		
Risk Management	Financial Risk	Advisory	Yes	Yes		Only if counterpart
	Non-Financial Risk	Advisory & Brokerage		Yes		
Corporate Lending	Lending	Investing & Advisory		Yes	Yes	Yes

3.10   Organizational strategies within corporate and international investment banking

Usually IBs organize their business according to three different dimensions:

1. Customers
2. Products
3. Markets/countries.

With reference to these dimensions, there are three different approaches:

a) Being a global player: offering all types of products to all kinds of customers in all the markets/countries. Example: JP Morgan or Goldman Sachs.

b) Being an international player: offering all types of products to all kinds of customers but only in certain markets. Example: BNP Paribas, Unicredit.

c) Being a local player: offering all products to all customers, but only in one market/country. Example: MedioBanca.

Strategies and strategic models of IBs are based on positioning relative to three different parameters/variables (CPM model, **Figure 3.3**).

Figure 3.3   **CPM model**

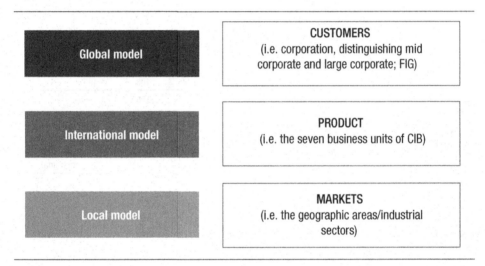

3.11 Different types of international investment banks: some examples

One should keep in mind that not all IBs are equal. Indeed, this last section of the chapter is just to give the reader some examples in the vast world of international investment banking. Below are the names of some institutions, grouped by their specific type. The most recent league tables, ranking banks on the basis of their activities and fees per product, region and industry as well as for deals, bonds, loans and equity are also reported. These tables are a good starting point to understand the global landscape of the most prominent names, and the sectors or areas in which they are market leaders. This is also invaluable information for students who want to apply to an IB for summer internships or off-cycles.[3]

---

[3] Be sure to keep an eye on IBs and check the most recent updates here: https://markets.ft.com/data/league-tables/tables-and-trends.

Table 3.4   **Types of IBs**

"Surviving" Global Investment Banks	Large International Investment Banks	Boutique/Local Investment Banks (focus on M&A business)	Retail Brokerage Firms (focus on client investments)
Bank of America	Natixis	Evercore Partners	Charles Schwab
Barclays	ABN AMRO	Greenhill & Co	Commonwealth
Citigroup	Macquarie	Houlihan Lokey	Financial Network
Credit Suisse	MUFG	Jefferies & Co	E*Trade
Deutsche Bank	Nomura	Lazard	Edward Jones
Goldman Sachs	Royal Bank of Canada	Moelis & Co	LPL Financial
J.P. Morgan	(RBC)	Perella Weinberg-	Royal Alliance
Morgan Stanley	Royal Bank of Scotland	Partners	Scottrade
UBS	Société Générale	Robert W. Baird & Co	TD Ameritrade
BNP Paribas	Wells Fargo	Rothschild & Co	
HSBC	Banca IMI	William Blair	
	Nordea	PJT Partners	
	Santander	Alantra	
	UniCredit	Centerview Partners	

Concerning the groups and types of IBs, it is essential to remember that they come in all shapes and sizes. The largest firms are usually referred to as the bulge bracket. The institutions that are not in the bulge bracket fall into second or third tier of banks; then come regional institutions and boutiques that specialize in a few selected services. The organization and structure of these IBs varies considerably.

3.12 Conclusions

Nowadays, international investment banks are increasingly key players in the financial system. IBs may be involved in a wide range of business areas, but the main function that has characterized them since their inception is probably the underwriting and sale of stocks and bonds. In this chapter, we have traversed the history of these types of financial institutions from their founding to the last years after the economic crises of 2007-2009 and 2011-2013.

We have deepened our knowledge about the different business areas in which IBs are involved. One of the main ones is the capital market. It is divided into primary and secondary markets. In the former, the main activities are initial public offerings (IPOs), seasonal offerings (SEOs), and private placements (PPs), while in the latter it is dealing and brokerage. We also examined the role of an IB in corporate finance, particularly with respect to the services offered in mergers and acquisitions (M&As), and analyzed the direct and indirect interventions of private equity (PE) IBs.

Table 3.5   Asset Class M&A

Rank by value YoY Δ	YTD Advisor	Rank Value per Advisor (US$ m)	Rank Value per Advisor YoY Δ	Rank Value per Advisor Market Share %	Rank Value per Advisor Market Share YoY Δ	Number of Deals per Advisor # of Deals	Number of Deals per Advisor YoY Δ
+1	Goldman Sachs & Co	94,375.7	+367.6%	36.2	+21.3%	36	+21
+6	Bofa Securities Inc	45,929.6	+441.1%	17.2	+11.3%	16	+3
-2	JP Morgan	44,922.9	+42.9%	17.3	-5.9%	32	+7
+11	Barclays	35,869.8	+688.1%	13.8	+10.4%	21	+15
-2	Morgan Stanley	24,885.9	+35.4%	9.6	-4.0%	13	-5
-2	Credit Suisse	21,817.8	+20.5%	8.4	-5.0%	10	+3
+25	Jefferies LLC	19,947.0	+1343.8%	7.7	+6.7%	25	+11
-2	Citi	18,800.3	+22.7%	7.2	-4.1%	13	+1
-4	Evercore Partners	12,188.4	-23.1%	4.7	-7.0%	7	-10
+17	Centerview Partners LLC	119,69.9	+521.7%	4.6	+3.2%	6	-1
	Subtotal with Financial Advisor	197,363.9	+123.2%	75.8	+10.6%	421	-371
	Subtotal without Financial Advisor	63,056.3	+33.8%	24.2	-10.6%	1692	-1,010
	Industry Total	260,420.2	+92.1%	100	0%	2113	-1,381

Source: All data retrieved from Refinitiv (League Tables) as of 27 January 2021.

Table 3.6   Asset Class Bonds

Book Runner	Proceeds per Book Runner	Proceeds per Book Runner	Proceeds per Book Runner	Proceeds per Book Runner	Number of Issues per Book Runner	Number of Issues per Book Runner
	Proceeds (US$ m)	Proceeds YoY Δ	Market Share %	Market Share YoY Δ	# of Issues	YoY Δ
JP Morgan	43,267.8	−18.8%	6.1	−0.3%	178	−36
Citi	38,660.0	−19.3%	5.5	−0.3%	144	−26
Deutsche Bank	33,323.6	+37.8%	4.7	+1.8%	114	−21
HSBC Holdings PLC	29,138.5	+13.7%	4.1	+1%	114	−17
Bofa Securities Inc	29,122.8	−21.6%	4.1	−0.4%	130	−25
Barclays	27,175.7	−30.8%	3.9	−0.8%	112	−41
BNP Paribas SA	26,143.2	+22.5%	3.7	+1.1%	105	=
Morgan Stanley	24,581.3	−14.8%	3.5	0.0%	117	−14
Goldman Sachs & Co	22,686.9	−32.6%	3.2	−0.9%	93	−28
Societe Generale	17,126.6	+7.9%	2.4	+0.5%	39	−15
Subtotal with Book Runner	704809,7	−15.2%	100	0.0%	1535	−483
Subtotal without Book Runner	0		0	0.0%	0	=
Industry Total	704809,7	−15.2%	100	0.0%	1535	−483

Table 3.7   Asset Class Equity

Book Runner	Proceeds per Book Runner	Proceeds per Book Runner	Proceeds per Book Runner	Proceeds per Book Runner	Number of Issues per Book Runner	Number of Issues per Book Runner
	Proceeds (US$ m)	Proceeds YoY Δ	Market Share %	Market Share YoY Δ	# of Issues	YoY Δ
Morgan Stanley	9,514.6	+68.7%	12.7	−0.4%	42	+15
Goldman Sachs & Co	6,635.6	+100.5%	8.9	+1.2%	42	+19
JP Morgan	5,456.5	+44.3%	7.3	−1.5%	31	+4
Citi	4,678.7	+35.7%	6.2	−1.8%	24	+1
Credit Suisse	3,956.7	+368.7%	5.3	+3.3%	23	+14
UBS	3,944.3	+274.2%	5.3	+2.8%	20	+10
Goutai Junan Securities	3,643.2	+1,852.9%	4.9	+4.5%	6	−1
Bofa Securities Inc	2,724.8	+33.8%	3.6	−1.1%	26	+11
Barclays	2,661.2	+76.2%	3.6	+0.1%	21	+9
China International Capital Co	2,249.9	−6.3%	3	−2.6%	8	−4
Subtotal with Book Runner	74,909	+74.3%	100	0.0%	400	+150
Subtotal without Book Runner	0		0	0.0%	0	=
Industry Total	74,909	+74.3%	100	0.0%	400	+150

In addition, we studied the different types of structured finance, seeing the main features of securitization, project finance and leveraged buy-out (LBO) transactions. In terms of asset management, as seen, IB deals with the allocation, protection and investment of financial assets for high-net-worth individuals, corporations, pension funds and mutual funds. Finally, IBs offer risk management and lending services.

At the end of the chapter, we presented the three dimensions (customer, product, market) by which IBs organize their business model: global model, international model, and local model.

4   Corporate Valuation: Domestic Analysis

The following two chapters will be devoted to company valuation and the relative tools, perks, advantages and soft spots. The valuation process is never an easy task. It requires analytical and technical abilities, historical and prospective data and a set of fully explained assumptions.

As we will discover in this chapter, there are several approaches when it comes to assessing the value of a target company. We will only cover two of them: the financial one, which is called the Discounted Cash Flow model, and the comparative one which uses market and transaction multiples.

The most-used valuation method is certainly the analytical DCF model, which requires detailed cash flow forecasting and the estimation of other subjective parameters such as the company's terminal value, future debt, growth rate and cost of capital. The last item, represented by the Weighted Average Cost of Capital (WACC), calls for additional calculations and hypotheses which make the valuation more complex, especially when dealing with MNCs. Once we have the DCF result, we can carry out a control method, based on market multiples or transactions related to similar companies in the market. These relative approaches also take into consideration the market perception of the firm's value and its growth opportunities.

Although the market offers a single price for each company, considering the large number of valuation methods and the great variety of assumptions that can be made, there will never actually be a single value for a company. In any case, let's start with the reading and explore company valuation.

4.1   Valuation methods and the life cycle of a company

Before dealing with the two central approaches to valuation, namely the financial and comparative models, it is worth looking at how different methodologies can be most suited for various life stages of a company (Damodaran, 2012). As a general note, free cash flows, and the ability of the firm to produce sustainable cash flow throughout the years, are the main variables that help us determine the life cycle of our firm (**Figure 4.1**):

1. *Startup*: There are no revenues at this point; the cash burning rate decreases up until we reach breakeven.

→ It is difficult to assign a cost of capital or evaluate future cash flows, therefore the most common way to value this company is the Venture Capital Method, used by venture capitalists when weighing whether or not to invest in what could become a unicorn.

2. *Development*: The firm keeps on growing at a sustained pace, cash flows start to increase and the road can now lead to mature growth or decline.
   → The best methodology in this case, as we will see in the chapter, is the DCF model, together with multiples.

3. *Maturity*: The firm consolidates both growth and cash flows.
   → LBO model or Adjusted Present Value method works best.

4. *Decline*: Cash flows can decline or even become negative, so the firm needs a restructuring or a turnaround.
   → Here we would use the capital approach.

Figure 4.1   Cash flows across the company life cycle

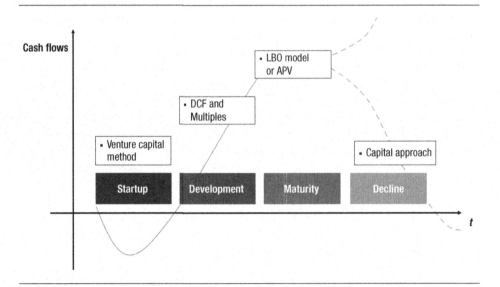

4.2   Asset side and equity side valuation: EV to equity bridge

There are two approaches to valuation: the asset side and the equity side. To remember this easily, one could argue that from the point of view of an investor investing in a firm means obtaining the right to a portion of its future cash flows. If I am a majority investor and I plan to buy out the company, I can decide on the financial structure, so I want to look at the firm as if it had no debt (asset side). If instead I am a minority investor, I will have no influence on any structural decisions, so I will look at the firm and how it is priced on the stock market (equity side). In other words, if I have an asset side approach, I am looking at the firm from the point of view of capital invested. Otherwise, if I am looking for an equity side evaluation, what I am evaluating is the net capital of the firm. The diagram in **Figure 4.2** should make things easier to understand (FCFO stands for Free Cash Flows from Operations; FCFE stands for Free Cash Flows from Equity; NFP stands for Net Financial Position). Clearly, this fundamental equation must always hold:

Enterprise Value − Net Financial Position = Equity Value

Figure 4.2   **Relationship between enterprise value and equity value**

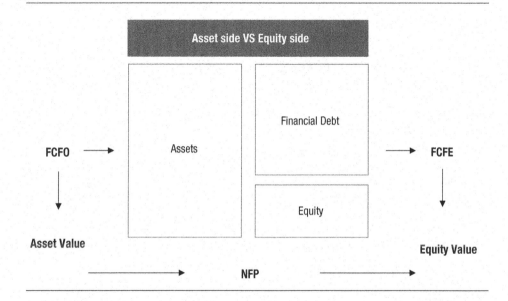

4.3   Financial method: discounted cash flow model

The most popular way for calculating the equity value and consequently the enterprise value of a company is represented by Discounted Cash Flow (DCF). The rationale behind this model rests on the assumption that the value of the company is made up by the present value of the free cash flows that the company will generate in the years to come, discounted using the Weighted Average Cost of Capital (WACC).

DCF is a simple model, based on the generation of cash flow and a few other variables we will look at in a moment. How do you calculate cash flows for upcoming years? The estimation is based on a sound and reliable Business Plan provided by the management of the firm or produced by the analyst using personal assumptions regarding the firm's future development. The main advantage of DCF is that this is a detailed forecast analysis. It helps clarify the main drivers of value; it includes the firm's future prospects in determining the Equity Value; it can be used to evaluate start-ups or firms with losses but also with high growth opportunities; it allows us to easily develop sensitivity analysis and scenario analysis. The major disadvantages include the fact that we need to make assumptions; it is labor-data intensive; it is difficult to evaluate firms with little historical data; detailed CF forecasting can be obtained only for a short period of time.

The general equation to calculate the equity value for an n-maturity perspective of investment is:

$$Equity = \underbrace{\sum_{t=1}^{n} \frac{CF_t}{(1+WACC)^t} + TV_n}_{\text{Enterprise Value}} + (SA - M - NFP)$$

Where:
TV is the Terminal Value at time n;
SA are Surplus (non-operating) Assets;
M represents the equity held by Minority shareholders;
NFP is the Net Financial Position.

Main variables to take into account in the model are:
a) *Cash-flows*: We need to present a financial statement.
b) *Time-horizon*: This refers to the number of years for which we want to predict cash-flows. If the time horizon is either too long or too short, the valuation may be meaningless. Usually five years is the time horizon adopted worldwide.
c) *Debt*: We need to prepay already-existing debt and try to predict its future evolution.
d) *WACC*: We need to calculate the appropriate cost of capital of the firm, considering the target financial structure.
e) *Terminal Value*: We need to predict the value of the corporation after the time horizon; this may be considered the "exit" value.
f) Finally, we adjust the final value considering *surplus assets and minorities*.

Figure 4.3   Discounted cash flow method

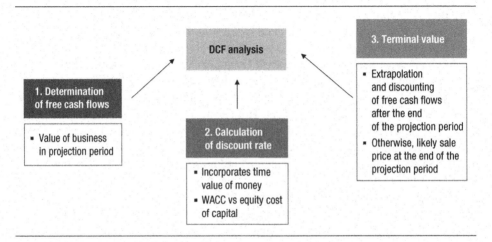

4.3.1   Cash flow analysis

Starting from the financial statement (**Figure 4.4**), we have to be able to compute the Unlevered Free Cash Flow (UFCF) and the Levered Free Cash Flow (LFCF).

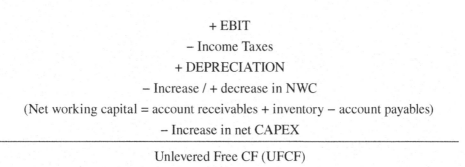

+ EBIT

– Income Taxes

+ DEPRECIATION

– Increase / + decrease in NWC

(Net working capital = account receivables + inventory – account payables)

– Increase in net CAPEX

Unlevered Free CF (UFCF)

Figure 4.4   P&L and cash flow statement

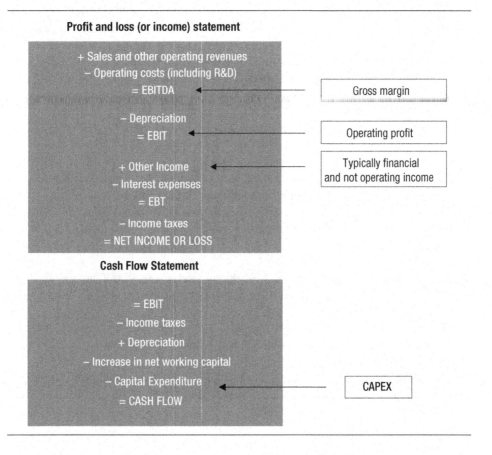

UFCF gives us information about the *cash flows produced from all of the assets of the corporation*; as such, these flows are available also to debtholders. So the suitable discount rate will be the WACC, the cost of both equity and debt capital. To understand the impact of actual and future debt to the cash flows produced:

$$+ \text{UFCF}$$
$$- \text{Interest expenses}$$
$$+ \text{New DEBT}$$
$$\underline{- \text{Debt Repayments}}$$
$$\text{Levered Free CF (LFCF)}$$

LCFCs are available to equity shareholders.

4.3.2   Debt analysis

In predicting the future evolution of debt, we can consider two options:

* *Option 1*: Rely on future cash flows already net of future DEBT (at the level of the numerator). However, the problem is that we need to predict exactly the amount and costs of future debt, and this is not an easy task except with a corporation that knows exactly how the debt will be repaid or raised in the near future (an SPV, either with project finance or an LBO).
  When LFCFs are used in the formula, Option 1 can be applied in the estimation of future debt.
  What is the risk associated with these CFs available to equity shareholders? Once the company pays its creditors, there may not be enough cash to repay shareholders. Therefore, in Option 1 the discount rate is represented by k_e. This equates to the opportunity cost for the shareholders to invest in the target firm rather than use money for other investments with similar risk characteristics.
* *Option 2*: Rely on the discount rate, which reflects the global financial structure of the company. The discount rate can address the risk of the business (k_e) or the risk of the debt (k_d).

With UFCF in the formula, Option 2 can be applied, using WACC as the discount rate. In this case, we consider both the risk of the business and of debt because WACC is a weighted average of k_d and k_e.

This is the most common way to calculate the free CFs for the firm (i.e. the cash flows available for financers and shareholders without considering a new debt issuance or old debt repayment).

We use the term Unlevered Cash Flows (UCF) or cash flows for the firm to highlight the fact that this parameter does not provide any information about the capital structure (D/E).

4.3.3   Cost of capital: Weighted Average Cost of Capital (WACC)

To obtain the Weighted Average Cost of Capital (WACC), we need to estimate k_d, k_e and then apply the following formula:

$$K_{WACC} = k_d^* \times \left(\frac{D}{(D+E)} \right) + i_e \times \left(\frac{E}{(D+E)} \right)$$

Let us see how to calculate the two variables, after tax cost of debt (k_d^*) and cost of equity (k_e).

Cost of debt

There are two ways to evaluate this:

1. We can address k_d using a *synthetic formula*:

$$k_d^* = k_d \, (1 - t)$$

Where:
    – k_d stands for the average weighted pre tax cost of capital calculated either by dividing the interest expenses by the financial liabilities or by taking into consideration every single rate referring to different financings in the company;
    – t stands for the corporate tax rate.

    This is a quick, objective formula but it does not tell us anything about the future evolution of the debt. What's more, some financial contracts don't have a single specific rate.
2. We can use the *analytical formula*, considering all costs paid on debt, so dealing with the different maturities of *debt exposures*.
    It helps to predict the evolution of debt and to include it in the company valuation. But this is a long, subjective, risky procedure: subjective because of the assumptions we must make, and risky because they can be wrong.

Cost of equity

This is computed through the Capital Asset Pricing Model (CAPM) formula:

$$k_e = r_f + \beta \, (r_m - r_f)$$

Where:
* r_f stands for the risk-free rate (the rate of return yielded by a risk-free investment consistent in terms of maturity with the investment itself). We usually refer to Germany's 10-year bund yield.
* $r_m = r_f + risk \ premium$ is the surplus return investors expect from the stock market, measured with historical series, with respect to a risk-free investment.

- Beta (β) stands for the degree of correlation between the investment in the company and the market. This reflects the systematic risk that we have in our well-diversified market portfolio if we invest in that specific stock. If β = 1, the risk that we should support investing in that specific corporation reflects exactly the risk that we observe in the market. If β > 1, we are adding market risk in our market portfolio by investing in that specific stock. If β < 1, we are doing the opposite – reducing market risk in our market portfolio by investing in it. This is all related to the concept of volatility, which is higher when β > 1, lower when β < 1. A β of 0 indicates that the portfolio is uncorrelated with the market. Beta is an important measure of the firm's risk: shareholders could leave the corporation and look for another one to invest in when they can find a higher return at their level of accepted risk or the same return taking a lower risk.

The Beta coefficient of a stock is a regression of returns of that stock against the returns on a market index. So to calculate the Beta, we need a significant amount of historical data derived from market activities.

When a company is not listed, we have to compute the Beta using the data of the comparable listed companies. Here are the steps to follow:

a) Search for companies similar to the target firm, in terms of business model, business risk, geographical markets;
b) Identify the comparable companies' Betas;
c) Unlever the Beta with data from comparable companies;
d) Relever the Beta using the target company data.

"Unlever" means to exclude the effect of capital structure while "relever" means to re-calculate the Beta coefficient using the capital structure of the firm. The aim is to eliminate the risk deriving from the financial structure of the comparable companies and consider only the business risk.

The procedure to unlever is:

$$\beta_u = \frac{\beta}{1 - (1 - t)\,(D/E)}$$

where D and E are the market value of debt and equity of the chosen comparable companies.

And the procedure to relever is:

$$\beta^* = \beta_u \times [1 + (1 - t)\,(D/E)]$$

In this case, we use the market value of D and E referring to the target's optimal structure, not the current one.

WACC

Once we get the k_e, we can calculate the WACC:

$$K_{WACC} = k_d^* \times \left(\frac{D}{(D+E)}\right) + i_e \times \left(\frac{E}{(D+E)}\right)$$

WACC represents an effective measure of the cost of all liabilities for the company.

4.3.4   Terminal Value

The Terminal Value (TV) is crucial for calculating the equity value. Representing the value of the company after the analytical forecasting period, it is approximately equal to the exit value. The formula is as follows:

$$TV_n = \times \frac{\dfrac{CF_n \times (1+g)}{(WACC-g)}}{(1+WACC)^n} \approx \frac{EBIDTA_n \times Exit\ Multiple}{(1+WACC)^n}$$

Where g represents the perpetual growth rate, that is, how fast the company is projected to grow every year.

4.3.5   Surplus assets, minorities and NFP

In the end, to obtain the equity value, we need to deduct from the enterprise value the net financial position of the target company (financial debts – cash equivalents) and, if they exist, we need to add surplus assets (non-core net assets) and deduct minority equity (non-controlling interests)

4.3.6   Global CAPM

The most complex aspect of the DCF method is calculating the discount rate (WACC) implementing the CAPM model, which takes several steps and the market data we just saw. Since we are dealing with MNC, an international version of the CAPM model could be used vis à vis a local one. Moreover, it is crucial to include the country risk of the target firm in the cost of capital calculation. We can either use the Goldman Model or we can modify the firm's cost of debt considering an additional default risk.

Global or local CAPM

When valuing MNCs, we need to consider how the return of the company we're investing in behaves against a global capital market, in other words, the correlation between the two. In order to understand a project's risk, we need a *global equity index*. We have to apply a Beta that reflects the covariance between the foreign project/company return (in the emerging market) and the world market portfolio of equity.

However, using a global market, we are likely to underestimate the β because emerging markets move in different ways with respect to developed markets. In fact, there is a negative correlation (β < 1), which implies that investing in an emerging market will decrease the overall risk of global equity portfolio. This could lead to a cost of equity (and WACC) of the corporation that is lower than less risky investments.

The more clever approach is to run a regression on the local market, applying the *local CAPM*. We do this by considering an equity portfolio including stocks of the foreign (target) market. However, sometimes this is not feasible because there may not be enough listed companies to generalize the trends of the local equity market, or there may not be any at all.

Goldman Model or additional default risk

When dealing with an MNC, we also have to consider the country risk in our valuation: this is the risk of investing in a foreign country rather than our domestic market. This risk includes all of the possible changes in the business environment that may adversely affect operating profits or the firm's value. Changes can derive from several factors, such as currency controls, regulatory changes or stability issues (mass riots, civil war).

The *Goldman Model* used by a number of prominent investment banks and consulting firms addresses country-specific risk in two steps (Mariscal & Lee, 1993):

1. Calculating the cost of debt and the cost of equity using the domestic (US) market as reference;
2. Adding the difference between the yields on local (target, foreign) government bonds and US treasury bonds to the discount factor. This is the sovereign debt spread, used as an approximation for local risk.

This approach is usually preferred when the target company is operating in an *emerging market*.

Another option is to include the *default spread in calculating the cost of debt*. This is based on the observation of EBIT coverage ratios of comparables, which are "sanity checks" that help us understand the capability of the corporation to repay debt in a certain period (a fiscal year). According to the risk the company is assuming in terms of EBIT coverage, the market demands a certain return, which determines the cost of debt. We can observe the ratio and the cost of debt of comparables; the latter are likely to be approximately the same as the company we are evaluating.

The EBIT coverage ratio (ECR) is calculated as EBIT/interest expenses – over a time period of one year.

Here is an example: we observe a ratio of 3x for comparables: ECR=3x (=ECR in my company). For companies like this, the market applies a default spread of about 300 bps. This means that if the corporation we are evaluating has a ratio equal to 3x, we can address its default risk by adding this same spread to our discount factor, that is the cost of debt. This value is firm-specific and increases (or decreases) the final WACC.

We could decide whether to consider company-specific risk (as in the AES case which we will see in the next chapter) i.e. to focus on adjusting the discount rate, or on country risk. Non-diversifiable risk must be inserted in the analysis too. It is worth looking back at what country risk consists of:

a) *Risk of expropriation by the local government.* Take, for example, a U.S. multinational investing in a South American country, e.g., Brazil, to acquire a foreign company. The valuation can be initiated using the Goldman Model to see if the investment has a positive NPV. The risk with this integrated approach is to not properly account for the point probability that an expropriation risk will actually occur. If the company in question is an industry giant and given the fact that this expropriation eventuality has almost never occurred in the history of the various Brazilian governments, this probability of expropriation can be considered very low indeed and the risk can probably be overlooked.

b) *Risk of currency devaluation.* Some South American countries in the past have not respected the maturities of their debts, exposing foreign companies operating there to an enormous risk of devaluation and deflation. Also in this case, however, it must be understood whether the devaluation of the local currency actually has a negative impact on the economic and financial balance sheet of the multinational. In a nutshell, if in the foreign country exposed to the event of a collapse in the value of the local currency, the multinational concentrates only production plants for goods then destined for export on the world market with prices denominated in its own home currency, then for the MNC the impact in terms of cash flows would not only not be negative but even positive due to a reduction in production costs in the local currency where the production plant is located.

c) *Tax increases in the foreign country can be a significant risk.* In this case, the multinational must do some scenario analysis assessing the impact of marginal tax increases in the foreign country on the production of its cash flows.

d) *Risk of reduced local demand.* Crisis phenomena in economies, especially in emerging economies, actually have an impact on the performance of sales and profits at local level. Once again, however, it must be investigated whether the output of production in the foreign country experiencing an economic crisis is destined for the local market or the international market. In this second hypothesis, once again, the crisis in the local economy will not necessarily have a negative impact on the financial performance of the multinational.

As an MNC, often country risk can improve the outcome of an investment. Case in point, in 2001, when Argentina suffered a severe crisis in the 2000s, many MNCs experienced a positive return on their local investments in the Country, both during and after the crisis for some of the reasons explained above (depreciation of the local currency did not affect international players having production plants in Argentina but exporting most of the products abroad).

4.4   Multiples method

Having looked at the DCF model, it is now time to consider another popular method: comparables. This takes into consideration the company together with its peers and looks at both market multiples and transaction multiples. We will now take a closer look into the understanding of both these types of multiples, as well as on the general and delicate process of selecting a set of them.

The value of a company can be determined by examining how comparable companies are valued (comparable in terms of industry, size, customers, and so on). As you can understand, determining the set of comparables is probably the most difficult and subjective part of this process as it is not always immediately intuitive. Think, for example, of an automotive company like Ferrari that would have been natural to compare with another company operating in the same automotive sector (e.g. Porsche or Lamborghini) but that, instead, for a broader analysis of brand perception similarity was instead approached and analyzed for its IPO by selecting comparables taken from the fashion and luxury sector like Hermes or Valentino.

The same can be done by looking at the sales price for companies in comparable transactions. The reasoning for the choice of comparables here applies similarly. Once this set of comparables has been established, stock or deal multiples are applied and the value of the company is determined. Comparable multiples are easily found on most finance websites (Yahoo Finance, Google Finance) and are calculated daily based on market prices. An alternative is using databases of transactions involving similar companies in the past. These databases (such as Bloomberg, Thomson One Banker, etc.) provide the Enterprise Value (EV) of the deal and its relative multiples.

4.4.1   The methodology

As mentioned, there are two ways of applying the comparable approach:

a) *identifying comparable companies*, by looking at stock or market multiples, or
b) *identifying comparable valuations*, by looking at past transaction or deal multiples.

How can we select similar companies and past transactions on which to base the analysis of comparables? A basic but effective approach is to start by selecting which companies and transactions to include in the analysis, taking care to consider the following aspects:

1. Classification of the industries in which they operate;
2. Financial considerations in terms of, for example, type of revenue and level of margins;
3. Geographical details about the location of their business and trading activities.

The most essential criterion is certainly the business sector, which is always used to filter companies and transactions; the others may or may not be included depending on how deep you want to go in an initial analysis.

When it comes to previous transactions, we often restrict the set by date and look only at transactions that have occurred in the recent past, being careful not to include transactions that occurred too far back in time and could have a distorting effect on the comparative analysis. For this reason we usually do not go beyond the last 3-5 years prior to the time of valuation because otherwise market, regulatory and competitors characteristics may have changed too much over time.

Let us now go a little deeper into the analysis of the two evaluation methods.

Stock or market multiples

As for *identifying comparable companies*, here is a list of questions that you should be able to answer:

- Industry: The target company's overall industry should be as similar to those of comparable firms as feasible. You don't want to compare integrated firms to outsourced companies, and you don't want to compare manufacturers to pure retailers.
- Statistical significance of sample: Creating a good sample is an essential part of the analysis. If the population of listed comparable firms in your local stock market is insufficient, try broadening the research to include similar companies listed in overseas stock markets. If there aren't still enough comparables, think about widening the industry definition. This last option should be used cautiously since it is clearly preferable to concentrate on the same exact industry and/or sub-sector.
- Size: Choose targets that are comparable in size (i.e. in terms of revenue, number of employees) and avoid comparing large and small firms.
- Other criteria to consider for consistency involve comparables with the same amount of leverage, the same degree of expected growth, and the same operational cost and R&D spending structure.

To sum up, to properly identify the most suitable comparables, we first have to analyze the main features of the target company in terms of business model and business risk, financial risk, size, geographical markets, operational risk, etc. Then we can choose among the target firm's competitors the set of comparables.

How to proceed with stock multiples?

a) Select a group of listed companies that can be considered "comparables" (the same sector, size, business mix, geography, etc).
b) Conduct a ratio analysis.
c) Compare valuation measure (numerator) to the company's performance measure (denominator) as indicated in **Figure 4.5**.

There can be asset side multiples:

a) EV/EBITDA: How many times do I have to multiply the EBITDA to buy the company?
b) EV/EBIT: How many times do I have to multiply the EBIT to buy the company?
c) EV/Sales: How many times do I have to multiply the sales to buy the company?

Figure 4.5   **Key input variables for multiples**

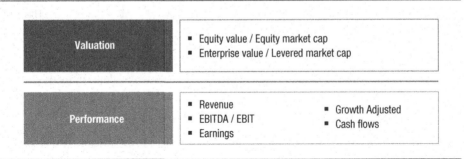

The result of the calculations with these multiples will be the enterprise value of the company. So, to obtain the equity value we will have to subtract net financial position, minorities and surplus assets. These kinds of multiples are used especially for industrial corporations, whose businesses are based on sales and operative margins. When valuing a loss-making enterprise, the EV/Sales multiple is the best and in fact the most common choice.

There are also equity side multiples:

a) P/E: How many times do I have to multiply the earnings to buy the company?
b) P/BV: How many times do I have to multiply the book value to buy the company?
c) P/CASH FLOW: How many times do I have to multiply the cash flow to buy the company?

These multiples give us information directly about the company's equity value.

Past transactions or deal multiples

When valuing a non-listed company, it would be better to use previous transactions analysis. In this case, a summary of acquisitions in a particular industry helps us ascertain the value of a business in the market (we call this deal comparison). In other words, we compare the company we're interested in to others that have recently been sold or acquired in the same industry. However, one thing to consider is that the transaction price also includes the *takeover premium*, which is usually firm-specific and negotiation-based, so it doesn't reflect the firm's real value.

The values obtained with this method are useful for M&A transactions but can easily become outdated and no longer reflective of the current market as time passes. Therefore, they are less commonly used than multiples of comparables.

The goals of this approach are to:

• value a business by determining relevant sector valuation metrics and identifying multiples paid in similar transactions;
• ascertain sector conditions by determining demand for business types and facilitating discussion of industry trends.

There is no quick way to put up a list of similar deals. The most typical strategy is to consult many sources, such as:

- M&A databases;
- Sector research studies;
- Acquisition and divestment history of the target and its comparables;
- Fairness opinions (within merger proxies or merger-related filings with the regulators);
- Previous deal analysis and/or pitch books (pitches made to potential investors);
- Publication of news.

Identifying comparable valuations means to find comparable metrics for valuing a company by:

1. Examining the value put on publicly listed companies: Using publicly traded company information to generate our collection of comparables is highly fascinating since the data is easily accessible but does not always allow for the accurate values to be determined. We may overlook the fact that firms are often listed when they are stable and profitable, assuming that they are in their maturity stage of life. This implies that the underlying features of the sample of similar listed firms may include companies that are substantially different from the company we are examining and may not be listed, for example. To highlight some of these distinctions, public firms do not face the illiquidity risk that unlisted companies do. An investor who purchases shares in a publicly traded company does not have to be concerned about the prospect of disposing of the investment in a short period of time and at relatively low transaction costs by reselling the shares on the secondary market. The investor in unlisted shares does not have a secondary market to resort to, making this investment significantly riskier. Furthermore, as previously said, listed corporations are mature and frequently extremely successful medium to large-sized businesses. When analyzing a firm that is still a startup or at the start of its development path, we cannot consider turnover and size characteristics that are comparable to those of publicly listed companies, and this element exposes the investor to more risk. In brief, when utilizing multiples derived on publicly traded firms, it should always be feasible to find discount factors that account for the risk of size, turnover, and liquidity that differentiates the sample of companies from the unlisted company that we are evaluating.

2. Examining prices paid for related private companies when they are the target of an acquisition: When compared to using data from public companies, this approach has the advantage of looking at the value attributed to a private company; in many cases, doing so means eliminating shortcomings, such as the unlisted company's different size and lack of liquidity. However, data on M&A transactions involving private firms is not as easily accessible as data on public corporations. This indicates that the acquirer of the similar transaction may have been ready to incorporate extra value for synergies and control in its acquisition price that we should not found in the firm we need to value on a stand-alone basis. But

how can we separate the price paid in similar transactions from these premiums that relied on and were only relevant to the specific transaction itself? This approach is not always straightforward to apply or appropriate since disclosure of the various components of the purchase price is not always made in M&A transactions, particularly when unlisted firms are involved.

Finally, although utilizing multiples for stock values may be quietly rewarding, they can also be too conservative at times. One significant downside of this valuation measure is, in fact, that there is no forward looking, no future predicting taken into consideration when computing multiples. Clearly, relying just on multiples without regard for future data, particularly when an ambitious future growth rate is expected, is essentially blind.

4.5   Conclusions

By now you should have all the introductory tools you need to understand and eventually perform a valuation of a target company, aimed at assessing its intrinsic value. There are several methodologies that have been developed over the time to evaluate a corporation. Just to list a few: Equity, Income-based, Mixed, Financial and Market Multiples. Throughout the chapter we focused on the most important ones used in mergers & acquisitions, private equity, investment banking, equity research, corporate development, and leveraged buyouts, namely:

- The Financial Method: Discounted Cash Flow (DCF) model, which considers the value of the company based on future discounted cash flows;
- Comparable methods:
  - Trading comparables: a relative valuation method that compares the current value of a business to other similar businesses by looking at trading multiples;
  - Transaction comparables: another relative valuation that takes into consideration other businesses that have recently been sold or acquired in the same industry and compares them to the target company.

Sometimes, especially during particular moments in the lifetime of a company, such as its early beginning or mature phase, the Venture Capital Method and Liquidation Methodology are considered. As we've seen in the chapter, the valuation of a company, the so-called target company, is a very sensitive and sometimes rather difficult process. This is not so much due to the underlying calculations, but rather the set of assumptions that underpin the analyst's forecasting and decisions. We saw a few valuation methodologies and given the sensitivity of the issue in question these techniques are generally compared to check the soundness of results.

  The most common approach to valuation is building a DCF model, probably the most objective and reliable method, but one that is very sensitive to assumptions. Indeed, there are several value drivers that must be estimated, on which most of the result of the valuation depend: future cash flows, weighted average cost of capital, terminal value of the firm, final adjustments. This chapter has given you insights on how to calculate each of them in an appropriate way and avoid biases. Remember, it's always best to prepare a sensitivity analysis too, to check how slight changes in parameters affect the overall value of the firm.

To further validate the results coming from the financial model constructed by analysts, a good way is to use a relative valuation, based on market multiples or transactions' prices of companies similar to the target firm. These methods allow the analyst to include information about the market's perception of the company value and growth opportunities as well. In doing so, the model incorporates a more subjective valuation, driven by irrational components such market sentiment or additional considerations like premiums for majority sale or discounts for minority sales and so on. When developing this analysis, there are different multiples that can be chosen and several steps that have to be followed. All of the decisions are usually driven by a meticulous investigation of the target firm. It helps to understand the suitable kind of multiple that has to be used and the firms, among competitors, that can be considered comparables.

In the next chapter, we will dive deeper into what all this theory means in terms of evaluating multinationals and how it can be applied in an international context.

5 The Cost of Capital
for Multinational Corporations

Having introduced corporate valuations in the previous chapter, it is now time to better understand the cost of capital. As we will discover, the cost of capital and its structure can severely impact the value of an enterprise or project and can determine whether companies choose to invest in business opportunities. Indeed, to finance daily and extraordinary operations, a firm has two tools at its disposal: debt and equity. Depending on the decisions made about these two sources of financing, the weighted average cost of capital (WACC) and value of the firm can differ.

There is no perfect capital structure, and more importantly, the optimal level of capital is never static but rather dynamic. For this reason, several drivers in decision-making regarding capital structure must be constantly checked. Among the most vital there are the initial debt and equity levels of the firm, its possibility of accessing capital markets, and current market conditions. In the context of MNCs, the political conditions of the host country, the favorable or unfavorable policies of domestic or international governing bodies, and exchange rate risks should also be considered. Indeed, as we will see the cost of capital, and more specifically the cost of debt and equity, can vary from country to country.

The weighted average cost of capital represents (WACC) the minimum acceptable rate of return on new investments. As such, it is the main indicator used to evaluate investment projects. The basic factors underlying the WACC for a firm or project are the degree of risk associated with it, the relative tax burden, and the supply and demand of various types of financing. Considering two equally profitable investments, the riskier one will have a relatively higher cost of capital and therefore will be less profitable (i.e., have a lower present value).

These are the topics that will be taken up by this second chapter on corporate valuation, widening the perspective to an international dimension typical in the valuation of companies operating in more than one country and called upon to evaluate the opportunity to invest in projects abroad. At the end of the chapter, a case study and a series of self-assessment questions will help readers reflect on and check their understandings of the concepts presented.

5.1   The cost of capital and cost structure

Capital budgeting at the multinational level establishes a logical and scientific framework for calculating the cost of capital in international transactions. By discounting cash flows, this methodology upholds the same concepts and reference models as classic investment research methodologies. Its distinction from more traditional models resides in the form of analysis used and the treatment of factors unique to international business projects.

A multinational company project can be assessed from two perspectives using the Multinational Capital Budgeting approach: the MNC perspective and the subsidiary perspective. The MNC perspective is based on a simulation of the influence of the foreign business's riskiness on the investor's domestic market. The subsidiary perspective is an analysis of the same business's riskiness from a purely local perspective. The primary distinction between the two approaches is in how the cost of capital is defined. In the MNC perspective, the cost of capital is determined by adding a factor indicative of country risk gained through new foreign activities to the risk factors already estimated for the domestic capital market. In the subsidiary perspective, the cost of capital is derived directly by extrapolating individual risk factors from the local financial market (Dell'Acqua et al., 2010). Both perspectives are analyzed in this chapter.

As it is commonly noted, the cost of capital is the most complicated and widely used variable for evaluating investments and businesses. Numerous other methods for evaluating the cost of capital in foreign transactions have been identified in the scholarly literature, and several of the more well-known ones will be examined in this chapter.

As we saw in the previous chapter, the term *cost of capital* can be understood as the minimum rate of return a firm must earn on its investments to keep the value of the enterprise intact. Put another way, the cost of capital represents the rate of return the firm must pay to the suppliers of capital for using their funds.

To calculate their cost of capital, corporations usually compute the weighted average cost of capital, which is also known as the WACC.

$$WACC = \frac{Debt}{Debt + Equity} \times Cost\ of\ Debt \times (+ 1 - Tax\ Rate) + \frac{Equity}{Debt + Equity} \times Cost\ of\ Equity$$

To finance their operations, MNCs need capital which usually consists of *equity capital* (earnings retained, and funds obtained by issuing stocks) and *debt capital* (borrowed funds). Using capital incurs some costs: the cost of equity reflects the opportunity cost for investors of investing in other projects, while the cost of debt is the cost a company incurs to borrow money and depends on the current level of interest rates, the risk of default by the company, and the tax benefit associated with the debt.

The percentage of debt and equity, i.e., the capital structure of the firm, is decided based on certain considerations. Firms want a capital structure that minimizes their cost of capital in order to maximize the value of the MNC. In the previous chapter, we discussed how to calculate the cost of capital or WACC, a value that depends on the cost of debt and the cost of equity. The WACC varies according to the amount of debt a firm has. This means that the WACC impacts the overall value of the firm, which we can measure with the DCF formula that discounts cash flows for the firm's WACC.

The graph in **Figure 5.1** illustrates this mechanism. If we start from a situation of zero debt (where the Kd line intercepts the y-axis), the more we add debt, the lower

Figure 5.1   The relation between cost of capital and debt

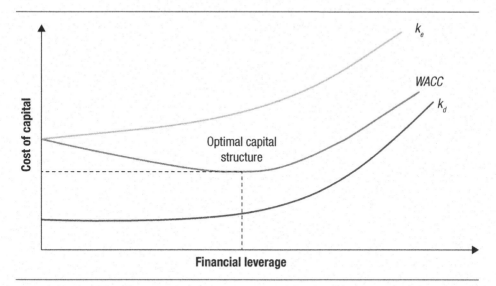

the WACC will fall. Yet this holds true only up to a certain point, since the WACC curve inverts and starts sloping upward when the level of debt reaches a point that allows the firm to proceed with its daily operations by partially financing them with debt, taking advantage of interest rate payments on that debt which are tax-deductible. This represents an optimal capital structure. The underlying mechanism leverages tax-deductible interest rate payments, since this means a higher debt ratio will result in a lower cost of capital for the firm. However, having too much debt will also augment the firm's risk of bankruptcy, which in turn increases the cost of both debt and equity. MNCs therefore need to find the optimal mix between debt and equity in order to achieve the most efficient capital structure. The theoretical optimum is obtained when the present value of tax savings associated with more debt is offset by increases in the present value of financial distress costs associated with excessive leverage. This is referred to as the *trade-off* theory of capital structure (Brealey et al., 2011).

As the graph demonstrates, we must ascertain the cost of debt to evaluate whether it is lower than the cost of equity. While the calculation of the cost of equity will be covered in Section 5.4, here it is important to point out how we determine the *cost of debt* in the WACC for a company. First, we should note that companies can acquire debt in the form of loans from commercial banks or securities sold to debt markets (i.e., notes and bonds). The normal procedure for measuring the cost of debt requires a forecast of interest rates for the next few years, the proportions of various classes of debt the firm expects to use, and the corporate income tax rate. The interest costs of the different debt components are then averaged according to their proportion in the debt structure. This before-tax average cost of debt is then adjusted for corporate income taxes (as seen in the above WACC formula) by multiplying it by (1-tax rate) to obtain the weighted average after-tax cost of debt.

Why is the WACC calculation so important? Determination of the firm's cost of capital is the starting point for several considerations. First, it is a measure of how much it costs a company to finance itself in light of its financial structure and it provides a base line for determining whether new capital expenditures can be made and in what proportion. The WACC can also be used to forecast the capitalization of the firm in the near future. Moreover, it helps managers understand what the optimal financial structure might be, or rather, the level of debt that will maximize the value of the firm. Relatedly, the WACC can also serve as an evaluation tool for top management, whose compensation could eventually even be linked to some financial parameters. Lastly, the WACC can have an impact on decisions about the dividend policy.

5.2   The MNC's cost structure decision

As we have just mentioned, firms face a trade-off when they want to raise capital to finance their operations. The optimal capital structure is, in fact, the mix of debt and equity that results in the lowest capital costs. On the one hand, by leveraging the company and contracting additional debt, the firm's shareholders may benefit from the tax shield effect, since interest payments are tax-deductible. On the other hand, contracting additional debt might compound the firm's bankruptcy risk and thereby increase its cost of capital, which in turn reduces the company's value. Nonetheless, the advantages of using debt as opposed to equity vary in relation to characteristics specific to each MNC and the features of the countries where it established subsidiaries so that the capital structure of companies operating in the same industry could vary significantly among countries due to a variety of environmental circumstances (Suk H. Kim et al., 2006).

5.2.1   The influence of a MNC's corporate characteristics

The capital structure of a multinational corporation (MNC) might be affected by characteristics that are unique to that organization. International business, it seems logical to believe, is riskier than domestic business. This is not always the case, since foreign investment returns are not always closely connected with domestic investment returns. In other words, multinational corporations may be less risky than enterprises operating completely inside the borders of a single country also because MNC could diversify not just among local projects but also between nations in order to mitigate risk (Suk H. Kim et al., 2006).

As presented by Madura (2015), there are then some specific features that impact the capital structure of a multinational company which should be kept in mind when analyzing its cost of capital. First and foremost, multinationals are large companies that experience a period in their life cycle that is usually represented by strong growth and/or otherwise stable cash flows that make it easier to manage a higher level of debt. The operational history of the company also makes it possible to easily access information about the company itself and the market, along with the presence of operational assets that participate in the creation of value. All of this then explains why creditors price as lower the risk that the cash flows generated by the MNC will not allow them to recover interest and principal. Secondly, there is evidence that MNCs gain greater money as they expand their presence in international markets thanks also to the economies of scale that can be experienced, together with the possibility that the expansion of a company's activities beyond its national borders also allows it to acquire essential managerial skills not available in the local market, with a further impact on the ability to generate greater cash flows. As a result, multinational companies with operations spread across multiple countries can have even more stable cash flows than just large domestic companies also because the adverse circumstances of a specific nation should have less impact on their cash flows. In addition, multinationals with lower credit risk (default risk) have more access to loans than those with higher risk. A variety of variables influence a multinational's credit risk and, consequently, its decision to raise debt rather than equity. For example, if a multinational's top management is seen as strong and professional, the company's credit risk may be low, allowing for more affordable access to loans. A multinational corporation that owns assets that can be used as collateral (such as real estate and other tangible assets) is also more likely to be able to borrow and is more likely to choose debt financing over other forms of financing. The ability to have profits, and therefore retain earnings, also influences capital structure. Mature and established multinationals may be able to finance most of their investments for the development of new projects with retained earnings at a positive IRR (Madura, 2015).

5.2.2 The impact of country-specific characteristics

Jong, Abe et al. (2008) discovered that various business-specific parameters such as firm size, risk, growth, and profitability had a considerable effect on cross-country capital structure, consistent with the predictions of standard capital structure theories. By examining the direct effect of country-specific variables on leverage, they demonstrate that creditor rights protection, bond market development, and GDP growth rate all have a major impact on corporate capital structure. They discover evidence for the relevance of legal enforcement, creditor/shareholder rights protection, and macroeconomic variables such as capital creation and GDP growth rate via indirect effect measurement. These findings imply that in nations with a more favorable legal environment and more stable and healthy economic circumstances, enterprises not only take on more debt, but also enhance the impact of firm-level drivers of leverage. Their conclusion is that country-specific variables do matter in determining and altering leverage decision globally, and that for the MNC is beneficial to adequately account for these aspects in corporate capital structure analyses.

Let's then review some specific national characteristics that could influence a multinational's choice of whether to use equity or debt financing (Madura, 2015). In some nations, governments limit the ability of local investors to invest their funds in anything other than domestic equities. Capital controls are enacted to restrict financial flows into and out of a country's capital account from the capital markets. These limitations might be applied throughout the economy or to a particular area or industry. Capital restrictions may be implemented by government monetary policy. They may impose restrictions on domestic people capacity to acquire foreign assets, referred to as capital outflow controls. Capital restrictions are often implemented during an economic downturn to prevent local individuals and international investors from withdrawing cash from a country. This creates an implicit barrier to cross-border investment opportunities. Some local investors may have fewer equity investment options than others because of these global investment barriers. A multinational company operating in countries where investors have fewer investment choices may therefore be able to obtain equity capital at a relatively low cost in these nations (because the supply of funds is high). To finance its activities, the multinational may decide to issue additional equity in these nations, thereby increasing the amount of equity it uses. For a variety of reasons, as Kim et al. (2006) point out, parent loans to overseas subsidiaries are more common than equity contributions. For instance, parent loans allow a parent business to repatriate cash from a foreign subsidiary with more freedom. Another argument for selecting parent loans over equity contributions is tax concerns. Interest on internal loans is usually tax deductible in the host nation, but profits are not. Furthermore, unlike dividend payments, principal payments are not usually considered taxable income. By employing loans instead of stock contributions, a parent and its subsidiaries may be able to save money on taxes.

In some countries, MNCs may be able to borrow money (debt) at a reasonably low cost, but the cost of debt in other nations can be quite expensive. As a result, a multinational's choice of debt may be influenced by the cost of debt in the countries in which it operates. When a multinational corporation is concerned about the possibility of weakening currencies in the domestic markets of its subsidiaries, it may attempt to finance a significant portion of its international operations by borrowing in those currencies rather than relying on funds from the parent company. As a result, the subsidiaries will send back less money in profits because they will pay interest on local borrowings rather than transfer profits to the holding company. The multinational corporation's exposure to exchange rate risk is reduced using this approach.

However, when considering politically unstable nations (see Chapter 8 on Country Risk) in which host governments may impose restrictions (e.g., prohibit capital flows across borders and/or seize assets) it is also important to take into account the negative impact such actions might have on subsidiaries. For example, if there is a high likelihood that the host government will impose a temporary freeze on funds to be remitted from the subsidiary to the parent company, it may be preferable for the multinational to use local debt financing to reduce the amount of the funds that would be temporarily blocked (i.e., the subsidiary can use these funds to pay interest and principal on the debt locally). In such cases, it would be preferable for the subsidiary to use more local financing, even if there is the possibility that a foreign government will confiscate its assets, since the creditors who lent funds to the subsidiary are likely interested in ensuring that the subsidiary is treated fairly by the host government. Subsidiaries may also issue stocks in the host nation to decrease their exposure to a high degree of country risk, as explained above. In this method, if the subsidiary becomes profitable, the minority shareholders (local investors) will reap the benefits directly. They could lobby their government to refrain from implementing exorbitant taxes, environmental restrictions, or other laws that would negatively impact the subsidiary's profits. A subsidiary owned by local investors with a minority stake may also provide some security from the potential risk of unwanted actions by the host government. Overall, increased political risk has been scientifically shown to raise the cost of equity capital for international firms (Kesternich and Schnitzer, 2010). This is because such constraints reduce the returns on investment projects while maintaining the same amount of expenditure. The rationale for debt capital is relatively ambiguous. The ideal degree of debt financing provided by the parent company is reduced when political risk in the form of complete or progressive expropriation grows, since the latter entails higher default risks (Tsyganov et al., 2015).

Finally, dividends to foreign stockholders are often subject to both local income taxes and withholding taxes. When local profits are remitted overseas as dividends, withholding taxes are imposed. This explains why many multinational corporations are hesitant to invest significant ownership in their overseas operations depending mostly on local debt financing.

5.3   The cost of capital for MNCs

International capital budgeting is influenced by a broader range of factors than those that affect domestic investments. The increased complexity of the analysis is due to a variety of factors.

Cash flows of the parent firm and the project
Here there are two perspectives to consider: one represented by the cash flows of the parent company in the home country, the other is represented by the project's cash flows in the host country. While parent cash flows represent the consolidated entity's operations, project cash flows focus only on the overseas project's enterprises.

Changes in the value of foreign currencies
Foreign exchange rate variations influence the foreign investment's future cash flows. From the parent company's perspective, it is necessary to forecast future exchange rates and conduct a sensitivity analysis of the project's feasibility under various exchange rate scenarios to understand the impact of foreign currencies on company as a whole when cash flows are converted to the home currency and funds are remitted to the parent.

Inflation
Inflation in the foreign nation will influence local operational cash flows, in terms of both raw material costs and revenue as well as parent company cash flows because of their effect on foreign exchange rates and the actual cost of financing in the foreign country.

Financing on a subsidized basis
When a host government subsidizes the project's financing at below-market rates, the amount of the subsidy must be expressly included in the capital budgeting analysis.

Geopolitical risk
Changes in government policy can have a variety of effects on a project's future cash flows in the host nation. For example, some countries may impose duties on imported goods to benefit local producers by protecting them from international competition, thereby reducing the earnings of multinational firms. Political risks then come in the form of price controls, industry regulation, or the application of restrictions and tariffs on critical inputs. Finally, a major concern of MNCs is that the political atmosphere in the host nation may deteriorate, leading to foreign closures and political adjustments that could take the form of trade barriers intended to limit or impede international trade.

Rate of discount
The discount rate is established to account for the extra risks associated with foreign currency and nation risk. MNCs must have publicly accessible data and, when feasible, perform historical analysis in order to make these changes. Otherwise, support from local managers who are familiar with the sorts of risks that exist in a foreign location may be required to make rational judgments.

Values at the end
Terminal values are much more difficult to calculate in a multinational setting because of the extra complexity of elements associated with assets located in a foreign jurisdiction, which may ultimately have segmented capital markets due to limitations on the movement of physical or financial assets

Source: Goel, S. (2015). *Capital Budgeting*. Business Expert Press.

Following Madura (2015), the concept of cost of capital and the methodology used to compute it are the same for both domestic firms and MNCs, yet they differ in practice because of several features particular to MNCs, which are outlined below. The first three factors (scale, access to international capital markets, and international diversification) are favorable for a MNC, since they result in a reduced cost of capital. The last two factors (exchange rate risk and country risk) are instead unfavorable, since they are likely to result in a higher cost of capital.

Moreover, it would be natural to wonder whether the weighted average cost of capital for MNCs is higher or lower than for their domestic counterparts. The answer to this question varies, since it is a function of the aspects described below, which must also be taken into consideration.

5.3.1   Favorable factors reducing the cost of capital

As we saw in the previous section, the capital structure of multinational firms today is influenced by a variety of variables, both country-specific and firm-specific. Most of them are based on existing theories of corporate capital structure and have been studied extensively in the academic literature. Other variables, however, do not have such a basic magnitude and are only the subject of separate empirical data (Tsyganov et al., 2015). In this part, we will divide the study of these variables that impact the capital structure of MNCs according to Madura (2015) based on their nature and effect into favorable factors that lower the cost of capital for MNCs and unfavorable factors that increase the cost of capital for MNCs. We begin by analyzing the favorable ones.

First, multinational corporations are often larger than domestic corporations. Because MNCs are given preferential treatment due to their scale, they may be in a better position to raise capital through stocks and bonds at a reduced cost. As a result, operations size can have a favorable impact on the WACC.

Second, MNCs can receive funding at cheaper prices than local enterprises if they have easy access to foreign capital markets. Furthermore, MNCs can take advantage of the benefits of having subsidiaries in countries with low interest rates, since they may be able to fund themselves at cheaper costs than the parent entity. Because of their global presence and strong capital position, the world's largest firms, such as Apple, Microsoft, and Alphabet (Google), can raise funds at a reduced effective cost, which gives them easy access to important financial markets. Furthermore, in cases of illiquidity in certain home markets, accessing money from overseas capital markets is critical. MNCs can avoid the dangers associated with firms in illiquid markets (such as tiny domestic firms or family-owned firms), since they have access to global markets. Multinationals can boost market liquidity by raising funds in euro-markets (money, bond, and stock), selling security issues abroad, and entering local capital markets through foreign subsidiaries. Such operations should increase their potential to raise funds in the short run compared to if they were constrained to domestic capital markets.

Thirdly, MNCs, due to their wide range of activities, are in a better position to lower their costs of capital than domestic firms. The following are two benefits of international diversification (Madura, 2015):

• A firm with cash inflows from various sources around the world enjoys relatively greater stability, as it has less cash flow volatility since the impact of a single economy on its revenues is reduced.
• International diversification (by country and by product) should reduce the firm's systematic risk, lowering its Beta coefficient and, as a result, the cost of equity. The benefits experienced by companies with diverse and international operations are linked to the *Portfolio Risk Reduction Theory*. To understand this theory, we must remember that the risk of a portfolio is measured by the Beta of the cost of equity (see Section 5.4.1). When an investor increases the number of securities in a portfolio, the portfolio's risk at first decreases rapidly, then asymptotically as it approaches the market's level of systematic risk. Any portfolio's total risk is thus made up of systematic risk (the market) and unsystematic risk (the individual securities). Increasing the number of securities in the portfolio reduces the unsystematic risk component while maintaining the systematic risk component constant. The Beta of a fully diversified domestic portfolio would be 1.0.

International diversification enables the cost of capital of a company to decrease. Benefits derived from internationalizing operations and diversifying can be associated with the *International Portfolio and Diversification Theory*. Its principles are grounded in the *Portfolio Risk Reduction Theory* described above and in the foreign exchange risk theory.

Grubel (1968) identifies international portfolio diversification as a "source of welfare gains from international economic relations". International portfolio theory typically concludes that adding international securities to a domestic portfolio will reduce the portfolio's risks (and thus its cost of capital). Although this idea is fundamental to much international financial theory, it still is based on individual firms in individual markets. Depending on the firm, its line of business, the country it calls home, and the domestic and global industry in which it competes, the global Beta may go up or down.

The foreign *exchange risk* of a portfolio is reduced via international diversification for the following reasons:

1. International portfolios, like typical domestic portfolios, combine assets that are not completely connected, lowering the portfolio's overall risk. In addition to typical portfolios, the investor can tap into a bigger pool of prospective investments by including assets from outside the local market (assets that were previously unable to be averaged into the portfolio's predicted returns and risks).
2. In contrast to typical domestic portfolios, when an investor or MNC purchases assets in another host country market, they may be purchasing a foreign-currency denominated asset and thus acquiring two assets: the currency denomination and the asset acquired with the currency. Though the purchase entails one asset in concept, it gains two in terms of projected returns and risks.

Fourth, most studies confirm that multinational corporations use significantly less debt in their capital structure than domestic corporations (Lee and Kwok, 1988). This is because they possess unique specific assets such as technology, patents, and brands, as well as the ability to create such assets, which enables them to compete successfully in international markets (Rogach, 2005). According to Tsyganov et al. (2015), this statement of assumptions allows for the expectation that multinationals must have relatively low debt capital ratios because the availability of these specific assets affects increasing returns and growth potential, as well as high market-to-book equity ratios that are characteristic of firms that use little debt (Park et al., 2013).

5.3.2   Unfavorable factors increasing the cost of capital

The aforementioned factors, including MNCs' access to capital and international diversification, enable these corporations to have a lower cost of capital than most domestic firms while maintaining a desired debt ratio – even when significant amounts of new funds must be raised. Nonetheless, some empirical studies have come to different conclusions, identifying some elements that in fact raise the cost of capital for MNCs.

To begin with, MNC operations and cash flows are more vulnerable to exchange rate fluctuations than those of domestic firms, implying a higher risk of bankruptcy. As a result, creditors and stockholders demand a higher rate of return, which increases the MNC's cost of capital. Thus, the greater the exchange rate risk, the greater the WACC.

Similar logic can be applied to exposure to country risk. The total country risk of a foreign investment is higher than that of a comparable domestic investment because of the additional cultural, political, and financial risks associated with foreign investments. Such risks amplify the volatility of returns on foreign investment, frequently to the detriment of the MNC (Madura, 2015).

Other risks faced by MNCs with a negative impact on their cost of capital include higher agency costs, political risk, and asymmetric information. Several factors influence how much these exposures affect capital costs. When a firm's investments are concentrated in a single economy and markets are partially segmented from other capital markets, country-specific and currency-specific risks cannot be diversified, meaning the firm's exposure to these risks cannot be eliminated. In contrast, a firm with globally diversified investors, particularly in integrated financial markets, can eliminate these risks, and its cost of capital will be lower. A large body of literature suggests that MNCs have lower systematic risk in relatively integrated financial markets than comparable domestic companies, owing to the benefits of international diversification. As pointed out by Tsyganov et al. (2015), the development stage and conditions of domestic capital markets then have a significant role on multinational corporations' capital structure. Multinational affiliates are known to employ less external funding and more internal financing in nations with limited capital market growth and inadequate creditor rights protection. This is because raising capital in such markets is highly costly (Desai et al., 2004). Internal funding may therefore be used in lieu of more costly external borrowing. As a consequence, global corporations would have a competitive edge over domestic firms that can only raise capital in domestic markets.

Other studies, on the other hand, find that some MNCs have a higher level of systematic risk than their domestic counterparts because the increased standard deviation of cash flows from internationalization outweighs the lower correlation from diversification. Aybar et al. (2005) , however, have shown that internationalization actually enables emerging-market MNCs to reduce their systematic risk enjoying higher firm value. This is because MNCs from emerging markets invest in international economies that are more stable than their home markets. This strategy reduces their operational, financial, foreign exchange, and political risks. The lower risk more than compensates for such firms' higher agency costs, allowing the firms to enjoy higher leverage and lower systematic risk than their US-based MNC counterparts.

Finally, there are some company-specific factors that can raise the cost of capital for MNCs. Companies with a high proportion of fixed costs have higher Betas, as do companies in cyclical industries. As a result, the firm's type can have a negative impact on its cost of capital. As Tsyganov et al. (2015) highlight, another critical aspect affecting international firms' capital structure is the tangibility of their assets. According to Hart et al. (1994), intangible assets are more vulnerable to company failures, resulting in decreased investor value during times of financial hardship or bankruptcy. This statement is intended to convey that intangible assets have a lower

Figure 5.2   **Cost of capital composition**

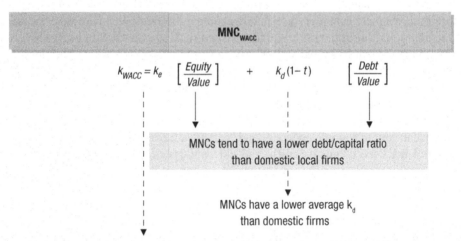

When it comes to the cost of capital and leverage, financial theory predicts that multinational businesses (MNCs) will have a lower cost of capital and a higher leverage level than their domestic counterparts. However, empirical evidence reveals that the answer is dependent on factors like as the development of the capital market, the institutional framework, and the political stability of the MNCs' home and host countries.

liquidation value. This indicates that businesses with a greater proportion of physical assets may afford to raise more debt financing, since tangible assets have a higher liquidation value. For multinational corporations, the existence of intangible assets is a critical element that enables them to compete on a global scale and gives them a competitive edge over local firms due to their unique capacity to produce new assets of this type. Over two-thirds of the global technology market is internal to MNCs, and technology is a direct result of MNC-specific intangible assets. This attribute could have detrimental effect on multinational corporations' cost of capital in case of financial distress.

Do MNCs then have higher or lower WACCs than their domestic counterparts?

It is difficult to generalize and say that MNCs always have lower costs of capital. Every MNC should evaluate the implications of each of the above factors on its cost of capital to determine the net outcome. **Figure 5.2** illustrates a few conclusions about the cost of capital for MNCs compared to domestic firms (Eiteman, 2010).

Example The WACC calculation of three multinational companies

Let us take the following three American companies as examples:
- Boeing
- (BA): Large, multinational corporation active in the aerospace sector.
- PepsiCo (PEP): Large, multinational food & beverage corporation.
- Walmart (WMT): Huge, multinational retail corporation.

Data available (as of 2021):
- T = Medium-term, five years
- US Treasuries (k_f): 1.54%
- S&P 500 return (k_m): 5.92%
- Tax rate (t): 27.0%

The formula:

$$k_c = \frac{D}{(E+D)} \, k_d \, (1-t) + \frac{E}{(E+D)} \, k_e$$

	E	D	Rating	Spread	Beta	K_d	K_e	WACC
BA	122.5	43.4	BBB-	171	1.47	3.25	7.98	6.51
PEP	230.6	36.4	A	118	0.65	2.72	4.39	4.06
WMT	371.6	42.4	AA	85	0.53	2.39	3.86	3.64

Let us compare the results for the same companies in November 2006, before the financial crisis, using the following numbers:
- US Treasuries (k_f): 4.25%
- S&P 500 return (k_m): 9.02% (1976-2006)
- Tax rate (t): 25.0%

	E	D	Rating	Spread	Beta	K_d	K_e	WACC
BA	69.2	3.4	A+	107	1.22	5.32	10.07	9.78
PEP	102.8	0.9	A-	133	0.50	5.58	6.64	6.61
WMT	191	24.6	AA	85	0.34	5.10	5.87	5.64

The increase in Beta, in this example, is not entirely unexpected as also shown by Slimane et al. (2017) who identify in their study how the impact of the global financial crisis in the region of North America and Western Europe is identified with an increase in Beta leading to a direct impact on systematic risk for most of the companies analyzed during the crisis period.

5.3.3   Dimensions of the cost and availability of capital strategy

Some of the favorable and unfavorable conditions that increase or decrease a multinational company's cost of capital have been outlined above. It is important to note that companies can best deal with the market conditions they face – and achieve lower global costs and greater capital availability – through a *properly designed and implemented market strategy*.

For instance, global integration of capital markets has given many firms (especially MNCs) access to new and cheaper sources of funds, beyond those available in their home markets. However, a series of characteristics pertaining to the local or global market can impact the availability of capital and the cost at which this capital can be sourced. These characteristics should be contemplated when devising a cost of capital strategy, as **Figure 5.3** illustrates (Eiteman, 2010).

Figure 5.3   **Analysis of cost of capital approaches**

A firm that must raise long-term debt and equity in a highly illiquid domestic securities market will almost certainly have a high cost of capital and limited access to that capital. This reduces its competitiveness both internationally and in relation to foreign firms entering the domestic market. Firms facing this situation include those located in developing countries with underdeveloped capital markets and those that are too small to access their own domestic securities markets. Many family-owned businesses fall into this category because they refuse to use securities markets to meet their long-term capital requirements. Such companies could strengthen their competitive advantage in sourcing capital by tapping into highly liquid global markets.

The current increasing globalization of the securities markets has two effects. The first is that market segmentation has significantly shrunk. The second is instead that the correlation among securities markets has multiplied, thereby reducing, but not eliminating, the benefits of international portfolio diversification. Many methods for estimating the cost of capital in foreign transactions have been presented in the scholarly literature. The most popular ones fall into two broad "families" (Hoang et al., 2017):

- approaches based on the Capital Asset Pricing Model (CAPM)
- straightforward methods for estimating the cost of capital

Many financial executives and investors believe that when determining the cost of capital for foreign investment, a company's cost of capital estimated using the standard CAPM is inappropriate since it is too low. The international CAPM structure is used in conjunction with global parameters, including a global risk-free rate, a global market risk premium, and a Beta evaluated against the global market. If it employs this strategy, the investor thinks that any non-diversifiable risk is appropriately reflected by the security's Beta component when compared to a global index (e.g., MSCI World). One reason to exercise caution when utilizing the international CAPM to evaluate enterprises in foreign (i.e., emerging) markets is that it frequently produces a lower-than-expected estimate of the cost of capital. Inappropriately low (per-ceived) cost of capital estimates originate from the inability of many investors to adequately diversify the idiosyncratic risk associated with developing markets investing. Investors may seek larger returns than those anticipated by the worldwide CAPM because of this potential imperfect diversification of systematic risk. Diversification is restricted for a variety of reasons, including but not limited to market obstacles and fragmented markets. Market impediments, such as discriminatory taxes and/or national legal or institutional frameworks, can result in segmentation of the market and a reduction in total diversification (Carrieri et al., 2013). In addition, measurement of international CAPM Betas in segmented markets can be confounded by the low correlation between domestic and overseas markets, which can result in a considerable reduction in the Beta (Erb et al., 1997). Even if global markets are integrated – and risk can be dispersed internationally as a result – the average investor may be "home biased," resulting in excessive exposure to familiar markets and severely limiting global diversification (Damodaran, 2013). The approaches used most often to determine the CAPM are adjustments to the market risk premium estimated for comparable enterprises in stable currency countries. They include the following:

• Adjusted hybrid CAPM
• Godfrey-Espinosa model
• Practitioner techniques

The adjusted hybrid CAPM method identifies the risk-free rate in hard currency (e.g., dollars) as a compo-nent of the cost of capital, along with credit spreads on government bonds denominated in hard currency with a longer maturity in the emerging country than government bonds with the same maturity issued in the country to which the hard currency refers. It also includes the equity risk premium adjusted for the incremental riskiness of the foreign country's stock market.
The Godfrey-Espinosa model is similar in that it calculates the foreign country Beta coefficient and the coefficient for estimating the volatility of equity returns in response to changes in an emerging country's government debt rating.
Practitioner techniques are based on the professional practices of prominent international investment banks. For the sake of brevity, we will discuss two of the most frequently utilized methods of practitioners. The first method, called "adjusted MRP," entails simply boosting the discount rate which would apply to a matching firm operating in a hard currency area by a factor equal to the credit spread on the emerging country's hard currency government bonds at the time. The second method, called "estimated MRP," is distinguished by its treatment of the credit spread and equity risk premium. This strategy considers the credit spread implicit in the yields on municipal government bonds. The equity risk premium is calculated primarily to compensate for the absence or insignificance of data in countries with developing equity markets by indirectly estimating the following key variables: a) the foreign country's expected GDP growth rate; b) the foreign country's expected inflation rate; and c) the average market dividend yield. The divi-dend yield is determined using historical data or, in the absence of such data, a predicted future dividend growth rate (Dell'Acqua et al., 2010).

Moreover, firms based in countries with *segmented capital markets* must devise strategies to eschew dependence on that market for their long-term debt and equity needs. A national capital market is segmented if the required rate of return on secu-rities in that market differs from the return and risk that would be expected if it were traded in other securities markets. Capital markets can become segmented for a va-riety of reasons, including excessive regulatory control, perceived political risk, anticipated foreign exchange risk, lack of transparency, asymmetric availability of information, insider trading, and other market imperfections. Firms constrained by any of these conditions must develop a strategy for getting out of their own limited capital markets to source long-term capital abroad (e.g., by attracting international portfolio investors).

5.4   The cost of capital across countries

In principle, the international CAPM (ICAPM) more accurately captures the characteristics of today's world than the classic domestic Capital Asset Pricing Model (CAPM). Unlike the local CAPM, the ICAPM assumes the interconnected of global financial markets and takes into account the consequences of unanticipated changes in foreign exchange (FX) rates. As a result, the ICAPM should be a better valuation tool than the CAPM. Capturing foreign exchange risk exposure in the broader sense of the ICAPM involves various foreign exchange risk variables. However, for professionals tasked with determining a company's cost of capital, the ICAPM provides no suggestion on how to estimate foreign exchange risk premiums. As a result, the ICAPM is commonly used in one of two simple ways. The first is as a global CAPM (GCAPM), which differs from the CAPM in that it uses the world market index and does not account for foreign currency risk. The second is as a two-factor ICAPM that combines a currency index (rather than a collection of bilateral FX rates) with the global market index (Ejara et al., 2017).
We will focus on Foreign/Local, Global, and Domestic/Home CAPMs.

Foreign/Local CAPMs
The so-called "Foreign/Local CAPM" methodology is based on target country variables (local variables) and assumes market segmentation. This method is based on the country in which an investment is made and is used when cash flows are denominated in the foreign currency of the target country. A country risk adjustment is included in the foreign CAPM.
The Foreign/Local CAPM technique is based on four components: (1) the foreign risk-free rate, (2) the country risk premium (CRP-target), (3) the foreign EMRP, and (4) the foreign Beta (Ogier et al., 2004).

(1) Target company country risk-free rate (Rf-foreign);
(2) Country risk premium (CRP-target): not applicable (already incorporated in the foreign Rf);
(3) Beta (β-foreign): Regressions of returns of peer companies in the target country against the target country index;
(4) Equity Market Risk Premium (EMRP): Equity risk premium for the target investment (should not be an additional country risk premium factor for the target if already embedded in the foreign Rf).

Global CAPM
The "Global CAPM" approach focuses on global variables and the assumption of global capital supply and demand. This approach considers the perspective of a global investor or a target company with global exposure (e.g., oil and gas, mining) that exports primarily to global markets. Calculation of the risk-free rate in this approach must ensure that cash flows are denominated in the same currency as the discount rate and that the risk-free rate is denominated in nominal terms when cash flows are nominal.
One of the difficulties inherent to this approach is estimating the EMRP on a global scale. One approach is to estimate the EMRP of a "mature" market (e.g., Germany) first, and then to add a country risk premium to the cost of capital, assuming that all companies are exposed to country risk equally (Ogier et al., 2004).

The Global CAPM approach is based on the (1) global risk-free rate, (2) country risk premium, (3) single global EMRP, and (4) global Beta.

(1) Risk-free rate: German government bond yield for example (Rf-global);
(2) Country risk premium (CRP-target): additional risk of investing in the target country;

(3) Beta (β-global): Measured against the global market portfolio (Damodaran, 2012);
(4) Equity market risk premium (EMRP): global EMRP = German EMRP/correlation of the German market to the global market portfolio.

The Home/Local CAPM approach is based on (1) the home risk-free rate, (2) the home risk premium, (3) the home EMRP, and (4) the home Beta (Ogier et al., 2004).

(1) Investor's home risk-free rate (Rf-home);
(2) Country risk premium (CRP-target): additional risk of investing in the target country;
(3) Beta (β-home): Regression of returns of peer companies in the target country relative to the country index;
(4) Equity market risk premium (EMRP-home): Premium for equity risk in the investor's home country (should not count twice as the same country risk embedded in Rf-home).

Each approach has some practical implications. Local CAPM approaches can result in an overestimation of the CRP due to the inclusion of country risk in both Rf and EMRP. However, if the CRP component of Rf is removed, the foreign country's Rf may be lower than that of a developed country.
Global EMRP is a theoretical concept rarely used in practice in the global CAPM approach. In this case, the Fisher equation can be used to convert the real rate of return into the currency-specific nominal rate.

Source: https://www.pwc.fi/en/services/deals/valuations/blog-three-approaches-to-apply-capm.html

If an emerging market investor uses the domestic CAPM approach, it may overestimate the CRP. In this case, the CRP can serve as the dividing line between the two countries.

Understanding why the cost of capital varies across different countries provides an insight into the competitive superiority of some MNCs in some countries. Knowing the differences in cost of capital in different countries may enable an MNC to formulate suitable strategies for the procurement of funds from markets where the cost is lower.

MNCs use the weighted average cost of capital to assess their cost of capital. The cost of equity found in the standard formula for the weighted average cost of capital and is calculated through the Capital Asset Pricing Model, also known as the CAPM and identified with the following formula:

Cost of equity = Risk free rate + Beta × Market premium

The cost of equity is the equivalent risk-free interest rate that shareholders could have earned on their investment, plus a premium to reflect the firm's risk. It represents the shareholders' opportunity cost. As stated above, risk-free interest rates differ by country, as does the cost of equity. According to McCauley et al. (1991), the cost of equity of a country can be calculated by first applying the price/earnings multiple to a stream of earnings. This multiple is related to the cost of capital. A high price/earnings multiple indicates that the company receives a high price when selling new stock shares for a given level of earnings, implying that the cost of equity financing is low. However, price/earnings multiples must be adjusted to account for inflation, earnings growth, and other factors in a given country.

Remember that the CAPM can be either domestic (if the firm's equity trades only in its domestic market) or international (if the firm's equity trades in a global market, reflecting its global portfolio). The risk-free rate (i.e., the yield on a US treasury note on which, to be practical, there is no default risk nor uncertainty about the reinvestment rates of intermediate flows) can be assumed to be the same in an international CAPM, but the market premium will need to shift to reflect the average expected global market returns for the upcoming financial periods. Furthermore, the firm's Beta will change in relation to changes in its larger global portfolio. This raises the question of whether we should use a global or a local CAPM. The answer is dependent on the situation. The appropriate equity risk premium should reference a global benchmark if capital markets are integrated or if shareholders are globally diversified. However, if markets are segmented or if shareholders hold domestic portfolios, a domestic benchmark should be used to determine the appropriate equity risk premium. The market premium measures then the additional return required on average by investors to move from a risk-free investment to an average risky investment derived from investors' risk aversion and the riskiness of the market portfolio. The greater the risk aversion and the greater the riskiness of the average risky investment, the greater the premium required by investors (Damodaran, 2012).

After weighting debt and equity in terms of their respective proportions, the cost of debt and equity can be combined to obtain an overall cost of capital. For firms located in countries with a low risk-free interest rate, the weighted cost of capital computed in this manner will be comparatively lower.

5.4.1   Cost of equity variations among countries

A few other considerations need to be made in the context of MNCs, in addition to those highlighted in the previous chapter:

- The *Risk-Free Rate* is the expected rate of return obtained by investing in a local riskless security. The return on U.S. government securities (such as T-Bills, T-Notes, and T-Bonds) is usually considered an accurate estimation of the risk-free rate because those securities are backed by the full faith of the U.S. federal government. However, T-Bills, T-Notes, and T-Bonds have very different maturities. An MNC should use a security with a maturity comparable to the expected life of the project or company. Differences in the risk-free interest rate across countries may depend on the supply and demand for funds.

   Moreover, tax laws in various countries differ in terms of rates, exemptions, and incentives. This influences the supply of funds to the corporate sector – and hence interest rates – differently. Some developing countries often make a number of concessions to attract multinationals. Most concessions come in the form of a full tax exemption for the first few years, called a "tax vacation". Additional temporary tax benefits include reduced income tax rates, investment tax credits, tax deferrals, and the reduction or removal of certain indirect taxes. These advantages, along with lower labor costs than in developed countries, have attracted many industries to several developing countries. Along with low tax rates, tax holiday countries must have (1) a stable administration, (2) adequate communications infrastructure, (3) currency freedom, and (4) availability of financial services (Suk H. Kim et al., 2006).

Demographic conditions in a country also affect the supply and demand for funds and, in turn, the interest rate. On this topic, Papetti (2020) identifies two factors that explain why aging has a downward impact on the natural real rate of interest in countries with a relative majority of older people: 1) labor as a production input becomes scarcer, and 2) individuals increase their willingness to save in anticipation of a longer life expectancy. It turns out that both variables account for almost equal amounts of the natural real interest rate's decreasing trend over the predicted horizon. For instance, countries with a high proportion of young adults, meanwhile, will have higher interest rates, as this demographic is relatively less thrifty and demands more money to satisfy its needs. Moreover, the monetary policy of the Central Bank of a country directly influences the interest rate at which funds can be borrowed by MNCs. A Central Bank that follows tight monetary policy to curb inflationary tendencies in the country will raise rates and hence the reference interest rates.

- The *Market Premium* is the spread of the expected market return over the risk-free rate. Due to the difficulty of estimating the returns of the world portfolio of equities, practitioners usually use broad indexes such as the S&P 500 as a market return approximation. In general, risk premiums are estimated with some degree of uncertainty. To address this issue, it is important to look at historical data (going as far back as possible) to construct the long-run average. When this is not possible due to a lack of data, a well-established developed market premium needs to be established. This can be done in several ways: (1) using the country risk approach, which involves multiplying the market risk premium by a country risk factor; (2) using the relative equity market approach, which involves modifying the market premium by the volatility of the country's equity market compared to the volatility of the developed market; or (3) using the mixed approach, which combines the previous two methodologies. This premium may depend on different factors, such as the level of financial leverage, government intervention, a country's economic situation, or interactions among creditors and corporations. A few considerations should be noted when observing differences among countries (Madura, 2015):

  - When a country's economy is stable, the likelihood of experiencing recession is relatively low. As a result, the probability of borrowers defaulting on repayment is also low. Under such circumstances, the risk premium is also likely to be low.

  - Governments in some countries actively intervene to rescue failing businesses (particularly those that are partially state-owned), providing a variety of forms of financial assistance such as through direct subsidies and long-term loans. However, in other countries the likelihood of government intervention to rescue firms from impending disaster is remote. As a result, risk premiums for the former will be lower than for the latter.

- Additionally, risk premiums vary across countries due to the varying degrees of financial leverage employed by firms in those countries. For example, due to the particular relationship between creditors and the government in Germany, German firms have a higher degree of financial leverage than firms in the United States also because German banks commonly hold bonds and shares in companies. Obviously, this increases risk tolerance because creditors have the ability to take control of the company in the event of financial problems by removing and replacing managers.

- The *Beta* is a measure of the covariance between the rates of return on a company's stock and the overall market. Similarly, a project's Beta represents the sensitivity of its cash flows to market conditions. This measure captures the systematic risk of a company or project (i.e., it is a measure of how the firm's returns vary with those of the market in which it trades). A company with a low Beta has low systematic risk; this means a low cost of capital if its unsystematic risk can be diversified away. For example, the Beta will be less than 1.0 for a firm with returns that are less volatile than the market; it will be 1.0 if the firm's returns are the same as the market; and it will be greater than 1.0 if its returns are more volatile (or risky) than the market.

Example WACC Calculation

Foxconn, a leading manufacturer of Apple's iPhones, has planned to invest about 40,705 Indian rupees ($542 million) in India in the next five years. This investment is targeted at boosting manufacturing of Apple devices in India. The investment will be financed with a debt of $300 million (22,530 rupees).

The portion financed with equity will then be 44.6%. To determine the cost of the project $= k_c$, we need to calculate the WACC of Foxconn.

Cost of debt (k_d)
The India 5-year government bond has a yield of 5.921%.
Given that Foxconn has a rating of A-, its spread over the Indian Treasuries would be 133bsp.
The cost of debt for Foxconn is then
$k_d = k_f + \text{spread} = 0.05921 + 0.0133 = 0.0725$ (7.251%).

Cost of equity (k_e)
Foxconn opts for a domestic CAPM.
The return of the Indian stock market (SENSEX) in the past year has been 11.31%.
The Beta for similar companies operating in India (Electronical equipment sector) is 1.40.
$k_e = k_f + \text{Beta} * (k_m - k_f) = 0.05921 + 1.40 * (0.1131 - 0.05921) = 0.1347$ (13.47%)

Cost of capital
India's marginal tax-rate is 25.17%.
$k_c = 0.446 * 0.1347 + 0.554 * 0.0725 * (1 - 0.2517) = 0.0901$ (9.01%)

This rate represents the WACC and hence the required rate of return of Foxconn. The firm will use this rate to discount the cash flows related to its investment in India.

Example Migos's estimation of WACC

The CFO of Migos, a Spanish MNC, has to decide how to finance a new project in Colombia. He could either issue new debt in euros or in Colombian pesos. The CFO prepares four scenarios with different capital structures:

- 30% of the project financed with euro-denominated debt and 70% equity;
- 50% equity and 50% of Spanish debt;
- 50% equity and debt split 25% in Spain and 25% in Colombia;
- 50% equity and 50% Colombian debt.

The Spanish debt cost and the Colombian debt cost are estimated by taking a 10-year treasury bond for each country. The cost of equity for Migos is 18%. The WACC is estimated using the weights defined in the previous scenarios. Results are shown in **Table 5.1**).

Table 5.1 **Capital structure scenario**

Possible Capital Structure	Spain Debt Cost (=1.245%)	Colombia Debt Cost (=9.014%)	Equity Cost (=18%)	Estimated WACC (in %)
30% Spain Debt 70% Equity	0.4%		12.6%	13.0%
50% Spain Debt 50% Equity	0.6%		9.0%	9.6%
25% Spain Debt 25% Colombia Debt 50% Equity	0.3%	2.3%	9.0%	11.6%
50% Colombia Debt 50% Equity		4.5%	9.0%	13.5%

As highlighted by the table, the most convenient option is financing the project with 50% Spanish debt and 50% equity. In fact, the cost of financing is much lower in Spain than in Colombia, while using more equity is, as usual, a more expensive option. To maximize the value of the project then, the CFO should opt for the second scenario. One possible drawback is increased exposure to exchange rate fluctuations, since the MNC is financing a project in Colombia with a euro-denominated loan. The impact of exchange rates on capital budgeting analysis will be discussed further in the next chapters.

5.5   The cost of capital methodology for addressing international projects

As previously seen, capital budgeting is the process of evaluating potential investment opportunities and allocating cash to favored projects. Capital expenditures are long-term financial commitments that are projected to generate cash flows beyond one year. Capital expenditures are used to acquire fixed assets, such as machines, factories, or entire businesses. Given the high sums of money involved in such long-term commitments, meticulous planning is essential to choosing which capital assets to acquire. Capital budgets are typically used to describe capital expenditure plans. Multinational corporations contemplating international investment prospects have a more challenging dilemma than domestic corporations.

Foreign ventures entail currency risk, political risk, and compliance with foreign tax legislation. Comparing projects across countries necessitates an examination of how all variables will vary across countries. There are several alternative approaches to capital budgeting (Melvin et al., 2017).

A MNC can propose an investment in a foreign project with the same risk that the MNC itself faces and use its weighted average cost of capital as the required rate of return for the project. However, many foreign projects could present different risk levels than the overall risk of the MNC.

Every time the cost of capital goes up, the NPV of projects goes down. Anything that affects k_c will also impact the profitability (NPV) of a project.

There are various ways in which a MNC can account for the different levels of risk in its capital budgeting process:

1. NPV (Adjusting Cash Flows): the MNC's cost of capital is engaged at a discount rate and cash flows are therefore adjusted to properly capture the risk of the project (Scenario Analysis).
2. Adjusted Weighted Average Capital Cost (Working at the Discount Rate Level): if the project is riskier, add a risk premium to the WACC to derive the required rate of return on the project; for example, adding 3% to capture exchange rate movements (Arbitrary Methodology).
3. Adjusted NPV (Levered Free Cash Flows): calculate the interest expenses in order to address the netted cash flows available for equity shareholders. These cash flows can be discounted directly by engaging the cost of equity capital.

The first method, the NPV technique, is a useful tool for international corporations. It utilizes present value because a dollar received today is more valuable than a dollar obtained in the future, i.e., one year from now. As a result, the amount of future cash flows must be discounted to reflect the fact that the value today will decline in proportion to the time required to realize the cash flows.

Estimation issues include determining whether to include all cash flows directed to the subsidiary housing the project or simply those paid to the parent company. A prudent mix of financial flows might result in tax savings for both the parent and subsidiary. Numerous financing effects should be considered, including depreciation charges associated with the capital expenditure, financial subsidies, concessionary credit terms extended to the subsidiary by a government or official agency, deferred or reduced taxes offered to encourage undertaking the expenditure, or a new ability to circumvent exchange controls on remittances (Melvin et al., 2017).

The second method, *adjusting the weighted average cost of capital for the risk differential*, is the most commonly used. With this methodology, if the foreign project is thought to exhibit more risk than the MNC, a premium can be added to the WACC to derive the required rate of return on the project. The capital budgeting process will then incorporate this required rate of return as the discount rate. If the foreign project shows lower risk, the MNC will use a required rate of return on the project that is less than its WACC.

As stated in Butler (2016), the total operational risks associated with international investments are higher than those associated with comparable domestic investments, because of the foreign market's cultural, political, and financial hazards. These risks increase the uncertainty surrounding the outcomes of international investments, frequently to the detriment of the multinational firm. International marketplaces are never fully integrated with the multinational corporation's global or domestic market. As a result, an increase in total risk associated with overseas investments may or may not be mitigated by a decline in the correlation between investment and market returns. Country-specific risk diversification, in turn, is contingent upon the degree of capital market segmentation and the degree to which the firm's investors are diversified locally or globally. For investors that are solely diversified within a single local economy, country-specific risks are systematic and cannot be hedged. This is true for markets that are segmented in part by other capital markets. In comparison, globally diversified investors participating in an integrated capital market can avoid many country-specific risks that are not diversifiable and thus systemic for a local investor. Take the example of a country-specific political event that is unrelated to events occurring outside the local economy. In such cases, political risks at the local level raise the overall volatility of foreign investment returns. However, from the perspective of a globally diversified investor, the increase in risk has no effect on required returns because it is compensated by a decrease in the correlation between local and global returns. On the other hand, from the perspective of investors confined to a single market, local political risks are not diversifiable and will affect required returns in that market. Similarly, while currency risks linked to a particular country are diversifiable for a global investor, they may not be for investors who hold only local assets. The diversification of currency risks within a domestic portfolio is contingent upon the country's industrial diversity. In economies with few industries, the value of domestic equities may be inextricably connected to the local currency's value. In more diversified countries with a large number of importers and exporters, the value of domestic stocks may be unrelated to the local currency's value. Yet while this may be true at an aggregate level, the fortunes of individual importers and exporters may be extremely susceptible to the value of the local currency (Butler, 2016).

Usually, investment banks adjust the MNC's cost of capital to account for:

- *Financial Risks*: financial risks are often associated with a money-related issue (i.e., the difficulty of easily repatriating revenues to the home nation, counterparty default risk). Currency risk is arguably the most well-known of these risks. Currency risk is a financial risk associated with the possibility that exchange rates (the value of one currency in relation to another) will fluctuate suddenly. For this reason, the cost of capital for a foreign project may be adjusted by the average rate of appreciation (depreciation) of the host country's currency during the lifetime of that project. If the home currency is expected to appreciate against the host currency, the cost of capital will be adjusted upward because a smaller amount of profits produced by the project in the local currency will be repatriated to the parent company in its home currency. A depreciation of the home currency, on the other hand, will result in the opposite effect and thus the cost of capital will be adjusted downward.

- *Political Risks*: government instability, expropriation, bureaucratic inefficiency, corruption, and even war are all examples of political risk. Political risk, according to Tsyganov et al. (2015), may have both micro and macro dimensions. Macropolitical risk affects all firms operating on the territory of a foreign nation, regardless of their area of business. The expropriation by a country's government of foreign-controlled businesses in the natural resource sector is a good illustration of the potential impacts of macropolitical risk. Micropolitical risk is more prevalent

among MNCs and often occurs as a consequence of corruption and a misalignment of MNC and local government objectives (Tsyganov et al., 2015). Such circumstances erode the country's attractiveness to foreign investors, who will almost
certainly demand a considerably higher expected return in exchange for future
investment in that nation – thus increasing their estimates of the cost of capital
for country-specific projects. The risk premium to be incorporated into the cost of
capital for a project in a country with elevated political risk will be higher than in
the case of a country with lower political risk.

- *Fragmentation of Capital Markets*: a capital market is said to be integrated when
  the actual returns required on assets of comparable risk traded in that market are
  identical everywhere. Because the law of one price applies, a multinational cannot raise funds more cheaply in one location or currency than in another in an
  integrated market. Rather, a market is segmented if the needed rate of return for
  identical risk assets in other markets is unrelated to the required rate of return in
  that market. Segmentation of capital markets is caused by government control of
  the flow of capital across borders, the existence of varying degrees of depth and
  development of capital markets, and a dearth of accurate information on investment and lending opportunities in different markets: all these factors drive the
  cost of capital for a MNC upward or downward. The cost of capital for a project
  in a segmented host country capital market has to be adjusted downward because
  restrictions are applied to capital outflows which results in the availability of
  funds in the host country at a lower interest rate than in the MNC's home country.
  However, sometimes the segmentation of capital markets can lead to higher capital costs than if these markets were fully integrated due to their inefficiencies,
  asymmetric information distortions, and higher levels of illiquidity.
- *International Diversification Effect*: the beneficial impact of international diversification is reflected in reduced exchange rate and country risks. In general, a
  MNC with a portfolio of subsidiaries across different countries will tend to have a
  relatively lower cost of capital because multinationals can reduce the volatility of
  their cash flows due to the fact that returns from different countries are less correlated (Hughes et al., 1975). However, diversification does not always lead to lower
  WACCs and, despite the favorable effect of international diversification on cash
  flows, bankruptcy risk could be about the same for MNCs and domestic firms.
  This is because MNCs face higher agency costs, political risk, foreign exchange
  risk, and asymmetric information – all factors shown to lead to lower debt ratios
  as well as a higher cost of long-term debt for MNCs.

The third method, the Adjusted NPV (APV), as mentioned, is the net present value calculated by considering only the cost of equity. It was first proposed by Myers
in 1973 and the method is very similar to the traditional discounted cash flow (DCF)
model, but the fundamental idea is that APV disaggregates the various components
of value and analyzes each separately. In contrast, WACC lumps all of the financing effects into the discount rate. Thus, the APV allows you to focus on the amount
of cash flows that will remain available to shareholders, stripping them of the debt

component. In this step, the difficult application of the method itself emerges, which consists precisely in the possibility of being able to predict the exact evolution of the company's leverage and, therefore, of the interest expenses in the projected horizon of the cash flow analysis.

5.6   Case study: FINA Italian Group goes internationally

5.6.1   Context

The cost of capital is a financial indicator that is considered with other variables in the valuation of multinational corporations. This statistic summarizes a number of factors that play a role in the success of foreign-based business activities, such as political and macroeconomic stability, and may have a significant impact on the success of new foreign international projects. Oftentimes, these factors are viewed solely qualitatively or without enough contextualization. This establishes a possible overestimation of the risks inherent in the development of international projects. Several foreign countries demonstrate risks that are greater than or equal to those anticipated. The following case will enable us to focus on a few key factors and illustrate how different variables contribute to increasing the cost of capital in specific countries. A careful examination of these risk factors, as well as some of the considerations outlined in this chapter, can help improve a company's valuation stance and the impact of international risk on the value of an MNC. In many cases, the risk is related to the brevity of the period during which the highest rates of return are guaranteed in certain foreign countries, to the low cost of production in some countries in exchange for the low cost of raw materials, and to the fluctuation of exchange rates. The opportunity to take advantage of such differential rates of return in a short period of time should be weighed against the risk of the same factors cancelling out the benefits accrued in the short run. As a result, a capital cost estimate is thus a useful tool for conducting an accurate evaluation of an international project (Dell'Acqua et al., 2010).

The FINA Group[1] is involved in the research, manufacturing, and distribution of technical, pure, and medicinal gases, as well as home care services, biotechnology, and the renewable energy.

FINA was created in 1930 by Giovanni Annoni and Aldo Gavazzi to construct two oxygen and acetylene facilities in central Italy. Since then, the group has developed steadily thanks to its globalization and diversification strategy in the home care market. In the 1980s, FINA shifted from a regional to a national strategy, capitalizing on significant changes in Europe's technical gases industry. The FINA Group expanded beyond Europe in 2011, establishing collaborative partnerships in India, Turkey, and Morocco.

---

[1] This case was fully elaborated by the author with the help of Giulia Zanetello.

With the introduction of new laws and significant modifications to the European gas sector, the FINA Group was able to develop a solid supply of money and plethora of investment options in gas-related enterprises. Foreign governments offered incentives to encourage foreign direct investment in infrastructure projects, and multinational banks were open to investing in volatile regions of the world, reducing the danger of expropriation and increasing cash availability. The risks associated with expansion were primarily related to the unpredictable nature of such investments and their possible impact on the group's financial stability. As a result, FINA was forced to reassess the company's assets and develop a new approach to determining the cost of capital. When FINA focused just on national contracts and the risk of changes in input and product prices was low, all projects were viewed as equally hazardous and the same discount rate was used uniformly. FINA's cost of capital model became progressively inadequate, however, as it expanded across Europe and, more specifically, into locations such as India, Turkey, and Morocco – in other words, into operations in nations that were markedly different from Italy in terms of risk.

As a result, FINA needed to develop a new model for calculating the cost of capital for each of its business lines dislocated in different geographic locations so that it could treat each investment as a unique opportunity with individual risks.

5.6.2   FINA's weighted average cost of capital for international projects

Multinationals have three options for determining the cost of capital for their projects: (1) the parent company's cost of capital, (2) the subsidiary/project's cost of capital, or (3) a weighted average of the two. If a parent company finances its foreign project entirely on its own, the parent company's cost of capital may be considered the acceptable cost of capital. If its foreign subsidiary finances the project entirely with foreign money, the foreign cost of capital can be considered as the acceptable cost of capital. However, in most situations, the multinational exploits the whole world as a common source of capital. Thus, the acceptable cost of capital is often calculated as the weighted average of the two (Kim et al., 2006).

To assess the risk of each investment, FINA decided to compute the project's weighted average cost of capital used to discount the forecasted cash flows.

$$WACC = \frac{E}{V} \times R_E + \frac{D}{V} \times R_D \times (1 - t)$$

Looking at the equation, to compute the WACC, FINA needed:

1. The cost of debt;
2. The target capital structure;
3. The local country tax rate;
4. The cost of equity.

Cost of debt calculations

Estimate the cost of debt. Multinationals such as FINA must account for a plethora of complex elements when calculating the cost of debt. To begin, global corporations may borrow money on international money markets, international bond markets, or local capital markets. Thus, they must estimate interest rates and the percentage of debt to be raised in each market in order to calculate the pre-tax cost of debt. Second, multinationals must estimate the tax rates in each market in which they want to borrow and evaluate the deductibility of interest by each domestic tax body in order to calculate the after-tax cost of debt. Third, when multinationals issue debt denominated in foreign currencies, the nominal cost of capital and interest must be adjusted for exchange rate gains or losses. For instance, the pre-tax cost of foreign currency debt is equal to the pre-tax cost of principal and interest repayment in the parent company's currency. This pre-tax cost of capital comprises the nominal foreign currency cost of principal and interest, adjusted for any foreign currency gain or loss (Suk H. Kim et al., 2006). The cost of debt is then going to be addressed in FINA as the sum of the risk-free rate and the default spread. Projects in nations with low credit ratings and high default risk may face the brunt of country default risk, particularly if they depend entirely on domestic revenue (Damodaran, 2013):

$$Cost\ of\ Debt = R_F + Default\ Spread$$

Cost of equity calculations

For a company, the cost of equity is the minimum rate of return required to entice investors to buy or hold the company's common stock. This required rate of return is the discount rate used to calculate the present value of all future dividends per share relative to the current stock price.

The price-earnings ratio is another way to calculate the cost of capital. It is calculated by dividing the price per share by the earnings per share. More specifically, the price-earnings ratio can be used to ascertain the rate of return that shareholders are seeking.

Finally, an alternative method to the above cost of capital valuation models is the capital price model (CAPM), which we described in detail in Chapter 4 and whose formula is given as a reminder below.

Reminder: Cost of Equity = Risk-free rate + Beta × (Market premium)

To find the cost of equity with the CAPM, FINA first needed to estimate a reasonable equity Beta representing the degree of correlation between the investment and the stock market.

$$Equity\ Beta = \frac{Covariance\ (R_S, R_M)}{Variance\ (R_M)}$$

To accurately estimate the Beta of a specific investment, corporations need to define the market portfolio benchmark. To estimate the cost of equity that would be calculated for foreign projects, FINA collected the equity Beta(s) of multiple Italian projects. It then unlevered those Beta(s) in order to neutralize the impact of the financial structure of the former projects (highly levered projects have higher Betas, since they are riskier for equity holders). The Betas need to be unlevered to make them comparable with one another.

$$B_{Unlevered} = \frac{Beta_{Levered}}{1 + (1 - t) \times \frac{D}{E}}$$

FINA then averaged the Betas belonging to the same business lines to yield one unlevered Beta for each business division. However, the equity Beta should reflect not only the market risk associated with each project or business line but also the different effects of leverage. Therefore, FINA had to re-lever the average equity Beta of each business line to account for the target capital structure of the project.

$$B_{Releveled} = Average\ B_{Unlevered} \times (1 + (1 - t) \times \frac{D^*}{E^*}$$

Using the re-levered equity Beta, FINA could calculate the cost of equity using the traditional CAPM equation:

$$Cost\ of\ Equity = R_F + B \times (R_M - R_F)$$

Could the WACC now be computed? Now that FINA had both the cost of debt and the cost of equity, could it compute the weighted average cost of capital to assess the foreign projects? No! These calculations still did not factor in the country-specific risk for the cost of equity and the project-specific risk.

5.6.3   Country-specific risk and project-specific risk

Country-Specific Risk

Country risk is an umbrella term that covers many different risks, including all the extra risks that come with doing business outside of the home country. It can be understood as the economic, political and business risks that are unique to a specific country and which might result in unexpected investment losses. Simplification of the decision to pursue a business opportunity in a foreign country is contingent upon two factors: the rate of return on the investment and the level of risk. These are the primary components of risk that investors may face:

- *Economic risk*: a considerable change in the economic structure or growth rate that significantly alters the projected return on an investment.
- *Risk of transfer*: resulting from a foreign government's decision to restrict capital flows.
- *Exchange rate risk*: a currency's exchange rate moves in an unexpectedly negative direction.

- *Location risk*: the impacts of spillovers produced by issues in a region, a country's trading partner, or countries with perceived similar characteristics.
- *Political risk*: the possibility that political institutions will change due to shifts in government power, social organization, or other non-economic causes.

These are just some of the components of country risk, which will be discussed in further detail in Chapter 8.

It was critical for FINA then to adjust its Italian-based cost of equity to reflect country-specific risk, since its projects in emerging markets were riskier than those in Italy (due to political regimes, regulation, expropriation, currency devaluations, etc.). Country risk implies a separate premium, comparable to the premium for a lack of liquidity, that should be included to the cost of stock. Higher levels of national risk will result in higher equity costs. Most premiums are calculated using sovereign ratings and/or CDS spreads.

As a result, FINA assumed that the spread between the yields on local government bonds and corresponding Italian Treasury bonds, referred to as the sovereign spread, accurately approximated the incremental costs (and market risk) in the local country.

FINA added the sovereign spread to the cost of equity to generate a WACC for each project.

$$Cost\ of\ Equity_{ADJUSTED} = Cost\ of\ Equity + Sovereign\ Spread$$

Project-Specific Risk

The above *approach* could provide FINA with a useful WACC reflective of the systematic risk associated with each project in relation to its local market. However, FINA also needed to consider the unsystematic risk of each project. This is known as non-systematic risk, specific risk or residual risk. Different categories of project-level risk were identified, each ranked and weighted according to FINA's ability to anticipate and mitigate the relative risks. Then projects were graded on their level of exposure to each risk category. Each level of risk led a certain spread to be added to the overall cost of capital.

5.6.4   FINA's strategy for making its cost of capital more adequate for the valuation of international projects

To sum up, in order to find the correct approach to calculate the cost of capital, FINA implemented the following procedure:

1. Compute the cost of equity and the cost of debt:

$$Cost\ of\ Equity = R_F + B_{Relevered} \times (R_M - R_F)$$
$$Cost\ of\ Debt = R_F + Default\ Spread$$

2. Add the sovereign spread to the cost of equity:

$$Cost\ of\ Equity_{ADJUSTED} = Cost\ of\ Equity + Sovereign\ Spread$$

3. Add project-specific risk:

$$WACC = \frac{E}{V} \times Cost\ of\ Equity\ (Adjusted) + \frac{D}{V} \times Cost\ of\ Debt \times (1-t) + Project\text{-}Specific\ Risk$$

Is this method of adjusting the cost of capital perfect? No. If we think carefully about the country-specific risk and project-specific risk, some overlaps become clear. Some risks, such as the exchange rate one, may be accounted for twice or more during the various phases of capital budgeting (i.e., both in calculating the risk components of equity and, therefore, in considering the specific riskiness of the project), leading to an overestimation of the discount rate and therefore the exclusion of initiatives that could be interesting from an industrial point of view but too financially depressed in the dynamics of the net present value of cash flows. Another limitation is that adding a country risk premium to the single factor CAPM model (the Ke) results in the application of the same country risk premium to all projects eventually established in the country, despite evidence that country risk is also dependent on a number of factors, including the line of business and the location of the project's revenues.

Case Nestlé, the globalization of capital markets and the cost of capital

The Nestlé case published by Stulz in the 1995 highlights two main opposing effects on the cost of capital that result from the globalization of capital markets.

On the one hand, the removal of barriers to foreign investment means that risk premiums on securities in general fall, because the risk of these securities can be shared more efficiently among investors with globally diversified portfolios – and spreading risks more efficiently among investors with globally diversified portfolios means lower required returns and thus higher stock prices. Over the last two decades, the progressive integration of international financial markets has resulted in a significant drop in the cost of capital for public firms all over the world.

On the other hand, the increasing level of integration of both capital markets and real business activity resulting from the global expansion of multinationals implies a higher degree of synchronization (correlation) among various international capital markets. This means there is a greater tendency for all markets to move together. One consequence of this phenomenon is that investors enjoy fewer benefits from global diversification and face larger risks connected with global events, which results in a higher cost of capital because of increased risk premiums.

Stulz (1995) in his study starts from analyzing as until 1988 Nestlé had two types of shares that were exactly the same in terms of voting rights and dividends but which differed in terms of ownership restrictions:

- Bearer Shares: available to all investors worldwide (both Swiss and foreign); investors could buy them anonymously;
- Registered Shares: available only to Swiss investors, who needed to be registered with the company.

Assuming that restrictions on foreign ownership have no effect on share values, both types of shares should have sold for roughly the same price. However, this was not the case. Registered shares were sold for approximately half the price of bearer shares, implying a discount since local investors demanded higher expected returns to compensate for bearing more risk in their portfolios than if they could diversify their holdings across international markets.

Nestlé removed restrictions on foreign ownership of registered shares in 1988, leading to a rise in the company's share price/equity capitalization. As a result, Nestlé benefited from market globalization by lowering its cost of capital. The rise was due to two factors in particular:

- The price of restricted shares climbed as limitations were eliminated, allowing Swiss investors to sell their shares to overseas investors. Swiss investors demanded a lower risk premium because they held fewer of these shares.
- The price of bearer shares decreased (though less significantly). This second effect was partly caused by the lack of integration in global financial markets in 1988. The lifting of ownership limits meant that the supply of Nestlé shares available to foreign investors suddenly significantly outstripped the demand for those shares at the price at that time. As a result, the bearer share price had to fall. This would not have happened in today's highly interconnected global marketplace.

Global CAPM

Given today's market globalization, many public corporations (particularly those outside the United States) may wish to reconsider their standard practice for estimating cost of capital to better reflect the reality of globally determined capital costs. Rather than using a foreign CAPM that assesses a company's risk in relation to local markets, it is recommended to use a global CAPM that views a company as a component of a global portfolio of stocks.

For instance, in the case of Nestlé, the author proved that using a global CAPM rather than a Swiss CAPM significantly alters cost of capital estimates. If it is used the local Swiss CAPM for Nestlé, its Beta will be very close to 1 (since Nestlé dominates Swiss capital markets). However, if it is used the global CAPM, its Beta will be lower. Overall, if it is used a global CAPM rather than a local one, the cost of equity for Nestlé will be lower, increasing the company's overall capitalization value.

Keep in mind that, as national economies become more interconnected, this effect of descending capital costs will decrease (i.e., the cost of capital will increase) as risks increase (due to the increased interrelation of global economies).

Source: Stulz, R.M. (1995). Globalization of Capital Markets and the Cost of Capital: The Case of Nestlé. *Journal of Applied Corporate Finance, Morgan Stanley*, 8(3), 30-38.

5.7   Conclusions

Though the concept of the cost of capital and how to compute it is the same for domestic firms and MNCs, how it is applied in practice differs because of several features particular to MNCs. In fact, whereas domestic firms are only exposed to the risks of their home markets, MNCs operate in various countries which all have unique risks impacting their cost of capital.

Computing the cost of capital accurately is essential to valuing and assessing investments in new projects. Usually, certain adjustments must be made in the MNC's cost of capital estimation typically due to:

1. exchange risk;
2. political risk;

3. segmentation of capital markets;
4. international diversification effects.

Moreover, we should also remember a few key points regarding the optimal cost structure and its main drivers. As we saw in the chapter, building an efficient financial structure means choosing the amount of debt that minimizes the WACC level and maximizes the overall value of the enterprise. The optimal structure is a dynamic rather than a static model and thus changes over time. Regardless of whether it is an MNC, every firm should carefully monitor its financials and make decisions that adjust for present conditions, rather than simply hoping to find a magic formula or level that will always work.

To assess your understanding of the chapter, try to answer the following self-assessment questions:

a) Why does the cost of capital for a MNC differ from that of a domestic firm?
b) How do the internationally diversified operations of a MNC affect its cost of capital?
c) Why is the cost of capital different across countries?
d) What factors contribute to differences in the risk-free rate and risk premium?
e) How should you set the cost of capital for a MNC evaluating a foreign project?
f) What specific adjustments need to be made?

6   Introduction to Foreign Direct Investment

Foreign direct investments (FDI) are a common means by which multinational firms exploit foreign business opportunities. FDIs can take the form of joint ventures with foreign firms, acquisitions of foreign assets (e.g., land, buildings, existing plants, etc.) or the establishment of new foreign subsidiaries. Financial managers must understand the potential returns and risks associated with FDI so they can make investment decisions that maximize the MNC's value.

This chapter aims to provide a definition and overview of FDI, focusing on the main motivations for seeking returns abroad and the benefits that investors might acquire from these activities. The chapter will then be divided in two parts, the first will discuss the perspective of an investor seeking to expand abroad and the analysis and research he or she must perform before committing to an FDI. The second part of the chapter will instead take up the perspective of host countries and governments, highlighting the main incentives and barriers they can enact to invite foreign investors. This theoretical discussion will be coupled with examples that help illustrate the topics described.

6.1   An introduction to FDIs

The definition of FDI

For simplicity's sake, FDI is defined as a relationship in which an investor obtains ownership interest in an enterprise located in a foreign economy. To be classified as FDI, this investment must give its owner a significant degree of influence or control over the management of the foreign enterprise. This is the most straightforward definition. However, due to the dynamism of MNCs and FDIs, it is worth considering a few more definitions. For instance, FDI can also denote corporate activity that grants the status of 'multinational' to a firm (Kozlow, 2011); in this sense, FDIs are how MNCs become multinational. Indeed, FDI is a major category of cross-border investments. It is also a financial activity that normally consists in an international capital flow from one country (home) to another (host). The purpose of this transfer is to acquire partial or full ownership of a business entity, which could be a branch, an entire business unit, and so on.

Moreover, FDIs also play a fundamental role in both international and national economic accounts. In the former case, it represents a primary category of classifying data on financial transactions, positions, and income. In the latter case, FDI earnings are large components of property income from abroad, since the net property income from abroad is added to GDP (Kozlow, 2011).

FDIs and MNCs are closely linked concepts. We have already defined MNCs in the previous chapters. Before more thoroughly defining FDIs, it is worth pointing out that neither MNCs or FDIs are static phenomena and that assigning one single definition is often difficult. Multinationals are constantly adapting and exploiting economic and market condition changes, and they often do so through FDIs, which are likewise flexible and continuously transforming. That being said, let us look more closely at FDI.

We can distinguish between more qualitative or quantitative definitions of FDIs. Qualitatively, FDI signifies ownership and control: the main goal of this type of investment is to obtain sufficient ownership to ensure partial or total control of an entity located in a foreign country. The type of relationship and control are often established with the aim of creating a long-term interest. Quantitatively, the nearly universally accepted definition of FDI is ownership of at least 10% of the common (voting) stock of a business operating in a country other than the one in which the investing company is headquartered. In most countries, this 10% enables participation in managerial decisions.

FDI relationships usually involve three main players: the direct investor, the direct investment enterprise, and (sometimes) a fellow enterprise. A *direct investor* is the entity that has a significant degree of influence or control over a foreign entity, which instead represents the *direct investment enterprise*. When an investor does not reach the threshold for equity investment in another enterprise, it is called a *fellow enterprise*.

Finally, Kozlow (2011) maintains that it is possible to distinguish between inward and outward direct investments:

- *Inward direct investment* refers to investments made by foreign companies to bring foreign money into local economies. They are also called direct investment in the reporting economy.
- *Outward direct investment* refers to an outflow of investment capital from local entities to foreign economies. It is also called direct investment abroad.

Foreign direct investment is a type of inward investment that includes mergers and acquisitions or the creation of new operations for already established businesses.

6.1.1   Modes of FDIs

It is conceptually useful to consider FDIs as involving a two-stage investment process: in the first step, the firm has to choose whether or not to invest in a foreign country; in the second, it has to decide upon the mode of FDI through which to enter the country (Alba et al., 2010). There are different modes through which firms undertake foreign direct investment (FDI): a merger and acquisition (M&A), establishment of new subsidiaries, and others. Each mode presents its own unique advantages and disadvantages.

FDIs can take several different forms. A foreign subsidiary can be a completely new entity or it can be formed through mergers and acquisitions with existing companies in the local country. In the first case, we speak of an organic internal growth strategy when companies decide to expand into new markets by establishing new entities in other countries to produce and sell new items. Some companies may choose internal growth because it allows them to customize international operations to suit their needs. Pirelli, for example, has expanded its overseas operations mainly by setting up factories abroad, as it did in Romania in 2004 through the establishment of the company "Pirelli Tyres Romania" and the creation of jobs and highly qualified staff in the foreign country. Pirelli also has several hundred local suppliers in Romania, which are Romanian companies that are growing together with Pirelli.

While internal growth is often more natural and less dangerous, the process can be slow. Nowadays, many multinationals buy other companies in other countries to gain access to new markets, rather than building plants that may take years to build by implementing a so-called external growth strategy through mergers and acquisitions. Multinationals often buy foreign companies to gain immediate access to the market they serve by lowering competition and accelerating international expansion. Luxottica, the largest eyewear company in the world, is a model of aggressive expansion through acquisitions and mergers. If we examine its track record, we find that after acquiring the renowned Ray-Ban in 1999, Oakley in 2007 and Brazil's Grupo Tecnol in 2011, it set its sights on France's Alain Mikli International in 2012 until its merger with Essilor in 2018. Some other common forms of FDI are listed below.

- *Licensing* is a business arrangement in which a firm authorizes another company to access its intellectual property rights (e.g., copyright, brand name, patent, technology, etc.) by issuing a license that lasts for a limited period of time. This is the safest way to establish FDI, since the MNC bears a minimum risk if the foreign producer is wholly locally owned. Also, the initial commitment required is low. For these reasons, licensing is very popular among multinational firms. However, firms typically experience lower gains with licensing, since fees obtained from licensing are usually small.
- A *joint venture* (JV) is a business arrangement in which two or more parties share their resources for the purpose of accomplishing a specific task, which could be a new project or a foreign business. Since the MNC collaborates with a local partner, it is able to better understand the customers, institutions, and culture of the local environment, and thus avoid possible misunderstandings due to integration. In addition, it can benefit from managerial and technological capabilities that best fit that foreign market.
- *Strategic alliances* can take several forms. Two firms may exchange a share of ownership with one another to develop and manufacture a product or service. They may even engage in joint marketing and servicing agreements in which certain markets are covered by the first partner and others by the second.

6.1.2 Types of FDIs

While FDI is judged similarly to domestic investments, it is subject to extra risks that may or may not be compensated by increased revenues or cost savings. Because they include significant cash and time inputs, these investments should be carefully evaluated and their different types and potential outcomes should be analyzed.

After having defined properly foreign direct investments, it is important now to highlight the different classifications of this type of investments. FDIs are diverse and can be differentiated on the basis of some key criteria, namely the goal behind the establishment of the foreign subsidiary, the role of the parent company in the subsidiary's global strategy, and the way the foreign subsidiary is established. Two additional criteria used to classify FDIs include the method of financing the new investment and the extent of the foreign ownership. However, below we will discuss only the first three criteria in detail.

As we classify FDIs according to these criteria, it is important to remember that these investments can take on so many distinct forms that they do not conform to a single model of behavior or effects.

The goal of the foreign subsidiary

In looking at why a foreign subsidiary is established, or the objectives and motivations driving its creation, we can distinguish among (Dunning, 1993):

- Exploration of resources. Until World War II, these investments accounted for the bulk of FDIs. The choice to go overseas was primarily motivated by the destination's geological and climatic characteristics. The aim was to select areas rich in minerals and metals or with appropriate climate conditions.
- Search for new markets. The choice to move beyond national boundaries is usually made to defend or grow the market, usually after a large surge of exports to that location. This type of FDI is expected to benefit local and regional economies. In particular, if the intention of the MNCs is to sell through the subsidiary goods and purchase inputs in the local market, this approach will have a favorable influence on the productivity of local companies and the host country economy in general. In the case where the objective of the subsidiary is only to develop an "export platform," where all production will be directed to foreign markets then it is less likely to produce positive externalities in the host country (Farole et al., 2013).
- Search for efficiencies. This kind of investment is driven by the desire to establish a subsidiary in a low-wage nation and gain economies of scale. Efficiency-seeking FDI can also result in knowledge and technology transfers, thereby encouraging R&D and economic upgrading in the local country. Mexico, for example, created its aerospace sector in less than two decades. Aerospace goods were very limited in 2000, but by 2015 the sector had evolved into a $5 billion export business that employs about 30,000 people, with an annual growth rate of about 20 percent. Connections between companies, both local and international, have helped the sector develop and maintain investment.
  In this context, efficiency-seeking FDI has been instrumental in launching the development of a "technology-intensive sector." Foreign investment helped channel technological and material know-how into production processes, facilitating the creation of a large industry (Fruman, 2016).

- Strategic Asset Acquisition. In this situation, the motivating rationale derives from the need to purchase strategic assets that are critical to the company's positioning and competitive advantage with respect to rivals. This strategy may enable a business to acquire a rival, diversify its product line, enhance the technology contained in its goods, or prevent a third party from purchasing the assets at stake.

The role of the parent company's global production strategy

To classify FDIs according to this criterion, we need to distinguish between *horizontal and vertical FDIs,* which in turn allows us to further differentiate between two broad production strategies to which a foreign subsidiary may contribute. The former refers to a horizontal transfer of a portion of home country production to overseas subsidiaries for the purpose of strengthening the firm's global competitiveness. Horizontal FDI happens then when a multinational company invests in many countries to carry out the same production process. The latter instead refers to the idea of dividing the manufacturing process into segments in which various parts of a finished product are made by two or more subsidiaries in two or more countries anywhere in the world. Vertical FDI therefore occurs when a multinational company divides its production process across the globe, placing each stage of production in the lowest cost country.

How is the foreign subsidiary established?

FDIs can also be characterized according to the method used to create the foreign subsidiary or affiliate. There are three distinct alternatives, each with its own cost-benefit analysis. The vast majority of new FDIs are greenfield or brownfield investments (through M&A). The first involves the formation and establishment of a new local business, which potentially includes the construction of a new facility on an open grassy field (hence the term 'greenfield'). The second refers to a foreign company acquiring managerial control of an existing company in a host nation by purchasing voting shares in the local organization. Alternatively, a foreign subsidiary can also be established through privatization, which includes the acquisition of a state-owned enterprise, utility, or transportation system.

The most significant difference in economic effect between FDI established through greenfield facilities and FDI acquired through M&A or privatization resides in their different contributions to the local economy. The acquisition of an established business organization does not generate the extra economic activity, employment, and tax income in host nations that greenfield firms do. At first, mergers, acquisitions, and privatizations all involve a change in ownership. Although the foreign firm may later decide to increase production in its newly acquired foreign subsidiary, it may first undertake a cost-cutting campaign or catalyze a contraction of the local workforce.

Greenfield vs. brownfield projects in foreign direct investment

Both investment strategies have advantages and disadvantages.

Because cross-border purchases sometimes include pricing rivalry among foreign corporations for control, multinationals that join a foreign market through greenfield investments may generate larger profits than those that enter through cross-border acquisitions.

On the other hand, there are many advantages to pursuing an acquisition strategy, including risk sharing and quick market access. The ability to take advantage of opportunities coming from trade liberalization and the development and dissemination of technologies on a global scale both justify foreign acquisitions. In terms of competition and social welfare, these two entry techniques have varied ramifications for the host country's economy. In some circumstances, the best solution for a firm does not match the best solution for the host country, hence the MNC's choices are influenced by the host government's FDI policies. Qui and Wang (2011) developed a model to forecast the sort of entrance method that MNCs will pick based on the host country's FDI policies. Market size, cost differential, degree of market competition, and fixed setup costs associated with greenfield investment all influence entry choice, according to the model.

6.1.3   Theories on the birth of FDIs

The question of why companies invest abroad is at the center of many academic debates. The timeline proposed below is just one of several attempts to explain the complex FDI phenomena characterizing our global economy in the past and the present.

At first, economic theorists did not try to explain why companies set up subsidiaries in other countries. FDI was classified as an undifferentiated flow of international capital, meaning that it was handled similarly to any other type of cross-border money movement. According to scholars, the phenomenon began to expand in scale and relevance in the world economic system after World War II (around the 1960s). Multinational corporations and foreign direct investment existed long before 1960, but there was no accepted theory to explain their existence other than the so-called Portfolio Theory. This notion, which came from the domain of finance, suggested that the 'why' behind international investment was located in the convenience of interest rates. Yet is this the only explanation? Hymer (1960) and Kindleberger (2002) have instead emphasized that global expansion involves taking risks, acquiring new habits, and encountering new cultures – which they call the passivity of foreignness. Such complications, however, have not dissuaded companies from investing abroad, which, according to Hymer (1960) and Kindleberger (2002), suggests that the choice to expand abroad was motivated by benefits outweighing these disadvantages. First, there are the benefits of ownership (also known as firm-specific advantages) related to technology, brand, marketing, and organizational capabilities that outweigh the disadvantages and dangers associated with competing with international firms in foreign nations. Hymer has contended that ownership advantage operates globally only in the absence of perfect competition and ideal markets (Cohen, 2007). Market imperfections (e.g., technical exclusivity protected by patents, better managerial and marketing know-how, product specialization or differentiation, and government measures such as tariffs, quotas, and subsidies) are necessary for FDI to flourish, because the firm "internalises or supersedes" these market failures through foreign expansion (Hymer, 1960, 1968).

In the 1970s, Oliver Williamsons, who was not convinced by the theory of ownership advantage, developed a new thesis: transaction cost theory. Williamsons maintained that firms make it possible to internalize the transactions that take place in the market in a single organization. Applying this reasoning to multinationals allows us to internalize inefficient transactions in different countries. The key to doing so is to internalize cross-border operations within a single entity. An internalization advantage exists when management determines its ownership advantages are formidable or sensitive enough that it does not need to rely on sources external to the company or risk sharing proprietary assets.

OLI: A paradigm for global expansion

Mithun Sridharan has summarized the OLI paradigm based on internalization theory and developed by researcher John H. Dunning in 1979.

Companies look to internalization to pursue access to foreign natural or strategic resources, whether physical, financial, technical, or human. In some cases, internalization entails strategic expansion choices to seek new customers by expanding product and service offerings. Moreover, growth on a large scale can impact efficiency by achieving economies of scale. The OLI paradigm therefore allows for identification of the optimal option for effectively developing a foreign direct investment strategy by leveraging three possible advantages: ownership, localization, and internationalization.

Ownership advantage
First, a company must have a competitive advantage to overcome the obstacles encountered in the foreign country, such as inability to communicate in the local language or lack of understanding of the local culture and customs.

Ownership benefits relate to highly desirable intangible characteristics that are uncommon, difficult to replicate, and anchored at the organizational level and which enable a company to achieve competitive advantage over international competitors. Companies need to consider whether they have a specific competitive advantage that can be transferred externally to offset foreign risk. This could be a strong brand image with an excellent reputation.

Location advantage
These types of advantages may be purely geographic or may be the result of widely accessible and inexpensive raw resources, low labor costs, tax incentives, lack of tariffs, or other geopolitical features of the host country that attract the interest and attention of the multinational. In the absence of these specific advantages, multinationals should carefully consider whether they should maintain domestic production or instead export goods, leveraging the demand for their goods and services in the world market.

The benefit of internalization
Outsourcing only makes financial sense if the contracting company can meet the multinational company's rules, standards, and quality criteria at a much lower cost. Alternatively, a foreign partner could provide market knowledge or more qualified personnel who will help create a superior product.

Source: OLI: A framework for international expansion. *Think Insights.* Available at https://thinkinsights.net/strategy/oli-framework/

In the 1980s, John Dunning took a different perspective: he maintained that going abroad is risky but necessary for MNCs since their competitors are doing it. This results in the so-called *location advantage*: the host country can be so attractive that, even though companies know it is dangerous, they still want to be present there. What characteristics of a country might be so attractive to motivate such foreign investments? Dunning highlights location advantages in the form of simple market imperfections: low labor costs, natural resources, or different and more advantageous tax systems. Indeed, when they exist in sufficient magnitude, these advantages designate a foreign country as the production site most likely to maximize profits from overseas sales.

Putting these three pieces together offers a more complete picture of why a multinational chooses to go abroad, namely because it wants to master certain abilities and reinforce its competitive positioning. The mix of ownership, location, and internalization advantages constitute the *OLI paradigm*.[1] Assuming that the conditions of ownership and internalization are satisfied, a company will opt to build and operate its own subsidiaries abroad if it also identifies the existence of location-specific advantages.

Finally, since the 1990s, scholars have been advancing the idea that setting up a business abroad could also be the outcome of the desire to belong to a network of companies, the so-called *network advantage*. According to Chen et al. (1998), the network approach views FDI as the establishment of a link between a domestic network and a foreign network, where linkages via FDI are viewed as a strategic choice that enhances, maintains, or restores the investor's competitiveness in a global market, rather than a profit-seeking motive aimed at extracting surplus value from a foreign market by exploiting its own strategic assets.

6.1.4   The relevance of FDIs: trends and data

The power and financial stakes involved in the spread of big international enterprises are so great that the executive and legislative branches of many countries find themselves directly engaging in FDI-related issues. This suggests the magnitude of the phenomenon. A bit more context on the impact of FDIs for the global and local economies might be helpful.

Statistically speaking, the prominence of MNCs in the international economy is demonstrated by the fact that for more than twenty years FDI has regularly grown faster than the world GDP (output) and other macroeconomic measures of activity.

---

[1] According to economist John Dunning's OLI paradigm (ownership, location, internalization), a company can benefit from specific advantages associated with owning or opening a foreign branch (ownership advantages). These advantages are inextricably linked to the territory and thus difficult to transfer (location advantages), and the company benefits more from these advantages by directly utilizing them rather than transferring them to other companies (internalization advantages).

FDI has become an increasingly vital driver of economic growth, stimulating the economies of both home and host countries. The relevance of FDI is also evident in the corporate sphere. Simply consider the essential core of most business strategies: production and sales in more than one country that grow sales and profits while cutting production costs. Not only are these two points a priority, but they can almost be considered a means of corporate survival. We used to say that globalization is no longer merely an option but an imperative. Is this assertion still valid today?

FDI trends (flows and stocks) are extremely relevant for understanding the relationship between a country's economy and the global economy as a whole. Not only are they barometers of a country's attractiveness for foreign investments, they can also gauge the vitality of a country's industrial structure and its competitiveness on a global scale, as well as its technological capabilities. At the aggregate level, FDIs

---

Measuring FDIs

Before discussing historical and recent trends in FDI, it is important to note that collecting high-quality data on FDIs at both a national and international level is a complex task. Indeed, there are a number of challenges in measuring FDIs. The first pertains to the correct identification of the entities that fall under the category of direct investor, direct investment enterprise, and fellow enterprise. Next, it is critical to detect possible divergences in the level of consolidation among business registers in data compiling and data consolidation practices, especially if different registers are used for international and national accounting purposes. One way to overcome such issues is to create a survey structured in a way such that all respondents are required to answer and provide data that follow the generally accepted standards used in direct investments. Data regarding the direct investment equity position of the direct investor should be based on the direct investment enterprise's financial books. Finally, it is essential to estimate on a quarterly basis the direct investment enterprises' earnings that are reinvested.

Because of the many challenges that arise in measuring, collecting, and consolidating data on FDIs, much effort has been directed at addressing these issues. There is urgent need to have data on FDIs that are consistent with the revised standards. One example of an intervention in this field is the development of a European project called the FDI network, which exchanges confidential data on FDI transactions. A second initiative implemented to favor comprehensive reporting to national authorities is the EuroGroup Register (EGR), which collects information on major MNCs operating in the E.U. and their legal entities and controlling investors. Moreover, an OECD Working Group on International Investment Statistics has been established to tackle the problem of harmonization and integration of data and FDI statistics regarding MNCs.

Finally, in 2009 the Coordinated Direct Investment Survey (CDIS) was launched by the IMF in collaboration with other institutions such as the ECB, Eurostat, the OECD, the United Nations Conference for Trade and Development (UNCTAD), and the World Bank. This survey promises to significantly improve statistics on both inward and outward FDIs in terms of accuracy and harmonization by using valuation principles in line with the BPM6 (IMF's Balance of Payments and International Investment Position Manual). This means that all debt positions will be carried at nominal value while listed equity will be reported using public market prices; unlisted equity instead will be reported on a "own funds at book value" basis, where the value of the enterprise as recorded in the books of the direct investment enterprise is considered a good proxy for market value.

Source: Kozlow, R. (2011). Multinational Enterprises, Foreign Direct Investment and Related Income Flows. *United Nations Economic Commission for Europe, Chapter 3.*

also tell us much about global economic, political, and geopolitical trends. In fact, a strict relationship seems to exist between FDI trends and globalization waves.

- From 1990 to 2001: Events such as the rise of globalization, the fall of the Berlin Wall, and privatizations brought about an increase in investments.
- 2001: 9/11 triggered a drop in FDIs due to issues of international security.
- 2007 and the subsequent financial crisis spurred a reduction in FDIs, since people had little money to invest abroad and instead wanted to keep their money in their home countries.
- 2018 saw another slight decrease in FDIs due to changes in the geopolitical environment which are still taking place.

The effects of FDIs on international trade

Over the years, FDIs have become the first way through that many multinational corporations sell their goods in foreign countries – often at the expense of foreign trade, which is perceived as a less convenient business strategy. Overseas production has therefore determined a change in how international trade is conducted, affecting not only the export and import levels of individual countries but also the type of goods those countries decide to trade. For example, Japan reduced its car exports towards the U.S. after the 1980s because many subsidiaries of Japanese MNCs were established in the United States. It is obviously more convenient for those subsidiaries to target local customers directly through their assembly plants in the U.S. Generally, an increase in FDIs is associated with a reduction in traditional imports, since goods that were previously imported from the MNC's home country are now produced locally by its foreign subsidiary. This argument has led to a controversial debate regarding the negative impacts of FDIs on the MNC's home country, especially the drop in exported goods and reduction of job needs in those areas. In fact, as soon as production is transferred overseas, the local workers who previously manufactured the MNC's goods are likely to lose their jobs. However, it is impossible to generalize this argument, since usually the effects of FDIs depend on specific case-by-case circumstances. For instance, Ireland and Singapore are two examples of countries that have increased levels of sophisticated and capital-intensive exports due to FDIs: in fact, around 90% of their exports of manufactured goods in the last two decades are the consequence of the impressive assemblage of world-class MNCs operating there (Cohen, 2007).

As mentioned above, FDI trends are extremely revealing in terms of the relationship between a country's economy and the global economy as a whole. Indeed, analyzing FDI developments allows us to understand global economic, political, and geopolitical phenomena. In this section, we will therefore examine the state of FDIs today in order to obtain a better picture of global trends.

The Covid-19 pandemic has deeply altered health, economic, social, and geopolitical stability across the globe. Inevitably, the pandemic has caused disruptions with significant impacts on global FDI. Indeed, FDI flows plummeted by 38% year-on-year (to $364 billion) in the first half of 2020 alone and fell by 50% if compared to the second half of 2019, as shown in **Figure 6.1**. FDI flows in the first quarter of 2020 were the lowest since the first quarter of 2013. This sharp decline was largely due to lower investment rates in the United States and in 18 other OECD countries, together with disinvestments from Switzerland, the Netherlands, the U.K., and Norway.

However, 2020 was not the first year that FDIs registered significant drops in flows. Indeed, the situation only seemed to worsen and accelerate a steady decline that had been underway for the previous five years.

Figure 6.1   Global FDI flows, Q1 2013 – Q2 2020 (USD billion)

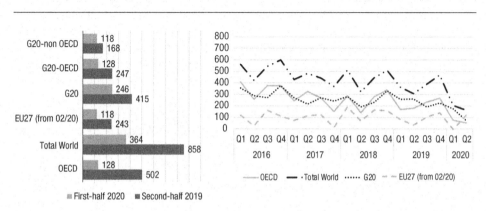

Source: OECD International Direct Investment Statistics database.

Figures 6.2 and **6.3** provide an overview of inflows and outflows of FDIs for selected areas.

Figure 6.2   FDI inflows for selected areas, Q1 2016 – Q2 2020 (USD billion)

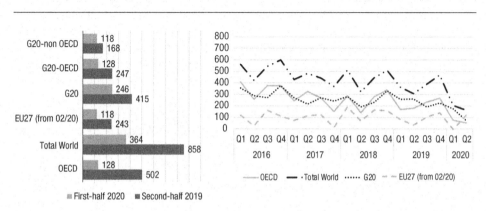

Source: OECD International Direct Investment Statistics database.

Figure 6.3   **FDI outflows from selected areas, Q1 2016 – Q2 2020 (USD billion)**

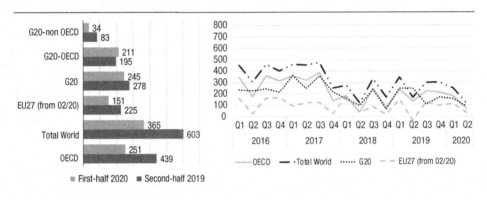

Source: OECD International Direct Investment Statistics database.

FDI inflows to the OECD area in the first half of 2020 bottomed out by 74%, includ-
ing by 51% in the EU27 countries and by 41% in the G20 economies, mostly due to
major drops in the U.S. (to approximately half of its 2019 value), the Netherlands,
Switzerland, the U.K., and Norway. On the contrary, FDI inflows rose in France,
Germany, Spain, and Sweden. Regardless of these declines, the first half of 2020 saw
Ireland as the top FDI recipient worldwide, followed by China, the United States, and
Luxembourg.

In terms of FDI outflows, in the first half of 2020 the OECD area experienced a
drop of 43%, while the EU27 countries dove by 33% and the G20 economies fell by
12%. This was mostly due to a downturn in Japan, Canada, and Italy with disinvest-
ments from the Netherlands that offset the rise in outflows of FDI from Luxembourg,
Germany, Sweden, Spain, France, and the United States. In the first half of 2020,
major sources of outward FDI worldwide were Luxembourg, the United States, Japan, Germany, and China.

According to UNCTAD's Investment Trends Monitor Global,[2] FDI increased in
2021, but recovery is severely uneven. Infrastructure financing increased due to economic stimulus packages, but greenfield industrial projects remained scarce. Global
foreign direct investment flows increased 77% to $1.65 trillion in 2021, surpassing
pre-Covid-19 levels but the largest increases occurred in developed nations, where
FDI reached $777 billion in 2021.

On the other hand, FDI flows in emerging nations increased only 30% (to about
$870 billion), with growth accelerating in East and Southeast Asia (+20%), and Latin
America and the Caribbean recovering to pre-Covid-19 levels, and West Asia increasing. Africa also saw an increase in inflows. More than $500 billion, or nearly

---

[2] Global Investment Trend Monitor, No. 40, 2022. Available at: https://unctad.org/webflyer/glob-
al-investment-trend-monitor-no-40.

three-quarters, of the increase in global FDI flows in 2021 ($718 billion) was reported in developed nations. Developing economies, especially the least developed countries (LDCs), saw a much smaller rebound.

Global FDI surged in 2021, but the recovery was severely unequal.

Figures 6.4 and **6.5** report *Outward* and *Inward* FDI financial flows in U.S. million dollars from 2020 to the third quarter of 2021 (OECD source).

Effects of FDIs on less developed countries

One argument that has recently emerged regarding FDIs is their effect on the economies of less developed countries (LDCs). This is an extremely controversial issue which is far from being resolved. The resulting absence of clear answers leaves policymakers in LDCs receiving mixed signals regarding how much or how little FDI they should allow. Two main currents of thought have arisen (Cohen, 2007).

The first one is critical of international business, advancing the idea that the maximization of profits that motivates MNCs to establish FDIs in less developed economies often has a negative impact on the local economic and social environment. The extent of this harmful effect depends on how weak the LDC's political and economic system is and therefore it is influenced by the power and money of MNCs. This negative view of MNCs is rooted in memories of the colonial experience and associates modern multinational firms with the raw-material-extracting foreign companies that used to establish one-sided, long-term deals with compliant colonial rulers. As a result, critics of international business strongly encourage tight regulation or even the banning of MNCs from less developed countries. They believe that inward FDI can only contribute to the further impoverishment of LDC populations via unemployment, unequal income distribution, and capital outflows that exploit workers, natural resources, and weak regulatory environments.

An opposing strand of thought supports international business as beneficial to LDCs and their economies. This perspective maintains that FDIs can create additional jobs and give local workers better training and wages or provide local economies the necessary support to develop advanced technologies which increase productivity and quality control and produce higher value-added goods. They also suggest that local businesses benefit from the presence of MNCs, since the latter often rely on local suppliers for components, equipment, and the provision of ancillary services. Vice versa, MNCs can also offer their technical and financial assistance to locals and thereby increase their quality standards or managerial capabilities. FDIs are often associated with higher capital investments, increased export levels, and higher foreign exchange earnings. Additionally, most of the relevant literature highlights the potential for high-quality FDIs to produce the following secondary advantages: increased competitiveness of local firms, a larger pool of highly trained workers, the attraction of additional investments, the rise of new businesses, better environmental protections.

As a result, LDCs can exploit the efficiency and know-how of MNCs' foreign subsidiaries to sustain economic growth and the social development of local economies by raising living standards and workers' skills and technological capabilities. Especially since the globalization of the 1990s, FDI has become a way for local decisionmakers to increase the standard of living and reduce the gap of knowledge they have with developed countries.

A final theory worth mentioning maintains that, in some cases, economic and political conditions in a host country are the independent variables determining the effects of incoming direct investment, not the other way around.

Source: Cohen, S.D. (2007). *Multinational Corporations and Foreign Direct Investments: Avoiding Simplicity, Embracing Complexity.* Oxford University Press.

Figure 6.4   **FDI outflows from selected areas, Q1 2020 – Q3 2021 (USD Millions)**

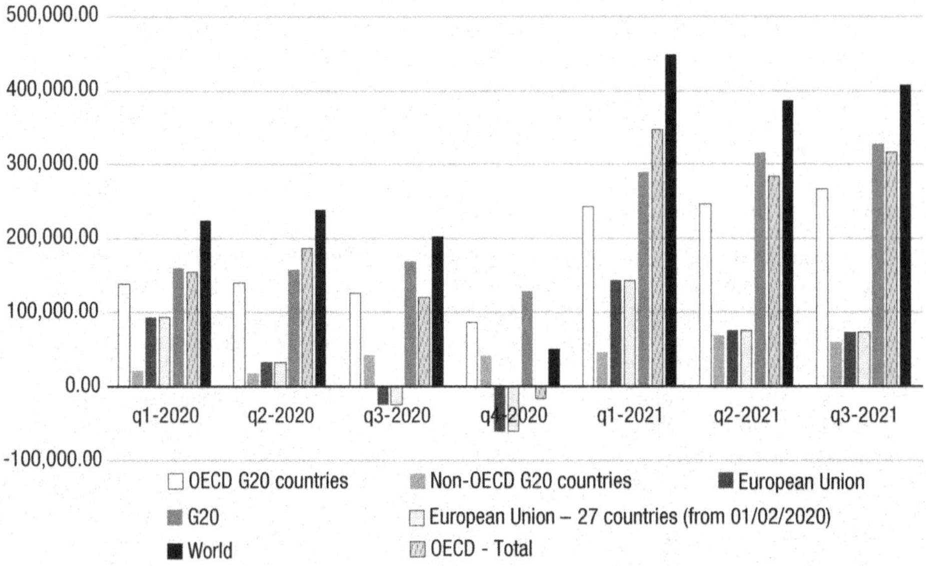

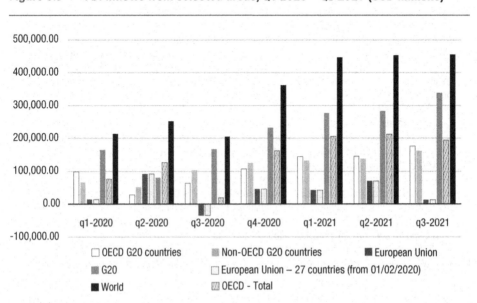

Source: OECD International Direct Investment Statistics database.

Figure 6.5   **FDI inflows from selected areas, Q1 2020 – Q3 2021 (USD Millions)**

Source: OECD International Direct Investment Statistics database.

6.2   The MNC perspective

6.2.1   The FDI decision-making process and motives

The decision to grow internationally is critical and could prove incredibly profitable, but it is also extremely risky and could threaten the entire company. A mistake in the international arena could mean the extinction of a thriving domestic company. As a result, multinationals must carefully consider whether or not to expand their operations. The analyses outlined below can help determine whether it makes sense to expand or restructure current overseas operations:

1. Identify the correct motivations. Examine the various revenue and cost motives for FDI and see which ones apply and prevail.
2. Feasibility Analysis. Determine the feasibility of the proposed project.
3. Corporate Control. Examine existing corporate control within the parent company and possible corporate control in foreign countries.
4. Country Risk Analysis. Analyze country risk in countries where the multinational does business now and in countries where it plans to expand. If country risk affects cash flows or the cost of financing projects, incorporate any findings into the capital budgeting process.
5. Capitalization. Review the MNC's current capital structure and decide if it is appropriate in light of its current operations and ability to repay loans. Estimate the cost of capital that could be raised to fund new foreign projects and factor that into the capital budgeting analysis.
6. Long-term financing. Consider international sources of long-term funds. Determine whether to adjust financing to minimize the cost of capital or to hedge foreign exchange risk (match the currency of loan repayment with the currency of cash entry).

Product life cycle theory, portfolio theory, and the *oligopoly model* have all been proposed as explanations and justifications for foreign investment (Kim et al., 2006). In determining whether foreign direct investment is appropriate for a multinational corporation, the following factors might influence the decision-making process. Indeed, multinationals typically participate in FDI to increase revenue, cut expenses, or do both capitalizing sometimes their oligopolistic advantages. These advantages include proprietary technology, management expertise, global distribution networks, access to scarce raw resources, scale efficiencies of manufacturing and finance, and ownership of a strong brand or trade name. By using such oligopolistic advantages, an MNC may be able to lower its cost of capital and raise its profitability, hence enhancing the firm's value (Kim et al., 2006).

According to Madura (2015), there are five revenue-related motivations for FDI. A first reason to pursue FDIs is to gain access to more profitable markets. When a multinational company notices that its competitors are generating exceptional earnings in a specific market, it may want to exploit the same opportunities by entering the same market at a lower price. One disadvantage of this strategy is represented by the possible takeover measures available to first movers. In some cases, a firm may exploit first-mover or monopolistic benefits. If the MNC owns resources or skills that are unique, such as technologies or specific know-how, it may attempt to exploit them not only in its local market but also internationally.

Another motivation for companies to engage in FDI is the creation of new sources of demand by taking advantage of countries with higher levels of economic growth where the population is willing to consume more. A firm may also pursue FDI to benefit from diversification. Net cash flow from sales of products across several different countries should be more stable than comparable product sales in a single country. Moreover, the MNC may reap the benefits of a possible lower cost of capital if shareholders and creditors perceive the company's risk to be lower thanks to less volatile cash flows.

Finally, FDI can be a reaction to trade limitations and constraints: a multinational company can undertake FDI simply to avoid trade barriers. In this regard, Burton et al. (1987) examine precisely the penetration of Japanese firms in the 1970s into the color television markets of the United States and Western Europe, initially through exports and then predominantly through local production as a defensive response to trade barriers erected in these markets to relocate Japanese factories from Japan and other Asian locations.

Continuing with Madura (2015), MNCs also engage in FDI for cost-related motives. Firms can benefit from using foreign raw materials, foreign factors of production, or foreign technology. The latter is becoming an increasingly common motivation, as MNCs establish overseas plants or acquire existing ones to access to unique technological capabilities and improve their production efficiency. The acquisition of foreign raw materials is often motivated by the need to reduce transportation expenses, which arise when the firm has to import goods from a country different from the one where it is going to sell its final products. In the past, FDI was pursued to benefit from lower labor and land costs, especially in less developed countries.

Another reason for FDI are the economies of scale represented by attempting to sell products in new markets, since higher production results in lower costs per unit of product and increased income and shareholder value. Finally, exchange rates are without a doubt one of the most researched FDI factors. Volatility, levels, and expectations have all been addressed in the literature. In terms of the magnitude of exchange rate volatility, both positive and negative impacts on the quantity of inbound FDI have been discovered, indicating a hazy influence of exchange rate volatility on FDI decision-making. In terms of exchange rate levels, current study generally finds a positive association between local currency depreciation and FDI. A third stream of empirical research has shown that a rise in the projected exchange rate may result in a drop in the quantity of FDI presently conducted (Franco et al., 2010).

6.2.2   Diversification analysis of international projects

Another way to look at FDIs is through diversification analysis, which suggests a multinational company should base the decision to pursue a foreign project on the benefits that can be obtained across countries. There are two main types of diversification: diversification across projects and diversification across geographic areas (Madura, 2012).

When a multinational company has several investments around the world, its main concern is not only the risk-return profiles of individual projects but also the performance of its overall portfolio of projects. In such cases, projects with high levels of return may be feasible despite their high risks, because the MNC does not undertake these projects alone but can combine them with safer projects. In other words, instead of focusing on only one project, it is better to develop a portfolio of projects through which the MNC can achieve a better risk-return tradeoff.

As shown by Tabova (2013), less risky countries receive higher investment shares than riskier countries, reading this result as evidence that investors take diversification opportunities into account, not only for portfolio investment decisions but also for foreign direct investment decisions. As suggested by asset allocation theory, starting from two projects it is always possible to build a frontier of efficient project portfolios in a risk-return environment. All portfolios on the efficient frontier are made of projects that minimize the risk for a given level of expected return. Project portfolios outperform individual projects thanks to the diversification benefit. In fact, the lower the correlation in project returns over time, the lower the overall risk. The portfolio that should be chosen by a multinational depends on the firm's attitude towards risk: the more conservative the MNC, the lower the risk-return combination it will pick (near the bottom of the efficient frontier).

The position of the frontier depends on the business in which the firm operates. Some MNCs have frontiers of possible project portfolios with better positions than others. Doukas (2003) finds, for example, evidence that geographic diversification increases shareholder value and improves long-term performance when firms engage in direct foreign investment related to the core business. His research also shows that, regardless of the industrial structure of the firm, foreign direct investment outside the core business can lead to a loss of shareholder value. Unrelated foreign diversification, on the other hand, is less damaging to already diversified (multi-segment) firms than to specialized (single segment) firms.

So far, we have discussed how essential it is to create a well-balanced portfolio of projects to avoid incurring excessive, correlated risks. As we dive deeper into this topic, we should also differentiate among the geographies and countries in which a firm decides to invest. Indeed, the potential benefits and risks of FDI vary from country to country.

For example, countries in Western Europe have well-established markets where the demand for most products and services represents substantial *benefits* to MNCs. Thus, these countries may appeal to MNCs when they have better products than those currently being offered. Countries in Eastern Europe, Asia, and Latin America tend to have relatively low costs for land and labor. Yet if a multinational wants to establish a low-cost production facility, it should also consider other factors such as the work ethic and skills of the local people, the availability of labor, and local cultural and political characteristics.

On the other hand, by diversifying its business among several countries rather than focusing on only one, a firm reduces its *risk* exposure to any single foreign country (Madura, 2012). However, since economic conditions among countries have become integrated over time, the weakness of one country may spread to other countries. Thus, diversification across economies may not be as effective when there are global economic conditions that adversely affect most countries.[3]

Having discussed project and geographic diversification, we can now confidently say that MNCs can achieve more desirable risk-return characteristics from their project portfolios if they sufficiently diversify among products and geographic markets. This also relates to the advantages MNCs have over purely domestic firms that serve only a local market; in such cases, the MNC may be able to develop a more efficient portfolio of projects than its domestic counterpart. These international projects can reduce the firm's overall risk thanks to international diversification benefits. However, selecting foreign projects whose performance levels are not highly correlated over time is key. This will ensure that various international projects do not experience poor performance simultaneously.

6.2.3 Risks of operating abroad

Unlike purely domestic companies, the operations of international/multinational companies are subject to at least four levels of risk, as shown in **Table 6.1** (the y-axis shows the location of the operation, i.e., domestic vs abroad, and the x-axis shows the source of risk, i.e., inside or outside the country):

1. Risk at home when operating at home.
2. Risk at home when operating abroad.
3. Risk in the host country when operating in the host country.
4. Risk in the host country due to geopolitical issues.

---

[3] Russia's invasion of Ukraine on February 24, 2022 has produced a series of enormous risks to a world economy that has not yet fully recovered from the shocks of the Covid-19 pandemic. International geopolitics have a strong impact on economies, exports, and imports, and therefore on international, economic, and financial trade across Europe and beyond. The Russian assault followed weeks of tensions that had already shaken the world economy by sending energy prices skyrocketing – with oil rising above $100 a barrel on the day of the Russian attack (for the first time since 2014) and European natural gas jumping as much as 62%.

Table 6.1   Location source of risk

Company Operating Abroad with Risk Linked to the Country of Origin	Multinationals Having Operations Abroad in Another Country (with Risk Coming from Abroad)
An example: Trump effect (Apple in China risks repercussions for Trump's policies of repatriating profits).	• Geopolitical risk • War or revolution (the case of the war in Ukraine) • Third party risk • FertiNitro in Venezuela
Domestic Company and Risk Coming from Inside	**Domestic Company in Home Country Damaged by Something Decided Abroad**
• Government and political instability • Nationalization • Reputational risk • Default of the state • Governmental trade policies	• Supranational regulations: EU regulation • Dumping/unfair competition • Sanctions decided by the European Union against Russia and the firm is selling in Russia

---

Example Venezuela, the Nationalization of FertiNitro

On October 11, 2010, the Venezuelan government took control of Fertilizantes Nitrogenados de Oriente, or FertiNitro, a fertilizer company with one of the world's largest nitrogen-based ferti- lizer factories. The American Koch Industries owns a portion of the corporation, while Saipem, a subsidiary of the Italian firm Eni, owns the rest. Pequiven, a Venezuelan state-controlled firm, owned 35% of FertiNitro prior to the takeover. Venezuela's President Chavez had been step- ping up nationalizations since his Socialist Party won a reduced majority in the September 2010 legislative elections. The week before, the government had taken over the agricultural supply company Agroislena.

6.3   Host government perspective

Each local authority has to identify all possible advantages and disadvantages to FDI in its country and weigh them. Typically, foreign direct investment may assist host nations, particularly developing ones, in a variety of ways:

1. Facilitates the transfer of technology and skills that are frequently in limited supply on the domestic market;
2. Boosts domestic employment and income;
3. Facilitates the development of managerial abilities among indigenous personnel;
4. Contributes to tax collections and aids in the balance of payments on a global scale (Kim et al., 2006).

However, if the finished products are sold in the same country, this may take market share away from other local competitors and cause layoffs. Some types of FDI could eliminate as many local jobs as they create. Therefore, depending on the forms of FDI in question, governments might provide incentives to encourage them, erect barriers to prevent them, or impose conditions to regulate them (Madura, 2012).

Politicians and governments are often at odds over laws and regulations affecting multinationals and their FDI. Indeed, two political factions have developed over time, one condemning such investments and another defending them, as perspectives on their costs versus benefits differ. The issue of whether free market or government regulation is more desirable is far from binary – indeed, it depends on a plethora of variables and particular circumstances.

It is worth noting that one factor influencing companies' decisions to invest in other countries is the favorable or unfavorable investment climate for business in the potential host country. One of the most important factors in a country's investment climate is the cumulative effect of national government attitudes, actions, and inactions. Indeed, government policies alter the quantity, quality, size, and mix of incoming FDI over time, depending on whether they are overtly accommodative, neutral, mildly discouraging, implicitly unfavorable, or deliberately hostile.

6.3.1 Incentives for FDI

The magnitude of FDI incentives is determined on a case-by-case basis and is often a consequence of the relative negotiation power of the two parties involved (the host government and the MNC). These benefits are usually classified into three categories (Cohen, 2007): fiscal incentives, financial incentives, and other incentives.

Ideally, FDI solves problems such as unemployment and lack of technology without taking business away from local firms. Following the same logic, governments should focus on incentivizing activities that create the strongest potential for spill overs between foreign-owned and domestic firms, education, training, and R&D (Blomstrom, 2003). It could be advantageous for the local government to offer incentives to MNCs to attract FDI. The three main categories of incentives are analyzed below (Cohen, 2007):

a) *Fiscal Incentives.* These aim at decreasing the multinational's tax liabilities through various measures, including tax breaks or tax exemptions on the income derived from exports, tax holidays to defer corporate income and property taxes for a fixed number of years, tax credits for profits that are reinvested locally, reductions in the standard corporate tax rates, accelerated depreciation allowances, and exemptions in the value-added tax for capital goods and raw materials purchases. Recently, for example, a number of tax measures have been implemented to make France more attractive to foreign investors. In particular, Macron's government has decided to gradually lower the French corporate income tax rate to 25% by 2022 (from 33.3%) and to develop tax incentives for innovation.

b) *Financial Incentives.* These help MNCs to establish subsidiaries and run their everyday operations by defraying expenses. A government may offer non-repayable subsidies in the form of rent-free land and buildings or direct grants to finance worker training and factory equipment. There are several examples of national or municipal governments selling property or buildings to foreign investors at below-market prices. Other common practices for host government are guarantees of MNC's loans or subsidized loans. Authorities may occasionally contribute to marketing and development expenditures, as well as day-to-day operational costs, in addition to assisting investors with start-up costs. Cost participation might be offered directly or indirectly via suppliers of products and services to the investor (OECD, 2003).

c) *Other.* This category includes a number of miscellaneous incentives that governments can provide to multiply FDIs, for instance subsidizing water and energy, establishing a well-functioning telecommunications infrastructure, modern transportation networks, and reduced environmental regulations such as exemption from import duties on raw material (Cohen, 2007). This category includes processes that facilitate getting government contracts, pre-investment feasibility studies, and closing the domestic market to future direct investment by competing foreign companies.

As reported by EY,[4] in reaction to the Covid-19 pandemic event, governments throughout the globe have engaged a variety of financial, fiscal, and other incentives to encourage foreign direct investment. Governments in Europe, India, and Africa, in particular, are giving a variety of incentives to attract firms from all over the globe.

Most European governments provide R&D tax incentives to most enterprises who do R&D in fields ranging from technology to pharmaceutical to food and financial services.

In India, state-level incentives are classified into three types: those connected to capital, those related to costs, and those related to taxes.

With capital-related incentives, 20% to 25% of the project cost might be returned to the corporation as an incentive. Expense-related incentives include, for example, lower power and water rates, as well as lower property and stamp taxes. The most crucial, though, are tax breaks. Taxes paid to the state government over a 10- to 12-year period are refunded to the company as a subsidy, up to a maximum of 60% to 70% of the project cost.

African incentives are being offered at the national level, in the form of tax relief or a decrease in the tax rate, and are tailored to each country's degree of development. They are aimed at creating jobs in the extractive industry, exports, infrastructure, and manufacturing. In some cases, incentives can have a more indirect nature. For instance, a country with high quality governance, political stability, developed physical and human infrastructure, and an adequate level of law protection will attract more investments from MNCs. On this point, see the study by Appiah-Kubi et al. (2020) that examined the link between corporate governance structures at the national level and foreign direct investment, with a focus on West African countries from 2009 to 2018. The results of the study show that nations that better safeguard the interests of non-controlling parties are able to attract more FDI. Economies with strong ethical standards often produce more foreign direct investment, and the presence of effective boards of directors significantly increases domestic FDI inflows.

---

[4] Smith, B. (2021, July 29). How Europe, India and Africa are incentivizing foreign investment. EY. Available at https://www.ey.com/en_gl/tax/how-europe-india-and-africa-are-incentivizing-foreign-investment

The study also suggests that West African nations build corporate governance frameworks that are completely independent of political pressures to ensure that FDI inflows that effectively impact the nations' well-being.

The impact of taxes on the location and investment choices of businesses

As stated in the introduction and conclusions of the report prepared by the *Swedish Agency for Growth Policy Analysis*, understanding which factors influence a company's location and investment choices is critical for a variety of reasons. Investment generates employment possibilities and the potential for economic development, which may be further boosted by productivity gains brought about by the concentration of economic activity. A good business and investment environment also has a beneficial impact on government budgets.

The Swedish report outlines several variables that determine where businesses are located and where they choose to invest. Aside from merely geographic considerations, market size, access to a qualified staff, and proximity to other businesses may all play a role. Taxes are regarded as significant policy measures to attract firms and stimulate investment, with corporate taxation being especially important for company location and investment choices. In addition to influencing where a company chooses to locate and how much money it invests, taxes may also affect where earnings are declared and whether new companies are formed.

According to the fundamental model for capital flows and taxes, an increase in the tax rate will result in a capital outflow, which will have a negative effect on a country's economy. Capital mobility to some degree influences the susceptibility of capital flows to changes in tax rates. Capital is one of the most flexible tax bases because of the increased globalization and liberalization of international markets – where the integration of capital markets has been the most comprehensive. As a result, there has been discussion of the possible negative repercussions of international tax rivalries, in which governments compete for capital by providing increasingly lower capital tax rates. One issue that has been raised is the possibility that tax competition will lead to tax rates falling below optimal levels, eroding the capacity of individual nations to pursue autonomous tax policies. Corporate taxes are crucial in determining where businesses should be located, where international investments should be undertaken, and where earnings should be declared.

Corporate tax rates also significantly affect the amount of foreign investment a nation draws, especially new E.U. member states. On the other hand, the forces of agglomeration are considerably more relevant for more established E.U. member states. As a result, lower corporate tax rates may compensate for the absence of agglomeration factors in the new member states. A lower company tax rate might potentially be a competitive advantage, helping to offset the disadvantages of potentially less desirable geographic locations or smaller sizes.

The quantity of foreign direct investment and the placement of business headquarters are both affected by labor income taxation. Again, findings vary between old and new E.U. member states: labor taxation has a bigger impact inside the EU15, but corporate taxes have a greater impact ion new member state investment.

Finally, the report identifies that dividend taxation has an impact on investment and the formation of new businesses. When opposed to smaller, younger enterprises that rely on outside funding, high-dividend tax rates benefit investment in established firms that have more chances to finance their operations by reinvesting earnings. Property taxes tend to be more crucial for new enterprises than corporate taxes, proportionally. To foster more dynamic business environments, the unusually high personal capital taxes (from an international viewpoint) in some nations may need to be reconsidered.

Source: Swedish Agency for Growth Policy Analysis (2014). *How Taxation Influences Business Location and Investment Decisions.* Available at https://www.tillvaxtanalys.se/download/18.62dd45451715a006 66f2100b/1586366214684/pm_2014_18_ENG.pdf

6.3.2 Barriers to FDI

Governments that are hostile towards FDI adversely impact locally owned companies. They impose tight regulation on any FDI that may affect local firms or economic conditions.
There are an extensive number of barriers to FDI that governments can implement to protect local enterprises. The most common are defensive barriers, regulatory barriers, national legislation and bureaucracy, political conditions, ethical and environmental regulations, and mass expropriation (Madura, 2012).

While FDI often provides host countries with the resources they need, emerging countries in particular view it with suspicion. There are several justifications for opposing foreign investment. Most of these disagreements relate to conflicts between the goals of the multinational corporation and the aspirations of the host government, and in particular the possibility that foreign investment can be read as the loss of political and economic sovereignty as well as control of key industries in the country with indiscriminate exploitation of natural resources and local unskilled labor (Kim et al., 2006). The most effective policy to repel FDI is to ban it outright, at least in sectors where sensitivity to foreign control is especially acute – either through *constitutional amendments or national legislation* (Cohen, 2007). These statutes and policies are intended to protect specific business sectors of public interest by preventing foreigners from having controlling interests in firms operating there. This practice is used by local authorities both in rich and poor countries: for instance, the United States limits foreign participation in domestic airlines, radio and TV stations (regulatory practices in telecommunications in the European Union also function to contain FDI), and nuclear energy sectors. Absolute, across-the-board bans on incoming FDI are no longer used since they are deemed prohibitively expensive.

A further barrier is represented by *bureaucracy*. Indeed, MNCs pursuing FDI are subject to different sets of procedures in each country. This makes it difficult for firms to become experts in bureaucratic processes in every market. Dar et al. (2020) investigated the relationship between bureaucratic quality and FDI inflows for selected South Asian countries (Pakistan, India, Sri Lanka, and Bangladesh) between 1995 and 2015, controlling for inward investment, economic development, human capital, exchange rate, financial development, and inflation, concluding that bureaucratic quality plays an important role in attracting FDI inflows to those countries. Furthermore, in addition, each country also has its own *regulatory barriers*. These come in the form of taxes, and regulations related to currency convertibility, earnings remittance, employee rights, and other policies that influence the profitability and liquidity of a subsidiary in a foreign country. Regulations in foreign countries are a complex subject for MNCs to consider, since they can be onerous, can change over time via surprise announcements, are subject to contrasting interpretations, and can pose challenges to the firm's business operations.

Among the most common methods used by government agencies that control M&As operations are *defensive/protective barriers*, which can prevent MNCs from pursuing acquisitions deemed harmful to local workers. A more extreme approach could entail restricting foreign ownership of local firms. One example is Japan, whose control system has effectively prevented or discouraged foreign direct investment in the country in the past.

The *political conditions* of a foreign country can also present barriers for MNC subsidiaries. Specifically, if a country is characterized by political instability due to unexpected changes in government or political conflicts, the outcomes of FDI could be at risk. Other barriers are represented by *environmental and ethical concerns:* some countries may impose environmental restrictions on subsidiaries, for instance through building codes, pollution controls, or policies regarding the disposal of waste material. Haeyeon et al. (2017) explore the influence of environmental regulations on foreign direct investment (FDI) in the manufacturing sector using Korean outbound FDI data from 2009 to 2015. When analyzing the degree of environmental control in the host nation, the research takes into account not only the stringency but also the implementation of environmental rules. The major findings of an FDI model estimation show that the stronger the rules in host nations, the lower the FDI to such countries. Moreover, each country possesses different ethical codes regarding business conduct. In particular, in some countries, bribes to government officials are common practice, so if MNCs do not act similarly, they might find themselves at a competitive disadvantage (Madura, 2012). Many academics have shown through their research that most nations that rank poorly on the Corruption Perception Index (CPI) tend to attract less direct investment. Nations toward the bottom of the CPI, on the other hand, tend to have additional problems that could reduce FDI flows even more, such as low GDP per capita, higher poverty rates, and less stable regimes. Research by Habib et al. (2002) investigates the influence of corruption on foreign direct investment (FDI). First, the amount of corruption in the host nation is assessed. Second, the absolute difference in corruption levels between the host and home nation is studied. The study confirms the detrimental effects of both. According to the results, international investors often avoid corruption because it is considered unethical and could result in operational inefficiencies.

Finally, a very effective means of discouraging FDIs is for a government to engage in *mass expropriation* (*nationalization*) of foreign-held companies.

Special requirements

In some cases, international acquisitions are allowed by governments but MNCs are subject to special requirements, often called performance requirements (Cohen, 2007). These are operational limitations imposed by the host government on MNCs wanting to establish foreign subsidiaries in their country. Such measures are aimed at finding a balance between the MNCs' interests and the local country's development goals and strategies. For instance, forcing a firm to have a minimum percentage of its production performed locally is a common way of increasing domestic production and creating new jobs. Additionally, MNCs could be obliged to export their finished goods so as to avoid harming local firms or guaranteeing a certain level of pollution control for manufacturing. Another common requirement is the retention of all the employees of the target firm to avoid potential discontent and protect general economic conditions in the country. It should be noted that these government-imposed conditions do not necessarily prevent a multinational company from pursuing FDI, though they may make such investments more expensive. The MNC will decide to implement such investments only if its expected benefits outweigh such costs.

Banking deregulation, the cost of capital, and FDI

Intriguing 2016 research examined the influence of bank deregulation on the foreign direct investment activities of firms in the United States. Kandilov et al. (2016) show that interstate bank
deregulation lowers the cost of credit (measured as the return on loans), increases the level of
competition in the banking industry, and increases the share of assets held by large banks in de-
regulated states. This is consistent with previous research (Cetorelli and Strahan, 2006). Using
interstate banking deregulation as a proxy for changes in the banking environment, Kandilov et
al. (2016) also find that lower lending rates are related to more foreign entry and lower transaction values. The same results are related to increased bank competition and the proportion of
large bank assets. The influence of credit constraints on foreign economic activity, especially
international investment, is the subject of a growing body of studies. Klein et al. (2002), for instance, demonstrate that changes in the availability of home country bank financing are important determinants of both the incidence and magnitude of FDI activity. Antras et al. (2009) have
developed a theoretical model of multinational corporations and imperfect capital markets that
predicts that weak financial institutions discourage overseas investment and force firms to rely
more on parent company financing. Finally, Bilir et al. (2014) show that the financial development
of the host country affects the activity of U.S. multinationals investing abroad; in particular, more
financially developed countries are able to recruit more U.S. multinational affiliates, and the effect is greater when the firm works in industries that are more dependent on external financing.

6.4 Conclusions

Though FDIs seem to represent a straightforward phenomenon, these investments
hide several complications. We discussed the reasons MNCs decide to go abroad and
the benefits, dangers, and risks involved in a global world.

We started by exploring the concept of FDI and its close relation to the theory of
MNCs and how they act in a global context. For the sake of simplicity, we defined
FDI as a financial process associated with companies operating in and controlling
income-generating facilities in at least one country outside their country of origin.
We analyzed the forms of FDI and ways of entering a foreign country, highlighting
the goals motivating MNCs. Then, we looked into the origins and reasons behind the
birth of direct foreign investment more qualitatively, touching on central concepts
such as the liability represented by foreignness, the internationalization advantage,
and the location and network advantage, which are summarize in the so-called OLI
paradigm.

The chapter was then divided in two perspectives: that of the MNC and that of
the host government. As we have seen, MNCs do not operate in a vacuum but instead
have to consider a variety of stakeholders in their decisions, above all the policies of
the government of the country where it wants to invest. First, we examined the specific reasons motivating MNCs to seek investment opportunities abroad. Among the
many motivations, it is worth mentioning revenue-related and cost-related ones. We
outlined the importance of diversification analysis in dealing with risks and expected
returns. To dive deeper into this idea, we also briefly considered an example of feasibility analysis by comparing two sets of portfolios. To show the host government

perspective, we provided an overview of the incentives, barriers, and special requirements often imposed by governments in exchange for the green light to operate in
their countries.

By considering FDIs from these two perspectives, readers should more easily
understand the repercussions of these activities on a variety of stakeholders and how
they can be perceived differently depending on one's position. Now that we have had
a general overview of FDI, we are ready to explore another interesting, more specific
topic concerning investments abroad: international acquisitions.

7 International Acquisitions

There are various ways in which a MNC can expand or reorganize. International acquisitions are one possibility and are largely the most popular, including international partial acquisitions, international acquisitions of privatized firms, international acquisitions (via international licensing or joint ventures), and international divestitures.

With overseas acquisitions, it is important to perform a thorough analysis of the target and determine its fit with the parent company. In a normal acquisition process, the MNC evaluates prospective targets to generate a list of potential acquisitions. Afterwards, the MNC eliminates the candidates whose shareholders are unwilling to sell or whose financial performance falls short of the acquirer's expectations (too expensive, substantial political risk, etc.). Then, each potential target is evaluated by assessing and forecasting its cash flows (taking into account the target's unique qualities and its home nation's characteristics) and discounting those predicted cash flows to the current value. Finally, the target's achieved valuation is compared to its value on the market (in the case of a public company) to assess if the company can be potentially acquired at a discount.

Determining the target's value is a critical step in the process of a foreign acquisition. The heart of the analysis is the estimation of the foreign target's cash flows. MNCs must carefully evaluate each element affecting the target's future cash flows to prevent over- or underestimating the profits that will be remitted to the parent and avoid mispricing the acquisition. MNCs should examine target-specific factors such as the target's prior cash flows and management talent pool, as well as country-specific factors such as economic, political, and currency risks, and stock market conditions. These elements are particularly significant as they have material impact on a foreign firm's operations.

Different prospective acquirers may produce divergent valuations of the same foreign target due to target cash flow projection differences, individual rates of return, or predictions of currency changes. Indeed, acquirers may have a range of projects in mind for the targets, each with a unique set of predicted synergies. Potential acquirers' countries may also be different and as such may be exposed to uneven exchange rate changes or have differing degrees of access to financing with different costs.

This chapter will focus on overseas acquisitions by first identifying key terminology and some recent developments in the market for multinational M&As and FDIs. It will then discuss in depth the process of selecting a target, with a particular emphasis on the economic and financial assessment of the target-parent company match. Finally, the key trends and main challenges of cross-border acquisitions will be presented, since these topics are highly relevant for the complex international environment multinationals currently have to navigate – from the 2020 global Covid-19 pandemic to the Russia-Ukraine conflict that exploded in Europe in 2022.

7.1   Types of multinational transactions

According to DePamphilis (2012), international external growth provides rapid access to new markets outside of one's domestic borders, however such growth presents unique challenges due to potentially significant cultural differences or local political and regulatory concerns. At the same time, they are also subject to many of the same problems as domestic M&As.

When considering international external growth, there are several expansion solutions that can be pursued:

- Greenfield investment through which the multinational company establishes a new business in a foreign nation while maintaining complete control over the product's proprietary technology, production, marketing, and distribution.
- Joint ventures can be used to share the risks and expenses of foreign growth by creating new expertise and gaining access to strategic resources. Most strategic alliances are formed with a local company that is already familiar with the country's competitive realities, legal and social conventions, and cultural standards. Local companies may be interested in forming partnerships to gain access to the foreign company's technology, brand recognition, or new products.
- Exporting is a further solution and it does not require any special investment abroad. However, downsides to exporting include high shipping costs, fluctuating exchange rates, and possibly taxes on imports into the local nation. In addition, the exporter has little influence over the marketing and distribution of its items in the foreign market.
- Licenses allow a company to buy the right to produce and sell another company's goods in a given nation or group of countries. Typically, the licensor receives a royalty for each item sold. The licensee bears the risks and invests in facilities to produce, market, and distribute products and services. As a result, licensing is often the most cost-effective method of international growth. However, the loss of control over the production and promotion of goods in other countries is one of its disadvantages.

Source: DePamphilis, D. (2012). *Mergers, Acquisitions, and Other Restructuring Activities: An Integrated Approach to Process, Tools, Cases, and Solutions eBook*. Academic Press.

M&As are corporate financial deals used to implement growth strategies and restructuring. M&A transactions can be structured in many different ways but are most commonly implemented by *establishing a new subsidiary, acquiring a company, or selling an existing division* (Spin-Offs or Carve-Outs). The most typical M&A deals for MNCs are those that enable the expansion of operations overseas. In this regard, MNCs can either establish a *foreign subsidiary*, create an *alliance/joint venture* with a local corporation, or *acquire a foreign business* (either fully or partially).

Among the types of transactions MNCs can consider for international expansion, the least expensive are alliances such as joint ventures and licensing agreements with foreign firms. Today, companies or business units form strategic alliances for many reasons: to gain new capabilities, obtain access to specific markets, or reduce financial and political risk. Other strategic motivations include the possibility of exploiting

---

Joint Ventures vs. International Acquisitions

Some nations oblige foreign investors to partner with a domestic player for them to be able to operate in such markets. However, joint ventures (JVs) should not be viewed as merely defensive tools. They can be a viable alternative to acquisitions in any local or international business strategy.

In JVs, foreign investors are required to share ownership and control with local businesses and individuals in growing economies. This supports the development of national economic capabilities and long-term national independence of critical sectors. When countries lack or have limited capabilities, forming JVs allows them to import skills and technology. Indeed, JVs have a number of advantages if compared with acquisitions, including the fact that the co-owner can provide local expertise and assets to help accelerate development. JVs can serve as a first step in developing a long-term market entry plan. It is fascinating to examine how national plans for joint ventures and acquisitions are interconnected, how they differ among nations, and how they evolve over time. The rise of China's automotive sector exemplifies the JV approach, as does Brazil's opening to international investment in the 1950s. Both required a high percentage of local content (about 90%) in the JV. However, due to competition, domestic manufacturers were eventually shut down or bought out by foreign companies. For instance, foreign companies now dominate the Brazilian market.

Despite the many advantages of JVs, acquisitions may be favored because the governance model is more transparent, decision-making is easier, and choices can be made more quickly (Whitaker, 2016).

---

better and faster access to technologies, gaining competitive advantage over rivals by consolidating forces, overcoming protective obstacles, or saving on labor costs (Uddin, 2011). While a full acquisition is often a long, difficult, and expensive process, in joint ventures the initial investment is typically smaller and less risky, although the cash flows that result are typically smaller too. However, Joint Ventures are not always the right solution and may not work for a number of reasons related to financial, industrial, cultural, and country-specific aspects. The case discussing the dissolution of the JV between the multinationals Fiat and General Motors below highlights some of the complexities that can prevent a JV from functioning successfully. In this case, an independent structure for Fiat proved to be the right strategic choice.

When strategic alliances don't work:
The dissolution of the Joint Venture between Fiat Group and General Motors

In March 2000, the American car manufacturer General Motors (GM) and the Turin-based automobile group Fiat SpA (Fiat) signed a joint venture with the aim of enabling both companies to achieve economies of scale and permitting Fiat to reduce its debt exposure. The terms and conditions of the alliance can be summarized as follows:

- Fiat sold 20% of Fiat Auto (the group's operating subsidiary) to GM in exchange for 5.1% of GM;
- All activities were combined into a JV (all raw material acquisition, purchasing, transmissions, etc.);
- Fiat put an option on the remaining capital of Fiat Auto that could be exercised between January and July 2004.

In 2003, the rating agencies were threatening GM not to buy Fiat Auto (which was considered a loss-making business) or they would have downgraded GM's debt. GM was very concerned that Fiat would exercise the put. In October 2003, the two companies entered into a standstill agreement that postponed the period for exercising the put. At the same time, Fiat Group's new CEO, Sergio Marchionne, had been given a mandate to sell the remaining 80% stake in Fiat Auto to the Americans or to try to restructure the company. To restructure, Marchionne needed a robust financial plan and a lot of liquidity but above all did not want interference in the governance; he aspired to recover full control of the company by buying back the 20% in the hands of the Americans. However, the JV was based on a put option for Fiat towards GM and not on the possibility of repurchase. Leveraging GM's fear of being downgraded if they were forced to buy the remaining 80% of the shares of the Italian company, which was losing 250 million euros a month at the time, Marchionne was able to convince GM that it was better for everyone to terminate the put option and return the remaining 20% of shares of Fiat Auto to Fiat.

Thus, in January 2005, Fiat and GM terminated the agreement with a payment to Fiat of 1.55 billion euros and GM's return of its shares to Fiat. All alliances were dissolved.

This cash injection from GM ending the deal financed the restructuring of Fiat's business, increasing revenues and reducing debt. Fiat made it clear that it no longer had need of a capital increase, and its net financial position (NFP) improved significantly in just 5 years (from -€10 billion to a neutral NFP). This was one of the largest turnarounds in the automotive industry. In 2007, the financially restructured Fiat returned to profitability and even survived the global financial crisis of 2007-2009 unscathed – though many of its automotive competitors experienced serious crises, including GM, which had to file for Chapter 11 bankruptcy.

The dissolution of the alliance was ultimately the right strategic choice for Fiat.

To rapidly implement envisioned growth strategies, MNCs typically opt for the acquisition strategy to either penetrate foreign markets and increase their global market share or capitalize on economies of scale through global consolidation that lowers cost of production. These companies view acquisitions as a better form of foreign direct investment (FDI) than establishing a subsidiary or a strategic alliance, since the target is already in place and benefits from established customer relationships. Indeed, acquisitions allow firms to have full control over the foreign subsidiary and quickly obtain a large proportion of foreign market shares. By acquiring a foreign target, an MNC will be able to obtain larger cash flows faster than the time it would require to establish a new subsidiary. On the other hand, complexities might arise in relation to the integration of the parent company's management style to the target. Acquisitions also require a larger initial investment. For this reason, an MNC may consider acquiring only a part of a firm (a *partial acquisition*) by purchasing only a portion of the existing shares of the target. In that way, the MNC can gain control over the target's management and operations (if it purchases above 51% of the total amount of shares issued) with substantially fewer funds.

Valuation of the target depends on whether a MNC plans to acquire enough shares to control the firm or not. If a MNC considers purchasing more than 51% of the firm's equity, the valuation is conducted as if the acquiring company planned to purchase the entire firm. This is because the company will then have to consolidate the target into its financial statements and therefore will have to account for all its assets and liabilities in its balance sheet. More specifically, the MNC may have to factor in the "control premium" it might have to pay to the target's shareholders. However, if the MNC buys only a small proportion of the firm's shares (hence gaining no control), it will only register a passive investment and therefore must estimate cash flows from the perspective of a passive investor.

A trend that has developed recently, especially in developing countries, is the privatization of companies previously owned by local governments. Such acquisitions are usually especially complex to value because of the uncertainty surrounding the firm's future cash flows. In fact, in these countries, economic and political conditions are often volatile during the transition to free market-oriented economies. Policies implemented by governments in such contexts are therefore exposed to unexpected changes and often unclear. Moreover, in these cases it may be difficult to find benchmarks for valuation because there are few publicly traded companies and there has been limited disclosure about prices paid in previous acquisitions. Also, the estimation of sales and volumes is highly unreliable since, given their public nature, these firms experienced little or no competition within their sector.

Finally, corporate divestment is an adjustment of the ownership and asset portfolio of the company that involves the partial or complete disposal of an asset or business unit. At an international level, divestures may occur when FDIs are no longer a feasible and profitable investment for the MNC. This may result from a change in expected exchange rates, an increase in the firm's cost of capital, an increase in the cost of labor, sudden tax hikes imposed by the host government, strong environmental regulations, or an intensified political and economic risk in the foreign country (Madura, 2012). International disinvestment is a significant global phenomenon. It may have an impact on the success of both parent and affiliate companies, as well as on the economies in which they operate. This impact can take many forms, including the following:

- Spin-offs;
- Equity carve-outs;
- Tracking stocks.

A Spin-off is a form of divestiture resulting in a subsidiary or division becoming an independent company. Ordinarily, shares in the new company are distributed to the parent company's shareholders on a pro rata basis. For example, a company might spin off one of its more mature business units that is experiencing little or no growth so it can focus on a product or service with higher growth prospects. The spun-off companies are usually expected to be worth more as independent entities than as parts of a larger business. An example was the demerger that took place in Fiat Group in 2011 (see the following box).

The sale of stock in a subsidiary in which the parent usually retains majority control is called equity carve-out. Sometimes also known as a partial spinoff, a carve out occurs when a parent company sells a minority (usually 20% or less) stake in a subsidiary for an IPO or rights offering. In most cases, the parent company will spin-off the remaining interests to existing shareholders at a later date when the stock price is much higher.

Spin-off: The Fiat case

In 2010, Fiat's business consisted of two separate and distinct subsidiary divisions: Auto and Industrial (the latter made up of trucks and farm equipment). These businesses had different earnings cycles, degrees of volatility, and non-comparable capital and ROCE requirements. Fiat's top management believed that the market did not understand the full value of the group and discounted its conglomerate structure. As a result, Fiat management proposed the division of the two businesses in order to:

- Provide greater strategic and financial clarity;
- Allow each business line to develop independently and according to its own needs.

In 2009 Fiat was trading at 2.9x EBITDA, and thus was fully in line with other comparable automotive companies. Similar companies in the industrial line of business were meanwhile trading at higher multiples in the between of 7x and 9x. Obviously, the market was not fully appreciating the value of the industrial segment, but in the overall valuation of the group only the automotive sector stood out. What were the reasons for this undervaluation and the discount applied to the Fiat group conglomerate? Let us try to analyse them:

- Lack of concentration from a managerial standpoint: if it is engaged in many different activities, management can be perceived as distracted and the company as lacking focus. As a result, the market penalizes this type of structure;
- Lack of clarity regarding the fact that they had other businesses besides cars;
- Investors prefer an investment that focuses on 'one' thing. This is because individuals prefer to personally diversify investment portfolios instead of buying diversified companies;
- Approach to risk: the high risks of the auto sector exposed even the most profitable sector (i.e., the industrial division) to risk;
- Experienced automotive analysts probably anchor their valuation in Fiat's traditional, historical business, automotive, while neglecting the other businesses.

To overcome this impasse in market valuation, the Fiat group was divided into two separate businesses. Each shareholder in the group was assigned a share of the automotive business (Fiat Auto) and a share of the new FIAT industrial business (called CNH). When the deal was announced, the market reacted very positively, and FIAT outperformed all other companies in the sector by 11%. The divorce lasted 8 months, and the multiples of the auto business fell (to 1.7x) – in line with the most comparable car companies – while the multiples of Fiat's industrial business rose (7.6x). The market immediately recognized the value of the two companies and started trading them in line with true peers, allowing the split group to pave the way for value creation. The group discount (10-15%) was permanently eliminated through this demerger, which had the effect of creating clarity and separating two de facto different businesses by solving the so-called conglomerate dilemma.

Lastly, tracking stocks are common stocks issued by a parent company that track the performance of a particular division without having claim on the assets of the division or the parent company. This is sometimes also known as issuing "designer stock." When a parent company issues a tracking stock, all revenues and expenses of the applicable division are separated from the parent company's financial statements and bound to the tracking stock. Oftentimes, this is undertaken to separate a subsidiary's high-growth division from a larger parent company that is experiencing losses. The parent company and its shareholders, however, still control the operations of the subsidiary.

Having described typical M&A deals relevant for MNCs, this chapter will now focus on international acquisitions and the valuation methodology implied by these transactions. While these considerations are customized for international acquisitions, the same methodologies apply to other cases of acquisition, albeit with some small differences. Before addressing the key considerations for M&As, we will first recall the different reasons a company might choose to invest overseas already introduced in Chapter 6 and where MNCs prefer to invest.

7.1.1　Theoretical paradigms and practical approaches regarding the motivation of International Investments

International mergers and acquisitions are frequently cited as one of the most effective ways for companies to gain access to new markets (Andersen, 1997). A company that wants to expand abroad, perhaps because it is experiencing or expects to experience a slowdown in its domestic business, can use new markets to balance and diversify its revenue sources, reduce country-specific risk, and boost growth (Penrose, 1995). Though mergers and acquisitions are an expensive and risky mode of entry (due to potential integration issues), they provide speed and access to complementary resources that are critical to the acquiring firm (Caves, 1996), such as specific knowledge and networks, which can vary by country. According to DePamphilis (2012), companies grow internationally for at least seven reasons. First, companies can diversify by investing in multiple countries or different industries in different nations, lowering the overall volatility of their consolidated earnings and cash flows. By improving the predictability of their revenues and cash flows, these companies may be able to minimize their cost of capital. Second, overseas markets offer local firms the opportunity to grow, especially larger firms that suffer from slower internal development. Such firms are more inclined to pursue international acquisitions, particularly in rapidly developing countries. Third, overcapacity is often the driving factor behind cross-border M&A activity, as companies seek greater economies of scale and scope, as well as pricing power with customers and suppliers. Fourth, some developing markets may be particularly attractive, since they often provide low labor costs, access to inexpensive raw resources, and minimal levels of regulation. As a result, moving production overseas allows companies to save on operating costs and improve their competitiveness in global markets. Fifth, organizations with extensive experience and unique technologies seek to grow into new industries by leveraging these advantages. Foreign buyers may seek to acquire companies with intellectual property in order to leverage these assets in their home markets. Sixth, companies in high-tax countries can shift production and reported profits by founding or acquiring firms in low-tax countries. Finally, changes in currency prices can have a significant impact on where and when foreign direct investment is made, as buyers may want to take advantage of foreign exchange opportunities (DePamphilis, 2012).

In short, a company invests overseas to add production facilities and boost its profits, so an economic rationale motivates most internationalization and choice to develop operations abroad. Still, given the number and different kinds of MNCs operating internationally, it would be too simplistic to consider profit as the sole driver of international expansion.

As we have seen in previous chapters, there are three main theoretical paradigms that attempt to identify what motivates companies to invest abroad (John Dunning's eclectic model, the so-called product life-cycle hypothesis established by Raymond Vernon, and the industrial organization theory of Stephen Hymer), but it is also important to consider the practical, real-world reasoning behind this approach. Economists sometimes overlook the simple fact that overseas expansion often results from the need for growth and value creation by shareholders. There is a widespread assumption that increasing or maintaining a current export market or building a new foreign market requires moving abroad. Moreover, tariff hopping is a classic reason for firms to produce in foreign markets, since tariffs are literally taxes designed to reduce or eliminate the price advantages of imported goods.

More complex reasons for international growth include objectives related to risk diversification. Geographically relocating production sites helps protect against unforeseen events such as worker strikes, natural disasters, adverse changes in laws and regulatory processes, fires, or plant sabotage. As we have seen in the Covid-19 pandemic, the more diversified a company is, the better it will be able to withstand unforeseen and unusual catastrophes. Another point worth exploring is the company's position in the competitive environment. Having to choose between being a leader and first mover or following other competitors could be a source of anxiety. In some cases, having a local manufacturing presence is a legal prerequisite to selling aggressively in overseas markets. Alternatively, companies may be enticed to establish an overseas subsidiary to begin a marketing campaign in the market of a key competitor in an attempt to erode their market share. Finally, a company may want to be seen as a local benefactor, so it might decide to invest overseas to support the local community and attempt to solve social issues.

In addition, certain structural developments in world trade can force companies to move portions of their operations abroad. With the introduction of a floating exchange rate system in 1973, nations with a chronic surplus saw their currencies appreciate, making their exports more expensive to foreigners, all other things being equal. In the early 1980s, this led to record FDI outflows. The information technology revolution that began in the United States in the early 1990s was another source of structural change in the global economic and business environment that influenced FDI. An increase in strategic direct investment seeking assets in the United States was one of its first effects. Growing concern about global access to oil and other essential commodities is a new pragmatic reason to invest abroad. Because of this fear, some governments have recently encouraged their domestic corporations to buy foreign-based natural resource companies.

7.1.2   Where do MNCs prefer to invest

Entering certain nations brings a slew of additional hurdles, including a variety of political and economic dangers.

It can be difficult to discern between political and economic dangers since they are often inextricably linked. Excessive local government control, confiscatory tax policies, limits on money transfers, currency inconvertibility, restrictive employment policies, seizure of the assets of foreign enterprises, civil war or local insurgencies, and corruption are examples of political and economic hazards.

Many of these hazards manifest themselves as shifting currency rates, raising the amount of risk involved with foreign direct investment in a foreign nation. Unexpected changes in currency rates may have a significant impact on the competitiveness of items manufactured in the domestic market for export to the global market. Furthermore, currency rate fluctuations affect the value of assets invested in the local nation as well as revenue repatriation from local operations to the parent firm in the home country. Foreign direct investment is strongly connected with economic and political freedom.

Before investing overseas, it is vital to perform research via local consultants and the findings of major credit rating agencies such as Standard & Poor's, Moody's, and Fitch IBCA. The decision to buy political risk insurance may be heavily influenced by the magnitude of the investment and the perceived degree of risk (DePamphilis, 2012).

Following a theoretical perspective, Eiteman et al. (2013) explain that the decision of where to invest should be based on a comparison between the expected risk-adjusted return and the firm's hurdle rate: the MNC should only choose countries where the former is higher. However, the lack of perfect information and data often precludes such a rational approach to decision making. Two additional practical theories have emerged recently in response to this problem. The first one is the *network perspective theory*, in which MNCs are considered part of an international network made by the parent company and its foreign subsidiaries. All the "nodes" in this network compete with each other for the firm's resources and to influence on the firm's strategy. The second theory is the *cultural distance theory*, which states that firms are less likely to expand in culturally distant locations. If they do, they prefer greenfield investments. MNCs more frequently integrate branches via the transfer of management practices (Beugelsdijk et al., 2017).

A more practical approach to understanding where MNCs prefer to invest considers which countries attract FDIs and which ones do not. Indeed, when deciding where to invest, companies first estimate total production costs to determine the financial appeal of an investment. They go on to consider the specificities of the *investment climate*. Indeed, according to a study by En Xie et al. (2017), if the host country's institutional regulations regarding financial markets, taxes, and corporate governance are stronger, the number of inward acquisitions will increase. The study underscores that the geopolitical, legal, and cultural distances between established and developing countries are more likely to be mitigated by the target country's market size, natural resource base, and lax institutional rules, particularly corporation and capital gains taxes.

7.2   Key considerations for M&As

As we saw in the beginning of this chapter, mergers and acquisitions are corporate finance transactions that companies use to execute both growth and divestment strategies. M&A refers to a variety of transactions in which beneficial ownership and control of a business are transferred from one or more parties to another. The bidder, i.e., the acquiring company that pays to acquire control of the target, and the seller, i.e., the target company that must be acquired, are the two actors. The bidder's objective is to establish the target company's fair value in order to maximize the value of the acquiring company's shareholders, while the target's objective is to establish an acquisition price at which the company can be sold. M&A transactions are managed by advisors on both the buy-side and sell-side who assist with the process, from identifying a target or buyer, to pricing and projecting the companies' integration policies.

A critical factor to consider is the target company's status as a private or public company. Private companies are sold through private transactions in which the parties involved are limited to the bidder and the seller; as a result, no information is required to be disclosed to the market until the deal is signed. On the other hand, when the target firm's status is public, a tender offer could be made by the bidder directly to the target's shareholders for the purpose of purchasing some or all of their shares in the corporation. The tender offer establishes a price and a time period during which shareholders can sell their own stock to the bidder. Tender offers are regulated by specific market rules. For example, in the United States, they are governed by the Williams Act[1], which requires mandatory information disclosure. The "put-up shut-up" rule, which aims to avoid market manipulation and insider trading, is a popular defensive proxy for protecting public targets. According to this rule, the bidder must "put an offer on the table" or disappear for a specified period of time, giving the target the opportunity to increase its value by improving its capital structure and/or management and thereby potentially increasing the value of any future transaction. As a result of this regulation, the bidder is prevented from making another offer until the end of the "shut-up" period.

M&A transactions may be classified geographically depending on whether the target is a domestic or foreign firm. The latter case is commonly referred to as a cross-border acquisition, and involves additional factors, such as the relevant exchange rate, taxes, blocked funds restrictions, and the costs associated with overcoming local government-imposed barriers. In general, market reactions vary when a deal is announced. Typically, the acquirer's stock price has a negative effect on a domestic transaction, whereas the bidder's stock price has a neutral or slightly positive effect on a foreign target. If the target company is publicly traded, its share price

---

[1] The Williams Act was adopted in the U.S. in 1968 in response to a series of hostile takeovers by large corporations that put shareholders and executives at danger. It is a federal law that defines the rules of acquisitions and tender offers.

frequently exhibits a large positive response as a result of the positive signal sent to the market by the high premium paid.

M&A transactions are costly and can be financed through either debt or equity. Debt financing involves the raising of debt: bank loans, syndicated loans, and bond issuance are the most common methods of debt financing for businesses. Instead, in equity financing, the consideration is paid through the sale of equity, and when the bidder is a public company the most common transaction is a seasoned offering. Occasionally, a company will go public (IPO) in order to raise the necessary funds to complete an M&A transaction in the near future. Another critical factor is the method of payment used to acquire the target: the bidder may pay the seller in cash or with its own shares in exchange for the target's shares. Often, these two methods are combined, resulting in a mixed payment. Cash offerings utilize cash from a variety of sources, including the balance sheet of the acquiring company, debt issuances, disposals, and capital increases. The primary advantage of cash offerings is governance, while the primary disadvantage is the financial instability that results from utilizing significant amounts of cash. The advantages of capital increases include the fact that equity may be overvalued, which results in a potentially favorable source of financing for the issuer. In a securities offering, the acquirer's common stock (or preferred stock) is distributed to the target shareholders. The exchange ratio is calculated, and it specifies the quantity of securities received by the seller in exchange for a share of the target company. The primary benefit is that no liquidity is consumed, while the primary disadvantages are governance and the negative signal sent to both the market and the target; indeed, it may appear as though the bidder believes its own stocks are overpriced, at which point the target will probably demand a bigger acquisition premium. Additionally, engaging in a securities offering may appear as though the acquirer does not trust the transaction because it is unlikely to generate synergies or a premium for control, which are the factors that contribute to the M&A transaction's value.

7.2.1   Reasons for M&As

As previously stated, external growth has become a primary way for multinational corporations to achieve dimensional growth and other objectives as quickly as possible. Companies can easily gain access to new distribution channels and market shares through M&A operations in shorter amounts of time than via internal or organic operations (such as expanding production capacity, expanding distribution platforms, innovating final products, or changing commercial/marketing strategies).

Indeed, companies today view the ability to offer new products and services, expand their markets and capabilities, or become sector leaders as critical factors for survival in a globalized world characterized by intense competition. The ability to achieve such advantages quickly is the primary reason for moving toward this type of corporate strategy.

Along with time constraints, another factor influencing an M&A decision is the desire to create value for the company; indeed, by combining multiple companies, it is possible to achieve a higher total value than if those companies remained separate (or at least this is one of the underlying assumptions of mergers and acquisitions).

In summary, the primary objectives of mergers and acquisitions are:

- Size and revenue expansions;
- Market share expansion;
- Competitive edge;
- Expansion into previously untapped foreign markets by the counterparty;
- Increased pricing leverage;
- Internal rate of return: if the bidder is a financial investor (such as a private equity firm or hedge fund), the bidder is looking for a specific financial return. It accomplishes this by increasing the target market's value in order to resell it at a higher price in the future.

The most common reasons for undertaking an M&A transaction are strategic reasons, with the primary objective of generating synergies. The strategic aims motivating these transactions can be classified as sensible or dubious (Brealey et al., 2006). Sensible reasons for mergers are those that add economic value to the transaction and are sufficient to proceed, whereas dubious reasons for mergers are still important factors to consider but are insufficient to initiate an M&A transaction. The following are the primary rationales usually classified as sensible (Brealey et al., 2006):

- *Economies of scale*: This refers to the cost advantages reaped by businesses when production becomes more efficient, which can be accomplished by increasing the firm's size while decreasing per-unit costs. This occurs because fixed costs can be spread across a greater quantity of goods. Economies of scale is frequently the logical outcome of a horizontal merger.
- *Vertical integration economies*: This occurs when a business merges with one of its customers/suppliers, which may result in cost savings and increased efficiency as a result of the company's increased market power and easier coordination and administration. However, certain historical transactions demonstrate that excessive integration can have the opposite effect.
- *Complementary resources*: This occurs when each company has what the other requires. It could occur, for instance, as a result of the merger of a small business with a unique product or service and a larger, more mature firm with organized sales and distribution channels.
- *Reducing inefficiencies*: Through an M&A transaction, a target company may be able to capitalize on previously untapped opportunities to eliminate inefficiencies because of a more efficient parent. The primary example is cost cutting to increase earnings.
- *Consolidation of industries*: M&A transactions can be beneficial for businesses operating in mature sectors, such as those with an excess of capacity and too many firms.
- *Funds in excess*: If a business operates in a mature sector with few, if any, pro-

jects with a positive net present value, the best use of its funds may be to acquire another business able to guarantee a positive return. On the other hand, if a business has excess funds but a scarcity of profitable investment opportunities, it will typically pursue a cash-financed merger to reallocate its capital.

The following are the primary dubious reasons (Brealey et al., 2006):

- *Diversification*: By diversifying its business lines, a corporation can manage its risks more effectively. A frequent misunderstanding is that investors pay a premium for diversification, which is incorrect because investors can diversify their portfolios independently.
- *The so-called "Bootstrap game"*: This creates a false impression of economic benefit from the merger, which becomes apparent only after a few years. It increases earnings per share in the short term, even if the transaction results in no real gain and the combined company's value is actually equal to the sum of the value of the separate firms. A company may have a high price-earnings ratio if its investors anticipate rapid earnings growth, which is accomplished through acquisitions of slow-growing companies with low P/E ratios. However, the outcome of this strategy is quite different. If the bidder acquires 100% of target equity exclusively through shares, the combined corporation's outstanding shares will be reduced. Thus, because earnings remain constant but the number of stocks decrease, EPS increases in the short term. Certain investors may be unable to see the artificial growth resulting from this strategy. They are misled by the higher EPS achieved without a decline in the price-earnings ratio. This in turn makes postmerger stock prices increase. However, to keep the EPS ratio at a high level, the company should continue to expand by merging at the same rate. Evidence shows that such a strategy is not feasible in the long run. Once expansion stops, EPS will decline together with the stock price. Therefore, a long-term acquirer has slower than normal EPS growth due to share dilution and a depressed P/E ratio.

Obviously, it is impossible to make a clear distinction among the reasons for pursuing a merger or acquisition, since underlying reasons are numerous and include not only financial or strategic considerations but also concerns about the company's image and overall reputation. Indeed, an M&A transaction inevitably results in an increase in a company's notoriety and prestige.

7.2.2   The M&A process

Acquisitions can be classified into several types based on what happens to the target company after the transaction is completed:

- A *statutory merger* occurs when an acquired company (B) merges with its parent company (A), transferring all its assets and liabilities. The target company ceases to exist (A + B = A);

- A *consolidation* is a merger in which all existing companies are merged into a single newly established company (A + B = C);
- *Acquisition of target* happens when the buyer acquires control of the target by purchasing (for cash or stock) shares directly from the target's shareholder; the acquired company therefore continues to exist as a subsidiary of the bidder.
- *Acquisition of assets* occurs when a buyer acquires a selection of a corporation's assets and liabilities. This acquisition technique avoids the potential problem of minority shareholders that sometimes occurs in the acquisition of stocks. However, this process is quite complex and involves the costly legal process of transferring titles.

There are several other classifications based on the type of M&A. For instance, horizontal mergers occur when two or more companies operating in the same line of business merge with the goal of consolidating the current competitive position in the market. Vertical mergers are possible if companies operate at different stages of the production process, with the goal of streamlining the value chain. Vertical mergers can be "forward" if the acquired company operates at a later stage or "backward" if the acquired company operates at a previous stage of the production process. Conglomerate mergers, on the other hand, are between companies that are not related in terms of operations or business activities. The companies involved in pure conglomerates have nothing in common, whereas in mixed conglomerates, the companies may want to expand their product lines – as in the case of Pizza Hut, which in 1977 merged with PepsiCo to become a division of the global soft drink conglomerate.

If the target's executives welcome or even seek out the deal, the acquisition process may take the form of a friendly takeover. Hostile acquisition, instead, consists in the investor talking directly to the target's stockholders or trying to replace the management with one that would approve the acquisition. The key feature of a hostile takeover is the unwillingness of target's management to sell the company. However, most hostile acquisitions are withdrawn at some point because they end up being too expensive and risky. Hostile acquisitions can be carried out through a tender offer or a proxy fight. A tender offer is a type of public takeover bid: it is an offer to buy some or all of the stockholders' shares in a company. Tender offers are usually public; they invite stockholders to sell their stocks within a specified period of time for a fixed price, which is set at a premium to the firm's market price.

The M&A process consists of several steps that can take anywhere from six months to several years, depending on the size and complexity of the transaction. Target, seller, buyer, financial advisor, legal advisor, accounting advisor (accounting firm), and other experts are all involved. The M&A process has several goals: all parties involved should have all the information they need to make a decision, while avoiding information misuse.

The M&A process of a buyer-initiated negotiated sale can be broken down into several steps that can be summarized as follows:

- *Definition of an Acquisition Strategy*: Defining an acquisition strategy and iden-

tifying objectives are the first steps in the investment process. While financial acquirers focus on determining appropriate returns for investors at this stage, strategic buyers need to understand how the M&A will complement organic growth
and fit into the acquirer's strategy. While the acquirers' objectives may differ, it's
important to remember that a well-defined acquisition strategy should include information on M&A objectives and selection criteria, as well as specific business
objectives for the potential target's future (Holterman et al., 2016).

- *Deal Origination*: Acquirers reach a point where they must conduct research, investigate, and select or identify appropriate targets in accordance with their acquisition strategies. This stage is referred to as deal origination or deal sourcing,
and it is critical for both strategic and financial acquirers because the greater the
deal flow (i.e., the number of potential targets to consider), the more likely the
target will be aligned with the investment criteria in the case of a financial investor or be appropriate for integration with the acquirer, in the case of a strategic
acquirer (Dallocchio et al., 2015).

- *Screening and Due Diligence*: Next, the acquirer approaches one or a few other
selected firms that have passed the initial screening to begin conversations and
conduct more detailed due diligence. Buyers use the due diligence process to gain
a better understanding of the target company's market, positioning, financials,
and management, as well as to identify potential risks, weaknesses, opportunities,
and strengths. The analysis of potential synergies that may be generated as a result of the transaction is a critical aspect on which industrial buyers focus during
a due diligence process that does not involve financial investors. If the realization
of synergies is critical to the transaction's success, it's critical that they are quantified and subjected to rigorous due diligence (Holterman et al., 2016).

- *Execution of the Transaction*: The transaction's execution involves multiple steps,
including valuing the business, finalizing the acquisition contract, and determining an acquisition financing strategy. In terms of valuation, much emphasis will
be placed on projections and discounted cash flow methodology, as well as on the
proper assessment of synergies, which can be overly optimistic at times and become a major source of post-deal value destruction.

- *Post Deal Monitoring or Integration*: Following the completion of the transaction,
acquirers should consider post-deal monitoring or integration, which is a critical
period for effectively creating value for shareholders and investors. This phase is
known as post-deal integration for strategic buyers, and successful integration is
the most important way to value a transaction. This phase necessitates meticulous
and comprehensive planning, including the management of any cultural diversity
through effective communication with employees and stakeholders, which is critical to the M&A's success.

In light of what is said above, properly managing the entire process is extremely important in order to avoid the risk of destroying value during the M&A process.

7.3   Valuation of a target

Discounted cash flows analysis and relative valuation are the two most frequent methods used for valuing a target company (see Chapter 4). The former is used to determine an investment's current value based on its future cash flows. The discount rate that is typically used to calculate the investment present value is the weighted average cost of capital, since it takes the expected rate of return of shareholders into account. If the DCF is greater than the initial investment cost, the opportunity may result in positive returns. The primary shortcoming of the DCF is that it is dependent on estimates of future cash flows that may prove to be inaccurate. Estimated cash flows may be impacted by target-specific factors (such as the target's historical cash flows or the acquirer's strategy for managing the target's managerial talent in the future) or country-specific factors (like local economic, political, and stock market conditions, as well as industry or exchange rates conditions).

Relative valuation, or comparable companies' analysis, is a technique for determining a business's financial worth by comparing its value to that of its competitors or industry peers. Multiples are standardized estimates of price; the most common trading multiples are the price-to-earnings (P/E) ratio, Enterprise Value/EBITDA and Enterprise Value/Sales. The main limit of trading multiples is that they compare a firm only with listed firms which are already large, mature, and with high liquidity (due to their public status). It is perhaps impossible to find two or more firms with same fundamentals that share the same risks, growth, and cash flow characteristics. Transaction multiples is another comparative valuation technique which instead looks at prices paid in past Merger & Acquisition transactions to value a comparable company. Here the main drawback is that there is less disclosed information. It is also important to note that, in this case, multiples can be skewed as a result of competitive bidding processes, premiums for control, and synergies paid by buyers.

Naturally, the valuation of a target may vary among multinational companies interested in acquiring it, as each may have distinct plans for managing the target's operations or integrating it into the parent structure, resulting in different perceived risks. Additionally, a bidder may be subject to varying taxation or currency exchange rates.

Synergies are a critical factor in determining M&A policies and are often factored in the valuation analysis and price paid for the target. Synergies are defined as the additional value created by combining two businesses, thereby creating opportunities not available to stand-alone firms prior to the merger; they can also be considered the difference between the sum of the independent companies' values and the combined firm's value after the merger. Synergies can be tangible, or they can be intangible and represented by knowledge and skills.

Synergies are classified into two categories: operational and financial (Damodaran, 2003). Operating synergies are those that enable businesses to increase operating income (through cost reductions), accelerate growth, or both. Additionally, it is critical to consider when synergies will begin to affect cashflows in order to discount their estimated values appropriately. We could categorize operational synergies as follows:

- Economies of scale enable the combined company to be more cost-effective and profitable. This is a common occurrence in horizontal mergers.
- Increased pricing power resulting from decreased competition and increased market share. As a result, margins and EBIT should improve. this is characteristic of mergers between firms in the same industry, particularly when there are only a few large firms, which allows for the formation of an oligopoly.
- Synergy of disparate functional strengths, such as when a firm with strong marketing capabilities acquires another with a strong product line.
- Increased growth in new or existing markets, such as when a firm producing consumer goods established in a developed economy acquires a firm with a stable distribution network and a strong reputation in an emerging market.

On the other hand, financial synergies can result in increased cash flows or a lower cost of capital, or both. These can be classified as follows (Damodaran, 2003):

- Tax benefits, which can result from tax laws that allow a target's depreciable assets to be revalued during acquisitions, ensuring higher depreciable costs in the future, or from the use of operating losses in the target to offset the acquirer's income.
  Thanks to the diversification effect, with increased debt capacity the combined cash flows and earnings of the two firms can become more predictable and stable, lowering the risk of default. Thus, the combined firm resulting from the transaction can increase its debt while maintaining a constant cost of capital.
- Combining a company with excess cash or cash slack (but limited investment opportunities) and one with high-yielding projects (but limited cash) can result in additional value for the combined firm.

Another factor to consider when determining the acquisition price is the premium for control. This is the value added as a result of altering the way the target is managed, and thus the difference between the firm's value with and without restructuring.

The following are common errors in valuing synergies (Damodaran, 2003):

- Subsidizing target shareholders for gains and strengths that they did not create; indeed, a fair share of synergies should allocate at least some of the additional value created to the acquiring company's shareholders.
- Conflating the concept of synergies (which necessitates the presence of two entities) with the value of control (which resides solely in the target).
- Using the incorrect discount rate. Cash flows generated by synergies are discounted using the combined firm's cost of capital, since they benefit the new entity, whereas cash flows generated by the target firm must be discounted using the target firm's own WACC. Furthermore, tax savings should never be discounted at the risk-free rate, as synergy-generated cashflows are not risk-free.

In general, the most common errors in M&A transactions continued to be repeated, for instance bidders paying excessive acquisition prices, overestimating the value of synergies and control, and having difficulty delivering promised benefits due to integration issues.

7.3.1   Main steps to evaluate a target into an international context

Businesses interested in acquiring overseas assets must follow the following steps: identify potential foreign targets, evaluate those targets, negotiate the transaction, and implement the integration of the target into the acquirer.

First, the acquirer assesses possible targets across different nations and produces a list of candidates. Then, the list is whittled down by removing targets that do not meet the necessary criteria to guarantee the success of the transaction. At this point, differences in accounting standards, fluctuating exchange rates across countries, and a potential overvaluation of the local stock exchange market can cause difficulties in properly valuing the opportunity to target a specific foreign company. At the domestic and industry level, the due diligence process must provide an understanding of the attitudes of the target's shareholders about the deal (are they against the transaction?) and a precise overview of institutional environment in which the target company is located (such as government regulations), in order to effectively respond to potential local constraints. The latter point is particularly significant in specific industries, especially those with high technological standards, where regulations can be particularly rigid (Ahammad M., 2009).

After shortlisting possible targets, the acquirer should conduct in depth due diligence on the remaining candidates to ascertain their predicted cash flows and evaluate if their worth surpasses the initial investment necessary to buy them. The choice to pursue a certain target over another will be highly dependent on these characteristics.

Negotiating and post deal integration of a cross-border M&A are extremely complex processes that are made even more difficult by lack of information and because of cultural differences (Buckley et al., 2002).

Value the target

Once the acquirer has completed the initial vetting, it conducts a valuation of all targets that passed the screening process. To derive a valuation, the company must estimate the present value of future cash flows that would result from acquiring the target. The discounted cash flow analysis approach used to value cross-border deals is similar to the one used when both the purchasing and target enterprises are located in the same nation. According to DePamphilis, D. (2012), the primary distinction between in-country and cross-border valuation approaches is that the latter require translating cash flows across currencies and changing the discount rate for risks that are not normally encountered when the acquiring and target firms are located in the same country. Cash flows for the target firm may be stated in its own currency with predicted inflation included (i.e., in nominal terms), in its own currency without inflation included (i.e., in real terms), or in the buyer's currency. Inflation in the target nation may have a varying impact on the various components of a target company's cash flows. It is thus prudent to predict the target's cash flows in its own currency first, and then convert them to the buyer's currency. This necessitates forecasting future exchange rates between the target's (local) currency and the buyer's currency (domestic).

As a subsequent step, assumptions about the target's future performance are necessary to be conducted. The first assumption involves the estimation of revenues and their expected growth rate. The cost of goods sold with selling and administrative expenses have to be estimated matching them with the synergies analysis (i.e. the cost synergies). The next assumption involves cash-flows, which are computed by adding the depreciation and amortization expenses back to the after-tax earnings. Finally, the target's future terminal value must be forecasted. The terminal value will depend on its expected future cash flows from that point forward, even though those cash flows will in general be related to the target's performance prior to that time.

7.3.2 Valuation changes over time and among different MNCs

Before moving to the next topic, we should briefly remark on changes affecting valuation. In fact, a valuation approach will never provide the same number for all MNCs for the same target (even though the processes used to value a target are similar among most MNCs), nor will a valuation of that target remain stable across time. Time and differences in the estimation of key parameters affect a given target's valuation. Changes can derive from divergent estimates of synergies and premium for control, the required return when investing in the target, and exchange rate effects on funds remitted to the MNC parent (Madura, 2015). The three factors listed below can potentially cause divergent valuations of the same target for MNCs.

First, MNCs will have different estimations of the target's expected future cash flows simply because they are characterized by specific post-acquisition synergies affected by how MNCs manage the target's operations. Consequently, the premium for control paid by the target will vary among MNCs. Starting from consideration of the target's business plan and subsequently embedding merger synergies that would result from the transaction (different across bidders) allows us to obtain what is known as the fair value of the target. Specifically, this corresponds to the *likely market price* that would be paid by a generic investor to obtain the target company. With the objective of defining the acquisition value of a company and understanding how it is different from the fair value, we can refer to the *value stratification model* (Massari et al., 2016), according to which:

$$W_{acq} = W_{standalone} + W_{synergies} + W_{PBOC}$$

Whereby the standalone value $W_{standalone}$ is defined as the company value attached to the business plan of the firm as a going concern, disregarding any transformational changes deriving from strategic acquisitions and consequent changes of control (Massari et al., 2016). Furthermore, $W_{synergies}$ is the additional value driven by synergies, which should be considered as additional flows generated by the target as a result of the transaction that directly accrue to earnings. Those same synergies will be shared on a pro rata basis among target shareholders and are therefore defined as *divisible* benefits. Lastly, W_{PBOC} is the further incremental value generated by a different type of synergic effects: those that benefit only the controlling shareholders and which are therefore called *indivisible* (Massari et al., 2016) or *private* (Dyck & Zingales, 2004). By considering this last item, the acquisition value can be seen as the value that a given bidder would attach to a specific investment, which could change from one bidder to another.

Secondly, discrepancies could also arise in the required rate of return for the acquiror. According to the negotiating power of the parties and the transaction type (public or private, entailing different levels of competition), the bidder will obtain a return on the investment equal to:

$$NPV_{acq} = W_{acq} - P$$

where:

NPV_{acq} is the NPV of the transaction;
W_{acq} is the present value of cash flows expected by the bidder pro-forma;
P is the price paid for the target.

According to the magnitude of the competition, the bidder will adjust the offer price to win the transaction in a competitive bidding process and, eventually, may even be ready to achieve a lower level of returns with respect to its bidding competitors. This may be because the risk connected to the plans of different bidders vary, thus changing their expected rates of return on debt and equity financing.

Thirdly, the valuation of the target could also vary among potential acquirers because they are exposed to different exchange rate fluctuations. For example, $/€ exchange rate fluctuations may differ from the fluctuations between the dollar and yen, since the dollar may appreciate against the yen but not necessarily against the euro (Madura, 2015).

In the end it should be considered how valuations become outdated quickly. In fact, when changes occur in the factors affecting expected cash flows (revenue growth, cost levels, etc.) or the required rate of return from investing in the target (cost of debt, tax rate, cost of equity), the value of the target changes too. In addition to variations in assumptions (revenue growth, cost levels, etc.), other general factors could also result in alterations in valuations over time. Some of these factors include the impact of the stock market, market sentiment, and anticipation. First, since changes in the stock market affect the price per share of each stock listed, and thus the value of publicly traded firms, the price the acquirer will have to pay for the target could be affected (recall that Target Price = Market Price + Acquisition Premium). An improvement in stock market conditions thus will increase the price of all targets. Finally, market sentiment and anticipation may affect the target's stock price.

If investors in the market anticipate a possible acquisition, the stock of the target may increase. In fact, it is common knowledge in the market that a target's shareholders are those who benefit the most from an acquisition due to the high premium paid by the acquiror. For this reason, stock prices of targets rise abruptly after a bid by an acquiring firm is announced.

7.3.3 A formula for evaluating international acquisitions

The acquisition decision should be based on a comparison of the benefits and costs as measured by the *net present value*. If the estimated present value of the cash flows ultimately received from the target over time exceeds the initial investment necessary to purchase the target itself, the company should in theory proceed with the international acquisition.

The NPV of a company from the acquiring firm's perspective NPV_a is:

$$NPV_a = -P_a + \sum_{t=1}^{n} \frac{CF_{a,t}}{(1+k)^t} + \frac{TV_a}{(1+k)^n}$$

where:

P_a = Initial investment needed by the acquiring firm to buy the target (Acquisition Price);
$CF_{a,t}$ = Cash flow to be generated by the target and transferred to the parent company;
k = Required rate of return on the acquisition;
TV_a = Terminal value of the target (expected selling price of the target at a point in the future);
n = Time when the target will be sold by the acquiring firm.

A more accurate estimation, however, takes into consideration the effect of exchange rates on the target's cash flows. Accounting for exchange rates, the net present value of a foreign target is given by the following formula (Madura, 2015):

$$NPV_a = -P_a + \sum_{t=1}^{n} \frac{CF_{a,t}}{(1+k)^t} + \frac{TV_a}{(1+k)^n} = -(P_f) \times S + \sum_{t=1}^{n} \frac{(CF_{f,t}) \times S_t}{(1+k)^t} + \frac{(TV_f) \times S_n}{(1+k)^n}$$

Looking at the equation above, the NPV of an acquisition depends on the initial investment, the cash flows that the target will generate in the future, and its terminal value. Both the acquisition price and the cash flows generated by the target are denominated in foreign currency (P_f, $CF_{f,t}$ and TV_f), so estimation of the current and future spot rate is required (S and S_t). If the initial investment is lower, or the cash flows and terminal value increase, the foreign targets should become more attractive for MNCs. Those estimations depend on multiple variables, including *exchange rate movements* ($S; S_t; S_n$).

This analysis is complicated by a series of issues that every firm faces when analyzing a target.

In the following two sections, we will outline how exchange rates (currency movements) can boost international acquisitions in specific countries and how to face uncertainty in the valuation process by incorporating risk into the acquisition analysis.

The British pound devaluation post-Brexit

Despite the uncertainties surrounding Brexit, the United Kingdom acquisition market grew significantly in 2018 as overseas acquirers took advantage of illogical devaluations of U.K. firms (i.e., lower initial investments). Investors began depreciating British firms in anticipation of a post-Brexit devaluation of the pound sterling, which would have reduced U.K. cash flows repatriated to overseas parents. Even firms that generated a significant amount of their overall income outside the U.K., and were therefore 'immune' to pound depreciation, were devalued.

Confident in the U.K.'s long-term stability (and the re-appreciation of the pound), various MNCs across the globe capitalized on discounted U.K. assets that were cheaper due to the pound's depreciation. For instance, Comcast paid $38.8 billion (£29.8 billion) for Sky U.K., while Vantiv paid $12.1 billion (£9.3 billion) for World-Pay. As the bar chart illustrates (**Figure 7.1**), despite the uncertainties surrounding Brexit, the number of acquisition transactions that took place in the United Kingdom between 2017 and 2018 increased by 10%. Similar conclusions can be derived looking at **Figure 7.2**.

Uncertainty and risk-adjusted analysis

When the terminal value is uncertain, the MNC may incorporate various possible outcomes and estimate the NPV based on each of them. One possible analysis is the estimation of the terminal value to have a NPV equal to zero; the so-called break-even terminal value. This value should be compared with the actual terminal value and, if the latter is equal or higher, the project should, in theory, be undertaken.

When facing uncertainty, a MNC has to adjust its acquisition analysis to incorporate the risk. There are two main methodologies for doing so (DePamphilis, 2012):

- *Risk-adjusted discount rate*: the greater the uncertainty about a project's forecasted cash flows, the larger the discount rate applied to those cash flows should be, all other conditions being equal. Numerous developing economies lack publicly listed corporations and mergers and acquisitions transactions to use as a benchmark for appraising businesses. In such situations, rather than arbitrarily adjusting the target company's cost of capital, the acquirer might factor risk into the value by evaluating various factors (e.g., GDP growth, inflation rates, interest rates, and exchange rates).
- *Sensitivity analysis*: after having forecasted the NPV of a proposed project, it may be advisable to consider alternative estimates for input variables. The primary ben-

Figure 7.1   U.K. M&A deals

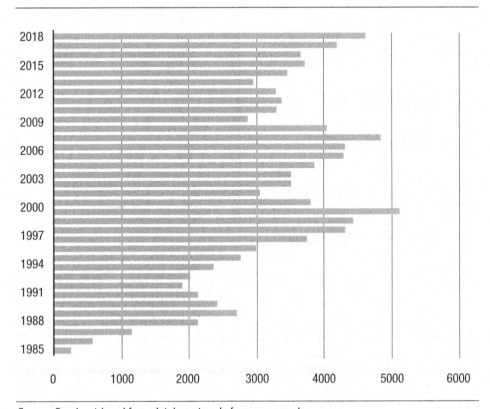

Source: Graph retrieved from database trends from ons.gov.uk

Figure 7.2   M&As involving U.K. companies

Source: Graph retrieved from database trends from ons.gov.uk

efit of using a scenario method is that it pushes the analyst to consider a broader variety of potential outcomes, such as the number of scenarios required to adequately
incorporate risk into projections or the probability that each scenario will occur. Its
primary downside is that it combines them through an analysis hampered by the
need to make assumptions that may be subject to a high degree of subjectivity.

7.4   Cross-border M&As and trends

7.4.1   Drivers and processes

Over the years, in the context of more globalized and competitive markets worldwide, MNCs increasingly undertake cross-border M&As. Cross-border M&As are a
type of foreign direct investment in which transactions occur between firms based in
different countries (Kang & Johansson, 2000), i.e., the acquiring company from Nation A purchases a target in Nation B.

    MNCs undertake cross-border mergers and acquisitions for a variety of reasons.
For example, the move may be a cost-effective and relatively fast way of gaining
competitive advantages (technology, brand names, etc.) or market position. In addition, international economic, political, and foreign exchange conditions may create market imperfections resulting in international target firms being undervalued.
Some further motivations for cross-border buying include gaining access to important proprietary assets, gaining strength and market dominance, alleviating competitive pressures, or addressing market changes. Creating synergies between local and
global operations, as well as across industries by increasing size through economies
of scale, diversification (i.e., expanding into new areas, consumers, goods, and so
on), and spreading risk by taking advantage of possible financial synergies are other
possible motivations for cross-border expansion.

    External market variables can also influence the number of cross-border acquisi-
tions that take place in a given period of time. Liberalization policies and increased
globalization, for example, have resulted in an increasing number of cross-border
transactions. On the other hand, uncertainty, protectionism, and periods of recession
have a detrimental influence on these types of M&As (Kang & Johansson, 2000),
which, for example, witnessed a steep fall after the 2008 financial crisis (Dallocchio,
Lucchini, & Scarpellini, 2015).

    Buying a company in another country is a three-step procedure:

- *Origination*: Identifying the target market and prospective company or companies of interest for the acquisition are critical first steps. When entering a mature
  market for instance, there are a wider selection of targets to choose from. After
  the target has been identified, it must be valued via either using basic approaches,
  such as discounted cash flow (DCF) or multiples (earnings and cash flows), or
  with industry-specific measurements that highlight the characteristics unique to
  the target's business.

- *Arrangement and Closing*: Once an acquisition target has been selected and appraised, the acquiror must seek approval from local regulatory agencies as well as from the targets' management. If the latter agrees to the purchase, the acquisition can be defined as a "friendly takeover," which is characterized by a more flexible and dynamic procedure than a "hostile takeover." In the context of a cross-border transaction, it is important to note that hostile transactions can be much harder to manage than in a domestic context, particularly in specific strategic sectors. On the contrary, friendly cross-border transactions are facilitated by the involvement of local banks, other financial institutions, or investment funds that aim to safeguard national interests and foster the development of the country's most significant MNCs (often called "national champions"). These transactions benefit from the direct and indirect assistance of local governments or political entities, as well as public opinion and the media (Whitaker, 2016). As a closing step, a compensation technique must be selected and approved by relevant stakeholders.
- *Post-Deal Execution*: This important stage, which is sometimes overlooked, aims at realizing the transaction's full value. The most difficult challenge is often bridging the gap between two distinct company cultures that have unexpectedly merged.

7.4.2   Challenges and characteristics

To promote the creation of shareholder value, M&As always involve complicated procedures and often face obstacles. Specifically, cross-border acquisitions have a series of characteristics and technicalities that more so increase the degree of complexity and challenges faced by the involved companies. Indeed, as a result of such difficulties, cross-border acquisitions may encounter undesirable circumstances such as target overpayment, excessive financial burdens, incompatible corporate cultures, and serious social consequences (e.g., because of laying off employees in the name of cost rationalization). It is essential to comprehend the key issues and challenges in cross-border mergers and acquisitions to try to mitigate the possible materialization of unfavorable repercussions.

Country risk is the initial barrier to cross-border mergers and acquisitions. Country risk refers to all the dangers that do not exist when investing in one's own country but do apply when investing abroad. Country risk can also be viewed through the lens of a lender, since lending across borders adds a level of complexity to a financial institution's portfolio, exposing it to a variety of extra hazards (Dallocchio, Lucchini, & Scarpellini, 2015). Country risk requires quantitative and qualitative assessment of the host country's circumstances. Country risk includes:

- Transfer risk, which is associated with the risk of the host foreign country government imposing blocked funds restrictions or barriers on the conversion of its local currency into a foreign currency;
- Currency risk, which is associated with the risk of the host foreign country government imposing blocked funds restrictions or barriers on the conversion of its local currency into a foreign currency;

- Exchange rate risk, which is associated with the risk of the host foreign country government imposing blocked funds restrictions or barriers on the conversion of its local currency into a foreign currency;
- Risks related to the country's geographic position;
- Sovereign risk stemming from the government's creditworthiness as a borrower or guarantor;
- The nation's economic risk;
- Political risk, which encompasses all political concerns that may impede company operations (e.g., nationalization, expropriation, corruption).

The importance of performing precise and extensive corporate due diligence represents a second difficulty. This is because, in addition to the country risk mentioned above, local companies in developing markets may overestimate their capabilities in order to attract M&A investors (Juneja, 2020). Due to greater information asymmetries, performing due diligence on overseas targets may be more difficult. This could lead to misidentification of synergies and payment of higher than appropriate premiums, resulting in unsuccessful value generation (Aybar & Ficici, 2009).

Government and political commitment to acquisitions is a third problem inherent in cross-border M&As. Cross-border mergers and acquisitions often need not only regulatory permission but also political support to proceed (Juneja, 2020). Government backing is beneficial in general, but required in some specific nations. In fact, different national governments have varying degrees of openness to foreign direct investments and diverse regulations governing such transactions. This influences the types of investment instruments that can be employed. Local legislation may impose restrictions on purchase price allocation or ownership percentages, and legal systems may decide the established legal form of the final entity (Dallocchio, Lucchini, & Scarpellini, 2015). If governments of target firm nations interfere more radically in pricing, workforce protection, finance, and overall national preferences, cross-border acquisitions could become radically more complex and difficult to implement.

A final problem with cross-border mergers and acquisitions is post-acquisition integration. In any acquisition, the integration of the target entity could jeopardize the entire success of the deal. However, this problem is more common in multinational transactions. These transactions are particularly vulnerable to the liability of foreignness (i.e., the expenses that foreign firms incur in host nations as a result of their foreign status) and double-layer acculturation (i.e., when an acquired company is required to adopt both the culture of the foreign country and that of the new company). These risks are undeniably linked to cultural and historical variations in tastes, business attitudes, and beliefs that must be checked and carefully monitored to effectively execute M&As and generate value (Aybar & Ficici, 2009). As an example is when in 1998 Daimler-Benz and Chrysler decided to merge with the goal of becoming one of the world's leading automotive companies. The differences and cultural distances (both organizationally and domestically) between the companies resulted in the failure of their merger after several years of post-merger integration.

7.4.3   Political risk classification

The interdependence of politics and cross-border integration

Stakeholder mapping is critical to identifying all public and political groups that may be interested in the M&A transaction, both domestically and internationally, and anticipating the integration features that will be of interest to them after the expansion is complete. Political stakeholders will be more concerned with the public, social, environmental, and domestic repercussions of a foreign corporation expanding into their nation than with simple economic considerations such as the number of synergies and the terms of the contract.

Political involvement in cross-border M&A is often focused on any negative influence on the status quo, especially when confronted with foreign buyers planning cost synergies via job cutbacks in the domestic market that pose serious political and/or economic danger to the host nation. While some consolidations are politically acceptable, mass closures of offices or operational sites and employment relocations will be passionately opposed unless there are no other viable solutions and those jobs would have been lost regardless. Another factor, especially when conducting business in developing economies, is the examination of the targets' political relations and dependencies on politicians and political authorities, which should be governed by globally accepted ethical business norms. Obtaining the backing of non-governmental groups, trade associations, and elected officials is a viable way of bolstering the company's public relations efforts around a M&A transaction and throughout the post-acquisition integration process (Whitaker, 2016). The acquisition of Chrysler Automobiles by Fiat in 2009 was the result of a strategy focused on relationships and collaboration between the management of the Italian automaker, the U.S. government, and major U.S. and Canadian pension funds. The deal was a win for all parties involved, ensuring Chrysler's continuity and as well as its workers while also allowing Fiat to create shareholder value through an international expansion strategy.

As mentioned above, there are many elements of country risk that a company faces when investing in or acquiring a company in a foreign country. Political risk, one of the major components of country risk, can be further classified to allow MNCs to best anticipate such risk and manage it appropriately.

Political risks can be divided into the following categories. For instance, at the project or company level, *firm-specific risk* (or *micro risk*) impacts MNCs. This risk is tied to the industry in which the business works and is unique to each company. Identifying firm-specific risk requires estimating the effect of changes in the local political climate on the target's operations. The subjective nature of this risk necessitates an in-house evaluation. Governance and foreign exchange risks are the most common firm-specific issues. When there is a perception that the foreign corporation has too much power over the host country's economy, when there is a violation of national sovereignty, or when the MNC is seen to have too much control over vital sectors, governance concerns are common. The best (and most typical) way to reduce these risks is for the MNC to arrange investment agreements and insurances with the host nation government ahead of time. *Nation-specific risk*, as the name implies, is risk unique to a country that affects all enterprises (local and foreign) operating there. Transfer risk, cultural risk, and institutional risk all fall under this category. Transfer risk may be mitigated in a variety of ways. A corporation may, for example, shift commodities across linked business divisions, fund its investment with local borrowing, and use strategies to minimize local currency risk. Terrorism, anti-globalization movements, environmental concerns, poverty, and cyber-attacks are all examples of *global risk*. Firms find it difficult to quantify this risk because of the ambiguity surrounding such infrequent situations.

7.4.4   Recent trends and developments in cross-border M&As

Now that we have seen the specifics of cross-border M&A transactions, we can discuss the trends and changes shaping the cross-border market for deal-making.

Cross-border transactions are often susceptible to geopolitical upheaval, and enterprises must be prepared for this. Any significant international shift that affects the economy, access to resources, foreign investment rules, or the emergence of new markets may either stimulate or stymie the growth of cross-border partnerships. Changes at the local level will be immediately apparent at the global level. There are several examples of such geopolitical shifts currently taking place, including the recent 2022 conflict between Ukraine and Russia on Europe's eastern border. Geographic political hazards are not limited to their own boundaries. They have significant domino effects on neighboring nations, and can generate new dangers in distant lands (i.e., terrorism), and influence public opinion, economies, and business environments in their native countries (Whitaker, 2016).

The years 2019 and 2020 were not fruitful for cross-border transactions. Indeed, geopolitical uncertainty arose in 2019 because of rising protectionist policies throughout the globe, trade tensions between the U.S. and China, and fears about Brexit, which resulted in a 13% drop in cross-border M&As year over year. In China, cross-border mergers and acquisitions fell by 25% year over year.

The situation worsened in 2020 due to the Covid-19 pandemic, which disrupted the global order and caused a 14.2% drop in cross-border M&A activity compared to 2019 levels. Furthermore, increasing nationalist feeling in the United States and Asia in 2020 resulted in rules and limits on foreign investments aimed at safeguarding domestic firms and sectors from opportunistic investors and emphasizing at-home investments.

Geographically, the Asia-Pacific (APAC) region had a 24.4% drop in outbound M&As in 2020, while Europe predominantly saw a slowdown in incoming M&As, which accounted for just 15.4% of overall E.U. M&A volume (the lowest share since 2009). On a more positive note, despite the overall reduction in cross-border M&A activity, an increase in mega-deals (i.e., agreements worth $5 billion or more) in 2020 meant numerous transactions were nonetheless able to proceed.

For a more fine-grained overview of regional M&A comparisons, see **Figure 7.3**.

2021 was the busiest year on record for M&As. There is no other way to describe the relentless boom in mergers and acquisitions that occurred in the twelve months ending on December 31, 2021, when global M&A volume surpassed $5.8 trillion. Each of the four quarters of 2021 ranked among the top six most active quarters in global M&A by volume since 2010.

Figure 7.3   Regional M&A comparison

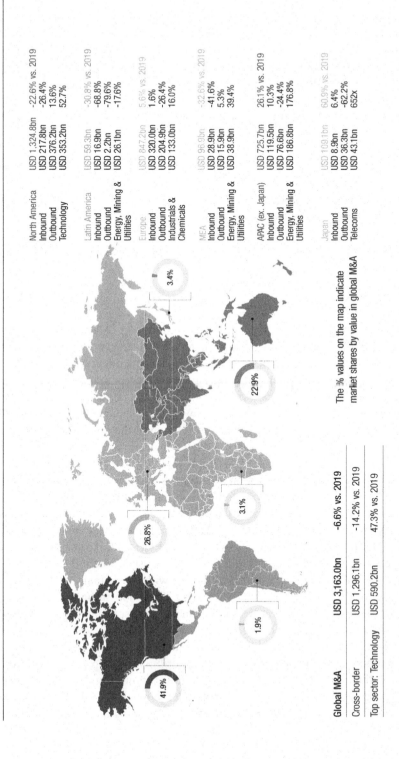

North America	USD 1,324.8bn	-22.6% vs. 2019
Inbound	USD 217.8bn	-26.4%
Outbound	USD 376.2bn	13.6%
Technology	USD 353.2bn	52.7%
Latin America	USD 59.3bn	-30.8% vs. 2019
Inbound	USD 16.9bn	-68.8%
Outbound	USD 2.2bn	-79.6%
Energy, Mining & Utilities	USD 26.1bn	-17.6%
Europe	USD 847.2bn	5.6% vs. 2019
Inbound	USD 320.0bn	1.6%
Outbound	USD 204.9bn	-26.4%
Industrials & Chemicals	USD 133.0bn	16.0%
MEA	USD 96.9bn	-32.6% vs. 2019
Inbound	USD 28.9bn	-41.6%
Outbound	USD 15.9bn	5.3%
Energy, Mining & Utilities	USD 38.9bn	39.4%
APAC (ex. Japan)	USD 725.7bn	26.1% vs. 2019
Inbound	USD 119.5bn	10.3%
Outbound	USD 76.6bn	-24.4%
Energy, Mining & Utilities	USD 186.8bn	176.8%
Japan	USD 109.1bn	60.9% vs. 2019
Inbound	USD 8.9bn	6.4%
Outbound	USD 36.3bn	-62.2%
Telecoms	USD 43.1bn	652x

The % values on the map indicate market shares by value in global M&A

Global M&A	USD 3,163.0bn	-6.6% vs. 2019
Cross-border	USD 1,296.1bn	-14.2% vs. 2019
Top sector: Technology	USD 590.2bn	47.3% vs. 2019

Source: Graph retrieved from Mergermarket report "Global and Regional M&A league tables 2020" (for more information visit mergermarket.com)

Cash remains a common payment form in U.S. cross-border transactions, accounting for more than 48% of the total transaction volume in 2021. Stock payments remain highly appreciated, since the world's stock markets have never been more globalized, and investor appetite for geographic diversity has never been greater. Debt played a significant role in terms of financing, with both high-yield bond and new loan issuance volumes setting full-year records.

Cross-border transactions totaled $2.1 trillion in 2021, up from $1.3 trillion on average over the previous ten years. Non-U.S. acquirers accounted for roughly 20% of the $2.6 trillion in U.S. deal volume in 2021. Acquirors from Canada, France, Germany, Japan, and the United Kingdom accounted for roughly 40% of cross-border deals involving U.S. targets, while acquirors from China, India, and other emerging economies accounted for about 3%.

Since the crisis sparked by the Russia-Ukraine war, we have seen bidders postpone and withdraw from transactions. The volume of cross-border deals in Q1 2022 was the lowest since Q2 2020. If cross-border deal volume continues to decline, global M&A totals are likely to suffer a visible decline as well during 2022.

7.5   Conclusions

The continuous evolution of markets on a global scale is a phenomenon that has resulted in a significant shift in business behaviors. Corporations are constantly transforming and adapting to these new dynamic and increasingly competitive environments, where growth and value creation have become fundamental requirements. The aim to maximize shareholder value can be reached either boosting the size of the company or increasing its sales. This growth can occur internally or externally. Merger and acquisition operations are a viable option in the second case. Indeed, by acquiring an existing reality, businesses can quickly acquire new resources and skills that can aid in the implementation of a specific strategy. The purpose of this chapter was to examine merger and acquisition transactions and to analyze different types of international transactions: developing a new subsidiary, acquiring a company (fully or partially), establishing joint ventures and finally selling existing divisions through spin-offs, equity carve-outs and tracking stocks. We discussed the main reasons why companies decide to invest abroad by engaging in FDIs and, more specifically, reasons for M&As and international acquisitions. The most common reasons for undertaking an M&A transaction are strategic reasons, with the primary objective of generating synergies. We have seen that the strategic aims motivating these transactions can be classified as sensible reasons, like economies of scale and industry consolidation, or dubious reasons, such as diversification or the so-called "bootstrap game." We then listed the main steps a MNC has to take when entering an M&A transaction: definition of an acquisition strategy, deal origination, screening and due diligence, execution of the transaction and post dealing monitoring. We then studied the valuation process a MNC follows to evaluate international acquisitions, highlighting how it starts with the identification of potential targets using a shortlist based on certain criteria. Afterwards, the MNC attributes a value to the shortlisted targets, generally based on the present value of their future cash flows. This value might change, as we have seen, due to a number of external factors. We also analyzed the main factors MNCs need to consider and the potential risks that might affect their international acquisitions. Finally, we deepened our understanding of cross-border M&A trends, with a particular focus on the impact of Covid-19 on the global M&A market.

8 Country Risk Analysis

Country risk represents the potentially adverse impact of a nation's economic environment on a MNC's cash flows. Within the spectrum of risks a MNC incurs when expanding abroad, country risk pertains to the economic and financial characteristics of a country that make it different from others. Such differences may come from a variety of historical, cultural, or geographical sources. They may also be inherent to the country's financial systems and government policies.

In this chapter, we will look more closely at two types of risk: political and economic. Political risk refers to any political condition that might prevent the MNC from operating in a given foreign country or might make it difficult or unpleasant to do so. Examples include adverse tax systems or fiscal policies that strongly discourage foreign players. More specifically, political risk can entail micro- and macro-risks, with the former affecting only specific industries and the latter applying more generally to all aspects and sectors impacted by foreign investors.

Economic risk should not be underestimated either. These risks generally pertain to the probability that a country will become insolvent and thus not pay back its debts or liabilities. Such circumstances of course have implications for the monetary policies that the country will put in place to maintain sustainable levels of unemployment or inflation.

Naturally, the higher a country's economic and political risk, the more insecure and uncertain investments there will be. The perceptions of investors regarding these two dimensions is crucial for countries wanting to attract or discourage foreign investments. This is where country risk assessment comes into play. It is worth noting that country risk assessments are currently performed on both developed and developing countries – though this has not always been the case. The stereotypical belief that Western economies are safe havens for investment is no longer true and should always be challenged. Indeed, with the recent debt crises in developed countries and significant trade deficits in many nations, no country is immune to risk. Looking at the famous PIIGS countries (Portugal, Ireland, Italy, Greece and Spain), we realize that the equation of Western with absence of risk is not always accurate. Still, it is true that Western economies have stable infrastructures and institutions that developing economies cannot always ensure; still, this does not always shield them from political or social turmoil. Uncertainty cannot be eliminated from the business environment, but it can be managed and transformed into *planned* uncertainty.

Evaluating country risk is a crucial exercise when selecting sites for international business, particularly if investments are expected. Each corporation confronts a unique set of country risks, so assessing and mitigating risk must be performed on a case-by-case basis. There are many issues and analytical frameworks for a business to examine as it develops its evaluation of country risk and creates a strategy for managing the uncertainties such risk entails. This chapter illustrates the most popular framework for comprehensive assessment of country risk.

In summary, country risk is a crucial factor when deciding to invest abroad, from both a financial and an economic point of view. MNCs conduct country risk analysis when they apply capital budgeting: financial managers must understand how to measure country risk and incorporate this risk within their capital budgeting analyses in order to make investment decisions that maximize the MNC's value.

8.1   Country risk

For García (2017), country risk has gained prominence and notoriety since the early 1980s, when the South American debt crisis erupted in response to the second oil crisis in 1979. At that time, many Latin American countries that had borrowed from both official and commercial sources began to struggle to meet their foreign payment obligations, with Mexico being the first to suspend payments in the early 1980s. Numerous bank failures in the United States followed the Latin American country defaults. Since then, the idea of nation risk has grown in prominence, resulting in the establishment of unique procedures and legislation (García, 2017). Country risk is an umbrella notion that encompasses economic, financial, political, historical, and sociological dimensions, as well as a collection of interrelated macroeconomic, institutional, and sociopolitical issues. Country risk can be aggregated by geographic region, even if the globalized economic system eliminates the traditional distinction between emerging and industrial countries, which is no longer appropriate given the structural financial weaknesses of many OECD countries and the contagious nature of financial crises – such as the one that occurred between 2007 and 2009, which revealed systemic vulnerability due to the structural links of the OECD. Strictly speaking, country risk refers to the sovereign risk of default on government debt or on debt guaranteed by the government. Sovereign debt defaults may occur for a number of reasons, including political ones, as a result of a government's decision to fail on its commitments. Nation risk is a general term referring to the risk that emerges when unanticipated changes in money flows or asset prices occur in a foreign country in which one is conducting business as a result of changes in local circumstances. This wide definition of nation risk is usually further specified in terms of two components: financial risk and political risk. Financial risk relates to unforeseen changes in the economic and financial environment, while political risk is the danger that a foreign country's government will alter the regulations governing the transaction, such as asset expropriation, money freezing, or changes to the tax system. The dangers covered by nation risk concept are not distinct entities but rather are inextricably linked and even overlap. The main components of nation risk are as follows (Bouchet et al., 2018):

- *Macroeconomic risk*: This refers to macroeconomic imbalances and their effects on the welfare of local and international economic actors.
- *Currency risk*: An overvalued currency has a detrimental effect on pricing competitiveness and the attractiveness of foreign investment. Exchange rate depreciation, on the other hand, erodes the buying power of domestic economic actors and raises the price of imported goods and services, including inputs for exports.
- *Sovereign and transfer risk*: This risk is unique to international transactions, including foreign direct investment. Investors and creditors are literally reliant on the sovereign borrower's "goodwill," since

> the borrower's legal and financial systems, including its central bank, are inaccessible to private international economic operators.
> - *Legal and Regulatory Risk*: This risk includes contract repudiation and incapacity to enforce contracts, as well as indirect risks such as bribery, regulatory opacity, or arbitrary rule and regulation changes.
> - *Political risk*: This risk is related to the country's institutions and governance, particularly the independence of its executive, legislative, and judicial branches.
> - *Socio-cultural risk*: This risk results from a radical shift in a country's cultural, ideological, or religious values, which in some cases result in social reforms or nationalizations that initially imply higher taxes, higher labor costs, declines in investment, and a massive flight of capital.
> - *Exogenous and systemic risk*: Contagion risk occurs when a nation's economic health is impacted by the volatility of a nearby country or area, while systemic risk results from issues such as global crises, global warming, and terrorism.

Country risk is a broad concept that encompasses both the potentially adverse effects of a country's political environment and its economic and financial environment. Understanding country risk and political risk is essential to international capital budgeting and managing operations in other countries, especially developing ones. Since these concepts also affect shareholder wealth, they are also of interest to global portfolio managers.

Country risk entails a variety of issues. It can be represented by labor strikes by dockworkers or truckers, or clashes between ethnic or religious groups that prevent people from going to work. It not only affects MNCs but also can have additional consequences on investors buying emerging market securities or banks lending this money.

Several indexes can help monitor country risk. The Index of Economic Freedom, which can be considered a risk-return analysis, highlights various ways that a government may seize potential profits. The Corruption Perception Index warns that doing business in certain countries will require clear corporate protocols regarding bribery. The Ease of Doing Business Index provides a general assessment of the institutions and rule of law in each country.

What is "risk"?

As Bouchet et al. (2018) demonstrate, "risk" is a term that refers to what could happen in the future as the result of unpredictable circumstances. It is the consequence of any activity with an uncertain conclusion that has the potential to create both huge financial advantages and losses. A smart place to start when trying to properly understand risk is identifying the kind and degree of uncertainty inherent in each decision. "Risk" is "quantifiable" when it is a component of uncertainty about which we can forecast the set of potential outcomes and their associated probabilities. "Ambiguity" is a subset of uncertainty in which the list of potential outcomes is known but their probabilities are unknown. When we are uncertain about the nature and scope of possible outcomes, we refer to this as "fundamental ambiguity." This form of uncertainty may be triggered by a number of factors, including innovation and technological advancement, as well as changes in cultural, social, and political circumstances.

For the authors, fundamental uncertainty coexists with a related concept known as "procedural uncertainty," which develops when a company's computational and cognitive skills are tested in the presence of specific future choices. Procedural uncertainty may occur when computing or cognitive assessment abilities are inadequate, or when a situation is so complex that even the most robust computational or cognitive capacities are incapable of properly analyzing it. No cross-border strategy can afford to ignore nation risk, and no investment can be undertaken without thoroughly assessing the socioeconomic, financial, and political climate of a country. Managers often want to minimize uncertainty by focusing their strategies on local markets, given the expensive complexity of nation risk. The problems inherent to outsourcing manufacturing to low-cost countries and establishing global value chains are well-known. This is because decreased labor costs do not always offset political insecurity, regulatory unpredictability, and logistical issues. Occasionally, the terms "cross-border risk" or "sovereign risk" are used synonymously with "country risk" to refer to the risk connected with foreign investment. As early as the mid-1970s, country risk was recognized as a significant component of cross-border strategy, first during the 1973 oil crisis and later during the Iranian Islamic revolution of 1978-1979. In the 1980s, a combination of fluctuating exchange rates, commodity price volatility, and sociopolitical unrest prompted an increasing number of multinational corporations to establish dedicated country risk analysis teams charged with assessing, forecasting, and mitigating the risks associated with cross-border investments. Foreign direct investment and outsourcing practices in the early 1990s shifted the emphasis of nation risk studies to low-wage developing countries and those with substantial raw material resources. The nature and consequences of national risk changed drastically over the 1990s. As the traditional divide between developed and developing countries was erased, new dimensions became apparent. Indeed, liquidity and solvency issues migrated from developing to developed nations with solvency ratios (i.e., public debt to GDP) near or beyond 100%, such as Italy, Spain, Greece, and Japan. Meanwhile, several developing economies have experienced sizable current account surpluses since the late 1990s. Since the beginning of the global financial crisis in the early 2000s, the ratings downgrades of developed countries have often been triggered by political risk in developed countries with complex legal, regulatory, and institutional structures that are no longer immune to social unrest. The risks faced by nations thus became a consequence of the complicated interconnections between the public and private sectors.

Authors also highlight as, for example, vulnerabilities in the banking sector have created a new source of nation risk, not only in emerging countries, but also in more established and ostensibly regulated markets. Country risk cannot be defined just by the financial and macroeconomic features of a country. Substantial risks – including legal, regulatory, reputational, and cross-cultural risks – may jeopardize a business's strategy and chances for success and profit. For far too long, the idea of nation risk analysis was restricted to assessing a foreign entity's capacity and desire to meet its external obligations completely and on time. This restrictive definition only took into account economic and political uncertainties in the value of cross-border investments, export revenues, and loan repayments. It was confined to international economic operators and excluded nations with a high risk of terrorism. For example, Brexit-related uncertainty will have a long-term effect on the U.K.'s commercial and financial relations with the E.U., as well as on the domestic business environment. Increased instability in the Brexit process will have a detrimental impact on investment, employment, and inflation, eroding consumer buying power. Growth is anticipated to continue to be sluggish, indicating that the country's risk is being absorbed by more than just foreign creditors, exporters, importers, and investors. Domestic inhabitants (households, investors, and the business sector) face nation risk as a consequence of their country's socioeconomic and political situation, since a country's government has the ability to make arbitrary decisions that influence its people's economic and sociopolitical well-being. Private enterprises, banks, insurance companies, and families all face heightened uncertainty and an unpredictable economic environment, which will influence profit, investment, and income possibilities. Consequently, country risk is shared by local residents who save, invest, and consume, as well as global managers and international bankers who construct complex organizational structures and sophisticated quantitative econometric models to reduce risk. Finally, national risk managers have traditionally concentrated on country-specific risk characteristics, such as balance of payment deficits, inflation, currency exchange rates, debt ratios, and political instability.

The global market economy, on the other hand, has added a new risk element for countries: the contamination effect of crises. Indeed, the breadth of the range of threats confronting economic participants in the global economy is a consequence of the sector's global reach. Without institutional stabilizers, such as a lender-of-last-resort fund, the global economy is more susceptible to shocks than at any other point in history.

Source: Bouchet, M. & Fishkin, C. & Goguel, A. (2018). *Managing Country Risk in an Age of Globalization: A Practical Guide to Overcoming Challenges in a Complex World*. Palgrave Macmillan.

8.1.1   An example of country risk: host government takeovers

Country-specific risks

Gaillard (2020) believes that the most severe kind of political risk is expropriation, which occurs when a foreign government seizes or confiscates a company's physical and/or financial assets. Expropriation is possible anytime unusual events such as rebellions, revolutions, or insurrections occur in the host nation. Expropriation risk is quite simple to handle conceptually. While no one enjoys asset forfeiture, it is possible to prepare for it in advance if you are aware it is a possibility. Expropriation risk can be included in multinational capital planning by assuming that expropriation is diversifiable and hence has no effect on the needed rate of return on investment, and then modifying predicted future cash flows to account for the possibility of expropriation. In reality, however, expropriation is often a convoluted process that involves short-term operational interruptions, medium-term talks with the host government and related parties, and long-term litigation in international tribunals.

As governments execute their fiscal, monetary, and social objectives, disruptions in operations are unavoidable. These are often placed on multinational corporations via tariffs, local content requirements that require a specific proportion of the final product be created locally, foreign currency controls, restrictions on expatriate labor, and host country taxes and regulations. Without significant changes in the business climate, each of these burdens essentially becomes a cost of doing business abroad. Sometimes, host governments provide additional incentives for foreign direct investment, such as subsidized financing, import subsidies, or preferential access to limited markets. If the amount of costs or incentives is subject to sudden change for political reasons, this uncertainty generates a political risk in the host nation. Thus despite globalization, several protectionist restrictions impacting foreign investment remain in effect across the globe. Some examples include bailouts, state aid, competitive devaluation, consumption subsidies, export incentives, import bans, quotas, tariffs, intellectual property protections, expropriation, investment restrictions, localization requirements, "national content" preferences, sanitary rules, technical trade barriers, funding facilities, trade defense measures, and immigration restrictions (Gaillard, 2020).

Blocked money is the consequence of host government limitations on remittances to the parent corporation. This extreme type of restriction occurs when a host government prohibits its money from being easily converted or swapped for other currencies. Such currency inconvertibility essentially prevents money from entering the foreign economy from foreign sources. More often, the host government imposes capital outflow limits to prevent capital flight and maintain the local currency. Local rates of return are likely to be lower in this case than rates of return available elsewhere. Unless unexpected changes in repatriation regulations or currency convertibility occur, frozen money is just a cost of doing business abroad.

According to Butler (2016), foreign enterprises often have to overcome host country suspicion and animosity. Local inhabitants often have a strong preference for indigenous goods and services, and this economic expression of nationalism known as protectionism is sometimes institutionalized in the host country's laws, rules, and tax policies. Governments often enact rules to safeguard specific sectors of the domestic economy from foreign competition. For instance, several countries implement "local content" requirements specifying the proportion of items that must be manufactured locally.

Another type of country risk is a multinational company's possible loss of intellectual property rights to rivals or former local business partners because of government action or inaction. Businesses safeguard their intellectual property by enforcing access restrictions on goods, technology, and procedures. If a host government enables one or more local enterprises to misappropriate the MNC's intellectual property rights, that company faces risk. If the MNC does not exert diligence in managing, controlling, and transferring its intellectual property rights, it may find itself competing in international markets or even in its own domestic market with former partners.

Source: Butler, K.C. (2016). *Multinational Finance: Evaluating Opportunities, Costs, and Risks of Operations.* Wiley Finance.

Assuming the MNC has little negotiating power in the host nation, a takeover by the host government could result in significant losses. There are several popular methods for reducing this type of risk. For instance, the use of particular technologies and raw materials that are not present in the host country but are necessary for the proper functioning of the subsidiary makes it disadvantageous and potentially useless for the local government to take control of the subsidiary, since it would have difficulty obtaining the same supplies without the MNC's headquarters; this means the MNC would maintain strong control over the local government even in the event of expropriation. Use of the host country's workforce can also serve as a disincentive for the local government, since a hostile takeover would put the jobs of its own citizens at risk. Financing from local banks has the same effect, since in the event of expropriation those banks might not be able to recover their exposures abroad from the multinational's headquarters. Risk mitigation can also be managed through insurance policies with investment guarantee schemes specifically designed to protect against the risk of expropriation (Fox et al., 2017). The implementation of structured finance operations and project financing strategies that shift the investment risks to the balance sheet of a new company (Newco) whose equity is controlled by the MNC can also be effective. These types of operations finance the activities of the Newco through extensive recourse to bank debt, the repayment of which is counter-guaranteed solely by the cash flow capacity of the Newco itself; this protects the balance sheet of the multinational, which cannot be involved in requests for the repayment of exposures and therefore of the debt assumed by the Newco. In the event of expropriation, the multinational can decide to cancel the project and liquidate the vehicle company (Newco), which will be the only entity attacked by creditors. This risk of having the project cancelled by the multinational in the event of expropriation might represent a strong point of dissuasion for the local government, which would risk jeopardizing the ability of the various stakeholders (not only banks) of Newco to recover their credits (Fox et al., 2017).

8.1.2   Techniques for measuring country risk

Gaillard (2020) argues that companies that analyze nation risk often perform macro- and micro-level evaluations. Macro-risks influence all businesses operating in a host nation. Unexpected changes in a host nation's monetary or fiscal policies, banking system, tax rates, capital restrictions, exchange rates, or bankruptcy and property laws all represent international monetary, financial, debt, fiscal, and trade risks that affect the MNC's activities abroad. A change in any of these policy factors influences multinational corporations operating in the country.

Micro-risks, on the other hand, are industry-, company-, or project-specific and must also be taken into account in measuring a MNC's country risk exposure. They include social and labor risks, capital risks, and boycotts, to name just a few. Foreign firms that breach fundamental social standards in their host countries risk worker unrest, which might interrupt operations and destroy their brand. Strikes and lock-outs are another form of risk. The third type of labor-related risk is the cost of labor and the possibility of being unable to attract, hire, and retain a sufficiently skilled workforce. Changes in immigration rules are an example of a political risk with a differential impact on the operations of some firms in a foreign country compared to others. Most states put harsh limitations on foreign labor within their national boundaries. Employers seeking to recruit labor in a host country may find themselves at a competitive disadvantage compared to domestic competitors if the barred imported staff is comprised of senior executives moved from headquarters. There are also risks associated with internal fraud, which include, but are not limited to, asset theft and false financial reporting in a foreign subsidiary. External fraud hazards include industrial espionage, racketeering, extortion, and violation of partnership agreements, among others. Apart from the customer preference shifts resulting from global trends and technology advancements, demand for products and services offered by international firms may be weakened by negative publicity and boycotts. The latter are ideological in nature and are often a reaction to a company's perceived ethical faults. Business circles have created innovative techniques to assist in mitigating microeconomic hazards. For example, an increasing number of businesses are issuing public statements about corporate social responsibility (CSR) and codifying company ethics (Gaillard, 2020).

As per Butler (2016), generally, nation risk evaluations must include evaluation of a country's financial or economic risks. Financial risk factors include both quantitative macroeconomic parameters and qualitative indicators of a country's financial or economic position. Quantitative macroeconomic factors include, but are not limited to, currency risk, interest rate risk, inflation risk, and host country trade balance exposure. They are directly influenced by a government's monetary, fiscal, and trade policies, as well as by numerous domestic and international events beyond the government's control. Other variables – such as the rate of loan defaults or restructurings, the average payment delay, and the percentage of contract cancellations by the host government – all have a direct effect on the financial climate. Ratings should also consider the degree to which businesses are subject to restrictive business practices, trade tariffs or restrictions, and the status of private property and bankruptcy laws. Research should be conducted to quantify the MNC's exposure to these types of issues and condense them into a few indices that accurately represent the local financial climate.

Another form of nation risk is political risk, which represents the danger of unanticipated changes in a foreign country's political, legal, or regulatory environment. Political risks generally develop from unforeseen changes in the host country's political climate or its ties with other nations. Political risk is mainly associated with a government's or policy's volatility. Stable administrations are more likely to pursue stable policies. Unstable governments are more prone to modify policy, posing political risk to multinational corporations. Along with the stability of government policies, multinational corporations must examine whether a policy change is likely to be beneficial or detrimental to the corporation. When a change in faction occurs as a consequence of an armed struggle (i.e., a war, revolution, insurgency, or coup), political stability is reduced. Corporations face political risks in part because political leaders are accountable to the public good while corporate leaders are accountable to the private welfare of their stakeholders. It is thus unsurprising that governments and companies often find themselves at odds. All of these political risk evaluations must be quantified and ultimately converted into a political risk rating (Butler, 2016).

First, it is important to acknowledge that there are two levels of country risk assessment. A *macro-assessment* of country risk considers all the variables affecting the country risk except those specific to a particular firm or industry. This type of assessment is uniform for a given country regardless of the firm or industry of concern, but it excludes some information that could improve the accuracy of the assessment. A *micro-assessment* of country risk involves assessing a country in relation to the MNC's type of business. It is used to determine how the country risk relates to the specific MNC. The impact of a country risk can affect MNCs and their specific projects in different ways, which is why micro-assessment of country risk is needed.

Before analyzing the methodologies available to evaluate macro- and micro-factors relevant to country risk, it is important to note that the multiple origins of country risk require a multidisciplinary approach. There are several different risk models, but they all share some key components:

1. *Political Analysis* of country risk, which considers the experience and preparedness of government officials, policy interventionism in economic management issues, political relations with foreign partners, or ethnic conflicts.
2. *Economic Analysis* of country risk, which considers the probable future economic performance of the nation to ascertain the likelihood that the country will repay its foreign debt, as well as assessment of monetary and fiscal policy, overall economic climate, GDP growth, and inflation rates.
3. *Financial Analysis* of country risk, which considers liquidity indicators and factors such as external debt and exchange rate stability.

Fox et al. (2017) suggest that the following specific methodologies can be used:

- The *scoring approach*, which provides scores to a list of financial and political indicators that are then compiled to produce an overall assessment of the risk associated with a nation. Some items can be objectively quantified using accessible statistics, while others must be subjectively estimated based on available information. Their effect on nation risk is then transformed into a numerical assessment and weighted according to their relative impact. In this technique, it is possible to create an overall evaluation of nation risk from separate assessments of political and financial risk. First, the political and economic aspects are given values that fall within a certain range. Next, weights (which should add up to 100 percent) are given to each of the factors in relation to the relative importance of each component. The nation's total risk rating will be determined by multiplying the political and financial ratings by their corresponding weights and averaging the results. Depending on the objectives of the MNC, the importance of political risk relative to financial risk varies: if the foreign investment is intended to expand the customer base in the foreign country, the MNC must pay close attention to financial risk; on the other hand, if the MNC wishes to establish a production facility abroad, the MNC must pay close attention to political risk.
- *Modeling Quantitative Analysis* uncovers the drivers of country risk. It involves regression models, which can involve measuring a company's performance, meas-

uring its increase in revenues, or evaluating its performance relative to a national index, per capita wealth, or a previous period. The results of these types of analysis reveal the relationship between a company and the economy of the nation in which it operates. These types of analysis obviously cannot foresee the problems of a country before they materialize, since predictions of the future based on analysis of the past do not always prove correct.

• Some features, such as links between countries, can be difficult to analyze without visiting the host country. Inspection trips can help clarify any ambiguous judgments about a country. A multinational company may also assess country risk in a number of nations at once. One technique used to compare political and financial assessments across nations is the *Foreign Investment Risk Matrix* (FIRM) methodology. This model illustrates financial and political risk as ranging from "bad" to "excellent", with ranges corresponding to different levels of risk. Each country is assigned a position in the matrix based on the political and financial ratings assigned to it. Many industrialized nations have high ratings, suggesting a low level of danger; on the other hand, many developing countries have lower ratings, indicating a higher level of risk. As a result of these variables, country risk ratings fluctuate over time, and multinational corporations must regularly update their risk ratings for each country in which they do business to maintain their competitive advantage.

Many MNCs do not use a formal method for assessing country risk. This does not mean that they neglect to do so, but rather highlights that there is no proven method or method that is deemed most appropriate. Most country risk analysis constitutes an effort to quantify risk, but this effort is never complete and cannot measure all hazards. Indeed, country risk does not behave like other, more predictable risks. Data used in the model might not be accurate or easy to find, and changes in reporting methods can impact model calculations. Moreover, the data used in quantitative models are historical and thus backward looking. In short, such models tend to oversimplify complex realities.

Lastly, many international projects last for 20 years or more. Consequently, MNCs need a proper *governance* system to ensure that managers effectively evaluate country risk when assessing potential projects. Major long-term projects should use input from external sources, and country-risk assessments should be incorporated in long-term analyses of these project.

8.2   Political risk

Political risk represents the danger that an investment's profits in a given country will deteriorate because of political upheaval or instability. Instability in investment returns might be caused by a change in administration, legislative bodies, foreign politicians, or military command (Lessambo, 2021).

Country risk is a broad concept that encompasses both the potentially adverse effects of a country's political situation and its economic and financial environment. Understanding country risk and political risk is an important aspect of international capital budgeting and managing operations in other countries, especially developing countries.

The biggest country risk is probably political, since these risks can completely undermine the performance of a local subsidiary. More generally, political risk refers to the possibility that political decisions or events in a country will affect the business climate in such a way that investors will lose money or not make as much money as they originally expected. Political risk is unavoidable in the global marketplace, even in developed countries. It may appear in the form of tightened regulations, taxation changes, and protectionism. In many emerging markets, the levels of political risk can be much higher than in more mature economies.

Political risks include changes in laws and regulations, breaches of contract by foreign governments, import or export restrictions, expropriation, foreign exchange restrictions, and political violence. **Table 8.1** summarizes some of the effects of such risks on investors.

Table 8.1   Effects of the risks

Type of risk	Effect on investors
Changes in laws and regulations	Increased expense of meeting local standards leads to lower profitability.
Import or export restrictions	The operations of foreign affiliates are disrupted with possible total loss of investment.
Foreign exchange restrictions	Foreign affiliates cannot make payments in hard currency to the parent company; the value of cash held in the foreign market depreciates while these restrictions are in place.
Breach of contract by government counterparty	Contract breaches cause losses for a foreign affiliate that can make it economically unviable.
Expropriation	The parent company loses its equity investment and income stream from the foreign affiliate and cannot meet loan covenants and financial obligations.
Political violence	Unsafe conditions lead to abandonment, resulting in physical assets potentially being destroyed and possible default on payments.

Source: Author's elaboration of *Managing Political Risk: A Guide for Canadian Businesses that Invest in or Export to Emerging Markets*, available at EDC.ca.

To illustrate the effects listed in this table, we will look at two real-world cases of MNCs reporting these types of risks in their annual reports. Such risks may seem distant and extreme, but they actually happen more often than we might expect.

A host country can indeed take over a subsidiary, either providing it with compensation for this *expropriation* or refusing to do so. This event can take place peacefully or by force.

According to a study by Oxford Analytica and Willis Towers Watson, these two scenarios were the main political risk concerns for MNCs in 2019. **Table 8.2** gives an idea of how vast the problem is and how many potential political risks can arise when operating abroad.

Table 8.2   **Main political risk concerns**

Risk	% total responses
Trade sanctions or embargos	31
Political violence or forced abandonment	22
Currency transfer or inconvertibility	17
Expropriation	14
Sovereign non-payment	9
Others	7

Source: Author's elaboration based on Oxford Analytica & Willis Towers Watson (2019).

This table summarizes a survey of a group of MNCs from different industries in developed countries (the U.S., Europe, and Japan). It included mostly Fortune 500 companies. 61% of the firms in this sample affirmed that their levels of political risk have increased since 2018, mainly due to the imposition of economic sanctions on countries such as Iran, Russia, and Venezuela. It will be evident in the next sections how these sanctions can intensify political risk and discourage investments.

Building on the data displayed in this table, we can intuit that certain countries tend to experience more conflicts and internal turmoil. This can affect the safety of those who work for the MNC and its subsidiaries. In addition, in such countries, business is volatile and cash flows are more uncertain. Due to political tensions, in some countries large MNCs can become symbols of their home countries and therefore be more exposed to terrorist attacks, incurring costs for ensuring the safety of their employees.

Case Eni and the dangers of continuing political unrest in North Africa and the Middle East

At the end of 2013, North Africa and the Middle East accounted for about 30% of the Company's proven oil and gas reserves. Several oil-producing nations in North Africa and the Middle East faced considerable political instability in 2011, resulting in government changes, unrest and bloodshed, and resulting economic repercussions. The volatility of those nations' sociopolitical frameworks is a source of worry, implying risks and uncertainties in the near future; in particular, the internal situation in Libya continues to provide a challenge to Eni's management. Eni's production performance in Libya was significantly affected by force majeure events in 2013, reflecting the continuing instability of the country's socio-political environment. It is worth noting that Eni is currently working to restore full production at its production assets in the country, following an internal conflict in 2011 that forced the Company to shut down almost all of its production facilities, including gas exports, for approximately 8 months, with a material impact on production volumes and operating results for that year. Due to the complexities of the country's transition era, Eni is still in the process of recovering the entire production plateau of its Libyan assets. For the entire year of 2013, Eni's Libyan operations produced 228 kboe/d, much lower than the pre-crisis output peak of 273 kboe/d set in 2010.

Source: Annual Report 2013 – Political Considerations, Eni. Available at https://report.eni.com/annual-report-2013/en/annual-report/financial-review-and-other-information/risk-factors-and-uncertainties/political-considerations.html

---

Case **GM is forced to cease operations in Venezuela after the illegal seizure of its plant (April 2017)**

General Motors Venezolana (GMV), the country's oldest and most traditional carmaker and market leader for more than 35 years, has been forced to halt operations in Venezuela owing to an unlawful court seizure of its assets. GMV's factory was abruptly seized by governmental authorities yesterday, interrupting regular operations. In addition, the company's assets, such as automobiles, were unlawfully removed from its premises. The seizure was allowed and carried out with complete disrespect for GMV's right to due process, inflicting irreparable harm to the firm, its 2,678 employees, its 79 dealers (the country's biggest service network with over 3,900 employees), and its suppliers (representing more than 55% of the auto parts industry in Venezuela). As a consequence, GMV announces the immediate end of its operations in the country and guarantees (to the extent permitted by the authorities) the payment of employee separation benefits arising from the termination of employment for causes beyond the parties' control.

Source: GM's press release (2017, April 20). Available at https://media.gm.com/media/us/en/gm/home.detail.html/content/Pages/news/us/en/2017/apr/0420-venezuela.html

---

Another dimension of political risk pertains to *economic and trade sanctions* that might be imposed on the foreign country by other states but which end up affecting anyone who does business there. International economic sanctions with an extraterritorial reach are increasingly being imposed by foreign governments and other international entities for political purposes. Developing countries are seen as targets for these measures. Economic sanctions are usually used by the United Nations or other supranational organizations to obtain political or humanitarian changes and threaten economic consequences if these changes do not take place. Between 1914 and 2000 (Hufbauer et al., 2007), the most common purpose of these sanctions (in 39.22% of instances) was to catalyze regime change and democratization, particularly against governments that maintained a hostile posture toward the sanctioning organizations. There are also other types of sanctions, such as trade sanctions, which limit trade contacts with the targeted country and result in decreased exports, or the implementation of trade quotas or higher tariffs. Financial sanctions seek to take the target's assets overseas, restrict current financial investments or transactions, and halt payments related to the target. Another targeted form of punishment is travel bans. Finally, there are embargoes, which restrict any dealings with the country subject to such penalties (Yoel, 2020).

U.S. Sanctions on Russia

Congress, the Biden Administration, and other stakeholders are discussing fresh sanctions against Russia in early 2022. In reaction to Russia's military buildup near and in Ukraine, the U.S. and its European allies have stated they will apply more sanctions if Russia attacks Ukraine again. Sanctions may include tighter limits on dealings with Russian financial institutions and technology exports from the United States, as well as the suspension of Russia's upcoming Nord Stream 2 natural gas pipeline project. Additional sanctions, including those targeting Russia's energy industry and secondary market transactions in Russian government debt, may also be considered.

Sanctions are a key component of U.S. strategy to confront and prevent malicious Russian behavior. The U.S. maintains sanctions on Russia primarily in response to Russia's invasion of Ukraine beginning in 2014, in order to reverse and discourage future Russian aggression in Ukraine, as well as to deter Russian aggression against other countries. The U.S. also maintains sanctions against Russia in response to (and to deter) malicious cyber-enabled activities and operations (including election meddling), the use of a chemical weapon, human rights violations, the use of energy exports as a coercive or political tool, weapons proliferation, illicit trade with North Korea, and support for the governments of Syria and Venezuela. Many members of Congress favor the implementation of strong sanctions in light of Russia's international actions and geostrategic goals. The United States has coordinated many of its moves against Russia with the European Union (E.U.) and others. As the invasion of Ukraine advanced in 2014, the Obama Administration saw E.U. support for sanctions as critical, owing to the E.U.'s stronger commercial and investment links with Russia than the U.S. Many officials and observers see continuous U.S.-E.U. collaboration in imposing sanctions as a visible demonstration of U.S.-European unity, thwarting Russian attempts to sever ties between transatlantic allies. In terms of economic effect, research indicate that sanctions have had a negative but minor influence on Russia's economy. Changes in global oil prices and the Coronavirus Disease 2019 (Covid-19) pandemic seem to have had a bigger effect on the Russian economy than sanctions. Following the rise in oil prices in 2016, Russia's economy started to improve even though sanctions remained in place and, in some cases, were reinforced. The Obama Administration and the E.U. established sanctions in response to Russia's invasion of Ukraine in part to exert longer-term constraints on Russia's economy while limiting collateral harm to the Russian people and the nations applying sanctions.

Source: U.S. Sanctions on Russia, CRS Report (2022, January 18). Available at https://sgp.fas.org/crs/row/R45415.pdf

It is important to distinguish these kinds of sanctions implemented for political aims from sanctions that emerge due to international trade breaches. Moreover, new sanction proposals have been developed based on violations pertaining to environmental agreements, such as the 2016 Paris Climate Agreement.

Paris Climate Agreement

It is a legally enforceable international climate change accord. It was accepted by 196 Parties at COP 21 in Paris on December 12, 2015, and went into effect on November 4, 2016. Its objective is to keep global warming considerably below 2 degrees Celsius, ideally 1.5 degrees Celsius, relative to pre-industrial levels. Countries aspire to accomplish this long-term temperature objective by peaking global greenhouse gas emissions as soon as feasible in order to establish a climate-neutral planet by mid-century. The Paris Pact is a watershed moment in the international climate change process because, for the first time, a binding agreement binds all countries together in a common cause to undertake aggressive measures to battle and adapt to the consequences of climate change.

Source: United Nations Climate Change. Available at https://unfccc.int/process-and-meetings/the-paris-agreement/the-paris-agreement

Other issues pertaining to political risk have to do with the specific characteristics of the host country. More specifically, the *actions of governments* can have a huge impact. Changes in the philosophy of government may be considered a proxy for a country's political risk, with an impact on the MNC's future cash flows. A subsidiary will not necessarily feel the repercussions of changing governments; however, it can be affected by new policies undertaken by the host country government or by altered attitudes towards the subsidiary's home country.

A host government can express its disagreement with or hostility to the MNC in several ways. It may impose pollution control regulations (which influence expenses) as well as extra corporation taxes (which effect after-tax profits), withholding taxes, and money transfer limitations (which affect after-tax cash flows sent to the parent). In some cases, a host government may obstruct financial transfers, causing subsidiaries to pursue less-than-ideal initiatives. MNC subsidiaries often transfer cash back to headquarters for debt repayments, supply purchases, administrative fees, or remitted profits. Alternatively, the MNC can invest such cash in local stocks, which may provide a lower return than the subsidiary might have received on money transferred to the parent. Some governments may even prohibit the exchange of their currency for another. As a result, profits earned by a subsidiary cannot be transferred to the parent through currency conversion. The parent company of a MNC may need to swap earnings for commodities in order to reap the advantages of projects in that nation. A host government can also use various means to align the MNC's operations to the country's goals: by requiring the company to hire local employees for managerial positions, requiring specific permits, imposing extra taxes, subsidizing competitors, and/or imposing restrictions to protect local competition.

A government's *bureaucracy* can also complicate the MNC's business, especially in emerging countries. In fact, red tape can delay a MNC's efforts to establish a new subsidiary or expand its business in a country. In some cases, government employees expect "gifts" before they approve applications by MNCs; in others, the lack of government organization can delay the development of a new business. In some circumstances, MNCs are adversely affected by a *lack of restrictions* in a host country that allows illegitimate business behavior to flourish. A common example is when a host government fails to enforce copyright laws against local firms that illegally replicate the MNC's product. The legal systems in some countries do not adequately protect firms against such behaviors. *Corruption* can increase the cost of conducting business or reduce revenues. Various forms of corruption can occur at the firm level or in firm-government interactions: a MNC may lose revenues because a government contract is instead awarded to a local firm that paid off a government official. To further complicate matters, laws defining corruption and their enforcement vary among countries.

Lastly, consumer attitudes in the host nation may lead to the emergence of an alternative type of political risk. Attitude is defined as a psychological disposition expressed by assessing certain things favorably or unfavorably (Eagly & Chaiken, 1993). There is a general trend in all countries to pressure resident customers to buy from local businesses. Multinational corporations that are considering entering a foreign market must keep an eye on the general level of customer loyalty to locally produced items in that market. It is possible that a joint venture with a local company is more practical than an export approach in some circumstances (Fox et al., 2017).

Despite the number of potential sources of political risk, if a project's potential return is substantial enough, it is usually considered worth undertaking and no risk is deemed too high. By contrast, when employee safety is a concern, the project may be rejected.

8.2.1   Benefits of managing political risk

There are several benefits to correctly managing political risks:

- Firms can forecast the impact of political events on their investments or exports more accurately. If a nation seems to be too dangerous, they may depart before anybody is harmed. Certain political upheavals may have a beneficial influence and disclose previously undiscovered commercial prospects.
- Effective political risk management enables businesses to join new markets that may be extremely lucrative but also include greater dangers.
- Firms that understand political risks may make more informed judgments on how to mitigate them, as detailed in the next section.

How political risk management enhances global business performance

- Political risk management should begin with top management, and responsibility for monitoring should be delegated to both the board of directors and management. The risk tolerance of the business should be conveyed across the organization. Additionally, it is critical to designate key personnel who will be accountable for risk management.
- Political risk management has a direct effect on performance and may have a financial impact by enabling the organization to predict leadership changes, influence legislation, and engage in social change, as well as to monitor the effects of regulatory, social, and economic change. These dangers are especially significant for businesses working in highly regulated sectors.
- Assessing political risk optimizes decision-making in terms of the overall management of several interacting risks and may also assist businesses in evaluating their political risks worldwide by determining if risks in various nations balance one another. This technique of diversification enables managers to track global shifts in political risks and capitalize on opportunities.
- Assessing risks before action adds value if they are systematically analyzed according to risk exposure. A risk manager should supervise the process, which should include all relevant data, both qualitative and quantitative.
- Systematic political risk management safeguards investments. This process should continue until project completion, since political risk might impact future operations and divestment choices. Establishing a structured risk communication network is critical to ensuring that information is successfully shared across the company for numerous objectives.

Source: PwC Advisory and Eurasia Group Research Report. Available at https://erm.ncsu.edu/az/erm/i/chan/m-articles/documents/PoliticalRisksummary.pdf

8.2.2   Managing political risk

All companies operating abroad should have a clear and simple framework for managing risks they might incur in their operations. An effective checklist includes the following:

1. Identify political risk exposure.
2. Measure risk exposure and its potential impacts.
3. Mitigate effects.
4. Monitor over time.

Main tools for mitigating political risks

Political Risk Insurance and Guarantees (PRI)
These tools allow investors and lenders to transfer political risks to a third party in order to mitigate political risks such as expropriation, breach of contract, currency inconvertibility, political violence, and failure to comply with an arbitration award. They include:

- Political Risk Assurance;
- Political Risk Guarantees;
- Credit guarantees.

Joint ventures or alliances with local companies
These tools allow investors to partner with local counterparts that have a better understanding of the local market, political system, and specific risks, thus allowing foreign investors to increase their knowledge of the market in question. Foreign lenders can similarly seek to co-finance large infrastructure investments with local banks.

Consultations with governments and political leaders
These tools enable investors and lenders to get informed about national development plans, infrastructure goals, and policy changes that could affect infrastructure investments. They allow private stakeholders to express their perspectives on public policy to improve the investment climate.

Risk analysis
These tools manage risks throughout the lifecycle of a project by analyzing the risk profile of an infrastructure project to identify key risks and optimal solutions to mitigate their negative impacts.

Source: OECD Asean. Available at http://rmid-oecd.asean.org/project-risks-mitigation/risk-mitigation-instruments/political-risk-mitigation/

A risk manager should be identified to coordinate and carry out these steps. When *identifying political risk exposure*, the company should first collect information, then pinpoint risks. Specifically, the risk manager should gather pertinent information about each type of political risk the company faces, or is likely to face, in the target country. The objective should be to find out how political conditions or factors may affect the company's goals in the market. Once all the information is collected, the risk manager should identify the political risks that most threaten the company's goals in the country. Seizure of assets might be a low-ranked hazard for an exporter but a more serious one if a company is considering a major investment or bringing valuable equipment into an emerging market to perform contract work.

When *measuring risk exposure* and its impact, risk managers apply the scenario outcomes they have developed to rank the risks and measure the company's exposure to each one. This involves assigning numerical values to each risk that reflect the potential impacts of the firm's exposure wherever possible. Some common measurement tools include Discounted Cash Flows (DCF), Organizational Network Analysis, or Diagnostic Tools.

- DCF is a way of assessing an investment's attractiveness by discounting future cash flow estimates to arrive at the present value.
- Organizational network analysis calculates the impact of a risk occurrence on a company's operations.
- Enterprise Risk Management is a tool that uses diagnostic technologies to detect and assess dangers.

The next step is *mitigating political risk exposure*, first by reducing the probability of a risky event and then by minimizing its effects if it becomes a reality. Further comments on this process will be presented below. The last step is *monitoring political risk exposure:* once the risk manager has established how the risk management process will work in practice, he or she can assign responsibilities and set up routines for reporting, evaluation, and review.

8.2.3   Mitigating strategies in political risk

It is crucial to understand risk mitigation strategies, since any MNC might find itself in a position to need to use them to reduce the uncertainty of an investment and increase its odds of success. Let's take the example of economic sanctions discussed above. Companies typically use one of two following approaches to mitigate the risks associated with economic sanctions. First, they use *holistic techniques* aimed at limiting the negative effect of political risk factors by lowering their likelihood of occurrence. This is primarily accomplished through lobbying activities against host governments. In these cases, multinationals work from within the local system, adapting their methods to the circumstances and legislation of the local market to minimize the likelihood of local hostility. *Safety measures*, on the other hand, seek to mitigate the extent of overall losses caused by political events in the host nation, such as expropriation, confiscation, or currency restrictions. In these cases, the MNC aims to reduce aggregate losses by distributing its functional areas and supply networks across many countries globally.

For example, if economic sanctions were to be put in place, using *alternative suppliers* from non-sanctioned countries might be an effective mechanism, depending on the characteristics of the MNC's goods or services. This practice is advisable for the procurement of non-commodity goods and services whose origins can be easily tracked by parties related to the sanctioning body. However, when sanctions have extraterritoriality features, this is impossible.

Shipment-based triangular trade transactions

The Russian-based MNC sells with its controlled firm in India to a U.K. firm. This triangle trade results in the following transactions:
- The MNC submits a sales order to its Indian subsidiary.
- The Indian subsidiary sends an invoice to the MNC and sells goods from the U.K.
- The Indian subsidiary sends a cargo ship to the U.K. to satisfy the order.

Another way of avoiding sanctions is engaging in so-called *trading triangulation transactions* to avoid direct linkages with sanctioned targets. In these cases, MNCs purchase goods or services through a vehicular non-sanctioned party under their control that is able to trade with the target in question. The non-sanctioned party arranges for the delivery of supplies to MNCs operating under the sanctioning body's jurisdictional reach.

Naturally, there are extensive worldwide initiatives aimed at uncovering and prosecuting the use of such methods. Huawei, a Chinese multinational corporation, was charged by U.S. officials in 2018 with utilizing unregistered associate businesses in Hong Kong and Mauritius to sell equipment containing U.S. components directly to Iran and Syria. Under U.S. sanctions, these components were prohibited from being sold to these two nations.[1]

Notably, a multinational corporation may also safeguard its interests by entering into an investment protection treaty with the destination country. In general, these treaties seek investment protection guarantees for multinationals from the foreign country's government that minimize dangers such as expropriation and confiscation while operating in their territory. Multinationals also use loopholes and ambiguous language in economic sanctions to continue to trade. Multinationals can moreover obtain exemptions from sanctions by lobbying local officials.

To address the demands of foreign investors, most OECD countries and many non-OECD nations offer investment guarantees and political risk insurance. Such services are also provided by private insurers. Typically, the overseas investment projects that need such insurance are in underdeveloped nations. Investment guarantees include a broad variety of goods and may be described as any guarantee and/or insurance product related to overseas investment. One such assurance is political risk (PR) insurance. Political risk is defined by the World Bank Group's Multilateral Investment Guarantee Agency (MIGA) as government acts that reject or limit an investor's or owner's ability to utilize or profit from its assets or that lower the company's value. From this perspective, war, revolution, government seizure of property, and acts that limit the flow of profits or other revenue inside a nation are all examples of political risks (Gordon, 2009).

---

[1] "For years, Chinese firms have broken our export laws and undermined sanctions, often using U.S. financial systems to facilitate their illegal activities," said Secretary Ross, US Department of Justice. Available at https://www.justice.gov/opa/pr/chinese-telecommunications-conglomerate-huawei-and-huawei-cfo-wanzhou-meng-charged-financial

Similarly, political risk insurance may help minimize the losses incurred by MNCs in relation to trade flows and investments in target countries, but it is a more expensive risk transfer mechanism than investment protection treaties. Providers of this type of insurance include the World Bank Group's MIGA (Multilateral Investment Guarantee Agency), the Asian Development Bank, the Inter-American Development Bank, ICIEC (Islamic Corporation for Investment and Export Credit), Lloyd's of London syndicates, and numerous country-specific export credit agencies (ECAs), as well as private insurers such as American International Group, Zurich Re, Munich Re, and Hannover Re. Most of these institutions are members of the Berne Union,[2] which currently counts more than 80 members.

The worst-case scenario occurs when a MNC chooses to leave the host nation.[3] This is the worst outcome since it can jeopardize the sale of local operations to prospective bidders. However, this downside will not necessarily keep a MNC from exiting if that is the least expensive option. Some escape methods are worth highlighting. For instance, local operations can be sold to non-affected domestic or foreign players to complete the withdrawal. Another possibility is to sell to local workers via an employee buyout (EBO) transaction or similar methods involving local stakeholders. Alternatively, the MNC might liquidate the various assets associated with its local activities. In all circumstances, it is to be expected that such sales would conclude at low prices, which means leaving the host country is typically seen as a last resort.

In conclusion, it is important for MNCs to take into account the elements that may lead to economic sanctions, as well as those that might increase the odds of political risks ruining their investment opportunities abroad. Both prevention and mismanagement of such risks might also expose the MNC to further losses.

8.3 Financial risk

According to Kirikkaleli (2020), political instability has a significant impact on a country's financial sector since it worsens its financial system. Political unrest is likely to have an impact on a country's risk-reward profile, as well as on the needed rate of return on existing and future investments. Because of the growing costs of domestic and international borrowing resulting from such unrest, governments typically increase taxes and cut government expenditure. The consequent slowdown in market economic activity in turn reduces people's spending capacities, further reducing the economy. Numerous empirical studies have shown that increased political tension in both domestic markets and the international arena has a negative impact on stock markets, as Kirikkaleli (2020) points out, and that, in times of political turmoil, risk-averse entrepreneurs are likely to shift their investments to countries that offer more relative safety and less risk.

[2] The International Union of Credit and Investment Insurers (Berne Union) is the international association for the export credit and investment insurance industry. It is a not-for-profit association, representing the global export credit and investment insurance industry since 1934. For more information see https://www.berneunion.org/Stub/Display/8

[3] Subsidiary closures are not uncommon. They are sometimes part of a multinational corporation's reconfiguration of foreign assets to optimize performance by investing in certain places and divesting in others (Chakrabarti et al., 2011).

In addition to political aspects, financial characteristics need to be taken into consideration when assessing country risk. Investors use a number of economic variables to discriminate between financially sound and financially troubled countries, including the following:

- the ratio of a country's external debt to its gross domestic product (GDP);
- the ratio of a country's debt service payments to its exports;
- the ratio of a country's imports to its official international reserves;
- a country's terms of trade (the ratio of its export to import prices);
- a country's current account deficit or current account deficit to GDP ratio.

These variables are directly related to a country's ability to generate inflows of foreign exchange and thus can signal the presence of financial risk.

The current European sovereign debt crisis has highlighted the relevance of government budget deficits and public debt-to-GDP ratios as predictors of sovereign risk, even in wealthy countries that are not considered financially dangerous. Indeed, it is important to note that a government's fiscal policy may alter financial risk characteristics: expansionary fiscal policies entail enormous spending and low taxation in order to promote the economy. On the other hand, this strategy results in a big national budget deficits, which increases the amount borrowed by the government. Long-term negative consequences may result if government borrowing is so high that it raises questions about the government's capacity to repay its debt.

Inflation and real economic growth are also crucial indicators. Indeed, one of the most visible financial aspects of a country is the status of its economy (both existing and prospective), as well as its demand for the MNC's goods. Recent gross domestic product (GDP) levels may be used to gauge a country's real economic growth and estimate future growth tendencies. In general, three factors can be used to determine a country's economic growth rate: interest rates, exchange rates, and inflation. In terms of interest rates, higher rates hinder an economy's growth and diminish demand. This explains why governments often aim to maintain low interest rates in order to promote the economy and encourage enterprises and consumers to borrow more. Exchange rates instead alter demand for a country's exports, and thus affect the country's output and income levels. A strong currency may lower demand for a country's exports, increase the number of items it imports, and thus reduce output and national revenue. Finally, inflation may influence customers' purchasing power and demand for the MNC's products. Inflation can also affect a country's financial situation through interest rates and currency value.

8.4   Adjusting capital budgeting for country risk

The growth of financial markets in Asia and Latin America and the allure of globalization have made the analysis and assessment of country risk a critical component of valuation in recent years. As companies and investors globalize and financial markets expand around the world, we are increasingly faced with estimation questions about the associated risks. In practical terms, should we adjust for this additional risk? If so, how?

In assessing the feasibility of a project, country risk can be incorporated in the capital budgeting analysis by adjusting the discount rate or by adjusting the estimated cash flows. If a company chooses not to purchase political risk insurance, when it forecasts future cash flows it must incorporate into the calculation how these cash flows might be affected by various political risks, such as expropriation, unexpected taxation, and so forth. Fox et al. (2017) outline a series of adjustments that should be made.

8.4.1   Adjusting the discount rate

The discount rate used in a project is intended to represent the needed rate of return on the investment. As a result, it can be modified to take into account nation risk. The lower a nation's risk rating, the greater its perceived risk and the higher the discount rate used in the project's cash flow projections. Because of its arbitrary nature, the discount rate may result in the rejection of possible initiatives and the acceptance of unfeasible proposals. Still, this technique is popular because it enables us to disregard political risk at first and forecast cash flows under the best case scenario (i.e., when no expropriation occurs), before then applying a discount rate that is scaled up to account for political risk towards the end of the projection.

The question of how to calculate the discount rate for emerging markets remains. Indeed, scholars argue that the simple CAPM method used for Western countries might not entirely capture the risks of other nations. Since many emerging markets show relatively low correlations with the global market, the standard CAPM procedure may lead to relatively low discount rates for emerging market investments, which strikes many practitioners and economists as counterintuitive. Emerging markets are not yet fully integrated with global capital markets, and therefore, it is possible that the CAPM does not capture all systematic risk factors, including political risk. One potential corrective might be to view political risk as a country-specific risk that can be diversified away by global investors. This would mean not adjusting the discount rate for pure political risk and instead only using business risk to augment the magnitude of the discount rate above the risk-free rate (Fox et al., 2017).

8.4.2   Adjusting estimated cash flows

The most effective way of adding different types of nation risk into a capital budgeting study is to predict how each kind of country risk will influence cash flows and, therefore, the net present value (NPV) of the project in question. The MNC can establish the probability distribution of net present values (NPVs) for the project by examining each conceivable effect. The choice to accept or reject the project will next be based on the company's evaluation of the probability that the project will create a positive NPV, as well as on the magnitude of the conceivable NPV outcomes, among other considerations (Fox et al., 2017).

8.4.3   Analysis of existing projects

MNCs should not only consider country risk when assessing new projects but also review this risk periodically after the project has been implemented. If a MNC has a subsidiary in a country experiencing adverse political conditions, it may need to reassess the feasibility of maintaining this subsidiary by considering various scenarios. MNCs commonly respond to adverse country risk conditions by restructuring their operations to reduce their exposure. Strategies such as selling a subsidiary can instead be difficult and costly.

8.5   Country risk analysis

The capital budgeting analysis discussed in the previous section requires information about political risk probabilities and alternative expropriation scenarios. Many organizations come up with ratings for most countries. Of course, the importance of these ratings is mainly dependent on the level of interaction and interconnection between the MNC and the specific country where it operates. For example, an MNC that establishes a foreign manufacturing plant to capitalize on cheap production costs and export the goods it produces there to other countries will be relatively less subject to local economic risk, because its customers are primarily outside the country. This example illustrates how ratings that do not distinguish between political and economic risk are not useful unless the MNC is equally subject to both hazards. Now, let's distinguish between these two types of risk.

8.5.1   Political risk analysis

Political risk analysis can be approached in a variety of ways. One of the first is the attribute technique. When studying political risk using this technique, numerous indicators need to be considered, including the following:

- political instability;
- ethnic and religious instability, as well as the strength of various ethnic or religious groupings;
- protection of property rights;
- the extent to which violence and armed insurrections occur;
- the degree to which xenophobia and nationalism exist.

These political indicators can be weighted and combined to produce a hypothetical political risk score. The weightings should be adjusted to account for the MNC's degree of involvement with the nation and the features particular to the instance at hand. While this technique may seem imprecise, it allows for comparisons of many nations using the same method for computing the final score.

Another approach is to examine the findings of the Political Risk Services Group (PRS), a New York-based firm that estimates the three administrations most likely to assume power in a given nation in the next five years. The more political instability a nation suffers, the more unreliable and vulnerable to change its PRS findings will be.

There are other ratings services to keep in mind. Institutional Investor provides a biennial country credit rating based on data from top world banks. The rating is based on a scale of 0 to 100, with 0 signifying nations with the lowest likelihood of default. A country's economic and financial outlook, financial reserves, debt payments, and current and trade account balances with other nations are the primary criteria used to assign credit ratings. Alternatively, Euromoney publishes an overall nation risk score based on nine weighted criteria, the two most significant of which are political risk and economic performance – both with a 30% weighting. The Economist Intelligence Unit (EIU) also provides a helpful indicator, which groups risk into four categories: political, economic policy, economic structure, and liquidity. It updates the indicator quarterly.

8.5.2   Economic risk analysis

According to Kirikkaleli (2020), experts have placed much emphasis on the fact that there is agreement regarding the detrimental effects of political instability on macroeconomic dynamics. Political uncertainty, on the one hand, alters kinds of investment, influences demand for components, and alters spending patterns – all of which have a direct impact on economic development. Economic development is expected to be harmed by drops in investment resulting from worsening political climates. Moreover, political uncertainty is viewed as an unfavorable situation for investors because it has a negative impact on economic performance. Because political uncertainty can shorten the life of a government, an unstable political environment narrows politicians' horizons, resulting in ineffective economic policies that harm the economy and financial sector. According to Kirikkaleli (2020), a number of recent studies have linked higher political conflict in the domestic market to slower economic development.

Economic risk assessment may seem simpler to implement than political risk assessment, since the latter is more difficult to predict and the former is based on the collection of objective economic facts. These facts can be grouped into economic and financial. Components of financial risk include foreign debt as a percentage of GDP, foreign debt service as a percentage of exports of goods, current account as a percentage of exports, net liquidity as months of import cover, and exchange rate stability. GDP per capita, real annual GDP growth, annual inflation rate, budget balance as a percentage of GDP, and current account balance as a percentage of GDP are all economic components. Clearly, financial risk is a proxy for a country's capacity to repay foreign debt, and it is heavily impacted by economic risk, which is a proxy for the host country's economic health.

8.5.3   Country credit rating

MNCs can also simply monitor, in a strategic way, the sovereign credit ratings that major international rating agencies assign to countries. In fact, Moody's, Standard & Poor's, and Fitch are increasingly rating sovereign bond issues to give an indication of the strength and reliability of the issuing country. Most developed countries are rated as investment grade, as are countries involved in the debt crisis (but not AAA). Most developing countries are instead considered unreliable (their debt is called junk debt), so they fall below the investment grade threshold.

Of course, sovereign defaults are not like corporate ones. There are no formal bankruptcy proceedings, and the consequences of defaulting influence relations among nations, since they imply serious difficulty in borrowing funds in the future. Countries that default will also find it complicated to engage in international trade. Lastly, defaults will only make the economic crisis worse, exacerbating capital flight and the response of banks. Still, the benefit of defaulting is that the debt service rules are modified, and potential deals may be struck to alleviate the debt burden, if not completely eliminate it. There are some protections for investors against the risk of countries becoming insolvent. Bilateral Investment Treaties (BITs[4]) serve exactly this purpose.

8.6   An excursus on the debt crisis

The 1980s debt crisis was one of the seminal historical events that established country risk analysis as a vital component of international banking and capital budgeting. Let us take a quick look at this historical episode and evaluate how it was handled. Afterwards, we will focus on two case studies that illustrate the implications of the crisis.

---

[4] "A bilateral investment treaty (BIT) is an agreement that specifies the terms and conditions for private investment in the territory of another state by persons and firms of one state. This is referred to as Foreign Direct Investment (FDI). Numerous BITs give a variety of protections to investors from one contracting state making an investment in the territory of the other, often including fair and impartial treatment, protection against expropriation, free transfer of means of production, and complete protection and security. Many of these agreements are notable in that they provide for an alternative dispute resolution mechanism in the event that an investor whose rights are protected by the BIT wishes to pursue international arbitration, frequently under the auspices of the International Center for the Resolution of Investment Disputes (ICSID, a World Bank organ), rather than proceeding to trial in the host state's court. There are now over 2,000 BITs in force, covering the majority of the world's nations. Capital-exporting governments often negotiate treaties under the same economic-legal paradigm as their own. The earliest of them goes all the way back to 1959, when Germany and Pakistan signed a treaty." See https://www.law.cornell.edu/wex/bilateral_investment_treaty

8.6.1   History of the debt crisis

Sovereign risk indicators during the Eurozone crisis of 2009-2013

The European debt crisis, often known as the eurozone crisis or the European sovereign debt crisis, is a multi-year financial crisis that has afflicted the European Union since the end of 2009. Several eurozone member countries (Greece, Portugal, Ireland, Spain, and Cyprus) were unable to repay or refinance their government debt or bail out over-indebted banks under national supervision without the assistance of third parties, such as other eurozone countries, the European Central Bank (ECB), or the International Monetary Fund (IMF).

As Gaillard (2020) has pointed out, Greece's newly elected Prime Minister, George Papandreou, sparked the Eurozone debt crisis in October 2009, when he raised the country's planned budget deficit to 12.5% – more than twice the prior prediction. Greek bond rates and credit default swaps surged in the months that followed, and the country's credit rating was lowered. A 110-billion-euro financial package was created to assist Greece in fulfilling its financial requirements in May 2010; this was part of a three-year program developed jointly by the European Monetary Union and the IMF. In June 2010, the European Financial Stability Facility (EFSF) was established to help two more countries: Ireland and Portugal (in 2010 and 2011 respectively). In 2012, Greece was bailed out once again. The European Stability Mechanism (ESM), which succeeded the EFSF in October 2012, bailed out Spain in 2012 and Cyprus in 2013.

As Gaillard (2020) mentions, the total foreign debt of oil-importing developing nations climbed to $436.9 billion between 1973 and 1981. This growth was fueled by the 1973 and 1979 oil crises, as well as the rise in worldwide interest rates that followed the 1979 shift in U.S. monetary policy. Although U.S. bank lending overseas had established specialized nation risk assessments in the late 1970s, they were unable to predict the 1982 debt crisis. The financial crisis began in August 1982, when Mexico's Treasury Secretary informed the country's international creditors that the government would stop principal payments on its debt.

For a long period after World War II, crude oil was the center of the economic system. Despite recent environmental protests, it continues to play an important role in many developments in the world economy.

The Organization of Petroleum Exporting Countries (OPEC) was established in 1960 to prohibit crude oil speculation and control its price. OPEC cut production in 1973, sending oil prices from $3.00 per barrel to more than $12.00 per barrel by the end of 1974. In the years that followed, developments in Iran and Iraq triggered another round of crude oil price hikes, with prices finally hitting $35.00 per barrel in 1981. When adjusted for inflation, this meant that oil prices hit $85.00 per barrel in 2010 dollars.

How did the surge in demand from oil-producing nations result in a debt problem in most industrialized countries? OPEC countries started making loans to international banks with the extra money they were earning from the escalated demand for crude oil and consequent skyrocketing prices. The banks in turn loaned what were called *petrodollars* to developing countries. This worked in the aftermath of the oil shock in 1973, when inflation was high and there were low interest rates and booming economies. However, as soon as the situation pivoted in the aftermath of the oil shock of 1979, these conditions were completely upended: inflation fell, interest rates soared, and economies started recessing. This new scenario led to a rise in real debt and a drop in overall exports – both trends which were unsustainable for developing countries, making them insolvent.

Banks had previously considered petrodollar loans attractive and virtually risk-free for three reasons. To start, the loans were issued at a premium above the banks' borrowing rates. Banks were therefore not exposed to interest rate risk. Second, since both deposits and loans were in dollars, the banks had no currency risk. Third, the loans were syndicated by the banks themselves. This resulted in banks in the developed world owning an exponential amount of non-OPEC developing nation debt by the end of the 1970s. External shocks to the industrialized world, as well as macro-economic mismanagement in the developing world in the early 1980s, sparked the debt crisis. Ironically, however, the debt crisis actually started in Mexico, an oil-exporting country.

The Organization of Petroleum Exporting Countries (OPEC)

Essentially an economic cartel, OPEC was created in 1960 when thirteen countries banded together to negotiate elements of oil production, pricing, and concessions with oil firms. On September 1, 1965, OPEC's headquarters were relocated from Geneva to Vienna. OPEC member countries possess about 79% of the world's proven oil reserves and approximately 35% of the world's natural gas reserves; they contribute 39% of the world's oil output and approximately 16% of the world's natural gas production. OPEC was formed as a reaction by crude-oil-producing nations to the economic domination of foreign oil firms, mostly Anglo-American, which had exerted near total control over the production chain from the 1920s through the 1940s thanks to a series of extraction concessions (reserves, extraction, refining, marketing). In 1928, the world's main oil firms signed an agreement in Achnacarry to form a cartel, with the goal of defining extraction zones and crude oil sales prices and prevent competition among the businesses themselves. Between the end of the 1940s and the beginning of the 1960s, these companies, known as the "seven sisters" – a term coined by Italian Enrico Mattei, a manager of Agip – came to control almost all Middle Eastern oil, unilaterally defining extraction quotas and prices. To minimize unfavorable price swings and maintain profits, the seven sisters often set extraction limits lower than their full production capacities, with clear repercussions for their income. It is worth noting that oil exports historically constituted, and continue to represent, almost the entire export production of several oil-producing nations, particularly those in the Persian Gulf.

8.6.2 Managing the debt crisis

At the start of the debt crisis, banks misunderstood this liquidity crisis; they wagered that developing nations would be only temporarily unable to repay their loans and that the economic situation would soon improve. They negotiated for debt rescheduling and granted fresh credit. By 1987, it had become evident that the banks would not be fully repaid. Many governments began implementing debt-reduction measures. Debt buybacks and debt-equity swaps became popular, owing to an active secondary market for developing national debt. Several of the debt-relief accords struck during the financial crisis included development assistance for impoverished nations.

In 1989, the Brady Plan, devised by then-U.S. Treasury Secretary Nicholas Brady, compelled banks to grant developing nations some type of debt relief. They ultimately decided to securitize the debt by issuing readily marketable bonds known as Brady bonds.[5] For many nations, the Brady bond market quickly supplanted the secondary bank loan market, fostering the growth of a vibrant bond market.

Case Dollarization as a solution to reduce sovereign risk

Following the two 1970s oil shocks, several Latin American countries had financial problems that required assistance from foreign financial institutions. In the early 1980s, the U.S. Treasury took the lead in bailing out these nations by assisting them in issuing so-called Brady bonds. Latin America, on the other hand, did not see the degree of recovery anticipated or the economic success achieved by other nations during that decade.

Latin America followed Chile's lead in the early 1990s and adopted neoliberal policies. This policy package included the privatization of governmental firms, the elimination of trade obstacles, and capital account liberalization. Capital flows increased rapidly because of such financial market deregulation, and the possibility of an "unexpected inflation" created an element of financial fragility that manifested itself in the mid-to-late 1990s.

One of the main characteristics of the crisis in Latin America in the second half of the 1990s was the public's flight from their native currency in search of the inflation protection offered by a stronger currency, the dollar. This approach, however, presented a conundrum for macroeconomic policymakers across Latin America. As demand for local currency fell below supply, the danger of devaluation grew, and monetary policy became ineffective. In the late 1990s, several academics and politicians argued that abolishing their own currency and replacing it with the U.S. dollar as legal tender would alleviate Latin America's monetary volatility and impose a solution to the region's chronic fiscal imbalance. Among the promises attributed to dollarization were the lowering of sovereign risk associated with developing country debt. This would result in a reduction in the cost of financing economic expansion. However, Ecuador's history demonstrates that dollarization has not had a significant influence on decreasing sovereign risk, which is a critical issue given the critical role sovereign risk plays in determining finance costs and real economic cycles. Determining the factors that influence sovereign risk and financial cost may aid in developing future policy prescriptions, particularly regarding exchange rates and dollarization in nations such as Ecuador.

Source: Pierre, J. & Rhodd, R. (2008). Sovereign Risk and Dollarization: The Case of Ecuador. International Trade and Finance Association, International Trade and Finance Association Conference Papers.

---

[5] Along with the Brady Plan, in July 1989 the World Bank launched an Expanded Co-financing Operations initiative. ECOs were established to aid borrowers in getting or expanding access to foreign capital markets, particularly via private placements and public bond offerings. Credit improvements available via the ECO program might take the following forms: commercial loan guarantees in the context of funding World Bank-approved projects; guarantees in connection with medium- and long-term debt issuance; contingent liabilities, such as bond issuances, with a specified option to "put" them to the World Bank; and assistance with limited recourse project financing.

Case Asian contagion 1997-98

The Asian crisis started as a currency crisis in July 1997, when Bangkok decoupled the Thai baht from the U.S. dollar, precipitating a series of currency devaluations and major capital flight. Between 1985 and 1995, Thailand's currency was tied to a basket of currencies led by the U.S. dollar. By 1997, Thailand's economy was running a current account deficit, experiencing poor consumer demand, and experiencing high inflation. The banking industry attempted to rehabilitate the economy by borrowing cheaply from overseas and lending at a higher rate locally, believing that the fixed exchange rate would shield it from danger.[6] Excessive speculation finally resulted in the baht's overvaluation. When the government's ability to sustain the baht ceased, the currency was free to float.[7]

The Indonesian rupiah's value plummeted by 80% in the first six months, the Thai baht fell by more than 50%, the South Korean won dropped by about 50%, and the Malaysian ringgit decreased by 45%. Capital inflows into the hardest-hit countries fell by more than $100 billion in the first year of the crisis. The Asian financial crisis, which was significant in both scale and breadth, became a worldwide catastrophe when it expanded to the Russian and Brazilian economies.

The crisis' rapid spread was precipitated by a series of unfortunate convergences: a sharp decline in global commodity prices, exacerbated by declining growth and demand in much of Asia; political instability in key countries such as Japan and Russia; doubts about the IMF's ability to act; and the global spread of financial panic. Exchange rates unfairly pegged to the dollar, current account deficits, very frail and poorly monitored banking institutions, and real estate speculation were all warning indicators. Western and Japanese financial firms panicked after years of seeing Asia as a potential area of prospective development. No one predicted the magnitude of the collapse catalyzed by the Thai currency devaluation. Banks were caught off guard, because they fundamentally misjudged political risk in some countries and placed too much emphasis on the former Asian economic "miracle" – relying too much on ratings and failing to comprehend the opacity of financial markets.

The last two cases exemplify that the consequences of poor country risk analysis are enormous. It is crucial to realize that globalization has forever changed the world, creating more volatility and risk. In this new context, transparency and disclosure are critical, as are greater awareness of political linkages and improved regulations.

8.7   Conclusions

In this chapter we analyzed the impact that country risk and economics risk might have on MNC. Country risk might vary from strike to political disorders to government takeovers. The MNC can adopt different strategies, as seen in the chapter, to mitigate the risk. The wide variety of model used to measure this risk are based on political, economic, and financial analysis. The most impacting one is probably polit-

---

[6] For more information see https://www.britannica.com/event/Asian-financial-crisis
[7] Rajshekar, N. & Bhavika, N. (2004). *The 1997 Devaluation of the Thai Baht and After*. IBS Case Development Center. Available at https://www.thecasecentre.org/products/view?id=19362#

ical risk, which includes change of regulations and laws. Political risk covers a broad range of factors such as trade sanctions to foreign countries, bureaucracy, lack of restriction and corruption. The MNC can adopt two different approaches to mitigate these risks: integrated strategy and protective strategy. In the financial risk analysis MNC should consider, using different indicators, the ability of a country to generate inflows of foreign exchange. The indicators, might include the level of debt to GDP, the deficit as well as inflation and real economic growth. Both political and economic risk should be taken into account in the capital budgeting. Finally, to better assimilate these two concepts we have deepened the debt crisis.

9 Exchange Rate Risk Management

Engaging in international and overseas operations represents a huge source of profits for MNCs, but it may come at a cost. As we saw in previous chapters, the number and degree of risks a company faces in foreign countries can be larger than in its own. This chapter will deal with one of the most salient risks that MNCs face abroad, namely exchange rate risk. The first part will review the politics of exchange rates and different types of exchange rate arrangements from a historical perspective. Next, we will focus on exposure to exchange rate fluctuations and the ways that companies can hedge against them. We will also dive deeper into the different types of exposure, techniques for protecting against it, and the main factors influencing these techniques as well as how companies can create well-designed risk management frameworks. We will then discuss the forecasting of exchange rates, including the motivations behind this practice, techniques, and common mistakes. Finally, we will consider the case of Kering, a French luxury group, to illustrate some of the notions addressed in the chapter and how they play out in practice.

9.1 Exchange rate policy

The currency and exchange rate policies implemented in each country have a significant impact on the global economy. The economic activity of each country is also influenced by the policies established by other governments. Government policies represent domestic as well as foreign interests and directly or indirectly affect exchange rates.

Given their critical influence and role, currency policies can lead to the emergence of tensions both between and within developed countries. One famous example is the creation of a single European currency in 1999,[1] which aimed to regulate the currencies of each European member state. Other initiatives implemented by governments of developing countries include tying currency to the dollar or letting

---

[1] The euro was introduced on January 1, 1999, after a decade of preparations; for the first three years, it was an "invisible" currency, used solely for accounting and electronic payments. On January 1, 2002, coins and banknotes were introduced, and the largest cash switchover in history occurred in 12 EU countries. For more information see https://european-union.europa.eu/institutions-law-budget/euro/history-and-purpose_en

it float freely. In general, governments choose strategies with the objective to keep their currencies relatively weak in order to boost their own exports and economic growth. Summaries of the key types of exchange rate structures are listed below.

The Russian ruble's recent history under several exchange rate regimes

A floating exchange rate system is one in which the forex market determines the price of a country's currency based on supply and demand in comparison to other currencies. By contrast, fixed or pegged exchange rates are systems in which a monetary authority publishes rates for buying and selling a currency in terms of a foreign one and commits to trading in limitless quantities at that rate. While the purchasing and selling rates shall in theory be the same, they vary in the majority of systems, creating (typically small) ranges within which even "fixed" exchange rates may fluctuate.

Throughout history, nations used a variety of approaches to currency exchange. The recent history of the Russian ruble is particularly illuminating. As Sohag (2021) notes, Russian paper money is currently produced by the Moscow-based Goznak State Company, which was founded on June 6, 1919. The coins are struck in the Monetnyj Dvor mint in St. Petersburg, which has been in operation since 1724, and in Moscow. Russia has seen significant currency fluctuations since 1991, when it adopted a market economy. Specifically, between 1992 and 1995, the currency rate fluctuated between RUB 125 per USD to around RUB 5,000, accompanied by severe levels of inflation. Russia adopted a fixed currency rate in 1995, which minimized exchange rate volatility until 1998, when the Central Bank implemented a redenomination scheme, converting RUB 1,000 to RUB 1. As a result, the exchange rate versus the dollar fell from 5,900 to 5.90. Russia adopted a controlled floating exchange rate system in 1998. The rate remained relatively stable at around RUB 30 per USD until 2014, when the country was hit by international economic sanctions in response to its activities in Crimea and Ukraine. This prompted the country to switch to a fully floating exchange rate system, which, combined with the collapse of oil prices, pushed the rate to around RUB 60 per USD.

Finally, as the author states, the ruble was devalued in 2016 because of continued decline in international oil prices and in 2020, during the global Covid-19 pandemic, the exchange rate increased slightly before collapsing following the outbreak of war in Ukraine in February 2022, when the ruble dropped nearly 40% with respect to its November 2021 value (0.0144) in relation to the dollar.

Source: Sohag, K., Gainetdinova, A., & Mariev, O. (2021). *The reaction of currency rates to economic policy uncertainty: Evidence from Russia*. Borsa Istanbul Review, 22(1). https://doi.org/10.1016/j.bir.2021.07.002

Fixed exchange rates

In *Principles of International Finance and Open Economy Macroeconomics* (2015), Cristina Terra[2] defines fixed exchange rates as follows: "The exchange rate ceases to fluctuate with respect to the reference currency in fixed exchange rate or currency board regimes." What the author wants to highlight is the fact that, when a country accepts a fixed exchange rate regime, it abandons its monetary policy autonomy,

---

[2] Terra, C. (2015). Exchange Rate Regimes. In *Principles of International Finance and Open Economy Macroeconomics* (pp. 265-295). Academic Press.

since this will be decided by the country to which the national currency is tied. However, this does not happen within a monetary union. As Terra (2015) says, "When a set of nations adopts a single currency, a common central bank is formed and decision-making rules are developed that take into account the interests of each member of the union." A similar definition of fixed exchange rates is provided in *International Money and Finance* (2017), by Michael Melvin and Stefan Norrbin.[3] According to them, "With fixed exchange rates, the national central bank loses its independence from the rest of the world regarding monetary policy. If domestic and international assets are perfect substitutes, they must provide investors with the same rate of return. It is clear that central banks cannot undertake an independent monetary policy with fixed exchange rates." A fixed exchange rate system is therefore similar to a gold standard, where all currencies are fixed to another currency, like the dollar, and exchange rates are set previously against such currency and then against all the others. It is immediate to notice that such structure obliges each nation to follow the monetary policy of the major currency, to maintain stable levels of inflations and exchange rates (Melvin & Norrbin, 2017). Finally, a different approach is taken by Victor A. Canto and Andy Wiese in *Economic Disturbances and Equilibrium in an Integrated Global Economy* (2018).[4] They define exchange rates in terms of Purchasing Power Parity (PPP), according to which "Under a fixed exchange rate regime, the inflation rate for traded goods will converge across nations. Because the exchange rate is constant and inflation rates tend to converge, the impact of terms of trade, i.e., the relative change in prices of non-traded items relative to traded goods, results in deviations from the PPP rate in the national inflation rate." In a fixed exchange system, the price of one currency is expressed in terms of another one. This means that in theory, because exchange rates are fixed, there should be an equivalence between the units of different currencies and therefore individuals shall be able to exchange as many units of a country's currency as they want (Canto & Wiese, 2018).

To sum up, a fixed exchange rate is thus a regime in which rates are kept stable or at most allowed to fluctuate within a very narrow band. The Bretton Woods Agreement (1944-1971) is an example of a fixed exchange rate system. Under this system, the values of all currencies were tied to the price of gold (Eiteman et al., 2013).

There are obviously many advantages related to the use of fixed exchange rates, especially reduction in the volatility of exchange rates, which lowers risk and encourages investment. In fact, with reduced uncertainty regarding exchange rates fluctuations, multinational firms can set up FDIs without needing to worry about expected future rates. Those direct investments will also benefit local businesses, opening them to additional revenue sources and enabling them to collect significant amounts of capital.

---

[3] Melvin, M. & Norrbin, S. (2017). The IS-LM-BP Approach. In M. Melvin & S. Norrbin (eds.), *International Money and Finance* (9th ed., pp. 251-275). Academic Press.

[4] Canto, V.A., & Wiese, A. (2018). Examining China: Purchasing Power Parity, Terms of Trade, and Real Exchange Rates. In V.A. Canto & A. Wiese (eds.), *Economic Disturbances and Equilibrium in an Integrated Global Economy* (pp. 387-391). Academic Press.

However, if a country's currency is fixed, its economy will be highly dependent on the government measures taken to preserve the value of the currency. Foreign investors could raise doubts about the quality of the currency if the local central bank keeps intervening in the foreign exchange market. Moreover, a fixed exchange rate system is extremely costly for a government, because it has to guarantee sufficient foreign exchange reserves to maintain such a policy.

Floating exchange rates

In *Economic Disturbances and Equilibrium in a Globalized Economy* (2018), Victor A. Canto and Andy Wiese explain floating exchange rates in the following way: "A trade deficit in a floating exchange rate system entails an inflow of capital or borrowing from one's international trading partners. For wealthy countries, experts fear that a trade imbalance indicates that a country is living above its means and has passed its prime. If that is the true, we should expect the market to anticipate this and decline in value relative to the rest of the world if the trade balance deteriorates. The implication is clear: it forecasts a positive association between the trade deficit and the stock market, as well as the rate of real GDP growth relative to the rest of the globe. Governments and central banks do not participate in the foreign exchange market in a free exchange rate system. The link between governments and central banks and foreign exchange markets, on the one hand, and stock markets, on the other, is strikingly similar. Governments may control stock markets to avoid fraud, but stock prices are let to float freely in the market."

As the name implies, floating exchange rates are characteristic of systems in which the value of a country's currency fluctuates in reaction to market factors. As a result, the exchange rate is governed by the relative supply and demand of other currencies. Their worth is thus not constant but fluctuates over time. However, we have to bear in mind that a totally floating exchange rate system is a purely theoretical concept. In practice, all governments and central banks intervene in some small ways in foreign exchange markets in an attempt to influence currency exchange rates. Being a self-regulating system is an advantage of a free-floating system. For instance, if a significant shift in global tastes results in a significant increase in demand for goods and services produced in the United States, this would increase demand for U.S. dollars, raise the U.S. exchange rate, and increase the cost of purchasing U.S. products and services for foreigners. A rising currency rate would then absorb some of the impact of shifting international demand.

The primary disadvantage of floating exchange rates is their unpredictable nature. Contracts between buyers and sellers in various countries must account not only for possible price and other changes throughout the duration of the contract but also for the possibility of currency exchange rate fluctuations. This system is diametrically opposed to the fixed exchange rate system in that the government is prohibited from intervening in the market since its currency is supposed to float freely. However, central banks may intervene on rare occasions to accomplish certain objectives, such as raising or lowering exchange rates through the purchase or sale of their currencies. Typically, the purpose of such intervention is to avoid big, abrupt changes in the value of a nation's currency, possibly by sale of the currency by the central bank to increase the supply of the currency and maintain a low exchange rate.[5] Floating exchange rates offer the following benefits:[6]

1. *Self-stabilization*: Any balance of payments mismatch would be immediately rectified through a change in the exchange rate. For instance, if a country's balance of payments is in deficit, then, all other factors being equal, the country's currency should devalue.
2. *Domestic Policy Announcement*: A country's balance of payments deficit can be remedied in a floating exchange rate system by adjusting the currency's price. Reduced deficits in countries with fixed exchange rate policies may result in broad deflationary policies for their economies with unfavorable implications, such as unemployment and excess capacity.
3. *Elimination of crises*: Central banks that devalue a currency by releasing insufficient amounts of it in exchange for other currencies will quickly find themselves inundated by those currencies due to the relatively large amounts they receive. Such changes occur automatically in a floating exchange rate system. The danger of an international monetary crises caused by exchange rate fluctuations are therefore addressed automatically.
4. *Defending Against Inflation*: If a country maintains a stable exchange rate, inflation is "imported" via increasing import prices. A country with a payment surplus and a stable exchange rate is more likely to 'import' inflation from countries with deficits.
5. *Reserves are diminished*: Flexible exchange rates should eliminate the need for substantial reserves to support economic development. These reserves can then be used to import capital goods and other commodities that will help the economy grow quicker.

The following are the major drawbacks of floating exchange rates:

1. *Insufficient investment*: Foreign direct investment (i.e., investment by multinational companies) may be discouraged by the uncertainty created by shifting currency rates.
2. *Speculation*: Daily currency changes might stimulate speculative flows of 'hot money' between countries, resulting in an increasing number of currency fluctuations.
3. *Indulgence*: Exchange rate stability exerts discipline on the domestic economy. It is possible that with a fluctuating currency rate, short-term concerns such as domestic inflation will be overlooked until they develop into crises.

---

[5] For more information see https://open.lib.umn.edu/principleseconomics/chapter/30-3-exchange-rate-systems/

[6] See also https://www.economicsdiscussion.net/international-trade/finance/floating-exchange-rates-advantages-and-disadvantages-currencies/26267

4. *Uncertainty*: As Butler (2012) notes, the primary disadvantage of a floating exchange rate system is that, because rates fluctuate continuously, forecasting how much a future flow of money in a foreign currency will be worth in the domestic currency is difficult unless market participants hedge their foreign exchange risk exposures through financial instruments (forwards, futures, options, and currency swaps).

A floating exchange rate system was established in 1971, following the major oil crisis of the 1970s, since IMF leaders were convinced that floating rates would enable most countries to better adapt to fluctuations in oil prices (IMF, 1999). Despite initial fears, the end of the Bretton Woods Agreement did not negatively impact the market, and the transition towards a floating system was relatively smooth and natural.

To summarize, the advantages of floating exchange rate regimes include better protection from other countries' macroeconomic shocks, such as unemployment and inflation. However, a floating system may be counterproductive if the country itself is experiencing those problems since it may be difficult for it to recover. A second advantage is the limited intervention of central banks in floating systems since exchange rates are determined only by the market. Government policies can therefore be implemented without needing to consider their impact on exchange rates. However, one major drawback of a floating exchange rate system is increased uncertainty regarding the value of a currency, especially in the short-term (Evrensel, 2020).

Pegged exchange rates

A pegged exchange rate system is a particular type of fixed exchange rate regime in which the value of a currency is tied to a single foreign currency or to a combination of foreign currencies. Pegged currencies are therefore not fixed but fluctuate in accordance with one or more other currencies. Countries usually peg their currencies to those of stronger or more advanced economies so that domestic businesses can enter larger markets with less volatility (Banton, 2020). Today, approximately one-fourth of all countries have their currencies pegged to some other major currency, such as the U.S. dollar or the euro (Juneja, 2020).

This practice had gained popularity since the dissolution of the end of Bretton Woods system. For instance, China decided to link its national currency, the yuan, to the U.S. dollar from 1996 to 2005. However, since 2005 its currency is no longer pegged and has been allowed to fluctuate within narrow boundaries. Several governments assume that China's central bank deliberately maintains a low yuan value to boost exports. Another country that adopted the pegged rate system is Venezuela, which has traditionally tied its bolivar to the U.S. dollar. Also in this case, occasional adjustments were made by the government to weaken the currency value in order to incentivize exports.

As with fixed and floating rates, a pegged exchange rate system has advantages and disadvantages. These regimes are often linked to a reduction in the degree of currency volatility, thus improving the country's economic and political conditions.

In fact, since local firms know the future prices of their goods on these local markets, they can easily predict demand and consequently adjust their supply needs. Additionally, pegged exchange rates can be used by local governments to increase the stability of their own currencies or as a tool to stabilize cross-border financial flows (Butler, 2012). Since the U.S. dollar is typically viewed as one of the most stable currencies, pegging to it often makes other currencies look more resilient. In these cases, local monetary policy also benefits from an increased level of trustworthiness by adopting pegged rates. This may occur because local authorities, especially in developing countries, are not considered reliable in implementing monetary policies, so outsourcing their policies to more developed nations through a pegged system may seem a more rational decision.

In terms of potential drawbacks, it is important to note the higher amount of foreign meddling that local governments with pegged currencies are subject to, since their monetary policies are largely influenced by those of the foreign country. Maintaining a fixed currency rate is also difficult for a central bank, especially if the country is suffering economic or political hardships. Indeed, in such situations, the central bank will have to continuously intervene in the foreign exchange market to protect its currency, and most multinationals and international investors may withdraw funds from the country out of fear that the peg will collapse. On the other hand, a floating currency system causes deficits to be automatically adjusted. For example, if a country imports excessively, it will be forced to pay a high price. This will result in a reduction in its money supply, resulting in deflation. Low prices result from deflation, and these low prices will make the country's exports competitive. As a result, an increase in imports will lead to an increase in exports! Free-floating systems tend to reach equilibrium. Currency pegs instead tend to worsen imbalances. Moreover, speculative attacks on a currency are only possible when it deviates too far from its intrinsic worth. Free-floating currencies do not stray far from their intrinsic worth. The market mechanism is initiated as soon as there is a divergence, and the correction occurs instantly. Currency pegs, on the other hand, might allow for a significant disparity between a currency's inherent worth and its market value.

9.2 Foreign exchange risk management

Before discussing the various foreign exchange risk exposures and how to manage them, we will review some studies on the benefits and drawbacks of hedging.

The cash flows o MNCs are undeniably affected by and sensitive to exchange rates and thus face currency risk. As a result, many businesses attempt to control currency fluctuations and risks through hedging procedures that protect the owner of a hedging asset or instrument against loss. Hedging requires the corporation to take a position (i.e., an asset, contract, or derivative) whose value will increase or fall in the opposite direction of the present position's value change (i.e., the exposure). Hedging can help businesses mitigate currency risk and cash flow volatility, but not without a cost.

9.2.1   Theories of hedging

There is no unequivocal agreement in the literature on whether currency risk should be managed or not by hedging against changes in exchange rates. There are several arguments for and against hedging (Dufey et al., 1983). All relate to the corporate management of currency risk. The consensus seems to be that there is no need to manage currency risk in an efficient currency market if the requirements of purchasing power parity, interest rate parity, and the international Fisher effect are met. When one or more of these international parity conditions are violated, firms face foreign exchange risk. As we discuss later in the chapter, this risk can affect transaction gains or losses, the economic value of a firm or project, or the consolidated accounts of multinationals, resulting in three types of foreign exchange exposure: transaction exposure, economic exposure, and accounting or translation exposure (Wang, 2020).

Dufey et al. (1983) in their study advance a very interesting picture of the need to hedge against foreign exchange risk underscored by the following statement, from which it is clear that such need is overestimated. According to them, "Foreign exchange risk does not exist; even if it did, firms should not hedge it." In support of their reasoning, the authors refer to a series of arguments which are particularly explanatory and among which we would like to highlight the Purchasing Power Parity Theory, the Capital Price Model, the Modigliani and Miller Theory.

The Purchasing Power Parity (PPP) Theory states that exposure to exchange rate risk should be zero, since exchange rate fluctuations are offset by price movements, resulting in zero sensitivity to exchange rate risk. However, the theory is too simplistic and does not take into account some relevant factors. Indeed, even if PPP is true, a particular firm may still be exposed to exchange rate risk because its input and output prices may change. Moreover, adjustments to changes in prices and exchange rates occur with a time lag – they are not immediate as PPP theory claims. Thus, the empirical validity of PPP increases the longer the time horizon. In shorter time periods, the firm is subject to exchange rate variability. Consequently, corporate managers should prepare for deviations from short-term PPP while planning long-term operating strategies.

According to the Capital Asset Pricing Model (CAPM), the only risk to consider is systematic risk, as it is not diversifiable. Companies can go to the foreign exchange or capital markets to hedge foreign exchange risk. What companies need to consider are the financial distress costs they may incur in the event of large shifts in exchange rates. Hedging currency exposure can be a good option to reduce the risk of default.

For Modigliani and Miller, hedging for the individual investor is much more effective than hedging activities pursued at the firm level. This is because market risk management can be easily handled by individual investors. However, while investors may face many barriers to their hedging activities, firms usually get good deals, especially because management can leverage its low-cost access to acquire inside information.

Through the proposed keys, the objective of the study by Dufey et al. (1983) was thus to identify various perspectives to understand the relevance or otherwise of foreign exchange management at the firm level.

9.2.2   The pros and cons of hedging

To summarize then, the views on hedging listed above represent an interesting starting point for many arguments made by proponents and opponents of hedging techniques. The question that many academics and practitioners have tried to answer is whether mitigating the risk of cash flow variability is a sufficient reason for managing currency risk. Eiteman (2013) provides a useful overview of the pros and cons of hedging techniques. On the one hand, hedging can help a company lower the risk posed by fluctuations in future cash flows, allowing it to better estimate future earnings and prospective investment activities, as well as prevent financial difficulties by ensuring that it can always meet its debt service obligations. Hedging gives management a competitive advantage over shareholders in terms of understanding the company's real and actual currency risks, as well as recognizing market disequilibrium and capitalizing on opportunities to create value through selective hedging (i.e., hedging only exceptional exposures).

On the other hand, hedging also makes it easier for shareholders to diversify currency risk in relation to business operations and according to their own risk preferences. Hedging is thus seen as a mechanism that burns corporate resources and reduces cash flows, ultimately producing agency risk and implying that management may participate in hedging transactions for its own gain and at the expense of shareholders. Moreover, efficient market theorists think that investors can see through the "accounting curtain" and thus they have already included the impact of foreign exchange in the market price of the company. In this perspective, hedging is therefore only an extra expense.

9.3   Exposure to exchange risk fluctuations: types and measurements

Having looked at a wide range of arguments for and against hedging, it is now the time to explore different types of exposure and the techniques that can be used to hedge against them. Exchange rates cannot be forecasted with perfect accuracy, but the firm can at least measure its exposure to exchange rate fluctuations. If the firm is highly exposed to such fluctuations, it can consider techniques to reduce this exposure. Measuring its degree of exposure is crucial to deciding which technique to use.

Figure 9.1 provides a brief overview of the main types of exposure.

Figure 9.1   Main types of foreign exchange exposure

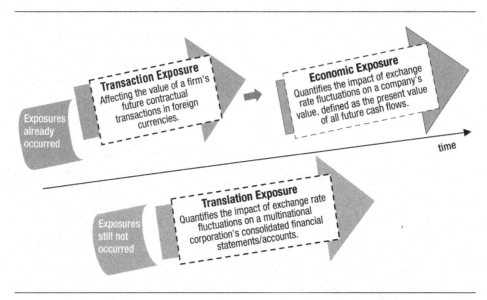

9.3.1   Transaction exposure

Fluctuations in exchange rates are one important factor affecting the value of a firm's future contractual transactions in foreign currencies. Transaction exposure defines the sensitivity of those transactions to exchange rate movements. García (2017) defines transaction exposure as the potential for a change in profit, or in other words, the risk associated with a change in the exchange rate that may occur during a transaction (often an international transaction). This perspective takes into consideration only the foreign currency risk associated with a given transaction. Put differently, transaction exposure measures potential adjustments in future cash flows resulting from existing financial commitments that have been incurred but were not settled prior to the exchange rate fluctuation. The settlement of these commitments can cause a gain or a loss to the firm because of the currency fluctuations. Indeed, transaction exposure is the most visible way that most multinationals are vulnerable to exchange rate risk. Transaction risk usually arises from activities such as importing or exporting and borrowing or investing, which generate payables or receivables in foreign currencies from customers of suppliers.

Wang (2020) explains that cash flows denominated in a foreign currency may be classified into two types: cash inflows or receivables and cash outflows or payables. In the first case, cash flows denominated in a foreign currency are received and converted into the domestic currency, and there is thus uncertainty about the value of the cash flows as measured in the domestic currency – but no uncertainty about their value as measured in the foreign currency. In the second case, there is ambiguity regarding the number of local currency units required to pay for a given, fixed number of foreign currency units. Because of exchange rate fluctuations, a corporation may pay more or less in home currency in a transaction that involves a foreign currency. Both cash inflows and cash outflows represent examples of transaction exposure. **Figure 9.2** provides an example the various timeframes that make up transaction exposure. Indeed, a transaction exposure (also known as *quotation exposure*) is established the instant (t₁) that a seller proposes a price in a foreign currency to a potential buyer. As soon as the buyer places the order (t₂), the potential quotation exposure is converted into an actual exposure (usually called *backlog exposure* to capture the fact that the product has not yet been delivered or billed). At the time of shipping and billing (t₃), the exposure now becomes a *billing exposure* until the moment of payment to the seller.

Figure 9.2   The lifespan of a transaction exposure

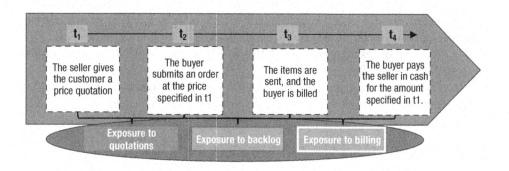

To assess transaction exposure, the MNC needs to estimate its net cash flows in each currency and measure the potential impact of the currency exposure. To do so, the MNC must prepare a projection of the consolidated net amount in currency inflows and outflows for each of its subsidiaries.

The further into the future a multinational company attempts to measure its transaction exposure, the less accurate the measurement will be due to the greater uncertainty regarding inflows or outflows in each foreign currency, as well as future exchange rates. The firm's overall exposure can be assessed only after considering each currency's variability and the correlations among currencies.

There are different ways to measure a firm's exposure. On the one hand, we can use the *standard deviation* of the portfolio, which indicates how much its value may deviate from the expectation. For instance, if a multinational will receive payments in two foreign currencies, the standard deviation of the monthly percentage changes of a two-currency portfolio could be a reasonable proxy of its risk. As a measure of exchange rate volatility, empirical researchers very often use the standard deviation of the moving average of the logarithm of the exchange rate. Tsounis & Serenis (2012) found that, for a sample of E.U. nations, exchange rate volatility had a minor influence on the volume of exports when it was assessed as the simple standard deviation of the log of the exchange rate. However, when other metrics that capture the impacts of high and low exchange rate values are utilized, there is evidence of a

bigger influence from exchange rate swings on the amount of exports. As a consequence, they discovered an overall statistically significant link showing a negative
relationship between sectoral exports and exchange rate volatility.

Another method of determining a firm's risk exposure is through value at risk
(VAR). As Garcia (2017) notes, VAR can be defined as a measure of the maximum
conceivable change in the value of a portfolio over a certain period of time and
with a specified probability, in this case a probability that depends on changes in
exchange rates. Exchange rate dynamics follow the same logic as stock prices, in
that today's price incorporates all available market information and thus provides the
most accurate projection for the future value. Tomorrow's price is therefore today's
price plus a little noise to account for any new information that enters the market
between now and tomorrow. As with many macroeconomic variables, the exchange
rate occasionally experiences what is called a structural change. This occurs when a
country's currency is devalued due to a crisis or for some other reasons, causing an
abrupt change in the exchange rate quotation that is not consistent with the dynamics
observed up to that point.

In general, the VAR can then be used to estimate the maximum one-day loss that
a global company could suffer due to exchange rate fluctuations.

9.3.2   Economic exposure

Considering all a company's activities, as well as its geographic location and the currency in which its
exposures are denominated, García (2017) suggests estimating its economic exposure to the exchange
rate in terms of impact on revenue, gross profit or gross income, and the relative risk associated with the
exchange rate fluctuations. Exchange rate movements can thus have a substantial impact on the value
of a company's cash flows if it has established transactions in foreign currencies (such as revenue from
foreign customers) or if it faces competition from foreign companies. The economic exposure of any
company depends on its functional structure and competitive environment. The functional (or organizational) structure of a company governs how the company is managed and thus how it functions globally.
This structure reaches increasing levels of complexity as the company becomes more international, with
the need to manage transfers of cash flows, revenues, taxes, and liabilities denominated in a variety of
different currencies. The company's competitive environment, on the other hand, is constituted by the
dynamics of its product markets and the reactions of its competitors to exchange rate movements. The
sensitivity of a company's cash flows to unexpected changes in exchange rates is also referred to as
operational or strategic and competitive exposure.

Economic exposure quantifies the impact of exchange rate fluctuations on a
company's value, which is defined as the present value of all future cash flows.
Economic exposure management refers to the process of seeking to contain and
mitigate the negative impact of exchange rate fluctuations on a company's value.
Transaction exposure is therefore a subset of economic exposure. The most common international business transactions to create transactional and economic exposure to foreign exchange risk for multinational companies are foreign currency exports and imports, interest received from foreign investments, and interest due on
foreign loans.

Wang (2020) explains that changes or fluctuations in exchange rates thus influence the cash/value flows of both foreign and domestic firms. Economic exposure to foreign competition in domestic and local markets can affect a firm's value, even if it is exclusively domestic. When the domestic currency appreciates, foreign goods become cheaper and more competitive, causing a firm's domestic sales to decline in the domestic market, where domestic goods compete with imported foreign goods. This reduces the domestic firm's cash flows. When the domestic currency depreciates, foreign goods become more expensive and less competitive, resulting in an increase in the firm's domestic sales and cash flows in the domestic market, since its local goods become more competitive than imported foreign goods. Changes in the relative value of a currency will have a comparable effect on a firm's foreign sales.

By contrast, international firms with a higher proportion of international costs to foreign revenues will be negatively affected by stronger foreign currencies, while firms with a higher proportion of foreign revenues to foreign costs will be negatively affected by weaker foreign currencies. For example, when the domestic currency appreciates, export items denominated in the domestic currency become more expensive in the foreign currency and therefore less competitive in the international market. Foreign sales and cash flows decrease as a result of domestic currency appreciation. Thus, an appreciation of the local currency can cause a reduction in both cash inflows and cash outflows. Local customers will be able to purchase foreign substitutes at a lower cost with their enhanced currency, while foreign importers will reduce their spending, since they need more of their own currency to pay for these products. These two factors will result in reduced cash inflows. With respect to cash outflows, an appreciation of the local currency will result in a decrease in the cost of imported supplies denominated in the foreign currency. A multinational company could reduce its foreign currency-denominated interest by simply exchanging the strong local currency for the foreign currency to make payments.

On the other hand, a depreciation of the local currency makes goods to sale abroad cheaper and more competitive, resulting in more foreign sales. Thus, a depreciation of the local currency results in an increase in both cash inflows and cash outflows. The multinational could benefit from less foreign competition because local customers will prefer goods denominated in a weak currency. For the same reason, the company's exports will seem cheap to importers, thus leading to an escalation in foreign demand for those products. The downside of this scenario is increased cash outlays: a depreciated local currency will make imported supplies denominated in a foreign currency more expensive, and foreign currency interest payments will also increase because more local currency will be needed. This has been the case for American tech giants (e.g., Apple Inc.), which after the financial crisis were able to leverage a weak U.S. dollar by strongly pushing the sale of their products (e.g., iPhones) abroad. However, these American multinationals typically source their components from abroad and have seen their supply costs rise.

Finally, income from foreign investments, like income from direct and portfolio investments and interest payments, is affected by price fluctuations. When the domestic currency appreciates, interest payments on bonds, loans, and other funds denominated in foreign currency also decline, resulting in a reduction in cash outlays – which generally has a favorable impact on the value of the business. When the domestic currency depreciates, interest payments increase, which has a negative influence on firm value (Wang, 2020).

Given the relative importance of protecting against economic exposure versus transaction exposure, many business areas have strategies to manage such risk. **Table 9.1** shows three of these approaches summarized by Wang (2020): market strategy, production approach, and financial strategy. Wang explains that the goal of market strategy is to minimize and manage sales exposure to currency risk by trying to understand and predict the extent to which a change in exchange rates will affect price adjustments. In these cases, it is necessary to develop a pricing plan that maximizes market share gains from favorable exchange rates and minimizes market share losses from adverse exchange rate conditions. The company can proactively target a specific consumer base and modify its products and production appropriately to maximize cash flows or maintain a predetermined level of cash flows in the event of currency fluctuations. Wang describes the production approach as instead focusing on containing and managing the foreign exchange risk associated with manufacturing costs. Finally, financial strategy is described as the effort to lower the cost of capital for the company while maintaining a particular level of future cash flows. Hedging can help organizations stabilize their contractual cash flows and eliminate uncertainty about their performance. To better understand the need for the application of these strategies, we suggest reading the case: "The Italian Diversified Company (IDS) and Foreign Exchange Risk Management in Canada" in paragraph 9.4.2.

Madura (2012) qualifies two methods for measuring the economic exposure of a multinational corporation. The first is to separately consider how sales and expense categories are affected by various exchange rate scenarios. A general rule of thumb is that firms with more foreign costs than foreign revenues will be unfavorably affected by a stronger foreign currency, and vice versa. A second technique is to apply regression analysis to historical cash flows and exchange rate data to

Table 9.1   Strategies to protect against economic exposure

Type of strategy	Recommended action when a foreign currency has a greater impact on cash inflows	Recommended action when a foreign currency has a greater impact on cash outflows
Market strategy	Pricing Plan to Maximize Revenues	Pricing Plan to Minimize Costs
Production approach	Increase foreign supply orders	Reduce foreign supply orders
Financial strategy	Restructure debt to increase debt payments in foreign currency	Restructure debt to reduce debt payments in foreign currency

understand the effect of a percentage change in the direct exchange rate of a given currency on cash flows measured in the firm's domestic currency, adjusted for inflation. As explained by the author, the coefficient estimated by the regression analysis is a measure of the sensitivity of the change in cash flows to changes in exchange rates. If this coefficient has a positive (and significant) value, it means that a positive change in the value of the currency will have a positive impact on the multinational company's cash flows. In the event of a negative coefficient, a positive change in the value of the currency will have an unfavorable effect on cash flows. Regression analysis can also be calculated using the MNC's stock price as a proxy for the value of the company to evaluate its changes relative to currency movements. See the case: "The Italian Diversified Company (IDS) and Foreign Exchange Risk Management in Canada" in paragraph 9.4.2 for this regression approach.

9.3.3   Translation exposure

Accounting exposure, also known as translation exposure, quantifies the impact of exchange rate fluctuations on a multinational corporation's consolidated financial statements/accounts. As a result, accounting exposure has no direct effect on cash flows. Accounting exposure management is concerned with the possible consequences of data consolidation for multinational corporations.

When preparing its financial statements, a multinational company is required to consolidate data from all its subsidiaries, which are usually presented in their local currencies. This means the parent has to translate each subsidiary's financial statement into its own currency, making it subject to fluctuations in exchange rates over the accounting period. Translation exposure indicates the exposure of the MNC's consolidated financial statements to changes in the exchange rate. Subsidiary earnings that are reported in the consolidated income statement are affected by those movements in the exchange rate. As a result, the periodic consolidation or merger of parent and affiliate balance sheets and reporting can result in exchange gains or losses of a non-cash flow nature. Although translation exposure does not affect a company's cash flows, it can have a major impact on its reported earnings and hence its market value by increasing or decreasing the parent's net worth and the size and activities of its foreign subsidiaries.

Madura (2012) outlines how a multinational firm's degree of translation exposure depends on the following factors: where its subsidiaries are located, the percentage of business they conduct, and the accounting method that is used. If a multinational company derives the majority of its business from foreign subsidiaries, the proportion of its financial statements affected by translation exposure will be higher. Location, conversely, determines the currency in which the financial statements of subsidiaries are denominated.

For consolidation purposes, each parent company has to translate both the balance sheet and the income statement of all its subsidiaries. The only financial statement that does not require translation is the cash flows statement, since it can be easily constructed from the previous two. Consolidation presents a challenge because different line items on individual statements are not necessarily translated by applying the same exchange rate. Because of the different exchange rates used in remeasuring different line items, imbalances can arise, which raises questions regarding how to deal with them from an accounting perspective. The translation method to be used is often related to the type of operations conducted by a foreign subsidiary. It is therefore useful to recall the two different categories into which subsidiaries can be divided:

1. An *integrated foreign entity*, or simple extension of the parent company, which has a high correlation with the parent's cash flows and general business activity; or
2. A *self-sustaining foreign entity*, which operates in the local economic environment in a manner independent of the parent company.

As mentioned above, at the core of the consolidation process is the issue of how the financial statement accounts of foreign subsidiaries should be translated. In this context, there are four main methods for translating the accounts and accounting items of a multinational corporation's foreign subsidiary, each one with a specific impact on the MNC's consolidated financial statements: the current rate method, the time method, the monetary-non monetary method, and the current/non-current method.

Using the *current rate method* (Statement of Financial Accounting Standards No. 52), all items are translated at the "current" exchange rate except for capital items. This is the method most used by firms globally. Below we have listed the classification rules to be followed for different items:

• All *assets and liabilities* are translated from the local currency into the reporting currency at the balance sheet date, or in other words, at the current exchange rate.
• All *income statement* items are translated either at the actual exchange rate on the day the revenues or expenses were incurred or at a weighted average exchange rate for the period. Moreover, the current rate method features any translation gain or loss that does not flow into net profit as an addition or subtraction of stockholder equity in an equity reserve account.
• *Dividends* are translated at the exchange rate on the date of the payment.
• *Equity items* are translated at historical rates, while retained earnings for the year end are obtained by adding the original year-beginning retained earnings to any income or loss for the year.

Assets and liabilities are also classified and translated according to their maturities using the *current/non-current approach*. This is because the value of current account goods, or those that will accumulate in the short run, is more likely to fluctuate in response to currency fluctuations. In other words, all current account items are translated using the current exchange rate, whereas noncurrent account items are translated using the historical exchange rate in effect at the time the item was initially entered into the register. Items on the income statement are translated using the exchange rate in effect on the day each item was incurred.

Statement No. 52 Summary

"The financial reporting of most enterprises operating in foreign nations will be affected by the application of this Statement. In order to account for them, different types of international operations will have different operating and economic features. Currency exchange rate fluctuations are omitted from net income for those that have no influence on cash flows but are included for those that do. These general conclusions are reflected in the requirements: The economic impacts of a change in the exchange rate on a largely self-contained and integrated activity within a foreign country are related to the operation's net investment. Translation adjustments resulting from the consolidation of that foreign enterprise have no effect on cash flows and are therefore not reflected in net income. The economic implications of a change in the exchange rate on a foreign business that is a branch of the parent's domestic operations are based on individual assets and liabilities and have a direct impact on the parent's cash flows. As a result, the gains and losses from such a transaction are included in net income. Contracts, transactions, or balances that are effective hedges of foreign exchange risk, regardless of their form, will be accounted for as hedges. This Statement replaces FASB Statement No. 8, Accounting for the Translation of Foreign Currency Transactions and Foreign Currency Financial Statements, and updates the existing accounting and reporting rules for foreign currency transactions and financial statements. It outlines foreign currency translation standards that are intended to (1) provide information that is generally consistent with the expected economic effects of a rate change on an enterprise's cash flows and equity, and (2) reflect financial results and relationships in the primary currency in which each entity conducts business in consolidated statements (referred to as its "functional currency"). The functional currency of an entity is the currency in which it functions in its principal economic setting. Depending on the facts, the functional currency may be the dollar or a foreign currency. It is usually the currency of the economic context in which the company generates and expends cash. Any type of activity, such as a subsidiary, division, branch, or joint venture, might be considered an entity. The Statement provides direction for this critical decision, which relies heavily on management's judgment in examining the facts. In a highly inflationary environment (3-year inflation rate of around 100% or more), a currency is not regarded stable enough to serve as a functioning currency, and the reporting parent's more stable currency is used instead. The following are the components of the functional currency translation approach used in this Statement: 1) Identifying the entity's economic environment's functional currency; 2) Measuring all financial statement elements in the functional currency; 3) If the functional currency and the reporting currency are different, use the current exchange rate for translation; 4) Differentiating the economic impact of exchange rate changes on a net investment from the impact of exchange rate fluctuations on individual assets and liabilities receivable or payable in currencies other than the functional currency. The process of translating a foreign entity's financial statements from the functioning currency to US dollars results in translation adjustments. Translation adjustments are not included in calculating net income for the quarter, but are disclosed and accumulated in a distinct component of consolidated equity until the net interest in the foreign firm is sold or liquidated completely or partially. The effect of exchange rate fluctuations on transactions denominated in currencies other than the functional currency results in transaction profits and losses (for example, a U.S. company may borrow Swiss francs or a French subsidiary may have a receivable denominated in kroner from a Danish customer). Unless the transaction hedges a foreign currency commitment or is a net investment in a foreign firm, gains and losses on those foreign currency transactions are normally included in assessing net income for the period in which exchange rates change. Long-term investment intercompany transactions are considered part of a parent's net investment and hence do not result in gains or losses."

Source: Statement of Financial Accounting Standards No. 52. Available at https://www.fasb.org/summary/stsum52.shtml

The *monetary/non-monetary technique* assumes that when the exchange rate changes, the value of monetary objects will change but the value of non-monetary items
will remain unchanged. Maturity is therefore not always an adequate criterion when
a subsidiary's accounts are translated into another currency. The monetary/non-mon-
etary method translates monetary balance sheet items such as cash, accounts receivable, accounts payable, and long-term debt at current exchange rates; it translates non-monetary balance sheet items such as inventory, plants and equipment, and
long-term investments at historical exchange rates. Income statement components
are translated using the period's average exchange rate – except for depreciation and
cost of goods sold, which are translated using their historical exchange rates. Capital
goods are converted using their historical exchange rates. As in the current/non-cur-
rent method, translation gains or losses may be recognized in the consolidated statement of income.

Using the *time method* (Statement of Financial Accounting Standards No. 8),[7]
some selected assets and liabilities are translated at the exchange rate at the time of
the creation of the item in question. This methodology assumes that many items (e.g.,
inventory and PPE) are regularly reassessed to reflect their value on the market. The
definition of different items can be found below:

- Current assets and liabilities are translated at the exchange rate in effect on the
  date of the financial statements; monetary assets and liabilities are translated at
  current exchange rates, whereas long-term assets and liabilities, as well as non-
  cash assets and liabilities, are translated at the historical exchange rate (i.e., the
  rate in effect when the asset was acquired or the liability was incurred). In this
  method, translation adjustments are reflected in the income statement rather than
  in capital reserves, so foreign exchange gains and losses introduce volatility into
  consolidated earnings.
- Income statement components are translated using the period's average exchange
  rate. However, because of their tight relationship with non-cash assets and liabilities, elements such as cost of goods sold and depreciation are translated at their
  historical rate.
- Dividends are calculated using the currency rate in effect on the date of payment.
- Equity items are translated at their historical rates, whereas retained earnings at
  the end of the year are calculated by adding the original retained earnings at the
  beginning of the year to any income or loss for the year. Yet unlike the current
  rate method, any translation imbalance also needs to be included.

In summary, all assets and liabilities are deemed exposed under the current rate
technique. The current/non-current method exposes only current assets and liabilities. The monetary/non-monetary technique exposes only monetary assets and liabil-

---

[7] "All sums measured in a foreign currency must be translated at the exchange rate in force on the
date the foreign currency transaction was measured, according to this Statement. All foreign exchange
profits and losses were to be reported in the period in which they occurred, i.e. when the rates changed."
Available at https://www.fasb.org/summary/stsum8.shtml

ities. The time approach exposes assets and liabilities calculated at current cost, but not those evaluated at historical cost.

It is important to note that, regardless of the methodology, a translation approach should not only specify the exchange rate to apply to each item in the statement but also designate the specific way of recording any imbalances that arise.

9.4   Exposure to exchange risk fluctuations: hedging techniques

9.4.1   Managing transaction exposure

As mentioned above, transaction exposure arises each time the expected future cash transactions of a firm are impacted by changes in exchange rates.

Thus, transaction risk arises whenever a firm has a foreign currency-denominated payable or receivable, investment, or loan. A firm facing transaction exposure has three major tasks:

1. It must first determine the extent of its transaction exposure.
2. It must then decide whether or not to hedge this risk.
3. Finally, if it decides to hedge part or all of the exposure, it must choose among the various hedging techniques available.

In general, firms face two options when managing transaction exposure: they can hedge the exposure or decide to remain unhedged. Each MNC should draw up the reduction strategy most appropriate to its currency risk exposure. The choice of whether to hedge is a subjective decision that depends on several factors, including the firm's attitude towards currency risk and its expectations concerning exchange rate fluctuations over the transaction exposure period.

A multinational company may choose to hedge most of its exposure, none of it, or to selectively hedge. The first solution is usually pursued to avoid the MNC's value being influenced by movements in exchange rates. Even though MNCs are never certain that hedging will be beneficial, knowing the amount of future cash inflows and outflows in terms of their home currency helps them to improve corporate planning. Vice versa, MNCs with businesses that are well diversified across many countries do not need to hedge themselves against exchange rate fluctuations. In fact, diversification limits the impact of exchange rates on cash flows. Finally, a third alternative is to hedge only if the MNC expects fluctuations in the currency's future value that will make it convenient to have some control over its exposure (Madura, 2012).

It is interesting to refer to Tscheke (2016) who found that when imports and exports are denominated in currencies that move in tandem, firms' exchange rate vulnerability is reduced. Domestic currency appreciations thus reduce marginal costs by increasing foreign currency export prices, allowing firms to offset international price increases. The author has built a structural model using firm-level data from seven European nations, showing that exchange rate pass-through in sales depends on both intermediate imports and the co-movement of currency rates associated with exports and imports. He found that operational hedging requires firms to deliberately select export and import areas with currencies that move in tandem.

Take a look at the following in-depth box on financial risk management at Eni.

Financial risk management at Eni

Eni is a global energy company that operates worldwide across the entire value chain, from oil and gas exploration, development, and extraction to electricity generation from cogeneration and renewables, traditional biorefining and chemicals, and the development of circular economy processes. Eni expands its end-market reach by selling gas, energy, and goods to consumers, businesses, and local markets around the world. The fact that Eni's operations are conducted in currencies other than the euro (primarily the U.S. dollar) exposes it to foreign exchange risk. Exchange rate fluctuations can have a significant impact on revenues and costs denominated in foreign currencies due to translation differences on individual transactions caused by the time lag between the execution and definition of the relevant contractual terms (economic risk) and the conversion of trade and financial payables and receivables denominated in foreign currencies (transactional risk). As the financial statements of subsidiaries denominated in currencies other than the euro are translated from their functional currency into euros, exchange rate movements have an impact on the reported results and shareholders' equity. In general, an increase in the value of the U.S. dollar against the euro has a favorable influence on Eni's operating performance and vice versa. Eni's foreign exchange risk management strategy seeks to reduce transactional exposures from foreign currency fluctuations by optimizing commodity risk exposures. Except for individual transactions to be evaluated on a case-by-case basis, Eni does not engage in any hedging activities for risks arising from the translation of earnings or assets and liabilities denominated in the foreign currencies of subsidiaries that prepare financial statements in a currency other than the euro. Eni's financial divisions effectively manage foreign exchange risk by pooling the holdings of its subsidiaries and hedging the Group's net exposure using derivatives such as currency swaps, futures, and options.

Source: Eni Annual Report 2020, publicly available at: https://www.eni.com/assets/documents/eng/reports/2020/Annual-Report-2020.pdf

---

Internal vs. external hedging

Before it makes any decisions related to hedging, a multinational company must determine the individual net transaction exposure for each currency in which it operates. This exposure is "net", since it represents the consolidation of all expected inflows and outflows registered in a given period. A crucial role in accomplishing this task is played by the management of each subsidiary, which has to report its expected inflows and outflows to a centralized group within the MNC. This group then consolidates the reports to determine the firm's overall exposure to each foreign currency.

Firms can choose among several techniques to hedge their transaction exposure. An initial distinction can be made between two different techniques: internal hedging (i.e., *operational hedging*) and external hedging (i.e., *financial hedging*). This general division is an essential starting point for understanding the various instruments available to companies.

We will start with internal or operational hedging. There are two different definitions of operational hedging that can be found in the academic research on operational management. The first was introduced by Huchzermeier (1991) and states that operational hedging strategies can be viewed as real options exercised in response to demand, price, and exchange rate contingencies faced by firms in the context of a global supply chain. These real options include switching among supply chain network structures and switching production and sourcing strategies based on demand and exchange rate uncertainties. The second definition of operational hedging is developed in Van Mieghem (2003), which defines it as mitigating risks by counterbalancing actions in a processing network that do not involve financial instruments. In finance literature, operational hedging is instead defined as the course of action of hedging a firm's risk exposure with non-financial instruments, particularly operational activities (Boyabatlı, 2004). Operational flexibility in the form of switching production or sourcing locations is the most prevalent type of operational hedging strategy.

As the definition above suggests, *operational hedging* is a kind of internal hedging technique in which a firm makes internal adjustments to certain business activities in order to hedge some of its currency exposure. Due to the substantial bargaining power and extensive amount of research it requires, this hedging strategy may be difficult to implement of for an individual firm. In fact, even though the techniques adopted are simple in principle, they may require some effort. Below we analyze the most common ones reported also extensively in literature:

- *Netting*: a first way to reduce currency risk consists in netting out currency exposures. This means matching a subsidiary's receivables and payables denominated in a foreign currency before transferring them to the parent company, so that the firm's net exposure is minimized and transfer costs are reduced.
- *Invoicing*: this is probably the simplest hedging technique, since it only requires that firms invoice in their own domestic currency. This means that foreign importers will be obliged to pay in the exporter's domestic currency and thus that they will be the only ones bearing the exposure to foreign exchange risk. This represents the major challenge of this technique, since it may be difficult for a firm to find a counterparty willing to accept such conditions, and any potential counterparty would presumably demand a payment for assuming the currency risk. Usually, the transaction exposure is transferred to the business that can manage it at the lowest possible expense. The price of the deal is negotiated in a way that incorporates such risk.
- *Leading and Lagging*: in this technique, a firm is able to reduce its transaction exposure by shifting the timing of its payment claims or outlays according to expected changes in exchange rates. If the MNC expects a depreciation of a foreign currency, it will try to collect its receivables denominated in that currency as soon as possible (i.e., leading), while it will probably delay respective liabilities to reduce future cash outflows (i.e., lagging).

Financial hedging is a risk management strategy employed to offset losses in investments by taking an opposite position in a related asset. In other words, financial hedging serves as a buffer to allow for the planning and implementation of operative adjustments in the face of significant exchange rate movements (Hommel, 2003). Risk reduction can be obtained by different financial strategies. Typically, firms use derivatives for risk reduction or to benefit from market timing (Geyer-Klingeberg et al., 2019). Unlike internal hedging, in this case of *external hedges* the company does not rely on internal operations but rather uses different instruments available in financial markets. The best-known are *forwards, futures, options, money market hedges, and swaps.* A brief description of these tools is provided below.

- *Options*: These are contracts that give the buyer the right but not the obligation to buy (call option) or to sell (put option) a foreign exchange sum at a pre-determined price, also known as the strike. The subscriber of such options pays an up-front fee. There is some debate over whether such contracts are opportune or not for companies, since the option premium and transaction costs must be paid in any case. In theory, options should be undertaken if the costs are lower than the potential loss a multinational company would bear if it remained unhedged. In addition to the classical distinction between put and call options, there is a second way to classify these instruments: over the counter options and exchange-traded options. The former enable the two parties to specify the contract terms on their own, while the latter are very standardized.
- *Forward contracts*: In these contracts a company agrees to buy (long position) or sell (short position) a certain amount of a foreign currency at a predetermined exchange rate at a specified date in the future. In this way, a firm is able to hedge its transaction exposure by locking in a specific exchange rate. Forward contracts are traded on over the counter (OTC) markets; there are several forward contracts for different currencies, with different maturities (up to twelve months). Contractual terms like the maturity and principal sum can be chosen arbitrarily by the two parties. Forward contracts are often not available for small and uncreditworthy companies, since banks fear they will not be able to fulfil their future commitments and therefore quote forwards at extremely high prices. Those companies may thus be forced to hedge their transaction exposure through futures.
- *Future contracts*: Though they are substantially similar to forward contracts, future contracts are more standardized, with limited and fixed contract sizes, maturity dates, and original collateral. For this reason, it may be difficult for a firm to find a contract that perfectly matches in size its currency exposure; in this case, it will only be able to engage in partial hedging. However, the presence of a liquid secondary market enables a company to close its position if a mismatch between the timing of the contract and the timing of the exposure arises. Futures are exchange traded: this means that there is a clearing house whose main role is to back these contracts. A firm willing to underwrite a future contract has to open a margin account with the clearing house and make a deposit of cash or other liquid securities in order to mitigate its credit risk. Future contracts are marked to market daily, but there is an imbalance between losses, which must be paid immediately in cash, and gains, which instead are delayed until the trade actually takes place. This may cause liquidity problems, especially for small firms.

- *Foreign Exchange Swap*: This contract involves a deal between two companies to trade a specified amount of money in a currency now and then trade it back at some pre-determined future date. In other words, it is a bundle of forward contracts. The two parties can specify the amount, maturity, principal, and delivery date of the swap contract. The exchange rate for the offsetting purchase or sale is called the swap rate. Setting such a contract requires the intermediation of a swap bank or swap dealer to reduce credit risk. In this way, the risk of default on the currency swap by one of the two parties is born by the broker. The advantage of a swap contract is that firms can raise a loan in their home country's domestic currency at better lending terms than those that would apply to a loan in a foreign currency at a foreign bank. It is far easier for them to then swap the respective loans with each other.
- *Money Market Hedge (or balance sheet hedge)*: This instrument involves borrowing or lending in the short-term money market so a firm can hedge its future receivables or payables at the current spot rate. In other words, the company borrows a sum of capital today and simultaneously exchanges it for another currency at the spot rate: if it has to hedge a foreign currency payment, it will borrow the home currency; vice versa, it will expect a future receipt denominated in a foreign currency if it needs to borrow foreign currency. In this way, it will convert the foreign currency transaction into a home currency payable or receivable, thus reducing its exchange risk exposure. Usually, companies implement a money-market hedging strategy when future contracts involve too high of an insolvency risk and forward contracts are not available on the market.

The limitations of hedging and alternative techniques

There are some limitations to hedging to be aware of: first, if the amount of goods the MNC is expected to export is unknown, it may be difficult to estimate how much it will need to hedge its exposure to the foreign currency. In this case, the MNC bears the risk of over-hedging, that is, hedging an amount in a foreign currency that is above the overall value of the transactions. To avoid such a scenario, the best option is to hedge only a portion of these transactions and not their complete value.

Another limitation of hedging pertains to so-called "*short-term hedging*": if a multinational company keeps hedging repeated transactions that are expected to happen in the near future, the benefit of hedging is reduced in the long run. Greater effectiveness can be achieved if hedging is instead applied to longer periods. Nevertheless, many MNCs seem to ignore this fact, given their tendency to hedge more receivables or payables that will occur in the short-term.

When it is impossible for a multinational company to fully eliminate transaction exposure through perfect hedging, alternative solutions may be pursued to decrease it. One possible method could be *currency diversification*[8]: like portfolio theory,

---

[8] *Currency diversification* stays for: "Using more than one currency as an investing or financing strategy. Exposure to a diversified currency portfolio typically entails less exchange rate risk than if

a firm can reduce its exposure to a single foreign currency simply by establishing transactions denominated in different currencies. If the correlation among those currencies is low or moderate, the value of future foreign currency inflows will be less variable, thus reducing its risk exposure to exchange rates.

An alternative hedging technique is *cross-hedging*, which is often used for currencies for which traditional hedging contracts are not available. This strategy consists in the identification of a third currency, highly correlated with the one to which the MNC is exposed, in order to exchange it at a given point in the future. This technique is also called a "proxy hedge", since the third currency becomes a sort of proxy for the currency in which the MNC has a risk exposure. The more the two currencies are positively correlated, the more effective the *cross-hedging* is. As Broll (1996) points out, there are really two typical methods for currency risk cross-hedging. The first, just mentioned above, is the possibility of cross-currency hedging through forward exchange contracts. Naturally, effective cross hedging requires that the two currencies act similarly. The US and Canadian dollars, as well as a large number of European Union currencies, are all good examples of connected currencies. The second method of risk management through cross hedging is to compute a regression between the spot exchange rate and the spot price of a correlated domestic financial asset.

Hedging long-term transactions

Multinational corporations are exposed to foreign currency transactions when they incur financial obligations that must be settled in foreign currency. For instance, a multinational firm may require payment in foreign currency at some point in the future for commodities supplied and exported (long-term transactions). When the payment is received in foreign currency, it must be changed to the multinational's domestic currency. If the value of the multinational's domestic currency has gained compared to the foreign currency during the interim period, the multinational will get less domestic currency for each unit of foreign currency. Depending on the amount of the multinational's domestic currency appreciation, this can be a very costly transaction. The multinational can avoid this outcome by managing the risk through one of a variety of available choices. The best possible way to avoid this risk is for the business to prevent the exposure in the first place. This might be accomplished by the global firm invoicing the buyer directly in its own native currency. The transaction's exposure risk is subsequently shifted to the buyer. Yet this may not be a viable option for a variety of reasons.

Assuming that a company does face exposure, it can choose between internal and external hedges (McCarthy, 2003). Internal hedges include the anticipation and postponement of foreign currency payments and accounts, while external hedges include derivatives such as forwards, futures, options, and swaps. Forward contracts are the simplest and most regularly utilized external hedges. Their popularity is due in part to their simplicity of usage, since they involve over-the-counter trading that allows for precise specification of dates and amounts as well as a low explicit cost. A back-to-back loan could be another attractive solution. This is an agreement between two parties to exchange currencies at the start of the contract, with the commitment to do so again at a specified exchange rate in the future. In practice, it is comparable to two currency exchange contracts.

---

all the portfolio exposure were in a single foreign currency." Available in the Nasdaq glossary, https://www.nasdaq.com/glossary/c/currency-diversification

9.4.2   Managing economic exposure

As mentioned above, economic exposure includes any impact of exchange rate fluctuations on a firm's future cash flows. Economic exposure for a firm stems then from
the competitiveness of its line of business as a result of future unanticipated exchange
rate swings and not only from the settlement of present or anticipated transactions
(Moffett & Karlsen, 2007). The way exchange rate movements influence a firm's
cash flows are not always linked to foreign transactions. Therefore, firms not only have to set an effective hedging policy for payables and receivables, but they also
have to think about other possible ways their cash flows can be affected by exchange
rate fluctuations.

Before managing economic exposure, it is fundamental for any firm to estimate
its overall exposure to each currency in terms of cash inflows and outflows by gathering relevant information from each subsidiary. One effective way to manage economic exposure is through *operational restructuring*. This means changing the locations in which revenues and costs are generated in order to match cash inflows and
outflows that are denominated in the same foreign currency. For instance, MNCs
that have production and marketing facilities in various countries may be able to
minimize the adverse impact of any economic exposure by shifting how their operations are allocated.

Such activity is far more complex than hedging a single foreign currency transaction. For this reason, most firms find managing economic exposure more difficult
than dealing with transaction exposure. In the latter case, the firm must only consider
each expected foreign currency transaction separately, since this reduces the impact
on its overall business. Conversely, managing economic exposure through restructuring affects the MNC in the long term: since reversing or eliminating restructuring is
very expensive, the company should think carefully before deciding to implement it
(Kallianiotis, 2013).

How the company specifically does this depends on the form of exposure to
which it is subject: if the exposure to exchange rate movements is higher for revenues
than for expenses, a firm will probably opt for a reduction in the level of revenues
vulnerable to exchange rates or for an increase in the respective expenses.

However, some revenues or expenses could be more exposed to fluctuations in
exchange rates. For this reason, it may not be sufficient for a multinational company
to match the amount of vulnerable revenue to an expense completely hedged against
exchange rate risk. In this regard, it might be useful to recall how Moffett (2007)
defined a MNC's competitive exposure as determined by its overseas operations and
competitive environment. More precisely, according to the author, the multinational firm competes for market share and revenues/costs in local currency and defines
three types of markets: those of fixed-price goods (usually regulated markets), those
of non-diversified goods and, finally, markets of specialized or niche goods. In fixed-
price goods markets, changes in exchange rates could cause the price to be altered to
protect consumers. If exchange rates move in an unfavorable direction for the multinational firm, price increases may be required in local currency markets, resulting

in large negative swings in the exchange rate combined with stringent regulatory requirements that could cause the company to leave the market. Undifferentiated goods markets are those in which producers compete for limited margins and focus on cost leadership. Because of the high level of competition in the industry and the cost-based pricing structure characterized by low margins, the company risks to incur unit losses if it does not raise its prices. If the exchange rate fluctuates significantly, the company may lose considerable market share. The third is the market for specialized goods. Firms in these markets can adjust product prices based on tactical or environmental reasons. Their products are sufficiently distinct to allow self-determination of prices. Continuing with Moffett, the author then identifies three types of exposure:

- *Expected exposure*: The parent company believes to have a certain foreign currency market share. Volume and price changes are small, leading to predictable net profits on foreign exchange. Exchange rate fluctuations are reflected in the market price only when it is officially allowed, and product differentiation and high price elasticity lead to consistent sales volumes. The future flow of money in foreign currency is sufficiently known.
- *Direct economic exposure*: The parent company is engaged in a market where high competition limits both revenue assurance and the choice of how exchange rate changes are reflected into end market prices (homogeneous goods). Despite the lack of managerial discretion, given its global structure, it is possible for the multinational firm to respond to rival firms with its own diversification capabilities resulting from its international structure.
- *Competitive exposure*: The parent company's market share and earnings are in jeopardy. The ability to pass rate changes is limited by two factors: first, the degree of differentiation between the company's products and close substitutes; secondly, the anticipated price response from rivals. Understanding the behavior of competitors is therefore crucial.

Overall, we can then say that the most important concern for a multinational company is certainly the impact of exchange rate fluctuations on its overall value and performance. However, its economic exposure can be effectively hedged if the MNC is able to pinpoint the underlying source of its exposure. Though this procedure may still not guarantee that the MNC is perfectly hedged, the firm can decide to implement a set of actions to reduce its exposure to a tolerable level, as illustrated in the following example.

Case The Italian Diversified Company (IDS) and foreign exchange risk management in Canada

As IDS expanded around the world, so did the extent of its exposure to different foreign currencies, and in the late 2000s it began to worry about its exposure to the Canadian dollar. In fact, IDS had several branches in Canada, with various commercial agreements with local companies based on the product lines offered. IDS was not entirely sure that the different branches all supported the same economic exposure. The first thing that the CFO of the parent company in Italy had to do was to try to assess how the cash flows of each subsidiary were related to the movements of the Canadian dollar through a regression analysis that assessed the link between the percentage change in the total cash flows of the operations versus the percentage change in the Canadian dollar over time. By analyzing the past, it was possible to determine how fluctuations in the Canadian currency had impacted IDS's results. A point-in-time regression analysis of each branch was necessary to identify whether all branches in Canada suffered from economic exposure and, if so, to what extent. This made it possible to discover how only some of the branches had exposure to the fluctuation of the Canadian dollar while others were not affected. Once the branches detecting exposure were identified, IDS could rethink its business operations and financial reporting. For example, the key components that influenced branch cash flows were income statement items (such as euro revenue, cost of goods sold, and operating expenses). If all manufacturing activity was assumed to be based in Italy, the IDS parent company would first determine the impact of each income statement item on the cash flows of the branches under analysis and then apply a regression analysis to assess the relationship between the percentage change in weight and each income statement item in those quarters for each specific branch.

If after the analysis IDS had found a significant positive relationship between the revenues of the various subsidiaries involved and the value of the Canadian dollar, it would have implied no relationship between the cost of goods sold by the subsidiaries and the value of the Canadian dollar – and therefore no relationship between the operating expenses of the subsidiary and the value of the Canadian dollar.

The findings of the analysis led to the conclusion that a depreciation of the Canadian dollar would result in a decline in IDS revenue. In addition, there would have been an increase in foreign competition, as Canadian customers would have shifted to cheaper goods than the Italian goods produced by IDS. There are several measures the firm could have implemented to reduce its risk exposure. It could, for example, have implemented a pricing strategy in which it reduced its prices when the Canadian dollar weakened against the euro. Alternatively, to avoid reducing its revenue, IDS could have set up futures contracts by selling Canadian dollars forward for the period it expected the currency to depreciate. In this way, while reducing its operating cash flows, IDS would have had a gain on the forward contract at the end date; this would have enabled it to buy Canadian dollars at a lower exchange rate and sell them back through the forward contract at a higher price, profiting from the difference. Another potential way of hedging would be to match the currency of the income with the expenses, buying materials for their production in Italy directly from Canada and thus reducing the cost of raw materials. However, the effectiveness of this strategy is actually reduced by the cost of transporting raw materials from Canada to Italy. Finally, IDS could have decided to take out a loan denominated in Canadian dollars, which would have then been repaid with cash flows from the portion of its revenues denominated in euros. In this way, a depreciation of the Canadian dollar would have resulted in lower debt repayments, thus partially offsetting the negative effect of the depreciation on sales in the various branches in Canada.

9.4.3   Managing translation exposure

As we have seen, translation exposure occurs when a multinational company translates each subsidiary's financial data into its home currency to compile the consolidated financial statements. The impact of translation exposure on a firm's cash flows is therefore indirect, though it is still fundamental for many MNCs to manage their translation exposure, since it may cause a reduction in their consolidated earnings and thus in their share price. Very interesting on this subject is the research of Bonini et al. (2016), who examined multinational companies' translation risk hedging strategy over a four-year period (2003–2006) using a sample of 622 companies in 25 countries. They discovered that a significant percentage of companies (47 percent) actively manage their translation risk. Northern Europe is dominated by hedgers, whilst Southern Europe, South America, and Asia are dominated by non-hedgers. A positive credit rating greatly boosts the chance of corporations adopting and sustaining a hedging program, as firms strive to prevent translation losses that might raise leverage ratios and could negatively influence their credit rating. Accounting standards are also critical, since corporations who use IFRS hedge more than those that use merely national standards. Authors also highlight that hedgers use a number of different tools for their scope, ranging from balance sheet to derivatives hedging. Derivatives are more prevalent among corporations that adhere to US GAAP, while loans and blended solutions are favored by companies that use IFRS or local accounting rules.

Forward or futures contracts can be used to hedge translation exposure: the MNC can commit itself to sell forward the currency that their foreign subsidiaries receive as earnings so that the relative earnings are counterbalanced by the cash outflow in the same currency. The more accurate the estimation of future exchange rates, the better protection a firm is able to obtain through this technique.

A common approach to managing translation exposure is the so-called *balance sheet hedge*, which involves equalizing the amount of assets exposed to a foreign currency to the liabilities exposed to the same foreign currency in the MNC's consolidated balance sheet. By doing this, a firm will reach a net translation exposure of zero.

Translation risk is much more complex to hedge. This practice is therefore usually not as widespread among companies as transaction risk hedging. One big limitation in hedging translation exposure is the estimation error in earnings forecasts, since there is no certainty that forecasted earnings will be available at the end of the year. Another issue pertains to forward contracts, which may not exist for some specific foreign currencies and thus are not an available option for MNCs with subsidiaries in such countries.

Accounting distortions also complicate translation risk hedging: translation gains and losses result from fluctuations in the exchange rate over the accounting period, while forward rate gains and losses arise because of changes between the future spot rate and the forward rate. The results of Bonini et al. (2016) also indicate that firms' decision to hedge translation risk has a long-term effect, consistent with what we have said above.

However, translation gains are not real gains, just gains on paper. In fact, the reported dollar value of the subsidiary's earnings increases solely because of the foreign currency's appreciation, without affecting the parent's cash flows. On the contrary, a transaction loss will result in a real loss for the parent, thus decreasing its net cash flows. It may not be opportune for a multinational company to decrease its translation exposure at the expense of higher transaction exposure (Madura, 2012). Following this path, according to some of the research cited (Nazarboland, 2003), translation exposure is an insufficient notion for managing foreign exchange risk, since it is solely an accounting measure of currency exposure that is unrelated to cash flows (Shapiro, 1993). However, the absence of a link between translation exposure and cash flow is debatable, since the rising impact of public accounting results over cash flows encourages financial managers to prioritize translation exposure appropriately and prudently (Ensor & Muller, 1981). This degree of sensitivity is supported by the fact that financial managers must meet the needs of a variety of stakeholders and hence prefer to borrow in their own currency rather than in a foreign currency, incurring in higher interest expenses but not reporting a foreign exchange loss (Haseltine, 1981).

9.5   Factors influencing foreign exchange hedging strategies

Hedging techniques implemented by businesses are influenced by various factors shaping the context in which the corporation operates and are by definition either *external* to the corporation or *within* it.

The *external corporate environment* refers to all the political and macroeconomic factors characterizing the market in which the company operates. More precisely, this environment is made up of two elements: *regulatory mechanisms* and the *market structures* under which the organization functions (Edelshain, 1995).

1. *Regulatory mechanisms* refer to the accounting principles and procedures mandated by each country with which MNCs must comply. MNCs must adjust their hedging strategies in response to such factors. For instance, capital controls established in the 1970s incentivized the use of domestic financial markets and the local retention of foreign earnings. The later elimination of exchange controls in many developed nations, instead, encouraged firms to use foreign currency in pricing transactions even for domestic deals.
2. *Market structure* became a relevant factor in the late 1970s, mainly because of the increasing interest on operating exposure. Each MNC must forecast the possible growth of the industry in which it operates and predict to what extent its competitors in foreign markets are likely to grow with respect to its domestic rivals. Another important forecast pertains to the possible foreign expansion of its product categories. In fact, markets that are growing fast usually imply a higher level of currency volatility, thus impacting the funding and sourcing strategies of firms. Market structure is therefore essential for both demand and competition in the industry.

In terms of a firm's *internal corporate environment*, two main factors influence how a firm reacts to currency exposure: organizational structure and management strategies (Edelshain, 1995).

1. *Organizational structure* refers to the fact that a firm's hedging strategies are a function of some structural variables that influence its vulnerability to currency fluctuations. These are mainly size, concentration of authority, and col-

lection of information. Today most scholars agrees that vulnerability to foreign exchange movements is directly proportional to the firm's size and standing. In fact, as a company's business gets more complex, it becomes necessary to maximize efficiency and react to changes in the competitive arena. Inevitably, certain decisions may have to be delegated, even though better management of fluctuating exchange rates is best achieved with highly centralized financial decision making. However, incorporating the knowledge sourced from different divisions may still allow a company to implement successful foreign exchange management.

2. *Development of a risk management plan* in line with organizational goals highly influences a firm's response to currency fluctuations. Management can use different techniques to do this: for instance, balancing out the effect of changes in the exchange rates on corporate results, eliminating the volatility of the currency exposure, or using such volatility to profit from exchange rate fluctuations as if they were standard operations. An important starting point for each firm before implementing exchange risk management techniques is to fully understand which factors most impact their currency risk hedging strategies.

9.6   Forecasting exchange rates

9.6.1   The importance of forecasting exchange rates

Multinational firms use forecasting approaches to compare and assess the different interactions among variables produced by the continuous fluctuation of rates in the foreign currency market and their own increasing globalization. As Giddy & Dufey (1975) state, forecasting techniques are based on formal models and can be premised in an assumed sequence of random relationships (e.g., simulation models) or in data-driven statistical relationships between the variable of interest and previous values in the same series (intrinsic or extrinsic models). The extrinsic and intrinsic predictive performance of both exploratory and causal statistical models is based on the assumption that associations formed in the past will remain relatively unchanged in the future. The international monetary environment also plays a role, as Znaczko (2013) reports, because national monetary authorities have committed themselves over time to keeping exchange rates within tiny margins around a target rate or "parity value." When a country's balance of payments becomes unbalanced and it is apparent that alternative approaches are ineffective, this value can be adjusted. The forecasting procedures developed in this environment follow a three-step process: 1) examine the balance of payments and other trends associated with currency pressures; 2) determine the tipping point of a situation based on the foreign exchange reserves of the central bank (including lending facilities); and 3) predict which of the relatively few policy options will be available to economic decision-makers in times of crisis.

Changes in currency rates can influence almost every aspect of a multinational corporation's operations. Exchange rate estimates, for example, influence whether or not to hedge future foreign currency payables and receivables. Both short- and long-term financing choices are another company activity for which exchange rate estimates are required. Indeed, global firms will want to borrow money in a currency with a low interest rate that will depreciate over the course of the financing term. The same argument holds true for bond issuance: multinationals prefer bonds denominated in a currency that is likely to fall in value over time in comparison to the currency they earn from sales. Other tasks impacted by foreign currency estimates include capital budgeting and investment choices.

When choosing to engage in a foreign project, it is important for the company to assess its cash flows in the parent company's native currency, which requires a forecast of future exchange rates. The multinational must pick a currency with a high interest rate and a value that is predicted to rise over the investment period, even for short-term investments, such as surplus cash left in deposits. Moreover, the value of foreign branch profits is influenced by future exchange rates: if the local currency is predicted to depreciate against the parent currency, the multinational may elect to transfer earnings back to the parent before the depreciation occurs. In the case of a strong currency, it may be preferable to reinvest profits (Madura, 2012).

Figure 9.3 outlines the many reasons why a multinational corporation might decide to undertake a prediction study. Predicting exchange rates, on the other hand, is far from straightforward, since variations are influenced by a variety of variables. As Benlaria & Boubekeur (2021) explain, researchers have attempted to solve the problems of forecasting exchange rates by studying various methods, ranging from the most basic methods – such as moving averages (Brown, 1963) and exponential touch (Trigg & Leach, 1967) – to autoregressive integrated moving average (ARIMA) models (Box & Jenkins, 1970), which were widely used until the 1980s, when Chen & Leung (2003) instead proposed a vector error correction model (VECM)[9] to forecast exchange rates. Researchers have been able to engage in financial forecasting studies based on artificial neural networks (ANN) thanks to the fast growth of artificial intelligence (AI) computer capabilities in recent decades. The neural networks technique is distinguished by its strong capacity to represent nonlinear interactions by scouring existing data for hidden links among variables. This approach does not rest upon any a priori assumptions about the variables; if a mathematical link exists between the dependent and independent variables, the neural network method will identify it via a particular training and learning process. The findings of research by Benlaria & Boubekeur (2021) have demonstrated the great effectiveness of the neural network model in forecasting Algerian dinar exchange rates. Because this approach does not involve many constraints or limits, it might be difficult to create statistical

---

[9] "Vector-error correction (VEC) models, or *cointegrated VAR models*, address nonstationarity in multivariate time series resulting from co-movements of multiple response series." Available at https://www.mathworks.com/help/econ/vector-error-correction-models.html

Figure 9.3   **Reasons to implement a forecasting analysis**

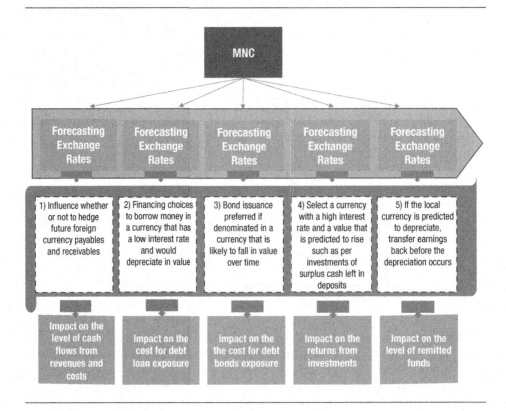

models appropriate for the data. In addition, the neural networks employed in the Benlaria & Boubekeur (2021) research to forecast future exchange rates are based on a univariate series of the exchange rate of the Algerian dinar versus the U.S. dollar. Because of the ongoing reduction in the dinar's value, its exchange rate is directly impacted by prior values and thus it is established on the basis of monetary and financial reasons that ignore the country's actual economy.

9.6.2   Forecasting techniques

In this section, we will analyze techniques that MNCs can use to forecast exchange rates. This practice has straightforward importance for any MNC aiming to minimize its risks and maximize returns. We present the three most used methods for forecasting exchange rates: the *fundamental approach*, *technical approach*, and *market approach*. We analyze these approaches below, together with some empirical findings.

The fundamental analysis approach

As the name implies, fundamental forecasting is based on the relationship between economic variables and exchange rates. Fundamental forex research is not limited to comparing current and historical data for specific economic indicators but rather involves multiple economic theories – all of which aim to contextualize and compare various kinds of economic data. For instance, a prediction can be constructed by evaluating the projected impact on exchange rates of general economic movements such as GDP, inflation rates, productivity, interest rates, money, and production differentials (Rossi, 2013). The most widely accepted economic theories underpinning fundamental currency analysis are founded on the concept of parity: the pricing condition at which currencies should trade when settled, depending on domestic economic characteristics such as inflation and interest rates.

From a statistical standpoint, a fundamental forecasting prediction provides a quantitative assessment of the impact of various variables on exchange rates. The underlying assumption is that the true worth of a currency will eventually be realized, which makes this strategy well suited to long-term investments. The three primary economic indicators employed in fundamental forex analysis are therefore interest rates, inflation, and GDP. These factors are unmatched in terms of economic impact compared to macroeconomic and geopolitical variables such as retail sales, capital flows, trade balance, bond prices, or other factors.

Source: Forex Fundamental Analysis: An Introduction (2021, August 17), Admiral Markets. Available at https://admiralmarkets.com/education/articles/forex-analysis/introduction-to-forex-fundamental-analysis

As this definition suggests, fundamental forecasting allows us to evaluate the fundamental relationship between factors and currency values. However, we must bear in mind that the precise timing of the impact of some factors on a currency's value is not known, and some factors may have an immediate impact on exchange rates. Building models based on fundamentals is thus a very complex task. To start, a firm has to identify the relevant factors that need to be considered in the forecasting process, then apply several techniques to estimate exchange rates. The main techniques used are the following:

- *Econometric models*: This method is used to forecast exchange rates by gathering all relevant factors that may affect a certain currency and connecting them. The output is usually obtained through a regression analysis. The main advantage of this method is that any variable can be added if required. However, MNCs should consider that coefficients derived from regression analysis will not necessarily remain constant over time. When forecasting is performed through a regression model but the impact of influential factors on exchange rates lags, it is possible to use their actual value as input for the forecast. On the other hand, only a forecast is possible for factors that have an instantaneous impact on exchange rates, since it is impossible to know their actual value.

- *PPP fundamental forecasting*: According to the theory of purchasing power parity (PPP), the real price of comparable commodity baskets in two countries should be the same. This means that the price level in the home country, converted to the currency of the foreign country by the nominal exchange rate, should equal the price level of the foreign country – or in other words, they should have the same purchasing power (Cassel, 1918). Following this definition, the percentage change in a foreign currency's value should reflect the differential between the home inflation rate and the foreign inflation rate. However, it may not always be possible to estimate exchange rates accurately with PPP, since nominal exchange rates tend toward PPP only in the long run and short run deviations from PPP tend to be substantial (Rogoff, 1996).

The technical approach

By technical forecasting we mean a method in which historical exchange rate data are used to predict future values. The rationale undergirding this approach is that past behavior and price patters can affect and influence the future. Usually, technical forecasting is performed through time-series-based prediction modelling of foreign currency rates. Many econometrics models have been developed in the scholarly literature (Box & Jenkins, 1976), i.e., the autoregressive integrated moving average process (ARIMA). ARIMA is a statistical analysis model that utilizes time series data to better understand a data set or anticipate future trends. If a statistical model predicts future values from previous values, it is called autoregressive. An ARIMA model may, for example, try to estimate a company's profitability based on previous periods or predict a stock's future pricing based on its historical performance. The time series model is completely technical and does not include any economic theory.

Technical forecasting is rarely used by MNCs since it is focused on the near future and thus not very helpful in developing long-term corporate policies. Also, the assumption that future rates will resemble past behavior with only small adjustments is only valid considering short time horizons. For this reason, most technical forecasts apply to very short-term periods (such as one day), because patterns in exchange rate movements are more systematic in that timeframe. An additional weakness is that the technical approach does not provide point estimates or a range of possible future values, and this reduces its predictive explanatory power. In fact, a technical forecasting model may work well in one period but produce a completely wrong prediction in another one.

The market approach

Market-based forecasting is usually premised in either the spot rate or the forward rate (Madura, 2012). Corporations can use the spot rate as a forecast since it represents the market's expectation of the spot rate in the near future. On the other hand, a forward rate quoted for a specific date in the future is commonly used as the forecasted spot rate on that date. In other words, a 30-day forward rate provides a forecast for the spot rate in 30 days, and so on. However, the general consensus is that forward exchange rates have little if any power as forecasts of future spot exchange rates (Fama, 1984).

If corporations are convinced that the forward rate is a reliable indicator of the future spot rate, they can simply monitor this publicly quoted rate to develop exchange rate projections. Long-term forward rates can be used to derive long-term exchange rate forecasts. These rates can be easily computed for a period of 2-5 years, although the bid/ask spread is wide because their trading volume is limited. Despite the dearth of quotes in financial newspapers, the quoted interest rates on risk-free assets for different countries can be used to calculate the correct value of forward rates implied by the interest rate parity (IRP).

This theory dates back to Fisher (1896), who provided a general analysis of the relationship between interest rates and expected changes in the relative value of international currencies. IRP states that the difference in interest rates between two countries will equal the differential between the forward exchange rate and the spot exchange rate over the same period. However, scholars have found no empirical evidence supporting the use of such technique. In fact, Meese & Rogoff (1988) found that a random walk model is a better proxy to estimate exchange rates.

As we can conclude from the discussion above, forecasting the exchange rate is an important but difficult task for MNCs. Moreover, the decision about which type of forecasting techniques should be used is never simple. For this reason, *mixed forecasting* is common. This approach involves using different forecasting approaches, assigning each a specific weight, with the more reliable methods given higher weights (and the sum of the weights equal to one). Using this method, it is possible to exploit the advantages of different techniques and overcome their possible weaknesses. However, there can still be changes in exchange rates unanticipated by any method; ta subjective assessment of conditions in a particular country should therefore be implemented.

Forecasting under market efficiency

According to Rossi (2013), building on the efficient market hypothesis, in the absence of risk premia or if they manifest only a small time variation compared to variations in fundamental pricing factors, the best approximation for the relative fundamental value of two currencies is given by bilateral exchange rates based on the information available at the given time. In this case, forecasting is affected by the efficiency of the foreign exchange market: if it is weakly efficient, then no information can be extracted from historical and current exchange rates to forecast exchange rate movements. As Madura (2012) maintains, if the foreign exchange market is semi-efficient or strongly efficient, then today's exchange rates already reflect all public information regarding expected interest rate movements. If historical trends are reflected in today's exchange rates but not in other public information on expected rate fluctuations, the market's efficiency is still weak. According to research, foreign exchange markets appear to be weak and semi-strong in terms of efficiency. Finally, in strongly efficient markets all relevant public and private information is already incorporated into current exchange rates. Given that private information is not available, it is impossible to test this form of efficiency. MNCs usually prefer to compute their own forecasts over time rather than to rely on market-based rates for forecasts of future rates. To assess proposed policies, they develop various scenarios and assess how exchange rates may change for each one.

9.6.3   Forecasting error

As mentioned above, a forecast represents an expectation about a future value of a variable, in our case the exchange rate, given the information available at the time of forecasting. It is immediate to notice that each forecast has an associated forecasting error, which is calculated as the difference between the effective value of the exchange rate once it is realized in the future and its correspondent expectation. The forecasting error is a measure of the overall quality of the forecast. A typical metrics used in econometric analysis is the Mean Square Error (MSE), defined as the sum of squared errors, divided by the number of observations considered in the sample. The higher is the MSE, the less accurate is the model.

We can distinguish between two kinds of forecasts: *in-sample* and *out-of-sample*. The former implies the usage of today's information to forecast what today's spot rate should be. For instance, the fitted values estimated in a regression are in-sample forecasts. Conversely, out-of-sample forecasting means using today's information to guess the future behavior of exchange rates. Of course, in order to make a reliable out-of-sample forecast, it will be necessary to make a bunch of assumptions about the future value assumed by fundamental economic variables.

In general, we have to acknowledge that a large proportion of the movement in the exchange rate cannot be forecasted by any technique, thus resulting in a higher forecasting error. Additionally, if the exchange rate moves away from the economic fundamentals, for instance in the case of a speculative bubble, then the forecast errors will be much larger. Therefore, a large proportion of the movement in the spot rate is unpredictable with any model. In such a situation, the random walk represents a useful benchmark: investors try to predict the change in the exchange rate, on the basis of the current spot rate, with an error term that should, under the hypothesis of efficient markets, be purely random. This hypothesis requires the error not necessarily to be small, but unbiased, that is, equal to zero on average. Recall that in the random walk model the exchange rate is assumed to be independent of its past history. To test the efficiency of exchange rate markets, simple linear regression analysis are usually implemented. However, Bilson (1990) points out that linear comparisons are meaningless, since technical analysis rely on nonlinearities.

An interesting study is the one recently made by Amat et al. (2018), which demonstrate that the use of methods stemming from the field of machine learning can lead to improved exchange rate forecasts with respect to simple exchange rate models based on OLS regression. They applied a sequential ridge regression and the exponentially weighted average strategy both with discount factors to a sample of different currencies over the period 1973-2014, with the aim of doing a 1-month forecasting of the exchange rate. Using such techniques, the authors found that fundamentals from simple exchange rate models (PPP or UIRP) contained useful information and that exchange rates were forecastable even for short horizons. In conclusion, by using machine-learning techniques, the authors proved that it is possible to detect a short-term relationship between classic fundamentals and exchange rates that goes beyond the simple random walk hypothesis.

There are several variables that can affect the quality of forecast error: the two most important ones are the currency's volatility and the investment horizon. More volatile currencies will have a larger forecast error, as their spot rates could easily deviate from any forecasted value in the future. Another variable to consider is the investment horizon: a spot rate forecast for tomorrow will have a relatively small error, as its deviations from today's value will be less than one percent. In contrast, a rate forecast for a month from now is more difficult to predict correctly, as the value of the currency has more time to deviate from the current level. For this reason, long-term projects are the ones most affected by exchange rate movements. Interesting on this point is the reference to the research of Macdonald & Nagayasu (2013), which shows that exchange rate projections are homogeneous across different types of sectors when the projection time horizon is the same, while they diverge within the same sector when the projection time horizon is different. In particular, the authors show that investors tend to underestimate future exchange rates over long-term projection horizons, but overestimate future exchange rates in the short term.

Before implementing decisions, MNCs should consider the impact of the potential error and monitor the performance of their projects over time. In some approaches, like the MSE presented above, the error is calculated with an absolute or squared value to account for the presence of negative values that may offset the calculation of the average forecast error. Negative errors are the result of underestimating exchange rates, while positive errors arise if forecasts overestimate exchange rates. If positive or negative errors persist over time, then the MNC has a bias in its forecasting procedure. Detecting bias is fundamental for a multinational company to improve its estimation accuracy. Since a forecast error results from events that have not been incorporated into the existing information used for forecasting, a common way of assessing the existence of forecast bias is to compute a regression of the spot exchange rate on an intercept and on the forward rate of the previous period in time. If the latter is unbiased, the intercept should be null and the regression coefficient should be equal to 1. If the regression coefficient is significantly less than 1, there has been an overestimation of the exchange rate; vice versa if the coefficient is greater than 1, this implies that the forward rate is systematically underestimating the spot rate. If errors are consistently positive, for instance, the company can adjust today's forward rate downward to reflect the bias.

9.7 Case study: the Kering Group and exchange risk management

To conclude, we will consider an example of the theoretical concepts discussed in this chapter. The case concerns the Kering Group, which, as an international company, is a good example of the techniques a multinational company should use to reduce its net currency exposure and minimize vulnerability to foreign exchange risk.

9.7.1 The Kering Group

Since its foundation in 1962, the Kering Group has become one of the leading luxury goods holding companies globally. It now operates in more than 120 countries and is headquartered in Paris. The Group brings together a pool of brands which are divided into three divisions: Luxury, Sport & Lifestyle, and Eyewear. Brands like Gucci, Yves Saint Laurent, Bottega Veneta, and Balenciaga form only a small part of its international portfolio. The markets and product categories in which the Group operates are highly concentrated: for instance, the Kering Group has a leading position in the luxury goods market thanks to firms such as LVMH, Richemont, and Hermès.

In terms of financial performance, 2019 saw incredible double-digit growth in revenues (16.2%) for the Group, reaching nearly €16 billion. However, the Group registered a drop of 37.4% in net profit (€2.3 billion) due to the negative impact of a tax settlement of about €1.25 billion with the Italian treasury, which took place in May 2019, combined with the extraordinary gain obtained in 2018 from the sale of Puma (€1.2 billion).

Though Western Europe has historically been the largest market for Kering in terms of personal luxury goods, 2019 saw an inverted trend, with APAC sales surpassing those from Europe for the first time. This was a result of a significant rise in revenues, which was 22.7% higher for APAC than 2018, while it was only 14.5% for Western Europe. This same trend characterizes the comparison between developed and emerging markets, with the former sub-total rising by 13.6% and the latter growing by 20.3%.

9.7.2 The Group's currency risk exposure

To understand Kering's exposure to currency risk, we have to consider the company's breakdown of borrowings denominated in different currencies, as shown in **Table 9.2**. In 2019, the total amount of gross borrowing was €5.1 billion, split into bonds, bank loans, and money market instruments. The majority of those borrowings were denominated in euro, while the amounts in other currencies were allocated to subsidiaries for local financing purposes. The two main foreign currency borrowings were Japanese yen-denominated and U.S. dollar-denominated. While the former increased from an equivalent of €362.8 in 2018 to €469.4 million, borrowings denominated in U.S. dollars declined from €315.8 to €277.0 million in the same period.

Table 9.2   Breakdown of the Kering Group's borrowings by repayment currency

(in millions €)	31 Dec 2019	Non-current borrowings	Current borrowings	%	31 Dec 2018	%
EUR	4,308.5	2,905.7	1,402.8	84.5%	3,188.3	81.2%
JPY	469.4	69.9	399.5	9.2%	362.8	9.2%
USD	277.0	133.4	143.6	5.4%	315.8	8.0%
CHF	14.3	13.2	1.1	0.3%	29.5	0.8%
TWD	10.2	–	10.2	0.2%	9.8	0.2%
Other currencies	18.7	–	18.7	0.4%	21.8	0.6%
TOTAL	5,098.1	3,122.2	1,975.9	100.0%	3,928.0	100.0%

Source: Kering Annual Report 2019.

Table 9.3 shows Kering's exposure to foreign exchange rates. Before hedging, the Group had a net exposure greater than €7.3 billion (it was €6.0 billion in 2018). This means that 46.2% of its total revenues were subject to exchange rate movements. That €7.3 billion can be divided into a net exposure (the difference between monetary assets and liabilities) and forecast exposure. With regard to the former, Kering registered an amount of €3.2 billion in 2019. This exposure arose from the fact that all its monetary items were denominated in the functional currencies used by subsidiaries to operate: assets included, for instance, loans and receivables, cash equivalents, and short-maturity investments; liabilities were made of loans and operating payables.

Considering the different currencies, the U.S. dollar represented the currency to which the Kering Group was most exposed (€1.9 billion), followed by the Chinese yuan (€1.3 billion), and the British pound (€0.7 billion).

In the last two lines of Table 9.3, the effect of hedging is accounted for to calculate the final net exposure of the Group. We will discuss the hedging techniques applied by Kering in the next paragraph.

Table 9.3   Breakdown of the Kering Group's exposure to each functional currency

(in millions €)	31 Dec 2019	USD	GBP	CNY
Monetary assets	4,207.9	982.9	285.8	677.4
Monetary liabilities	994.9	410.1	9.7	0.1
Net exposure on the balance sheet	3,213.0	572.8	276.1	677.3
Forecast exposure	4,103.2	1,344.4	425.5	677.0
Net exposure before hedging	7,316.2	1,917.2	701.6	1,354.3
Hedging instruments	(6,166.4)	(1,705.1)	(591.4)	(980.4)
Net exposure after hedging	1,149.8	212.1	110.2	373.9

Source: Kering Annual Report 2019.

9.7.3   How to manage currency risk

Currency risk management at Kering primarily includes the use of financial instruments addressed at hedging risks coming from inter-company transactions and international trade (i.e., exports and imports). In 2019, the Group invested €6.1 billion (+14.3% with respect to 2018) in hedging instruments such as currency swaps, currency options, and currency forwards. Table 9.4 shows the breakdown of those instruments. Given their customizability and flexibility, forward contracts accounted for almost 92% of the overall amount of derivatives used by Kering.

At the end of the 2019 fiscal year, most of the derivative instruments that qualified as cash flow hedges had a remaining maturity of less than one year. They accounted for almost €6 billion. Kering used them to hedge cash balances expected to

Table 9.4   **Breakdown of the Kering Group's derivative instruments by type**

(in million €)	31 December 2019	31 December 2018
Currency forwards	(5,669.4)	(5,036.4)
Cross currency swaps	(109.1)	(105.7)
Currency options – export tunnels	(233.2)	(160.7)
Currency options – purchases	(154.7)	(92.1)
TOTAL	(6,1664)	(5,394.9)

Source: Kering Annual Report 2019.

be realized the following year. The remaining portion of €100 million was constituted by currency swaps with a maturity of more than one year. On the other hand,
derivatives qualifying as fair value hedges were used to hedge items identified in the
balance sheet as at fair value.

Due to foreign exchange risk management, the Kering Group was able to reduce
its exposure by €6.2 billion, to a final value of €1.1 billion – just 7% of total sales.
Together with financial techniques, operational ones are a fundamental instrument
for hedging foreign risk exposure, even if they do not appear explicitly on balance
sheet figures. Given the uncertainty every MNC faces, it is crucial to build flexible
risk management strategies and financial instruments that enable the firm to adapt
quickly to evolving situations and effectively hedge its foreign exchange risk.

9.8   Conclusions

Currency exposure management is fundamental for corporations operating worldwide. One reason why firms may decide not to hedge concerns the costs of the operation, which sometimes outweigh the benefits. Firms adopt different approaches to
currency hedging depending on their objectives and forecasts. The goal of this chapter was to provide an overview of the basic tools necessary to develop an informed
opinion about the advantages and disadvantages of hedging in different currency environments.

When deciding to go abroad, a multinational firm cannot underestimate the impact that exchange rates might have on its profitability. Accurate risk management
of exchange rate fluctuations could save a business from dangerous outcomes. This
chapter aimed to provide readers with a sense of what it means to face exchange
rate risk and to outline three key exchange rate systems: fixed, floating, and pegged.
Under a fixed exchange rate system, rates are either kept stable or allowed to fluctuate only within tight boundaries. A floating exchange rate arrangement means that
exchange rate values are determined by market forces. In a pegged exchange rate
system, the value of a country's home currency is pegged to a foreign currency or to
a combination of currencies. A few additional notions were also introduced to help

clarify the long-standing debate over hedging and highlight three arguments against it: the purchasing power parity theory, the capital asset pricing model and the Modigliani Miller theory.

By the end of the chapter, readers should have a better sense of the three types of exposure to exchange risk that exist and the relevant techniques for hedging against it. We discussed transaction exposure when the value of a firm's future contractual transactions in foreign currencies are affected by exchange rate movements. Two ways of measuring this exposure emerged: through the standard deviation of the portfolio and through use of the value-at-risk method. Next we discussed economic exposure, which occurs when the value of a firm's cash flows are affected by exchange rate movements if it executes transactions in foreign currencies, receives revenue from foreign customers, or is subject to foreign competition. Economic exposure can relate to local currency appreciation and depreciation. The measurement technique used for economic exposure is either looking at sales and expenses categories affected by the risk or conducting a regression analysis using historical cash flows and exchange rate data. Lastly, we considered translation exposure, which occurs when a subsidiary's financial statement must be translated into the currency of the MNC parent company. In this section, we also outlined specific hedging techniques for each exposure and the internal and external factors influencing these techniques, the importance of forecasting exchange rates and the reasons for doing so, and the errors inherent to forecasting techniques (which can be technical, fundamental, market-based, or mixed).

Lastly, to demonstrate how these concepts work in practice, we analyze hedging in the Kering Group, a multinational business exposed to currency variations. We saw that in order to mitigate this risk, Kering offsets the largest portion of its currency exposure by using financial derivatives.

10 Equity Financing

The process of "going public" is a crucial one for a company and it might be surrounded by complexities and difficulties along the way. To multiply the probability of success and make sure these difficulties disappear, corporations usually request the help and advice of experts: Investment Banks. These financial institutions assist the client in the entire listing process.

Given the importance and delicacy of the task, when choosing an investment bank, an issuer usually does not go for the cheapest option in terms of fees. Instead, it looks for the most reliable and highly reputed expert, even though this should not be the only criteria used to decide on advisors. In the real world, the investment banks that lead the market are Goldman Sachs, JP Morgan, Morgan Stanley and Bank of America Merrill-Lynch. This quartet shares most of the market, but there are dozens of other participants that might potentially be best suited to a company that wants to get listed. In the end, what is really important is to find an ally who has your best interests at heart.

As you might have realized from these first few lines, the topic of this chapter is the equity capital market and more specifically Initial Public Offerings and Seasoned Offerings. We will devote most of our time to talking about the former, and make sure that all the concepts we discuss in theory are then clearly understood and reflected in practice, with the case of the Ferrari IPO. We will then turn to Seasoned Offers, and touch on the definition and main features of this process too. Lastly, we will look at an additional example of right issuance by Unicredit.

10.1 Equity Capital Markets (ECM)

In equity capital markets, the special kind of "product" is *equity*, which can be sold in *public* or *private transactions*.

A *public transaction* occurs when an issuer sells its equity to investors and the company becomes listed on a certain stock market, which we refer to as the stock exchange. This procedure happens through *IPOs* and *SEOs*:

- *IPOs* (*Initial Public Offerings*): also referred to as unseasoned offerings, are public offerings in which the equity of a company is listed and sold on the stock market for the first time.

- *SEOs (Seasoned Offerings)*: additional equity of an already-listed company is sold into the stock market. This can happen in two ways, differing in the time required for the transaction. The "American way" of increasing capital is allowed solely in the U.S. where the execution can take only a few days through either an *accelerated book building* or a *bought deal transaction*. On the other hand, according to the "European way," the transaction usually takes 3-6 months as companies have to give the rights issue to their current shareholders. In other words, the issuer gives the right to its pre-existing shareholders to participate in the increase of capital before other potential investors can do so. In the American way, we don't need to give this right to existing shareholders and we can dilute existing shares. Therefore, in Europe, SEOs are longer, more complex procedures.

A *private equity transaction* is when the equity is sold to investors but the company is not listed on the stock market. There are two types of investors in these transactions, institutional investors such as PE investors, and other retail investors such as high net worth individuals.

IPOs and SEOs are the most profitable services that an Investment Bank (IB) can offer to its clients. Therefore, IBs are happy to receive a mandate from a company to go public with an IPO or SEO. Fees for IBs are very high because these transactions have an elevated risk for the advisor. For example, in a recent transaction that was carried out by one of the oldest banks operating in Italy, there was the surprise in the media when it became known that the advisor selected was paid almost €400 million in fees for six months of work. What journalists did not properly take into account was the fact that there was a huge risk in the mandate for the advisor: the commitment to buy all the unsold shares, with a total exposure of €8 billion.

In any case, let's start our analysis with IPOs.

10.2 Initial Public Offerings (IPOs)

An IPO is the very first time a firm is publicly listed in a stock market. It is very common to see big celebrations and news coverage surrounding the stock markets, such as the NYSE, during the day of an IPO. These events are watched all around the globe and are the center of economic attention of the day that they take place. This is because firms raise a considerable amount of capital on IPO day so these occasions represent an important opportunity to investors around the world. According to the New York Stock Exchange: "IPOs are a proven method of connecting companies, employees and economies with the capital they need to expand their businesses, build more jobs in their communities, retain top employees and elevate their brands. It's a process that fuels innovation, drives growth and encourages healthy competition."

IPO (*Initial Public Offering*), as we said, is when the equity of a company is sold on the stock market for the first time. An IPO occurs when a privately-held company decides to go public. This is one of the most complex transactions for a corporation because it is difficult to properly target investors and sell this special kind of product (equity) for the first time into the market. It is also an expensive transaction, in terms of fees paid to advisors, since such transactions may involve high risks to Investment Banks (i.e. 7%-9% of the issued amount paid to advisors). For this reason, it is extremely important to properly evaluate an IPO before going ahead. So, what are the main reasons for an IPO? There are usually three: *Financial*, *Strategic* and *Corporate Governance*.

Financial reasons are when the issuer needs to collect new resources for financing new investments. A company might be faced with profitable investment opportunities that are risky and require an enormous amount of money to be financed. But these transactions might actually be too big, risky and expensive in terms of regulatory capital to be financed only through simple banks or with debt. Before deciding to opt for an IPO, the company must, however, make sure that the transaction cannot be financed either by bank loans or by other debt instruments. To assess whether debt can be used, it is important to know how heathy the debt market is in the domestic country relative to the international market. Another financial reason could be the need to reduce the cost of debt for the issuer. If the company increases its level of equity, its D/E capital ratio decreases. As a consequence, the firm is perceived as less risky, which results in an improvement of its credit rating which in turn reduces its cost of debt. In the end, a final financial reason is expanding the opportunity for new leverage. New equity injected in the capital structure means the company is expanding its capability to augment its future debt capacity.

Strategic reasons relate to the necessity to sustain a corporate/business strategy. It is possible to finance part of the acquisition price with stocks. Target shareholders are more willing to accept stocks of a listed company compared to stocks of an unlisted company, which are less attractive, because the latter does not have the liquidity or pricing advantage of the former. Therefore, the likelihood of acceptance by target shareholders of listed shares is much higher. This probability is even higher still if the stocks are issued in the same country of the target shareholders as it reduces their exposure to foreign factors such as exchange rates, political risks, etc.

In addition, when a company decides to enter new markets, it will be subject to costs to reach new customers and market its products and services. An IPO can facilitate the entrance into a new market as it improves visibility (in terms of marketing/brand) by exposing the firm to the financial community in the country where the IPO will happen: it is an indirect way to make the company's brand available in the country it wants to enter. By promoting the IPO, by law to retail investors and not only institutional investors, the company is also promoting its brand. Therefore, to understand if this is a strong enough reason, it is essential to make a comparison between marketing costs and IPO costs.

Luxottica raised funds in US market by managing an IPO there to reach American customers. The CEO not only wanted to expand via internal growth but also via M&As.

Prada went for an IPO in Asia, where the fashion industry was growing, in order to promote the brand and support expansion in that continent. Managing an IPO directly in Asia meant that Prada met the standards to be listed in the Asian market. This implies that Prada has good quality products, thereby promoting the brand's image in Asia (brand marketing).

Supporting growth in new countries is simply a matter of expanding the number of clients or promoting a new product. By listing in another country, the newly-public firm proves it is reliable as it must have complied with many formal procedures. Furthermore, the listed corporation will also acquire a more valuable currency to pursue growth opportunities in the form of what's called an acquisition currency. To better understand the reasons behind an acquisition currency: American investors will never accept Italian shares as payment because they may feel not protected enough by accepting foreign shares, or because there might be restrictions for American investors to invest in foreign listed corporation. Therefore, there must be an acquisition currency available to pay for the transactions.

When the Italian eyeglasses producer entered the US market, it was still a private company. Luxottica decided to support growth there by listing the company in the NY Stock Exchange, in order to convince the country that it was a trustable company with a quality product, because it had to go through formal procedures to do so. This also helped Luxottica to pay part of the acquisition price of Ray-Ban and support the promotion costs.

Corporate governance reasons can be engaged to support an IPO transaction when a company needs to find an exit strategy for pre-existing shareholders. In other words, an IPO could represent a way out for pre-existing shareholders who want to liquidate their investment. However, this cannot be the only reason for going public, or at least the official one, since new investors would like to see that existing shareholders believe that the company has a future. Evidence of this can be found in the Prada Case.

Certain shareholders of Prada, such as Banca Intesa, would have used IPOs as a way to liquidate part of their participation in the company.

Going public is always an important step in the history of a corporation, also because the transaction gives enormous visibility to the founders of the company, improving their own reputation together with that of the company itself.

Attracting the best managers in the sector could also be another way to justify an IPO. If you are a listed company, you can seduce managers with the proposal of stock option compensation. Also, CEOs want international exposure that can be more easily achieved through a listed company.

Probably corporate governance reasons are not enough to justify an IPO; instead, a combination of reasons should prompt a company to make this move.

The Facebook IPO was an exception to this assertion. In fact, in this case the IPO was justified solely for corporate governance reasons, as shareholders were private equity investors who entered when Facebook was first created, and were looking for an exit strategy that was easily implemented with the IPO.

A company does not require all the listed reasons to go for an IPO; a single strong reason might be enough.

> For the Ferrari IPO, the main strategic reasons were to increase the brand visibility and to change its perception, by positioning the company as a global competitor in the luxury goods sector, and no longer in the automotive industry. From a financial point of view, €870 million were raised and corporate debt was reduced by approximately €1 million. This transaction was part of a "separation" plan whose purpose was first to separate Ferrari from the FCA group, then to change the company's shareholders structure. The initial corporate governance (90% of shares held by FCA, the remaining 10% by Piero Ferrari) was revised during the IPO phase (80% of shares held by FCA, 10% by Piero Ferrari, 10% by public share-holders) and finally defined after the execution of the separation plan (24% of shares held by Exor – i.e. Agnelli family –, 10% by Piero Ferrari and 66% by public shareholders). In 2018, Ferrari's EV/EBITDA multiple was 29.36 thus achieving the strategic objective of being priced by the market in line with the multiples of other companies operating in the luxury goods sector.

10.2.1   The IPO process

When dealing with an IPO, there are four issues to resolve: *where to sell shares, in which market, which shares* and *to whom.*

Where to sell shares

First of all, "where to sell shares" does not refer to the stock market where the corporation will be listed; the reference is to the investors that the shares will ultimately be sold to.

First, there are domestic (retail) offers, also known as *domestic public offers* where the company decides to sell its shares to local/national investors (e.g. an Italian incorporated company decides to sell shares to Italian investors). Usually, in domestic offers, shares are sold to both retail and institutional investors.

Secondly, international/global (institutional) offers, also known as *international private offers* are those where the company decides to sell its shares to foreign investors (e.g. an Italian incorporated company decides to sell shares to foreign investors). Usually, in international offers, shares are sold only to institutional investors, as it is expensive and time consuming to sell the shares of a company, which might be an unknown entity, to retail investors.

Multiple offer is what happens in reality, where a mix of domestic (retail offers) and international (institutional offers) is executed.

In which market?

The question "which financial markets to sell shares in" refers to the market where the company will be listed.

Usually companies get listed in their *home market* (*single listing*). In this transaction the equity will be proposed where the company is actually incorporated. This alternative is the least expensive and the easiest one because it is less complicated to adhere to all the laws and rules that are imposed by the local stock exchange as they are regulations applied in the home country of the company (e.g. when a company incorporated in Italy lists its equity in Italy).

Otherwise, *foreign market (single listing)* is another option where the equity will be proposed in a country which is not where the company is incorporated. This alternative is more expensive and more complex. There are several reasons why a company might want to opt for a foreign market transaction.

First, it may need to expand the investor base. If the company wants to do so by targeting foreign investors, it could be a smart idea to list the stock in the country where those foreign investors are located, overcoming all the problems they would be subject to, such as exchange rate risks, differences in corporate governance rules and taxation.

Second, as we have seen, an IPO can also aim at sustaining a business strategy. For example, an issuer can be interested in an IPO if the company is looking to pursue an M&A strategy; probably, a cross-border M&A. One example might be an Italian incorporated company that wants to acquire a competitor in the US; an IPO in the US is a way to acquire funds in that country's currency.

Third, it might just be that the home market of the issuer is small and inefficient.

Fourth, if the issuer believes that the company will be able to attract the attention of international investors, but thinks that they won't invest in the home stock exchange (that of the issuer), one option to consider is listing in a foreign market to not miss the opportunity of having large institutional investors among the shareholder base. Notice that in some smaller markets it is harder to attract international investors.

Fifth, going public abroad could be a necessity when the company operates in a specific niche. In order to be considered credible in that specific sector firms have to be admitted in a specific index/market; ex. NASDAQ: if you operate in the social media business. If you want to compete, you need to be listed where your competitors are.

Sixth, when the issuer doesn't meet the requirements to be listed in the home market it must go abroad to be listed.

Last but not least, this "foreign listing option" should also be taken into consideration when the equity is differently evaluated depending on the stock exchange market on which it is listed. Some stock markets in which the demand for equity securities is higher will usually accept higher stock prices than other foreign markets.

Together with home and foreign market listing options, we also need to investigate *dual listing transactions*. A company can decide to list its own shares in two different markets, probably its own market and a foreign one. It is a complex and expensive solution because the company has to abide by the system of rules of different markets. Very few companies file for a dual listing because they have to deal with a large number of related issues. This is the case of ENI (*Ente Nazionale Indrocarburi*, a multinational corporation operating in the oil and gas sector) which is now in New York and Milan. Fiat Chrysler Automobiles (FCA), before merging on January 16, 2021 with Groupe PSA to form Stellantis Group, was also initially dual listed in Milan and New York.

Ferrari is an Italian incorporated company that managed to be listed first on the U.S. stock exchange and only later in Italy. Fiat was dual listed at the beginning, but then the CEO, Marchionne, decided to delist it from the Italian stock exchange because Fiat was no longer producing or selling most of its cars in Italy. Marchionne was trying to convince the market that Fiat was no longer an Italian brand because, due to the debt crisis in the government, being an Italian company meant paying a huge country risk discount. However, the problem with Fiat was that the market did not understand that it was not exposed to country risk. To convince the market to properly appreciate the value of Fiat, Fiat Chrysler Automobiles N.V. was created (FCA), which became the parent company of the new group and was registered in the Netherlands. FCA listed its shares first in New York and only later in Milan. The country risk discount was finally eliminated creating value for the shareholders. Moral: when deciding on a single or dual listing, remember that the final aim is creating value for shareholders.

Which shares

Answering to the question "which shares" means understanding where the money from the transaction is going. Let's clarify that there are *primary offerings* and *secondary offerings*.

Primary offerings involve newly issued shares. In this case, proceeds go directly in the balance sheet of the company because a piece of equity is sold on the market.

In *secondary offerings*, existing shares of pre-existing shareholders are sold on the market and proceeds are cashed in by these shareholders.

In both cases, we are dealing with an IPO because neither company was listed before the transaction. The market does not appreciate secondary offerings too much because when shareholders sell their shares normally it is because they believe those shares are overvalued.

To whom?

To whom are you going to sell shares is the last question to answer. We can differentiate between *retail* and *institutional tranches*.

Retail tranches are transactions where shares are sold to retail investors. When targeting retail investors, a document must be drawn up called the *Prospectus* which includes all the information/risks of the company. This is a very long and complex document, which serves to give transparency and information to investors. The main advantages are that retail investors are not qualified, therefore, through the use of asymmetric information, there is a chance of *making arbitrage*, i.e. selling shares at a higher price. Disadvantages are that it is time consuming and expensive due to the fact that many investors need to be targeted in order to cover the entire issue.

With an *institutional tranche* shares are sold to institutional investors. In this case, a document called an *Offering Circular* is drawn up, a lighter version of the Prospectus, to distribute to these potential investors. This is because these investors understand the risks underlying the transaction. The advantages of this type of transaction are that the process is faster and less expensive, as each institutional investor has the power to subscribe a substantial portion of the issue. The fact that these investors are qualified is an advantage here too, but by the same token a disadvantage, in the sense that there is no chance to make use of arbitrage. Actually, as institutional investors have strong bargaining power, the issuing company needs to accept the conditions imposed by them, and propose the transaction at a discount.

However, in reality, retail and institutional investors are often targeted at the same time and offered shares at the same price. Generally, a majority (on average 80%-85%) of shares are proposed to institutional while a minority (on average 15%-20%) to retail investors. But this is not a written rule and, for example, it did not occur with Facebook, when Morgan Stanley proposed a percentage greater than 15%-20% (26% to be precise) of shares to retail investors, mostly because FB wanted to target investors who were also the main users of the platform.

In summary:

- Where to sell shares: domestic vs international offering.
- Which market: single vs dual listing.
- Use of proceeds: primary vs secondary offering.
- To whom: retail/public vs institutional/private offering.

10.2.2 Legal framework

In order to implement an IPO, it is necessary to check the norms to adhere to in the country where the company will go public without forgetting the rules that are imposed by the owner of the market. (i.e. Borsa Italiana Spa is the owner of the stock market in Italy and has been part of the London Stock Exchange Group since 2007, when they merged). In the financial system, together with the financial markets and with financial intermediaries, there are other important players as well: *authorities* and *supervisors*. When a company wants to be listed and admitted to a stock exchange, it must ask permission from the supervisors. In Italy, Commissione Nazionale per le Società e la Borsa (CONSOB) is the authority that supervises the activities of listed companies within the financial market, while Bank of Italy oversees the activity of financial intermediaries.

10.2.3 Key steps of an IPO process

The IPO process can be divided in three different steps: *Preparation*, *Pre-Launch* and *Execution*.

Preparation

This first phase, *preparation*, takes place approximately 4-6 months before the IPO launch. The IB receives a call from a client that is interested in an IPO. If the right reasons exist for taking this step, the IB accepts the mandate and becomes the *Global Coordinator* (GC): the leader of the IPO process, aka the book-runner, i.e. the bank with the role of allocating shares.

Figure 10.1   **Syndacate structure**

The Global Coordinator starts working on what we call the *Syndicate*, a group of banks made up of the GC, leading the group, and below it a certain number of *Co-leader Banks* and, at the bottom, the *Seller Banks*. The global coordinator is an investment bank; co-leaders are also investment banks, while seller banks can be both investment banks and commercial banks (**Figure 10.1**). All these banks help the global coordinator to target investors situated in different parts of the world and to sell equity.

For example, if Mediobanca receives the mandate from Prada, which wants to be listed in a foreign market, this bank must create a syndicate with banks that cover the world in terms of international offerings. So, for example, Goldman Sachs (GS) will try to sell to Chinese investors, while Santander would target investors in South America.

Usually, there is only one Global Coordinator. However, there are cases in which there is more than one, which are called *Joint Global Coordinators*. Why wouldn't a global bank want to have global coordinators that are also global banks? Because all global banks compete against one another to be the best in their field, so they would never want to give a competitor the upper hand by inviting it to participate as a global coordinator. So, we would have: GS with Mediobanca, GS with Santander, or GS with Unicredit. However, it is extremely difficult to find GS partnering with JP Morgan or with Morgan Stanley, because they are direct competitors and don't want to share points in the league table.

The syndicate is needed to guarantee the sale of all the shares, for distribution reasons, and also because the syndicate acts as a sort of certification (a signal to the market about the quality of the issue).

Corporations want to be sure to receive all the money they have requested from the issuance. Typically, the GC also acts as an *underwriter.* There are several underwriting services that can be offered to clients: *best effort commitment, full underwriting commitment* and *partial underwriting commitment.*

- *Best effort commitment*: This is the cheapest mandate in terms of fees. It means that the IB must do its best to place the entire issue, but it doesn't have obligations to subscribe unsold shares. This is the best mandate an IB can receive if it isn't sure it can sell the whole issue, even for a cheap mandate. It is also the service usually chosen by the best companies, which only need IBs to take care of the procedure and have no doubt that they will be able to place all the shares, so, this is a way they can save on fees. However, the best effort mandate is also chosen by smaller companies that don't want to spend too much money to pay the fees. These are complex transactions because even though the IB does not risk money, it does risk its reputation.
- *Full underwriting commitment*: The IB guarantees the entire transaction, which means that if the IB doesn't manage to sell the shares to the market, it will underwrite the remaining part of the issue and insert it in the balance sheet. This commitment entails a high level of financial risk for the bank. In fact, if the IB isn't able to place the entire issue, it wouldn't want to take part in the governance of the company and it will sell the shares to the market at a discount.
- *Partial underwriting commitment*: The IB guarantees only part of the transaction; for instance, with a total issuance of 2 million shares, the IB might guarantee to sell 1 million.

The main difference among these commitments is the amount of fees paid by the issuer to the IB: best effort is the cheapest, while full underwriting is the most expensive in terms of fees (7%-9% of total issue). Specifically, the main fees in this kind of transaction are *gross spread fees*: total amount of fees paid by the client to the global coordinator, usually a fixed percentage of the total issue. These fees are split into *managing, underwriting* and *selling fees*. Managing (or arranging) fees (usually 20%): fees for managing the transaction to those who lead, so to both global coordinators and co-leaders; underwriting fees (usually 20%) to remunerate the risk taken by the global coordinator and co-leaders to underwrite the transaction; selling fees (usually 60%) paid for the selling activity and are proportional to the number of shares sold.

The book runner (another name for global coordinator) retains most of the fees because this player is the one to decide how to allocate shares (usually first to its own investors and then to the investors contacted by other banks).

> Morgan Stanley, to assist Facebook in a full underwriting commitment, accepted 1.1% in fees, a huge discount compared to the fees usually applied to issuers, because it did not want to miss out on such a big opportunity as there were other competitors willing to serve as advisor on the transaction.

Advisors make money when the value of the issue rises, that is when there is an increase the price or the number of shares to sell.

In this preparation phase, before going ahead with the IPO, the key is to understand from the very beginning the intrinsic value of the issuer (DCF). This is calculated by comparing the value with a DCF methodology with multiples; therefore, it is important to consider market trends as well. Whenever the market is willing to offer a lower price to competitors than the one computed by the advisor, that should set the new price threshold for the IPO. If instead the client does not agree to go public at a lower price, the advisor can withdraw from the mandate (there is a clause specifying this in case of disagreement between client and investment bank). It is essential from the very beginning to agree with the client about the price. The advisor first identifies the total amount of proceeds that the client wants to raise from the transaction, and then proposes an issue price and a number of shares:

$$Total \ amount \ of \ proceeds = Issue \ price \times Number \ of \ shares$$

So, increasing the total amount of proceeds means either increasing the issue price or the number of shares. As an example, Morgan Stanley upgraded Facebook's share price from $[28-34] per share to $[34-38], and the number of shares from 19 to 24 million.

Pre-launch

The second phase, the *pre-launch*, takes place approximately 3-4 months before the IPO. The pre-launch involves the filing of mandatory documentations to register the transaction with public authorities. This phase consists of two crucial steps: *creating the Prospectus* and *filing for the IPO*.

- *Creating the Prospectus*: a (public) legal document drawn up to accurately describe the details of the issuing corporation and the proposed offering to potential investors, from a financial, fiscal and legal perspective. It includes business due diligence (the Business Plan), and legal due diligence (fiscal/legal issues) which is required information to disclose to the market before the IPO. If a corporation fails to disclose mandatory information prior to the IPO, it could be sued.
  When preparing the Prospectus before the launch of an IPO, all information about the business must be included both for institutional investors and for retail investors The preliminary Prospectus is sometimes called a "red herring". The Prospectus includes a description of the business in which the company operates, the corporate strategy, the quality of management, the company's future performance, and what the company is going to do with the proceeds raised from the issue. In a secondary offering, the proceeds must go in the hands of pre-existing shareholders and not to the company. However, remember it cannot be explicitly stated to the market that all the proceeds will be used to liquidate pre-existing shareholders; it must be a mix of the two.
  The global coordinator works on the Prospectus, together with a law firm and an auditing firm. After the transaction has occurred, the global coordinator will be jointly liable in front of the market of the content of the prospectus together with the law and auditing firms. Therefore, it is essential to choose the best legal and auditing advisors to prevent legal action once the IPO has occurred. Only once the transaction is disclosed to the market, the Prospectus can be published.
  Embedded in the Prospectus is business and legal due diligence, but they are not represented in a separate way in this document.

If the offering structure is organized with a private offering, instead of the Pro-spectus, a simplified document is required: the Offering Circular. This is a short document briefly describing, in a simplified version, the issuer and the transaction. It is not distributed to the entire market, but only to institutional investors. These investors already know the company, so there is no need to explain everything in detail. What is the reason for opting for a private offering? The chance to speed up the process, because the offering circular is quicker to prepare.

- In the second stage of the pre-launch phase, the *registration of the IPO*, the firm must prepare a registration statement and file it with appropriate institutions (Borsa Italiana and CONSOB in Italy, and with the owner of the stock exchange market, Borsa Italiana SpA). The registration statement discloses all material in-formation concerning the corporation making a public offering. When deemed necessary, Borsa Italiana has the authorization to refuse the transaction and inter-rupt it without any explanation to the issuer, even if both CONSOB and the owner of the stock exchange had accepted it previously. After receiving the "green light" from the authorities, marketing may begin and the company can officially start going public. If the authority does not authorize the IPO, the advisor would not reveal to the market that it had received the mandate, as this would damage its reputation. *Pilot Fishing* is the pre-marketing activity that starts even before re-ceiving IPO authorization targeting most loyal investors, usually institutional in-vestors, to start assessing their sentiment about the IPO.

Execution

The third phase, *execution*, takes place approximately 1-2 months before the IPO launch. It includes *pre-marketing activities, setting the price range* and *allocating the shares*.

In the *pre-marketing* phase the issue is presented to groups of investors around the world during the "Road Show." The Road Show stimulates interest in the com-pany among investors and allows the firm and its underwriters to gather information from them. So, the Global Coordinator calls the co-leaders and tells them to start meeting potential investors to get a feel for the market interest in the IPO. These are informal meetings to attempt to gauge the sentiment of potential investors: Is the market ready? What is the appetite towards that sector?

During the pre-marketing activities, what becomes clear is the price range to stay in to sell the issue. It is now necessary to enter in the *setting the price* stage, a minimum and a maximum price: the price range [Pmin;Pmax]. Securities are priced according to not only the estimated value of the company, but also the expected de-mand for the issue. When setting the price range, the IB must take into consideration the appetite of the market besides the interest of the issuer. In fact, in the end, the market makes the price, even if the issuer has a different value for the company in mind. As previously presented, the total amount of proceeds, that is, the total funds the company wants to raise for the issue, are given by the following formula:

Total amount of proceeds = Issue price × Number of shares

Notice that total proceeds are decided with the client, according to funding needs. What's more, the number of shares has an impact on dilution issues: existing shareholders have a smaller number of shares when new ones are issued. The issue price is linked to the company valuation. To reduce the price, the client must increase the number of shares, but it is necessary to consider the effects of this move in terms of dilution.

After the pre-marketing activities and setting the price range, the next step begins: allocating the shares to investors (the *allocation phase*). The day of the IPO a range of prices is no longer possible; there must by a single price. There are three different mechanisms to allocate shares:

1. Fixed price offer;
2. Dutch auction offer;
3. Book building offer.

When setting the price range, the request of the company/issuer/entrepreneur comes into play: if the issue price is distant from the expectations of the entrepreneur because the market is not willing to offer the price from the evaluation, the alternatives are to either stop the IPO process at that stage (setting the price range) or satisfy the customer and move forward at the price requested by the issuer. In this case, there is the risk of not being able to place the whole issue and therefore the IB might suffer a reputation loss. The highest number of IPOs happen when the market is in a bubble because companies do not want to sell at a discount when the market is facing bad times. A company might be willing to wait until the market conditions improve to raise more funds before proceeding with the IPO. For example, Prada did this twice because the market was too depressed when the company tried to schedule its IPO (in 2001 and in 2007).

Let's examine the different share allocation mechanisms.

With a *fixed price offer*, the book runner (BR) fixes the share price and proposes it to the market. This is very risky, because there is a range of possible prices, and the decision is made that the information collected in the pre-marketing activity is enough to price the issue: the allocation is made at a single, fixed price. In this case the IB is speculating on the price of the IPO based on market sentiment, even if the bank has no commitment to buy yet from the market. The price set by the IB can be:

• too high: not enough demand to place the whole issue at that price; or
• too low: leave the money on the table.

The fixed price offer is no longer used today; in the past it was used in France. The only advantage of this mechanism is that it is fast.

With a *Dutch Auction*, the auctioneer tries to find the optimal price for the issue, matching it with the lowest price acceptable by the issuer. The bidding process starts from an abnormally high price which gradually decreases until all the shares are spoken for. For example, the auction may start at an abnormal price of $150 per share, with the intention to sell 100 shares. So, the auctioneer starts collecting offers:

- Investor 1 → $100/share → 30 shares.
- Investor 2 → $90/share → 30 shares.
- Investor 3 → $85/share → 70 shares.

This process continues until the price is reached at which all the shares are spoken for; in this case, at Investor 3's price we can sell all the shares. If the price is set at $85, all three investors will buy, so $85/share is the maximum price for selling all 100 shares. The investor who offered more will be served first. This share allocation mechanism is usually used by reliable, well-trusted companies. The Dutch auction offering sees little involvement from the IB because there are no strict commitments and therefore it is very cheap. However, this method presents some problems. First of all, with this mechanism investors are not committed to buying shares from a legal point of view. What is more, it is a transparent procedure, as it is an auction, so the IB cannot allocate shares on a discretionary basis.

Google used the Dutch auction mechanism in 2004 (the last global and very well-known company to do so). On 19 August 2004, Google went public and came out with its initial public offering (IPO). It turned out to be the 25th largest IPO in corporate history and the biggest technology IPO to date. Before its release, the IPO had been the subject of several controversies and the target of much criticism.
The day before the IPO, Google knew that some investors were willing to buy at $115/share but didn't trust them, and started the IPO with a price of $85/share. At the end of the day, Google reached the price of $100 but could have gone to $115. Before the IPO, the company also reduced the number of shares it had planned to sell from 25.7 million to 19.6 million, to be sure to place the whole issue. The auction process for Google was divided into five stages: Qualification, Bidding (the bid had to specify the desired number of shares and a share purchase price), Auction Closing, Pricing, Allocation. On August 19, just a few hours after going public, Google's share price climbed to more than $100, an increase of almost 20% on the initial offer. A day later, the shares fetched nearly $108.31. The IPO managed to raise nearly $1.4 billion for Google, a remarkable feat, considering the poor performance of other technology shares. Of the $1.4 billion total proceeds, Google earned nearly $1.1 billion while its founders and the initial investors pocketed the rest. Despite all the speculation, the Google IPO had performed extremely well.

In *book-building offers*, everything starts with the one-week-long, pre-marketing phase: warming up the investors, testing the market sentiment for the offer, setting the indicative price range. Next the marketing phase begins with one-to-one meetings with potential investors. Then the books are given to the co-Lead banks and they are asked to collect offers from potential, mainly institutional, investors around the world for the issue. The revelation of price signals by institutional investors allows the book runner to price the offer fairly. This phase, which lasts one to two weeks, consists of building the books that define how to collect the bids. Orders, which are formally "non-binding," can be placed directly with the book runner or with other members of the syndicate. The unwritten rule is that orders can be withdrawn before the closing of the book building.

It is possible to collect three types of orders (**Figure 10.2**), *strike bids, limit orders* and *step orders*. With *strike bids*, investors say that on the day of the IPO they will either buy a certain number of shares, without saying the price, or that they will pay a certain price at which the investor is willing to participate, without indicating the

Figure 10.2   Type of orders

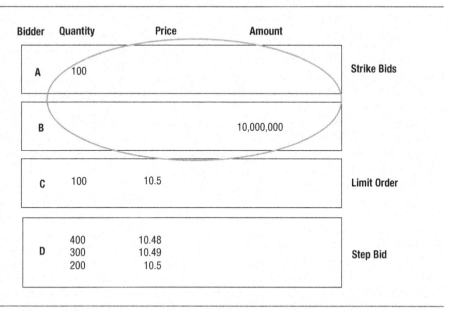

Bidder	Quantity	Price	Amount	
A	100			Strike Bids
B			10,000,000	
C	100	10.5		Limit Order
D	400 300 200	10.48 10.49 10.5		Step Bid

number of shares. With *limit orders*, investors state the number of shares that they are willing to buy at a certain price. With a *step order* an investor is willing to pay a certain price for a certain number of shares, but is also willing to buy a certain number of shares at a different price and also another number of shares at yet another price.

Advisors would like to cover the entire issue by collecting only step orders, because they can predict the reaction of the market to price changes. Limit orders are also desirable (albeit not as much). A better perception of investor appetite can be gained from limit orders and step orders, which are therefore the preferred methods.

Once the co-leaders have collected the orders, they give the books to the Global Coordinator; the co-leaders are not invited to price the issue. The Global Coordinator (i.e. the book runner) is the only one entitled to manage the books. The GC studies the books of the co-leaders and determines the price of the issue and the offer size, and decides how to allocate shares to retail and institutional investors. Through the book building methodology, the GC is able to allocate shares on a discretionary basis, as this is the only one who knows all the bids that have been collected. The book runner has enormous power in terms of deciding who to invite to the IPO. Usually, he or she will decide to allocate shares to:

- Strategic investors;
- Larger and qualified investors;
- Loyal customers/investors;

- Repetitive bidders;
- Investors who placed limit or step orders;
- Investors who placed the orders directly to the book runner;
- Buy and hold investors;
- Investors with long-term perspectives, to avoid the "underpricing puzzle."

Investors are committed to participate in the IPO at the price they stated during the book building. Though their commitment is not legally binding, it is a serious obligation. With respect to the book building methodology, it is important to deal with the underpricing puzzle, considering the price of the shares at the end of the IPO (after the transaction has occurred, on Day 1) and the initial price (IP) stated to the market:

$$UP = \frac{P1 - IP}{IP}$$

Where:
IP = Issue Price
P1 = Price at closing on the first day.

Relative underpricing: Absolute Underpricing (–) change of the relative market index. What does the "underpricing puzzle" explain?

- Ex-ante uncertainty;
- Inefficiency of the secondary market. (In reality, it's not the issue price that's wrong; it's the excessive euphoria of the secondary market on the first day of trading that determines underpricing.)

There are two possible scenarios that can occur. The first is that $P1 > IP$: the price at the end of Day 1 is higher than the issuing price proposed by the IB. The company will blame the IB for having left money on the table, setting the price too low. The second possible scenario is that $P1 < IP$: the price at the end of Day 1 is lower than the issuing price. The IB will not receive any thanks from the issuer, who would be happy in any case, and the IB might get calls from upset investors. In fact, an advisor like an IB is in the middle between two clients. In order to avoid the underpricing puzzle, investors need to understand that underpricing is given by the fact that the secondary market is not efficient: the secondary market must have some time to adjust and reflect the real price of the issue. However, the GC can say this to a certain kind of investor (strategic, larger, qualified, loyal investors). Therefore, having many retail investors for IPO issues is not ideal because they don't fully comprehend the IPO transaction; if the price goes down because of external factors, retail investors will not understand the reasons so they will sell, creating even bigger problems. Knowledgeable investors, on the other hand, are not concerned about the price going down a bit after the first day of trading. Besides the fact that the secondary market is not efficient, there is also ex-ante uncertainty related to IPO transactions.

Pension funds and insurance companies are very price sensitive because they are long term investors. This being the case, they tend to buy only at their (low) price. On the other end of the spectrum, hedge funds are not price sensitive because they are short-term investors, so they tend to buy even if the price is high because they probably have already shortened their positions.

> On the day of the IPO, the offer price should not be too high, because this would result in losing the most trustable investors (insurance companies and pension funds) that support the issue and avoid the underprizing puzzle. So, a viable option might be to go public at a discount compared to the competitors, to convince investors to switch from competitor's shares to the issue in question. If you are a qualified investor, you understand this and appreciate it; if you are a retail investor, you don't. This is called "Discount to peers."
> The general rule is to always dedicate only a very small part of the issue to retail investors because, not being qualified, they do not understand what they are buying and they might sell as soon as the price drops a little, causing further price reductions.
> For example, Facebook decided to sell its shares extensively to retail investors who panicked when they saw small reductions in price and started a massive sell off. If Facebook had sold its shares only to strategic investors, they wouldn't have cared. After some time, Facebook shares recovered the issue price and even exceeded it.
> Note that selling at a discount requires the agreement of the entrepreneur with regard to which investors to sell the shares to.

Ways to sustain the price after the IPO are the *green-shoe option, lock-up agreements* and *bonus shares*. The *green-shoe option* is the only case where the advisor is allowed to artificially influence the price on the market by buying back shares from the market or by selling additional shares. *Lock-up agreements* use contractual clauses with certain shareholders which oblige them to commit not to resell to the market within a six-month time period. But the problem with lock-up agreements is that, when the deadline expires, the price drops because all shareholders sell at the same time. So, the pricing problem is just shifted: in the short-term lock-up agreements act as price stabilizers, while in the medium-term they produce price instability. *Bonus shares* are the extra shares given to investors to prevent them from selling for a certain period of time.

The IPO of Prysmian

Prysmian, previously known as Pirelli Cables, is the former division of cables and optical fibers owned by both Pirelli Group and Telecom. In late 2001, management tried to undertake the sale of the firm in the M&A market, with no success. However, at the end of 2004, the private equity division of Goldman Sachs, valuing the deal as attractive, bought the company and changed its name to Prysmian.

In 2007, Goldman Sachs started to implement an exit strategy from the investment via an IPO of the company. The new owners offered the public around 72 million shares, representing about 40% of the total capital of the company. The offer was presented to investors as a way of participating in the upside of end-market growth by means of good execution, operating leverage and cash generation capabilities. Among the key takeaways of the equity story, Prysmian had a leading market share, growing fundamentals, a high level of investment in R&D and diversification (in terms of products, clients and geographies) and a solid management track record.

Figure 10.3   **Marketing activity for the IPO**

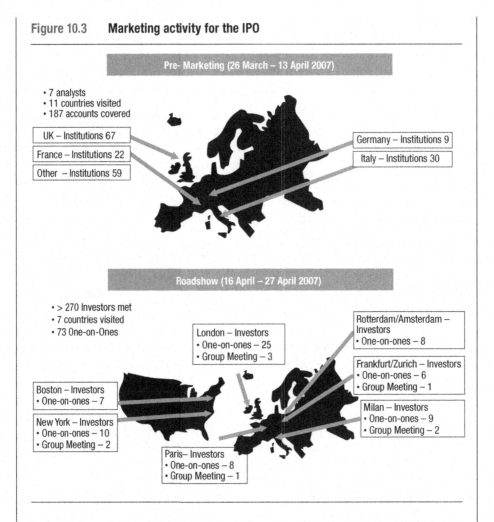

Results of the extensive marketing activity, which can be seen in **Figure 10.3**, showed that investors, while expressing concerns on the cyclicality of the cable business and on the future sustainability of margins and R&D expense level, highly regarded the good business diversification and exposure, the attractive sector trends, the high level of profitability (in terms of margins and ROIC), the top line and earnings growth and the high management credibility.
The final price for the offering, starting from an initial range of €13.25 and €16.75, was set at €15.00, which attributed the company an implied market capitalization of €2.7 billion.
The final allocation of demand saw about 15% of the offer going to retail investors, with the top 10 orders essentially dominated by long money investors.

10.3 Case study: Ferrari's IPO

An Initial Public Offer represents a fundamental moment for a company, as taking the decision to be listed on the stock exchange means exposing your company, all its data and its performance records to external investors. To summarize, this operation can take place for several reasons:

1. *Financial*: to attract new funds, to increase rating and debt capacity.
2. *Strategic*: to sustain a business strategy, to support the costs to enter a new market or to reach new customers, to support growth in new countries.
3. *Governance*: an IPO represents an exit for pre-existing shareholders, it can raise reputation of existing shareholders and it can be used to attract the best managers in the sector (by increasing visibility and through stock options compensations).

This case serves to explain the main reasons why Ferrari pursued an IPO and to describe the technical aspects that lie behind such an operation. The first part of this case will analyze the historical context in which Ferrari was born and developed, and then move on to depict the environment in which Ferrari operates, defining the position the company occupies within the automotive market. In the second part the reasons that Ferrari decided to opt for an IPO will be explored, together with the main factors that convinced the company's management to quote a part of the equity on the stock market (in the Ferrari case, 10% of the equity was listed). The third part of this case will outline the technical aspects of an IPO and study the financial results obtained by Ferrari after completing the IPO transaction.

10.3.1 History of Ferrari and its business

History

Enzo Ferrari, born in 1898, was a race car driver for Alfa Romeo with a passion for cars. This passion eventually led him to create a racing department within Alfa Romeo named "Scuderia Ferrari". But when the Great Depression came, it deeply affected the world of sport competition, and Alfa Romeo put an end to the partnership with Enzo Ferrari. After a hiatus due to the outbreak of World War II, Scuderia Ferrari came back on the scene stronger than ever. Since its early years, Ferrari immediately became a protagonist in the racing world. The core business of Ferrari, in fact, was the construction of engines and cars for motor racing competitions; the sale of road cars actually served the sole purpose of financing the sports projects of the racing department. Enzo Ferrari was initially reluctant to produce road cars but it was the only way to fund Scuderia Ferrari. He soon realized that Ferrari needed a more complete and efficient industrial structure and thus he decided to open the doors of his company to possible investors interested in Ferrari's growth. One of the companies most interested in the acquisition of Ferrari was Ford, the famous car company founded by Henry Ford in Michigan in 1903, but the two parties could not agree on the terms. Ferrari instead turned to the Italian industrial giant Fiat which in 1965 decided to create a partnership with Ferrari. This union gave Ferrari the opportunity to not only create an industrial structure able to guarantee the production of many more cars without altering Ferrari's sense of exclusivity, but also access to new funds and resources that allowed Enzo Ferrari to manage the racing department of his company with greater confidence.

The 1980s were the years that saw the explosion of sales and the birth of cars capable of marking an era to further enrich the aura of legend surrounding Ferrari and its tradition. In that same decade, however, the company lost its founder, Enzo Ferrari. At this point a new corporate structure was created, in which Fiat owned 90% of the shares, and the remaining 10% were held by Piero Lardi Ferrari, a son of Enzo. In the following years, Ferrari grew in terms of visibility, exploiting a brand that was now known all over the world.

Fiat decided, in June 2002, to sell 34% of Ferrari shares at a price of €775.2 million to a consortium led by Mediobanca, an Italian bank. In 2006, under the guidance of the new CEO Sergio Marchionne, negotiations between Fiat and Mediobanca started for the repurchase of 29% of the shares. Then slowly through the years, in 2010 the ownership structure went back to the original one where Fiat returned to holding 90% of the shares and the remaining 10 % remained in the hands of Piero Lardi Ferrari, a structure that has remained the same ever since.

These last ten years have definitively established Ferrari's standing in the world thanks to an increasing number of Ferrari Stores, now counting thirty-six. The business also expanded in emerging markets such as the Middle East, China, India and the Far East, without forgetting constant consolidation of historical markets such as US, Germany and the United Kingdom. In 2013, Sergio Marchione moved Ferrari headquarters to Holland and created a holding company, New Business Netherlands N.V., which he took over as president in 2014. This holding was partly quoted on the NYSE (10%) through an IPO, which will be detailed in the next sections.

Business

Ferrari's core business was now in the production and sale of sports and luxury cars. Luxury and exclusivity are diktats, and for this reason the company has always imposed a ceiling on the number cars produced over the years to avoid tarnishing the aura of legend that surrounds Ferrari.

As for internationality, Ferrari is a global player. Most of the cars sold are in the EMEA region, approximately 48.3%, followed by Americas with 28.6%, APAC region ex China-Hong Kong-Taiwan with 14.8% and lastly China-Hong Kong-Taiwan with 8.3%, as of the 2019 annual report.

Competitive landscape

Competition is a word that has always accompanied Ferrari, since the day of its foundation. The "prancing horse" symbol of Ferrari has become over the years the emblem of a team capable of obtaining victories in the most important competitions around the world.[1]

Turning to competitive players, in order to carry out an operation of this kind, however, a distinction must be made between companies operating in the same sector as Ferrari and which have similar production dimensions, such as Aston Martin, Lamborghini, McLaren and Bentley (**Table 10.1**) and companies operating in the same sector but with completely different production sizes, such as Porsche, BMW and Mercedes. The former were chosen for a question of consistency.

Table 10.1   Ferrari and its competitors

Company	Cars produced	Revenues (million)	Net profit (million)
Ferrari	10,131	€ 3,766	€ 699
Aston Martin	5,862	£ 997	£ 134.2
Lamborghini	8,205	€ 1,800	€ 271
McLaren	4,662	£ 1,485	£ 24
Bentley	11,631	€ 252,632	€ 16,960

Sources: Ferrari website, Aston Martin website, Lamborghini website, McLaren website, Bentley website as of 31 December 2019.

10.3.2   Main reasons for the IPO

As we mentioned above, the reasons for a company to perform an IPO are many and can be grouped in three distinct areas:

Financial reasons

An initial public offering is launched with the clear purpose of resolving financial concerns. More precisely, an IPO can provide a firm with additional funds to spend; it can also result in a reduction in the debt/equity ratio, allowing the company to increase its debt capacity and enhance its credit rating.

In the Ferrari situation, the initial public offering proved to be financially critical for the whole FCA company. Indeed, 10% of Ferrari shares enabled FCA to raise a total of 790 million euros (17,175 million shares), plus the green-shoe option (over allotment), which added about 1.7 million shares for an extra 78 million euros. FCA raised a total of 870 million euros during the IPO transaction. The placement of this Ferrari stake enabled FCA to lower its debt by around one billion dollars and it is part of a strategy termed "Separation" aimed at separating FCA from Ferrari.

---

[1] The symbol of the "prancing horse" is globally recognized and associated with the image of Ferrari; in 2013, Brand Finance deemed the Ferrari brand the "most powerful brand."

Strategic reasons

From a strategic point of view, the IPO for Ferrari was essential to enhance the visibility of the Ferrari brand; on 21 October 2015, the date of the Ferrari debut on the NYSE, all the attention of the financial world was focused on Ferrari and its imminent listing, thus generating an immediate media response.

Another effect of the IPO, which always comes with an increase in visibility, is an expected upsurge in sales in the country in which the company lists its shares (in Ferrari's case the United States). In fact, 33% of the Ferraris sold in the world are destined to end up in America, so an expansion of its brand through IPO would foster the growth of Ferrari business, that is, the sale of cars in that macro area.

The last aspect to consider at a strategic level is the perception that Sergio Marchionne, Ferrari N.V. CEO, wanted to create regarding Ferrari through this operation. Ferrari is principally a car manufacturing company, for all intents and purposes. But for the reasons previously mentioned related to the strength of the brand and the exclusivity of Ferrari, from the financial point of view this company is closer to the luxury sector. Sergio Marchionne, deeply convinced of Ferrari's strength, from the beginning spoke of Ferrari not as a car manufacturer but as a luxury goods manufacturer, similar to brands such as Prada, LVMH, Valentino, Hermes. There are no doubts, in fact, that Ferrari can be considered worldwide as a Luxury and iconic brand, enough to be awarded the world's strongest brand by Brand Finance Global 500 at the World Economic Forum at Davos.[2] Thanks to this correlation with luxury goods, Ferrari's valuation multiple is higher than that for the automotive industry. Before the entry of the Ferrari shares on the NYSE, analysts estimated the EV/EBITDA, a multiple valuation used in finance to estimate the value of a company, at a value between 9x and 12x. The stock, which started 2015 with an EV/EBITDA that stood at those values, is now at 29.36 (as of April 13, 2022).

Governance

One motive for an IPO is to reorganize the company's ownership structure. In the Ferrari situation, the NYSE IPO was just the first stage in a strategy to significantly change the company's governance. FCA had 90% of the shares throughout the pre-IPO period, while Piero Ferrari held the other 10%. Following the NYSE IPO, a new sharing structure was formed, which included public shareholders.

Guiding questions

There are some useful guiding questions that can help contextualize and plan an IPO.

[2] "Brand Finance Global 500 names Ferrari as the World's strongest brand for the second consecutive year," Ferrari Corporate (2020, January 22). Available at https://corporate.ferrari.com/en/brand-finance-global-500-names-ferrari-worlds-strongest-brand-second-consecutive-year

a. *Where to sell*

Two options are usually available: i) selling to domestic investors in the home market of the firm, allowing both retail and institutional investors to access the offer; ii) selling internationally, where institutional investors are favored to be targeted worldwide because of advantages in terms of speediness and limited costs of the process. Ferrari chose to sell shares with an international offering strategy, targeting institutional investors dislocated all around the world.

b. *Which market*

Another key point to consider is whether to be listed in the home or foreign market. Ferrari was listed in the NYSE for several reasons:

*   The New York Stock Exchange is the largest exchange for trading volume, granting Ferrari great visibility.
*   NYSE is located in a strategic position with respect to the most important institutional investors.
*   The parameters imposed by the U.S. Securities and Exchange Commission (SEC) for listing are very strict; for this reason, being admitted to an American stock exchange is a sign of great stability and security of any company.

c. *Which shares*

A distinction must be made between:

*   Newly issued shares (primary offering): actions specifically created for the IPO; and
*   Existing shares (secondary offering): shares owned by pre-existing shareholders.

In the Ferrari case there were already existing shares and specifically, the IPO was made possible thanks to the placement on the NYSE of 10% of the shares of Ferrari NV, the Dutch holding company which holds 100% of the Ferrari Spa shareholding, and is owned by the FCA Group, with 90% of the shareholding.

d. *To whom*

The last thing to consider before initiating an IPO is whether to seek public investors (retail and institutional) or private investors (only institutional investors). Ferrari chose to conduct a private offering for convenience and speed in carrying out the Initial Public Offering's operations; indeed, the primary advantage of this type of offering is the possibility to easily contact the financial institutions to whom we wish to propose the purchase of a portion of the shares. The primary drawback of the private offering is that, since it involves specialists in the equity industry, it is impossible to engage in any form of price arbitrage.

10.3.3 The IPO process

The fundamental steps in carrying out an operation of this kind are examined in the following box.

The IPO process

Preparation

- Choice of Global Coordinator: task of the GC is to create a syndicate of various investment banks with a broad customer coverage. This syndicate must guarantee the sale of the shares on the day of the IPO.
- The investment banks that make up the syndicate also act as guarantors towards the company. They sign an underwriting agreement that can be i) best effort, ii) full underwriting, or iii) partial underwriting.

- In 2015 Ferrari chose as Global Coordinator UBS Securities LLC, a Swiss financial services company, of which Sergio Marchionne was non-executive vice president from 2008 to 2010. UBS immediately started to create the syndicate and as joint bookrunners chose: Merrill Lynch, Pierce, Fenner & Smith Incorporated and Santander Investment Securities Inc.
- Ferrari opted for a partial underwriting commitment.

Pre-launch Prospectus

- The Prospectus is a legal document that presents to the supervisory authorities information on future performance, strategy, competitive advantage, quality of management, and the use of proceeds.
- The Prospectus contains all the information concerning the lock-up agreement, obliging some shareholders to retain their shares for a certain period of time to prevent huge drops in the stock price.

- The Prospectus was delivered to the SEC on 23 July 2015.
- Ferrari NV, FCA, Piero Ferrari and some directors, during the first 90 days of the IPO, were obligated not to sell or offer any of their actions without first asking for written permission from the Global Coordinator and Joint Book Runners.

Execution

1. *Pre-marketing activities*
The Road Show consists of a series of meetings that the selling shareholder organizes with potential investors, usually involving only institutional investors; this is the opportunity to present all the details of the transaction.

1. *Pre-marketing activities*
The Ferrari Road Show started in early October 2015. Sergio Marchionne, accompanied by representatives of the Global Coordinator and the joint book runners, started a series of presentations with the aim of presenting the Ferrari's IPO on the NYSE.

2. *Setting the price range*
The possible price range of the stock is determined, taking into account: the history and prospects of Ferrari, financial performance, future earnings, securities market condition, and recent market prices.

2. *Setting the price range*
Ferrari, after completing the Road Show and receiving a range of feedback from institutional investors, set a price range between $48 and $52 per share.

3. *Allocation*
In this phase, the shares are distributed to investors according to specific criteria. The book building offer consists of two phases, the first occurs during the Road Show and is called the "book building" and the second consists of "closing the book building", once all the offers submitted by the investors have been collected. The GC has to confirm the price of the sale of the stock, the size of the offer, and how to allocate the shares among the investors.

3. *Allocation*
Ferrari set a price range between $48 and $52. The Global Coordinator, on 13 October 2015, set the price of the stock at the maximum price range, $52 per share. On the day of the IPO, the sale of the entire stock package was recorded (9% of the total equity of Ferrari NV) with a gain of around €790 million. Ferrari, after registering the sale of all the shares offered to the market, accepted the green-shoe option; this allowed the sale of another 1.75 million shares, which were added to the 17,175 million shares already placed by the selling shareholder during the IPO.

10.4 Seasoned offerings (SEOs)

A firm can raise funds either *internally* or *externally*. If a company prefers to use *internal funds* it will have to refer to *retained earnings*, while if it prefers *external funds* it can decide either to choose *new debt* (using syndicated loans or corporate bonds) or *new equity*. Raising funds through equity is the last option available to companies, especially for public companies, because equity is more expensive with respect to the other two alternatives. Why then should a corporation opt for a SEO? The reason is straightforward: the company is probably already highly levered and cannot ask for new debt, and does not generate sufficient earnings. Therefore, the only possibility still open for raising funds, restructuring debt or supporting investments is through a capital increase. Note that public companies cannot use funds raised through SEOs to pay dividends. Taking into consideration the previous argument, it is very intuitive to understand why a SEO is a bad signal to the market. If a firm cannot raise more debt or does not generate sufficient earnings, both are signals of financial or operational difficulties, which in other words means bad management. The result of the announcement of a SEO is a decrease in the stock price, no matter what the reasons are.

Notwithstanding the fact that SEOs are much less difficult to carry out with respect to IPOs, because of fewer information asymmetries, still, the role of investment banks is crucial for the success or failure of this transaction. IBs need to present the deal in a very appealing way, given that the market already interprets it negatively.

Whether we are analyzing a SEO in the United States or in Europe, in both cases there is the possibility of *dilution effect*. When additional shares are issued investors' proportional ownership in the company is reduced. In other words, when the number of outstanding shares multiplies, each existing shareholder owns a smaller percentage of the company making each share less valuable. Dilution also reduces the value of existing shares by reducing the stock earnings per share (EPS). The potential benefit from a decrease in EPS is that the funds the company receives from the sale of new shares can boost the company's profitability and stock value.

A further distinction which is worth mentioning is the difference in the approaches we encounter in U.S. with respect to the European market. The main difference is that a European company must ask to its pre-existing shareholders if they are willing to subscribe to the capital increase and therefore participate in the issue or not. The main reason for the subscription of the SEO is to prevent existing shareholders to be diluted due to the issuing of new shares. This method is longer than the alternatives available in the U.S.; it lasts a minimum of two months to raise funds from pre-existing shareholders.

The American strategy gives the possibility to close the transaction in a few days since there is no obligation to ask to existing shareholders if they are willing to participate or not.

Because of the importance of raising funds to implement the necessary strategy, it is common practice for public companies to ask for the advisory services of investment banks. The role of these financial institutions is to assist the client in raising

funds. There is substantial difference in the role investment banks have in seasoned
equity offerings or IPOs. An IPO is much more difficult to conduct, therefore it requires more effort from the investment bank which translates into higher fees. Once
the company is public, it needs less assistance to raise new funds. In this case IBs are
called to ensure the soundness of the transaction and to identify the right target of
investors which are willing to buy the shares.

10.4.1 Different alternatives around the world for increasing capital

There are three different alternatives that can be applied by a corporation to raise
capital. Two of these alternatives (*bought deals* and *accelerated book building*) are
available for US listed companies and the last one (*rights issue*) applies to European
listed companies.

In *bought deals* we have the involvement of an IB that buys shares from the issuer, and then sells the shares as quickly as possible to institutional investors. The IB
buys the shares because it knows that it will be able to resell them in a few days, taking the risk to buy at a certain price to hopefully resell at a higher price.

Profit for the bank is given by the difference between Selling Price and Acquiring Price. The risk for the IB is to buy the issue without knowing exactly if there are
enough institutional investors willing to pay a higher price.

Accelerated book building (ABB) is a transaction which occurs in a very short
period of time. In order to implement a traditional book building during an IPO, a
minimum of a few of weeks is needed. However, if a company is already listed and
wants to use an ABB, the process is likely to take only a few days. This is achieved
through targeting a small group of institutional investors in order to implement a fast
book building procedure to sell/allocate all the shares of the company sold in the
SEO. Profits are represented by the gross spread (amount of fees paid to the advisor).

In both mechanisms (BO and ABB), it is possible to reach *only* institutional investors because of the time constraints and the amount of risk, which cannot be absorbed by retail investors.

While in the US and Canada, companies are authorized to sell additional shares
in a matter of a few days implementing these two strategies to increase the capital of
the company, in Europe it is necessary to follow the so-called *rights issue* procedure.
Here, pre-existing shareholders have the right to opt to participate, before any others,
in an SEO (capital increase). This right makes the process very long; usually it lasts
between three and six months. On the day of the launch, shareholders are offered
the chance to participate in the seasoned offering. In proportion with the number of
shares held by pre-existing shareholders before the capital increase, they have the
right to buy new shares in order to maintain their participation in the company. During the meeting with shareholders, the issuer, with the support of the advisor, offers
them a discounted price at which they can participate at the capital increase on the
day of the execution in the market. This usually happens within two months from the
shareholder meeting.

It is important to mention that the market does not react very well to the announcement of a capital increase, because, as said, in the end this means that the company is asking for money that it is unable to raise on its own by taking out loans, and it does not have enough profits available to cover the issue. In other words, the market understands that there is a problem. In fact, usually the launch of a capital increase is necessary because of growth that cannot be sustained with available resources (earnings) or because restructuring strategies need to be implemented.

Another reason for the bad market reaction can be explained by the fact that the participation in the capital increase is necessary for shareholders if they do not want to be diluted after the issue, which is what would happen if the new capital is bought by new investors.

For example, assume that the total number of shares of a firm before a capital increase is 100. If the firm sells another 100 shares, the total number of shares outstanding after the transaction would be 200. In this case, let's say Anne is an investor, and she is holding 5 shares (5%) out of the 100 shares before the capital increase. If she decides to not participate in the transaction, afterwards she will still have 5 shares, but out of an outstanding number of 200 shares, which now represents only 2.5% of the equity.

In Europe, dilution is prevented by offering to pre-existing shareholders the possibility to buy the number of shares that is necessary for them to maintain the same level of ownership after the capital increase. The transaction has to be approved with the favorable vote of pre-existing shareholders to whom must be given the chance to maintain the same share of equity after the completion of the process.

The incentive to participate in the transaction is given by offering to pre-existing shareholders an American[3] option that lasts three weeks from the day of the execution on the market. The option gives the possibility to buy a security at a strike price that will hopefully be below the (theoretically) expected trading price during the three weeks of execution.

The value of one share post-issue will be the average of the value of the old and new shares. This is called the *Theoretical Ex-Right Price*, or TERP:

$$TERP = \frac{n \times P + N \times S}{n + N}$$

Where:
n = number of outstanding shares
P = current market price
N = number of newly issued shares
S = issue price.

---

[3] European option: there is a specific day in the future on which holders are authorized to exercise the option. American option: holders have a time period to exercise the option.

Because the day of the execution in the market, the old share is split into two identical instruments, it is possible to calculate the value of one right as the difference between the market price (before the execution) and the price of the share ex-right:

$$RIGHT = Current\ market\ price - TERP = P - TERP$$

The TERP is referred to as theoretical because, when the EGM (Extraordinary General Meeting) is held with shareholders, this is in advance of at least two months with respect to the day when the execution will happen in the market. During the EGM, an option is offered to pre-existing shareholders that has to be "in the money" two months later. An option is in the money if the strike price is below the current market price. This means that during the EGM, shareholders must be offered a discount on the market price at which shares will be traded during the execution of the transaction. Therefore, the TERP is theoretical because it is simply a prediction the day of the shareholder meeting; it is called "ex-right" because at the time of the execution shares will be traded separately from the value of the right.

The issue price, in order for the option to be in the money, has to be given at a discount from the TERP. Different types of discounts in the ECM are Discount to Peers, Discount to TERP and Discount to Market. The first one, discount to peers, is applied the day before the company goes public. This is when the advisor must tell the entrepreneur to sell at a discount to peers, to give investors a reason to support the price of the shares the day of the IPO and beyond. This is because the investors know that even if the price partially drops, the value of what they bought is high, so they will not sell. The discount to TERP is the second discount that we find in the ECM. During the EGM, we must set a price that is below the current market price the day of the SEO. We must predict the future market price at the time of the issue, which is the TERP. The discounted price is the discount to TERP, so, the shareholders will have in their hands an option that is in the money.

If the price of the shares once the issue is made goes below the TERP, and the option is above the current market price, this is bad because shareholders won't exercise the right. In this case, the value of the right becomes 0. The issuer will sell no shares to pre-existing shareholders and all unsold rights are called RUMP.

$$RUMP = Number\ of\ rights\ that\ are\ not\ exercised$$

Rump is the number of new shares that are unsold. The company wants to avoid this risk, usually by offering a full underwriting mandate to the advisor. This means that the advisor is committed to buying all the rump at the strike price offered to shareholders even though the option is out of the money. This is the big risk of these transactions, and this is why fees requested by advisors are so high also for these capital markets transactions.

10.4.2 UniCredit: a €13 billion rights issue

This last section is about the capital increase of the UniCredit Group (UCG) announced on 13 December 2017. First of all, it is important to highlight the reasons which led the Italian banking conglomerate to approach the market once again, after previous attempts in 2008, 2009 and 2012:

- the need to improve capital base, considering the EU macroeconomic environment and the pressure from regulatory entities (banks were being obliged to increase their capital base);
- the need to cover an earnings shortfall accumulated over the previous few years.

Therefore, on 11 July 2017, the newly-appointed CEO Jean Pierre Mustier approached the media with a press release announcing his strategic restructuring plan. The plan focused on five main pillars:

a) *Strengthen & Optimize capital*: UCG needed to strengthen its capital base, being a Systemically Important Financial Institution with a CET1 ratio below the industry average.
b) *Improve Asset Quality*: UCG, due to the heavy burden of NPL in the Italian banking sector, needed to convey a signal to investors to restore their confidence in the banking institution. To do so, it planned to actively deal with NPLs on its balance sheet, mainly accumulated through the acquisition of Capitalia.
c) *Transform Operating Model*: UCG needed to convince investors that the Group planned to implement a radical chance of the business model in order to improve the profitability margin by reducing the cost base.
d) *Maximize Commercial Bank Value*: UCG aimed to expand the revenue base by leveraging on its existing client base.
e) *Adopt Lean but Steering Centre*: UCG set a target of high-level transparency so as to optimize the cost base at a corporate level.

The above-mentioned pillars were going to be achieved through the main operations below:

1. *Release of fresh capital via asset disposal* (6-7 billion):
   - *Sale of 30% stake in Fineco*: Management depicted this as a great opportunity since the deal was trading at a good multiple, while at the same time stressing the importance of maintaining control notwithstanding the forced sale.
   - *Sale of Pekao*: Management agreed to dispose of the Polish unit mainly because of the controversies on regulatory matters which limited the possibility to exploit potential synergies within the Group; in addition to this, the sale also occurred at good multiples.
   - *Sale of Pioneer Investments*: UCG spotted a high growth rate implied in the trading multiple of the unit and therefore they decided to capture it by selling Pioneer to Amundi.
2. *Reducing the portion of NPLs by project FINO* ("Failure Is Not an Option"). Disposal through securitization of €17.7 billion (face value) of bad loans. Moreover, the CEO team introduced directives aimed at actively managing the remaining NPL exposure and avoiding future origination.

3. *Change in the operating model*: UCG needed to cut costs by closing branches and expanding the consumer base through online banking services; this in response to the wave of digitalization of the traditional banking industry. In addition to this, UCG wanted to leverage on existing client relationships by cross selling a wider range of products.

The section below highlights the relevance of the communication campaign promoting the transaction in the capital markets and in the media; these efforts were significant determinants of the huge success of the rights issue.

The operation was very delicate since UCG had raised capital several times before (13 billion between 2008 and 2017), and the financials were not very attractive in the eyes of investors given the low interest rate environment that was squeezing profitability. In addition, it must be stressed that already-public UCG was implementing a sort of "RE IPO," as the size of the rights issue was 13 billion, or 260% of the outstanding shares.

As a matter of fact, the top management, together with the investor relations team, succeeded in "selling the story" to investors, as demonstrated by the strong reaction in stock market price (+16%) at announcement date. The technical reason behind this shocking positive stock performance is that short sellers started closing their position as soon as they saw the market stock price experiencing positive returns (in order to minimize losses). Moreover, communication to the market in preparation to the announcement played an important role. These astounding results were achieved mainly by:

- providing investors with tangible proof of asset disposal ("binding agreements");
- credibility enhanced by the huge transformation plan financed by the capital increase;
- gradual timing of the release of information to the media in order not to scare off potential investors; in the early stages by monitoring the news media and by winning the consensus of the analysts and then on the day of the announcement with pre-alert media, wire calls, etc.

The transaction went through very smoothly, with a 38% discount to TERP for the ordinary shares, with very high turnover of the rights (a very strong signal of rights issue success) and an average synthetic discount of 1%.

UniCredit rights issuance in numbers

Let's recap all the information we have about the rights issuance:

- 13 billion rights issuance;
- Subscription Ratio: 13 – 5; 13 new shares for every 5 existing ordinary shares held;
- Subscription Price: €8.09 per share;
- Last share price before the deal: €25.92.

With all this information, we can calculate the TERP:

$$TERP = \frac{n \times P + N \times S}{n + N} = \frac{5 \times €25.92 + 13 \times €8.09}{5 + 13} = €13.04$$

With the TERP, we can compute the Rights Value:

$$RIGHT = Current\ Market\ Price - TERP = €25.92 - €13.04 = €12.88$$

This implies that pre-existing shareholders can either exercise their rights and buy 13 shares for each 5 shares held at €8.09, or sell their rights (1 right per share held) for €12.88 on the market. As this mechanism prevents pre-existing shareholders from being diluted, we should see that shareholders have the same economic value:

- before the transaction;
- if the shareholders exercise their rights;
- if the shareholders sell their rights on the market.

Let's assume that Marco had 10 shares of UniCredit's stock before the Rights Issuance. We can now compute Marco's economic value in the three scenarios mentioned above:

1. Before the transaction: 10 shares priced at €25.92:
   - €25.92 × 10 = €259.2
2. If Marco executes his rights: 10 shares + 26 shares from the rights issue priced at €13.04 less the issuance price (€8.09) for each of the new 26 shares he buys:
   - €13.04 × (10+26) − €8.09 × 26 = €469.44 − €210.34 = €259.1
3. If Marco decides to sell his 10 rights for €12.88 each on the market, he will hold only 10 shares, priced at €13.04 each:
   - €13.04 × 10 + €12.88 × 10 = €130.4 − €128.8 = €259.2

As we can see, no matter which scenario Marco opts for, he will not be diluted from an economic point of view. However, from a control perspective, if Marco decides to sell his rights on the market and therefore to not execute them, he will experience control dilution as he will hold a smaller fraction of the overall equity value of UniCredit.

10.5 Conclusions

This chapter covered the Equity Capital Markets and the two main ways to raise capital on them. The most popular use of the ECM is Initial Public Offerings.

As for IPOs, we looked at the process, key steps and an example of the Ferrari IPO. The Initial Public Offering process usually starts 5-6 months before the actual issue date. The success of the IPO is crucial for the long-term survival and reputation of the firm, thus the investment bank in charge of the process must pay particular attention to the details. First, the market outlook should be excellent, to avoid ending up contending with unfavorable selling conditions for placing shares. In fact, there are several examples of Initial Public Offers that were postponed at the very last moment due to unfavorable market conditions (i.e. Prada went public in 2012 after postponing its IPO twice). During the analysis of the issuer, the investment bank must carefully understand the *reasons that lead the client to sell its equity to the public*. Firms could decide to go public for *strategic reasons*. In this case, the company needs capital that is not obtainable from other sources (i.e. internally or via bank loans), to expand the business, finance new investments, or augment the availability of debt. Beyond this, a firm might need to be listed for *marketing reasons*. In fact, when a business becomes public, it dramatically enhances its visibility and reputation in that market, making future transactions easier to carry out and acquiring funding for these deals (i.e. Luxottica and Ray-Ban in the United States). Eventually, there could be corporate *governance reasons*; in other words, the Initial Public Offer can be seen as a good exit strategy for existing shareholders, or a way for the firm to gain notoriety and attract the best managers by offering them positions in a listed, well-reputed company. After an investment bank has been appointed by the client, it must decide on several issues, such as *where to sell the shares*, if it is better to target only institutional investors or to also include retail investors, etc.

The Initial Public Offering process is usually divided into three main phases: *preparation*, *pre-launch*, and *execution*. In the first step, the issuer appoints the global coordinator, that is, the investment bank which has obtained the mandate. The mandated investment bank must carefully analyze all the choices previously described create a syndicate with both co-leaders and selling banks. To put it simply, the team that will go through the process is set up. Most importantly, in this phase, the corporation is also valued. The valuation is crucial as it will give an indicative amount of the capital that will be raised at the end of the Initial Public Offer. The main methodologies used by financial analysts to value an enterprise are the Discounted Cash Flows analysis, based on the ability and probability of the firm to generate positive cash flows in the future. However, sometimes multiples analysis is also carried out to pair the company with a comparable enterprise that in most cases is already listed. Valuation is as crucial as it is complicated because these models are strongly influenced by the assumptions made in the preliminary phase. Hence, analysts should try to be as precise as possible to carry out a fair valuation, and similar values obtained through the use of different methods are always a positive indicator, as this means that the value is likely to be fair.

After this comes the *pre-launch phase*. Here, analysts of the investment banks carefully study any aspects of the firm and start writing the Prospectus. The Prospectus (or red herring) is a crucial document that is used to show all the information to potential investors; it is also required by regulatory agencies to obtain approval for listing. Usually, before receiving this approval, investment banks avoid doing marketing activities with potential investors, except for "pilot fishing," testing the waters for the IPO, which is conducted with loyal buying-side firms. Alongside the Prospectus, an offering circular (a simplified version of the Prospectus) is also drawn up to show to institutional investors that, of course, have far more knowledge than their retail counterparts.

As soon as the regulatory institutions give permission for the listing, the *execution period* starts with the marketing activities. During this phase, the global coordinator and the issuer organize road shows, events in which they meet potential institutional investors all around the world (i.e. London, New York, Boston, etc.) and start presenting the company and gathering information about investor interest in the enterprise. After this is probably the most critical phase: *allocation and price setting*. In order to fix the price, investment banks can either go for a *fixed price offer*, a *Dutch auction* or a *book building*. *Fixed price offers*, which are no longer used, are characterized by the offer price being fixed based on pure estimation of the demand; hence they can end up being very hazardous and, as such, not convenient for the issuer. With a *Dutch auction* (i.e. Google and JP Morgan case), the global coordinator sets a very high price and starts lowering it as soon as purchasing orders are submitted by investors, until the moment in which the offer is fully subscribed. However, Dutch auctions are not available to everyone as the company needs to be very well-known and must have a platform on which to receive offers. So the most used method is the *book building* process, in which the book runner collects all the commitments from potential investors, through three different types of order: *Straight bids* (also known as *strike bids*), *limit orders* and *step bids*. The *straight bid* is when the investor is prepared to buy a fixed number of shares at whatever price or vice-versa. *Limit orders* are when investors are willing to purchase a fixed number of shares, but at a determined offer price. Lastly, there is the *step order*, where investors show the intention to buy different quantities of shares depending on the offer price. This model has the advantage of discretion, because it is the Investment Bank that decides how to allocate shares and more importantly because it gives more information on investor appetite for the offering. Thanks to these bids, the book runner can price the issue fairly and guarantee the likely success of the Initial Public Offer. In this last phase, there are several conditions that should be met.

Of course, it is crucial that the offer is fully subscribed, hence that there are no unsold shares. In addition, investment banks usually leave a little bit of room to guarantee some liquidity in case of unfavorable or unexpected events and to ensure that the subscribers are beneficial to the issuer and its corporation. Usually, the focus is on including buy & hold investors, rather than short-term profit seekers such as hedge funds, in order to give stability on a longer-term horizon to the company. To understand and evaluate the level of success of the Initial Public Offer, the first days of trading need to be closely followed and analyzed. In fact, when a company's shares start trading, there is usually sizeable volatility that could determine either major upswings or downswings. IPO participants usually dislike big movements in either direction, as it means that either the issuer has left too much money on the table or that investors have not done a good deal. For these reasons, the investment bank is interested in stabilizing the price post-IPO. This stabilization is usually done through the use of lock-up agreements, which deny investors the chance to sell the shares for a pre-determined period after the IPO; bonus shares are also used by the Investment Bank to reduce the selling pressure on the share.

Another key use of ECM is Seasoned Offerings. Usually with an IPO, firms don't sell 100% of their equity, but only a certain part of it. During an SEO, firms sell an additional portion of their equity to raise extra capital.

Final remarks

In order to have a better understanding how IPOs and SEOs apply to the financial world, here's how Goldman Sachs defines their ECM activity: "The Equity Capital Markets team works closely with public and private companies, governments and financial sponsors to originate, structure and execute equity and equity-linked financings such as initial public offerings, follow on offerings, convertibles and derivatives." As we can see, initial public offerings and seasoned offerings (follow-on offerings) are integral parts of what investments bankers do on a daily basis.

In the NYSE's IPO Guide,[4] J.P. Morgan lists the advantages and potential issues of conducting an IPO in the following way:

- *Access to capital*: The most common reasons for going public are to raise primary capital to provide the company with working capital to fund organic growth, to repay debt or to fund acquisitions. Following the IPO, the company will be able to tap the equity markets via follow on offerings of primary and/ or secondary shares, or a mix thereof. After the company has been public for one year, it will be eligible to access the equity capital markets on demand via a shelf registration statement.
- *Liquidity event*: The IPO can be structured such that existing owners of the company can sell down their position and receive proceeds for their shares. In addition, once the company is public, the existing owners have a public marketplace through which they can monetize their holdings in a straightforward and orderly fashion.
- *Branding event and prestige*: By listing on the NYSE, the company will receive worldwide media coverage through the financial markets, which provide constant live coverage on publicly traded companies.
- *Public currency for acquisitions*: Once the company is public, it can use its publicly tradable common stock in whole or in part to acquire other public or private companies in conjunction with, or instead of, raising additional capital.
- *Enhanced benefits for current employees*: Stock-based compensation incentives align employees' interests with those of the company. By allowing employees to benefit alongside the company's financial success, these programs increase productivity and loyalty to the company and serve as a key selling mechanism when attracting top talent.
- *Loss of privacy and flexibility*: In order to comply with securities laws, public companies must disclose various forms of potentially sensitive information publicly, which regulatory agencies, as well as competitors, can then access.

---

[4] The *NYSE IPO Guide* (3rd ed.), published by Caxton Business & Legal, can be found at: https://www.nyse.com/publicdocs/nyse/listing/nyse_ipo_guide.pdf

- *Regulatory requirements and potential liability*: Correspondingly, public companies must regularly file various reports with the Securities and Exchange Commission (SEC) and other regulators.
- *Cost and distraction of management time and attention*: Going public is a relatively expensive process, incurring one-off and ongoing costs for legal counsel, accounting and auditing services, insurance, underwriting fees, printing, as well as for additional personnel to handle expanded reporting, compliance, and investor relations activities.

With the advent of social media, financial firms started to share their daily activity with their followers. A great way to keep up to date with NYSE IPOs for example, is to follow their Instagram feed where they publish all their day-to-day activity and interviews in which they explain the mechanics behind ECM.

11 Private Equity Financing Around the World

The following chapter is devoted to Private Equity (PE) and to analyzing its development across the world. It is important to have a global perspective, as different systems define private equity in slightly dissimilar ways. Indeed, when it comes to evaluating private equity funds, it is vital to distinguish between two distinct legal frameworks, the European Union format and the Anglo-Saxon format. In the EU, PE is considered a financial service and it is therefore supervised by financial authorities. This leads to greater protection for the investor but also to higher costs and lower flexibility for funds. In the Anglo-Saxon world, private equity is considered an entrepreneurial activity rather than a financial service. The difference between the two formats impacts the fundraising activity of the PE firm and the relationship between the sponsor group and the investors.

With these introductory remarks, that partly reveal what will be one of the most salient topics of the chapter, private equity will be considered from a number of different perspectives. The very first paragraphs of this chapter will be devoted to preliminary definitions and to contextualizing the phenomenon. The second section of the chapter will deal with the taxonomy and the various sources of financing according to the different stages of a lifecycle of a firm in need of funds. Diving deeper, the chapter then will explore the two approaches to private equity in the European and Anglo-Saxon systems. The analysis will be accompanied by the characterization of the different vehicles and economic mechanisms used in the two systems. Concluding remarks will highlight the trends in PE and what can be considered some alternatives (crowdfunding and Special Purpose Acquisition Companies, just to name a few).

11.1 Preliminary definitions

This introductory section is meant to provide all the necessary definitions to better understand the topics we will discuss. Firstly, a dual definition of private equity will be described, detailing its main phases and classifying venture capital and buyout. Next, the reasons and risks underpinning a private equity operation will be assessed.

11.1.1 The definition of private equity and its phases

The definition of private equity is based on two aspects, each related to the two main characteristics of the PE relationship. On one hand, PE is a *source of financing*: It is an alternative to other sources of liquidity, such as a loan or an IPO, for the company receiving the financing. By the same token, PE is an *investment* made by a financial institution, a Private Equity Investor (PEI), in the equity of a non-listed company (i.e. a company that is not public).

The nature of the PE business is to invest capital collected through fundraising in targeted non-listed companies and obtain a return on the investment by selling the portfolio of companies after having increased their equity value. Thus, private equity investments are characterized by a precise schedule and the process can be divided into four phases:

- *Fundraising.* This activity is performed by General Partners (GPs) or the Asset Management Company (AMC) to secure the commitment from investors to provide financial resources to the limited partnership or fund that will be the recipient of the investments. When all the committed funds have been collected, the investment vehicle is created.
- *Investing activity.* The GPs or the AMC invest the resources they have collected to acquire equity stakes into potentially fast-growing, value-creating companies. The target companies are selected after a process of market scouting, screening and negotiation.
- *Managing & Monitoring.* To create value, the investment professionals actively influence the business activity of their portfolio companies.
- *Exiting.* The private equity fund remunerates its investors by selling ownership stakes in the portfolio companies. The most common exit strategies are a trade sale to a strategic buyer, an IPO, or sale to another PE player.

11.1.2 Venture capital and buyout

In private equity, we can distinguish between Venture Capital (VC) and buyout investments. Both transactions are part of the private equity world, but usually a single operator specializes in only one of the two, due to the fact that they each require different sets of skills and aptitudes, given the different stages of the life cycle of the company they deal with (see the example of the acquisition of Valentino Fashion Group by Permira, a private equity firm specialized in buyouts).

- *Venture capital*, a very specific case of PE, is the investment realized by a private equity investor (PEI) at the *beginning* of the life of a company, in the start-up phase.
- *Buyout*: is when a PEI invests in *later* stages, when the company is mature.

How does the relationship work between the PEI and the venture-backed company (i.e. the company financed by the PEI)? On the one hand, in order to raise funds, the

Figure 11.1   PEI and venture-backed company

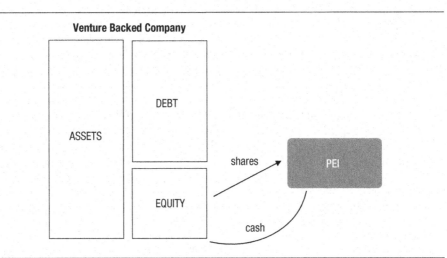

(venture-backed) company is willing to sell a portion of its unlisted equity, while on the other hand, there is a private equity investor willing to buy this equity. Thus, the investor gets shares of the equity of the company in return for the inflow of cash (**Figure 11.1**).

The transaction explained above can be justified by two main reasons:

- *Governance*: A company that decides to finance itself by selling unlisted equity must accept a PEI, a qualified investor, in its governance, and this investor might interfere with its decisions. It is therefore a kind of marriage in which both parties accept to share governance.
- *Return*: The return that PEI expects is not dividends, but only the appreciation of the equity: capital gains. Therefore, it is a marriage that will inevitably end, usually lasting 10 years.

In private equity there is a company needing money for a certain *clearly identified reason*. The company collects money by *issuing equity* on the private market. The PEI will not only become a shareholder but will contribute to the management of the company. The professional investor will gain a return only by generating capital gains. The most critical aspect in PE is the close relationship between the investor and the entrepreneur.

Indeed, the starting point for private equity is knowing what's behind the label: think of the story of a company and a private equity Investor. They are the two main players, with two different objectives clearly in mind:

- The Company needs to raise funds, and PE is a source of financing.
- The PEI is willing to finance this unlisted company. But this investor must be a

professional, because there are a number of issues and challenges (which will be assessed in the next section) to consider and deal with for every private equity investment.

To properly understand private equity, beyond the motivation of PEIs, we also have to understand why *companies* would accept a deal like this. From the financing perspective, they can gain:

- *Financial benefits*: increase in equity value, higher rating, decrease in cost of capital, buildup in debt capacity (A young company may not be able to raise a loan, because it has no collateral to offer or because it is not yet profitable and would not be able to repay the principal and interest in a timely manner; however, the same could happen to a mature company going through a crisis.)

From a managerial perspective instead, the key idea is that a private equity Investor brings in knowledge, network and certification.

- *Knowledge benefits*: A qualified investor has soft skills and hard skills necessary to properly manage the business and the company.
- *Networking benefits*: There are periods in the life of the company when there is a need to meet potential new customers, suppliers, lenders.
- *Certification benefits*: By having a PEI in its equity structure, the company proves to the market that it is a valuable enterprise with a good product/service, and that it was able to attract such an investor, which draws the attention of other investors as well.

A side note should be added here. *Minority* investments are done at the beginning of the life of the company; *majority* investments at the mature stages. In both cases, investors have to interact with the governance. Certain types of private investors are purely financial investors (*hands off*), and do not participate in management. However, most investors have a *hands-on* approach, which means they not only provide funds but are also interested in management; this is a great value added for any company.

11.1.3 The possible risks of private equity

When considering a private equity investment, there are a number of challenges and risks investors face. Indeed, there are three perspectives that a PEI must take into account when investing in private equity that make it special and different from public equity. These perspectives explain why one needs qualified investors for such investments. In particular, there are three risks to consider (Caselli et al., 2021):

1. *Pricing*: The company is not listed on the stock market, so there is no published price to refer to. Therefore, one starts a negotiation process with the counterparty: first identifying the value of the company (equity), then passing from this intrinsic valuation to the price that could be acceptable for the counterparty (a long

process). If the investor is not qualified, it is difficult to find the right sales price for the equity.

2. *Liquidity*: There is not a market to refer to and hence no market to resell the investment in. The possibility is either to find another private equity investor, which can be challenging as the potential acquirer is also an expert. This will probably lead to a long, complex and expensive negotiation. As a result, liquidity becomes an issue. Another possibility could be selling to a financial or strategic investor or opting for an IPO (but this would take at least six months).
3. *Monitoring*: In public markets, there are always supervisors and authorities to protect shareholders, but with private investments, there are none so investors have to protect themselves.

The points above can also be viewed as the main differences between public and private equity, differences which taken together justify the reasons why only *qualified* investors should and usually do operate in the private equity business.

11.2 The life cycle of a firm and its financing options

The life cycle of the company is essential information in order to understand if a company can use PE to satisfy its needs, and also to identify the different kinds of PE investment (and the right one). As mentioned before, the definition of PE is an *umbrella definition*. It identifies as many clusters as the number of the company's life cycle stages, as long as the company is not listed.

By means of introduction, there are six life stages of a company, each requiring different types of financing. The first three stages are part of the venture capital business while the last three pertain to the buyout world.

1. Development: There is nothing more than the business idea so money is needed to support R&D. ⇒ *Seed Financing*
2. Start-up: The business idea is translated into a service, so it is time to start working; money is needed to get the company going (investments in working capital and fixed assets). ⇒ *Start-Up Financing*
3. Early growth: There could be an equity gap with respect to the business plan, and capital is needed to ensure the company grows (additional investments in working capital and fixed assets). ⇒ *Early Growth Financing*
4. Expansion: Investments in new working capital and fixed assets. ⇒ *Expansion Financing*
5. Maturity: PEI investors enter the scene to solve a situation of generational change or discussion among shareholders, they bring funds but most of all managerial expertise. ⇒ *Replacement Financing*
6. Decline: Money is used to exit from crisis situations. ⇒ *Vulture Financing*

One single label (=private equity), six different businesses.

Example Casavo

Casavo is an Italian start-up, founded by Giorgio Tinacci, an ex-Bocconi student who graduated not long ago. Casavo is an instant buyer company and leverages on technology to make offers to buy real estate properties quickly. The tech platforms integrate an algorithm that evaluates homes and offers owners the best price.

Casavo is the Italian Instant Buyer: they buy houses, renovate them and put them back on the market. In maximum 30 days people can sell their homes and get 100% of the agreed amount. Why? Because selling a house can be hard and unpredictable, Casavo instead has helped dozens of owners through the selling process, making it easy and stress-free.

The revenue model is driven by two premiums: the liquidity premium (no direct cost for the consumer) and the renovation premium.

When Tinacci first had this idea, he could not access traditional means of funding such as bank loans, as no bank was willing to grant a loan on a project that was merely a business plan with no collateral. He managed to secure capital from a famous Silicon Valley Fund, as its second investment in Europe (the first startup this fund backed was Deliveroo). This sparked interest among other investors, as if this Silicon Valley fund had given a sort of *certificate of excellence of the idea*.

Example Acquisition of Valentino Fashion Group by Permira Investment Firm (2007)

This was one of the most iconic deals ever done in Italy, but a very complex one. Valentino was a phenomenal brand but it had aged a bit. In 2007, customers were mostly >47 years old. This very fact was a cause for some concern but also an opportunity. So Valentino undertook a huge transformation and put the brand back in touch with the customers.

Complexity came from different standpoints. By acquiring Valentino, Permira would be buying three different companies and at least two completely different business lines. In fact, Valentino Fashion Group (VFG) was made up of:

- Valentino, absolute luxury brand;
- Marlboro, causal and sportswear;
- Hugo Boss (52% control), accessible luxury.

Moreover, Valentino was experiencing some troubles:

- Intimidating firm for customers;
- Overpriced: three times higher than its luxury brand peers;
- Not much product consistency;
- Lack of shopping experience;
- Retail outdated; a lot to do to renovate the shopping experience.

The firm had a clear, solid brand image and heritage, but the reality was different, and the company was definitely underperforming in terms of financials. However, there was huge potential for value creation. Permira entered at a 17X multiple, a very high one. They appointed a new CEO, Stefano Sasso, with a clear vision, focalized on long term, working close with Fabrizio Carretti and the Permira team. Despite initial complications, the transaction was a success, the firm was re-organized and sold in 2012 to the fund of the royal family of Qatar for 25X.

How do you replace Valentino "the man"? Permira, after hiring the wrong person in 2007, eventually found the right people, Maria Grazia Chiuri and Pierpaolo Piccioli. So the Permira team took a good brand, revamped it, and resold it for $1 billion. The new owners "oiled the machine," and now it's worth $3 billion.

Figure 11.2   Stages life of a company

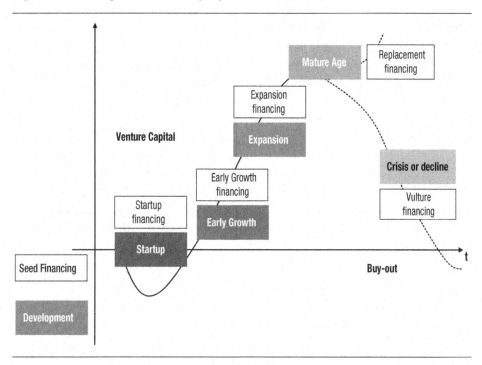

Before looking at each one of these phases, here are two examples that should help better understand the different needs of a firm in the stages of its life cycle. The first one deals with the first phases of life, while the second with the last ones.

There are six diverse types of investments relative to the stage of life of the company (**Figure 11.2**). In each stage, there is a different market and a different risk-return profile. The riskiest stage is the first one because the company has no history and no collateral.

This stage is when the idea is supported by the funds of the entrepreneurs and PEIs, who are willing to take on the risk even if the company does not yet exist. Another risky stage is vulture financing, because the entrepreneur has to be ready to bear the risk of having no guarantee that the company will be rescued. In other words, the risk is not being able to recover the company's investment. The six life stages each relate to a suitable private equity investment, as described below (Caselli et al., 2021).

Venture capital

Investments are characterized by a high level of risk; PEIs need to have a hands-on approach, and must develop a deep level of knowledge of the field where the company operates. **Table 11.1** shows the venture capital stages life.

Table 11.1   **Venture capital stages life**

Stage of life	PE cluster
Development The moment when founders start to formulate and develop the business idea.	**Seed financing** • The riskiest and most complex phase for the financing • Investment in an idea, R&D project: high uncertainty, the investor must believe in the idea of the entrepreneur • Two levels of risk: Can the idea generate an output and is the output marketable? • Support and bear the expenses of R&D (for example for a patent) • Most common sectors are biotech, tech, pharma • Rule 100/10/1: the PEI must screen around 100 projects, shortlist 10 of them, and only one will turn out to be successful • Investors must try to protect themselves from the possibility that the founder is suddenly unable to work • At this stage the solution is the *incubator strategy*, an ad hoc infrastructure where the inventor can work without worrying about his ideas being stolen • The commitment of the team of founders is fundamental at this stage.
Startup The business is actually starting; initial business plan is created; work on products to offer the market.	**Startup financing** • Investment in fixed asset and working capital • Still very risky • PEI inserts lots of covenants on specific issues (put-options, collaterals, stock options) to protect its investment and to deliver the proper set of incentives to the team of founders • Finding the right balance: the investor should not own too much or too little of the company (an optimal amount would be for example less than 50%, where the investor has the right to participate in governance, but the founder has the majority ownership). The central role must remain that of founders and entrepreneurs.
Early growth Usually this spans the first three years after start-up phase; the product is created; sales are generated; the company starts to grow.	**Early growth financing** • Funding the first phase of growth, now not only has the idea been translated into a product (or service) but it has also met the interest of the market that is beginning to demand it. You need to meet demand by increasing production • Need to close two gaps: money gap (cash flows needed to run the business; this can also be done through banks, as the company is starting to be considered a credible borrower) and industrial gap (PE has to intensify its activity in support of, the company that needs managerial support to properly handle the market).

Buyouts

Table 11.2 shows the buyout stages life.

Here is some further information on the last phases.

Table 11.2   Buyout stages life

Stage of life	PE cluster
Expansion Sales keep on growing extensively; product now has proved to be successful and there is the need of additional funds to support the expansion.	**Expansion financing** The fastest phase of growth of a company, where it needs to consolidate its market positioning. Investment is only done to sustain and reduce the cash gap. Level of risk is moderate and the stake held by PEI is not very high. Expansion can follow two paths: internal growth or external growth: • Internal growth strategies: expand by developing activities through investing in other functions of the company • External growth: targeting new customers by entering new markets and eventually in new Countries mostly with the engagement of M&As deals. • In the case of the startup Casavo (see the Box), this is exactly what happened. After an initial presence only in a limited local market (the cities of Milan, Rome and Turin) the company began a path of growth in the rest of Italy but also abroad where it made a series of acquisitions of local competitors entering the Spanish, Portuguese, Greek and French markets.
Maturity Sales growth is stable and the firm will be looking for a change, sooner or later.	**Replacement financing** • The company does not really need additional capital, this cluster mostly is when there is the replacement of current shareholders with the new ones (PE investor) and money flows from buying to selling shareholders • The intervention of the PEI can be justified by the support given also from a strategic point of view for the implementation of acquisition of new companies • Three important transactions are usually found at this stage: LBOs, Private investments in public equity (PIPE) and corporate governance deals • The level of risk is moderate and depends on the strategic process that it is needed to be implemented. See the Box on the intervention of the private equity fund Permira in Valentino Fashion Group: there the Buyout intervention was exactly justified by the need to replace the founder of the company and to implement a strategy able to confirm the possibility for the company to survive and evolve thanks to the strategic and also financial support of PEI.
Crisis/decline	**Vulture financing** • The type of risk that PEI has to bear is in line with and very similar to that which it has to face in case of intervention at the beginning of the life cycle of a company during seed and startup phases. This is because also in this case the risk for the PEI to lose all the investment made is very high, as there is an elevated probability that the company that is experiencing the crisis does not survive and defaults • Two different paths: restructuring financing to turnaround the business and distressed financing to liquidate the company.

Expansion phase

Internal growth:

- Provide R&D support (with money).
- Provide funds for additional working capital and assets.
- Provide managerial support (and networking).
- Quite an easy transaction, alternative to a loan (bringing more value on top of financing).

External growth: PEI are advisors for:

- Origination phase: scouting the market for potential targets.
- Arranging phase: equity value, negotiating price, setting up the transaction.
- Financing phase: deciding the best way to finance the transaction:
  - Directly: the PEI gives money to acquire the target, entering the equity of the acquirer. Pros: the target is merged with the company with synergies. Cons: the PEI also gets a portion of these synergies.
  - SPV: PEI creates an SPV (empty box) co-owned by the PEI and the acquirer, and the SPV acquires the target. Why is this done through an SPV?
    a) Isolation of the transaction from the PEI.
    b) Lower price (the target would ask for a higher price in the direct transaction due to synergies).
    c) Separation of risk of debt and the acquirer (if the SPV defaults, it is a separate entity from the acquirer).

However, this is a more expensive option and synergies might be lower. Synergies are constituted by the creation of additional value (2+2=5) through economies of scale, cuts in costs and so on. Moreover, the PEI can also provide fiscal and legal support in handling the M&A process, saving on costs and adopting a hands-on approach.

Replacement financing

Three important transactions that are classified as replacement financing:

1. LBOs (leveraged buyouts): The PEI is looking for a target company to buy 100% of its equity. The target usually has relevant cash flows, a low D/E ratio and assets which can easily be sold on the market. The purchase is done through an SPV which is injected with debt (up to 90% debt, 10% equity, very high leveraging); this debt will be repaid with the acquired company's cash flows. The purchase is aggressive insofar as the SPV is leveraged. The goal is not to manage the target company, but to resell it for capital gains to a:
   - strategic buyer who is searching for synergies as a source of value, or a
   - financial buyer who is seeking other sources of value.
2. PIPE (private investment in public equity): This is an investment in a minority stake of equity of a listed (public) company. Why? To resell it in a private transaction to a private buyer willing to pay a higher price (usually 3 to 4 times higher) for strategic reasons.

3. Corporate governance deals: This is an investment in a listed company. Such a company runs a reputational risk instead of a financial one. The aim here is to replace existing shareholders with private equity investors, because the company needs managerial support from the PEI who can reorganize the management of the company. This is a very typical case for a family firm that needs managerial support, or when a firm's owners want to be liquidated.

Vulture financing

There are two options in this phase:

1. Restructuring financing (turnaround)
   - Not a lot of PEIs are willing to invest given the risk and difficulty.
   - PEIs support companies in financial crisis with money (PEI as financier) and managerial expertise (PEI as advisor).
   - Majority shares are usually bought, so investors gain full control over governance matters and take a strong hands-on approach: appoint CEO and top management; define the strategy; work on the asset side and liabilities side. The asset side approach (the strategic one) consists in deciding to sell assets that are no longer strategic; the liabilities side approach (the financial one) entails debt equitization and amending or extending strategies. Debt equitization means trying to reach an agreement with lenders on missing and late payments (turn debt holders into equity holders). "Amending strategies" is intended as cancelling portions of debt to lenders, which they accept when there is a low recovery rate. "Extending strategies" means extending the maturity of the exposure so the company can pay it off without going into default.
2. Distress financing: contrary to restructuring, this is very common in PE. Distress financing is an investment in a company which is technically dead (going through a liquidation process); the aim here is to buy strategic assets or gain control of patent rights. The reasons for this are that first of all the PEI is a trader of assets and this investment is done precisely to sell assets to a third buyer and achieve capital gains. Second, the PEI can insert the assets in other venture-backed companies in its portfolio:
   - Assets are taken to the court and the procedure is overseen by a judge; the negotiation process is usually long.
   - To buy the company, some *poison pills* have to be taken, such as being obliged to employ all former employees in the new company too.
   - These deals work quite well in the U.S.

11.3 Private equity investors: two different formats

Regardless of where the deal occurs, there are two legal frameworks, each with its own regulations and players:

- The *European Union format*, regulated by an EU Directive;
- The *Anglo-Saxon format* regulated by US and UK laws.

Using one of the two formats does not necessarily mean that the deal occurs in that respective area. The European format has been adapted and is now used in Brazil, Russia and other countries, whereas the Anglo-Saxon format is also used in India and Australia. What is more imperative to consider is *where* the funds are raised.

Before diving into the two systems and examining their differences, we will define a fund (including the Anglo-Saxon model). A fund is like a bank account where all the investor money is collected. Asset Management Companies (AMCs) manage a series of funds. We will describe the role of AMCs further on.

According to the financial directive, a fund can be organized as open-end or closed-end:

- *Open-end* funds have greater levels of flexibility. In an open-end fund, investors can enter whenever they want to (not necessarily at the beginning) and can exit the fund before maturity. This means that the fund manager has to be ready to liquidate investors before maturity if they wish. These funds are mostly used in the Anglo-Saxon world, but not often in Europe.
- *Closed-end* funds mean that investors enter the fund at the very beginning, when it is launched on the market (during the fund-raising period), and exit at maturity. With this type of fund, investors can exit only when they are replaced (in the secondary market). The investors have to be ready to accept long-term investments and have to trust their AMC completely.

  Investors are usually very wealthy private individuals, but also pension funds, insurance companies and banks. The least engaged of the three are banks, because they spend regulatory capital by investing in risky activities. PE is the riskiest business that bank can invest in.

  In venture capital funds (typical of the Anglo-Saxon format), general partners manage the limited partnership (vehicle) to decide how to use the money collected from limited partners. "Limited partner" take this name because the maximum amount they risk is equal to the funds they invest. General partners instead can risk more than what they injected. The first difference with respect to the European framework (closed-end fund) is that general partners have to be ready to invest at least the 1% of the funds collected. Another difference is that in Europe the fund cannot leverage its own position. In the US (VCF), instead, the limited partnership is allowed to do so.

In Europe the relation between AMC and investors is regulated by the so-called "internal code of activity"; in US there is a "limited partnership agreement." Both are contracts establishing how to manage the fund/limited partnership and the relative economic mechanisms. However, the difference is that the limited partnership agreement is a *private* agreement, while for the internal code of activity the two parties need the approval of the local central bank.

11.4 The European system

In the European Union, there are two Directives regulating PE activity and, in fact, the entire financial system:

1. The Banking Directive;
2. The European Financial Services Directive.

Behind these directives lies the idea that the financial system in Europe has to be managed with stability. For this reason, before a financial institution opens for business, it must earn approval by both the local and central authorities.

In Europe, private equity firms are considered financial services/institutions. These entities have to follow a set of rules to guarantee that their business is organized with efficiency and stability. So, when starting business in Europe, PE firms need to ask for authorization from the local central bank and accept oversight by local supervisors. The three legal entities that can ask permission to start their own activity to the local supervisor are:

- Banks;
- Closed-end funds;
- Investment firms.

Investment firms and closed-end funds are regulated by the financial services directive and the new AIFM (Alternative Investment Fund Managers) directive, while banks are regulated by the banking directive.

11.4.1 Banks

In Europe, banks are universal, i.e. they can conduct any kind of financial transaction except:

- collective asset management (but they can own equity in AMCs);
- insurance activity (again, they can own equity in insurance companies);
- non-financial activities (but they can own equity in non-financial firms).

When a bank wants to invest in private equity, it has two options:

- Direct investment – which is very rare because when a bank directly invests, it has to set aside a significant amount of regulatory capital (which consequently it cannot reinvest) due to Basel rules, because PE is a risky investment. For that reason, any capital gains obtained from the investment are diminished. The only time when the bank invests in PE directly is when it is an urgent investment to save a company, or because the company is of particular importance to the bank (it has extended loans to that company and this is the only way to recover the investment, i.e. equity is the only way the company can pay the bank back).
  - *Prada case*: In 2006, Banca Intesa accepted entering into the Prada equity

structure as a means of repayment of Prada's debt, i.e. debt equitization. However, in 2012, when Prada went public, Banca Intesa sold its shares on the
stock exchange.
- Investment through closed-end funds: the bank invests in a closed-end fund (managed by the AMC which the bank itself owns); in this case, the bank has to set
aside regulatory capital for only 2% which the AMC has to invest, and the rest
of the investment is actually provided by the bank's clients. But when there are
capital gains, the bank gets a percentage (through carried interest charged to the
investors) and earns management fees.
  - Entering as an investor – generates a hurdle rate and capital gains.

11.4.2 Closed-end funds

When referring to closed-end funds, there are three subjects to consider (**Figure 11.3**):

1. *The Asset Management Company* (AMC): A financial institution that can host
   many funds at the same time (they can be both closed and open-end) and it can
   manage financial services as defined by the Financial Services Act (i.e., personal
   management of savings, dealing, brokerage, advisory).

2. *Closed-end fund*: A separate entity that invests money for a pool of investors. It is
   non-floating: the investors can invest only in the fundraising phase and can exit
   only at the end of the life cycle of the fund.

3. *Investors*.

Figure 11.3   Mechanism of closed-end funds

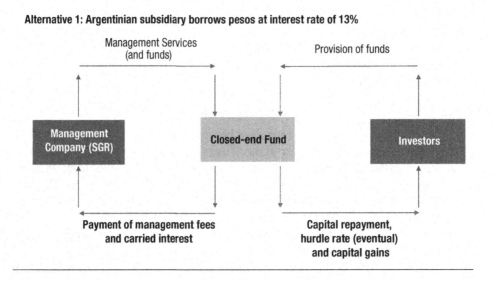

Alternative 1: Argentinian subsidiary borrows pesos at interest rate of 13%

Management Services
(and funds)

Provision of funds

Management
Company (SGR)

Closed-end Fund

Investors

Payment of management fees
and carried interest

Capital repayment,
hurdle rate (eventual)
and capital gains

What is an AMC? First of all, it is that organization that manages funds. The AMC is a consulting company that decides to enter the private equity business and the first thing that it has to do is to ask for the authorization of the local central bank. Shareholders of AMC can be states, banks and private individuals with certain characteristics. AMC shareholders are also requested by legislators to be ready to invest back into the consulting company at least the 2% of the total funds that they raise from investors.

The *economic mechanisms* meant as remuneration for the AMC are *management fees* which consist of a fixed percentage paid on a yearly basis, calculated on the basis of the *committed capital* (the money committed by the investors). The fee is usually 2% of committed capital.

> *Example:*
> C.C.=$100 m; MF=2%/yearly $\Rightarrow$ $20 m; maturity=10 years.
> At time 0, the breakeven point (to pay back investors) = 20/80=25%.
> The management of the vehicle also earns carried interest: paid on the ability to perform well, in order to incentivate the performance. This is expressed as a percentage of the IRR (usually 25%-35%).

11.4.3 Lifetime of a closed-end fund

In the lifetime of a closed-end fund, the following moments are the most important:

- $Time_0$
- $Time_3$
- $Time_N$ (where N is the end of the fund)
- $Time_{N+3}$

There are four phases, as evident from the timeline in **Figure 11.4**:

1. Fundraising.
2. Draw-down.
3. Getting to N.
4. Extra time.

Figure 11.4   **Lifetime of a closed fund**

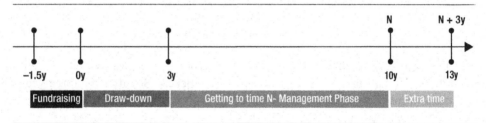

First of all comes *fundraising*. Before launching any activity, the AMC needs approval by the authority, which depends on three criteria.

a) The size of the fund:
  - The AMC must specify to the supervisor the target amount, e.g. 100 million euros (in Europe, average size is from 100 to 300 million euros).
  - If the target approved by the central bank was 100 million euros, and the AMC manages to raise only 99 million, it must start the process all over again.

b) The value of every ticket:
  - This refers to the minimal amount of money which must be invested by each investor, typically 1 million euros – big investors are targeted instead of small retail ones.
  - The ticket is written in the Internal Code of Activity and once approved, it cannot be changed.

c) The investment target:
  - One or a small number of industries must be specified, because AMC must be specialized and have expertise to create value in a given sector.
  - This is supervised by the depository bank, which will not authorize any transaction contradicting the Internal Code of Activity and can notify the local central bank which investigates and can even replace the AMC in charge of the fund.

Once the approval is granted, the AMC has as a maximum 18 months to collect all of its money.

Generally, 4-5 months is the average time taken by an AMC to collect the whole sum that will be invested. As a matter of fact, if the AMC does not collect the money in the time allowed, they usually stop beforehand, otherwise they would lose their reputation. In fact, 50% of the funds all over Europe do not manage to get to time 0.

> Commitment is *not* investment, but money that investors promised to put in investments (the PE vehicle), this is a preliminary phase (when the opportunity arises, the investor will be made).

In the second stage, there is the *draw-down period*. At time 0, the fundraising phase comes to an end. In this period, the AMC has the possibility to ask the investors to deposit a percentage of their commitment (e.g. 10%). The time is set at 3 years, because collecting all the capital from the investors will take much more time than it does in capital markets. In the time going from time 0 to the third year, the closed-end fund has to call in all the money previously subscribed by the investors during the fundraising phase, who can also deposit their investment by installments.

The third stage is the *getting to time N*. At Time 3, the investors have to have entirely injected all the money equivalent to their tickets. So, after the three years, the AMC keeps on investing until the end of the fund. In fact, some investing activity can have already taken place before Time 3, but not using the entire amount.

The length of the fund can be defined by the AMC, as long as it is shorter than 30 years. Usually, 90% of the funds have a maturity of 10 years. As a matter of fact, for an AMC, 10 years is a long enough maturity to make two investments:

- Year 0-3: first investment.
- Year 3-5: exit from the first investment.
- Year 5-7: second investment.
- Year 7-10: exit from the second investment.

Finally, there is eventually the *extra time* (the grace period). After the end of the closed-end fund there is the possibility to use up to three year of extra time. PE tends to have low liquidity, so sometimes an AMC does not have the whole amount of cash it would need to pay off the investors right away. When the fund finally comes to an end, the AMC valuates the fund and spreads this value among all the investors consistent with the amount of the ticket bought by each investor in the beginning of the fund.

11.4.4 Investment firms

Investment firms are regulated by the Financial Directive; these financial institutions need approval from the supervisors (local central banks). They can be created by a small group of investors which do not want to comply to strict regulations and want to invest their own money ("family offices" – a group of family members who are potential investors). They can undertake the same activities as banks except collecting deposits but, they have a different liability side. (The bank's largest liability are deposits, which the investment firm cannot collect.)

The balance sheet of an investment firm can be represented as shown in **Figure 11.5**.

Figure 11.5   Balance sheet of an investment firm

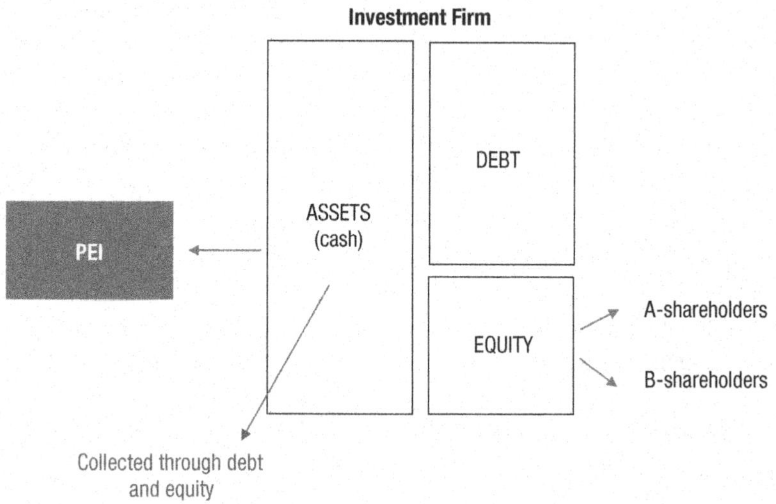

A-shareholders and B-shareholders replicate the relationship between AMC and in-vestors in closed-end funds.

- *A-shareholders*: act as an AMC – they manage how the cash is invested and are remunerated with yearly management fees and yearly carried interest (computed yearly because the investment firm does not come to an end as closed-end funds do).
- *B-shareholders*: act as investors – they do not participate in the management of the investment; they are remunerated with the difference between the profits and carried interest given to A-shareholders (these are small, private investors).

Investment firms are like corporations; they can raise debt.

Why then are investment firms used for PE investments? They can be leveraged, un-like closed-end funds which cannot raise debt. This is because if small, private enti-ties (typical investors in these firms) lose their money, it is not a problem on a large scale. But investors such as insurance companies and pension funds (involving ma-ny individuals' savings for their retirement, etc.) cannot afford to risk that much – it would be socially unacceptable.

11.5 The Anglo-Saxon system

In the Anglo-Saxon world, PE is not a financial service (as it is in Europe), rather it is an *entrepreneurial activity*, so the regulatory framework is made up of Common Law, ad hoc fiscal rules and special regulations for PE activity. In the end, in the An-glo-Saxon format, there is no authorization/supervision. You can start a PE business as long as it is not against the law, and there are different ways to organize it. The most common are *Venture Capital Funds* (VCF – the most important), *Small Busi-ness Investment Companies* (SBICs), *Corporate Ventures*, *Banks*, and *Business An-gels*.

Although the common idea underpinning the definition of PE is the same for both the US and the UK, it is worth taking the two separately and highlighting their different structures. For the US, there is a focus on:

- Venture Capital Funds;
- Small Business Investment Companies;
- Banks;
- Corporate Ventures;
- Business Angels.

For the United Kingdom instead, considerations rest on:

- Venture Capital Funds;
- Venture Capital Trusts;

- Local PPP (public private partnerships);
- Banks;
- Business Angels.

As both systems share business angels and banks, these two formats will be dealt with straight away.

Banks

Like in Europe, there are many constraints for banks in the US to invest directly in PE, so they rarely do so. Instead, they usually act as General Partners or Limited Partners in Venture Capital Funds.

Business angels

- These are PE investors without professional skills: foundations, charities, universities, high net worth individuals.
- In the US, for example, the main benefit is the QSBS rule (Qualified Small Business Stock) – if the capital gains received from one PE investment is immediately reinvested in another one, no taxes are levied – a huge incentive for such investments.

11.5.1 USA

(Venture) Capital Funds

This section will look at VCFs and how they work. The following characteristics will be considered:

- Main players;
- Contracts;
- Mechanisms;
- Lifetime.

Starting from the *main players*:

1. General partners (like the AMC in the EU format):
   - They are investment professionals who own the private equity firm (which sponsors the limited partnership (LLP).
   - They manage the vehicle (limited partnership).
   - They decide how to use the money they've raised.
   - They risk more than what they injected in the fund (they're fully liable for the LP's debts – worst case scenario, they lose everything).
   - They must invest at least 1% of the total amount collected in the fund (first difference from the closed-end fund).

   – They receive an annual management fee (1.9% to 2% of the committed capital) regardless of the investment performance and carried interest, which is a percentage of the capital gains (on average, 20%). After the exit is done and there are capital gains, 20% is paid out to general partners and the rest goes to limited partners.

2. Limited partnership (vehicle – like the closed-end fund in the EU format):
   – This is sponsored by a private equity firm (a small organization owned by few investors).
   – The limited partnership can be leveraged (i.e. it can raise debt) (the second difference from the closed-end fund).

3. Limited partners (like investors in the EU format):
   – They are simply investors.
   – They are called "limited" because their maximum risk exposure is the amount they invested in the fund. (They are not liable for more than what they invested.)
   – Typically, limited partners are:
   a) Banks;
   b) Pension funds;
   c) Insurance companies;
   d) Private investors.

Figure 11.6   Mechanism of VCF

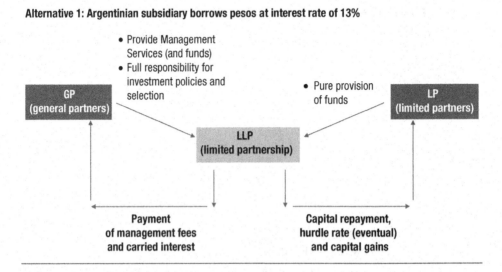

Alternative 1: Argentinian subsidiary borrows pesos at interest rate of 13%

Figure 11.6 represents the general *mechanism* illustrating how a VCF works. The main differences with respect to closed-end funds are the following:

1. A VCF is not a financial institution; it is an entrepreneurial activity. (An AMC in contrast is a financial institution and, as part of the financial system, must get permission to start operating.)
2. The limited partnership agreement does not have to be approved by a supervisor (a central bank); the Internal Code of Activity meanwhile does have to be approved.
3. A VCF must invest just 1% of the total fund value (as opposed to the 2% requirement for an AMC).
4. A VCF can raise debt (an AMC cannot).
5. Investors are free of taxes.

As for the *contract*, the relations between the limited partners and the general partners is regulated by a *limited partnership agreement* that specifies the terms of the investment, determines the management of the fund and relative economic mechanisms, and details the relationships between the limited partners and the general partners. It is a private agreement (which does not need to be approved by an authority such as a central bank) and contains information about size, sectors/industries in which the money will be invested, economic mechanisms, hurdle rate and capital gains for limited partners, and management fees and carried interest for general partners.

The success of a limited partnership is due to:

- Very simple operational model;
- Tax transparency (third difference from closed-end funds): No tax for investors if:
  - Fundraising lasts for 1 year;
  - Maturity is 10 years;
  - The maximum extra time is 2 years.

The *life of a venture capital fund* typically lasts from 10 to 12 years. The timeline in **Figure 11.7** should provide an idea of the phases.

Figure 11.7   Timeline of VCF

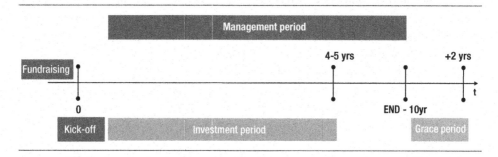

Before time 0:
- Fundraising:
  - Short and effective for big players;

   - Time for collecting commitments;
   - When the target amount is reached or oversubscribed, Phase 1 starts.

Phase 1:
- Investment period:
   - Lasts 4 to 5 years;
   - Commitments of the investors are requested;
   - In these 4 to 5 years, GPs must exhaust all the dry powder they have (fulfil the promise that they will invest).

Management period:
- Starts when the money is invested;
- Screen companies;
- Intervene in Board of Directors.

Extra grace period:
- Used to optimize the divestiture process (to make the exit more profitable, because currently there may be unfavorable market conditions or similar);
- Exit can be done from Year 5 to Year 10 or 12 – through an IPO or trade sale (to another PEI or to a strategic buyer).

Once the LPs sign the contract, they promise to give a certain amount of money called committed capital. Once the committed capital has been raised, the fund is closed and the screening and investment activity of the GPs starts.

   The nature of the PE business is to invest the committed capital in private companies, increase their equity value and then sell them to obtain a return (capital gains) on the investment. That is why PE business has a precise schedule and can be divided in four phases.

   Generally, for both venture funds (the vehicle is Limited Partnership – LLP) and closed-end funds, the process of private equity can be divided into:
- Fundraising:
   - GPs and AMCs collect commitments from investors;
   - When all the commitments have been collected, the investment vehicle is created.
- Investing:
   - Market scouting, screening, negotiation;
   - Equity stakes of target companies (with a high growth potential) are bought.
- Managing and monitoring:
   - Creating value by actively influencing the business activity (if a hands-on approach is used).
- Exiting:
   - Selling ownership stakes in the company to remunerate the investors;
   - Most common exit strategies: IPO, sale to a strategic buyer, sale to another PE fund.

SBIC (Small Business Investment Company)

Marking the beginning of PE development in the US is the SBIC. This corporate format was created through the Small Business Investment Company Act of 1958 to stimulate the venture capital market. These companies, which are public-private partnerships, are legal entities which consist of two shareholders:

- One must be a Public Administration (which invests 50%): this pure investor cannot manage the company (example: a US state, e.g. California, a municipality, e.g. New York City).
- The other one can be any shareholder (who invests 50%): usually a bank, a corporation or an individual with the right and the duty to manage the investments and the company as a whole.

Figure 11.8 is an example of the structure of a SBIC balance sheet.

Figure 11.8   **Balance sheet of a SBIC**

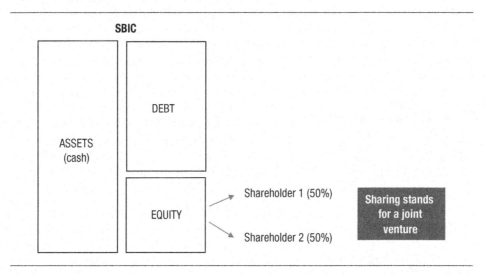

Both shareholders receive a management fee and profits (calculated by the carried interest approach) which are unevenly distributed. The PA can only receive profit remuneration up to a certain threshold (less than the 50% they invested), as stated in the SBIC agreement. The remaining profits go to the other shareholder. This is acceptable because the intent of the investment is to have a social impact and promote venture capital investments. Losses are shared equally between the public administration and the other shareholder. SBIC can raise debt – 33% of it can be borrowed from the Federal Reserve at a very low interest rate (the rate of T bills) which is set yearly. Capital gains and other revenues are free of tax; taxation starts with the distribution of earnings. This kind of "tax-free" vehicle cannot be implemented in the EU, even though both in Europe and Asia the introduction of such a vehicle is the topic of intense debate.

SBICs are very popular in the US, because with a partner belonging to the Public Administration, investors feel that they can invest in even riskier deals. Lastly, SBICs are considered one of the best models of PPP (Public-Private Partnerships).

Corporate ventures

Corporate ventures are not a proper legal entity, but a division or a department of a corporation which wants to invest in venture capital. Thus, they only do seed and start-up financing. The investment is undertaken to promote R&D, outputs, and patents. Unlike in venture capital funds, the goal is not to generate IRR, but to increase the value of the corporation by developing a product/service.

11.5.2 United Kingdom

The mechanisms in the UK are more similar to the US that the EU systems. The UK financial market is regulated by Common Law and great importance is placed on the courts. Regardless of that, in the UK it is possible to use schemes created under the European format (Banking Directive and Financial Services Directive); this allows for a greater variety of solutions for equity investors.

(Venture) Capital Funds

As mentioned before, VCFs are legal entities operating as limited partnerships just like in the US (i.e. not built under the European scheme of closed-end funds). Also like in the US, they aim to attract the same type of investors in terms of risk-return profile. Limited partners are generally private investors, banks, pension funds, insurance funds and corporate investors. VCFs are allowed to leverage and must have a maturity of 10 years.

Venture Capital Trust

These were introduced in the UK in 1997, and had great success in that market. Nowadays VCTs are gaining recognition as a format, and they can be found in India and Australia as well. VCTs are based on the old British concept of a trust (the first were established in the 11th and 12th centuries) and were created to contend with succession issues.

A VCT is an entity, not a company. The owner, namely the settlor, does not manage its assets, but a third party (trustee) does so for the settlor and is fully liable. If the VCT has a maturity, at the end of it the owner (settlor) gets back their assets from the trust. The VCT is like an "empty box" which does not publish any financial reports.

Figure 11.9 is an example of the structure of a VCT balance sheet.

Figure 11.9   Venture capital trust balance sheet

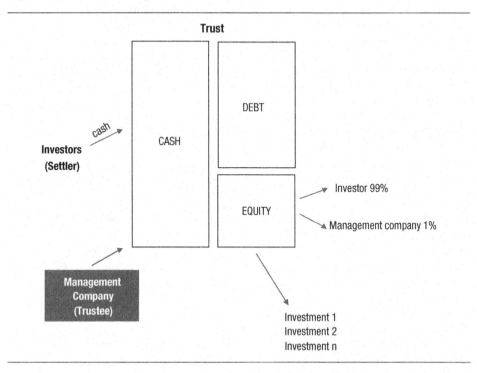

With respect to the applications of VCT in private equity:

• Connects retail investors with PE (unlike closed-end funds).
• General partners (GPs) create a trust with a term (the VCF term) and they set a portion of their assets aside which are used as a collateral to show the LPs their commitment to managing the fund.
• Investors = settlers:
  – inject 99% of the money in the fund;
  – receive a certificate of investment listed in the London Stock Exchange which solves the liquidity issue;
  – must trust the reputation of the trustee (the management company which will invest the injected cash);
  – are granted fiscal incentives in the end.
• Management company = trustee:
  – manages the money injected in the fund;
  – must inject 1% of the total funds injected in the fund;
  – at least 70% of the money injected must be invested in PE, the rest can be invested in something more liquid according to management's choice.
• Asset = cash (of which at least 70% will be invested in private equity).

- The trust does not own any assets, it just has the cash the investors (settlers) injected initially in order for it to be invested in venture capital.

Local PPPs (Public-Private Partnerships)

PPPs are not as popular as in the US (within the SBIC category); these entities operate at a local level and comply with local laws.

11.6 The economic mechanism of an AMC

In closed-end funds there is an interaction between the investors and the AMC. Investors will be paid, and a gain or loss will be generated at the end of the fund (i.e. either at time 10 or at time 13). But what about the managers of the funds? The goal of this section of the chapter is to understand how the AMC is remunerated over the fund's lifetime. Specifically, the AMC receives two different kinds of remunerations: management fees and carried interest. Please note that the rules that will be presented are also valid for fund managers operating in the US as long as they operate in PE deals.

11.6.1 Management fees

Management fees correspond to the amount of money an AMC receives every year from closed-end funds. Closed-end funds are vehicles generating:

- Revenues, in the form of capital gains;
- Dividends coming from the companies in which the investment is made;
- Losses, in case the deal is not successful.

The management fee is a fixed percentage of money calculated on the value of the closed-end fund in the beginning, when the fund is created. For instance, in the case of a closed-end fund worth €100 million bearing management fees at 2%, every year the AMC receives €2 million from the fund. The management fees must be precisely calculated because they have to cover:

- Operating costs;
- Remuneration of the advisor helping the AMC in the consulting activity;
- Remuneration of the technical committee.

The percentage of the management fees is in fact calculated with the capital budgeting approach. That means that it is computed by replying to the question: "Is the amount enough to properly cover all expenses?" The answer is not in fact in the percentage per se; rather it stands as the absolute value of these fees. In case an AMC belongs to a bank, all the above-listed costs will be easily covered. On the contrary, if the AMC is an independent entity, covering all the expenses can be very difficult. For instance, in venture capital, AMCs are owned by professionals and not by financial institutions, because they need a workforce who can fully be devoted to the venture-backed company.

11.6.2 Carried interest

The second source of remuneration for the AMC is made up of carried interest. *Maximizing the carried interest* is the ultimate goal of an AMC. It is computed only at the end of the closed-end fund's life cycle.

$$Carried\ Interest = \%\times(Final\ IRR-Hurdle\ IRR)$$

IRR is a discount rate that equals the investments with the present values of the future returns on said investments. The carried interest is the spread between the final IRR and a hurdle (a.k.a. threshold) IRR multiplied by a fixed percentage. Usually, the fixed percentage ranges between 25-30%; the hurdle rate ranges between 7- 8%. This means that, at the end of the fund, the AMC will receive a carried interest if and only if the final IRR is larger than 7-8%. The carried interest formula is also called *the waterfall mechanism*. This mechanism can be used either with or without catch-up, where the choice to calculate IRR one way or the other is up to the AMC and must be agreed in the Internal Code of Activity.

- *Without catch-up*: The carried interest is computed on the difference between the final IRR and the hurdle rate.
- *With catch-up*: The carried interest is directly computed on the final IRR.

Simple carried interest:

- Committed capital = €100 mln
- Total exit value = €200 mln
- Simple carried interest in place = 20% (applied to the positive internal rate of return of the vehicle)
- Carried interest = (200 – 100) × 20% = €20 mln

There are certain rules that can be applied and engaged in PE investments; one of these is the hurdle rate.

Carried interest with the Hurdle rate:

The hurdle rate is a threshold rate, a preferred return we want to pay to investors even before we pay the carried interest to GPs/asset management company.

- Committed capital = €100 mln
- Total exit value = €120 mln
- Carried interest = 20%
- Hurdle rate in place = 8%

The hurdle rate is 8% of the committed capital = 8% × (100) = €8 mln. Before paying a carried interest to the GPs/managers, we want to pay a preferred return to the investors, addressed on the committed capital.

The carried interest will be paid on what remains.
Therefore, the carried interest is: $(120 - 100 - 8) \times 20\% = €2.4$ mln

Carried interest with the catchup clause:

Once the hurdle rate is paid to investors, we can anticipate the payment of carried interest to managers and general partners.

- Committed capital = €100 mln
- Hurdle rate in place = 8%
- Carried interest = 20% on the IRR produced by the bank hold
- Catchup in place (this is a provision, a clause agreed upon with investors)
  - Multiple investments with different times of liquidation:
  - Time 1: liquidation of €109 mln
  - Time 2: €1 mln
  - Time 3: €10 mln
  - Total = €120 mln

We are simply changing the time when we will pay the carried interest:

- Time = 1: liquidate investment of 109 million; capital gain of 9 year 1 we have 109 million at our disposal and we pay 8 million to our investors (we are paying the hurdle rate = 8% × 100); (109 − 100) × 20% = 1.8 million (does not consider the 8 million for the hurdle rate; 1.8 is addressed directly to the committed capital-consider simple carried interest). We have 1 million at our disposal so we start paying just that 1 million.
- Time = 2: liquidate 1 million. Total cumulative proceeds = 110 million. Capital gain is 10 million. General partners should receive (110 − 100) = (10 million) × 20% = 2 million. We have already paid one million to them so at the end we should pay 2 million − 1 million (anticipated in year 1).
- Time = 3: liquidate 10 million. Total cumulative proceeds are 120 million; total capital gain = 20 million. (20 million × 20%) = 4 million − 2 million (paid in the previous years) = 2 million.

The difference with the simple carried interest is that here you can pay during the life of the fund/limited partnership, instead of doing the whole calculation at the very end.

11.7 Private equity trends and players

After having analyzed private equity in detail by describing its features and differences around the world, it is worth having a look at the dimensions of the phenomenon, how it evolved over time, who the main players are and the most recent trends shaping the market.

In terms of the dimensions of the global private equity market, the following graph gives an idea of the proportion of deals and their value. It also illustrates the main trends since 2005. Before looking at it, worth mentioning is the fact that since the 1980s, where there was a huge availability of debt, until 2007 (with the exception of 2001), there has always been stable and positive growth of the PE phenomenon. The maximum levels of deal value were reached in 2006 and 2007, values that as of yet have never been attained again.

In the past five years, the PE industry has raised, invested and distributed back to shareholders a record amount of funds like never before in its history. However, despite its positive recent performance, the global buyout share of the total M&A market represented solely approximately 15% in 2018, increasing to 18.8% in 2020. Nevertheless, PEs possessed unprecedented levels of cash to invest, where that year the whole industry (including venture capital) had a total value of $1.45 trillion.

Despite the high levels of liquidity, PE has been facing changing market dynamics that can pose some challenges to this activity. In particular, 2020 was a year of great disruption; the Covid-19 pandemic and its economic hardships have affected sectors and economies worldwide. Nevertheless, private equity dealmakers kept making deals in 2020, while exits and fund-raising fell in line with robust five-year averages. While initially PE activity declined in April and May 2020, it snapped back in the third and fourth quarters of 2020, demonstrating its resilience and generating $592 billion in buy-out deal volume (up 8% from 2019 levels). As described by many experts in the industry, in some respects, its quick rebound did not come as a surprise: one of PEs greatest strengths over time has been the ability to prosper in times of economic disruption.

If we look more closely at the situation in Europe, trends over time have been very similar to the situation in the rest of the world. We are witnessing an increasing amount of capital committed and a growing number of funds. In the midst of the pandemic, however, European private equity activity was slightly slower to rebound and lagged in both the second and third quarters while jumping back up in the fourth quarter.

As for the Italian market, recently there has been tremendous development in the sector (see **Figures 11.10** and **11.11**) and some investments topped out at around 7 bil-

Figure 11.10 **Italian private equity deal activity by quarter (2017-2020, Q1-Q3)**

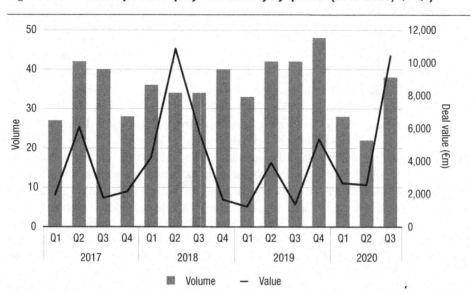

Source: Mergermarket (2020); for further information visit mergermarket.com.

Figure 11.11   **Evolution of PE investment activity**

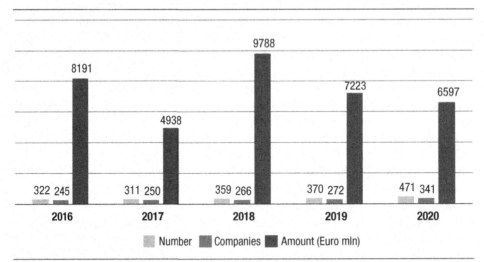

Source: Author's elaboration of AIFI Research 2019 Market overview; for further information visit https://www.aifi.it/en/home.

lion euros in 2019 and 2020. The Italian market has also registered some megadeals and an increase in the weight of international investors of late. Indeed, around 55% of PE and venture capital investments in 2019 in Italy were brought into the country by international operators, 30% of which do not even have a seat or an office in this country. Moreover, similarly to Europe and the rest of the world, the Italian PE market has been quite resilient to the economic disruption caused by the pandemic in 2020: although there was a reduction of 9% in the total amount invested, the number of investments and deals grew by 27%.

Current global developments have also impacted the outlook and expected trends of the private equity market. In particular three developments are important to mention. In the first place, recent market uncertainly established a greater need for deep sector and subsector expertise among investors. Indeed, the more knowledgeable PEIs are about a sector, the better they are expected to understand how a specific market is changing and how to take advantage of it. Moreover, greater attention is expected to be required with regards to due diligences and valuations. In particular, given that multiples for PE investments are at almost record highs, funds need to be able to engage in investments and targets that will be able to achieve revenue growth and multiple expansion with little margin for error. Finally, the changes experienced in a remote working environment in 2020 have pushed PE firms to accelerate their transition from analog to digital. Technology will not only impact in-house investments and transitions, but even targets and analyses.

Now that an overview of the trends that have affected the private equity market over time has been provided, with a subsequent analysis of the most recent developments and a focus on the EU-Italian situation, it is important to comprehend who the key players are that are shaping the market in today's environment.

If in 1980s, operations were mainly linked to conglomerates that were bought and then broken up and sold separately, and in 2000s PE was all about infrastructures, who are the big players now? The chart below (**Table 11.3**) lists the top players in the private equity world. With respect to the past, we can witness a shift towards fewer but bigger names.

Table 11.3   **PE top players companies**

2020	2019	Firm	Five-year Fundraising Total ($m)	Headquarter
1	1	Blackstone	95,951	New York
2	2	The Carlyle Group	61,719	Washington DC
3	3	KKR	54,760	New York
4	12	TPG	38,682	Fort Worth
5	5	Warburg Pincus	37,587	New York
6	10	NB Alternatives	36,505	New York
7	4	CVC Capital Partners	35,877	Luxembourg
8	7	EQT	34,461	Stockholm
9	19	Advent International	33,491	Boston
10	14	Vista Equity Partners	32,095	San Francisco

Finally, the last two tables provide an indication of the most recent deals and exits completed in the third quarter of 2020 globally. Many sectors and players have been actively involved in recent private equity activity, nevertheless, as previously mentioned, many of the larger fund names outlined in Table 11.3 can be identified as the key dealmakers in **Tables 11.4** and **11.5**.

As the figures in the tables show, therefore, the pandemic itself did not impede industry growth. On the contrary, the Covid-19 crisis resulted in an unprecedented injection of liquidity by governments and various central banks into economies around the world that not only helped companies, but also ensured that debt to finance purchases remained available and relatively affordable. So in 2021, private equity funds enjoyed their second highest fundraising year in the industry history, according to Bain's annual report, ending a five-year run that provided $1.8 trillion in fresh funding for purchases. Funds also increased payments to investors and continued to outperform all other asset classes. For the first time in history, the average transaction size exceeded $1 billion in 2021. Global growth initially provided the same positive stimulus in terms of high returns for early 2022 as well, but rising inflationary pressures and the onset of conflict in Europe between Ukraine and Russia could somewhat contract potential gains in 2022 and future years.

Table 11.4   PE deals Q3 2020

Target	Investor	Seller	Sector	Deal value ($m)	Closing
Thyssenkrupp Elevator AG	Civen Advent International	Thyssenkrupp	Industrials	17,200	31/07/20
Ellie Mae	Ice	Thomabravo	Technology	9,423	04/09/20
Adnoc Gas Pipeline Assets (49%)	Brookfield Ontario Teachers	Adnoc	Oil & Gas	8,941	15/07/20
58.com	General Atlantic Warburg Pincus	Listed (NYSE)	Technology	6,742	18/09/20
Cheniere (42%)	Brookfield Blackstone	Blackstone	Power & Utilities	5,896	24/09/20
Masmovil	Providence Equity KKR Civen	Listed (NYSE)	Telecom	4,724	11/09/20
Viridor	KKR Hermes	Pennon	Waste Management	4,555	08/07/20
Vertafore	Roper	Bain CapitalVista	Technology	4,526	03/09/20
LogMeIn	Francisco Partners Elliott	Listed (NASDAQ)	Industrials	3,822	31/08/20
Tower Infrasturcture Trust	Brookfield	Reliance Industries Limited	Infrastructure	3,267	01/09/20

Source: Author's elaboration of Mergermarket data.

Table 11.5   PE deals Q3 2020

Target	Investor	Seller	Sector	Deal value ($m)	Closing
Engineering	Bain Capital	Apax Neuberger Berman	Industrials	1,600	23/07/20
INWI	Ardian Canson	Tim	Telecom	1,346	02/10/20
Goolden Goose	The Carlyle Group	Permira	Consumer Goods	1,300	16/06/20
Sorgenia	Fondi Italiani per le infrastrutture Asterion	MPS BPM Intesa Sanpaolo Unicredit	Power & Utilities	1,000	06/10/20
Gamenet	Apollo	Trilantic Europe Intralot	Gaming	721	14/02/20
Nexi (10% stake)	Intesa Sanpaolo	Mercury	Finance	653	30/06/20
The dedica anthology	Covivio	Varde	Real Estate	573	07/09/20
Valagro	Syngenta	Metalmark Capital	Industrials	500	06/10/20
Permasteelisa Group	Atlas Holding	Lixil	Industrials	440	30/09/20
Renvico	Engie	KKR Mecquarie	Power & Utilities	400	10/03/20

Source: Author's elaboration of Mergermarket data.

11.8 New alternatives to private equity

This last section outlines the possible alternatives to private equity, focusing on SPACs, private debt funds, crowdfunding and venture philanthropy.

11.8.1 SPACs

Invented in the US about 10 years ago, Special Purpose Acquisition Companies (SPACs) emerged in Europe three or four years ago. A SPAC is an "empty shell" – a kind of SPV (a new corporation founded for the sole purpose of investing in PE, i.e. acquiring a specific company).

Working mechanism: Sponsors (very experienced professionals from investment banking or the corporate world) inject a small amount equity in the SPV; 20% of the vehicle is held by the promoter/sponsor, and the remaining 80% is listed in the stock exchange to raise capital. Although a SPAC is an empty shell, investors are notified that the money will be used to execute an acquisition as a form of PE investment (100% of equity is bought).

The investors buy stock in the SPAC in order to participate in the PE investment it makes. Funds are raised exclusively to make one single investment – the acquisition of a specific company. The promoters/sponsors have 24 months to find the potential target and complete the acquisition. If the SPAC succeeds, it merges with the target company in the end. If it doesn't, the investors get their money back and the SPAC is delisted (it is a "one-shot vehicle").

For more information about SPACs, see the box "SPAC regulations in Italy" at the end of this chapter.

11.8.2 Private debt funds

Private debt funds are the exact same vehicles as in private equity (closed-end funds, investment companies, banks). The only difference is here the investment is made in private debt and not in equity.

In Europe, there are many non-listed SMEs which don't want to collect funds though banks (or can't) and they would rather turn to the market. Thus, PDI (private debt investors) provide funds to them and also give them a two- to three-year grace period before the interest should be repaid – the company is given time to become profitable. PDIs can also provide support from the managerial point of view. Public companies can issue bonds on the market and collect debt in that way, but it is much harder to do so for private companies that can refer to PDI as a more flexible alternative of financing. The private debt sector has remained active even after the setbacks suffered in the early stages of the Covid-19 pandemic by rebounding in 2021, which has been rapid thanks to a growing economy, high liquidity in the credit markets, and companies avoiding insolvency for these reasons. **Figure 11.12** shows the geographic distribution of the world's largest private debt funds as of January 1, 2022.

Figure 11.12   **The geographic distribution of the world's largest private debt funds as of January 1, 2022 ($bn)**

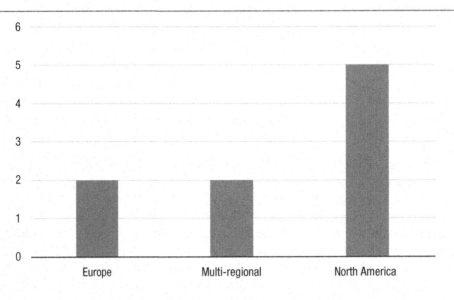

Source: Author's elaboration of Private Debt Investor data.

11.8.3 Crowdfunding

Crowdfunding is an alternative financing source (Gigante et al., 2021) in which individuals use an internet platform to participate directly in raising capital for an entrepreneurial project by providing a loan (lending-based model), underwriting shares of the company's risk capital (equity-based model), or offering a donation (reward and donation-based models). The phenomenon emerged in response to challenges in accessing capital through the traditional banking system, due to the "credit crunch" characterizing the early twentyfirst century. Different players launch then their financial needs directly on an on-line platform and raise funds from investors willing to participate. It works mostly for companies in their earliest stage in life. In the US, there is no need for authorization for starting such a platform while in Europe, authorization from supervisors is necessary to collect money on a crowdfunding platform.

11.8.4 Venture Philanthropy

When a PEI invests in businesses with a social purpose, that is called venture philanthropy. Investors and management here agree to get lower profits in terms of capital gains, management fees and carried interest, because of the social impact they want to support by investing in this business. Thus, venture philanthropy is a type of venture capital, and is often referred to as social venture capital, since it entails investing venture cash and offering managerial experience in business initiatives that seek creative solutions to social and environmental challenges. These investments are designed to provide solutions to social and environmental problems based on economic market principles.

11.9 Private equity as a growth opportunity for Italy

The mechanism of private equity and all the managerial – and financial – advantages that it brings can be seen as an enormous resource for Italy and its SMEs. Indeed, it is not infrequent within Italian companies to find succession problems, the desire to diversify portfolio of investments, misalignment between interests of shareholders, family disputes or the simple drive of managers to become entrepreneurs. All these circumstances call for the intervention of specialized, competent figures such as PEIs, who with their funds, knowledge and expertise can turnaround the situation for the best.

In this sense, private equity can truly be the key and main protagonist of the transformation and modernization of the Italian entrepreneurial system of small and medium enterprises. Management buy-outs in particular should be the tool for change, to revitalize the country's economy, ensure generational shifts, 'managerialize' and teach financial rigor and stability.

11.10 Conclusions

Private equity is a business with a broad definition. It is useful to remember the definition given by the SEC: "Whatever investment in *equity* instruments with an *active approach* by the investor and with a *definite exit strategy*." The definition of private equity is based on two different aspects we must keep in mind every time we deal with this issue. On one hand, private equity is a source of financing for a company. This means private equity is an alternative to other sources of financing like an IPO or bond issuing or obtaining a loan from the banking system. On the other hand, private equity is an investment made by a financial institution, a private equity investor.

Throughout the chapter many aspects that characterize the business of private equity were analyzed. First, we described PE according to the firm's life cycle, where the PE strategies can be very different. We might be investing in the same instrument (equity or semi-equity) but the kind of company is not the same. In the early-stage investments (venture capital) targeting very new businesses, entrepreneurs need money and competences. These are the riskiest forms of equity investments because there is high uncertainty. A hands-on approach here is fundamental to understand the investment. If instead the company is sufficiently credible and the product is already on the market and successful, then the uncertainty decreases and with it the riskiness of the

investment. Lastly, during expansion and late-stage investing, investments in private
firms with a good market potential and management team could be appealing. The
PE investor injects capital in the company to allow it to invest more in the business
and grow. The same can be said of distressed investing or special situations investing
in companies that are not doing well, but that can be bought at very low price and
then be the object of speculative trading.

In this chapter, we assessed how private equity is seen differently around the
world and how these differences reflect on the various PE tools. Indeed, when talking about the PE phenomenon, it is correct to distinguish between Anglo-Saxon and
European systems, as they entail a different legal definition of private equity. Still,
despite the fact that they have very different legal entities, the functioning of private
equity behind the legal entities is exactly the same, because it is based on two different players working together: on one hand, managers and on the other, investors
who decide to commit their money to certain legal entities. Next we focused on the
economic aspects of the phenomenon, looking at the remuneration mechanism for investors and managers. Moreover, the most recent private equity trends, volumes and
deals were discussed. Finally, the chapter concluded with final remarks on alternatives to PE and how PE can be seen as a tool for growth.

SPAC regulations in Italy

A SPAC (Special Purpose Acquisition Company) is a listed corporate vehicle (an "empty shell"),
formed and managed by a group of "promoters" (or "sponsors") for the specific purpose of carrying out a business combination with a private target company within a certain time horizon.
While in other countries (e.g. US) SPACs are specifically regulated, in Italy they are not subject to
an explicit legal framework. Thus, it is necessary to look at the broader picture of the corporate
regulations to understand how their specific features and events are regulated.

The corporate form

Under Italian law SPACs are incorporated as joint-stock companies, which are regulated by the
Civil Code and, if listed, also by precise regulations (Legislative Decree 58/1998 and Issuers'
Regulations, adopted by Consob).
According to the Civil law, within a joint-stock company we have three primary corporate bodies:

- A Shareholders' Meeting, composed by those who contributed to the share capital of the
  company. Shareholders decide on the internal organization (e.g. appointment and removal of
  directors) as well as on the most important matters within the company (e.g. dividend distributions, approval of certain extraordinary transactions).
- A Board of Directors, the body composed by a certain number of directors and responsible for
  managing the company. The fundamental duty of directors is to appoint, support and monitor
  executives, those who run day-to-day operations.
- A Supervisory Board, which ensures that the company is managed in compliance with the
  laws and the articles of incorporation and that suitable controls are in place.

In a SPAC we have two main categories of shareholders:

- The promoters, who formed the SPAC and serve as directors;
- Market investors, who contribute to the share capital of the SPAC at the IPO.

Promoters and investors have different categories of shares bearing different economic and administrative rights, which reflect the different roles they play within the SPAC. They are entitled to vote at the shareholders meeting based on their stake and on the limits set by the category of shares they hold. The main decision for which a shareholders' approval is required within a SPAC regards the execution of the business combination.

IPO and listing regulations

After the initial nominal capital contribution of the promoters, a SPAC raises additional capital to complete the business combination through an Initial Public Offering (IPO) of the shares. Following the IPO, the SPAC will become a listed vehicle whose shares are traded on a specific market. In Italy there is a specific legal framework governing IPOs. It includes transparency and disclosure obligations, among which the most important is the publication of the "prospectus," a document providing relevant information about the offering to the public.

The prospectus must comply with the requirements of European legislation, the CFA and Issuers' Regulations by Consob, thus its preparation and publication is a complex and time-consuming process. However, if the investment offering is addressed only to institutional (qualified) investors, the rules governing the content of the prospectus (and thus the complexity and extensive procedure) will not apply. This is one of the main reasons why SPAC IPOs are typically addressed only to institutional investors.

A SPAC must also respect the specific rules of the trading venue for the admission to trading, which requires filing an application complying with the provisions of the specific market:

- In regulated markets, a SPAC must comply with the requirements of the Issuers' and EU Regulations as well as with the rules of the specific market. The issuance of new securities is supervised by CONSOB. Moreover, SPACs are required to file and provide financial statements.
- In non-regulated markets, a SPAC is subject to less binding and stringent obligations (e.g. no prospectus is required).

In Italy there are two trading venues on which a SPAC can be listed:

- The Electronic Market for Investment Vehicles (MIV), which is a regulated market for listing investment vehicles such as SPACs. Access is reserved to institutional investors.
- The Alternative Investment Market (AIM), which is a non-regulated market (an MTF, Multi-lateral Trade Facility) mainly for SMEs.

While certain rules do not apply in specific markets (e.g. less binding obligations in an MTF), the issuer must always comply with the regulations regarding market abuse, independently of the trading venue. Indeed, the issuer is obliged to disclose, as soon as possible, inside information directly pertaining to the same issuer. Inside information is precise in nature, confidential (it has not been made public) and price-sensitive (if it were made public, it would influence the share price).

The business combination

The purpose of the SPAC is identifying and completing a business combination, which can take various forms:

- A stock acquisition, where the SPAC purchases a controlling stake in the target company, either by acquiring existing shares or by subscribing newly issued shares.
- An asset acquisition, where the SPAC purchases assets (e.g. a business unit) of the target company.
- A merger of the target company with and into the SPAC.

The last deal is the typical outcome since the main objective of the transaction is to maintain the listed status of the SPAC. However, this can also be achieved in several steps or through the combination of some of the above-mentioned forms.

Another type of business combination that can take place is a demerger, through which the SPAC is able to complete more than one business combination. However, SPAC demergers are more common in other international markets (there are only few cases in Italy).

Information about business combinations is subject to relevant disclosure to the market since it can be considered inside information. There are also disclosure requirements depending on the trading venue in which the SPAC is listed. For instance, in case of a merger of the target with and into a SPAC (reverse merger) listed in a regulated market, the publication of a new prospectus is required since the surviving entity is different.

Within the Italian regulatory framework there are two key rules:

- Shareholders who vote against the business combination at the time of the approval have a withdrawal right with cash reimbursement.
- The SPAC must implement the business combination within a certain time horizon (typically 18-24 months), otherwise it is dissolved and the invested capital is refunded to all shareholders.

Certain types of business combinations do not require shareholders' approval and thus shareholders cannot oppose them and they do not have an exit right. However, under Italian law, within a SPAC opposing shareholders have an exit right with reimbursement because the business combination determines a change of the corporate purpose. According to Article 2437 of the Italian Civil Code, the change of the corporate purpose is one of the few specific circumstances in which shareholders of listed companies can exercise the exit right and request the liquidation of the value of the shares they hold.

Regarding the second point, under Italian law SPACs typically either set a period of 18-24 months as the term of the company in the Articles of Incorporation, or introduce a specific term for winding-up.

Challenges among SPAC stakeholders

There are some issues that can arise among SPAC stakeholders.

As mentioned above, we have two main categories of stakeholders:

- Promoters, who formed the SPAC and represent the governance. They hold preferred shares with limited administrative and economic rights. These can be converted into common shares under specific conditions and give a right to the proportional allocation of warrants.
- Investors, who contributed to the SPAC share capital at the IPO stage. They hold common shares and they have the right to vote at the shareholders' meeting to approve the business combination.

There may be a potential conflict of interest of promoters. Given the structure of their remuneration, they may be incentivized to pursue any business combination, independently of whether it is aligned to investors' interests, or creates value for them.

There are certain rules which protect investors from promoters' misconduct and opportunistic behavior. For instance, to prevent promoters from being replaced, the preferred shares held by them cannot be transferred until the business combination is achieved. Moreover, investors are the ones who have the ultimate control over the business combination: they can decide to vote in favor of the transaction or they can oppose and exercise their cash-exit right.

The exercise of warrants which may be held by investors is also subject to restrictions (e.g. a lock-up period) as in the case of preferred shares in order to keep the interests of investors in line with those of the promoters.

Once a certain target company has been identified and negotiations have started, it is important to look at the legal structure of the transaction as well as to consider which market the SPAC is listed on.

Indeed, as we mentioned above, not all business combinations require shareholder approval. What typically happens in de-SPAC transactions (business combinations between the SPAC and the target company) is that they determine a change of the corporate purpose, which constitutes an amendment of the articles of incorporation requiring an enhanced threshold of shareholders' approval in an extraordinary shareholders' meeting.

The rationale behind this process is to avoid any opportunistic behavior of promoters and to ensure that sufficient funding will be available to complete the business combination. Indeed, requiring shareholders' approval with super-majority implies limited exercise of withdrawal rights with cash-exit.

Under Italian law, the structure of the shareholders' meeting and the required threshold depend on whether the company (SPAC) is listed on a regulated market or on some other trading venue. In particular, different rules apply depending on whether or not the company has access to the risk capital market (i.e. it is listed on a regulated market or its shares are widely distributed in the market).

- A SPAC listed in a regulated market (e.g. MIV) is always considered a company with access to the risk capital market, thus it must comply with the specific provisions of the Italian Civil Code that apply to this type of company.
- A SPAC listed in a non-regulated market (e.g. AIM), unless its shares are widely distributed in the market, is considered a company without access to the risk capital market and therefore it must comply with the specific provisions for these companies.

Regarding the required threshold to approve the business combination, we need to distinguish between whether or not the SPAC relies on the risk capital market. In case of SPACs that do not rely on the risk capital market (e.g. they are listed on a non-regulated market but do not have widely distributed shares), if the bylaws do not provide a higher threshold, in order for the business combination to be approved, a vote in favor by more than half of the share capital is needed.

In case of SPACs that do rely on the risk capital market (e.g. they are listed on a regulated market like the AIM or they have shares that are widely distributed in the market), approval for the business combination requires the favorable vote of at least two thirds of the share capital *represented at the shareholders'* meeting. In case the first call is not duly heeded, a second call is required with a lower quorum. In particular, at least one-third of the share capital must be represented at the shareholders' meeting and, in order for the business combination to be approved, the favorable vote of at least two-thirds of the share capital represented at the meeting is required.

In general, these thresholds apply independently of whether the SPAC has access to the risk capital market or not. However, in SPACs that do not rely on the risk capital market, for the approval of specific, important decisions (e.g. a change of the corporate purpose) the second call of the shareholders' meeting is subject to a larger majority, that is the vote in favor of more than one-third of the *total* share capital. The fact that different rules apply to the second call makes the approval of the business combination less difficult for SPACs relying on the risk capital market (e.g. SPACs listed on the MIV).

SPAC and private equity

SPACs and private equity vehicles, such as private equity closed-end fund, show certain similarities. They both raise funds from a number of investors, and they both have an investment policy.

private equity vehicles are subject to the regulations on collective savings management, since investors delegate the management of their own money and the investment activity is carried out in their interest and independently from them. The question is whether SPACs, which share some features with private equity vehicles, are also subject to these regulations. The Bank of Italy clarified that SPACs fall within the category of "holding companies" and do not have to comply with the regulations on investment services and activities. The rationale is that they have a different return mechanism and a different position of managers with respect to investors:

- In private equity vehicles the return for investors is determined by the capital gains generated by the divestiture of the previously acquired shareholding. On the contrary, in SPACs there is no divestiture, since the purpose is to merge with the target and the return is linked to the success and profitability of the target.
- In private equity vehicles managers are fully independent from investors, who delegate the management of their own money. On the contrary, in SPACs, managers (promoters) are not fully independent in their investment activity, since shareholders have the right to approve or reject the business combination.

Source: Gigante, G. & Conso, A. (2019). *Le SPAC in Italia: stato di un fenomeno in evoluzione*. Egea.

12 Structured Finance Deals: A Focus on LBOs

Recent innovations in technology and financial engineering have generated new kinds of financial tools and operations that fit the specific, unconventional needs of some market players: structured finance instruments. This chapter will cover most of what there is to know to gain a general understanding of structured finance and more specifically of leveraged buyouts (LBOs). We will start off with introductory definitions on structured finance, its features, the main actors and the advantages and disadvantages of such financial operations. We will then focus our attention on LBOs, identifying different typologies, looking at merger sales and asset sales specifically. The chapter will then consider what the best conditions are for an LBO and the requirements and suggested features of a good target. The last part of this chapter will be devoted to sources of value, capital structure of NewCos and profitability of LBOs. The chapter will conclude with final remarks on recent trends in LBO transactions.

12.1 Introductory definitions

12.1.1 Structured finance

Structured finance includes a set of financial deals that several kinds of market actors offer to borrowers whose needs are too sophisticated and unique to be satisfied through a simple loan. As a consequence, the finance instruments implemented in these cases are riskier and more complex. Usually, ad-hoc vehicles are created to support the main categories of transactions. In the case of securitization for example, a Special Purpose Vehicle (SPV) is established to issue bonds on the market against real or financial assets segregated in that same vehicle. The interest payments on these bonds will then be provided by the capacity of the assets included in the SPV to produce cash flows.

Project finance instead has to do with an industrial/infrastructure project segregated in an SPV in order to concentrate the risks and to separate the capital invested in the project from the firm's total capital. According to Gatti's definition (2012), project finance is then a term that refers to an industrial/infrastructure project that is financed off-balance sheet through a network of contractual arrangements with key counterparties (contractors, buyers, suppliers, operating agents, etc.). The borrower is an ad hoc created project company that is financially and legally distinct from the sponsors (separate incorporation) and represents a Newco, the SPV.

The term "project finance" therefore refers to the financing of a single particular project within a company formed solely for the purpose of designing, building and operating that specific infrastructure whereas in conventional corporate financing, a single company often undertakes many concurrent initiatives that are financed as a portfolio of projects. LBOs get their financing from an SPV (NewCo) that is in turn financed by a bank or an institutional investor for the purpose of taking over another company. Cash flows deriving from the acquired company are used both as collateral and as debt repayment for the loans and bonds issued by the SPV.

In all the previous three cases, the usual mechanism utilized for this kind of operation is the usage of an enormous amount of debt.

12.1.2 Common characteristics of structured finance operation

Structured finance transactions have some common characteristics:

- A *Special Purpose Vehicle* is the legal entity of the new corporation, designed to take over the initiative (project finance; LBO; securitization). The SPV is created to borrow funds, but it is different and separate from the sponsor, which is the company behind the project that handles project development. Therefore, all economic consequences generated by the initiative are attributed to the SPV. Lenders finance a venture, not an operating firm. For this reason, PF allows firms to isolate the specific project's risk, using the new legal entity. Furthermore, the assets of the SPV are the only collateral available to lenders together with the cash flow from the initiative (so this is a case of no-recourse financing). Thus, this is a very risky endeavor for lenders.

- *Economic consequences* are attributed exclusively to the SPV, so lenders will only focus their attention on this entity, which they are willing to finance. The sponsor company can go on with its main business, avoiding any impacts on its financial position.

- *Assets* of the SPV represent collateral for lenders, and are usually cash flows produced from the initiative.

- *Leverage* is used to an extreme, i.e. a high debt-to-equity ratio (much higher than in standard corporate settings). The SPV's balance sheet, in fact, is mostly made up of debt. Only a small amount of equity is raised (usually the minimum legal requirement). This aspect increases the riskiness of such operations, especially for lenders.

12.1.3 Market-oriented or bank-oriented deals

Structured finance transactions can be either *market-oriented* deals or *bank-oriented* deals.

- In market-oriented deals, a company resorts to the market to raise funds for the transaction. The SPV will be financed with bonds, so efficiency in distributing and placing these instruments is critical. Hence, the market is dominated by investment banks or large financial conglomerates.
- In bank-oriented deals, quickly-available funding is vital. So this market is dominated by large financial conglomerates or large, international commercial banks. These kinds of actors provide funds and also act as advisors and arrangers.

12.1.4 Benefits from assembling a financial transaction in a structured form

The clear legal and economic separation between the initiative and the sponsoring party means that the two can have very different creditworthiness before and after the operation. Several benefits are presented below, including the possibility to:

1. ensure the continuing financial flexibility of the sponsor (isolating the risk of the transaction). The sponsor invests money only as SPV equity capital, and the entire initiative is carried out using money deriving from the financing the SPV received.
2. experience a lower cost of funding compared to traditional corporate loans because all the risk is referred to the initiative and not to the financial exposure of the sponsor company. Thus, the sponsor company does not have to renounce to the initiative because of a high rating and cost of funding.
3. maintain unaltered the ability to raise funds. The company has to provide specific collateral (isolated from the risk) dedicated solely to repay the debt provided by the lenders of this transaction and to reduce contamination risk. Thus, the other assets of the sponsor are available for new financing.
4. enjoy other advantages, typical of every deal: reduced contamination risk, especially in project finance, and the constant ability to raise new cash, also in unfavorable market conditions (securitization).

12.2 Leveraged buyouts

A leveraged buyout (LBO) is the acquisition of an entire company or division drawing amply on borrowed money to cover the cost. The acquiring company uses the assets of the target company as collateral for the loans, so the whole acquisition is made without having to commit substantial capital.

When a company acquires an entire target, the LBO is a *merger sale* transaction; when only a division of the target company is acquired, the LBO represents an *asset sale* transaction. In both cases the acquirer pays most of the acquisition price with debt.

The high level of leverage involved, however, makes the transaction risky in terms of:

- Loss-given default (LGD): This represents the amount of money that the borrower can lose if the acquiring company defaults and fails to make its debt repayments. This value can be reduced if the SPV provides guarantees, usually in the form of assets.

- Probability of default (PD): This is the risk, in terms of historical-data based probability, that the SPV will not pay back the exposure (principal + interest). To predict the probability of default, one must define cash flows, which must be enough to repay the debt, but there also other alternatives such as:
  - Asset stripping: selling off company's non-operational assets in order to improve returns for equity investors, the cost of capital and, consequently, reduce the probability of default. Non-operational assets are those that are not essential for conducting the business, e.g. real-estate that is not necessary for the transaction.
  - Securitization: merging several financial assets, which are then sold to investors in financial markets. This can be implemented to reduce exposure to PD by referring to operational assets that can be separated from the balance sheet of the company. Commercial credits are usually considered assets that can be sold without affecting the business too much.

The main components of an LBO are represented by the *debt* (obtained to conduct the transaction), the change in the *control* of the target after the acquisition/merger, and shift from public to *private* transactions. Typically, LBOs focus on publicly traded companies that will be delisted once taken over.

12.2.1 LBO features

LBO deals can differ in terms of:

- Who carries out the acquisition;
- Whether this actor is inside or outside of the target.

In terms of these differences, we have:

- LBOs;
- MBOs (Management Buyouts): when the acquisition is executed by the target company's current management;
- MBIs (Management Buy-ins): when involves an external management group;
- FBOs (Family Buyouts) and FBIs (Family Buy-ins): when the acquirers are members of the controlling family or a new family.

The deal follows four basic steps:

1. Creating the SPV/NewCo.
2. Funding the SPV with little equity and high debt.
3. Acquiring 100% of the target shares.
4. Merging the target into the SPV (which changes its name to the target's original name).

Some differences can be underlined in some of these steps depending on whether we are dealing with an asset sale or a merger sale.

12.2.2 Merger sale

In a merger sale, the SPV is created using a small amount of equity (minimum capital requirements) and great deal of debt. Then, the SPV collect funds which are then used to acquire control of the target's equity.

Consider the case of a target firm with equity worth 2,000 (100%) and the following simplified balance sheet:

Target			
Assets	3000	Debt	2000
Goodwill	1000	Equity	2000
	4000		4000

Current management and a private equity investor opt for a capital structure for the acquisition as follows:

- Equity 30% (of which 40% management and 60% PE investors)
- Junior debt: 20%
- Senior debt: 50%

Here are the usual steps:

1. Creating and funding the NewCo. What is the total amount of funds needed to take control of the target? Management contributes 240 of the equity while the private equity investor provides 360.

NewCo			
Cash	2000	Senior Debt	1000
		Junior Debt	400
		Equity	600
	2000		2000

2. Acquiring the Target: Target shares are pledged to creditors until the merger is completed.

NewCo			
Target shares	2000	Senior Debt	1000
		Junior Debt	400
		Equity	600
	2000		2000

3. Incorporating/Merging the target into the SPV.

NewCo – Target			
Assets	3000	Existing Debt	2000
Goodwill	1000	Senior Debt	1000
		Junior Debt	400
		Equity	600
	4000		4000

Existing debt is usually refinanced with the senior debt facility. The bet equity investors make is that the target will have sufficient cash to repay the heavy debt load generated by the acquisition.

12.2.3 Asset sale

In an asset sale, the acquisition involves only a profitable business division of a company. Thus, the process is mainly focused on selecting the assets that can be acquired, and analyzing the main options that reduce the D/E and increase the financial structure efficiency. This kind of transaction is often much faster to complete because there is no need for a full due diligence of the target (as with a merger sale). The evaluation of the acquirer is focused on the asset characteristics and not on the fiscal/legal/financial characteristics of the company.

12.2.4 Good conditions for LBOs

Considering the high level of risk of the transaction, the acquirer must carefully assess some generic and specific conditions in order to determine whether the LBO will create or destroy value.

Generic conditions that refer to the target company:

- Maturity: It should be mature enough to guarantee the availability of abundant cash flows necessary for debt repayment.
- Availability of assets: The target company's balance sheets should be full of assets that can be easily used as debt collateral or as a cash source through asset stripping or securitization.
- The target company's pre-acquisition shareholders should be willing to sell their participation in the target company. This would help to reduce costs and time needed for negotiation and transaction activities.

Specific (target-related) conditions that are more related to the characteristics of the company:

- FCF unlevered > debt repayment: Annual Free Cash Flow Unlevered from the target company should be higher than the yearly reimbursement of the debt.

- EBIT > Interest Expenses: EBIT of the target company should be higher than the annual financial interests.
- Good rating: Company operations should guarantee that the post buyout rating of the company will improve as a result of a reduction in the cost of debt.

12.2.5 Good target companies

Good potential candidates for an LBO are firms flush with cash that have stable performance:

- Mature market.
- Strong market position.
- Good management.
- Stable/Low growth.
- Non-core assets eventually to be disposed.
- Low initial leverage.

Firms operating in markets with intense growth and offering high-tech products are not suitable for a buyout.

The ideal target company operates as a leader in a mature market, offers non-sophisticated products, and has a solid balance sheet with mostly material assets.

12.2.6 Sources of value in LBOs

What are the critical aspects of the LBO transaction that ensure a high level of final return for the acquirer?

- *Deleveraging.* This is the most opportunistic strategy, very often used by private equity investors with a financial background. Deleveraging can be conducted as a decrease in outstanding debt through strategic repayments over the years.

  Example: entry in t_0 EBITDA=100; multiple 6x; outstanding debt = 500; equity value = 100.
  The bet: at Year 5 debt is completely repaid; no growth and no new investments.
  Result: exit at t5 EBITDA=100; multiple 6x; outstanding debt = 0; equity value = 600.

- *Arbitrage.* The LBO transaction is implemented to acquire a target company that is undervalued by the market. The bet here is that the acquirer can increase the multiple without managing the company but instead by whetting the market appetite toward the target company. Hence, the acquirer gets the difference between the multiple paid and the multiple received.

  Example: entry at t_0 EBITDA=100; multiple 6x; outstanding debt = 500; equity value = 100.
  The bet: at Year 5 EV/EBITDA at exit is higher that the initial value of the multiple (debt can be refinanced).
  Result: exit at t_5 EBITDA=100; multiple 8x; outstanding debt = 500; equity value = 300.

- *Growth*. This represents a hands-on approach in the investment, aimed to obtain an uptick in EBITDA and profitability, necessitating a high level of involvement of the investor in firm management. This approach is usually chosen by private equity investors with an industrial background.

> *Example*: entry in t_0 EBITDA=100; multiple 6x; outstanding debt = 500; equity value = 100.
> The bet: at Year 5 EBITDA at exit is higher that the initial value (debt can be refinanced).
> Result: exit in t_5 EBITDA=133.3; multiple 6x; outstanding debt = 500; equity value = 300.

12.2.7 Capital structure of a NewCo

The breakdown of an LBO's financial sources follows a general ranking:

a) Bank Loans (First lien secured and second lien secured): 30%-50%.
b) High-yield Bonds (Senior unsecured and senior subordinated): 5%-15%.
c) Mezzanine Debt: (Unsecured and subordinated): 30%-50% (i.e. debt capital layer with the lowest ranking, highest flexibility and highest cost. This debt can be structured to offer equity upside potential in the form of purchased equity or detachable warrants that are exchangeable into common stocks of the issuer.)
d) Equity Contribution (Preferred stock and common stocks): 2%-10%.

It is necessary to find various alternative sources of funds to actually pay the acquisition price of the target.

12.2.8 Profitability of LBOs

Shareholders, mezzanine investors and senior lenders evaluate profitability using standard IRR methodologies, thus using the algebraic sum.

- For *Shareholders*: initial equity contribution and the periodic dividends (net of taxes) and final exit value (net of taxation on the capital gains).
- For *Senior Lenders*: initial debt drawdowns and spread on money market rates (net of taxes) and principal repayment.
- For *Mezzanine Investors*: initial contribution and periodic interest, principal repayment and equity kicker (right given to mezzanine holders to participate to the acquisition of the company's equity by buying a specific percentage of this equity).

12.3 Recent trends and developments in LBOs

In the previous chapter, recent developments concerning the private equity market were outlined. In particular we examined the trends in investment activity worldwide, with a focus on the EU and Italy. Then the chapter listed the largest and most prominent funds along with a few deals concluded in 2020. This section on trends will resume the discussion in the previous chapter, but with a focus on buyouts and buyout-specific developments.

Starting off with an analysis of the historical evolution of buyouts in Europe, since 2008, buyout-focused funds and deals have disappeared in European countries, which have felt severe effects of the financial crisis on their economies. Fundraising for Europe-focused buyout vehicles fell consistently because of a widespread erosion in confidence for making large deals and a lack of interest in distressed deals. As a consequence, deal numbers and values dropped considerably as well.

However, now that European economies are returning to pre-crisis levels, buyout activity is regaining prominence. Indeed, we can notice an overall upward trend since 2013. More specifically, buyouts represent the largest piece of the pie, followed by growth and venture capital investments. Of course, we have to keep in mind that European investments tend to have lower volumes with respect to American ones. This however is also due to more stringent regulations and unsuitable regulatory environments, which are long overdue to be modernized and tailored to new types of investments in Europe. For details on deal sizes and volumes, please refer to **Figure 12.1**. In general, however, we can state clearly that the deal value has increased steadily since 2013, surpassing the peak of 2007 in 2018.

Conversations about the fallout of the recent Covid-19 crisis and its impact on buyout activity and private equity investments in both the EU and globally were included in the previous chapter. Nevertheless, there are some current trends concerning the structure of buyout investments that are worth noting. In particular, in recent years, buyout leverage ratios (representing the amount of debt used for LBO transactions) have been trending upwards, registering an acceleration in pace in 2020. Indeed, in that year, almost 80% of deals were leveraged with more than 6x EBITDA.

When evaluating average multiples paid for LBO transactions, in 2020 the enterprise value to EBITDA multiple reached 11.4x in the United States and 12.6x in the European Union. Such multiples, which are even higher than those prior to the global financial crisis, put tremendous pressure on investors to select appropriate targets, and to produce growth and value prior to an LBO exit, in order to generate adequate returns. As LBOs are at historic highs in terms of multiples, similarly LBO performance is proving to be steady, giving more reliable returns if compared with the public stock market for over a decade.

It is important to note that many companies went into emergency mode during the Covid-19 outbreak, but subsequently concentrated on how to expand in a post-pandemic scenario in both the United States and Europe. European leveraged finance markets remain robust, and loan issuance for mergers and acquisitions (M&A) and leveraged buyouts (LBOs) increased significantly in the first half of 2021. In the first half of 2021, in fact, issuance of high-yield bonds and leveraged loans for buyout and M&A deals increased to $319.5 billion throughout North America and Western and Southern Europe, a 64 percent year-over-year rise from $194.6 billion in H1 2020. The $187.34 billion in Q2 2021 issuance marks the largest quarterly

Figure 12.1   2007-2020 European private equity investment activity

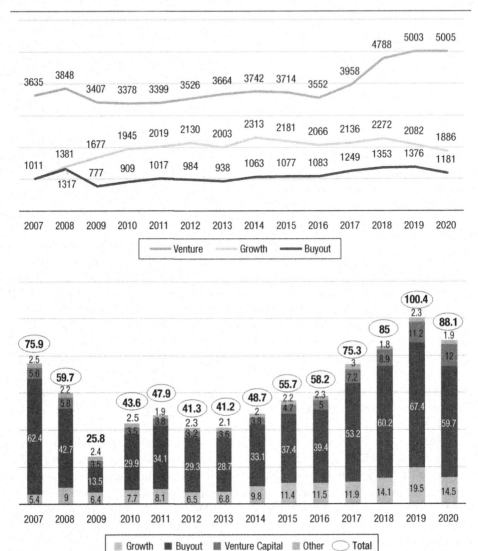

Source: retrieved from Invest Europe (2021); for further information visit investeurope.eu

amount for these areas since 2015. This trend has been slowing down a bit in the last two quarters of 2021, especially in Europe (see **Figure 12.2**). In Q4 2021, the volume of leveraged loan for both buyout and M&A was just €57 billion. However, leveraged loan issuance in the region climbed 28% in 2021, rising to €289.7 billion from €227 billion in 2020.

Figure 12.2   European Leveraged loan issuance (quarterly)

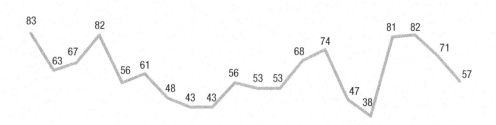

Source: data retrieved from Debtwire Par Restructuring Database (White & Case LLP, 2022)

Figure 12.3   European buyout Leveraged loan issuance (quarterly)

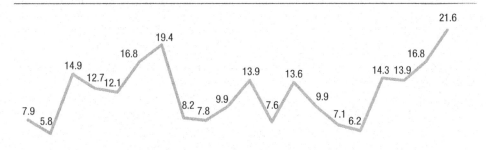

Source: data retrieved from Debtwire Par Restructuring Database (White & Case LLP, 2022)

On the contrary, if we focus just on European buyout issuance, there was an increase in the second half of the year, as shown by **Figure 12.3**. In Q4 2021, buyout leveraged loan issuances reached a peak of €21.6 billion, registering a growth of 51% with respect to the beginning of the year's value.

Finally, worth mentioning is an interesting market trend developing in the buyout market which we did not discuss in the previous chapter due to its strong implications for LBOs. This trend, affecting virtually every industry worldwide, concerns environmental, social and governance issues (ESG), which companies are now expected to be accountable for. Indeed, ESG considerations have made their way into the buyout market and are affecting LBO transactions on a global scale. The ESG approach to investing involves running relative screening in due diligence processes and requiring transparency of investments on related concerns. In particular, the EU has implemented sustainable finance action plans, requiring investors to disclose the way in which they support and implement ESG principles. Furthermore, the topic of positive impact is particularly significant, as more and more research is finding a positive correlation between the inclusion of ESG measures and improved financial results. Therefore, ESG is seen as a core driver in value creation and risk mitigation.

12.4 Conclusions

Structured finance products and operations can represent a good way to conduct specific, risky transactions isolating the risk through an ad-hoc vehicle (SPV). As highlighted in the chapter, these transactions share some common characteristics: a high level of leverage, an ad-hoc special purpose vehicle and the economic and legal consequences deriving from the ownership separation between the vehicle and the company that leads the transaction.

The core section of the chapter was devoted to the leveraged buyout, its features and characteristics. An LBO is one of the most common structured finance transactions, mostly used in M&A deals, when a company decides to acquire a target that produces consistent free cash flow, used as collateral for the leveraged operation. The high amount of debt involved makes the transaction very risky, both in terms of loss given default due to limited collateral provided, and probability of default.

Furthermore, the process that underpins this operation is quite long and complex both in terms of legal and financial requirements. However, if the target company succeeds in generating a sufficient amount of cash flow to repay the debts, the acquiring company increases its size and profitability with little use of funds. Throughout the chapter we looked at how to develop a successful operation. Indeed, the acquirer should evaluate some general conditions about target firm's earning stability and some specific financial aspects as well to ensure the effectiveness of the process. The ideal target company for an LBO operates as a leader in a mature market, offers non-sophisticated products, and has a solid balance sheet with mostly material assets. These critical aspects will lead to high returns, at the end of the transaction for all of the actors involved: shareholders, senior lenders and mezzanine investors.

Then, we reviewed the basic steps of an LBO transaction, namely creating a NewCo (SPV); funding the NewCo with a minimum amount of equity and a lot of debt; acquiring 100% of the target shares (merger sale) or a specific division (asset sale); merging the target into the NewCo. Finally, the latest trends and deal values of LBO transactions were outlined.

13 Debt Financing and Debt Capital Markets

Multinational corporations typically use long-term sources of funding – both domestic and foreign – to finance long-term projects. It is important to take a few things into consideration when determining what forms of financing can maximize the wealth of MNCs and in which cases. Indeed, one of the aims of the chapter is to introduce the matching strategy, which takes places when financing is issued in the currency of an overseas investment to offset part of the debt accumulated by this subsidiary with its own inflows, thus avoiding exchange rate risk. As we will see in the initial part of the chapter, this mechanism can usually be implemented by using currency swaps. The second part of the chapter will discuss the key decisions that need to be made when raising debt in terms of denomination currency, maturity, and fixed or floating rates. All these decisions can impact the cost of the debt, and therefore project feasibility.

Despite the volatility of markets and the complexity of available options, companies continue to have three fundamental funding alternatives: equity, loans and bonds. In debt-related financing, there are many instruments available to the financial managers of companies, including bank loans (bilateral vs. syndicated loans), commercial paper, bonds, and convertible securities. A corporation's financing mix will essentially reflect its financial manager's response to a number of questions:

- Should the corporation borrow for the short term or long term?
- Should the debt have a fixed or floating rate?
- Should the corporation borrow at home or abroad? In which currency?
    - Eurobonds, foreign bonds (e.g., Yankee, samurai).
- What terms should be agreed upon with lenders/investors?
    - Seniority, i.e., priority over junior or subordinated creditors.
    - Collateral, i.e., ring-fenced assets that the secured creditor can seize if the borrower defaults.
    - Covenants, i.e., restrictive clauses to prevent the borrower from undertaking actions that could be detrimental for the creditor and/or financial covenants (i.e., financial ratios that need to be met to avoid default).
    - Convertibility.
- How much should the corporation borrow?
- What are the main considerations implied in the Trade-off theory of financing choices?

- Tax shield: Interest payments are regarded as a cost and are deducted from taxable income (i.e., interest is paid from before-tax income).
- Cost of financial distress.
- And in the Pecking-order theory of financing choices?
  - Informational problems and conflicts of interest.

The objective of the third part of this chapter will be to dive deeper into debt financing, highlighting its characteristics with respect to equity and focusing on some specific types of debt. Banks loans will be discussed first, in conjunction with the limitations of traditional loans and some alternatives. Comparisons will also be made with syndicated loans, which will be distinguished from bank loans in terms of organizational process, syndication strategies, and fees or pricing strategy. Bonds will also be defined and their features, types, and mechanisms for issuing and pricing will be considered.

13.1 The debt market: trends and developments

Before we begin, we need to comprehend the trends that have recently been shaping debt capital markets. In particular, we will assess the post-2008 situation and the latest developments stemming from the Covid-19 pandemic.

After the 2008 global financial crisis and the 2009 relapse caused by the increased riskiness of some southern European sovereign bonds, the credit market experienced a crunch, with banks less willing to lend and individuals and companies reluctant to invest. In response, central banks worldwide implemented unconventional monetary policies, including zero interest policy rate plans, liquidity injections, and quantitative easing that have deeply affected the debt market. These measures have profoundly altered the relative convenience of debt as a financing tool, especially with respect to equity. The remarkable cost reductions in bond issuance and zero interest rate plans have made debt a more interesting and viable financing alternative for corporations. As a result, markets worldwide have witnessed an explosion in global debt – so much so that today we live in a much more leveraged world than we did just a decade ago.

This greater reliance on debt markets has given rise to new risks for investors and new emerging trends. Mainly, there has been a marked decrease in the issuer quality of bonds. Ease of access to the credit market has prompted many non-investment grade companies to issue corporate bonds, which, at approximately 15%, now represent a remarkably high percentage of total worldwide issuances. Moreover, BBB rated debt instruments (the lowest grade investment before the non-investment class) have peaked in the last few years: they surged from 38.9% of total investment grade emissions before the crisis to 53.1% in 2018 and sat just above 40% in 2021. This trend, associated with an apparent decline in the quality of covenant protections for investors, gives companies a stronger position while forcing investors to deal with financial claims with a higher intrinsic risk of failure.

The most recent shock to the debt market has been the global outbreak of the Covid-19 pandemic, which triggered major turmoil, volatility, and uncertainty worldwide. To provide some context for how the debt market has developed through this crisis, it is important to note that the ECB, U.S. Federal Reserve, the U.K., and other major economic powers have launched massive measures to support their economies, including QE (Quantitative Easing) programs and cutting short-term interest rates to grant greater liquidity to the markets. However, despite these measures, yields in government bond markets have remained above the February 2020 values (the spread between the BTPs and 10-year bonds averaged 205 basis points in March 2020, with respect to 140 points in February). Moreover, throughout the crisis, not only were highly rated debt instruments successfully placed on the market but so were BBB and lower rated bonds, due to the high level of liquidity in the markets.

Nevertheless, trading levels in the secondary market were greatly affected by the high levels of volatility and declining prices in most debt instruments. Another effect of the pandemic on debt has been the use of leverage by MNCs. In recent years, leverage has been implemented for development operations (investments and acquisitions) or to remunerate shareholders through dividends or share buy-back transactions. Indeed, requests for money to finance current activities have surged by 70%, while those for new investments have dropped by 40%. Overall, however, thanks to the active response of major central banks, interest rate levels have been contained and the general belief is that the relative convenience of debt, if compared with equity as a financing tool, will continue in subsequent periods. "The Russia-Ukraine conflict will have a big effect on economic activity and inflation," ECB President Christine Lagarde warned at a 2022 press conference, citing rising energy and commodity prices, disruptions to international trade, and a general loss of confidence. The ECB raised its inflation forecast for 2022 from 3.2% to 5.1% due to rising energy prices. This suggests that central banks will have to raise interest rates more slowly than previously expected to combat inflation while economic growth slows.

13.2 The matching strategy of MNCs

In the first section of this chapter, we will assess the methodologies used by MNCs to finance long-term projects. Since MNCs can access both foreign and domestic sources of funds, they need to consider all forms of potentially financing available to them before selecting the one that best maximizes the company's wealth and also possibly reduces its debt cost.

A common method MNCs use to deal with debt is called the *matching strategy*. Indeed, the subsidiaries of MNCs commonly finance their operations by employing this strategy using the same currency they use to invoice their products. The subsidiary's exposure to exchange rate movements is therefore lowered, since it uses a portion of its cash inflows to repay its debt.

For example, U.S. Company A can issue bonds denominated in euros, British pounds, Japanese yen and Mexican pesos to finance its foreign operations. Its subsidiaries in the U.K. can use British pound inflows to pay off their UK debt, while the other foreign subsidiaries do the same. By tapping various debt markets, Company A can match its cash inflows and outflows for each currency, and thereby lessen its exposure to exchange rate risk.

This strategy is particularly useful if the MNC has subsidiaries located in countries where interest rates are relatively low. In such cases, the firm's cash flows are more stable for two reasons: first, it can benefit from a lower financing rate; secondly, it reduces its exchange rate risk, since debt repayments are denominated in the same currency as that of its cash inflows.

This strategy can be performed by using *currency swaps*. A currency swap is an agreement between two parties to exchange periodic payment streams in two distinct currencies for principal and interest payments under certain contractual circumstances. A contract of this type entails: i) a spot exchange of a specified amount of one currency for another at the current exchange rate; ii) a forward exchange in the opposite direction (at the same exchange rate); iii) the payment of periodic interest accrued on the amount of currency exchanged by both parties during the life of the contract. In a currency swap, each of the counterparties holds a long-term position in relation to an asset generating interest income in the currency of denomination and a short-term position in relation to a liability, which earns interest in the currency of denomination of the short-term position.[1] The currency rate swap between IBM and the World Bank was the first conventional currency swap agreement. In this case, which took place in the late 1980s, the dollar's increase versus European currencies provided a chance for IBM to realize capital gains on existing loans in Swiss francs (CHF) and German marks (DEM). However, this was only possible if IBM traded its current CHF and DEM debts with another party. Salomon Brothers began seeking an interested party on behalf of IBM for this purpose. Finally, it determined that the World Bank was the best choice for the suggested swap. After a few initial stumbling blocks, the World Bank and IBM agreed to the first-ever standard swap transaction.[2]

An MNC might want to use this method to mitigate exchange rate risk when it is unable to borrow a currency that matches its invoice currency. Engaging in a currency swap may enable the MNC to have cash outflows in the same currency of its inflows at periodic intervals, thereby reducing its exposure to exchange rate movements.

Below are two example applications of the matching strategy using currency swaps.

---

[1] https://www.borsaitaliana.it/borsa/glossario/currency-swap.html
[2] Satish, D. & Agarwal, M. (2011). Currency Rate Swap Between IBM and World Bank, Case-Reference no. 111-076-1. https://www.thecasecentre.org/products/view?id=105320#

Example (1)   Using currency swaps

U.S.-based company Madison Co. has a U.K. subsidiary that wants to issue a British pound sterling bond so that it can make payments with money coming in from its existing U.K. business. U.K.-based Nell Co. wants to issue dollar-denominated bonds because most of its money comes from customers in the United States. If Madison is known in the dollar market and Nell is known in the pound market, bonds that are worth dollars can be issued by Madison, while bonds that are worth pounds can be issued by Nell. For the dollars, Madison will pay Nell in pounds using money from its subsidiaries in the United Kingdom. Nell will do the same with its subsidiaries in the U.S. to repay the debt issued in US dollars by Madison. In this case, the two multinationals will be protected from the risk that the exchange rate falls. The diagram in **Figure 13.1** shows how this works.

Figure 13.1   Currency swap

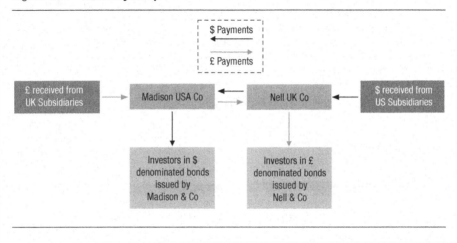

Example (2)   Currency Swaps at Walt Disney

1. The Case

The Walt Disney Company, headquartered in California, is a diversified international corporation that operates entertainment and recreation complexes, produces films, develops community real estate projects, and sells consumer products.

At the time of Tokyo Disneyland's opening in April 1983, Walt Disney's CFO was concerned about the company's potential exposure to future fluctuations in the yen/dollar exchange rate due to the influx of theme park royalty revenues. On the one hand, expectations suggested the yen (JPY) would depreciate against the U.S. dollar (USD). On the other hand, Japanese vacationers and foreign tourists visiting Tokyo were flocking to the new theme park. As a result, the exposure needed to be strategically managed and financially hedged in order to maximize the company's value.

2. The Resolution

Walt Disney had two options for mitigating the risk of currency fluctuations. First, Disney was considering a 15 billion JPY 10-year bullet loan, with the principal repaid at final maturity, 7.50%

interest paid semi-annually, and 0.75% in front-end fees. Second, a U.S. investment bank proposed arranging for Walt Disney and a French utility company to enter into a swap mediated by the Industrial Bank of Japan (IBJ), in which the French company would assume a liability in ECU (European Currency Unit) in exchange for future revenue in yen, and Disney would assume a liability in yen in exchange for future revenue in ECU.

Disney required USD for expansion purposes, which necessitated the conversion of JPY into USD. Because the amount of cash received in Japan was significant, JPY depreciation could severely disrupt Disney's financial plans. Given the volatility of the yen/dollar rate, this represented significant exposure that needed to be hedged. Given the long-term trend, if JPY appreciation was less than expected, Disney would suffer. As a result, full hedging was the best way to protect against future exchange fluctuations. There were basically two options: i) Establish a yen liability, i.e., a 15 billion JPY 10-year bullet loan or ii) perform a swap with a U.S. investment bank.

As shown in **Figure 13.2**, the French company had a comparative advantage in borrowing in both currencies, but Disney had a comparative advantage in ECU. If Disney borrowed in ECU and the French utility company borrowed in JPY, the combined interest rate would be lower (9.47 + 6.83 = 16.3%) than if Disney borrowed in JPY and the French utility company borrowed in ECU (7.75 + 9.37 = 17.12%). This suggests that it would be a good idea for Walt Disney and the French utility company to participate in a swap to exchange liabilities.

Figure 13.2   Swap Mechanism at Walt Disney

A – YTM of French Eurobonds in denominated currency of Yen of ten year maturity period
B – YTM of French Eurobonds in denominated currency of ECU of ten year maturity period

To summarize, the Walt Disney Company ultimately chose the ECU note offering combined with the swap into yen liability, as recommended by its American financial advisors.

Nonetheless, the yen appreciated dramatically over the next few years, and evidence of the yen's vast undervaluation was abundant. It is worth noting that the company's conservative nature was reflected in its hedging decision. In fact, the time lapse on which the hedging mechanism was built in retrospect may have been too long. Even though the unconventional hedging solution reduced Disney's exposure, it stood firm in its decision to hedge Tokyo Disneyland's royalties and later issued Swiss francs swapped into yen liabilities (see **Figure 13.3**).

Source: Adapted with the help of Giulia Zanetello from *Kester, W. Carl, and William B. Allen*. "Walt Disney Co.'s Yen Financing." Harvard Business School Case 287-058, January 1987.

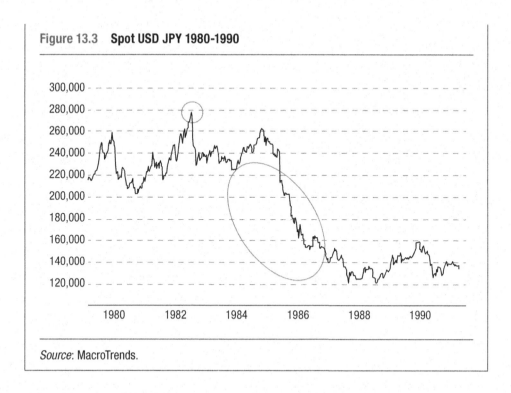

Figure 13.3 **Spot USD JPY 1980-1990**

Source: MacroTrends.

13.3 Key decisions when raising debt

When selecting financing options, MNCs must make a series of choices regarding which solutions are most appropriate to their business and needs. Among the many decisions involved in this process, some of which are assessed below, are the choice of debt currency denomination, debt maturity, and rate structures. Other important issues include the decision whether to use debt or equity and which type of debt is preferred (i.e., bank debt or bond). However, it is worth highlighting that it is increasingly common for MNCs to raise debt within the countries where their subsidiaries are located. As Henderson, Jegadeesh and Weisbach (2006) have demonstrated, approximately 20% of all capital raised through bond issuance comes from countries outside the issuing firm's home nation. However, companies that expect their subsidiaries to borrow locally need to provide sufficient initial equity capital or financial backing. In fact, local suppliers and creditors are likely to avoid providing debt financing in the absence of such conditions. Keloharju (2001) established that business entities may choose to raise foreign currency debt for three reasons. First, this strategy serves as a hedge against foreign currency risks. Hedging mitigates the effect of currency gains and losses on reported profits (Smith et al., 1985). Second, foreign currency borrowing may be less expensive than local currency borrowing. As Shapiro (1991) demonstrates, in certain nations tax policies incentivize enterprises to borrow in a foreign currency regardless of its strength or weakness. Thirdly, speculative considerations may make foreign currency debt an appealing option if the interest rate gap between two currencies does not precisely represent the predicted change in the exchange rate.

However, according to Stobaugh (1970), not all multinational corporations use the same approach to financial management. Annual international sales of a multinational corporation are a significant predictor of financial behavior. Small businesses often have little decision-making authority and make minimal efforts to get optimum financing. Medium-sized corporations are often centralized, with a strong emphasis on the net cost of each transaction. On the other hand, large multinationals often have centralized treasuries, and therefore tend to finance their subsidiaries directly so they can take advantage of the parent company's rating, which is usually higher than that of its subsidiaries due to their different sizes and levels of diversification. In addition, for companies with ratings, there are limits on how much debt can remain at subsidiary level in order to avoid structural subordination and negative impact on the rating itself. Large multinationals therefore may make use of local financing but in a more limited capacity.

13.3.1 Choice of debt-currencies for subsidiaries

The first decision to be made when subsidiaries are looking for a new long-term financing opportunity is in which currency the debt obligation should be set. There are many advantages for a subsidiary to borrow in the local currency. The main one is the possibility of reducing the MNC's foreign exchange exposure. In fact, subsidiaries can structure their liabilities in such a way as to match the currency they borrow with the currency used to manufacture their products. In this way, they can reduce their exposure to foreign exchange risk at no added cost to shareholders. The basic rule is to finance assets that generate cash-flows denominated in a foreign currency with liabilities denominated in the same currency. In other words, "currency-matching." An additional point made by Jang (2017) is that firms are more likely to obtain bank loans from overseas lenders in nations where foreign subsidiaries are situated. Presumably, foreign operations can lower information asymmetry and monitoring costs to a capital provider. A final advantage of borrowing in the local currency is related to interest rates. Since the subsidiary's cost of debt will depend on the local interest rate of their host country, the local interest rate may be lower than the one in the parent company's country, thus making it more convenient to raise funds abroad. Similarly, Keloharju and Niskanen (2001) discovered that a sample of Finnish enterprises was more likely to issue foreign bank debt when interest rates in Finland were quite high. Allen (2019) connects these decisions to monetary policy: when a central bank lowers interest rates in one country, multinational corporations from other nations are more likely to raise debt in that foreign country's currency (Erel et al., 2020).

In some cases, the situation may be the opposite: MNCs have to bear an additional risk related to local interest rates that are higher than those in the parent company's home country. In such a scenario, borrowing locally will expose the subsidiary to a higher country risk premium, thus increasing its cost of debt. This situation usually arises when the subsidiary is located in a developing country characterized by relatively high interest rates and unstable market conditions. As a result, parent companies in lower-interest rate markets (e.g., the U.S.) may consider providing a loan in their own currency to finance the subsidiary in order to avoid the high cost of local debt. However, this will force the subsidiary to convert some of its cash flows to the parent company's currency to repay the loan, which would entail exchange rate risk. To sum up, the choice to finance abroad may depend on several factors: the microeconomic characteristics of the foreign subsidiary, the macroeconomic environment, and the specific financial details of the transaction. According to Siegfried et al. (2007), the main motivation for issuing debt in foreign currency remains to reduce exposure to exchange rate volatility along with strategic choices and in response to regulatory constraints. The authors maintain that multinationals can be more active in issuing foreign currency debt for three strategic reasons: first, to diversify their investor base across different currency regions; second, to overcome any fundraising constraints imposed by their domestic markets; and third, to focus on increasing their recognition abroad and thereby lower their financing costs. Regulatory constraints appear to limit the issuance of debt instruments abroad, as this solution could entail significant fixed transaction costs due to legal advice on disclosure and taxation issues, as well as costs related to overcoming information asymmetry.

13.3.2 Choice of debt maturity

Another decision that an MNC needs to make regards the choice of debt maturity. Indeed, long-term maturity can be used for financing subsidiary operations over an extended period, while a shorter maturity might be a better option to finance working capital.

The MNC must decide whether to obtain a loan with a maturity that perfectly fits its needs or one with a shorter maturity that has a more favorable interest rate but requires seeking additional financing when the loan matures. This latter case poses some uncertainty pertaining to the interest rate to be paid for the additional financing: the so-called re-financing risk. As Chala A. (2018) demonstrates, refinancing risk is a significant determinant of firms' debt maturity decisions, even more so in times of high financial uncertainty. The study demonstrates that firms with a high risk of refinancing prefer longer maturities. This effect is more pronounced for high-yielding and low-cash-flow firms.

Before making any decisions related to maturity, the MNC first has to consider the shape of the yield curve of the country where it intends to finance. If the country shows an upward-sloping yield curve, it means that yields are lower for short-term maturities than for long-term maturities. One possible explanation is that investors want to be compensated for lower liquidity by asking for a higher rate of return on long-term debt. The curve typically slopes upward also because investors expect a higher reward for taking the risk that rising inflation will reduce expected returns on longer-dated bonds. Because a 10-year note has a longer duration, it typically yields more than a two-year note. Yields move in the opposite direction of prices.

It therefore could seem convenient for an MNC to finance its project with short-term debt, since it will experience a lower cost of debt financing. However, this choice implies that additional funding will be needed after the existing loan reaches maturity, and thus that the company may experience a higher cost of financing when it tries to obtain it. The shape of the yield curve is different across countries, even though an upward-sloping curve is usually quite common. The opposite case is rarer, and it is often the result of the implementation of government policies. Indeed, the government may decrease long-term interest rates in a phase of economic downturn or rise short-term rates in the opposite case to slow down the economy (Fox et al., 2017). Expectations of stronger economic activity, higher inflation, and higher interest rates are typically signaled by a steepening curve. A flattening curve can indicate the opposite: investors are expecting rate hikes in the near future and are losing faith in the economy's growth prospects.

13.3.3 Choice of debt rate

Another way MNCs can play to their advantage is by deciding upon a *fixed* or *floating* interest rate. Usually, floating rates are tied to some indices. One common index in Europe is the Sterling Overnight Index Average (SONIA), indicating the effective overnight interest rate paid by banks for unsecured transactions in the British sterling market.

When financing at a rate linked to the SONIA, the MNC must forecast the SONIA for each year, in order to determine the interest rate to which it will be subject. This estimation is also necessary to forecast the interest payments related to the loan and the annualized cost of financing. For a borrower, having a floating rate bond or loan is advantageous when interest rates are falling, as the firm is not tied to a higher coupon rate. On the other hand, having a fixed coupon may be a better option if the MNC expects interest rates to rise over the life of the bond. However, if the firm is concerned about increases in interest rates but does not want to set up a fixed bond, it may choose to hedge this risk with interest rate swaps. In this way, it will reduce its exposure to interest rate fluctuations and at the same time exploit the advantage of current low interest rates.

Interest rate swaps are one of the most widely used financial derivatives to manage interest rate risk for companies. Many existing theories shed light on their advantages while also highlighting some of their limitations (Mao et al., 2002).

There are two limitations in the use of swap contracts: first, the firm is exposed to the risk of default of the counterparty. Second, it may be dispendious in terms of time and resources to find a suitable candidate for the swap (Madura, 2008). Faced with the threat of rising or falling interest rates, multinationals must therefore care-fully choose whether to issue fixed- or floating-rate debt. This is because even small changes in interest rates can cost or save a company millions of dollars in interest costs to financing. Further decisions about which rate to choose for financing are therefore also strongly influenced by the characteristics of a subsidiary's business in cases of intercompany loans.

If the foreign subsidiary's performance matches the cyclical growth and contrac-tion of the local economy, it may benefit from more local variable interest rate debt because the company's ability to bear higher interest payments increases when the economy improves. Conversely, when circumstances are difficult, interest rates are often lower, making interest costs a lesser burden. Profits and cash flows, in fact, de-cline when the economy suffers, making fixed interest payments less attractive and more dangerous. In addition, the more debt a branch already has, the less tolerant it will be to interest rate fluctuations, so highly leveraged branches should create and maintain more fixed-rate debt than variable-rate debt for better financial exit plan-ning. In the same vein, if the foreign branch's cash flow coverage ratios are tight, a fixed interest rate should be favored for its predictability.

Real-life options available to MNCs

Up to this point, we have seen that MNCs have many decisions to make when con-sidering raising additional debt: whether to let the subsidiary finance itself on its own or provide the necessary funds from the parent company; in which currency the debt should be denominated; whether interest rates should be fixed or floating, whether it should issue long-term or short-term debt, and so on. It is now time to look at some specific forms of bond debt that have recently gained traction among MNCs. The most interesting types are listed below.

1. *Foreign bonds*: These are debt instruments denominated in a currency which is foreign to the borrower and sold in a country of that currency. For example, if a British firm is placing dollar denominated bonds in the U.S., it is said to be sell-ing foreign bonds.
2. *Fixed rate bonds*: Most bonds are issued using a fixed rate since investors do not want to be exposed to changes in rates. In this case, the MNC can opt for an inter-est rate swap to convert all or part of the fixed coupon into a floating one.
3. *Floating rate notes*: On these notes, interest rates are adjusted to reflect the pre-vailing rates. These are typically used for short term bonds for sub-investment grades companies.
4. *Foreign currency convertible bond* (FCCB): Foreign currency convertible bonds are issued by a MNC and underwritten by a non-resident in foreign currency. The main difference from a simple foreign bond is the fact that it can be converted into equity shares by the issuer company.

13.3.4 Choice of debt: other factors

There are many other considerations that MNCs need to keep in mind when devising their financing strategies and selecting debt instruments and their structures. These include:

- *Expectations*: Expectations play a significant part in multinational debt choices since they also impact markets. For example, if there is widespread consensus that interest rates will decline in a nation, borrowers might opt to fund a portion of their debt on a short-term basis. In the event of growing interest rate expectations, the converse is true.
- *Liquidity*: Liquidity refers to the ability of lenders or investors to sell debt instruments in the secondary market. The more liquidity, the lower the cost for borrowers.
- *Market Inflation*: If a given interest rate represents a good value for deciding on a financing choice, the same must be analyzed in relation to the inflation rate. The notion of the real interest rate, i.e., the nominal interest rate minus the inflation rate, can be useful in this regard. For example, if in period T1 interest rates are at 15% and inflation is at 10%, the real interest rate will be 5%. If in period T2 interest rates fall to 10% but inflation also falls to 3%, the real interest rate will be 7%. So even though nominal rates have fallen, real rates have risen due to inflation.
- *Credit Ratings*: Credit ratings have an impact on yield levels. In fact, the higher the credit rating of the borrower, the lower the credit spread that will be charged by the lender. There are a number of agencies involved in the credit rating business, but the three most important are Standard & Poor's, Moody's, and Fitch Ratings. Their ratings are based on the probability of default by the counterparty, the nature of the obligation, and the security offered in the event of bankruptcy.
- *Risk difference between parent and subsidiary*: Multinational subsidiaries typically face a higher risk premium if located in riskier countries. As a result, when considering local currency debt financing, estimates of the parent company's cost of financing must be revised upward.
- *Tax implications*: Taxes are a significant factor influencing debt financing decisions for multinationals. One scenario in which local currency lending could be detrimental is when the local subsidiary has a carry forward tax loss. Since the subsidiary will not be able to take advantage of the tax benefit of the interest deductions, parent company might opt to make a capital injection financed by borrowed funds.

Example   Factors influencing capital budgeting decisions

The choice of currency when selecting financing options affects other aspects of MNCs. In particular, when an MNC evaluates a set of new projects and is subject to budget constraints, it must consider several issues before coming up with a final decision. For instance, in what currency to borrow, to finance, interest rate levels in the different countries, the inflation rate, and so on (Madura J., 2008). The following cases exemplify these choices more clearly.

Case 1: Effects of inflation on capital budgeting decisions

The management of Oui R ND Enterprises is examining a pair of projects in foreign subsidiaries:
- The Holtz project offers a 14% return in a country with a 3% inflation rate.
- The Weiss project is expected to produce a 23% return in an economy that has a 12% inflation rate.

Because of limited resources, only one project will be funded, and the decision will be based on the real expected rate of return. The real expected rate of return on each project is
- Holtz: (14%–3%) /1.03 = 10.68%
- Weiss: (23%–12%)/1.12 = 9.82%

Case 2: How expectations about interest rates affect pricing contracts

A U.S. aerospace manufacturer is negotiating a $25 million contract with a Japanese airline. The items are scheduled for delivery and payment in six months (i.e., during the next budgetary period). The current spot rate, U.S. interest rate, and Japanese interest rate are respectively 96.37 yen/dollar, 6%, and 7%. Assuming that the interest rate parity holds, the forward exchange rate will be 97.28 yen/dollar. The contract will be priced in yen and coordinated through the U.S. firm's Tokyo sales operation. The minimum contract price that the U.S. firm should accept is 2,432,000 yen, using the forward exchange rate that coincides with the payment. Because leading Japanese economists predict that the Japanese interest rate will increase to 8% within the next six months, however, the forward exchange rate should adjust to 98.19 yen/dollar. This would establish a minimum contract price of 2,454,750,000 yen. The difference of 22,750 yen (i.e., 2,454,750,000 – 2,432,000,000) or $231,694 (calculated at the new expected forward exchange rate) would be lost if the new exchange rate were not used to price the contract. When developing the Tokyo sales budget for the next budgetary period, this specific contract should be valued at 2,454,750,000 yen, and the U.S. aerospace manufacturing firm's comprehensive budget should reflect a $25 million contract for the Tokyo sales operation. The cash budget would translate any resulting cash flow from the Tokyo office to the U.S. operation at a 98.19 yen/dollar forward exchange rate.

Source: Adapted with the help of Giulia Zanetello from the case in Rivera, J. and Milani, K. (2011). Budgeting for International Operations: Impact on and Integration with Strategic Planning. *Management Accounting Quarterly*.

13.4 Debt capital markets: debt financing, bank loans and others

This section will analyze debt financing by highlighting its characteristics with respect to equity. It will also define some specific types of debt, such as bank loans, syndicated loans, and bonds, and outline their particular features and main differences.

13.4.1 Debt financing and its features

In this introduction to debt financing, the key dimensions of a debt instrument and the trade-off between debt and equity will be considered. Then we will look at an example involving a difficult choice among several forms of financing that could apply.

Firstly, any debt instrument is defined along three key dimensions: the principal value, the periodic payments of interests, and the maturity date.

- The principal value (or face value, maturity value, or par value) represents the amount owed to the lender that must be repaid at some point during the life of the debt, commonly at maturity.
- The periodic interest payments, or coupons, are computed as a percentage of the principal amount.
- The maturity date is when the principal amount of a debt falls due.

Deciding among debt alternatives implies weighing pros and cons. The main pros can be summarized by financial benefits, added discipline, a high level of confidentiality, cost of capital, and impact of the debt for actual shareholders. Since it is tax deductible, the actual cost of debt is lower with respect to the nominal interest payment. The added discipline is that the debt can make managers more prudent about the investments they make (since debt requires the company to deal with interest payments and repay capital). In addition, confidentiality is high for bank loans or bond transactions compared to an ECM (Equity Capital Market), where more information must be disclosed. As for the cost of capital, the right mix of debt and equity improves the WACC (debt is less expensive than equity for shareholders) and upgrades the evaluation of a company and the returns of shareholders (since they can provide less in their equity contributions). Finally, debt is not dilutive for the shareholders compared to a potential capital increase or to convertible securities.

The main cons are the risk of future financial distress, deterioration of the company image, and reduction of future financial flexibility. In terms of the risk of future financial distress, it is not possible to add additional debt when there is already exposure to it. With equity, there are no obligations towards investors (payment of dividends is not mandatory). Equity is "patient capital," because there is a long-term horizon. With debt, there is instead the obligation to pay back interest and principal. In the case of excessive borrowing coupled with negative corporate performance, an MNC runs the risk of not being able to repay the debt entirely. In the case of financial distress, there is a negative impact on the image and reputation of the company as well. Finally, adding debt on top of the capital structure poses the risk of diminishing future financial flexibility.

Figure 13.4 shows different financing alternatives.

In the following example, we can see there may be several alternatives (with related advantages and disadvantages) that the financial manager of a MNC has to evaluate to develop a global perspective that identifies the best possible choices for the company.

Figure 13.4 Financing options

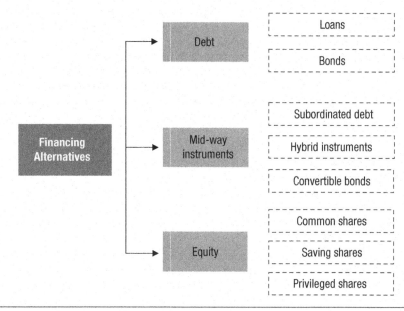

Source: Author's elaboration from JP Morgan.

Example   Prada

Suppose Prada's Chief Financial Officer (CFO) needs to consider raising 1 billion euros through the equity capital market (ECM) or through the debt capital market (DCM). What is the best way to approach this financial mix analysis? How should the CFO decide on the characteristics of the capital raising? Let's concentrate on the DCM alternative.

If the CFO decides to rely on bond issuance, the starting point would be to understand what is happening in the euro markets. Would the Euromarket, for example, finance Prada by buying its bonds? Understanding this requires studying how Prada's competitors use the DCM for their financing choices. In 2010, the competitor Bulgari raised 120 million euros on the Euromarket by selling 5-year bonds and paying a spread of 2.75%. In 2011, another competitor, LVMH, issued 4-year bonds with a spread of 1.85% over the LIBOR and 7-year bonds with a spread of 2%. Analysis of such competitors made it clear that the Euromarket was experiencing a deep crisis, especially for government bonds, but that corporate bonds still gave companies the opportunity to raise funds from the European bond markets.

Another financing possibility for Prada was to turn to the U.S. bond market and sell bonds directly there. No direct competitors of Prada had financed themselves on the U.S. bond market in the recent past, but the U.S. market was particularly receptive to corporate bond issues – despite a crisis with a spread similar to the European one – but offered a lower LIBOR rate.

Prada could also look at the possibility of raising capital in the form of debt on the Hong Kong (HK) bond market. At that time, the HK market was characterized by a particular trend: many companies were issuing so-called dim-sum bonds. As with the U.S. bond market, in the HK market Prada could not observe or analyze on-site financing choices by direct competitors, but the corporate bond market in Asian markets in general was attractive. In October 2012, McDonald's

had been able to sell bonds in Asia by paying a total cost of 3% (i = 3%). In other words, international investors were willing to buy bonds denominated in the local Chinese currency because
they expected to gain from the appreciation of the yuan/renminbi. At that time, 90% of dim-sum
bonds issued in Asia had a distinctive feature: a short-term maturity of less than 18 months. The
expectation of currency appreciation could not be realized in the long term; investors could only
speculate on a very short time period by accepting a particularly low return on the bonds. All the
technical features of such bond issues were acceptable to Prada except for the short-term maturity because this clause exposed the company to the risk of refinancing in a period of time that
was too short for Prada's financial and strategic needs.

Like all multinational companies, Prada was thus faced with different financing alternatives
whose characteristics had to be fully analyzed if it wanted to define their impact on the company's financial structure. It had to evaluate:

- Local Italian bank loans;
- The local Eurobond market;
- Foreign European bank loans;
- The foreign U.S. bond market;
- The foreign HK dim-sum bond market;
- The foreign HK USD bond market.

Source: Adapted from a recommended case study: Sapp, S. (2012), *Prada: To IPO or Not to IPO: That
Is the Question*, available at https://hbsp.harvard.edu/product/W12153-PDF-ENG

Main factors affecting the financing mix

Financing decisions are complicated, especially given the multiple options available (**Figure 13.5** shows the different alternatives of debt financing) and their repercussions on the optimal financial structure discussed in previous chapters. Here are
some issues that need to be taken into consideration when making decisions on this
topic:

- Cash position;
- Ability to access debt and equity capital markets;
- Maximum amount of debt and equity immediately available in case of new capi-
  tal market transactions;
- Initial capital structure;
- Rating considerations and impacts;
- Ability to generate cash flows to pay back the debt.

13.4.2 Bank loans

For many small (and medium) firms bank loans represent the only source of borrowing (debt). On the other hand, many multinational corporations prefer syndicated
loans and bond issuing. This divergence can also be explained by the fact that there
are various attitudes to debt financing in different geographic locations. In Europe,
for instance, 80% of the financing for corporation is covered on average by bank
debt, while in U.S. the opposite is true and bond transactions prevail.

Figure 13.5 Overview of most relevant debt instruments

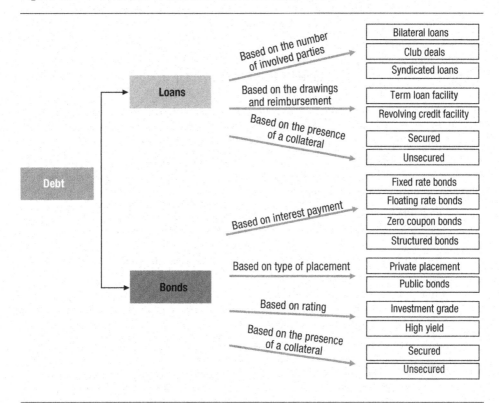

Source: Author's elaboration from JP Morgan.

There are several dimensions according to which loans can be classified:

- Banks can provide credit on either a *short-term* basis (i.e., uncommitted lines) or with *committed lines* (that cannot be suspended without notifying the borrower). Committed lines can take the form of a Term Loan or Revolving Credit Facilities (RCF):
  - A *Term Loan* has a scheduled repayment profile and, once repaid, cannot be redrawn.
  - *RCF* allow the customer to borrow up to an established limit with fixed maturity. In addition to paying interest on any amount borrowed, the borrower also pays a commitment fee on the unused amount.
- Banks can also provide loans with different *maturities*:
  - *Bridge loans*, typically have a short lifespan (12 months + 6 months) and are repaid with the proceeds of 1) asset disposals, 2) bond take-outs, and 3) capital increases.

- *Term loans* have a five-year maturity and amortizing repayment schedule or bullet payments (in one instalment) at maturity; they differ in terms of collateral, covenants, and fixed vs. floating rates.
- Most long-term loans are floaters with interest payments based on a *benchmark rate*, such as the Euribor (Euro Interbank Offered Rate), plus a spread which is a function of the implied creditworthiness of the company and the maturity of the loan. Floater loans can be repaid in advance with no cost.
- Longer term bank loans can be *secured* when a bank asks for collateral to mitigate credit risk (especially in cases of small and medium enterprises that are financing an acquisition, the building of a plant, or transactions with an implied high risk for the lenders, such as LBO transactions). Collateral can include pledges on shares, current accounts, receivables, inventories, mortgages on fixed assets, or corporate guarantees.
- Banks loans usually involve undertakings and financial *covenants*:
  - General undertakings: *pari passu*, negative pledges, restrictions on mergers, restrictions on asset disposals, no change of business, restrictions on dividend distributions (the most common), and restrictions on giving loans/providing guarantees.
  - Financial covenants maintain key figure ratios – such as the borrower's debt to equity ratio and debt to EBITDA ratio – below certain thresholds defined in the agreement or above in the case of the coverage ratio (EBITDA over interest payments). Covenants can be *positive* (e.g., financial ratios) or *negative* (e.g., to restrict the borrower's ability to do something).

In addition, early prepayment can be envisioned in cases of change of control (i.e., in the event the majority shareholders are replaced), cross default, insolvency proceedings, or non-compliance with undertakings/financial covenants.

Repayment schedules

Bank loans are generally repaid according to three alternative schedules (for simplicity, the example below uses fixed interest rates).

- *Constant instalments*: e.g., an amortizing loan of €1000 with a 4-year maturity. The borrower repays a *fixed amount* throughout the maturity of the instrument that is determined by a mix of interest and principal (**Table 13.1**).

Table 13.1   Repayment with constant installment

Year	Initial Balance	Interest	Instalment	Principal	Final Balance
1	1,000.0	100.0	315.5	215.5	784.5
2	784.5	78.5	315.5	237.0	547.5
3	547.5	54.8	315.5	260.7	286.8
4	286.8	28.7	315.5	286.8	0.0

- *Constant principal*: €1000, 4-year maturity. Here the principal is fixed (**Table 13.2**).

Table 13.2   Repayment with constant principal

Year	Initial Balance	Interest	Instalment	Principal	Final Balance
1	1,000.0	100.0	350.0	250.0	750.0
2	750.0	75.0	325.0	250.0	500.0
3	500.0	50.0	300.0	250.0	250.0
4	250.0	25.0	275.0	250.0	0.0

- *Bullet*: the principal is reimbursed in one instalment at maturity with a constant amount of interest (€100).

In the case of constant instalments and a constant principal, the repayment schedule can include an initial grace period when no payment of capital is due. After the grace period (if applicable), the repayment schedule is typically defined based on the business plan of the company. A bigger portion of repayment at maturity is called a final balloon payment.

Companies can also use *leasing* to finance the purchase of fixed assets or make investments in properties. A lease is an alternative way of financing the acquisition of an asset, where the lessee (user) pays monthly instalments (including interest and capital) to the lessor (owner) for the use of an asset and can gain ownership at the end of the lease period. The lessor is the legal owner during the duration of the lease, while the lessee not only has operational control over the asset but also bears the economic risks of the change in valuation of the underlying asset, since it is listed as an owned asset in the balance sheet. Firms often choose to lease assets rather than to buy them mainly for the tax benefits involved, since they can expense the interest paid on the lease each year and depreciate the cost of the asset over its life.

Limits of traditional bank loans

There are two limits to traditional bank loans:

1. The first limit is represented by the types of clients (borrowers) to be served. For certain types of clients (financial institutions, public authorities, and large corporations), direct financing from a single bank is not feasible due to the large size of the transaction.
2. The second limit involves regulatory issues. Banks are required to limit their exposure to a single counterparty at maximum 25% of their eligible capital, while the absorption of capital for banks is a function of the underlying rating (the lower it is, the higher the cost and the incentive to sell the loan in case of underwriting).

13.4.3 Syndicated loans

A syndicated loan is a loan provided by a group of banks in the form of a single contract to a borrower. Because these loans are issued in the market through an underwriting process, participating banks may be motivated to join a syndicate to fill a gap in origination capacity in specific geographic regions or industries. A small bank can enter indirectly into a relationship with a borrower it might not normally get as a customer and build a network with the larger banks that operate the syndicate by funding a portion of a syndicated loan. While bilateral bank loans remain the most common form of financing in Europe for companies below a certain size, bigger companies have become increasingly reliant on syndicated loans and bonds in recent years (Godlewski & Sanditov, 2015). Banks underwriting big loans receive compensation for taking this risk, while banks that are only participating receive lower fees. Typically underwriting banks define a syndication protocol to reach their desired final take (i.e., the amount of loan they want to retain on their books). Often the economic agreement includes a "flex," i.e., the possibility of increasing the price if there is not enough demand to reach the final take (for example, if market conditions have changed in the meantime).

As an alternative to bilateral bank loans or club deals (i.e., loans with a limited number of banks), two other forms of debt financing are worth mentioning: bond issues and syndicated loans. This section will provide a fine-grained account of syndicated loans, while the following will be devoted to bond issues.

Companies have employed syndicated loans for a long time. While syndicated loans were first used to fund LBOs and M&A transactions, today they cover a considerably larger variety of multinational operations. During the 1990s, the syndicated loan market developed at a rate of around 20% per year, and it has since grown to become the world's biggest private debt market.

A *syndicated loan* is a single (large) loan with a unique contract provided by a syndicate. A syndicate is a group or pool of banks with a clear hierarchical structure that is formed to provide substantial financing, generally to fund an M&A transaction or a specific capex plan. The loan is generally too big to be granted by a single bank. In a syndicate, a lead bank coordinates the pool of lenders. A syndicated loan is on one hand a form of relationship lending, in which the relationship between the lender and the borrower – typically institutions such as commercial banks – is of primary importance; on the other hand, it is also a form of transaction lending where the focus is on the transaction, as is typical of investment banks. In other words, syndicated loans are issued on the market (so they undergo underwriting by one or more banks), but they are also subject to very strong relationship aspects.

Advantages and disadvantages of syndicated loans

Table 13.3 and the paragraphs below exemplify *advantages and disadvantages of syndicated loans* from the perspectives of both clients (borrowers) and banks.

Why a syndicate? Over time, syndicated bonds have gained ground due to the benefits they present for both lenders and borrowers.

- *Lenders:* Banks create a syndicate to share the risk of a large loan (reduce their exposure to borrower-related risks), invest in different projects, and lend to di-

Table 13.3 **Pros and cons of syndicated loans**

	Client perspective	Bank perspective
	Syndicated loans	
Pros	• no need for public rating, no public disclosure of information	• insert covenants and control the client
Cons	• direct bank supervision and control • more restrictions in terms of covenants, security package, undertakings	• regulatory capital absorption (balance sheet at risk)

verse borrowers (increase portfolio diversification and revenue diversification), manage the regulatory impact of capital, and create a network among banks (for marketing and relationship reasons). Banks are also motivated to join syndicates to enhance their origination capabilities in certain geographies or industries where their origination capabilities are limited. The latter results from the opportunities presented for example to smaller banks that enter into relationships with borrower it normally would not have access to as clients.

- *Borrowers:* Companies can typically take advantage of lower costs compared to bond issues (while bilateral loans are generally cheaper since commercial banks might have other reasons to provide a loan, such as the management of current assets, providing guarantees, etc.).

Are there drawbacks and challenges? Of course, while syndicated loans offer many advantages for both parties, they also present some drawbacks.

- *Lenders:* A syndicate with many banks is difficult to manage. This why there is typically one coordinating bank (one or more of the underwriters) that helps the borrower to interact with all the banks participating in the transaction. Finally, syndicated loans can generate problems related to the interconnectedness of the banking system, since direct links between banks can be critical channels of crisis contagion (i.e., the 2008 financial crisis).
- *Borrower:* Borrowing from a syndicate usually limits the flexibility of the loan with respect to what the borrower would get in the framework of an exclusive bank relationship. Moreover, the borrower is forced to interact and share information with a large number of banks.

How to organize a syndicate

The syndication process involves many actors with various roles and tasks within the syndicate. A syndicated loan transaction is organized in the following way: there is a company that needs to raise funds (for example, to fund an M&A or an important capex plan). Investment banks often play the role of underwriters, while commercial banks invest their money once the transaction is underwritten. The underwriters invite other banks to join and reduce their risk. The process remains open until the underwriters reach their target or "final take" (i.e., the amount they are prepared to keep on their books). In certain conditions, the initial pricing can be increased if this objective is not reached in a defined timeframe ("market flex").

To describe the process of a syndicated loan in more detail, this section will outline the three main stages of the syndication process and then clarify the decision-making stages.

As mentioned above, the syndication process is composed of three main stages:

- *The Pre-Mandated Stage*: At this stage, the future borrower solicits competitive offers to arrange the syndication from one or more banks. If the company has a good bargaining position, it may draft a "term sheet" to be proposed to prospective arranging banks, who can modify the terms by balancing their acceptability on the market and the expectations of the borrower. After having examined the proposals of various banks, the borrower chooses one or more arrangers. The arranger will have the mandate of forming a syndicate and negotiating a preliminary loan agreement, and it may also agree to underwrite part of the transaction. In the case of a confidential transaction, the borrower relies on a limited number of banks that underwrite the transaction and avoids needing to involve other banks.
- *The Post-Mandated Stage*: At this point, the arranger prepares and distributes an informational memorandum for potential syndicate members containing information about borrower's creditworthiness and loan terms. A bank meeting can also be planned, with the arranger sending formal invitations to potential participants and determining the allocations. If other banks are interested in the deal, they are sent drafts of loan documents that have been previously negotiated by the arranger. If a deal is underwritten, other banks are involved once the transaction has become public.
- *The Post-Signing Stage*: Once the loan document is signed, the deal is active, the loan is operational, and the debt contract is legally binding. At this stage, the arranger's role is terminated, and the responsibilities of the agent bank commence. This latter role is typically given to the arranger if it also participates in the syndicate as a lender. The agent bank has the power and responsibility to administer the syndicated loan on behalf of all participant banks, which in turn must also monitor the borrower until the maturity of the loan.

To fully understand what is involved in the creation of a syndicate, we need to consider a number of questions:

1. How many banks are involved?
2. Which banks are involved?
3. What is the "final take" for a lead arranger or underwriter (the mandate lead arranger or the MLA)?

Figure 13.6 shows the debt financed by banks and the equity of the sponsor.

Figure 13.6   Financing of the syndicated loans

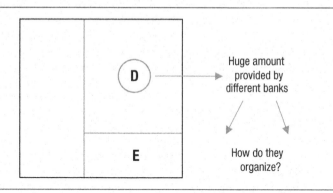

1. *Number of banks.* The number of banks is the first crucial question. Indeed, depending on the choices made by the borrower, the number of banks involved in a syndicated loan is related to a series of advantages in terms of economic convenience, confidentiality, bargaining power, and organizational costs. Thanks to risk allocation, in a syndicate with many banks it is possible to include smaller banks (mainly commercial ones) and the MLA can retain a portion of the fees to remunerate its activity. In underwritten deals, a limited number of banks (even 1) assume all the risk and are therefore paid underwriting fees. Banks joining the syndicate are paid via the fees: the underwriter retains a fee on the total size of the facility (the so-called "skin"), while participating banks are paid based on the amount they subscribe. Fees for participating banks are based on the size of the ticket and the role. **Table 13.4** provides a summary of the considerations to take into account when there are many vs few banks in the syndicate.

Table 13.4   Advantages and disadvantages related to the number of banks in syndicate loans

	Many Banks	Few Banks
Pros	• risk shared among many banks involved in the syndicate • smaller banks can be involved and they have lower bargaining power in the distribution of fees • smaller tickets = lower fees to pay to each bank invited to the syndicate	• degree of confidentiality is higher • reduction of coordination costs and decision-making processes
Cons	• higher coordination costs • more potential risks for confidentiality issues	• larger tickets = more fees to pay to each bank invited to the syndicate • greater risk for banks invited due to the necessity for them to underwrite larger portions of the loan

2. *Selection of banks.* Common practice in the capital markets arena is to reciprocate invitations to participate in deals: if the MLA invites a bank to join a syndicate, very likely the invited bank will return the favor when it gets a mandate. The specific characteristics of the loan, the offer, or the borrower could require certain institutions to be involved. In general, the borrower suggests that the MLA invite some banks with which it has relationships; for the rest the MLA typically calls banks with which it has a close relationship with or with which it wants to establish a relationship.

3. *Mandated Lead Arranger* (MLA). Together with the underwriters, the MLA determines the proportion of the loan to be sold in the market and how much to retain on its balance sheet. "Final take" is the technical term indicating the final amount the MLAs will keep on their books. (As mentioned above, MLAs assume all responsibility in relation to the client in the initial phase, but in the end retain only a small portion of this amount.) The tendency is to sell down a big portion of the loan (especially in the case of investment banks) to minimize the amount of absorbed capital. Only big commercial banks that have access to ECB funding have the credit to retain a larger portion of the loan. Some banks specialize in the underwriting and selling of corporate loans retaining a small portion of the loan or super senior RCF and selling down the exposure to institutional investors who are more prepared to bear the credit risk of the underlying asset and receive a high interest rate in exchange. Selling a high portion of the loan has *pros* and *cons*:
   - Pros: it transfers a larger part of the credit risk to third parties, frees up liquidity, and increases the return on capital employed.
   - Cons: it sends a bad signal to the market (i.e., that the MLA does not trust the borrower's ability to repay the debt).

Example Return for the shareholders of an MLA

There is a clear trade-off between lower exposure and maintaining a reasonable amount of final take. This is an example of the return for an MLA's shareholders. Let's suppose that at T_0 the arrangement fees are €10 million and exposure is €100 million (exposure is the capital invested). If the MLA invites other banks into the syndicate and cuts arrangement fees to €1 million, transferring the whole exposure to the market (so that it has 0 exposure), the MLA functions as a sort of money machine: €1m/0 (the return tends toward infinity, which of course is a temptation).

The problem is *trust*: as the MLA, it is hard to explain to the syndicate why you do not want to retain part of the loan on your books. This is a bad signal for the syndicate but also for the borrower who trusted you and will dissipate your chances of getting other mandates in the future. On the other hand, for the MLA's shareholders it is better to reduce the final take as much as possible to maximize returns.

The actors involved are the Mandated Lead Arrangers, Co-Lead Arrangers, Arrangers, Co-Arrangers, and Lead-Managers. The Mandated Lead Arranger (MLA) is the bank that receives the mandate. This bank is also called the book runner, since it "runs," or is in charge of, the books during the syndication process. The MLA is the lead actor: it designs the operation with the borrower and invites all the other banks, thus choosing the participants. The MLA receives the mandate on a fully committed basis, meaning it has to provide the bulk of financing requested by

> the borrower. For the MLA, the risk is not finding other banks willing to provide financing to the borrower (for various reasons, including risk/return). To avoid this risk, the MLA can assemble a very small group of large banks (referred to as Co-Arrangers or Co-Book Runners) to off-load part of the risk before launching the transaction on the market. Co-Lead Arrangers are mainly investment banks; together with the MLA, they provide the amount requested by the borrower. Once the group of underwriters is formed, the MLA and the CLAs try to sell down a portion of the loan to the market. They find the banks willing to participate in the loan. (Lending banks are organized in different tiers. Usually there are different titles corresponding to the level of commitment that they provide).

Arrangers are mainly Commercial Banks that lend the biggest portion of funding. Co-Arrangers are responsible for a smaller portion of funding. Lead Managers are at the bottom of the ladder, providing the least amount of funding. In other words, the various actors form a pyramid, with the MLA at the top, Co-Leaders (Joint Lead Arranger) in the middle, and Arrangers, Co-Arrangers, and Managers at the bottom. There are two additional players to mention: the documentation bank and the agent bank. The documentation bank participates in all the meetings of the syndicate; it negotiates the facility agreement that gets proposed by the lawyers on behalf of the lenders and the borrower and prepares the documentation supporting the credit applications of invited lenders. This is a complex task considering the number of banks involved in a syndicate. The agent bank plays an administrative role which consists in collecting money from the syndicate and transferring it to the borrower (the client). In the same way, repayment from the borrower is provided directly to the agent bank, which transfers the money to the other members of the syndicate. Usually, the agent bank and the documentation bank are part of the group of MLAs. **Figure 13.7** presents a diagram illustrating the structure of a syndicate.

After having analyzed the aspects shaping the process of syndicated loans, it is important to note that, considering how their market works, the characteristics of the parties involved are central, especially the reputations of the MLA and Co-Leaders. Indeed, they are responsible for due diligence and for making allocations to other syndicate members.

Syndication strategies

What differentiates strategies in a syndication process is how confident the MLA is in its ability to place big portions of the loan in market. Traditionally, MLAs have used two strategies to do this:

- *Single Stage Mandate*: High risk, high return. If the financial markets are very liquid and volatility is not a concern, the MLA can take on the mandate on its own, committing itself to underwrite the whole loan amount and then going to the market to sell a portion of the loan to other banks. This strategy does not involve creating a group of underwriters, so the MLA does not have to share the underwriting fees with other banks. It is the most profitable option for the MLA and the most suitable alternative in periods of higher liquidity for deals perceived as "sound."

Figure 13.7   Structure of a syndicate

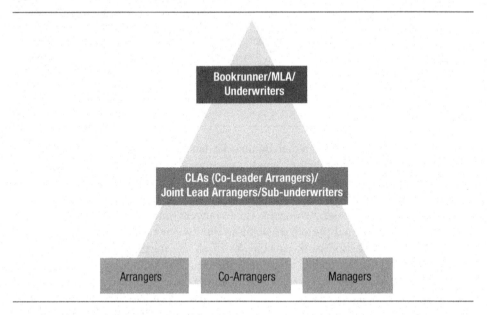

- *Dual Stage Mandate*: A longer process. In the first stage, the MLA shares the commitment to lend the bulk of funding with other big banks (underwriters). For example, if the commitment in question is of €1 billion, the MLA might call three other banks and ask them to commit to providing one-fourth of the loan. In the end, this would enable the MLA to make a commitment of only €250 million, since the remaining €750 million will be underwritten by the other underwriters. In the second stage (general syndication), after the group of underwriters is organized, the MLA and other underwriters allocate portions of the loan to other banks participating in the syndicate. The MLA shares the risk with the Co-Lead Arrangers, in order to deal with the volatility of the market. In this case, the return for the underwriter is lower because the risk is also lower. This strategy is most suitable in periods of higher uncertainty for deals with specific features or when the deal is perceived as "aggressive."

In situations of financial turmoil and increased volatility of the market, there is a need to speed up the process since there is a risk of receiving the mandate when the market is favorable and completing the syndication process after the market has turned negative. In such scenarios, the following strategy has become very common:

- *Club-Deal Mandate*: A *club deal* is a smaller loan (usually less than $150 million) that is pre-marketed to a select group (usually around 3-5) of relationship lenders with closer ties to the borrower. When a borrower requires funding, it asks a limited number of banks to join together and form a group. This syndicate has Joint MLAs, which is useful because it speeds up the process.

Borrowers pay various fees to participant lenders according to the syndicate fee structure. A significant amount of bank income in the syndicated loan market comes from such fees. The fees received by syndicate participants and the interest on the loan are the sources of potential income. Certain fees are shared among syndicate participants according to their roles and level of participation in the financing.

MLAs receive an upfront fee for originating the financing, arranging the syndicate, and underwriting the facility. This amount is split into:

- A *praecipium* paid to the MLA to remunerate the leading role this party plays (or arranging fees for banks coordinating the syndicate);
- *Underwriting fees* paid to underwriters based on underwritten amount;
- *Participation* (or *closing*) *fees* paid to lenders based on the total amount that they will provide;
- *An agency fee* paid to the Agent Bank, which is usually between €50,000 and €100,000 depending on how many banks take part in the deal;
- A *residual pool* paid to the MLA and Co-Lead Arrangers.

The difference between the underwriting fees earned and the portion given to the participating banks is called the "skim" and represents the gain for the underwriting banks.

Pricing of loans

The pricing of loans is a function of:

- The absorption of capital and required target remuneration (ROAC formula);
- The maturity;
- The cost of funding (lower in cases of ECB funds, such as Targeted Longer-Term Refinancing Operations, TLTROs).

The ROAC (Return on Allocated Capital) is a measure used to evaluate the marginal profitability of a single transaction.

$$ROAC = \frac{Income\ before\ taxes}{Risk\ Capital} \ VS\ Net\ cost\ of\ Capital\ (\%)$$

It is calculated as the ratio of income before taxes and allocated risk capital. Financial institutions set a target ROAC based on their cost of capital net of an internal return.

The income before taxes calculation is based on:

- + Interest income and upfront fees
- − Expected loss (which combines the exposure amount, PD (Probability of Default), and LGD (Loss Given Default)).

The risk capital (or regulatory capital) represents the capital absorption of the loan.

The Basel regulations define two different methodologies for calculating capital requirements:

- In the standard approach (STD), the regulatory weightings depend on the credit ratings assigned to the counterparty by external ratings agencies and on the characteristics of the exposure.
- Internal approaches (internal ratings-based approach-IRB) instead depend on the method used (the foundation internal ratings-based approach-FIRB or the advanced internal ratings-based approach-AIRB) and are based on the banks' own estimates on one or more parameters.

Below are the calculations used to determine the capital requirement based on the approach adopted.

1. Standard (STD):
- Requirement = 8%*RWA (Risk Weighted Assets), with RWA = exposure (exposure at default-EAD)* regulatory weighting factor

2. IRB (FIRB or AIRB):
- Requirement = 8%*RWA, with RWA = f(PD, LGD, EAD and, in some cases, Maturity-M)
- RWA = weighting function used for exposures, depends on type of portfolio.

13.4.4 Bonds

International bonds are debt securities issued in a foreign country by a non-resident entity that are denominated in the domestic currency of the issuing entity. A domestic bond is a debt obligation issued by a domestic issuer in a domestic currency that is sold and traded in the domestic market. Domestic bonds, unlike foreign bonds, are not subject to currency risk. A foreign bond is a debt instrument issued in the domestic market by a foreign entity in the currency of the domestic market to raise funds. Investors can buy international bonds in a way similar to how they buy domestic bonds: the broker provides clients with a list of available bonds, which they can purchase at the market price. Participants in the international bond market are those who engage in the issuance and trading of debt securities and can be classified into three categories: issuers, underwriters, and purchasers.

Finally, it is important to mention so-called global bonds, which are huge bonds that would be difficult to sell in only one nation or specific area of the world. For this reason, global bonds are sold at the same time in major markets around the world and then traded everywhere. The average issue size for these types of instruments typically exceeds $1 billion. Most are denominated in U.S. dollars.

- *Issuers of securities: Issuers* sell bonds or other financial instruments in the market to finance the activities of their organizations. The governments of different countries are usually the largest issuers and use the bond market to finance government operations, such as social programs and other critical expenditures. Corporations issuing debt for financing purposes are also significant issuers in the bond market.
- *Bond Underwriters or Bookrunners:* Historically, the underwriting segment of the bond market has consisted in investment banks and other financial institutions that assist issuers in marketing their issues.
- *Bond Buyers:* The final market participants are those who purchase issued debt. Governments often purchase debt from other nations if they hold excess reserves of that country's currency thanks to trade between countries. Banks are also important investors in bonds. Other investors are typically fund managers or insurance and hedge funds (Lessambo, 2021). Coupons on bonds are made by interest rates (generally fixed) and a spread that is a function of the value of the credit of the counterparty and the tenor of the transaction.

13 Debt Financing and Debt Capital Markets   393

Bonds are an alternative to bank loans. This section will offer an in-depth overview of the issuance of bonds.

Table 13.5 exemplifies some *advantages and disadvantages of bonds* from the perspectives of both clients and banks.

Table 13.5   **Pros and cons of bonds**

	Client perspective	Bank perspective
	Bonds	
Pros	• no direct control by banks • ability to extend maturities • quick access to a vast number of investors • diversification of funding sources • limited set of undertakings/covenants	• no regulatory capital absorbed • pure fees business
Cons	• need to prepare an offering circular • costs for selling	• reputational risk in case of low credit profile of the company (the risk that, in the end, the issuer will not repay the money)

Bonds are defined as long-term debt securities issued to investors by either a public offering or through a private placement (in both cases with an underwriting process).

Their main features are the following:

- The issue size generally ranges from 300 million to 1 billion (lower than that there is a risk of illiquidity).
- The most common maturities are generally 5, 7, and 10 years, but longer maturities are possible.
- The interest rate is usually fixed, and coupons are paid annually or semi-annually.
- Collateral security and the level of seniority protect bondholders from other creditors in case of default.
- Covenants are generally limited versus bank loans. Covenants can include Change of Control clauses: these give bondholders the possibility of putting the bond (asking for repayment) if there is a significant change in the shareholder structure that negatively impacts the credit rating of the company. A put is better than the default typical with bank debt, since it precludes cross default (the possibility that other debtholders will ask for a default under one agreement as a consequence of their default on another contract).

Bonds may or may not be rated. Ratings reflect the bond's probability of default and have a direct, measurable influence on its interest rate and on the cost to the firm of issuing debt. The greater the bond's default risk, the lower its rating and the greater the risk premium associated with the bond. Rated bonds require a high level of disclosure (since rating agencies review every extraordinary transaction and judge their impacts when making their assessments). They also require a payment to obtain and keep the rating. However, bonds allow the issuer to reach a high number of investors and subsequently to pay a lower coupon (typically, public bonds are rated). Rated bonds are issued by companies that are IG (Investment Grade), Sub-IG, or HY (High Yield/Speculative). Unrated bonds are more suitable for companies trying to sell themselves in the market with a better image than the one reflected in the assessment received from rating agencies. Unrated bonds are more expensive and more difficult to place in volatile market conditions.

Table 13.6 shows the main rating scales.

Table 13.6   **Rating scales**

Moody's	S&P	
Aaa	AAA	Investment Grade
Aa	AA	
A	A	
Baa	BBB	
Ba	BB	Sub Investment Grade
B	B	
Caa	CCC	
C	D	Speculative Grade

Source: Investment scale from Moody's and S&P.

Bond types

The different bond types are listed below.

- *Straight bond*: The name derives from the fact that it remains a bond until the end of its life. Straight bonds can be senior (secured or unsecured) bonds, subordinated bonds, or high yield bonds. A senior bond pays interests at regular intervals, and at maturity pays back the principal that was originally invested (the most common is the plain-vanilla bond: it reaches maturity between 5-10 years on average, with interest payments every 3, 6, or 12 months and the principal paid at maturity). Traditional bonds are typically fixed-rate instruments. In some cases, issuers place floating rate notes with shorter maturities than fixed-rate bonds and variable coupons depending on the base rate (e.g., Euribor + spread). The issuing entity of a straight bond can be a
  - municipality;
  - corporation;
  - government.
- *Subordinated bonds*: Here the payment of interest and principal is "subordinated" to senior bonds in the case of default. Some subordinated bonds include a PIK

(Payment in Kind) feature, meaning that interest might not be paid but instead added to the principal amount to be repaid at maturity.

- *High-Yield Bonds (HYs)*: These are senior bonds (typically secured) issued by sub-IG companies. They contain a call feature (i.e., the issuer can repay the bond after a certain number of years with a predetermined decreasing premium).
- *Index Linked Notes*: These are bonds in which the interest payment is linked to a specific price index – often the Consumer Price Index (i.e., it is an inflation-linked bond).
- *Zero Coupon Bonds*: These are debt securities that do not pay interest but are issued at a discount; all interest is paid at maturity, together with the principal.
- *Hybrid Bonds*: These bonds combine both equity and debt features. Like senior bonds, they pay a coupon (which could eventually be deferred) and generally have a stated maturity, which may even be very long. Hybrid bonds are subordinated to all classes of debt in case of default. Rating agencies usually consider hybrid bonds as 50% equity and 50% debt, meaning half of the amount issued is not included in all the financial ratios for corporations. The coupon is higher than the other senior debt of the issuer, because of the higher risk of default for the investor. The main features of hybrid bonds are
  - maturity: long dated (> 50 years) or perpetual;
  - coupon payment: could be discretionarily deferred or mandatory if specific metrics are not respected;
  - subordination compared to all other debt instruments;
  - can be replaced only with similar instruments.
- *Convertible bonds* include a provision giving the holder the right, but not the obligation, to convert the bond into a predetermined number of ordinary shares of the issuer (conversion ratio). These instruments benefit from the characteristic of traditional fixed income securities (since they regularly pay coupons and nominal value at maturity if they have not been converted previously). At the same time, they offer the chance to benefit from possible appreciation in the company's stock value. In some circumstances, the issuer can repay in cash to avoid the dilution of shareholders in case of conversion. These instruments are generally much cheaper (for the issuer) than senior bonds since they include the option of conversion into equity.
- *Bonds with warrant*: These bonds allow the holder to acquire shares of the issuing company at a specific price and within a specific time frame. Like convertible bonds, the warrant gives the holder the right but not the obligation to exercise the option at maturity, but unlike convertibles, when the holder exercises the warrant, they also retain ownership of the bond which will repay the notional amount at maturity. The embedded warrant can be detached and sold separately from the bond itself before it is exercised.

Types of issue

As mentioned above, bonds are long-term debt securities issued to investors either by
- Private Placement:
  - involves a limited number of investors (mainly institutional);
  - amounts between €30 and €250 million;
  - typically unlisted;
  - may have higher restrictions vs. public bonds;
  - in certain cases, involves longer maturities due to the specific needs of investors (e.g., insurance companies).
- Public Placement:
  - the audience is not known in advance;
  - the audience is > 100 investors.

Table 13.7 summarizes the pros and cons of the two different issuing strategies.

Table 13.7   **Advantages and disadvantages of public and private placement**

	Private Placement	**Public Placement**
Pros	• less disclosure • very limited information released to the market	• improve the size of the transaction • lower cost due to liquidity of the instrument • more counterparties involved
Cons	• higher cost of debt given illiquidity of the instrument	• cost (although limited) • requires a prospectus (although with a lower degree of complexity in terms of due diligence compared to equity offerings)

Bond offering mechanism

A bond offering is similar to an equity offering but less complex. The players involved are the issuer, the investors, and the book runners. Lawyers take care of the documentation, and auditors release the comfort letters.

The financial actors in a bond offering are

- *Global Coordinators/Underwriters*: are involved from the beginning in the advisory phase; they manage all the deal-making, putting their reputations on the line by placing the debt.
- *Bookrunners*: Global Coordinators and other banks that have an active or passive role in the placement of securities. The group of banks designated by the issuer to place the issue are considered active bookrunners. They are responsible for maintaining the investor order book and determining the final allocation to each investor. They also arrange investor calls and accompany the issuer on roadshows. Passive bookrunners, on the other hand, are not actively involved in the placement of bonds and therefore do not have access to book management.

- *Lead managers*: are responsible for the distribution of large portions of the new issue. In large issues, multiple lead managers are appointed, and they are known as Co-lead managers or Joint-lead Managers. Bookrunners are typically also lead managers.
- *Co-managers/Co-agents*: dealers mandated by issuers or invited by the lead managers to participate in the new issue. Co-managers are brought into a deal for their relevant niche expertise and distribution networks. They may distribute a fixed and pre-agreed percentage of the issuance, but they do not usually have an active role. This role is often covered by smaller banks.
- *Sellers-Commercial*: banks in charge of targeting retail investors when there is a dedicated retail tranche.

Remuneration fees

These are referred to as management fees and are paid to the Global Coordinator, who in turn splits them into various categories to remunerate the different players taking part in the syndicate. The highest remuneration is for the roles of Global Co-ordinators and Lead Managers. Co-managers are usually paid a more limited amount (i.e., 50k). Overall fees are a function of the (i) rating, (ii) maturity, (iii) frequency that the issuer taps into the market and of (iv) market conditions.

The selling process involves the following steps:

1. Setting up the memorandum (like the IPO prospectus but containing less information);
2. Conducting roadshows (less than for an IPO, and only in certain cases);
3. Book-building/selling;
4. Allocating orders to investors, privileging the "real money" investors: i.e., investors interested in keeping the bond for longer versus hedge funds/traders interested in reselling to earn profits in a short timeframe.

The success of a transaction can be judged based on its oversubscription (the number of orders collected versus the amount offered). The higher the percentage, the more the issuer can reduce the price versus the initial indications and the better the bond's performance on the secondary market after closing (more investors looking to buy if they receive lower allocations).

The execution of this type of transaction takes at least six to eight weeks from inception to completion. The diagram in **Figure 13.8** illustrates the process.

The most relevant documents required are:

- Offering memorandum (OM) – a marketing document that includes the following information:
  - summary of business description and industry overview;
  - risk factors;
  - financial information;

Figure 13.8   **Steps in a bond offering**

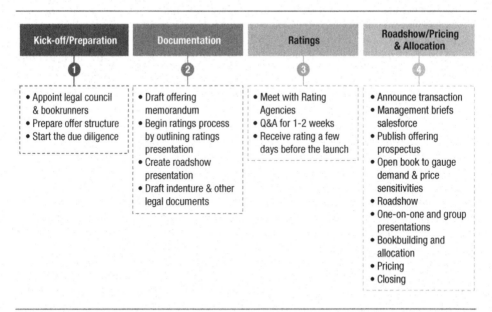

Source: Author's elaboration from Mediobanca.

  - – description of notes (structure/ranking, redemption provisions, covenants);
  - – company and management overview.
- Rating presentation – a confidential document providing detailed information on the company business; it includes both historical and projected financials.
- Roadshow presentation – derives from the presentation of the rating agency; no projections or estimates are included.
- Legal documentation – primarily consists of the description of notes, purchase agreement, and fee letters.
- Audited financials – the previous three years of audits, together with unaudited interims (reviewed by auditors); following the offering, the issuer provides quarterly and annual reports on an ongoing basis.

Execution strategies

Key bond execution strategies are:

- The *Best Efforts* strategy: a commitment to oversee – not to guarantee – the sale of the newly-issued bonds at the best possible conditions within a date agreed with the issuer. It does not imply any commitment to a specific size or to other terms of issue on the part of the bank. The bank is not liable for delivering a product that bears higher-than-expected costs for the issuer. Since this strategy is less risky for the bank, fees are also generally lower;

- The *Backstop* strategy: sets a maximum level of costs that the issuer is willing to bear. The bank commits itself to issuing a bond with a coupon not higher than the one agreed upon with the issuer. Should the coupon be higher than the maximum agreed upon level, the costs are covered by the bank itself; vice versa, if the coupon is lower than the expected range, the "extraordinary" proceeds are retained by the issuer;
- The *Underwriting* strategy: involves a slight variation and is almost never used in bond issuances. Issuers tend to choose backstop over underwriting for a simple reason: the underwriting process lets banks retain the extraordinary proceeds of the issue (e.g., if the issue bears a lower-than-expected coupon), whereas backstop pays these proceeds to the issuer.

Pricing bonds

The pricing of a bond is primarily a function of the credit quality of the borrower. The higher the probability of default, the higher the yield the investor will require. The following factors are considered by bankers when issuing price guidance for a new corporate bond:

- credit quality;
- comparables – CDS and cash levels;
- current and expected supply in the sector and wider market;
- event risk and external factors;
- regulatory risk;
- new issue premium.

The price of a new bond will also be dictated by the structure of the new issue, based on factors such as:

- size;
- maturity;
- covenants;
- subordination;
- coupon step-ups.

The pricing of bonds is therefore based on the sum of risk-free rate + risk premium. The base rate can be:

- an interbank market rate (e.g., Euribor for floaters);
- a mid-swap for fixed notes (with the same maturity as the bond's tenor).

The risk premium is calculated considering:

- the specific security (i.e., secured vs. unsecured);
- rating/implied rating;
- market conditions;
- tenor;
- liquidity;
- investors' knowledge of the issuer;
- presence of a secondary curve (i.e., existing bond trading on the market).

Measuring credit spreads

Measuring credit from the market price of a fixed-rate bond is not an easy task. In the market two main measures are used to price credit:

- *Spread over Swap curve* (measured in basis points – 1 bps is equivalent to 0.0001 or 0.01%): A swap is a contract in which two counterparties agree to exchange interest rate flows. The Swap Curve is an array of swap rates for each relevant maturity. The spread over the Swap Curve is the difference between the yield of the bond being evaluated and the Swap rate for a specific maturity;
- *Spread over Government curve* (measured in basis points – 1 bps is equivalent to 0.0001 or 0.01%): The Government Bond Curve is constructed by compiling the outstanding government on-the-run benchmarks. Prices taken from the major exchanges or markets via Bloomberg or Reuters. The spread over the Government Bond Curve is the difference between the yield of the bond being evaluated and the yield of the government bond for a specific maturity.

Environmental, social, and governance bonds

Since the European Investment Bank issued its first Environmental Social Governance (ESG) bond in 2007, numerous other companies and organizations have followed by issuing their own. Depending on their ultimate goals, ESG bonds are classified as green, social, sustainable, or sustainability-related. The first three are used to fund specific projects, while the last one is used to help a company achieve its sustainability goals. ESG bonds are attracting a wide range of investors and companies for motivations that can be summarized as follows[3]:

- Issuing an ESG bond allows for clear, direct, and factual communication about the company's role in improving industry efficiency, with a focus on the key projects/investment areas that will benefit from the funds raised. These topics pique the interest of bond investors, customers, employees, suppliers, regulators, and governments;
- Investors are increasingly incorporating ESG analysis into their portfolio construction, which allows issuers to attract mainstream investors interested in socially responsible investing, thereby expanding the universe of potential buyers and increasing demand;
- A sustainable and responsible development approach across the company's sphere of influence can be catalyzed by an ESG bond project, which can then improve communication of sustainability ambitions and Corporate Social Responsibility (CSR) reporting processes, as well as increase the company's capacity for future issues.

13.5 Conclusions

This chapter started with an introduction to long-term financing for multinational corporations. It highlighted that choices pertaining to long-term financing can have a significant impact on the success or failure of a project and can ensure stable and predictable cash flows for the parent company if well-designed. The chapter began by looking at the matching strategy, i.e., how to issue financing in the home currency of the subsidiary in order to pay back part of the subsidiary's debt with proceeds

[3] https://www.swissinfo.ch/eng/esg-bonds-and-their-use-cases-explained/47337504

made in-country – and therefore avoid exposure to exchange rate risk. The approach to this strategy assessed was the currency swaps methodology. The second section of the chapter was instead devoted to debt financing considerations, such as the denomination currency, the maturity of the debt, and the interest rate.

Building on this knowledge, the third section of the chapter discussed long-term financing. It explained that an MNC's financing options are many and can involve debt or equity. The final section of the chapter focused on debt financing tools, as well as their main features and characteristics. This section began with a description of the advantages and disadvantages of choosing debt over equity to raise funds for daily operations and overseas expansion. It then dove deeper into three important tools: bank loans, syndicated loans, and bonds.

Bank loans can provide credit on a short- or long-term basis and can be classified as committed or uncommitted lines. There is a difference between term loans, which have a scheduled repayment profile, and revolving credit facilities, which allow the customer to keep borrowing as needed. The maturities of loans can vary. There are so-called bridge loans – which usually have a short duration and are used to finance an acquisition – and term loans with maturities of several years and amortization payments. Interest rates can also be variable (floating or fixed), and loans are usually accompanied by covenants and undertakings. They can be repaid according to three different schedules: constant instalments, constant principals, or the bullet method.

Syndicated loans are contracted by a syndicate of several banks. Creating a syndicate is a way to share the risk of a loan and split the regulatory capital that would otherwise rest on the shoulders of a single bank. Within a syndicate, however, not all banks have the same roles. The Mandated Lead Arranger is the head of the group and coordinates the financing. Crucial concerns when building a syndicate include i) how many banks to involve, ii) which banks to involve, and iii) the final take for the lead arranger. The outcome of the financing can vary based on the decisions made regarding these issues.

Bonds are long-term debt securities issued by investors either through private or public placement. Their interest rates are usually fixed, and coupons are paid annually or semi-annually. Bonds can be rated or unrated according to rating agencies. We looked at several types of bonds in the chapter: straight, hybrid, and with warranties. The bond offering process is very similar to an equity offering (though less complex), and involves a global coordinator, co-leaders, sellers, and underwriters/ bookrunners. It also entails roadshows, like IPOs, as well as book building and bond allocations. The pricing of a bond is based on the sum of the risk-free rate and the risk premium.

With these concepts in mind, it is evident that the decision of how to finance a corporation is a challenging decision considering the variety of options available.

14 Corporate Governance and Shareholder Activism[*]

14.1 Introduction

As we approach the final chapter of this book, readers should have extensive knowledge of the basic notions of finance, as well as knowledge of some practical examples of how to apply them to real life cases associated with international finance and multinational companies.

The topic under discussion in this last chapter is crucial to making sound and rational investments in domestic markets or abroad: corporate governance. We will discuss its features and possible applications in the world of active and passive investing, and more specifically, when some shareholders become active participants in implementing governance changes through the so-called "shareholder activism." The chapter will begin with an introductory section devoted to key characteristics and definitions of corporate governance, agency problems, shareholders, and their relationships within the corporate governance structure of corporations. The following section will then assess what investing means from a passive and active point of view. Finally, the last section will be devoted to a specific cluster of active investors, namely shareholder activists, and the main features of their campaigns.

14.2 Corporate governance

Corporate governance is often treated by students as something mostly theoretical. In reality, corporate governance is the most important element to consider when taking investment decisions. Investing means taking exposure to an asset, directly or indirectly, by buying company shares (equity) or company debt (liabilities). In the first part of this chapter, we will focus on the introductory notions key to understanding corporate governance, including its main pillars and functioning mechanisms, as well as provide an overview of the agency problem of corporations and their inherent conflicts of interest.

---

[*] Written by Gimede Gigante and Stefano Sardo with the precious collaboration and support of Maria Vittoria Venezia.

14.2.1 Corporate governance definition and models

Corporate governance frameworks at the national level

As Butler (2012) has described, large firms are often controlled by one or more of the following stakeholders: the State (e.g. China), large families (e.g. Mexico), commercial banks (e.g. Germany) working with business partners (e.g. Japan), or the capital markets (e.g. in the U.K., U.S., Canada, and Australia). The author maintains that throughout the history of most nations, businesses have been created by individuals and cultivated and controlled by these founders and their family descendants. A country's corporate governance structure has a considerable impact on the success of these family businesses. While financial markets have largely supplanted governments as the primary source of financing for businesses in most developed economies and a growing number of emerging economies, governments continue to dominate economic activity in some regions. Commercial banks continue to play a critical role on the European continent and in Japan. On the other hand, capital markets are gaining traction in these countries and are therefore eroding the power of other stakeholders. National systems of corporate governance are influenced by a multitude of different laws (such as civil law, common law, and Sharia). The British empire traditionally relied on common law systems, which are built on judges' interpretations of prior rulings. Civil law systems date back to ancient Rome and are based on a codified collection of laws that are overseen by experienced judges. Sharia (or Islamic law) is a code of ethics developed from the Quran and other sacred texts.

As pointed out by Butler, developing economies have absorbed features of these legal systems while retaining important characteristics of their own, focusing on three distinct business sectors:

- A *state-owned sector* composed entirely of government-owned enterprises;
- A *listed sector* of firms that have been partially privatized and are publicly traded;
- An independent *private sector* composed of family-owned and publicly-owned enterprises.

In countries such as China, while the government continues to own and manage a substantial portion of the economy, much of the country's growth and prosperity also depend on the private sector, and China is rapidly moving toward a capital market-based system of corporate governance. Shanghai, Shenzhen, and Hong Kong all have stock exchanges that are among the largest and most active in the world. China maintains a two-tier supervisory structure for listed companies, similar to the German system, in which a supervisory board acts as a check on a board of directors. The supervisory board must have a minimum of three members, one of whom must represent employees and one of whom must represent shareholders. Managers of companies may not be members of the supervisory board. Many publicly traded companies are directly controlled or influenced by the government through members of the supervisory board (Butler, 2012).

Corporate governance pertains to the powers, rights, and duties of different corporate bodies (Shareholders' Meetings, Directors, and Boards of Supervisors) and the internal organizational structure of the corporation and its functions. More broadly, corporate governance includes all the rules that affect the governing bodies of the corporation.

There are three main corporate governance models:

1. *One tier* or the *Anglo-Saxon model,* in which the Board of Directors is appointed by a Shareholders' Meeting. Committees are established within the Board of

Directors by law or by best practice. The audit committee, for example, has the controlling function over the board and over financial issues.

2. *The two tier* or *German model*, in which the Board of Supervisors (i.e., Aufsichtstrat) is appointed by a Shareholders' Meeting and has mainly controlling functions; it can sometimes approve strategic plans and financial statements. The Board of Supervisors in turn appoints the Managing Board (i.e., Vorstand) that carries out day-to-day business.

3. *The traditional Latin model*, developed in France, Spain, and Italy (and adopted in China, Japan, and Taiwan). According to this model, the Shareholders' Meeting appoints both the Board of Directors and a separate body which has controlling function (in Italy it is called the "Collegio Sindacale").

Overview of the Alibaba Group's corporate governance

As Lin et al. (2020) represent, Alibaba, one of the world's biggest e-commerce platforms, has seen tremendous growth in its domestic market, as well as experiencing M&A expansion and structural reorganization. Founded in 1999, Alibaba has grown into an international corporation. Corporate governance has been variable and evolved over time for Alibaba. Its executive staff has been headed by founder Jack Ma since the company's inception but its ownership structure has evolved through three phases: an early phase marked by the company's openness to venture capital and private equity funds, a second phase marked by the entrance of Yahoo, and a third phase marked by its international stock market debut. Initially, Alibaba was funded by Jack Ma and his team and was rapidly opened to venture capital and private equity investors and other type of financers from the United States, Singaporean investment funds, and Sweden. Opening capital up to third parties has affected its determinations of the optimal mix of resources and dilution throughout its phases of growth. In 2005, Alibaba and Yahoo agreed upon an investment arrangement in which Yahoo bought Alibaba shares and allowed venture capital and private equity investors to withdraw. Yahoo then acquired a 40% stake in the Alibaba Group, which was equivalent to 35% of the voting rights. In 2007, the Alibaba Group's B2B subsidiary was listed on the Hong Kong Stock Exchange, providing an alternative exit strategy for the remaining venture capital backers. The Group was left with three significant stockholders: Yahoo, Jack Ma and his management team, and SoftBank.

As reconstructed by the authors, since October 2010, Yahoo's voting power has climbed from 35% to 39%, while the voting power of the Alibaba management team has declined from 35.7% to 31.7%. Yahoo obtained two board seats thanks to the influence exerted by Jack Ma and his management team on the founding group's governance, which resulted in a repurchase of 50% of Yahoo's shares in September 2012 for $6.3 billion in cash and $100 million in Alibaba Group preferred stock. Yahoo gave up the authority to choose a second board member and waived a number of vetoes over Alibaba Group's strategic and operational choices by agreeing to the transaction. Following this repurchasing, Jack Ma and his management team reclaimed control of the board. After its first public offering on the New York Stock Exchange, the ownership structure of the Alibaba Group changed to the following: SoftBank (32.4%), Yahoo (16.3%), and Jack Ma and his management team (13.1%) controlled overall the 61.8% of the Alibaba Group. With access to the world's biggest capital market, the United States, the Alibaba Group has been subject to a class action lawsuit in the United States initiated by seven law firms for alleged "regulatory concealment of investigations." Many Chinese firms has historically opted to list and seek funding in the United States, being one of world's most sophisticated financial capital markets also characterized by stringent market regulation that protects investors. The required additional laws and regulations imposed upon the overseas IPOs translates into higher legal risks and expenditures, as it was in the case of Alibaba and other international firms that have chosen to list in the United States.

The Alibaba Group, which has a dual-class share structure, was interested in the NYSE listing also because it enables firms to arrange themselves differently than the standard 'one share, one vote' structure. The rationale behind dual-class share arrangements is that founders of businesses want to retain control even after they are publicly traded. Dual-class shares may provide more voting rights to certain owners than others. Major organizations such as Google, Groupon, and Facebook, as well as other technology companies, have implemented dual-class shares. Prior to their popularity among technology businesses, dual-class shares were most prevalent among media organizations such as the *New York Times*, *Washington Post*, and News Corp. The dual-class structure was believed to aid in the preservation of the journalistic integrity of these media businesses. Proponents of dual-class shares claim that the structure enables them to prioritize long-term profits above short-term gains while on the other hand creates a discrepancy between economic exposure and actual influence (Lin et al., 2020).

In all three models, it is mandatory to have an external independent auditor that controls the financial statements of the company. An exception worth mentioning is the German "Co-Determination" governance model (*Mitbestimmung*), which involves mandatory employee representation on the Board of Supervisors of larger corporations. All corporations with more than 2,000 employees must have a supervisory board elected half by shareholders and half by employees. All corporations with more than 500 employees must have a supervisory board, one-third of whose members are elected by employees. Co-determination is not applicable to corporations with political, religious, charitable, scientific, artistic, or journalist purposes, out of respect for their freedom of speech, religion, and thought. The co-determination model is also used in Luxembourg, France, Sweden, Denmark, Austria, and the Netherlands. There was also a proposal to apply the model in the U.K., but it was rejected.

14.2.2 Corporate governance: key tools

Where in Europe are minorities best protected?

After examining different forms of shareholder protection legislation, it's natural to wonder whether there is a clear leader in terms of which regulatory frameworks best protect shareholders. Establishing a ranking based on theoretical norms may be ineffective, since how legislation plays out in practice often deviates from theory. Examining actual data to determine which European nations draw, for example, the most activists might represent a better indication of efficacy.

Several past empirical studies have attempted to address the subject in this way. For instance, Becht, Franks, Mayer, and Rossi (2009) analyze the Hermes U.K. Focus Fund's private engagements, concluding that U.K. regulatory and legal frameworks are particularly conducive to investor engagement. They cite 30 cases in the UK of strong performance by a single fund between 1998 and 2004. This assessment verifies Armour's and Skeel's (2007) findings that lobbying and legislation aimed at minority protection are highly beneficial for U.K. active investors. More recently, according to Activist Insight (2020), the number of publicly traded firms susceptible to activist participation expanded fast in 2020, 40% over the previous year; despite the significant impact of Covid-19 on investments, existing circumstances support a swift rebound. Additionally, the report's authors state that most enthusiasm stems from the Brexit referendum, which weakened the pound and pushed the FTSE 100 and FTSE 25 (two indices for U.K.-listed firms) higher. Indeed, from 2017 to 2020, political volatility was a significant factor impeding activity.

Germany is also regarded as a very "activist-friendly" nation. In 2017, Activist Insight stated that, though interactions had risen over the previous two years, they were still in their infancy. In 2021, Germany was considered one of the top European targets for activists. While Germany has always been a difficult environment for activist investors – with cultural and legislative barriers such as the popular two-tiered board structure and the predominance of family ownership in company equities – since 2017 German institutions and public opinion have become more receptive to activist interventions, seeing activists as supportive investors seeking to unlock value for shareholders rather than as adversaries seeking to strip companies of their valuable assets for personal gain. Moreover, the aforementioned legislative features provide a robust framework for minority protection, which activists applaud (Venezia, 2021).

Source: Venezia, M.V. (2021). *Corporate Ownership and Shareholder Activism: A Pan-European Analysis with a Focus on Italy*. Master Thesis in International Management, Bocconi University, Supervisor Prof. Gimede Gigante.

Since the General Meeting and the Board of Directors are two of the most important tools protecting investors and enabling proper corporate functioning, it is worth analyzing their roles more in detail:

- The *General Meeting* is where shareholders come together and cast their votes. This can, and generally is, an Annual General Meeting (AGM), where the Annual Report, remuneration, Board renewal, and other recurring events can also take place. If certain specific matters (such as a share class conversion) are on the agenda, this can also be called an Extraordinary General Meeting (EGM), where there is need of a reinforced majority. Otherwise, it is more simply called a General Meeting (GM). Depending on the company's by-laws and jurisdiction, such meetings can be called by any shareholder with at least 5% ownership to vote on non-extraordinary items (i.e., a Board change). For example, when a fund wants to promote a change, sometimes the matter is brought up to all shareholders to express their vote. This can be done by the Board of Directors, which decides the agenda of the general meeting, or by the fund itself, which, depending on by-laws and jurisdiction, can add an item to the agenda even with a 2% stake or can call a new General Meeting with a 5% stake.
- The *Board of Directors* is an additional tool for corporate governance and can be composed of different categories of directors:
  - *Chairman/President*: this figure is entrusted with the power and responsibility of calling and running meetings, setting the agenda, conducting the discussion, and enforcing voting procedures.
  - *Executive Directors*: these are employees with high-level managerial responsibilities.
  - *Non-Executive Directors*: these members have a seat on the board but do not have any specific role in the company.

- *Independent Directors*: these are board members who have no significant personal, financial, or professional relationship with the corporation. They are crucial in resolving situations in which other board members have conflicts of interests. Sometimes, these positions are mandated by law.

For example, in Italy the *"Testo Unico della Finanza"* requires that if the Board of a listed corporation has more than four members, at least one must meet independence requirements. These requirements (according to Article 148, Section 3) specify that:

- Independent Directors cannot be spouses or relatives up to the fourth degree of the Directors of the company (and controlled entities); or
- Persons linked to the company (or their controlled entity).

For the Italian Stock Exchange, these requirements are recommended to become a listed company but not mandatory:

- An adequate number of Independent Directors (on average, 4 out of 10, according to the 2013 survey of listed Italian corporations).[1]
- Stricter independence.

The number of directors appointed by minority shareholders should reflect the following formula:

$$min \ \# \ votes = \frac{\# \ directors_{wanted} \times shares_{present}}{\# \ vacancies + 1} + 1$$

According to Lin (2001), the tools described above provide only a skeletal structure for corporate governance, and the effectiveness – as well as the very existence – of corporate governance depends entirely on how this framework is fleshed out.

According to Lin (2001), the key elements are:

- Statutory provisions, particularly those relating to the definition and exercise of shareholders' rights.
- Monitoring, compliance, and enforceability of these legal and other statutory requirements.
- Ownership concentration or dispersal.
- Board attributes, such as the composition, representativeness, independence, and qualifications of board members, as well as the existence of sub-committees.
- Supporting checks and balances.
- Accounting standards.
- Product market competitiveness.
- Managerial job market competitiveness.

---

[1] For more information see Alvaro, S., Ciccaglioni, P. & Siciliano, G. (2013). *L'autodisciplina in materia di corporate governance: un'analisi dell'esperienza italiana.* Consob. Available at https://www.consob.it/documents/11973/201676/qg2.pdf/47a2d9ce-6165-4d1f-a746-62d5bbe889e1

- The efficiency and competitiveness of financial markets, and the provision of financial discipline and incentives, especially in equity markets where shareholders can exercise their "vote."
- Cultural and historical factors, which strongly influence business organizations, practices, and the passivity or activism of shareholders in governance.

14.2.3 The agency problem

Madoff's fraud

As Gupta et al. (2009) report, on December 10, 2008, Bernard Madoff, a well-known Wall Street trader and former NASDAQ chairman, admitted to running a $50 billion Ponzi scheme.[2] Madoff acknowledged conducting a Ponzi scam through his firm, Bernard L. Madoff Investment Securities LLC., which specialized in investment management and advisory services (BLMIS).

According to the federal complaint, the deception began in the 1980s, when BLMIS established its investment management and advisory department. The department was charged with investing clients' funds in common stocks, options, and other securities of well-known and prominent companies. Clients were also guaranteed that, if they desired, their principal amount of investment and profits earned to that point would be returned. Instead of investing the cash in the securities market, BLMIS's advisory and investment management arm would deposit the entire amount in an account at Chase Manhattan Bank. When redemption requests were received, they were handled using the bank account's pooled funds. On December 11, 2008, Madoff was arrested and admitted to the colossal scam, which the SEC and other authorities had failed to notice for years.

Source: Gupta, V. & Chakraborty, B. (2009). *The 'Bernard Madoff' Financial Scam*. IBS Center for Management Research.

Agency problem is a conflict of interest that occurs when agents do not fully represent the best interests of principals. In the framework of corporate governance outlined above, agency problems can emerge between management and the Board of Directors or between the Board and shareholders. There are famous examples of agency problems that became extremely damaging for companies, such as the Enron scandal in 2001 or the Bernie Madoff scam in 2008. Indeed, the administration structure of corporations presents the risk that directors put their interests before shareholder interests, especially when it comes to remuneration, poor efforts, transfer of corporate opportunities, free-riding, and so on. This is related to the very definition of the principal-agent relationship, which is a fiduciary relationship established when a person (i.e., the "principal") grants consent to another person (i.e., the "agent") to act on his/her behalf and under his/her general control, and the agent accepts this responsibility.

---

[2] A Ponzi scheme is a deceptive investment strategy that promises huge returns with no risk to investors. A Ponzi scheme is a kind of investment fraud in which money is collected from later investors to pay off previous investors. This is comparable to a pyramid scam in that both rely on money provided by new investors to pay back previous investors. When the influx of new investors slows and there is not enough money to go around, both Ponzi and pyramid schemes inevitably collapse. Available at https://www.investopedia.com/terms/p/ponzischeme.asp.

When management or the majority of the Board act in their own interests instead of in the interest of shareholders, detrimental choices can be made that put the financial soundness of the corporation at risk. Although the examples mentioned above of Enron and Bernie Madoff are indeed criminal, it is important to note that the actions of management do not necessarily have to be criminal to be damaging or negative for investors. In fact, there are several choices that could harm shareholders indirectly, though they are not against the law. For instance, top management can receive a very high remuneration (approved by the Board), irrespective of the actual performance of the company. More subtly, if the Board of a very large company sponsoring major events worldwide had access to free tickets, hospitality, etc., would the Board be willing to split the company in two if it were better for shareholders, even though that would mean losing most of these privileges and benefits?

Corporate governance also refers to the ways the agency problem is addressed. Indeed, to mitigate such issues a corporation can take a number of actions:

a.   Clearly set a limit on the actions of directors.
b.   Remunerate with stock options.
c.   Perform monitoring by other stakeholders (banks, law firms, etc.).
d.   Establish competition among companies.
e.   Adopt rules that align with corporate law.

As highlighted above, unsuitable corporate governance can cause serious damage to companies. Indeed, many of the biggest failures in corporate history have been related to failures in corporate governance. This can start from inappropriate management incentives or poor control of the Board of Directors by auditors. The problem of poor corporate governance is that investors do not have access to accurate representations of reality. With sound governance, investors can instead price risk and allow the "right" investor to own the "right" asset.

The Board's contribution to the failure of Enron Corp

As Maleki et al. (2004) pointed out, the deregulation of energy in the mid-1980s created enormous new potential for the young company Enron operating in the industry. The company was a pioneer in trading, marketing, and monetizing natural gas and electricity across a range of industries, from energy to the Internet. During Enron's heyday, the company was celebrated by the media, business and academia for gracefully transforming itself from a regional energy company to an innovative global player. By 2000, it was ranked seventh on the Fortune 500 list, with sales exceeding $100 billion.

However, when market values plummeted in early 2001, Enron's stock price also collapsed and in October of that year, Enron reported a third-quarter loss of $618 million, decreasing its net worth by $1.2 billion; in November 2001, the company filed a Form 8-K9 with the Securities and Exchange Commission, notifying the SEC of its plan to restate its financial accounts.

Enron's stock price then fell below $1 that month after Dynegy Corporation, which had agreed to acquire Enron for $10 billion, withdrew when Enron's debt was downgraded to "junk" and incorrect debt and cash flow figures were discovered in Enron's financial statements.

Enron filed for bankruptcy in December 2001, declaring $13.1 billion in debt for the main company and $18.1 billion in debt for its affiliates. Enron's internal and external control failures explain the company's demise, the seventh largest bankruptcy in U.S. history.

The reasons for Enron's downfall seem to be limitless and range from misleading accounting methods to the inability of external auditor Arthur Andersen LLP (Andersen) and the Securities and Exchange Commission (SEC) to oversee the company to the inability of banks and analysts to truly assess the risk of non-performing assets on Enron's balance sheet (very risky and unprofitable foreign investments and projects).

It appears that Enron's Board of Directors allowed the perpetuation of the factors that brought the company to its knees by remaining silent, even though it was the only body capable of overseeing both internal abuses at Enron and external abuses by the company's independent legal and accounting advisors. The Board of Directors, on the other hand, looked out for its own interests and protected itself by approving exorbitant compensation plans for the company's executives through its compensation committee, approving incentives to the last and totaling in 2001 more than $750 million in cash awarded for work completed in 2000, despite the fact that the company's total net income was $975 million in 2000.

Since Enron's inception in 1985, Andersen had served as both an independent auditor and an internal consultant. The Board never raised concerns about the company's non-accounting activities, which Andersen called "high-risk accounting procedures," and benefited from the audit firm's inherent conflict of interest.

Banks and analysts were the second source of external controls beyond the accounting firm, but routinely overlooked Enron's poor overseas operations and ever-increasing debt (despite low asset values) to preserve Enron's "investment-grade" credit rating.

Source: Maleki, A. & Schwalbach, J. (2004). *Enron: The Role of the Board in the Collapse of Enron Corporation.* Discussion Papers 2004, Humboldt-Universität zu Berlin, Institut für Management Malik.

14.2.4 The power of directors vs. shareholders

Another critical corporate governance topic relates to the power to manage the corporation, which is vested in the Board of Directors. The Board often delegates this power to executive directors and the managers of the corporation. There are differences in the power that directors or shareholders hold in given situations. For instance, the Shareholders' Meeting has some ability to manage the corporation in case of extraordinary transactions (M&As, spin-offs). Directors manage the corporation, while shareholders instead express their will by voting on fundamental corporate transactions and electing the directors who will represent them. Shareholders can also amend governing documents (Articles of Incorporation or Bylaws), though there are differences in this regard between the U.S. and civil law systems. More specifically, in the U.S. shareholder approval is necessary to amend the articles of incorporation, but these amendments need to be proposed by the directors. In Europe or Japan, on the other hand, shareholders have more power to amend the AOI or Bylaws. This is especially true in civil law systems with concentrated ownership structures.

14.3 Investing

The second section of this chapter will be dedicated to defining investing and the difference between passive and active investors. In order to start with the basics, we will devote an entire section to the topic of investing, since sometimes the media and film industry depict investors negatively as irresponsible gamblers. Think about Michael Douglas as the notorious Gordon Gekko in the movie *Wall Street* (1987), Danny de Vito in *Other People's Money* (1991), Ben Affleck in *Boiler Room* (2001), Leo Di Caprio as Jordan Belfort in the *Wolf of Wall Street* (2013) or Ryan Gosling as the Deutsche Bank banker in *The Big Short* (2015). These films share several common features, especially the depiction of investors as handsome, rich, and immoral men. From such movies, one gets the impression that investing is akin to gambling – or even worse, gambling with other people's money! Yet there is no worse offence for a real investor than being considered a gambler. Real-life investors share the same objectives as these fictional representations: maximizing profits, or more simply, making money. However, phrases such as "betting on a stock" strengthen erroneous views of investing. Gambling is based on luck, and, although some people buy and sell stocks by basing their decision on luck, we cannot call this investing. One key litmus test distinguishing investors from gamblers is consistency of returns over time. Some individuals may make stellar returns for a few years and then see terrible negative performance. This is probably a good indicator that such an individual is a (possibly very successful) gambler and not an investor.

As we explain below, investing leaves little room for luck and is instead based primarily on strategic thinking and concrete analysis.

14.3.1 The definition of investing

Before we approach the topic of investing, it is important to make some distinctions in terms of the definition of this activity.

Investing refers to the act of taking on risk exposure in relation to the asset of a corporation. Whether investors are buying equity or debt, what they receive is analogous: exposure to an asset. Although the risk profile of equity and debt varies, the primary focus is always the asset. Depending on how the risk of an asset is priced, an investor will choose to invest using either equity (more risk on the downside in exchange for the upside), debt (more protection but a more limited upside), or a broad range of financial instruments engineered to better fit the risk profile of the investor. Indeed, when selecting the investment instrument, an investor must keep in mind that equity and debt mirror of a company's assets and that the difference between them lies in their exposure to risk.

Some further distinctions can be made concerning investing. For instance, we can distinguish between primary and secondary investing. The former occurs when new capital is invested in exchange for exposure to an asset (i.e., debt or equity newly issued by a company). Secondary investing occurs when capital is invested to buy exposure to an asset previously held by somebody else (i.e., debt or equity sold by another lender or shareholder). Another distinction is represented by the difference between public and private investing: publicly traded exposures are represented by stocks and bonds, while privately traded ones include private equity or loans.

Investing therefore means buying exposure to an asset. Thus all investors – from the individual who owns one share of a company to the large investment fund managing trillions of dollars – believe that the value of the asset will generate value to remunerate their risk. As a company grows its assets, liabilities are secured by more assets and the cost of risk therefore decreases; the value of the equity increases by the same net amount of the cash paid to service the liabilities, in accordance to the balance sheet structure (**Figure 14.1**). In exchange for taking a higher risk, the equity holders (shareholders) are able to vote and appoint the Board of Directors – a power that debt holders generally do not possess. Therefore, by appointing directors to the Board so that the company can prosper, the shareholders have a responsibility towards both the company and its debt holders.

Figure 14.1   Balance sheet structure

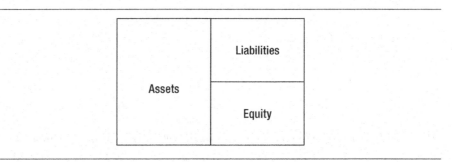

14.3.2 Principles of investing

Benjamin Graham (1959) – an economist, professor, and American entrepreneur – articulated a fundamental rule of investing: *do not lose money*. Another important concept to bear in mind is that there is a perfect correlation between risk and reward. The riskier the asset, the higher the upside (and the higher the probability of a downside). No risk implies no high return. Consider for instance a debt investor. If a company is large, with low leverage and stable growth, the price of risk will be low. This would be the right type of exposure for banks. Should this company experience financial distress, however, then the cost of risk would increase and the right lender would instead be one with higher risk tolerance, such as a high yield or even distressed investor.

14.3.3 Active vs. passive

Having described investing and its main features, it is time to look at a salient distinction in the investment world: active versus passive investing. According to Mäntysaari (2005) in the book *Comparative Corporate Governance: Shareholders as a*

Rule-maker, active shareholders are involved in the business of a company: they operate the business or at least have a say in how it should be run, and therefore influence company decisions and use voting and other rights. *Passive shareholders*, on the other hand, are only investors; they rely merely on the rules that govern corporate management. Applying this definition, most of today's financial investors are passive shareholders. The only exclusions would be controlling shareholders, who operate the business, and activist investors who are vocal in expressing their views.

On the other hand, if we consider financial intermediaries and operators, a much more interesting definition of active and passive funds emerges. A *passive fund* is an investment vehicle that tracks a market index to determine the security where it invests; a passively managed fund implies lower costs and allows investors to profit from the inevitable long-term success of the market. In a passive fund, there is no discretion in buying or selling securities, since the objective is to replicate the index. Also known as index funds, these vehicles cannot sell securities if they are unhappy with their strategies. The main advantage of these funds, and in part the reason for their success, is their low cost to investors.

In 1976, the first passive fund was created by John Bogle,[3] founder of The Vanguard Group (one of the biggest passive asset managers, managing $6.7 trillion as of February 2021). This passive fund or index fund revolutionized financial markets. The new format was a response to investors who were frustrated because they believed that actively managed funds failed to produce sufficient returns despite their high fees. The success of passive funds is such that Moody's Investors Service Inc. recently predicted that they would surpass actively managed assets by 2024.

In 2005, Warren Buffet, probably the world's most famous investor who runs and controls Berkshire Hathaway, argued that active investment managed by professionals – in aggregate – would over a period of years underperform the returns achieved by rank amateurs who simply sat still.

Subsequently, he offered to wager $500,000 that no investment professional could select a set of at least five hedge funds that over an extended period would have matched the performance of an unmanaged S&P-500 index fund charging only token fees in a ten-year period (picking the low-cost Vanguard S&P fund as contender).

Ted Seides[4] from a fund of funds called Protégé Partners picked five funds-of-funds whose results were to be averaged and compared them magainst Vanguard S&P index fund.

---

[3] John Clifton "Jack" Bogle (May 8, 1929 – January 16, 2019) was an American philanthropist, investor, and business entrepreneur. He founded and led The Vanguard Group and is credited with inventing the index fund. As an active investor and money manager, Bogle emphasized investing over speculation, long-term patience over quick action, and minimizing broker costs to the greatest extent feasible. Bogle's ideal investment vehicle was a low-cost index fund maintained for the duration of his life, with dividends reinvested and purchases made using dollar cost averaging. His 1999 book *Common Sense on Mutual Funds: New Imperatives for the Intelligent Investor* was a blockbuster and is widely regarded as a classic in the financial world.

[4] Ted Seides, CFA founded Capital Allocators LLC to research asset management best practices. He created the Capital Allocators podcast in 2017, and by December 2021, the program had amassed eight million downloads. The Brunswick Group dubbed it the best institutional investment podcast, while

The five funds-of-funds he selected had invested their money in more than 100 hedge funds, which meant that the overall performance of the funds-of-funds would not be distorted by the good or poor results of a single manager.

Each fund-of-funds operated with a layer of fees that sat above the fees charged by the hedge funds in which it had invested.

Results from Berkshire Hathaway 2016 Annual Report are shown in **Table 14.1**.

Many observations can be made here. We could argue that things would have been different if, instead of five FOFs, we picked five top hedge funds run by the world's best fund managers, but that was not the case.

Another interesting thing to consider is that this analysis includes no indication of volatility. Volatility is a metric that some investors see as critically important. Indeed, volatility reduction is among the many value propositions of a hedge fund. In the end, however, it is evident that buying into an S&P index fund would have allowed investors to double their investments.

Table 14.1   **Return of FoFs by year**

Year	Fund of Fund A	Fund of Fund B	Fund of Fund C	Fund of Fund D	Fund of Fund E	S&P Index
2008	−16.5%	−22.3%	−21.3%	−29.3%	−30.1%	−37.0%
2009	11.3%	14.5%	21.4%	16.5%	16.8%	26.6%
2010	5.9%	6.8%	13.3%	4.9%	11.9%	15.1%
2011	−6.3%	−1.3%	5.9%	−6.3%	−2.8%	2.1%
2012	3.4%	9.6%	5.7%	6.2%	9.1%	16.0%
2013	10.5%	15.2%	8.8%	14.2%	14.4%	32.3%
2014	4.7%	4.0%	18.9%	0.7%	−2.1%	13.6%
2015	1.6%	2.5%	5.4%	1.4%	−5.0%	1.4%
2016	−2.9%	1.7%	−1.4%	2.5%	4.4%	11.9%
Gain to date	8.7%	28.3%	62.8%	2.9%	7.5%	85.4%

Barron's, *Business Insider, Forbes*, and Value Walk all named it one of the best investing podcasts. Along with the show, Ted consults managers and allocators, using his experience and contacts to assist them in increasing their profits. In March 2021, he launched his second book, *Capital Allocators: How the World's Elite Money Managers Lead and Invest*, which distills essential lessons from the podcast's first 150 episodes. He founded Protégé Partners LLC in 2002 and served as President and Co-Chief Investment Officer from 2002 until 2015. Protégé was a multibillion-dollar alternative investment organization focused on seeding and investing in tiny hedge funds. Ted was covered in the 2010 book *Top Hedge Fund Investors* by Larry Kochard and Cathleen Rittereiser. Ted published his first book, *So You Want to Start a Hedge Fund: Lessons for Managers and Allocators*, in 2016 to share his expertise and lessons learned.

14.3.4 Passive funds and corporate governance

Appel et al. (2015) have hypothesized that, contrary to their initial suspicions, passive investors have incentive to be involved in the governance of the companies in which they hold shares, because they cannot sell their positions. This is becoming more evident as governance becomes increasingly important for passive funds. The summary in **Figure 14.2** by Lazard shows how the largest three passive funds work constructively towards better governance in the companies in which they invest.

Figure 14.2   **Example of investment in governance**

BlackRock	Vanguard	State Street
Reshaping Finance	**Principles of good governance**	**The importance of responsibility**
• BlackRock believes that **climate change is reshaping finance** and hence wants portfolio companies to: – Discuss UN Sustainable – Development Goals – Disclose climate risks – Follow Sustainability Accounting Board guidelines • **BlackRock will enforce this** by voting against directors who don't implement the above by 2020 • **Other actions by BlackRock on climate change**: – Sustainable investment strategies – ESG incorporated as core risk – Exit high risk sectors and double ESG offering – Improving Transparency	Vanguard established 4 principles of good governance: • **Board Composition**: incorporating independent directors, disclosing Board diversity and long-term board strategies • **Oversight of Strategy & Risk**: oversight is a Board responsibility – they should be involved in the execution; long-term risks should be disclosed appropriately • **Executive Compensation**: to be performance-linked to incentivize long-term performance • **Governance Structures**: to protect shareholder rights. Boards must also be held accountable to shareholders	• State Street believes that **ESG concerns are closely tied to shareholder value** • The company will implement the use of the **R-Factor** (i.e., responsibility factor) to evaluate the companies that respect ESG in the long term – The R-Factor is an ESG scoring system that measures the "performance of a company's business operations and governance as it relates to financially material ESG challenges facing the company's industry" • From 2020 SS took appropriate **voting action against companies with low R-Factors** who are not planning to improve it • From 2022 SS will **vote against Directors at companies whose R-Factor lags peers**

Source: Author's elaboration of *Lazard's Quarterly Review of Shareholder Activism – Q1 2020*.

14.3.5 Active funds

In active funds, the fund or portfolio manager decides in which securities to invest. In active funds a key role is played by the fund or *portfolio manager* (PM) who makes investment decisions. Depending on the fund strategy and its proposition to

investors, the spectrum of possible investments can be more or less wide. Many active funds have benchmarks which they aim to beat, mainly in terms of absolute performance or mitigation of volatility. For example, the PM of a long-only equity fund
that uses the S&P500 as a benchmark will be more likely to have the majority of its
portfolio invested in U.S. stocks with a relatively high weight in the S&P500, which
they believe will perform better than others. For a PM in a multi-strategy hedge fund,
on the contrary, the objective is to generate absolute returns, with no limitation on asset class or benchmark index. This PM will have a wider variety of options with regards to capital structure and the possibility of virtually taking long or short exposure to any investable asset in the world.
If we return to the Mäntysaari (2005) definition of active and passive shareholders,
within active funds most of investors are passive as they buy and sell stocks with little interaction with management, they partially diversify by not holding concentrated
portfolios (even though in sell-offs this correlations go to 1).

However, a more limited yet growing number of active funds take on the role of
active shareholders. The public perception of shareholder activism involves a precise investment strategy based on buying something that is undervalued and being
vocal in advocating changes to its managing board. However, this representation is
misleading, because activism, as defined above, is only one of the tools available to
active shareholders to create value for investors. The *active shareholder assumption*
holds that the fair value and market value of an asset can differ based on a multitude
of factors, including investors' appetites for certain industries and geographies or the
strategies taken by the Board, which may not maximize the asset's potential. This
assumption is based on the conviction that markets are not perfect. In other words,
markets do not price everything correctly, contrary to what many economists believe.

Consider for instance Company A, which has two divisions, one which generates
energy and the other which is a construction business. The two businesses follow two
different cycles: the energy business is stable and predictable, while the construction
business is much more cyclical. Given its higher predictability, the energy business is
also valued at higher multiples than the construction business. If we assume that the
two businesses have the exact same EBITDA, in theory the company should trade at
the average between the energy multiple and the construction multiple. In practice,
however, the implied trading multiple will be lower because of the so-called *holding
discount*. In simple terms, the holding discount arises from the fact that there is no
right investor for the asset: the energy investor will not like the exposure to the construction business, and the construction investor will not like paying a higher price
for the asset due to the energy business. Hence, it would be lucrative, at least theoretically, to separate the two businesses, for instance via a spin-off. Using this approach,
all investors will receive one share of the energy business and one of the construction
business; they can therefore decide to retain the business they like and sell the other.
This is sometimes called financial engineering.

Altering the example, what if the construction business becomes underinvested
because all its capital expenditures (i.e., Capex) are devoted to the more profitable energy segment? This would make perfect sense for a CEO and for a Board. However,

in the long term, the market share in the construction business would be lost, and at some point the division would cease to be profitable. As a result, the business might close, with serious consequences for its employees and stakeholders. The question is, why not sell the construction business beforehand to allow it to continue doing business? In such a case, middle management might be supportive but top management and the Board could oppose the move, since it would result in a company of half the size. This would not only mean less power and influence but also less diversification.

To take up another example, in companies with different shareholder remuneration policies, why might two (hypothetical) identical companies pay different dividends to shareholders? When companies are controlled by one shareholder, the Board follows the vision of that shareholder and other shareholders (minorities) follow. If the controlling shareholder does something in their own interest that operates against the interest of other shareholders, the minorities will fight to defend their rights. When companies are not controlled, the risk of an agency problem is high, since the Board is not accountable to a stable, solid counterpart.

When a controlling shareholder has significant influence and exerts accountability over top management, passive funds often argue that they represent a similar degree of influence and accountability over management, since as stable counterparts, they cannot sell their stakes in the company. While this may be true, in this case the issue is one of capacity. As passive funds reflect investments in thousands of stocks, it becomes impossible for them to monitor all those companies with the same depth as an investor managing a very concentrated portfolio of five stocks, for example. Moreover, the low fee charged to investors does not allow for the deep and detailed assessment necessary to determine whether the strategies taken by the boards of each company are in the best interest of all shareholders. Therefore, despite being increasingly important and useful, passive funds alone can fix only part of the agency problem.

14.3.6 Opponents

Opponents of activism, such as prominent corporate adviser Lipton (2013), argue that it is detrimental to the long-term interests of companies and their shareholders. Activism may pump-up short-term stock prices and benefit the activists (who, according to Lipton, do not stick around to "eat their own cooking"), but it harms shareholders in the long run. Lipton (2013), for example, has argued that what is most important for companies subject to hedge-fund activism is "the impact on their operational performance and stock price performance relative to the benchmark, not just in the short period after announcement of the activist interest, but after a 24-month period."

Is this claim true? In a comprehensive empirical study, *The Long-Term Effects of Hedge Fund Activism*, Bebchuk et al. (2015) find that it is not:

> During the five-year period following the intervention month, operating performance relative to peers improves consistently. We also examined whether, as opponents claim, the initial stock-price spike accompanying interventions, which we find to be

approximately 6%, is reversed in the long term. Using each of these methods, we look for evidence of the asserted long-term underperformance of companies that were the targets of activist interventions. As we discuss below, we find no evidence for the existence of the asserted long-term negative returns in the data.

14.4 Shareholder activism

14.4.1 Active shareholders

The backbone of value investing resides in evaluation of an asset's fair value. If, compared to the market value, there is enough gap to remunerate for the risk taken by the investor, then the investor identifies a path to value creation. The *path may or may not involve an active role for the investor*. For a passive shareholder, the target company will have to follow that path independently. For an active shareholder, engagement will begin between the investor and the management or the Board. The company may have very good reasons for not following that path, which from an outside perspective can be difficult to appreciate but may become clear through constructive dialogue. In some circumstances, there can be different views held by the investor and the Board or the management team. At this crossroad, most active investors will decide to sell the stock if they do not believe the company is on the right track. Others will work further to make their case, and this is when some funds use an additional tool called *shareholder activism*. Shareholder activism represents a range of activities fulfilled by one or more shareholders of a publicly traded company to determine changes in the corporation that will improve performances and create value. These methods include, among others, dialoguing with the management, using media channels to publicize their requests and pressure managers, and formally advancing proposals at shareholders' meetings.

Given that the fund involved in shareholder activism does not have control over the asset, it needs to convince other shareholders of the merits of its case. To use activism, the amount of work required to analyze an asset and have enough conviction to back the investment thesis is huge and often involves the aid of external professionals. This may include working with private consultants or consulting companies to obtain industry insights and better understand the sector and its competition dynamics. Important advice is often attained by engaging law firms, for instance, to understand if an envisioned path is achievable (consider an asset spin-off and the legal complexity involved). Nevertheless, though connection with consultants, lawyers, and bankers is extremely helpful, the ultimate call is always made by the fund or portfolio manager.

Considering the processes and parties described above, active funds are more expensive than passive funds for investors. Indeed, the typical fee structure of an active funds is based on a 2% management fee and 20% performance fee. The investor's judgement is essential to deciding which among thousands of active funds have the right to earn those fees.

It is common to have the wrong perception of shareholder activism. In fact, it can often remind people of political activism (which is very loud) and of terms such as "activist campaign," "board coup," etc., which can have a negative connotation. Even in funds that are known as activist, there is usually no hostility with the board or management. Moreover, due to the increased use of activist tools, boards and management teams are becoming increasingly willing to listen to such shareholders, and in most cases, an agreement is found among parties with no public disclosure. Dialogue between the investor and the company may even end up with the fund going public in support of the management and the Board of Directors. In some circumstances, activism involves making a public case and engaging with other shareholders to gather support for the envisioned path to value creation.

Sometimes, the activist's case has enough support to make the Board change paths; the company may even end up with a new Board and management. Other times, other shareholders do not agree with the activist's proposal and there is no change of path. Activism does not work without the broader shareholder base becoming engaged and convinced that the activist's position is in the interest of all shareholders (and stakeholders). The activist case must therefore be highly compelling.

14.4.2 A brief history of the evolution of shareholder activism

The origins and history of shareholder activism can be traced back to Isaac Le Marie,[5] a significant shareholder in the Dutch East India Company in the seventeenth century. Investors like Benjamin Graham,[6] and John Paul Getty[7] are more recent instances of shareholder activism. The so-called "Wall Street walk" was formerly the most popular tactic employed by investors who disagreed with management: the term was used to describe situations when a significant shareholder threatened to sell stocks and liquidate their stake because of discontent with the governance or company's strategy.

---

[5] Isaac Le Maire (c. 1558 in Tournai – 20 September 1624 in Egmond aan den Hoef) was a Walloon entrepreneur, investor, and significant stakeholder in the Dutch East India Company (VOC).

[6] Benjamin Graham was an American businessman, entrepreneur, and economist. Graham is widely regarded as the first economist to develop the concept of value investing, which he began teaching at Columbia Business School in 1928 and later improved with David Dodd in several versions of the book *Security Analysis*. Following this publishing success, Graham wrote a handbook for investors, *The Intelligent Investor*, which was first published in 1949. *The Intelligent Investor* established the foundation for investor activism.

[7] Jean Paul Getty was a businessman in the United States and the founder of the Getty Oil Company. In 1957, *Fortune* magazine labelled him the wealthiest American alive, and in 1966, the *Guinness Book of World Records* named him the world's wealthiest private individual, valued at about $9 billion in today's money. He authored many books, including the internationally successful *How to Be Rich* and autobiography, *As I See It*. He passed away in 1976.

Graham's golden rules for investing

Individual investors, according to Graham, "lack the time and temperament to monitor their assets frequently." As a result, amateur investors should invest with "simpler, longer-term goals" than professionals. Graham averages profits over a seven- to ten-year period to assess a company's true earning capacity. This prevents the investor from being taken advantage of by a company that uses insider knowledge to make earnings look bigger than they are. In assessing a company's success, Graham outlines essential criteria: profitability, stability, growth, financial health, dividends, and pricing history. The key principles identified in *The Intelligent Investor* can be simplified into seven golden rules for investing:

1) The company you invest in must be of sufficient size to provide some stability. Because investments are particularly vulnerable to economic circumstances, they should not be made in companies that are not adequately funded. Size is determined by turnover, which must be at least $100 million for industrial companies and no less than $50 million for utilities. Obviously, during those years everything had to be tied the U.S. stock market.
2) The financial status of the company must be stable. Companies with a high amount of debt and a poor payment record are not rewarded by the market. The ratio of total assets to total debt is one measure for determining financial strength. If it is greater than 2, it indicates that the company's obligations are covered primarily by capital.
3) The company's profits must be consistent over time. A company that earns a lot in one year and then fluctuates between profits and losses is not a reliable company that can provide assurance. Earnings must be consistent for at least ten years before a company can be considered truly profitable.
4) The company must pay dividends. A company that pays dividends is profitable and compensates its owners. Of course, consistency is required, so coupons must be paid regularly for at least 20 years.
5) Profits must increase steadily. A company must evolve and expand to avoid being absorbed by competitors over time. Accordingly, earnings must increase over time, at least by one-third over the previous ten years.
6) Multiples should be kept separate. A ratio greater than 15 on average for the previous three years between the price of shares traded in the market and expected earnings indicates that the company is overvalued. Another metric to consider is the inverse of the multiple, which is the ratio of expected earnings to price. If this is higher than the long-term rate of highly rated bonds, the stock should be evaluated for inclusion in the portfolio.
7) The stock price should not be high relative to assets. When the stock is valued at 1.5 times the value of the company's equity, the market may have overpriced the company.

The situation changed in the 1950s with the establishment of mutual funds. Mutual funds exacerbated the agency problem, supporting the growth of more "modern" shareholder activism. At the time, activism was mostly associated with the United States. Shareholder activism gained more international recognition in the 1980s, with activists called *corporate raiders*. These activists acquired huge ownership shares in public firms through hostile takeovers (i.e., takeovers not endorsed by the management) that replaced managers or forced them to change strategies. *White knights* emerged as a counterpart to corporate raiders. The task of these investors was to present a more palatable alternative to shareholders by proposing to purchase the firm.

Although the techniques of today's shareholder activists are markedly different from those of corporate raiders, many of the investment funds leading the current market were founded in the 1980s. Furthermore, shareholder activism is a much more prevalent phenomena nowadays; indeed, in the last decade, activism has become a prominent trend in Europe. According to research firm Insightia,[8] 810 publicly traded firms (127 of which were in Europe) were subject to public activist demands in 2020 – a significantly greater number than the 476 companies in 2014. One of the factors contributing to the rise of activism is the increased amount of capital coming into investment funds, which have become an attractive investment, particularly in today's low-interest climate.

In recent scenarios, active investors have tended to focus on companies with financial risks, underperformance, or governance difficulties. Qualified active investors identify issues and provide solutions to resolve them, raise the company's value, and earn a return on their investment. Although target firms may gain from the involvement of active investors, there have been numerous cases of managers opposing active investors by using defensive techniques to stave off hostile action. It is worth mentioning, however, that in the last few decades the relationship between firm management and active qualified investors seems to have become far less contentious. Indeed, activists have sought consensus and maintained a cordial dialogue wherever possible: according to PWC's 2020 Annual Corporate Directors Survey,[9] 87% of CEOs have seen a positive influence from proxy voting methods.

14.4.3 Types of activists and forms of shareholder activism

Private equity vs. hedge funds

To help the reader better understand hedge fund activism, it might be worth highlighting the distinctions between hedge funds and another comparable but distinct financial instrument, private equity (PE). In fact, private equity and hedge funds may seem almost identical but bear two significant distinctions. For starters, private equity often invests in illiquid, unlisted assets, but activist hedge fund investors typically target publicly traded companies and somewhat illiquid stakes in public stocks. Moreover, traditional PE firms are often buyout firms interested in the isolated control of the company in which they invest; they tend to resell the investment after a period that averages between 7 and 10 years. In contrast, hedge fund activists seek corporate influence rather than control and seek to maximize profit for all shareholders through a minority investment in the company, with no desire to acquire full ownership.

The typical PE model involves a cooperative relationship with the target company's Board of Directors and a series of private-sector negotiations in which the private equity firm acquires control or the entire stake of the company in exchange for its commitment to maintain the company as a portfolio for a specified period. This time is used by the private equity firm's experienced managers to implement operational and financial strategies designed to increase the efficiency

---

[8] For more information see https://www.activistinsight.com/research/Insightia_ShareholderActivism2020.pdf

[9] Available at https://www.pwc.com/us/en/services/governance-insights-center/library/annual-corporate-directors-survey.html

and stability of the investment company, with the goal of exiting the investment with a profit thanks to increased market value at the end of the holding period. In contrast, activist funds focus their efforts on advising and changing the strategic directions of undervalued companies, without taking control or buying them outright. These reforms must be implemented from a minority position, often 10% or less, using a variety of strategies to exert influence.

While the PE model reaps the benefits of greater efficiency exclusively for the PE firm, with hedge fund activism all shareholders benefit from these increased profits. The activist is entitled to the profits in proportion to their ownership, and all other shareholders of the target company will benefit from the value creations achieved. One final point must be made: the purer activist approach belongs to private equity firms, which own a company, know it intimately, and are fully involved in its administration. The work of hedge fund activists is distinct. They do not run companies, but they do exercise influence and authority because they have the support of other shareholders, whose backing is necessary to bring about any eventual change in management or strategy (Venezia, 2021).

After this introduction to shareholder activism and overview of its history and evolution, we should now consider the different types of activists and the various forms of activism. First, we should distinguish between levels of investment diversification and the levels of activism exerted by investors (**Figure 14.3**). Indeed, although an investment fund often depends on "stock picking" activities or duplicates a benchmark, a private equity fund implements more complicated strategies, accepts higher degrees of unpredictability and governance engagement, and opts for a considerably lower degree of diversification. Private equity funds typically complete the acquisi-

Figure 14.3   **Categories of funds**

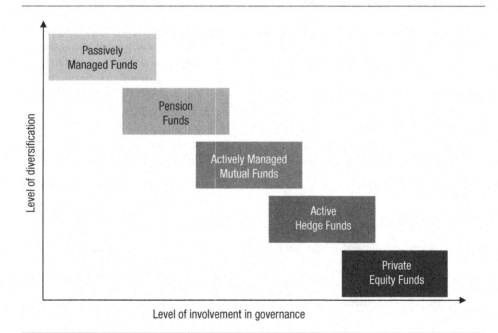

tion of a relevant ownership position in a firm and use their resources and talents to generate value by changing strategic aspects of the target or providing access to new channels of development. In the middle are pension funds, actively managed funds, and hedge funds, which can be distinguished by varying degrees of investment diversification and activity.

In this sense, we can define the so-called "buy-side" as any financial institution that attempts to generate value for the investor base they represent by purchasing investment instruments. Their techniques vary depending on the strategies characterizing the specific financial institution.

As Croci et al. (2012) point out, another important distinction is between *low-cost* and *high-cost* activism. Low-cost activism refers to measures taken by activists that do not require a significant ownership commitment (i.e., around 5%). This technique is comparable to shareholder proposals, "say on pay" campaigns, and private conversations with management – situations in which managers might decide to repurchase the shares of active investors in exchange for a high premium. "Say on pay" campaigns are also one of the most passive approaches. They often involve organizing meetings and writing letters to the firm in order to influence compensation plans or recommend changes to the company's communication strategies. On the other hand, shareholder proposals refer to tactics used by active investors to persuade other shareholders to join them in requesting changes to the board's governance policies/ practices or composition, the company's executive compensation plan, the oversight of specific functions (such as audit or risk management), or the company's corporate citizenship behavior (for example, in relation to ESG problems).

On the other hand, high-cost activism refers to a stake in capital that exceeds 5%. The primary objective of high-cost activists is to discover the target's "hidden value," which is determined by significant expenditures on legal, fiscal, and strategic advising services, as well as the engagement of headhunters and industry specialists. This type of activism is regarded as considerably more assertive: the objective is to resolve recognized problems within the firm in order to increase the company's worth. These investors do not rule out the possibility of potential conflicts with managers. Thus, while low-cost activism is generally preferred by investors who are unwilling to fight and prefer a friendly relationship with management (such as pension funds), high-cost activism is preferred by financial institutions that do not shy away from potential conflicts to achieve their objectives, such as hedge funds.

Environmental, social, and governance (ESG) factors in activist investing

A key current trend pertains to a company's ESG (environmental, social, and governmental) impact. Activists have always been outspoken about the acronym's G component: government and, in this context, governance. What is newer and increasingly trending now is the attention paid to the E and S components. Activist campaigns related to these issues continue to grow in popularity, and activists increasingly emphasize firms' insufficiency with regard to environmental and social norms.

For instance, as reminded in Gigante et al. (2021), Solvay[10] was recently approached by Bluebell Capital Partners[11] to clean the coastline of Rosignano,[12] which visitors refer to as the Italian Maldives and which the World Health Organization classified as a "priority pollution hotspot in the Mediterranean" two decades ago. Solvay has a AAA grade from MSCI for ESG risk and is a sector leader in chemical safety and water use, which should make think about the quality and soundness of these rankings.

As ESG activism has grown in popularity, so have calls for more sustainable growth and increased transparency. Both the European Union and the United States are pressing for increased regulation in this sphere. Finally, ESG is also used as a tool to assess a company's long-term viability and determine whether it is capable of creating value for its shareholders, and more importantly, for all stakeholders. The primary objective of investors is to maximize long-term value for stakeholders, and E and S are considered means to that end. The bulk of the market employs ESG screening as a technique for identifying "bad firms." Activists also employ those criteria to identify targets with which to engage and which they can revolutionize.

"Say on pay" mechanism

As Fisch et al. (2017) note, the Dodd-Frank Act – which was signed into law by President Barack Obama on July 21, 2010 in the aftermath of the Great Recession – significantly altered the regulatory mechanisms of U.S., finance with the goal of improving consumer protections through the imposition of a number of regulatory reforms, including requiring large U.S. public companies to provide shareholders the opportunity to vote on executive compensation on a non-binding basis. The say-on-pay vote is intended to rein in excessive executive salary and to urge boards to adopt compensation structures that tie executive income more closely to performance. Although the evidence is varied, most studies cast doubt on the effectiveness of this legislation. Most shareholders approve of remuneration packages, and compensation levels have remained consistently high. Although a lack of shareholder support for executive compensation is uncommon, many companies' say-on-pay votes have revealed low levels of shareholder support, which directors must consider when developing compensation plans; without total endorsement, the company and board may suffer reputational damage. While obtaining a bare majority is technically adequate, most businesses strive for far more.

Shareholder support for compensation programs is influenced by a variety of factors, the most important of which are the compensation amount, compensation methods, and stock price performance. According to the findings of Fisch et al. (2017), "say on pay" has limited effectiveness if it is only used to discipline managers who are underperforming. Moreover, to the extent that shareholder voting influences board behavior by signaling dissatisfaction with a company's financial performance, it can be counterproductive if it pushes directors to focus on short-term stock performance rather than long-term sustainable value creation.

Tröger et al. (2019) investigated the impact of say-on-pay legislation using a hand-collected dataset of 1,682 executive compensation packages at 34 companies in the main German stock market index (DAX) from 2009 to 2017. They discovered that when it comes to the design of

---

[10] Solvay Group is a Belgian company operating in the chemicals and plastics sector. It is listed on BEL20, the Belgian stock exchange. It was founded in 1863 by Ernest Solvay, whose heirs control it through Solvac SA.

[11] Bluebell Capital Partners is a long-term investor focused on European public equities.

[12] Rosignano Marittimo is an Italian town of 30 004 inhabitants in the province of Livorno in Tuscany on the sea.

compensation packages for newly hired employees, the supervisory board is responsive to say-on-pay votes, and that their findings are influenced by the relatively few pronouncedly dissatisfied say-on-pay votes that have occurred in corporate Germany. Nonetheless, the research is significant because it contributes to our understanding of how "say on pay" works. The observations of Tröger et al. (2019) apply more generally to say-on-pay regimes. Any evaluation of how a shareholder voice strategy regulates executive remuneration must pay close attention to the limits that contract law imposes on the adaptation of existing remuneration agreements, and thus must take a medium to long-term view that ideally extends to a full board-member turnover period (Tröger et al., 2019).

14.4.4 Activist campaigns

The campaigns of activists and their operations

Activists behave in a fairly predictable and consistent manner, beginning with a peaceful approach that can evolve into a more aggressive one if their demands and proposals are not met with approval by the present board. The efforts of activists span from private engagements and discussions with corporate management to written letters or inquiries from shareholders during meetings, direct proposals, proxy disputes, and lawsuits (Pozen, 1994; Partnoy and Thomas, 2006). The process is typically as follows: activists envision four viable avenues for making their voices known, the first of which is direct demand discussions with the executive board. Generally, hedge fund activists engage and speak with the Board of Directors to determine whether there is opportunity for negotiation about their requests and demands. Typically, such discussions take place secretly, behind the company's walls, but activists may feel compelled to share their desires with the public and may publish letters or written text with their requests that are distributed to the press. If these discussions with management fail and there is no common ground on which to begin a dialogue, the next step is to seek board participation – typically by exploiting minority representation legislation, such as list voting in Italy. If this continues to fail to produce the desired effects, activists can threaten and, if necessary, participate in genuine proxy wars with the backing of the remaining shareholders, mostly institutional investors. When a proxy war is initiated, dissident shareholders present a proposal to the management during a shareholder meeting to debate their concerns and offer suggestions. A proxy contest is typically used to exert pressure on management by making the activists' requests public and thus in more urgent need of resolution.

While the steps and procedure can be generalized as described above, activist campaigns and their engagement tactics vary by country due to a variety of factors, including the size of the hedge fund stake, the support garnered from other shareholders, and the institutional and legal system in each country. To categorize the objectives of shareholder activists, it may be helpful to turn to Becht et al. (2014), who identified four possible aims:

- Corporate governance (usually board member substitution);
- Takeovers;
- Policy on payouts;
- Corporate reorganization.

According to the authors, shareholder activism in public companies is frequently directed at changing the composition of the Board of Directors and removing directors who do not have the company's best interests at heart. The objectives of activists may also include assisting in a takeover to ensure that their shares are tendered at a more equitable and higher valuation than the bidders' first offer. Additionally, activists might advocate for an increase in dividends or other kinds of remuneration for shareholders by altering the company's business goals and strategic vision. More broadly, activists are concerned with corporate reorganization methods that enable people to participate in corporate governance matters, from electing directors to remedying a lack of information circulation inside the corporation.

Ideal target companies are often corporations with a low market value relative to book value but with a successful business. Typically, the payouts of these businesses are lower than those of rivals before activists interfere, while their takeover defenses, as well as CEO compensation, are typically higher than those of competitors. Moreover, ideal targets have a greater institutional investor ownership, which makes it easier for activists to enter and get support from a broader audience.

To summarize, the authors correctly point out that there is a widespread belief that activists initiate conflicts. However, campaigners maintain that the starting point should always be market and book value. If there is a mismatch, some funds sit and wait for the discrepancy to close, while activists encourage firms to create value. Selecting a target firm is always about determining how much value is buried and whether any of it can be extracted. It is critical for the activist to have the tools necessary to extract it.

An *activist campaign* entails several specific steps and characteristics. Usually, the activist's case is illustrated via a public letter or presentation (sometimes with an ad-hoc campaign website). The campaign outlines potentially disappointing past performance (or relatively poor performance) and introduces proposed actions to invert the performance trend, such as restructuring activities, M&As, or changes in remuneration. It also quantifies the potential value creation resulting from such activities.

When an event requiring a public vote occurs, a proxy advisor is typically hired by the activist to collect votes from shareholders. The Board, or another shareholder with an opposing view, can do the same by hiring another proxy advisor, beginning what's called a *proxy fight*.

During the period between the presentation of the activist case and the actual vote – which is at least 30 days – both the company and the activist fund separately engage with other shareholders to explain the merits of their case (or lack of one) for change. Attendance is important for a vote on an activist proposal, since the fund with a minority stake will try to win support from as many investors as possible. This is even more important when there is another minority shareholder with a large stake. Generally, between 60-70% of shareholders attend an annual general meeting (AGM). Indeed, attending and/or voting at a shareholders' meeting requires effort, meaning there must be compelling reasons to do so. AGMs have the highest attendance when the annual report is being approved, meaning this represents the best window for gathering investor support. At the AGM, shareholders can vote either physically or by proxy and, depending on the result, the Board will implement the will of the shareholders.

Shareholder activism in Italy

As outlined in Gigante et al. (2021), Italy ranks fifth in the EMEA region in terms of the number of activist campaigns, ranking behind the United Kingdom, Germany, Switzerland, and France – nations all known for their favorable investment climates and extensive regulation protecting minorities. However, the largest and most established participants in the Shareholder Activism sector, primarily hedge funds, also operate in Italy, and some smaller players have also entered the fray. The largest firms targeted are often those with a high market capitalization, and the majority of successful activist requests concern changes in board representation and management bodies. Italy is at an early stage of activism development, with mostly large enterprises touched by the phenomenon, which should continue to grow and could potentially help Italy's post-Covid-19 recovery.

14.4.5 Future trends

When it comes to future developments, many analysts focus on the growing number of SPACs (Special Purpose Acquisition Companies), mostly in the United States, and what has been dubbed "spactivism." Indeed, some U.S. investors are creating SPAC vehicles in the North American market. A SPAC is a special purpose entity that investors use to generate capital through an initial public offering whose proceeds are then used to execute an acquisition within two years. In 2020, SPACs raised $79.87 billion in gross funds from 237 transactions – significantly more than the $13.6 billion raised in 2019 (from 59 IPOs). In 2020, the number of these entities increased significantly in the United States, and this trend continued into 2021. With the increase of SPACs, new public firms will enter the market and may become targets of activists.

Private equity firms have also been relatively active in recent years in public markets: KKR filed a 13D in January 2020 and was appointed to the Board of Directors of Dave & Busters; Cerberus publicly addressed Commerzbank and was appointed to the board; Oaktree reported two public investments; and New Mountain publicly addressed Virtusa and was appointed to the board. According to Bruce Goldfarb of *Forbes*, today's crossover activist private equity investors combine the value-enhancing strategies of conventional activists with the features of private equity buyout financing.

Finally, considering the recent case of Gamestop, which shook the financial markets deeply, the issue of retail investors may be of interest. At the start of 2020, Gamestop's stock was trading between $3 and $4. Short sellers were drawn to this stock due to its very cheap price. The company was considered to rely on an outmoded business strategy which, particularly in the face of a pandemic, would inevitably result in stock declines. The participation of non-professional investors coordinated through Reddit's "WallStreetBets" channel, which has over 2 million subscribers, was instrumental in reversing the stock's value. In the final weeks of 2020, these non-professional investors planned a countermove, confronting institutional investors on the field and purchasing massive amounts of Gamestop shares via the subscription of "call options." Gamestop shares saw 20 billion transactions in a single day, making it the most traded stock worldwide.[13] The Gamestop story taught investors that retail can be critical and should not be overlooked. While activists may be cautious in targeting a corporation that has a significant portion of its ownership structure in retail, this might work to their favor if the point they are making gains traction. Retail investors are also extremely sensitive to the ESG issues outlined above and should be viewed as assets rather than threats by activists.

14.5 Conclusions

The aim of this final chapter was to introduce the topic of corporate governance and the world of active and passive investing, offering a deeper dive into the theme shareholder activism. Understanding these topics is paramount to possessing a well-rounded view of investing in both domestic and foreign markets and understanding the different forces affecting company actions and strategies worldwide.

The first section was devoted to corporate governance, a topic often disregarded in academic studies of business and finance but which is nevertheless fundamental. Corporate governance was first assessed by exploring the different models available worldwide, specifically the differences among Anglo-Saxon, German, and Latin models of governance. The main tools of corporate governance were outlined, including entities such as the General Meeting and Board of Directors. Finally, the agency problems faced by firms in relation to corporate governance and the difference between the power held by directors and shareholders were discussed. The second section of the chapter addressed the topic of investing, and more specifically, its definition, main principles, and the important distinction between active and passive investing as well as active and passive funds. The final section explored the activities of active investors and shareholder activism. We provided a brief history of the development of activism to better identify the significance of this phenomenon and the main types of activists and the characteristics of their campaigns.

---

[13] Available at https://www.am.pictet/it/blog/articoli/mercati-e-investimenti/il-caso-gamestop-cosa-e-accaduto-e-perche

About the Author

Gimede Gigante (PhD in Banking and Finance), Course Director of Principles of International Finance at Bocconi and Harvard Business Review advisory council member, has served as Academic Director of the Bocconi Summer School since 2019. Deputy Director of the Master of Science in Finance, he is also Deputy Director of the Bachelor's Degree Program in Economics and Finance at Bocconi University, where he holds the academic position of Lecturer in the Finance Department. He holds ITP qualification (International Teachers' Program) from SDA Bocconi. He has held visiting positions at the Finance Department of Columbia Business School and at the Salomon Brothers Center (Stern School of Business, NYU). He is a fellow of the Research Unit of Investment Banking & Structured Finance at the Baffi-Carefin Center (Centre for Applied Research on International Markets, Banking, Finance and Regulation). Since 2012 he has been teaching Financial Systems, International Finance and Investment Banking courses as a faculty member of the Master Program in International Management and the Master of Finance at Bocconi University in Milan. Professor of Investment Banking at SDA Bocconi in Mumbai (India) since 2014, he has been teaching Finance Lab & Private Equity at the Summer School of Bocconi University (since 2015), and Corporate Finance at Fudan University (Shanghai-China) as part of the Fudan-Bocconi Double Degree in International Management Program (DDIM) (since 2016). In 2022, his courses included Private Equity at SDA Bocconi's MBA Master Program with Seoul National University (SNU). Certified Public Accountant and professional auditor, his main areas of research are international finance, financial markets, corporate valuation, investment banking, fintech and private equity. He has published a variety of papers on banking and acts as a consultant and board member to several financial and non-financial institutions. Advisory Board Member of the international scientific journal *Corporate and Business Strategy Review* (since 2022), Associate Editor of the journals *International Journal of Economics and Finance* and of the *Rivista dei Dottori Commercialisti* (since 2021), Associate Editor of the journal *International Journal of Economics, Finance and Management Sciences* (since 2020) and Associate Editor of the international journal *Accounting and Finance Research* (since 2013). Winner of the Award for Excellence in Teaching at Bocconi in 2015-2016, 2016-2017, and 2019-2020.

About the Author of the Foreword

Matteo Arpe is the founder, Chairman and CEO of Sator, which controls CER –
Centro Europa Ricerche and Sator Capital Limited, asset manager of the same named
Private Equity Fund. He is also founder of Tinaba, an Italian fintech which has developed a digital ecosystem that enables users to manage, transfer and share money,
offers multichannel shopping experiences, and provides access to innovative financial services, social charity and crowdfunding. Thanks to his thirty years of experience, Matteo Arpe has risen to the top of the Italian banking and financial system.
He graduated in Business Economics at Bocconi University in Milan, and then began his professional career at Mediobanca, rising in the ranks until he was appointed Central Director, at the age of just 33. In 2001, he joined the banking group Banca
di Roma, taking on the role of Chief Executive Officer of Mediocredito Centrale. After one year he was appointed General Manager and later named Chief Executive Officer of the parent company, Capitalia, the third largest bank in Italy. He was one of
the first members of Young Global Leaders promoted by the World Economic Forum
and Professor of Economics at the University of Rome, LUISS Guido Carli.

Bibliography

Activist Monitor (2020). *Full Review 2020 Activism in Europe.* http://www.mergermarket.com/pdf/AM2020Europe.pdf

Adams, R.B., Almeida, H., & Ferreira, D. (2005). Powerful CEOs and their impact on corporate performance. *The Review of Financial Studies*, 18(4), 1403-1432.

Ahammad, M. (2009). *The Management of Cross Border Acquisitions and Performance.* Sheffield University Management School.

Alba, J.D., Park, D., & Wang, P. (2010). *Determinants of Different Modes of Japanese Foreign Direct Investment in the United States.* Asian Development Bank.

Allayannis, G.S. & Ofek, E. (2001). Exchange rate exposure, hedging and the use of foreign currency derivatives. *Journal of International Money and Finance*, 20, 273-296.

Allen, G.D. (2019). *Foreign Monetary Policy and the Currency Composition of Corporate Debt.* Working Paper, Ohio State University.

Amat, C., Michalski, T., & Stoltz, G. (2018). *Fundamentals and Exchange Rate Forecastability with Simple Machine Learning Methods.* HAL SHS, Sciences Humaines et Sociales, HEC Paris.

AMF (2020). *Report by the Autorité des Marchés Financiers on Shareholder Activism.*

Aminadav, G. & Papaioannou, E. (2020). Corporate control around the world. *The Journal of Finance*, 75(3), 1191-1246.

Andersen, O. (1997). Internationalization and market entry mode: A review of theories and conceptual framework. *Management International Review*, 37, 27-42.

Antràs, P., Desai, M., & Foley, F.C. (2009). Multinational firms, FDI flows and imperfect capital markets. *Quarterly Journal of Economics*, 124(3), 1171-1219.

Appel, I.R., Gormley, T.A., & Keim, D.B. (2016). Passive investors, not passive owners. *Journal of Financial Economics*, (121)1, 111-141.

Appel, I.R., Gormley, T.A., & Keim, D.B. (2019). Standing on the shoulders of giants: The effect of passive investors on activism. *The Review of Financial Studies*, 32.

Appiah-Kubi, S.N.K., Malec, K., Maitah, M., Kutin, S.B., Pánková, L., Phiri, J., & Zaganjori, O. (2020). The impact of corporate governance structures on foreign direct investment: A case study of West African countries. *Sustainability*, 12(9), 3715. doi:10.3390/su12093715

Armour, J. & Cheffins, B. (2009). *The Rise and Fall (?) of Shareholder Activism by Hedge Funds.* ECGI - Law Working Paper No. 136/2009.

Armour, J. & Skeel, D. (2007). *The Divergence of U.S. and UK Takeover Regulation.* Institute for Law and Economy Research Paper No. 08-24.

Atik, A. (2012). A strategic investment decision: "Internationalization of SMEs": A multiple appraisal approach and illustration with a case study. *iBusiness*, 4(2), 146-156. doi:10.4236/ib.2012.42017

Aybar, B. & Ficici, A. (2009). Cross-border acquisitions and firm value: An analysis of emerging-market multinationals. *Journal of International Business Studies.*

Aybar, B. & Thirunavukkarasu, A. (2005). Emerging market multinationals: An analysis of performance and risk characteristics. *Journal of Asia-Pacific Business*, 6(2), 5-39. doi:10.1300/J098v06n02_02

Bain & Company (2021). Global Private Equity Report 2021. https://www.bain.com/globalassets/noindex/2021/bain_report_2021-global-private-equity-report.pdf

Baird, R. (2021). Important Information about Initial Public Offerings. https://content.rwbaird.com/RWB/Content/PDF/Help/Important-information-about-IPOs.pdf

Banco de España (2003). Definitions of Foreign Direct Investment (FDI): A Methodological Note. https://www.bis.org/publ/cgfs22bde3.pdf

Banton, C. (2021, April 3). Understanding a currency peg and exchange rate policy. *Investopedia*. https://www.investopedia.com/terms/c/currency-peg.asp

Baracuhy, B. (2016). Geopolitical risks and the international business. *The Journal of Political Risk.* https://www.jpolrisk.com/geopolitical-risks-and-the-international-business-environment-challenges-for-transnational-corporations-and-their-global-supply-chai

Battilossi S. (2020). *Handbook of the History of Money and Currency.* Springer Nature. doi:10.1007/978-981-13-0596-2_56

Baxter, M. & Jermann, U. (1997). The international diversification puzzle is worse than you think. *The American Economic Review*, 87(1), 170-180.

Bebchuk, L., Brav, A., & Jiang, W. (2015). *The Long-Term Effects of Hedge Fund Activism.* NBER Working Papers 21227, National Bureau of Economic Research, Inc.

Becht, M., Franks, J., & Grant, J. (2010). *Hedge Fund Activism in Europe.* European Corporate Governance Institute ECGI.

Becht, M., Franks, J., Grant, J., & Rossi, S. (2009). Returns to shareholder activism: Evidence from a clinical study of the Hermes UK focus fund. *The Review of Financial Studies*, 22(8), 3093-3129.

Bekaert, G. & Hodrick, R. J. (2018). *International Financial Management* (3rd ed.). Cambridge University Press.

Belcredi, M. & Enriques, L. (2013). *Institutional Investor Activism in a Context of Concentrated Ownership and High Private Benefits of Control: The Case of Italy.* ECGI - Law Working Paper No. 225/2013.

Belcredi, M., Bozzi, S. & Ciavarella, A. (2017). Institutional investors' activism under concentrated ownership and the role of proxy advisors: Evidence from the Italian say-on-pay.

Benlaria, A. & Boubekeur, L. (2021). Forecasting exchange rates using artificial neural networks. مجلة البشائر الاقتصادية. 7(2). doi:10.33704/1748-007-002-045

Bernabò, F. (1969, June 22). Tra la Fiat e la Ferrari annunciato l'accordo. *La Stampa.*

Beugelsdijk, S., Kostova, T., Kunst, V.E., Spadafora, E., & van Essen, M. (2018). Cultural distance and firm internationalization: A meta-analytical review and theoretical implications. *Journal of Management,* 89-130. doi:10.1177/0149206317729027

Biagi, E. (1980). *Ferrari, the Drake, Storia di un instancabile sognatore.* Rizzoli.

Bilir, L.K., Chor, D., & Manova, K. (2014). *Host-Country Financial Development and Multinational Activity.* NBER Working Paper 20046.

Bilson, J. (1990). 'Technical' Currency Trading. In L. Thomas (Ed.), *The Currency-Gedging Debate* (pp. 257-275). IFR Publishing.

Binelli, M. (2003). *La quotazione in borsa della Ferrari. Cambiamenti organizzativi, rischi e fattori critici.* Angeli.

Blomstrom, M. & Kokko, A. (2003). *The Economics of Foreign Direct Investment Incentives.* NBER Working Papers 9489, National Bureau of Economic Research.

Bloomberg (2020, February 20). Currency Rates Matrix. https://www.bloomberg.com/markets/currencies/cross-rates

Bochner, S.E., Avina, J.C., & Cheng, C.Y. (2016). *Guide to the Initial Public Offering* (8th ed.). Merrill Corporation. https://www.wsgr.com/a/web/15354/ipoguide2016.pdf

Bodmer, E. (2014). *Corporate and Project Finance Modeling: Theory and Practice.* John Wiley & Sons.

Bonini, S., Dallocchio, M., Raimbourg, P., & Salvi, A. (2018). Do firms hedge translation risks? *Journal of Financial Management, Markets and Institutions.* doi:10.2139/ssrn.1063781

Booth, J. (1994, March 11). The IPO Underpricing Puzzle. *FRBSF Weekly Letter.* https://fraser.stlouisfed.org/files/docs/historical/frbsf/frbsf_let/frbsf_let_19940311.pdf

Bordo, M. (1993). The Gold Standard, Bretton Woods and other monetary regimes: A historical appraisal. *Federal Reserve Bank St Louis Rev, 75*(2), 123-191.

Bordo, M. (2003). *Exchange Rate Regime Choice in Historical Perspective.* NBER Working Paper Series. doi:10.3386/w9654

Borsa Italiana. *Currency Swap.* https://www.borsaitaliana.it/borsa/glossario/currency-swap.html

Boston Consulting Group. *Cross-Border PMI: Understanding and Overcoming the Challenges.* https://www.bcg.com/documents/file48163.pdf

Box, G. & Jenkins, G. (1970). *Time Series Analysis: Forecasting and Control.* Holden-Day.

Boyabatlı, O. (2004). *Operational Hedging: A Review with Discussion.* Working Paper Series, INSEAD, Faculty & Research.

Boyson, N.M. & Mooradian, R.M. (2011). Corporate governance and hedge fund activism. *Review of Derivatives Research, 14*(2).

Brand & Finance (2012). *Global 500 Ranking 2021.* https://brandirectory.com/rankings/global/2012/

Brau, J.C. & Fawcett, S.E. (2006). Initial Public Offerings: An analysis of theory and practice. *The Journal of Finance,* 1.

Brav, A. & Jiang, W. (2015). The long-term effects of hedge fund activism. *Columbia Law Review,* 115, 1085-1156.

Brav, A., Jiang, W., Partnoy, F., & Thomas, R. (2008). *The Return of Hedge Fund Activism.* ECGI-Law Working Paper N°.098/2008.

Brav, A., Jiang, W., Thomas, R.S., & Partnoy, F. (2008). Hedge fund activism, corporate governance, and firm performance. *Journal of Finance,* 63, 1729.

Brealey, R.A., Myers, S.C., & Allen, F. (200). *Principles of Corporate Finance: Global Edition* (10th ed.). McGraw-Hill.

Brewer, T. & Young, S. (2000). *The Multilateral Investment System and Multinational Enterprises.* Oxford University Press.

Britannica (2022). Gold-exchange standard monetary system. *Britannica.* https://www.britannica.com/topic/gold-exchange-standard

Broll, U. (1996). Cross hedging in currency forward markets, Diskussionsbeiträge - Serie II, No. 308, Universität Konstanz, Sonderforschungsbereich 178 - Internationalisierung der Wirtschaft, Konstanz.

Brown, G.W., Hu, W., & Zhang, J. (2020). The evolution of private equity fund value. *SSRN Electronic Journal.* doi:10.2139/ssrn.3621407

Brown, R.G. (1963). *Smoothing, Forecasting and Prediction of Discrete Time Series.* Prentice-Hall.

Bruno, S. (2015). Legal rules, shareholders and corporate governance. The European share-
    holder rights' directive and its impact on corporate governance of Italian listed compa-
    nies: The Telecom S.P.A. case. *Corporate Ownership & Control*, 12(2-3), 394-398.

Buckley, P.J. & Casson, M. (1976). *The Future of the Multinational Enterprise*. Macmillan.

Buckley, P.J., & Ghauri, P.N. (2002). *International Mergers and Acquisitions: A Reader*.
    Thomson.

Burton, F. N., & Saelens, F. H. (1987). Trade barriers and Japanese foreign direct investment
    in the color television industry. *Managerial and Decision Economics, 8(4)*, 285-293.
    http://www.jstor.org/stable/2560548)

Butler, K.C. (2012). *Multinational Finance: Evaluating Opportunities, Costs, and Risks of
    Operations*. John Wiley & Sons.

Canali, C. & Cianflone, M. (2017, September 09). Ferrari compie 70 anni: la storia di una
    leggenda dei motori tutta italiana. *IlSole24Ore*. http://www.ilsole24ore.com/art/mo-
    tori/2017-09-08/ferrari-compie-70-anni-storia-una-leggenda-motori-tutta-italiana-175617.
    shtml?uuid=AEEE80PC

Canto, V.A. & Wiese, A. (2018). Examining China: Purchasing Power Parity, Terms of Trade,
    and Real Exchange Rates. In *Economic Disturbances and Equilibrium in an Integrated
    Global Economy* (pp. 387-391). Academic Press. doi:10.1016/B978-0-12-813993-6.00045-3

Carleton, W., Nelson, J., & Weisbach, M. (1998). The influence of institutions on corporate
    governance through private negotiations: Evidence from TIAA-CREF. *The Journal of Fi-
    nance*.

Carletti, F. (2018, February 01). Per Ferrari utile netto 2017 a + 34%, in Borsa corre oltre quota
    100 euro. *IlSole24Ore*. http://www.ilsole24ore.com/art/finanza-e-mercati/2018-02-01/per-
    ferrari-utile-netto-2017-34percento-borsa-corre-oltre-quota-100-euro-124825_PRV.shtm-
    l?uuid=AEXtPksD

Carrieri, F., Chaieb, I., & Errunza, V. (2013). Do implicit barriers matter for globalization?
    Review of Financial Studies, 26 (7), 1694-1739. doi:10.1093/rfs/hht003

Caselli, S. & Gatti, S. (2004). *Banking for Family Business: A New Challenge for Wealth
    Management*. Springer.

Caselli, S. & Gatti, S. (2004). *Venture Capital: A Euro-System Approach*. Springer.

Caselli, S. & Gatti, S. (2005). *Structured Finance: Techniques, Products and Market*. Springer.

Caselli, S. & Negri, G. (2018). *Private Equity and Venture Capital in Europe*. Elsevier Aca-
    demic Press.

Caselli, S. & Gatti, S. (2021). Shareholders' ownership characteristics of Italian listed compa-
    nies: Do they really matter for firm's performance? Research in partnership with Equita.
    Bocconi University.

Caselli, S., & Negri G. (2021). *Private Equity and Venture Capital in Europe: Markets, Tech-
    niques, and Deals* (3rd ed.). Elsevier.

Caselli, S., Gigante, G., & Tortoroglio, A. (2021). *Corporate and Investment Banking*. Bocco-
    ni University Press.

Caselli, S., Gigante, G., Gatti, S., Chiarella, C., & Negri, G. (2020). *Investment Banking in
    Europe: Where We Are and Where We Are Going. Implications for Firms, Financial In-
    stitutions and Regulators*. Bocconi University BAFFI CAREFIN.

Cassel, G. (1918). Abnormal deviations in international exchanges. *Economic Journal*,
    28(112), 413-415. doi:2223329

Caves, R.E. (1996). *Multinational enterprise and economic analysis*. Cambridge University
    Press.

Cera, M. (2020). *Le società con azioni quotate nei mercati*. Zanichelli.

Cesario, G. & Gigante, G. (2021). What drives investment decisions on equity stake in private equity? The Italian case before and after the Great Financial Crisis. *Corporate Ownership & Control*, 18, 224-240. doi:10.22495/cocv18i3siart1

Cetorelli, N. & Strahan, P.E. (2006). Finance as a barrier to entry: Bank competition and industry structure in local U.S. markets. *The Journal of Finance*, 61, 437-461.

Chakrabarti, A., Vidal, E., & Mitchell, W. (2011). Business transformation in heterogeneous environments: The impact of market development and firm strength on retrenchment and growth reconfiguration. *Global Strategy Journal*, 1(1-2), 6-26.

Chala, A. T. (2018). *Refinancing Risk and Debt Maturity Choice during a Financial Crisis.* Working Papers 2018 No.33, Lund University, Department of Economics.

Chen, H., & Chen, T.J. (1998). Network linkages and location choice in foreign direct investment. *Journal of International Business Studies*, 29(3), 445-467. http://www.jstor.org/stable/155520

Chen, A.-S. & Leung, M.T. (2003). A Bayesian vector error correction model for forecasting exchange rates. *Computers & Operations Research*, 887-900.

Cianflone, M. (2013, May 8). Ferrari assume 250 dipendenti in Italia e limita la produzione per mantenere il valore del marchio. *IlSole24Ore*. http://www.ilsole24ore.com/art/motori/2013-05-08/ferrari-assume-250-dipendenti-italia-e-limita-produzione-mantenere-valore-marchio-- 141231.shtml?uuid=ACted8sB

Ciavarella (2017). *Board Diversity and Firm Performance across Europe*. Consob. https://www.consob.it/documents/46180/46181/wp85.pdf/b9172933-785c-4996-b065-3a04aacff33f

Claeys, G. (2017). *The Missing Pieces of the Euro Architecture*. Bruegel Policy Contribution No. 28.

Clark, E. (2004). *Currency Futures, Swaps and Hedging*. Greenwood Publishing.

Clifford Chance & The Economist Unit (2012). *Cross-border M&A: Perspectives on a changing world*. https://www.cliffordchance.com/content/dam/cliffordchance/PDF/Feature_topics/Cross_Border_Changing_World.pdf

Clifford, C.P. (2008). Value creation or destruction? Hedge funds as shareholder activists. *Journal of Corporate Finance*, 14(4).

Clingermayer, J. & Wood D.B. (1995). Disentangling patterns of state debt financing. *American Political Science Review*, 89(1), 108-120.

Coase, R.H. (1937). The nature of the firm. *Economica*, 386-405.

Cohen, S.D. (2007). *Multinational Corporations and Foreign Direct Investments: Avoiding Simplicity, Embracing Complexity*. Oxford University Press.

Conklin, D.W. (2002). Analyzing and managing country risk. *Ivey Business Journal*, 66(3), 36-41. https://iveybusinessjournal.com/publication/analyzing-and-managing-country-risks/

CONSOB (2013). 2013 Report on Corporate Governance of Italian Listed Companies. *Statistics and analyses*. https://www.consob.it/documents/46180/46181/rcg2013en.pdf/50cac-3cd-02d8-4a71-a054-268badb9e40f

Cooper, R.N. (1982). *The Gold Standard: Historical Facts and Future Prospects*. Harvard University. https://core.ac.uk/download/pdf/6252203.pdf

Corporate Finance Institute. *Managing Risks in Investment Banking*. https://corporatefinanceinstitute.com/resources/knowledge/strategy/managing-risks-in-investment-banking/

Cristoferi, C. & Gaia, M. (2007, May 16). Permira Buys Valentino Stake. *Reuters*. https://www.reuters.com/article/us-valentino-idUSL1663058320070516

Croci, E. (2007). Corporate raiders, performance and governance in Europe. *European Financial Management*.

Croci, E., Ehrhardt, O., & Nowak, E. (2012). The corporate governance endgame – An economic analysis of minority squeeze-out regulation in Germany. *SSRN*. doi:10.2139/ssrn.2080745

Czarnitzki, D. & Kraft, K. (2009). Capital control, debt financing and innovative activity. *Journal of Economic Behavior & Organization*, 71(2), 372-383.

Czarnitzki, D., Kraft, K., & Dunning, J.H. (2009). The eclectic paradigm of international production: A restatement and some possible extensions. *Journal of International Business Studies*, 19(1).

Dallocchio, M., Lucchini, G., & Scarpellini, M. (2015). *Mergers & Acquisitions*. Egea.

Damodaran, A. (2003). *Measuring Company Exposure to Country Risk: Theory and Practice Country Risk and Company Exposure: Theory and Practice*. New York Stern University. https://people.stern.nyu.edu/adamodar/pdfiles/papers/CountryRisk.pdf

Damodaran, A. (2012). *Investment Valuation: Tools and Techniques for Determining the Value of Any Asset*. John Wiley & Sons.

Damodaran, A. (2013). *Equity Risk Premiums (ERP): Determinants, Estimation and Implications – the 2013 Edition*. http://pages.stern.nyu.edu/~adamodar/

Dar, A.A., Taj, M., & Siddiqi, M.W. (2020). Link between bureaucratic quality and FDI inflows: A South Asian perspective. *Journal for Economic Forecasting, Institute for Economic Forecasting*, 0(3), 149-168.

Day, A. (2012). *Mastering Financial Modelling in Microsoft Excel: A Practitioner's Guide to Applied Corporate Finance* (3rd ed.). Pearson.

De Falco, S.E., Cucari, N., & Sorrentino, E. (2016). Voting dissent and corporate governance structures: The role of say on pay in a comparative analysis. *Corporate Ownership & Control*, 13(4-1), 188-197.

Dell'Acqua, A. & Etro, L. (2010). *La Valutazione delle Aziende*. Bocconi University.

Deloitte (2021). *Italy Private Equity Confidence Survey*. https://www2.deloitte.com/it/it/pages/private/articles/italy-private-equity-confidence-survey---deloitte-italy---deloitte.html

Demsetz, H. & Villalonga, B. (2001). Ownership structure and corporate performance. *Journal of Corporate Finance*, 7(3), 209-233.

DePamphilis, D. (2012). *Mergers, Acquisitions, and Other Restructuring Activities: An Integrated Approach to Process, Tools, Cases, and Solutions eBook*. Academic Press.

Desai, M.A., Foley, C.F., & Hines, J.R. Jr. (2004). A multinational perspective on capital structure choice and internal capital markets. *The Journal of Finance*, 59(6), 2451-2487.

Dyck, A. & Zingales, L. (2004). Private benefits of control: An international comparison. *The Journal of Finance*, 59(2), 537-600.

Di Nino, V., Habib, M., & Schmitz, M. (2020). Multinational enterprises, financial centres and their implications for external imbalances: A Euro area perspective. *ECB Economic Bulletin*, 2/2020. https://www.ecb.europa.eu/pub/economic-bulletin/articles/2020/html/ecb.ebart202002_01~1a58c02776.en.html

Doukas, J.A. & Lang, L.H.P. (2003). Foreign direct investment, diversification, and firm performance. *Journal of International Business Studies*, 34(2), 153-172. http://www.jstor.org/stable/3557150

Drummond, J. (2010, October 17). Mubadala Sells Ferrari Stake for €122m. *Financial Times*. https://www.ft.com/content/fc52bc74-eff4-11df-88db-00144feab49a

Dufey, G. & Srinivasulu, S. (1983). The case for corporate management of foreign exchange risk. *Financial Management Association International*, 12(4), 54-62.

Dunning, J. (1981). Explaining the international direct investment position of countries: Towards a dynamic or developmental approach. *Review of World Economics*, 117(1), 30-64.

Dunning, J.H. (1988). The eclectic paradigm of international production: A restatement and some possible extensions. *Journal of International Business Studies*, 19, 1-31.

Dunning, J.H. (1993). *Multinational Enterprises and the Global Economy*. Addison Wesley.

Dunning, J.H. (2009). Location and the multinational enterprise: John Dunning's thoughts on receiving the "Journal of International Business Studies" 2008 Decade Award. *Journal of International Business Studies*, 40(1), 20-34.

Durbin, E. & Ng, D. (2005). The sovereign ceiling and emerging market corporate bond spreads. *Journal of International Money and Finance*, 24(4), 631-649.

Eagly, A.H. & Chaiken, S. (1993). *The Psychology of Attitudes*. Cengage Learning.

EDC (2016). *Managing Political Risk: A Guide for Canadian Businesses that Invest in or Export to Emerging Market*. http://www.iberglobal.com/files/2016-2/managing-political-risk.pdf

Edelshain, D. (1995). *British Corporate Currency Exposure and Foreign Exchange Risk Management*. Ph.D. London Business School.

Eichengreen, B. (2011). *The New Monetary and Financial History*. Routledge.

Eichengreen, B. & Hausmann, R. (1999). Exchange Rates and Financial Fragility. In Federal Reserve Bank of Kansas City, *New Challenges for Monetary Policy*. https://www.kansascityfed.org/Jackson%20Hole/documents/3551/1999-S99eich.pdf

Eiteman, D., Stonehill, A., & Moffett, M. (2013). *Multinational Business Finance* (13th ed.). Pearson.

Ejara, D., Krapl, A., O'Brien, T., & Ruiz de Vargas, S. (2017). Comparison of Cost of Equity Models: New International Evidence. *SSRN Electronic Journal*. 10.2139/ssrn.3023501

Ellis, K., Michaely, R., & O'Hara, M. (1999). *A Guide to the Initial Public Offering Process*. https://www.academia.edu/download/44382331/Guide.pdf

Ensor, R. & Muller, P. (1981). *The Essentials of Treasury Management*. Euromoney Publications.

Epstein, S. (2001). *The Late Medieval Crisis as an 'Integration Crisis'*. Routledge.

Erb, C., Harvey, C.R., & Viskanta, T., (1996). Expected returns and volatility in 135 countries. *The Journal of Portfolio Management*, 22(3), 46-58.

Erel, I., Jang, Y. & Weisbach, M. (2020). *The Corporate Finance of Multinational Firms*. National Bureau of Economic Research.

Espinasse, P. (2014). *IPO: A Global Guide*. Hong Kong University Press.

Essilor (2017). *EssilorLuxottica: A Growth Story in the Eyewear Industry*. https://www.essilor.com/essilor-content/uploads/2017/01/Presentation-January-16-2017.pdf

European Commission (2018). *Essilor/Luxottica Merger Procedure Regulation*. https://ec.europa.eu/competition/mergers/cases/decisions/m8394_4217_3.pdf

Evrensel, A. (2020). Advantages and Disadvantages of Floating Exchange Rates. *Economics Discussion*. https://www.economicsdiscussion.net/international-trade/finance/floating-exchange-rates-advantages-and-disadvantages-currencies/26267

Facebook (2012). Facebook's IPO revised prospectus. Facebook Press Releases. https://etrade.com/rtpublish/images/Facebook_Revised_Prelim_Prospectus_and_FWP.pdf

Facebook (2014, February 01). Facebook to acquire Whatsapp. Facebook Press Releases. https://about.fb.com/news/2014/02/facebook-to-acquire-whatsapp/

Fagernäs, S. & Singh, A. (2007). Legal origin, shareholder protection and the stock market: New challenges from time series analysis. *Journal of Political Economy*, 106(6), 1113-1155.

Farole, T., Winckler, D. & Oliver, J. (2013). *Some Types of Foreign Investment Are Better Than Others: A Look at Factors That Help FDI Boost the Local Economy*. WP Published on the *trade post*, World Bank Blogs.

Fernández, P. (2012). *Valuation of an Expropriated Company: The Case of YPF and Repsol in Argentina*. IESE Research Papers D/1055, IESE Business School.

Ferrari (2015). *Ferrari's IPO prospectus*. Ferrari Press Releases https://corporate.ferrari.com/sites/ferrari15ipo/files/16_f-1_prospectus.pdf

Ferrari, G. & Sardo, S. (2021). Hedge Fund Activism: A European Perspective. *Bocconi Students for Capital Markets*.

Financial Times (1994, Mar 11). The IPO Underpricing Puzzle.

Financial Times (2007, May 20). UniCredit Buys Capitalia for €22 bn. https://www.ft.com/content/9bbdefba-06e0-11dc-93e1-000b5df10621

Financial Times (2021). League Tables: Investment Banking Review. https://markets.ft.com/data/league-tables/tables-and-trends

Fisch, J.E., Palia, D., & Davidoff, S. (2018). Is say on pay all about pay? The impact of firm performance. *Harvard Business Law Review*, 8(101).

Fisher, I. (1896). *Appreciation and Interest*. Macmillan for the American Economic Association.

Fama, E.F. (1984). Forward and spot exchange rates. *Journal of Monetary Economics*, 14(3), 319-338. doi:10.1016/0304-3932(84)90046-1

Fox, R.P. & Madura, J. (2017). *International Financial Management* (4th ed.). Cengage Learning.

Franco, C., Rentocchini, F., & Vittucci Marzetti, G. (2010). Why do firms invest abroad? An analysis of the motives underlying Foreign Direct Investment. *ICFAI University Journal of International Business Law. IX.*, 42-65.

Fruman, C. (2016). Why does efficiency-seeking FDI matter? *Private Sector Development Blog*, World Bank Blogs.

Gadanecz, B. (2004). The syndicated loan market: Structure, development and implications. *BIS Quarterly Review*, 75-89.

Gaillard, N. (2020). *Country Risk, The Bane of Foreign Investors*. Springer.

Gallarotti, G.M. (1995). *The Anatomy of an International Monetary Regime*. Oxford University Press.

Gapper, J, (2017, October 02). The Ferrari Files: How One Man's Obsession Saved Racing Car History. *Financial Times*. https://www.ft.com/content/9427424a-be97-11e7-9836-b25f8adaa111

García, F.J.P. (2017). *Financial Risk Management: Identification, Measurement and Management*. Palgrave McMillan.

Gatti, S. (2012). *Project Finance in Theory and Practice* (2nd ed.). Academic Press–Elsevier.

Gaughan, P.A. (2018). *Mergers, Acquisitions, & Corporate Restructuring* (7th ed.). John Wiley & Sons.

Geyer-Klingeberg, J., Hang, M., & Rathgeber, A.W. (2019). What drives financial hedging? A meta-regression analysis of corporate hedging determinants. *International Review of Financial Analysis*, 61, 203-221.

Giddy, I.H. & Dufey, G. (1975). The random behavior of flexible exchange rates: Implications for forecasting. *Journal of International Business Studies*, 6(1), 1-32.

Gigante, G. (2020). *Mergers & Acquisitions*. Aracne Editrice.

Gigante, G. & Bider, G. (2021). The effects of corporate venture capital on value creation and innovation of European public owned firms. *Corporate Ownership & Control*, 18(4), 117-133. doi:10.22495/cocv18i4art9

Gigante, G. & Cerri, A. (2021). *Finance Lab*. Egea.

Gigante, G., Conso, A., & Bocchino, E.M. (2020). *SPAC from the US to Italy: An Evolving Phenomenon*. Egea.

Gigante, G. & Cozzi, G. (2021). Equity crowdfunding: An empirical investigation of success factors in real estate crowdfunding. *Journal of Property Investment & Finance.* doi:10.1108/JPIF-06-2021-0055

Gigante, G. & Guidotti, G. (2021). Do Chinese-focused U.S. listed SPACs perform better than others do? *Investment Management and Financial Innovations*, 18 (3), 229-248.

Gigante, G. & Pambianco, R. (2020). Le banche italiane alla prova Covid-19. *Economia e Management.* https://emplus.egeaonline.it/it/396/emergenza-coronavirus/1165/le-banche-italiane-alla-prova-covid-19

Gigante, G. & Sottoriva, C. (2021). *Economia, gestione e finanza dei football club professionistici.* Egea.

Gigante, G. & Venezia, M.V. (2021). Corporate ownership and shareholder activism: The case of Italy. *Corporate Ownership & Control*, 19(1), pp. 159-168. doi:10.22495/cocv19i1art12

Gillan, S. & Starks, L. (1998). A survey of shareholder activism: Motivation and empirical evidence. *SSRN.* doi:10.2139/ssrn.663523

Gillan, S. & Starks, L. (2000). Corporate governance proposals and shareholder activism: The role of institutional investors. *Journal of Financial Economics.*

Gillan, S. & Starks, L. (2007). The evolution of shareholder activism in the United States. *Journal of Applied Corporate Finance.*

Gnutti, A.H., Martin, J.D, &. Ramsey, J.D. (2014). Predicting corporate voting outcomes for shareholder sponsored proposals. *Corporate Ownership & Control*, 12(1-8), 742-758.

Godlewski, C.J., Sanditov, B., & Burger-Helmchen, T. (2010). *Bank Lending Networks, Experience, Reputation, and Borrowing Costs.* Université de Strasbourg.

Gonzalez-Bravo, Y.M. (2020). Political risk management practices of multinational corporations: Their approaches to deal with developing countries under economic sanctions. *Journal of Evolutionary Studies in Business*, 5(2), 215-247. doi:10.1344/jesb2020.2.j081

Gordon, K. (2009). Investment guarantees and political risk insurance: Institutions, incentives and development. *SSRN Electronic Journal.* doi:10.2139/ssrn.1718484

Graham, B. (1959). *The Intelligent Investor: A Book of Practical Counsel.* Harper.

Greco, F. (2016, April 22). In Ferrari cinquemila euro di bonus. *IlSole24Ore.* https://st.ilsole-24ore.com/art/impresa-e-territori/2016-04-22/ferrari-premio-4570-euro-062850.shtml

Greenwood, R. & Schor, M. (2009). Investor activism and takeovers. *Journal of Financial Economics.*

Griseri, P. (2016, December 5). La metamorfosi della Ferrari. *Repubblica.it.* http://www.repubblica.it/economia/affari-e-finanza/2016/12/05/news/la_metamorfosi_della_ferrari-153547324/

Grubel, H.G. (1968). Internationally diversified portfolios: Welfare gains and capital flows. *American Economic Review*, 58, 1299-1314.

Habib, M. & Zurawicki, L. (2002). Corruption and foreign direct investment. *Journal of International Business Studies*, 33(2), 291-307. http://www.jstor.org/stable/3069545

Hart, J. (2017). Globalization and Multinational Corporations. In *The SAGE Handbook of International Corporate and Public Affairs.* SAGE.

Hart, O. & Moore, J. (1994). A theory of debt based on the inalienability of human capital. *The Quarterly Journal of Economics*, 109(4), 841-879.

Haseltine, J.B. (1981). A Longer-Term Approach. In R. Ensor & P. Muller (Eds.), *The Essentials of Treasury Management.* Euromoney Publications.

Henderson, B.J., Jegadeesh, N., & Weisbach, M. S. (2006). World markets for raising new capital. *Journal of Financial Economics*, 82(1), 63-101.

Hennart, J.F. (1982). *A Theory of Multinational Enterprise.* University of Michigan Press.

Hymer, S. (1960). *The International Operations of National Firms: A Study of Direct Foreign Investment.* Ph.D. dissertation, MIT, published by MIT Press under the same title in 1976.

Hoang, D., Horn, M., Emmel, H., Gatzer, S., Lahmann, A., & Schmidt, M. (2017). *Country Risk – Equity Costs: A Global Comparison: Methodologies and Implications.*

Holterman, W., & van de Pol, M. (2016). *Mergers & Acquisitions.* PricewaterhouseCoopers. http://dx.doi.org/10.1136/vr.m4879

Hommel, U. (2003). Financial versus operative hedging of currency risk. *Global Finance Journal,* 14(1), 1-18.

Horan, S. (2008, October 5). How institutions manage counterparty risk. *Financial Times.* https://www.ft.com/content/14692da0-917b-11dd-b5cd-0000779fd18c

Huchzermeier, A.H. (1991). *Global Manufacturing Strategy Planning Under Exchange Rate Uncertainty.* PhD Thesis, the Wharton School, University of Pennsylvania.

Hufbauer, G., Schott, J., Elliott, K., & Oegg, B. (2007). *Economic Sanctions Reconsidered* (3rd ed.). Institute for International Economics.

Hughes, J.E. & MacDonald, S.E. (2002). *International Banking: Text and Cases.* Addison Wesley.

Hughes, J.S., Logue, D.E., & Sweeney, R.J. (1975). Corporate international diversification and market assigned measures of risk and diversification. *Journal of Financial and Quantitative Analysis,* 10(4), 627-637.

Hymer, S.H. (1960). *The International Operations of National Firms: A Study of Direct Investment.* MIT Press.

Hymer, S.H. (1968). *The Large Multinational "Corporation."* Edward Elgar.

IMF (1999). *About the IMF: History: The End of the Bretton Woods System (1972–81).* https://www.imf.org/external/about/histend.htm

Insightia (2021). *Shareholder activism in 2020.* https://www.activistinsight.com/research/Insightia_ShareholderActivism2020.pdf

Invest Europe (2021). *Investing in Europe: Private Equity Activity 2020.* https://www.investeurope.eu/media/4004/investing-in-europe_private-equity-activity_2020_invest-europe_final.pdf

Isaac, K.S., Ibidunni, A., Kehinde, O.J., Ufua, D., Elizabeth, K.B., Oyo-Ita, D., & Mathias, C.M. (2020). The role of multinational corporations in global economic practice: Literature review. *Journal of Management Information and Decision Sciences,* 23(5), 619-628.

James, H. (2012). *Making the European Monetary Union: The Role of the Committee of Central Bank Governors and the Origins of the European Central Bank.* Harvard University Press.

Jang, Y. (2017). International corporate diversification and financial flexibility. *Review of Financial Studies,* 30(12), 4133-4178.

Jansson, A. (2014). No Exit!: The logic of defensive shareholder activism. *Corporate Board: Role, Duties and Composition,* 10(2), 16-31.

JP Morgan (2013). *Corporate Finance Post-Brexit.* https://www.jpmorgan.com/jpmpdf/1320725860498.pdf

JP Morgan (2017). *Japan Cross-Border M&A.* https://www.jpmorgan.com/jpmpdf/1320736622067.pdf

JP Morgan (2018). *Rethinking Capital Structure Today? A Fireside Q&A for Senior Decision-Makers.* https://www.jpmorgan.com/jpmpdf/1320726902318.pdf

JP Morgan (2020). *2020 Global M&A Outlook.* https://www.jpmorgan.com/solutions/cib/investment-banking/2020-global-ma-outlook

Juneja, P. (2020). Advantages and Disadvantages of Currency Pegs. *Management Study Guide.* https://www.managementstudyguide.com/advantages-and-disadvantages-of-currency-pegs.htm

Juneja, P. (2020). Cross Border Mergers and Acquisitions and Some Recent Trends in This Field. *Management Study Guide.* https://www.managementstudyguide.com/cross-border-mergers-and-acquisitions.htm

Kahan, M. & Rock, E.B. (2007). Hedge funds in corporate governance and corporate control. *University of Pennsylvania Law Review*, 155.

Kahn, C. & Winton, A. (1998). Ownership structure, speculation, and shareholder intervention. *The Journal of Finance*, 53, 99-129.

Kallianiotis, J. (2013). *Exchange Rates and International Financial Economics.* Palgrave Macmillan.

Kandilov, I., Leblebicioglu, A., & Neviana, P. (2016). The impact of banking deregulation on inbound foreign direct investment: Transaction-level evidence from the United States. *Journal of International Economics.* doi:100.10.1016/j.jinteco.2016.02.008

Kang, N. & Johansson, S. (2000). *Cross-Border Mergers and Acquisitions: Their Role in Industrial Globalisation.* OECD Science, Technology and Industry Working Papers.

Kaplan, S.N. & Stromberg, P. (2009). Leveraged buyouts and private equity. *Journal of Economic Perspectives*, 23(1), 121-146. doi:10.1257/jep.23.1.121

Karpoff, J. (2001). *The Impact of Shareholder Activism on Target Companies: A Survey of Empirical Findings.* ECGI European Corporate Governance Institute.

Karpoff, J., Malatesta, P., & Walkling, R. (1996). Corporate governance and shareholder initiatives: Empirical evidence. *Journal of Financial Economics.*

Keloharju, M. & Niskanen, M. (2001). Why do firms raise foreign currency denominated debt? Evidence from Finland. *European Financial Management*, 7, 481-496.

Kering (2020). *2019 Annual Report.* https://keringcorporate.dam.kering.com/m/5950e-4d285ac1f9a/original/2019-Financial-Document.pdf

Kesternich, I. & Schnitzer, M. (2010). Who is afraid of political risk? Multinational firms and their choice of capital structure. *Journal of International Economics*, 82(2), 208-218.

Kim, S.H. & Kim, S.H. (2006). *Global Corporate Finance: Text and Cases.* Blackwell Publishing.

Kim, S.W. (2018). *The Euromarket and the Making of the Transnational Network of Finance, 1959–1979.* PhD dissertation. University of Cambridge.

Kim, S.W. (2019). *Has the Euro-Dollar a Future? The Production of Knowledge, Contestation and Authority in the Eurodollar Market, 1959-1964.* Boydell and Brewer.

Kindleberger, C.P. (2002). Stephen Hymer and the multinational corporation. *Contributions to Political Economy*, 21(1), 5-7.

Kirikkaleli, D. (2020). Does political risk matter for economic and financial risks in Venezuela? *Economic Structures* 9, 3. doi:10.1186/s40008-020-0188-5

Klein, A. & Zur, E. (2007). Entrepreneurial Shareholder Activism: Hedge Funds and Other Private Investors. AAA 2007 Financial Accounting & Reporting Section (FARS) Meeting Paper, ECGI - Finance Working Paper No. 140/2006, NYU Law and Economics Research Paper No. 06-41, 1st Annual Conference on Empirical Legal Studies.

Klein, A. & Zur, E. (2011). The impact of hedge fund activism on the target firm's existing bondholders. *The Review of Financial Studies*, 24(5), 1735-1771.

Klein, M.W., Peek, J. & Rosengren, E.S. (2002). Troubled banks, impaired foreign direct investment: The role of relative access to credit. *American Economic Review*, 92, 664.

Kokkinis, A. (2014). Shareholder short-termism in the UK: The Kay Review and the potential role of corporate law. *Corporate Ownership & Control*, 11(3-1), 166-174.

Kozlow, R. (2011). Multinational Enterprises, Foreign Direct Investment and Related Income Flows. *United Nations Economic Commission for Europe, Chapter 3*.

KPMG (2018). *Basel 4 – A Brief Overview*. https://assets.kpmg/content/dam/kpmg/xx/pdf/2018/12/basel-4-an-overview.pdf

Kugler, P. (2016). *The Bretton Woods System: Design and Operation*. Oxford University Press.

Kugler, P. & Straumann, T. (2020). International Monetary Regimes: The Bretton Woods System. In S. Battilossi (Ed.), *Handbook of the History of Money and Currency* (pp. 1-21). Springer Singapore.

La Porta, R., F.Lopez-de-Silanes, F.A., Shleifer A., & Vishny R.W. (2000). Investor protection and corporate governance. *Journal of Financial Economics*, 58, 3-27.

Lardy, N. (1998, July 01). China and Asian contagion. *Foreign Affairs*. doi:10.2307/20048967

Lazard (2020). *Review of Shareholder Activism – Q1 2020*. https://www.lazard.com/perspective/lazards-quarterly-review-of-shareholder-activism-q1-2020/

Lee, K.C. & Kwok, C.C. (1988). Multinational corporations vs. domestic corporations: International environmental factors and determinants of capital structure. *Journal of International Business Studies*, 19(2), 195-217.

Legorano, G. (2016, September 14). Banca Monte dei Paschi Names Marco Morelli CEO. *Wall Street Journal*. https://www.wsj.com/articles/banca-monte-dei-paschi-names-marco-morelli-ceo-1473875989

Lerner, J., Hardymon, F., & Leamon, A. (2012). *Venture Capital & Private Equity: A Casebook* (5th ed.). John Wiley & Sons.

Lessambo, F.L. (2021). *International Finance*. Springer Books.

Lin, C. (2001). Corporatisation and corporate governance in China's economic transition. *Economics of planning*, 34(1), 5-35.

Lin, R., Chen, J., & Xie, L. (2020). Alibaba Group—The Evolution of Transnational Governance. In *Corporate Governance of Chinese Multinational Corporations*. Springer Singapore.

Lipton, M. (2013, February 26). Bite the Apple; Poison the Apple; Paralyze the Company; Wreck the Economy. *Harvard Law School Forum on Corporate Governance*. https://corpgov.law.harvard.edu/2013/02/26/bite-the-apple-poison-the-apple-paralyze-the-company-wreck-the-economy/

Macdonald, R. & Nagayasu, J. (2013). *Currency Forecast Errors at Times of Low Interest Rates: Evidence from Survey Data on the Yen/dollar Exchange Rate*. University of Strathclyde.

Madura, J. (2008). *International Financial Management* (9th ed.). Cengage Learning.

Madura, J. (2012). *International Financial Management* (11th ed.). Cengage Learning.

Madura, J. (2013). *International Financial Management* (12th ed.). Cengage Learning.

Madura, J. (2015). *International Financial Management* (13th ed.). Cengage Learning.

Malan, A. & Cianflone, M. (2015, March 3). Ferrari, Marchionne: Possibile Holding in Olanda. *IlSole24Ore*. https://st.ilsole24ore.com/art/impresa-e-territori/2015-03-03/ferrari-marchionne-possibile-holding-olanda-111714.shtml?uuid=ABBEVM3C

Mansi, S. & Reeb, D. (2002). Corporate international activity and debt financing. *Journal of International Business Studies*, 33, 129-147.

Mäntysaari, P. (2005). *Comparative Corporate Governance: Shareholders as a Rule-maker*. Springer.

Mao, C.X. & Li, H. (2002). *Corporate Use of Interest Rate Swaps: Theory and Evidence.* doi:10.2139/ssrn.327422

Mariscal, J.O. & Lee, R.M. (1993). *The Valuation of Mexican Stocks: An Extension of the Capital Asset Pricing Model.* Goldman Sachs.

Marsh Mercer Kroll (2008). *M&A Beyond Borders: Opportunities and Risks.* http://graphics.eiu.com/upload/eb/marsh_cross_border_report.pdf

Massari, M., Gianfrate, G., & Zanetti, L. (2016). *Corporate Valuation: Measuring the Value of Companies in Turbulent Times.* John Wiley & Sons.

Maug, E. (2006). Efficiency and fairness in minority freezeouts: Takeovers, overbidding, and the freeze-in problem. *International Review of Law and Economics*, 26, 355-379.

Mayer, D. & Jebe, R. (2010). *The Legal and Ethical Environment for Multinational Corporations.* Routledge.

McCarthy, S. (2003). *Hedging Versus not Hedging: Foreign Currency Transaction Exposure Management Techniques.* School of Economics and Finance, Queensland University of Technology Series of Discussion Papers and Working Papers.

McCauley, R.N. & Zimmer, S.A. (1991). Bank Cost of Capital and International Competition. *Federal Reserve Bank of New York Quarterly Review*, Winter, 33-59.

McKinsey & Company (2021). *A Year of Disruption in the Private Markets: McKinsey Global Private Markets Review 2021.* https://www.mckinsey.com/industries/private-equity-and-principal-investors/our-insights/mckinseys-private-markets-annual-review

McKinsey China (2017). *A Pocket Guide to Chinese Cross-Border M&A.* http://mckinseychina.com/wp-content/uploads/2017/04/McKinsey_A-Pocket-Guide-to-Chinese-Cross-Border-MA-English.pdf

Meese, R.A. & Rogoff K.S. (1988). Was it real? The exchange rate-interest differential relation over the modern floating-rate period. *Journal of Finance*, 43(4), 933-948.

Melin, L. (1992). Internationalization as a strategy process. *Strategic management journal*, 13(S2), 99-118.

Melvin, M. & Norrbin, S. (2017). Financial Management of the Multinational Firm. In *International Money and Finance* (9th ed., pp. 173-190). Academic Press.

Mergermarket (2020). *Global & Regional M&A Report 2020.* https://www.mergermarket.com/trendreports

Mergermarket (2020). *Value over Volume: Italian M&A and PE Activity in 2020.* https://www.gpblex.it/wp-content/uploads/2021/01/GPBL_H2_2020.pdf

Metrick, A. & Yasuda, A. (2010). The economics of private equity funds. *The Review of Financial Studies*, 23, 2303-2341. doi:10.1093/rfs/hhq020

Mills, R.H. & Terrell, H.S. (1984). The determination of front-end fees on syndicated eurocurrency credits. *International Finance Discussion Papers*, No. 250.

Moffett, M. & Karlsen, J.K. (2007). Managing foreign exchange rate economic exposure. *Journal of International Financial Management & Accounting*, 5, 157-175. doi:10.1111/j.1467-646X.1994.tb00040.x

Moody's Investor Relation (2018). *EssilorLuxottica Update to Credit Analysis.* https://www.essilorluxottica.com/sites/default/files/EssilorLuxottica%20Moody's%20Credit%20Opinion%205%20December%202018.pdf

Mourlon-Druol, E. (2012). *A Europe Made of Money: The Emergence of the European Monetary System.* Cornell University Press.

Mourlon-Druol, E. (2014). Don't blame the Euro: Historical reflections on the roots of the Eurozone crisis. *West Eur Polit*, 37, 1282-1296.

Mourlon-Druol, E. (2020). European Monetary Integration. In *Handbook of the History of Money and Currency*. Springer Singapore.

Nazarboland, G. (2003). The attitude of top UK multinationals towards translation exposure. *Journal of Management Research*, 3(3), 119-126.

Neal, L. (2016). *A Concise History of International Finance from Babylon to Bernanke*. University of Illinois at Urbana-Champaign, Cambridge University Press.

OECD (2002). *Foreign Direct Investment for Development*. http://www.oecd.org/investment/investmentfordevelopment/1959815.pdf

OECD (2003). *Checklist for Foreign Direct Investment Incentive Policies*. https://www.oecd.org/investment/investment-policy/2506900.pdf

Ong, S., Petrova M., & Spieler, A. (2010). Shareholder activism and director retirement plans repeals. *Corporate Ownership and Control*, 7(3).

Oxford Analytica & Willis Towers Watson (2019). *Political Risk Survey Report*. https://www.willistowerswatson.com/en-US/Insights/2019/12/2019-political-risk-survey-report

Pandit, S.A. (1971). The Asian dollar and free gold markets in Singapore. *Finance and Development*, 8(2).

Papaioannou, G.J. & Karagozoglu, A.K. (2017). *The New Issues Markets*. Academic Press.

Papetti, A. (2020). Demographics and the Natural Real Interest Rate: Historical and Projected Paths for the Euro Area. *Working Paper No. 1306,* Bank of Italy: Temi di Discussione. doi:10.2139/ssrn.3746172

Park, S.H., Suh, J., & Yeung, B. (2013). Do multinational and domestic corporations differ in their leverage policies? *Journal of Corporate Finance*, 20, 115-139.

Partnoy, F. & Thomas, R.S. (2007). Gap Filling, Hedge Funds, and Financial Innovation. In *New Financial Investments and Institutions*. Brooking Institution Press.

Penrose, J. (1995). Essential constructions? The 'cultural bases' of nationalist movements, *Nations and Nationalism*, 1, 391-417.

Phalippou, L. & Gottschalg, O. (2009). The performance of private equity funds. *The Review of Financial Studies*, 22(4), 1747-1776. doi:10.1093/rfs/hhn014

Pignataro, P. (2013). *Financial Modeling & Valuation: A Practical Guide to Investment Banking and Private Equity*. John Wiley & Sons.

Pitelis, C. N., Teece, D. J. (2018). The new MNE: 'Orchestration' theory as envelope of 'internalisation' theory. *Management International Review*, 58(4), 523-539.

Presciani, C. (2020). *La trasparenza degli azionisti istituzionali di società quotate*. Giappichelli.

Private Equity International (2020). *2020 PEI 300 Report*. https://www.privateequityinternational.com/the-pei-300-2020/

PWC (2020). *Annual Corporate Directors Survey*. https://www.pwc.com/us/en/services/governance-insights-center/library/annual-corporate-directors-survey.html

Qui, L. & Wang, S. (2011). FDI policy, greenfield investment and cross-border mergers. *Review of International Economics*, 19(5), 836-851.

Raja, K. & Kostyuk, A. (2015). Perspectives and obstacles of the shareholder activism implementation: A comparative analysis of civil and common law systems. *Corporate Ownership & Control*, 13(1-5), 520-533.

Reeb, D., Mansi, S., & Allee, J. (2001). Firm internationalization and the cost of debt financing: Evidence from non-provisional publicly traded debt. *The Journal of Financial and Quantitative Analysis,* 36(3), 395-414.

Ricardo, D. (1911). *The Principles of Political Economy & Taxation*. J.M. Dent, E.P. Dutton.

Rivera, J. and Milani, K. (2011). Budgeting for International Operations: Impact on and Integration with Strategic Planning. *Management Accounting Quarterly*.

Rogach, O.I. (2005). Transnatsionalni korporatsii v svitoviy ekonomitsi: Monographiya. Kyiv: Vydavnychopoligraphichniytsentr «Kyyivskiy universytet», 176.

Rogoff, K.S. (1996). The purchasing power parity puzzle. *Journal of Economic Literature*, 34(2), 647-68. https://scholar.harvard.edu/files/rogoff/files/51_jel1996.pdf

Rossi, B. (2013). Exchange rate predictability. *Journal of Economic Literature*, 51(4), 1063-1119.

Rugman, A. (2009). *The Oxford Handbook of International Business*. Oxford University Press.

Rugman, A. (2013). *Mastering Financial Modelling in Microsoft Excel: A Practitioner's Guide to Applied Corporate Finance* (3rd ed.). Pearson.

Sageder, M., & Feldbauer-Durstmüller, B. (2019). Management control in multinational companies: a systematic literature review. *Review of Managerial Science*, 13, 875-918. doi:10.1007/s11846-018-0276-1

Samll, C. (2011). Does Governance Travel Around the World? *HLS Forum on Corporate Governance and Financial Regulation*.

Sanford, J.G. & Hart, O. (1980). Takeover bids, the free-rider problem, and the theory of the corporation. *The Bell Journal of Economics*, 11(1), 42-64.

Sapp, S. (2012). *Prada: To IPO or not to IPO: That is the Question, Again*. Harvard.

Satish, D. & Agarwal, M. (2011). Currency rate swap between IBM and World Bank. *IBS Case Development Center*.

Schill, M.J. & Craddock, J. (2017, January 11). Ferrari: The 2015 Initial Public Offering. *Harvard Business Review*.

SEC (2015). PROJECT OWL DOCUMENT, Form F-1 Registration statement under the securities act of 1933: New Business Netherlands N.V. https://www.sec.gov/Archives/edgar/data/1648416/000164841615000004/newbusinessnetherlands.htm

Sercu, P. & Uppal, R. (1995). *International Financial Markets and the Firm*. South-Western.

Shapiro, A. (1991). *Foundation of Multinational Financial Management*.

Shapiro, A. (2010). *Multinational Financial Management* (9th ed.). Wiley & Sons.

Shengelia, T. (2016). *World Economy and International Economic Relations*. Universal.

Siegfried, N., Simeonova, E., & Vespro, C. (2007). Choice of currency in bond issuance and the international role of currencies. *ECB Working Paper No. 814*. doi:10.2139/ssrn.1015262

SIFMA (2020). *2020 Outlook – Trends in US Capital Market*. https://www.sifma.org/wp-content/uploads/2019/12/2020-SIFMA-Outlook.pdf

Sims, J. & Romero, J. (2013, November 22). Latin American Debt Crisis of the 1980s. *Federal Reserve History*. https://www.federalreservehistory.org/essays/latin-american-debt-crisis

Slaughter, M.J. (2009). How U.S. Multinational Companies Strengthen the U.S. Economy. *Business Roundtable and the United States Council Foundation*.

Slimane, I.B., Bellalah, M., & Rjiba, H. (2017). Time-varying beta during the 2008 financial crisis - Evidence from North America and Western Europe. *The Journal of Risk Finance*, 18(5). doi:10.1108/JRF-02-2017-0020

Smith, A. [1776] (1981). *An Inquiry into the Nature and Causes of the Wealth of Nations* (2 vols.). Liberty Fund.

Smith, C. & Stulz, R. (1985). The determinants of firms' hedging policies. *Journal of Financial and Quantitative Analysis*, 20, 391-405.

Sohag, K., Gainetdinova, A., & Mariev, O. (2021). The response of exchange rates to economic policy uncertainty: Evidence from Russia. *Borsa Istanbul Review*. doi:10.1016/j.bir.2021.07.002

Solnik, B. & McLeaver, D. (2009). *Global Investments* (6th ed.). Pearson.

Stecklow, S., Dehghanpisheh, B., & Pomfret, J. (2019, January 9). Exclusive: New documents link Huawei with suspected front companies in Iran, Syria. *Reuters.* https://www.reuters.com/article/huawei-iran-idINKCN1P21MK

Steinhauer, B., Mahler, F., Kronat, O., & Weitkamp, T. (2015). Germany – Upfront fees in syndicated lending in light of recent federal court of justice judgements. *Clifford Chance Newsletter.*

Stobaugh, R. (1970). Financing foreign subsidiaries of U.S.-controlled multinational enterprises. *Journal of International Business Studies*, 1, 43-64. doi:10.1057/palgrave.jibs.8490717

Stulz, R.M. (1995). Globalization of capital markets and the cost of capital: The case of Nestlé. *Journal of Applied Corporate Finance*, 8(3), 30-38.

Stulz, R.M. (2022). Globalization of capital markets and the cost of capital: The case of Nestlé. *Journal of Applied Corporate Finance*. doi:10.1111/jacf.12484

Tabova, A. (2013). Portfolio diversification and the cross-sectional distribution of foreign investment. *FRB International Finance Discussion Paper No. 1091.* doi:10.2139/ssrn.2364598

Terra, C. (2015). Exchange Rate Regimes. In *Principles of International Finance and Open Economy Macroeconomics* (pp. 265-295). Academic Press.

Thia, J.P. (2019). Bank lending—what has changed post-crisis? *Journal of Economics and Finance*, 43, 256-272.

Thomas R.S. & Cotter J.F. (2007). Shareholder proposals in the new millennium: Shareholder support, board response, and market reaction. *Journal of Corporate Finance*, 13(2-3), 368-391.

Tiwari, S. (2017). *Multinational Financial Management: An Overview.*

Tonello, M. (2012). Hedge Fund Activism: Findings and Recommendations for Corporations and Investors. The Conference Board Research Working Group Series. doi:10.2139/ssrn.1107027

Tovey, A. (2017, June 29). McLaren Races to Record Sales and Profits as Expansion Plan Takes Hold. *The Telegraph.* https://www.telegraph.co.uk/business/2017/06/29/mclaren-races-record-sales-profits-expansion-plan-takes-hold/

Trading Economics. *Average Interest Rates.* https://tradingeconomics.com/country-list/interest-rate

Trigg, D.W. & Leach, A.G. (2017). Exponential smoothing with an adaptive response rate. *Journal of the Operational Research Society*, 18(1), 53-59. doi:10.1057/jors.1967.5

Tröger, T.H. & Walz, U. (2019). Does say on pay matter? Evidence from Germany. *European Company and Financial Law Review*, 16(3), 381-414. doi:10.1515/ecfr-2019-0014

Tscheke, J. (2016). *Operational Hedging of Exchange Rate Risks.* Munich Discussion Paper, No. 2016-18, Ludwig-Maximilians-Universität München, Volkswirtschaftliche Fakultät, München. doi:10.5282/ubm/epub.30227

Tsounis, N. (2012). A new approach for measuring volatility of the exchange rate. *Procedia Economics and Finance*, 1, 374-382. doi:10.1016/S2212-5671(12)00043-3

Tsyganov, S., & Zalisko, O. (2015). Mne specific factors of corporate capital structure: Comparative Analysis in terms of financial resources demand and supply. *Baltic Journal of Economic Studies*, 1(2).

Uddin, M. & Akhter, B. (2011). Strategic alliance and competitiveness: Theoretical framework. *Journal of Arts Science & Commerce.*

UniCredit (2007). *Merger Deed of Capitalia into UniCredit Signed.* https://www.unicredit-group.eu/en/press-media/press-releases-price-sensitive/2007/PressRelease0183.html

UniCredit & Capitalia (2007). *Merger of UniCredit and Capitalia to Consolidate Italian Footprint and Create the No. 1 Eurozone bank by Market Capitalization.* https://www.unicreditgroup.eu/content/dam/unicreditgroup-eu/documents/en/press-and-media/press-releases/2007/Eng_Press_release_200507_Final.pdf

Valdez, S. & Molyneux, P. (2012). *An Introduction to Global Financial Markets* (7th ed.). Palgrave Macmillan.

Van der Elst, C. (2011). Shareholder activism in good and bad economic times. *Corporate Ownership and Control*, 8(2). ESCEM School of Business and Management.

Van Mieghem, J.A. (2003). Capacity management, investment, and hedging: Review and recent developments. *Manufacturing and Service Operations Management*, 5(4), 269-302.

Vernon, R. (1966). International Investment and International Trade in the Product Cycle. *Quarterly Journal of Economics*, 80, 190-207.

Vismara, A. (2019). *The Italian Corporate Bond Market: What is happening to the capital structure of italian non-financial companies?* Equita Group and Bocconi University. https://www.equita.eu/static/upload/eve/event-2019---the-italian-corporate-bond-market.pdf

Wang, P. (2020) Transaction Exposure. In: *The Economics of Foreign Exchange and Global Finance*. Springer.

Whitaker, S.C. (2016). *Cross-Border Mergers and Acquisitions*. John Wiley & Sons.

White, A. (2021, February 11). California State Teachers' Retirement System, Owning Approximately $300 Million of Exxon's Shares. *Top1000Funds*. https://www.top1000funds.com/2021/02/calstrs-takes-on-exxonmobil/

White & Case (2022). *European Leveraged Finance: From Survive to Thrive.* https://www.whitecase.com/sites/default/files/2022-01/white-case-european-leveraged-finance-2022-web.pdf

Wilkins, M. (2009). The History of Multinational Enterprise. In *The Oxford Handbook of International Business* (2nd ed., pp. 3-35). Oxford University Press.

Wilkins, M. (2009). US Business in Europe: An American perspective. *Librairie Droz.* doi:10.3917/droz.bonin.2008.01.0035

Williamson, O.E. (1981). The modern corporation: Origins, evolution, attributes. *Journal of Economic Literature*, 19(4), 1537-1569.

Williamson, O.E. (1985). *The Economics Institutions of Capitalism*. The Free Press.

Xie, E., Reddy, K.S., & Liang, J. (2017). Country-specific determinants of cross-border mergers and acquisitions: A comprehensive review and future research directions. *Journal of World Business*, 127-183. doi:10.1016/j.jwb.2016.12.005

Yan, A. (2006). Leasing and debt financing: Substitutes or complements? *The Journal of Financial and Quantitative Analysis*, 41(3), 709-731.

Yoon, H. & Heshmati, A. (2017). Do environmental regulations affect FDI decisions? The Pollution Haven Hypothesis Revisited. *GLO Discussion Paper Series*, 86.

Znaczko, T.M. (2013). *Forecasting Foreign Exchange Rates*. Applied Economics Theses. State University of New York Buffalo State.